Irish Orientalism

Irish Studies
James MacKillop, *Series Editor*

Other titles in Irish Studies

Irish Orientalism

A Literary and Intellectual History   Joseph Lennon

SYRACUSE UNIVERSITY PRESS

First Edition 2004
04   05   06   07   08   09   6   5   4   3   2   1

The paper used in this publication meets the minimum requirements of
American National Standard for Information Sciences—Permanence of
Paper for Printed Library Materials, ANSI Z39.48–1984.∞™

Library of Congress Cataloging-in-Publication Data

Lennon, Joseph (Joseph Allen)
    Irish orientalism : a literary and intellectual history / Joseph Lennon.— 1st ed.
        p. cm. — (Irish studies)
    Includes bibliographical references and index.
    ISBN 0-8156-3044-1 (alk. paper)
    1. English literature—Irish authors—History and criticism. 2. English literature—Irish authors—
Oriental influences. 3. Oriental literature—Appreciation—Ireland. 4. Literature, Comparative—
Irish and Oriental. 5. Literature, Comparative—Oriental and Irish. 6. Ireland—Intellectual life. 7.
Middle East—In literature. 8. Orientalism in literature. 9. Orientalism—Ireland. 10. Asia—In
literature. I. Title. II. Irish studies (Syracuse, N.Y.)
    PR8719.L46 2004
    820.9'9417—dc22
                                2004005263

To my mother and father,
and to Joanne with love

JOSEPH LENNON is an assistant professor of English at Manhattan College in New York City. He has published poetry and essays on Irish literature and culture in various books and journals.

Contents

Illustrations

Preface

I HAVE MANY TO THANK for help with the research and writing of this book. Foremost, I want to thank those people who have indulgently given me direction: J. Michael Lennon, Jerry Phillips, John Carey, Lee Jacobus, Philip O'Leary, Luke Gibbons, Kevin Whelan, Joep Leerssen, and the late Adele Dalsimer. For the basis of my pursuit here, I am indebted to the late Edward Said. For providing valuable feedback on my manuscript (part or whole), I thank Joanne Dittersdorf, J. Michael Lennon, Donna Pedro Lennon, Joep Leerssen, anonymous readers through Syracuse University Press, Peter Lennon, Robert Klaus, Yvonne Murphy, Lee Jacobus, Jerry Phillips, Rachel Lynch, Clare Carroll, John Waters, Casey Dwyer, Amy Farranto, James MacKillop, Annette Wenda, Theresa Litz, and the staff at Syracuse University Press. For helping with translation and research questions, I am grateful to Br. Patrick Horner, Ashley Cross, Robert Hasenfratz, Gauri Viswanathan, Anindya Ghoshal, Nitya Jacob, Debasis Bandyopadhyay, Brendan MacCarthaigh, Michael Silvestri, Breen Ó Conchubhair, Christopher Bayly, Patrick Colm Hogan, and Rolf Loeber.

The research for this book could not have been done without the generous support of a NEMLA (Northeast Modern Language Association) Summer Fellowship, support from Knox College's John and Elaine Fellowes Fund, a University of Connecticut Dissertation Fellowship, and, above all, a travel grant from Manhattan College. For help in applying for and securing funding, thanks must be given to Lee Jacobus; Rocco Marinaccio; June Dwyer; Mary Ann O'Donnell, the dean of arts of Manhattan College; and Weldon Jackson, the provost of Manhattan College.

I also thank the various organizations, groups, and their members that have heard presentations of this material: ACIS (American Conference for Irish Studies), ACIS Mid-Atlantic Region, MLA (Modern Language Association), Columbia Irish Studies Seminar, GRIAN (Graduate Irish Studies Association of New York), Galway Conference on Colonialism, GISC (Graduate Irish Studies Conference), SCLA (Southern Comparative Literature Association) Conference, Caxton Club of Knox College, Junior Faculty Research Forum and Dante Seminar at Manhattan College, and the "Home and the World: Rabindranath Tagore at the

End of the Millennium" conference sponsored by the Asian American Cultural Center and the Asian American Studies Institute at the University of Connecticut. I learned much from the many helpful suggestions made by panelists and audience members at these presentations. Sections of this work have appeared previously in the *Comparatist,* guest editor Michael Molino (spring 1996); *Rabindranath Tagore: Universality and Tradition,* edited by Patrick Colm Hogan and Lalita Pandit (Associated University Presses, 2003); and *Ireland and Postcolonial Theory,* edited by Clare Carroll and Patricia King (Cork University Press, 2003).

Enormous thanks to the many librarians and the various research institutions where they work: the New York Public Library (and the Henry W. and Albert A. Berg Collection and the Carl H. Pforzheimer Collection), Homer Babbidge Library at the University of Connecticut, Thomas P. O'Neill and John J. Burns Libraries at Boston College, Royal Irish Academy, National Library of Ireland, Rabindra Bhavan and Santiniketan, National Library in Calcutta, Asiatic Society in Calcutta, the British Library, and the International Headquarters of the Theosophical Society in Adyar, Chennai (Madras), India. Also I am grateful for the support and hospitality of the wonderful Irish studies programs that have made me feel at home: Boston College's Irish Studies Program, New York University's Glucksman Ireland House, and the University of Notre Dame's Keogh Center in Dublin. I also want to thank everyone at University Hall, S.J., on Leeson Street in Dublin for their hospitality.

For suggestions and inspiring conversation (in addition to the individuals above), my gratitude to: Daniel Collins, Clare Carroll, Eamon Grennan, Robin Metz, Norman Mailer, Roy Foster, Colum McCann, Chris Kelly, Stephen Kaplan, Catherine Candy, Jean Lutes, Jonathan Curley, Christian Langworthy, Chuck Morris, Seamus Heaney, Robert Hellenga, William Brady, Andrew and Jeanette Chernin, Tyler McDaniel, Jeffrey Jones, Maria Brandt, Kevin Kidd, Todd Hearon, Veerendra Lele, Seamus Carey, William Buse, Christopher Breiseth, Maureen O'-Connor, Helen "Tidi" Verner, Nathan Wallace, Sean O'Brien, Sam Smucker, Anke Pinkert, Jim Rogers, Gary Vena, Patrick Hogan, Jonathan Hufstader, Margaret Gibson, Stephanie Roach, Karen Cajka, Aaron Bremeyer, Jenny Spinner, Peter McGahey, Tom Shea, Maureen O'Connor, Karen Overbey, Spurgeon Thompson, Mary McGlynn, Martin Burke, Robert St. Cyr, Ed Hagan, John Atteberry, Bernadette Cunningham, Margaret Preston, James Smith, Robert Savage, Rich Murphy, Marjorie Howes, Mark Taylor, John Runions, Mark Palazzolo, Robbie Liben, Sharon Gregory, Ann-Marie Hendrickson, Bill Weinberg (and the Moorish Orthodox Radio Crusade at WBAI), Todd Davis, Ken Womack, William Baker, Rachel Scoazec, Michael Molino, Marika Beneventi, Massimo Baccigalupo, Norris Church Mailer, Tejinder Singh and his family, Michael Ferarro, Amy Hausmann, Catherine Phil MacCarthy, Susan Guaccero, Adrienne Rich,

Deirdre Bryan, Tony Perrottet, Janis Brody, Nancy Milford, Moloy Raushit, and Gwen Batten. And to Alexander Gargilis, my deep thanks. For their unremitting support, I greatly appreciated my colleagues over the years at Knox College, University of Connecticut, Boston College, Northern Illinois University, and Manhattan College.

For their support, belief, and hospitality, I have deep gratitude for my family: J. Michael and Donna Pedro Lennon; Anthony and Mary Pedro; Mary Mitchell Lennon; Jim Lennon; Stephen Lennon; Peter and Karen Lennon; Paul Pedro; Kathy Aruda; Maureen Macedo; Lester and Harriett Dittersdorf; Ira Dittersdorf; Betty Weisskopf; my uncles, aunts, and cousins in Newport, Somerset, and beyond; and the Nicholsons, particularly Sean, Mary, Seamus, Betty, Linda, and Marie. Thanks to the Wertheim Study Room at the New York Public Library and the Writers Room (and its indefatigable staff) in New York City, without which nothing would have been written. My profound thanks to all those named and unnamed, remembered or forgotten, who have helped research, assemble, edit, amend, and publish this labor of love. The mistakes I own alone. Last, Joanne Dittersdorf, my partner, love and thanks to you.

Introduction

Chapter I. Certainty of Early Keltic Settlements in Eire. Q. Where did the earliest races who first reached Ireland come from? A. From the East.

—Canon Ulick J. Bourke, *Pre-Christian Ireland*

SCOTA AND SCYTHIA; Erin and Iran; Milesian and Phoenician; Brehon and Brahmin; Sinn Féin and Swaraj—these pairings provide a shorthand history of Irish Orientalism, especially its forked claim to antiquity and barbarity. Long before it was treated as Celtic, Irish culture was linked to the "Orient." Ireland's ancient history and culture supposedly stemmed from Asian and Middle Eastern, or West Asian, cultures. This study traces literary and intellectual links between the Oriental and the Celt from the medieval period to the mid-twentieth century. Such connections emerged from Ireland's imagined place in Greek texts as a wild, remote borderland, existing well off the western coast of the great Eurasian continent, in the ocean that stretched around the sphere of the earth to the eastern end of the habitable world. Eventually, such representations gave birth to two antitheses of modern, enlightened Europe: the Celt and the Oriental.

Although Irishness is still linked with Asian images today (as in the 1990s image of the "Celtic Tiger"), rarely are such comparisons understood as springing from a genuinely Irish tradition. Nevertheless, such images, tropes, narratives, and arguments pervade Irish cultural and intellectual history from Dicuil, a medieval monk, to W. B. Yeats and beyond. This study traces this semiotic history from the earliest Irish texts to the twentieth century when cross-colonial ties developed between nationalists in Ireland and other parts of the former British Empire, particularly India.

A vital dynamic of Irish Orientalism is represented visually in a woodcut from Charles Vallancey's *Essay on the Antiquity of the Irish Language* (1772) (see fig. 1). The image portrays two round towers standing, as it first appears, side by side; the first— "Round Tower at Ardmore Ireland"—appears to be an abandoned structure. Nevertheless, it looks solidly intact. The second structure just further afield—"Round

xv

1. "Round Tower at Ardmore Ireland; Round Tower in India." Woodcut done for General Charles Vallancey. Published in *An Account of the Ancient Stone Amphitheatre Lately Discovered in the County of Kerry with Fragments of Irish History Relating Thereto, &c, &c, &c.* (1812).

Tower in India" (note the less specific place-name)—is shown as a piece of architecture that dialogues with its environment: a leafy tree and another building appear beside. The first slightly foregrounded tower appears austere, isolated, and obsolete in an otherwise empty field; moreover, with no external stairs, it cannot easily be accessed. The second more decorative tower seems to stand slightly upfield at the horizon. Its less specific place-name and more ornate bands signify common Orientalist generalizations, which were just becoming linked with imperial programs in the late eighteenth century. As a piece of architecture the Indian tower exists in a living context. Most important, however, a man stands at the top of its steps, pausing at its threshold, perhaps, we may imagine, looking toward the absent/present tower in far-off Ireland. This composite image of the towers is clearly synthetic, in both senses of that word, that is, put together and artificial. The contrast between the two is telling, signifying the broader dynamics of Irish Orientalism: the ancient and absent Celtic culture mirrors the living and present Orient.

This pairing of the towers both suggests an Indian origin for the round towers and indicates a significant impulse of Irish literary and intellectual history: that an ancient culture and somewhat inaccessible history can be accessed through a comparative study of the living Orient. It not only affirms an affinity between Ireland and the Orient, but also recognizes this bond as a strategy for the survival and resurgence of Irish culture. Because imperial pairings also gained prominence in England during its period of imperial expansion, the linking of the Oriental with the Irish has been understood as an extension of the logic of Empire, a mutual "othering" of the colonized periphery, which at times it was. But representation depends not only upon a dominant discourse such as Orientalism; the wielders and weavers of narratives have agency, however unacknowledged, however occasionally employed. Cultural nationalists were inspired by an Irish-Oriental connection; they created anti-imperial and cross-colonial narratives from this ancient semiotic connection, which had ancient roots, though not the ones that Vallancey suspected.

Much antiquarian pseudoscholarship, particularly the debate surrounding the origins of the round towers, resonated in Irish culture to a great extent because the ideas were based on medieval Irish Oriental origin legends. The towers seemed to confirm that Ireland was an ancient and remote Oriental settlement, not an uncivilized, degraded island off the coast of Europe. Moreover, the buildings captured the attention of the press and reading public, leaving a lasting impression on Irish nationalist iconography and the popular imagination. The Oriental shadow of the towers exists today perhaps only as a distant semiotic connection, felt only through a shared air of exoticism and antiquity in Celticism and Orientalism. Nevertheless, Irish Orientalism at one time helped imagine and actualize cross-colonial ties and decolonizing narratives around the globe.

In the eighteenth century, the term *Orient* signified Asian, West Asian, and North African cultures, which, in the European gaze, were collectively seen to resemble one another. Along with the rise of European imperialism, the study of these cultures developed into an academic discipline: Orientalism. Through this discipline, and through the growing number of literary and other representations of these cultures, the Orient gradually came to signify a host of attributes, behaviors, and perspectives, which were decidedly non-European and often the embodiment of European fears and fantasies. Edward Said argues in *Orientalism* (1978) that this body of representations and knowledge can best be understood as a discourse that became bound and determined by European imperialism (he focuses on British and French) and pervades Euro-American cultures. The discourse does not merely collect knowledge on Asian, West Asian, and North African cultures; it also collectivizes and molds them into a Western construction of the Orient, enabling Euro-American imperial control. Over the course of imperial history, Asian and West Asian cultures often identified with understandings promoted through Orientalism, and just as often when decolonizing, cultural nationalists reversed Orientalist stereotypes in an effort to overturn the colonial image of themselves. Throughout this study, the terms *Orient* and *Oriental* will refer to this Euro-American discourse. The term *Orient* is intended here to highlight the European discourse on Asia and West Asia and is not meant to signify those actual cultures, which are referenced by name.

The dominant imperial discourse of European Orientalism emerged in Britain and France; this discourse had considerable impact in Ireland, but Irish Orientalism has a distinct history. Native Irish representations of Asian and West Asian cultures date back to an Irish tradition in the ninth century. Many of these representations depict Irish ancestors migrating from Asia. Following these early narratives of the Orient, Ireland has been identified, compared, and contrasted with various Asian cultures. For early modern and medieval Irish writers, parts of the Orient signaled Ireland's ancient heritage. Later, because of Ireland's complex relationship with the British Empire, the Orient also came to signify another arm of British conquest for many Irish writers. Witnessing the process of cultural misrepresentation given by British commentators and historians of Ireland, Irish writers often highlighted the constructed nature of cultural representations when discussing both Irish history and the Orient. Imperial British texts had long compared Ireland with other Oriental cultures, at first in order to textually barbarize Ireland and later in order to discover intra-imperial strategies for governing its colonies. Such British representations further encouraged Irish writers to use the Orient allegorically and indirectly comment on cultural differences, nationalism, unionism, sectarianism, and imperialism. To study Irish writings on the Orient, therefore, is also to study Irish cultural narratives of antiquity, Celticism, and nation.

The pervasive nature of the Celtic-Oriental affinity has long been seen as an underlying tissue of Irish culture, based on legends of successive migrations to Ireland from the Orient recorded as Ireland's origin legends in the medieval chronicle *Lebor Gabála Érenn*. Evidence of such affinities has subsequently been claimed in race, language, and culture—and more particularly in music (Arabian-Moroccan-Celtic), knot work (Ethiopian-Arabic-Celtic), mysticism (Indian-Persian-Irish), travel and trade (Scythian-Phoenician-Celtic), architecture (Egyptian-Indian-Eskimo-Celtic), physiognomy (Mongol-African-Gael), ancient dress (Chinese-Scythian-Celtic), ancient law (Brahmin-Brehon), warfare (Egyptian-Scythian-Celtic), politics (Irish-Indian-Persian-Egyptian-Chinese), and, generally, sensibility (Oriental-Celtic). Irish literature and the writings on the Orient not only brought these comparisons to bear in their representations of the East but also integrated them into Irish perceptions of Ireland's place in both Empire and the world. In particular, the comparison between the Oriental and the Celt has long endured as a cultural force in Ireland. Over the past twelve centuries, transmutations of Irish Oriental origin legends appear in a variety of texts: grammatical texts, genealogies, histories and pseudohistories, pastoral dialogues, pseudo-letter collections, travel narratives, antiquarian studies, Orientalist romances, Celticist studies, popular fiction, anticolonial critiques, syncretic Irish-Asian works. Viewed apart, these texts have seemed idiosyncratic to literary scholars. Viewed together, they coalesce as a history and constitute an unacknowledged discourse in Irish culture and European imperialism—a discourse that seeded decolonizing critiques of imperialism around the globe.

Scholars have dismissed Irish Orientalist representations as significant because they seem provincial borrowings from British, French, and German Orientalism or because they are based in legend and speculation, not in science or modern historiography. Until recently, studies of Irish nationalism have also passed over Celtic-Oriental and Irish-Asian representations, dismissing them for being self-deprecating or reactionary, for merely reversing the imperial stereotypes of Orientalists and Celticists. Supposedly defined by the semiotic binary of imperial assertions and nationalist reversals, Irish Orientalism has been dismissed as a distinctive discourse, seen as an impossibility by nationalist critics in British, Irish, and postcolonial arenas. But this dismissal is valid only if the supremacy of the imperial-nationalist dynamic is admitted. Because arguments that dismiss Irish Orientalist writers as defensive joiners or opportunistic chancers (on either the imperial or the nationalist side) are discussed later, I will not discuss them here. This study itself runs the danger of also being dismissed as the latest in a long series of illogical discussions about connections between the Oriental and the Celt. But the goal of this work is not to reassert the legendary Oriental origins of the Irish. The goal is to reveal a semiotic history, as well as the cultural contexts and the ramifications of Ireland's Oriental imaginings.

Organization and Overview

This book is divided into two sections: the first concerns the development of Irish Orientalism before the Celtic Revival; the second explores the Orientalism of the Celtic Revival. The first three chapters survey the discourse chronologically: Chapter 1 discusses the emergence of the Oriental origin legends, exploring the influential Greco-Roman-border characterizations alongside early British impressions of Ireland. The second chapter traces the development of the origin legends as pseudohistory, as well as antiquarianism, philology, and early linguistics. Chapter 3 explores early literary representations of the Orient in Irish literature in the eighteenth and early nineteenth centuries, covering pseudo-Oriental letters, discovery narratives, Oriental romances, and parodic translations. Closing the first section, chapter 4 explores Irish representations complicit with Empire and discusses intra-imperial analogies in popular culture and politics, particularly between Ireland and India. The second section begins by surveying similar texts in chapter 5 but exploring the other side of these Oriental-Celtic comparisons: cross-colonial comparisons. The last three chapters offer readings of the Orientalist works of W. B. Yeats, George Russell (AE), James Stephens, and James Cousins.

In order to understand the roots of this discourse in Irish writing, a culturally based approach is needed. Until very recently, Irish studies scholars and critics have not recognized the existence of Irish Orientalism as even a peripheral discourse in Irish culture and literature. Attempting to understand Irish Orientalism broadly, this study examines texts across a wide variety of genres: origin legends, annals, pseudohistories, histories, topographies, chorographies, geographies, poetry, novels, romances, dramas, essays, histories, biographies, letters, textbooks, false memoirs, pseudotranslations, sectarian pamphlets, political tracts, cultural criticism, academic studies, popular stories, newspaper articles, book reviews, pseudo-Oriental letters, and speeches. In short, this work explores the wide variety of Irish texts that offer a significant representation of either the Orient or a specific Asian or West Asian culture. It explores the writings of Dicuil, Séathrun Céitinn, Roderic O'Flaherty, General Charles Vallancey, Oliver Goldsmith, Thomas Moore, James Clarence Mangan, Lady Augusta Gregory, Frederick Ryan, Roger Casement, and others, in addition to the four Revivalists. Through these writings, we trace the continuity (and development) of an affinity between the Celt and the Oriental, two synecdoches for cultural discourses in Ireland, England, and Europe.

In medieval and early modern Europe, the Scythians gradually came to signify the ancestors of the Gaelic Irish, as later would the Phoenicians, Milesians, and Celts. Eastern connections typify this multifaceted and layered history, one that often eludes simple textual influence and reference. No single explanation of a medieval etymological extrapolation, translation error, or transposed traits can account for the origin of Irish Orientalism, because many representations between the Irish and the Asians emerged in Irish and British texts. Moreover, this discourse both links the ancestors of the Irish with ancient Asian cultures and transmutes imperial representations of barbaric and wild Ireland. From these sources, real philological and linguistic theories, cultural narratives, and political models developed. Without imperial orientation and negative reinforcement, however, this semiotic connection might never have developed.

The Oriental and the Celtic acquired their modern attributes (and ideological bases) in the late seventeenth century. Even earlier representations of Ireland had depicted it as a remote borderland, inhabited by migrants from Scythia, Egypt, Greece, Spain, Britain, Phoenicia, and other lands. Ireland's traditional history is one of migration, settlement, and integration. The origin legends developed into cultural myths over many centuries in response to political exigencies and cultural shifts. Unlike Irish texts, British histories tended to focus on the absurdity of the origin legends, which, in turn, reinforced their continued appearance in Irish texts. By the time the legends had been clearly disproved in modern archaeological and historical terms, the cultural myth and Oriental affinity had become part of the Irish national story, encouraging its own logic.

Celticism and Orientalism developed along parallel lines in the same period, encouraged by similar concerns and often advanced by the very same scholars and writers. Consonant with the expansion of European colonialism, Orientalism developed as an academic discipline and knowledge base, as well as a set of cultural and political expectations about Asian and West Asian peoples and cultures. Scholarly interest in Celtic and Gaelic cultures and languages emerged in English and Anglo-Irish intellectual circles, to a great extent, through the emerging field of Celtic linguistics. Many investigations treated the Celtic languages (Irish, Welsh, Breton, Scots-Gaelic, Cornish, and Manx) as links to a primeval European language. Building on Irish histories, British histories, and classical Greek and Roman texts, these descriptions emphasized Ireland's antiquity and remoteness, often comparing Ireland, the Orient, and other "premodern" cultures. Later, in the literature of the nineteenth century, Irish Orientalism contributed to an increased use of allegory and linguistic play through which the Irish decolonizing and nationalist voices might exist. Strategically, Irish cultural nationalists increasingly undermined the expectations and colorings of Anglo-French Orientalism and bolstered Ireland's Oriental affinities and cross-colony identifications.

The Celtic Revival stands as the most recognized moment of Irish Orientalism. During this time, Irish cultural nationalists wrote plays, essays, stories, poems, and novels with Oriental themes, ideas, and images woven as leitmotifs to Celtic themes. James Stephens went as far as mingling Indian philosophy with versions of Irish legend (see Stephens 1924) and had Irish storytellers mix talk of karma with tales of "the seraph Cuchulain" (Stephens 1914, 143–223). Prominent Irish literary magazines published poems and stories based on Vedic texts, recasting Indian stories in Irish atmospheres. AE's "Krishna," for instance, published in a 1912 issue of the *Irish Review,* sets incarnations of the "Light of Lights" (Krishna) in stereotypical Irish settings: playing as a child in the grass outside a rural cottage and exiting a pub in a reverie, "the King of Kings outcast reel brawling through the starlit air." [1] Perhaps the best-known examples of the Revivalists' borrowings from Asian literature, however, are Yeats's Celtic "Noh" dramas based upon revived Cuchulain stories and traditional Japanese plays. Yet another powerful illustration is the lived and literary example of Irish poet, playwright, and essayist James Cousins, who spent half of his life in Ireland and the other half in India. Being involved in the literary and cultural revivals in both British colonies, Cousins mingled the Indian and Irish in his poetry, drama, and essays. Taken together, these examples have been examined for the influence of thought and writings of Theosophy, particularly of Madame Blavatsky (see Blavatsky 1888). As most any study on Theosophy will note, Blavatsky appropriated Indian and other Asian philosophies into her bizarre spiritual philosophies, but hers was not the only source of Orientalism for these Revivalists.

Theorizing Irish Orientalism as a Distinct Discourse

Irish writers have long understood the Orient within their own cultural moments and political realities, borrowing and building on antecedents. A basic assumption of this study is that elements in culture continue over time, transmuting through generations. This assumption is based in the reasoning of the semiotician pragmatist philosopher Charles Saunders Peirce, whose doctrine of synechism asserts that we expect the universe to exhibit continuities rather than discontinuities. Adopted into the realm of culture, the doctrine of synechism implies that our significant cultural tropes will develop new variations, mutate old forms, or revert to supposedly traditional forms without losing traceable historical strands, that elements of culture continue even when rejected. Moreover, a discourse is not only continuous but also cumulative—it gathers tropes, tendencies, and political strategies along the way, tropes that continue to help define the culture or help individuals within the culture make sense of the world. In order to understand experience, we make sense of it based on what made sense before—in philosophy, this has been referred to as coherentism.[2] Applied to culture, coherentist ideas imply that every generation re-creates the manner in which the previous generation(s) understood the world, using similar materials and justifications. In other words, despite massive cultural upheavals and demographic and linguistic shifts, cultural continuity is the rule, not the exception. With these assumptions of continuity, accumulation, and coherence recognized, other questions arise: What does the Oriental signify in different areas of knowledge? How does Irish Orientalism resemble and differ from Anglo-French Orientalism? Do origin legends continue to manifest themselves despite (beside) or in spite of (against) larger discourses such as Orientalism and Empire? How did Irish Orientalism develop from the origin legends, and how did its distinguishing characteristics develop? Why has the discourse remained unacknowledged as such? These questions have guided this project, but have not dominated its organization, which is primarily historical.

The body of Orientalist literature written by Irish writers is not monolithic, nor does it entirely lack cohesion. A number of common narratives stretch across the centuries, conjoining the works as a discourse. Whatever the connections, one thing is certain: the discourse is distinct from other European and American Orientalist projects. Whereas the Orientalist projects of English, French, American, and German authors have been distinctly explored in criticism, the works of Irish writers and intellectuals are usually considered as a subcategory of English Orientalism. For many Anglo-Irish Orientalists, who felt ties of consanguinity with the English as fellow Britons, this grouping makes a certain amount of sense. The colonial interests of many Anglocentric Irish intellectuals and Orientalists closely resembled the interests of their English colleagues; indeed, these Irish Orientalists usually viewed themselves as proud subjects of the British Empire. But more often than not, imperialism was an ambivalent issue for Irish writers and intellectuals, Gaelic, Anglo-Irish, or otherwise, and their discussions and representations of the Orient, examined as a tradition, reflect and embody this divide in its many permutations and variances.

Recently, Ireland's Celtic heritage has been interrogated and discussed as a cultural invention; even less validity exists for Ireland's Asian heritage, which was rigorously attacked in the nineteenth century. Nevertheless, medieval Irish monks recorded a number of legends about the Oriental origins of the Irish, and the legends were widely embraced in Irish culture for centuries. Images of the Orient allowed later Irish writers an avenue for indirectly representing Irish-English relations, colonialism, cultural resistance, and decolonization. Textual instances of Irish Orientalism often appear insignificant beside instances of other cultural Irish narratives such as patriotism, nationalism, and religion, in part because Orientalist images are not perceived, generally, as belonging to an "Irish tradition"—yet they certainly predate images of comely maidens and whitewashed cottages. These important representations enabled Irish writers to experiment with the dynamics of exoticism and autoexoticism (see Leerssen 1997) in a hybrid discourse that was neither entirely native nor entirely foreign. This liminal nature of Irish representations of the Orient has made it curiously uncontroversial and unexamined, able to be read as beneficial to both imperialism and native Irish culture.

During the rise of European imperialism, the Orient offered Irish writers some discursive control over an aspect of Empire: the representation of (other) colonized peoples. Although such texts at times shared knowledge and power with the dominant discourse of Anglo-French Orientalism, these representations also reveal the liminal position often occupied by Irish writers within the British Empire, that is, these writers could belong to both the imperial metropole and the colonized periphery. Although some pieces of literary Orientalism by Irish authors merely extended the discourse of Orientalism to Ireland (paralleling the Celticist study of the exotic Gael), a larger number worked against the dominant representations of Anglo-French Orientalism and Celticism, exposing the Orient's constructed and politicized nature. As Julia Kushigian notes in *Orientalism in the Hispanic Literary Tradition,* we should not expect all Orientalisms to "do no more than 'elaborate' on the 'major steps' of the Anglo-French position" (1991, 2). Similarly, Sheldon Pollack in his essay "Deep Orientalism?" argues for new understanding of German Indology within European Orientalism, arguing that "their 'othering' and orientalization were played out at home" as a form of internal colonialism (1993, 77). He also suggests that "[t]rying to conceptualize in larger terms the meanings and functions of German orientalism invites us to think differently, or at least more expansively, about orientalism in general. It directs our attention momentarily away from the periphery to the national political culture and the relationship of knowledge and power at the core—directs us, potentially, towards forms of internal colonialism, and certainly towards the domestic politics of scholarship" (82). Pollock's treatment of a distinct German Orientalism focuses on how knowledge and power generate and sustain power for German national culture, not for Anglo–French imperialism. Similarly, most Irish Orientalist authors, although often complicit in the creation of the discourse of European imperial domination, usually had a different agenda than imperial Orientalists in Britain and France. The goal was less often about imperial domination than about an escape from it.

Perhaps beginning with Edmund Burke's speech "On the Impeachment of Warren Hastings" in 1788, Irish writers wrote specific political critiques of the Orient and the imperial figures governing the Asian and West Asian cultures. Other more literary Oriental representations allowed Irish writers a discursive realm in which to explore colonialism, nationalism, and sectarianism. Such representations, though affiliated with European Orientalism, can be distinguished by their Irish intonations. Through their participation in imperialism, moreover, many Irish works challenged its internal dynamics, developing issues of Irish imperial complicity and Irish anticolonial resistance within representations of the Orient. In the nineteenth century, many writers clearly attempted to deflect, resist, or obviate imperial narratives by pairing Irish anticolonial narratives with popular representations of the Orient. Other writers had no such anti-imperial agendas but still revealed an ambivalence about Irish culture's place in Europe. Therefore, any study of Oriental representations in Irish letters needs to distinguish complicit repetitions of imperial representations of Asia and West Asia (as the "Orient") from strategic, anticolonial, or cross-colonial redirections of Orientalism. These conflicting strategies of representation constitute the strange, ambivalent tandem within the discourse of Irish Orientalism and at the heart of the twentieth century's Celtic Revival.

In *Orientalism,* Edward Said traces the development of the Orient as a European and American construct. Said's argument focuses on Anglo–French Orientalism and its nexus of "historical specificity, knowledge, and power" (to borrow from Lata Mani and Ruth Frankenberg's critique of *Orientalism,* 1985, 180). As noted, this nexus of Orientalism had much purchase in Ireland, as did many Anglo–French narratives, but it cannot account for the place of Orientalism in Irish culture. In theorizing Irish Orientalism, therefore, critiques of dominant Anglo-French Orientalisms are instructive but not always applicable. Other critics have also amended and critiqued Said's argument. One of the best overviews of Said's work in this field may be "The Challenge of *Orientalism*," by Mani and Frankenberg (1985), as well as Said's own "Orientalism Reconsidered" (1985), and his afterword in the 1995 edition of *Orientalism*. These overviews further, rather than challenge, the main conclusions of his work. In contrast to these developments and the many bland and specious critiques that have appeared in various journals over the past twenty-five years (for example, Windschuttle 1999), the most significant critiques of Said's work are by Aijaz Ahmad (1992), Dennis Porter (1983), and Carol A. Breckenridge and Peter van der Veer (1993). They make insightful and valid critiques of Said's use of Foucauldian terminology and concepts, attacking his sense of a "real Orient." But, as Bill Ashcroft and Pal Ahluwalia's explication (1999) of Said's work notes, Said's study is primarily a humanistic critique of the discipline of (Anglo-French) Orientalism and not actually a Foucauldian one that maps an all-encompassing discourse. Ashcroft and Ahluwalia convincingly argue that Said alters Foucault's theoretical conception of "discourse" to include the possibility for agency, claiming that a discourse can be altered through critique. Said argues that he borrowed from Foucault to construct his theoretical framework but that he does not subscribe to all of Foucault's conclusions. He asserts that a Foucauldian sense of discourse would not allow that a cultural force could alter a political reality articulated by the discourse; such a force would always already be part of the discourse and thus its course determined. Nor could the discourse be altered by a force outside of it, because to critique a discourse is to enter it.

Edward Said argues for the existence of a "real Orient" beyond the discourse of Orientalism—both outside it and within it—and thus a position with agency; evidence for this claim is in the full title of his 1978 study: *Orientalism: Western Conceptions of the Orient*—the Orient is a place that exists independent of Western conceptions. Orientalism, in other words, constructs an Orient, but a "real [if effaced] Orient" also exists outside the discourse, although Said never clearly defined it, perhaps because any representation of the "real Orient" would be reductive. Asian cultures presently labor under the long history of European constructions of the Orient; indeed, they have now been heavily shaped by such constructions. Nevertheless, numerous possibilities of altering the apparently totalizing discourse (especially by lessening its prevalence) have been posed by postcolonial writers and thinkers, Irish writers included, as this study notes. Ashcroft and Ahluwalia argue, in short, that we should not use Foucauldian criteria to critique Said's work; instead, we should use Said's own concept of "worldliness"—as in the ethical and efficacious cosmopolitanism of a critic—to understand his project.[3]

Because Irish Orientalism often directly claims allegiance to the narratives of both the colonizer and the colonized, the syncretistic narratives of writers such as James Cousins are often more than the expressions of an anticolonial perspective. Robert Young makes a pertinent point regarding the apparent impossibility of resisting Orientalism from within. "If it is necessary, as Said demonstrates, to be inside such structures in order to make any argument at all, it is also he argues, vital to be outside them in order to subvert them. But what kind of knowledge would this be?" (1989, 128). Perhaps a question for this study could be phrased: "What strategy of knowledge use would this be?" In a sense, the "both/and" strategy (to appropriate from Richard Kearney) of Irish Orientalism and its use of Orientalist knowledge in anti-British and anticolonial narratives offers an illustration of agency within and outside of the discourse of Orientalism. Writing from within a position of European imperial privilege, Irish Orientalism provides agency for Irish cultural decolonization and, at times, enables cultural decolonization in Asian and West Asian colonies.

Despite discrepancies between Irish and Indian proximity[4] to the center of Empire, the anticolonial strategies of both Irish and Indian cultural nationalism resemble one another. Both perspectives or strategies confront the "cultural caesura" and the "spatial-time of cultural difference" between the colonizer and the colonized (Bhabha 1990, 251). And both often attempt to seize the "value-coding" (to borrow from Spivak 1990 and 1999) of Empire and, with such cachet, promote colonized cultures. An attempt to theorize Irish representations of the Orient must recognize the liminal place of Irish culture in the British Empire, that is, with access to narratives of both the colonized and the colonizer.

Celtic-Oriental comparisons allowed Irish writers to rhetorically assert both their proximity to the metropole, or center of Empire, and their proximity to the periphery, depending on the context, audience, and purpose of their argument or representation. Cultural nationalists used this semiotic connection to assert an ancient Oriental past for the Irish and to differentiate Irish culture from English culture, just as unionists often used the connection to denigrate the Gaelic Irish and promote Anglicized culture. Although using tropes of the Orient did not require any immediate understanding of the actualities of colonial life in England's distant colonies, Celtic-Oriental connections often propelled Irish cultural nationalists beyond Orientalism toward an international critique of European colonialism. And occasionally, the connection coincided with a mutual and surprisingly personal (if not entirely factual or equitable) cross-colony identification between nationalists in both Ireland and non-European colonies, particularly India.

By "cross-colony identification" I mean a strategy for decolonization that obviates the imperial binary that has divided many ways over the centuries: East and West; civilization and barbarity; Christian and heathen; enlightened and savage; white and nonwhite, European and non-European; within the Pale and beyond the

Pale. At the edge of Empire, circumferential ties (real or imagined) can exist without the mediation of the imperial center—for example, when travelers from Ireland or India establish relations without the official mediation of the East India Company (EIC) or the British Raj.[5] Such connections may also develop when colonized individuals recognize an experience or representation in a distant colony as familiar, which may in fact have come to their attention through imperial comparisons. Although many cases of Irish cross-colony ties existed, Irish interactions with Asians and West Asians, which were mostly through the British Empire, were rarely intersubjective,[6] which is to say, it was rarely a relationship in which equals recognize equals, or, to borrow from Hegel, a relationship in which individuals recognize self-consciousness in the other.[7] Such intersubjectivity primarily came about through nationalist, anticolonialist, and Theosophical exchanges. Irish-Asian cross-colony identification was certainly a response to colonization, and, like all efforts at decolonization, successful or not (nationalism, abrogation, appropriation, nativism, collaboration, liberal and radical decolonization, adulteration, allegory, hybridity, strategic essentialism, and so on),[8] it attempted to alter colonial pathologies of power. Nevertheless, Ireland's liminal place in Empire at times hampered the identification, as did England's cultural influence in Ireland (especially on issues such as race and governance); exotic Orientalist impressions also distanced its audience from actual Asian cultures, and the pervasive doctrinal sphere of Orientalist knowledge in Europe—what Said has termed "latent Orientalism" (1995, 206)—limited understandings of Asian and West Asian cultures.[9] Despite such inhibitors, many cases of cross-colony identification thrived, and these distinguish the Irish discourse from the Anglo-French.

Through writers such as Richard Madden, who critiqued the excesses and inhumanities of European colonialism around the globe in the 1840s, cross-colony connections grew as anticolonial movements became international. We see this impulse in the first issues of the *Nation* in the early 1840s, which are filled with analyses of colonial situations in Asia. Before Irish independence, Irish cosmopolitan figures such as Frederick Ryan and Roger Casement wrote against imperialism and Orientalism. An early Revivalist, Ryan worked for an Egyptian nationalist paper before returning to Ireland to promote anticolonialism and trade unionism until his untimely death in 1911; significantly, he explicitly linked colonialism with the Western constructions of the Orient. Casement, while working as an imperial administrator in the Congo, began to promote human rights and nationalist struggles in Europe's colonies. He eventually vigorously promoted reforms in Africa, South America, and Ireland and later was executed by the English government, in part, for his preparatory role in Ireland's Easter Rising of 1916. Likewise, another prominent Irish figure who wrote about colonialism in the Orient, James Connolly, was also executed by the British in 1916. Connolly had learned about the operations of the

British imperial military firsthand before working as a labor agitator and Irish nationalist. These and other critics of imperialism link the cause of Irish nationalism with nationalist struggles in other colonies in their representations of the Orient.

In 1944, a Trinity Orientalist, Menahem Mansoor, coined the term *Irish Orientalism* in his significant study, *The Story of Irish Orientalism*, which gives a history of academic Orientalists in Ireland.[10] As someone who wrote about Irish scholarship on the East, Mansoor points out in the introductory section of his study that in English and Irish letters, "enough has been said to show that . . . an affinity with the East had long been part of the Irish temperament" (13). Indeed, so much literature has been written on or within the subject of an Irish "affinity" with the East that we can discern a tradition of narratives of Irish-Oriental affinities in Irish cultures throughout the eighteenth, nineteenth, and twentieth centuries. Historically, Irish Orientalism offered imaginative writers a discursive clutch to disengage from the standard power relations of English-Irish relations. They could then imaginatively reengage the colonial discourse through allegorical or other devices, readdressing Irish tensions from a suspended vantage that did not promote an "either/or" binary of center and periphery. Such works of Irish Orientalism engaged the colonial discourse from a perspective that could operate with an inclusive "both/and" perspective, that is, both the center and the periphery—rhetorically taking advantage of both the Orientalist perspective of the colonizer and the nationalist convictions of the colonized. Irish Orientalism implicated colonialist enterprises on both a macro- and a microlevel: macro because Orientalism and Celticism as knowledge bases were always already implicated in the power dynamics of British colonialism in the Orient and Ireland, and micro because Irish Orientalism often took a specific colonial moment or event (such as a Persian ambassador visiting England and Ireland) as its immediate subject matter. Edward Said's terms *latent* and *manifest* Orientalism describe a similar base-and-superstructure relationship within Orientalism, but these definitions do not allow for a rhetorical manipulation of established Orientalism to create an ironic critique of imperialism. On the microlevel, Irish cultural nationalists could create the voice of an Oriental speaking back to the metropole about issues relevant to Ireland. Although this voice was often riddled with Orientalist notions, it often imagined a new power dynamic for the colonized and colonizer and promoted an independent national culture.

We might best understand the discourse of Irish Orientalism as strategic in its deployment, if often complicit with the overall discourse of imperialism. Nevertheless, Irish writers who often recognized the transparency of Orientalism wrote to subvert impressions of the colonized Orient. This strategic complicity has often made their representations seem anomalous to critics. Many Irish writers turned to the Orient to project images of sameness onto the Orient as a mode of decolonization. The power to represent a colonized people is related to the power of self-representation, both of which run the danger of merely reproducing the power structure within which they operate. But access to representation is crucial in a colonial relationship, as Joep Leerssen, echoing Marx,[11] notes in his essay "Irish Studies and *Orientalism:* Ireland and the Orient": "In a colonial relationship, there are those who represent, and those who are represented; the former wield discourse, the latter do not" (1998, 173). Irish writers who wrote about an essentialized Orient, in a sense, both represented the East and represented themselves. Like similar representations of the "real Irish," this sort of strategic essentialism (to borrow from Gayatri Spivak)[12] loosens the fastened binary relations of colonizer and colonized.

In occupying the ambiguous position between the "First World" and the "Third," these writers reveal, unwittingly or not, the machinations of imperialism. In such a "both/and" space, the hegemony of Empire becomes more discernible for the simple reason that it is observed from multiple vantages. As Leerssen has astutely written:

> The ambiguous case of Ireland, both part of Europe and part of a denigrated colonial periphery, hugely complicates this straightforward binariness. Ireland is subject to hegemonistic representation, but also has access to it. English exoticism did not silence the Irish voice as it silenced the native voices from the colonies; conversely, when Ireland uses the language of exoticism, it does so in less ethnocentrist ways than in England. With Irish authors, it is not just a matter of watching or being watched, seeing or being seen: Ireland is in the Twilight between First and Third World, between the ones in the dark and the ones in the light, Ireland watches how it is watched by England; Ireland watches itself watching the Orient. (173)

Many Irish cultural nationalists and academic Irish Orientalists increasingly became fascinated with the construct of the Orient. In doing so, Irish Orientalists, especially those "Celticist Orientalists" of the Revival, gained insights about cultural representation and their own (constructed) Celtic identity. This is akin to observing oneself in folded tripartite mirrors, wherein one watches oneself observe oneself from a vantage not limited by the binariness of direct reflection. Such fresh vantages are crucial for decolonization, and, therefore, the strategies for producing it are valued and are, unfortunately, reified at times. This tripartite vantage helped Irish writers renegotiate their position in the British Empire. By witnessing how they saw themselves (and how the English operated elsewhere), they could imaginatively break from the colonial binary of colonizer and colonized, center and periphery.

Throughout the nineteenth century, missionaries, soldiers, sailors, and Orientalists from Ireland (such as Lafcadio Hearn and Stanley Lane-Poole) made an increasing number of contacts with West Asian and Asian cultures (many even "went native"). These Irish in the Orient, like the Irish authors of pseudo-Oriental letter collections, could easily occupy the role of both colonizer and native nationalist. For instance, James Cousins left Ireland as a youth but carried visions of his homeland with him throughout his life and occupied a nebulous position as an Irish-Indian cultural nationalist. Although stereotypes speckle the texts of these writers, they do not observe the strict code of most Euro-American Orientalists—that an "irreducible distance" exists between the white man and the Oriental (Said 1995, 228). Many Irish writers also explicitly compared the negative effects of colonial projects in Ireland and in Asia and West Asia. In a 1911 issue of the *Irish Review*, Frederick Ryan intelligently explores the "Persian Struggle" against foreign capital and concludes: "How entirely intelligible, one had almost written, how Irish, it all is" (286). J. Chartres Molony's comparison of India and Ireland in *The Riddle of the Irish* discusses this cross-colony recognition caused by imperialism: "Diwan Bahadur N. Subramaniam, once a well-known figure in South Indian life, remarked to me that Indian and Irishman should understand each other. 'Each,' he said, 'is one of a conquered race, and the conqueror is the same for both' " (1927, 158). This identification differs dramatically from the perspective of T. E. Lawrence or other British Orientalists, in which Occidentals and Orientals could never fully understand one another because the white man was always the observer, the Oriental always the subject.

Represented as being both of Europe and not of Europe, colonizer and colonized, also made the Irish a group with which other colonized groups could identify. Significantly, Menahem Mansoor, author of *The Story of Irish Orientalism,* was "not himself Irish" but was a "native speaker of Arabic," to quote the Trinity Orientalist R. M. Gwynn in the foreword to the study (1944, 5). I note this primarily in order to make clear that Mansoor described "the Irish" as a group exclusive of himself—he watched the Irish watching the Orient. Others in Asian and West Asian colonies also watched Ireland watching, particularly Bengali nationalists and cultural nationalists who read and reread Dan Breen's *My Fight for Irish Freedom* (1924) as a "Revolutionaries' Manual" (Silvestri 2000, 472). In *Gora* (1917), a novel of the Bengali thinker, nationalist, and writer Rabindranath Tagore, the titular character discovers that he himself is not an Indian Brahmin, but actually an Irish orphan. Unlike Kipling's Kim, another Irish orphan in India, he is initially distraught when he discovers that he is European and realizes, by extension, that he is racially complicit with the system of colonial oppression. These two characters, neither created by an Irish writer, could represent the two poles of Irish Orientalism—as imagined by an imperialist and by an anticolonialist.

As a discourse, Irish Orientalism both extended and deflected the broader and more well-known Orientalisms of Europe. The discourse includes many strategic locations of writers and intellectuals, a number of whom pursued knowledge of the East and created images of the Orient for purposes other than, or in addition to, the justification of European colonialism in Asia and West Asia. For nineteenth-century Anglocentric intellectuals, the Celtic-Oriental link could confirm the barbarity of the Irish; for Irish cultural nationalists, the Orient was a strategy to help obviate Empire. Historically, then, Irish Orientalism was both a way to participate in imperialism and a way to deny it. It offered a path of resistance (disguised or obvious) as well as, at times, a path of collusion. But Irish Orientalism as a discourse was not merely an extension of Anglo-French Orientalism, nor did it merely repeat and internalize British colonial stereotypes of the Oriental. During the Celtic Revival, when the Oriental shared the limelight with the Celtic, Irish Orientalism writers transformed colonial stereotypes and developed a millennium-old Irish narrative for asserting an independent and ancient culture in Ireland.

Part One ☙ Continuity and Development

THE IRISH TRADITION of Oriental motifs stretches back from characters such as Fu Manchu in the mid-twentieth century through the Theosophists of the Celtic Revival and the Romantic works of Aubrey de Vere, James Clarence Mangan, Lady Morgan, and Thomas Moore in the nineteenth century to the works of Frances Sheridan, Oliver Goldsmith, and Edmund Pery in the eighteenth. The discourse continues backward through conjectures in the seventeenth and sixteenth centuries about Irish history and affinities with the Orient to medieval European origin legends and classical Greek and Roman representations of barbaric cultures at the edges of the habitable world. On one hand, the interest stemmed from English, continental, and Greco-Roman ideas about the nature of civilization, culture, and Empire. On the other hand, textual links between Celtic and Oriental cultures existed independently in native Irish and Gaelic culture as far back as Irish writing extends. Throughout the course of Irish cultural history, this unacknowledged discourse of Orientalism has served as an important imaginative and allegorical realm for Irish writers and intellectuals.

The strategy for the first half of this study has been inspired and greatly informed by the techniques and scholarship of Irish studies scholar Joep Leerssen. His works trace images of Irishness and cultural and national identity throughout English and Irish texts from the Greeks to the nineteenth century. His foundational studies *Mere Irish and Fíor-Ghael* (1986; reprinted 1996) and *Remembrance and Imagination* (1996; reprinted 1997) laid the groundwork for literary and cultural historians and scholars. For this study, his tracing of cultural tropes through Irish and British texts has been particularly illustrative; even his following a seemingly insignificant trope, the representation of whiskey, *uisce beatha,* can reveal much:

> How important the impact of [sixteenth-century] descriptions of Ireland was for later attitudes and writings regarding the country and its inhabitants may be gathered from a small detail which can be traced, like a radioactive isotope, from text to text: it is Campion's short description of the Irish eau-de-vie, whiskey (then called "usquebaugh," fr. Gaelic *uisce beatha,* "aqua vitae"), which the Jesuit thought,

1

"dryeth more, and inflameth lesse" than the distilled cordials known in England.
. . . This particular little characterization became a formula that can be found in vir-
tually all English descriptions of Ireland up to (and even into) the eighteenth century. And this fact may in turn serve as an indication that such descriptions were
often as indebted to earlier descriptions as they were to the individual author's personal observations; or, in other words: that such descriptions may be regarded as belonging to a textual tradition with its own intertextual cohesion. (1996b, 40)

Similarly, the semiotic connection between Irish culture and Asian and West Asian
cultures has endured and distinguished Irish culture during the centuries of its perpetual reinvention. This connection has persevered as a comparison throughout
Irish history in both Irish and British texts; emerging in early texts as an ancestral
connection between Scythians and *Scotti,* the comparison developed through a
number of other permutations from legendary to racial and political: the Phoenician and the Magogian and the Gael; the Oriental and the Celt; the Chinese and the
Erse; the Swarajist and the Fenian; the Bengali and the Irish. Tracing this "radioac-
tive isotope" reveals the texts in which it appears, the course of a peripheral discourse, and the developments in Irish cultural identity throughout the centuries.

This first section of the book examines the construction and influence of early
Irish-Oriental origin stories on pseudohistories, antiquarianism, and literary Orientalism, following the abandonment of antiquarian suppositions about the Irish
origins in the East and the concomitant development of a literary mode employing
the Orient as an allegory of Irish issues. Strangely, profound historical upheavals and
sea-change disruptions in culture (poverty, famine, invasion, colonization, civil unrest, and focused oppression on religious, linguistic, and political identities) have affected this peripheral discourse in its changes in subject matter, but rarely did its
dominant modes and characteristics shift. Accumulation, continuity, and cohesion
rather than invention define the progress of most traditions and cultural discourses;
this one is no exception. Stories of Ireland's ancient past and legendary Asian origins
occupied a prominent place in Irish culture from the ninth through the eighteenth
centuries, offering political commentary since its first recording. As the debate surrounding the origins of Ireland's round towers pushed this dominant narrative into
less empirical realms, particularly poetry and politics, the political imperative of the
narrative (legitimating an Irish nation) had become bare and clearly evident to cultural nationalist writers such as Thomas Moore, who then helped develop Orientalist tropes to address imperial issues throughout the nineteenth century.

The semiotic connection between the Celt and the Oriental came to signify
the dynamics of Ireland within the British Empire—perhaps best understood in
gradations of resistance and complicity. The origin legends became foundational to
Irish cultural nationalism in the eighteenth century and developed into a literary

and mystical connection during the Celtic Revival in the early twentieth. Alongside this development, other strands of the connection appeared in texts within many developing fields of study—archaeology, linguistics, anthropology, historiography, Orientalism, and Celticism—as well as in literary texts that used the connection variously to exoticize, valorize, or denigrate. Last, both intra-imperial and cross-colonial analogies emerged as inheritors of this semiotic connection; both imperial sympathizers and nationalist writers rediscovered and manipulated the cumulative, connotative values attributed to both Ireland and European colonies in Asia and West Asia in order to create models for governing policies and, conversely, for organizing decolonizing movements around the globe.

The first major development after the creation of the origin legends, the shift from the origin legends to antiquarian suppositions about ancient Irish history, occurred after major English incursions in Ireland in the late seventeenth century. Growing justifications for Irish national autonomy fueled these arguments. Irish antiquarianism fell from prominence in part because of the lack of source criticism[1] in its circles during the eighteenth century, and the disciplines of archaeology, philology, and the new historiography eclipsed its place. Perhaps because of the establishment of universities throughout western Europe and Britain from the fifteenth through the seventeenth centuries, as the Gaelic order lost significant authority in Ireland, the learned Irish fell out of step with other European trends. Arguments asserting an ancient consanguinity between the Irish and various Asian and West Asian cultures collapsed in the early nineteenth century, but the tropes of the Oriental and the Celt had been established already, and comparisons were increasingly made in a variety of popular, literary, and political texts through the Celtic Revival.

As mentioned in the introduction, this study extends Charles Saunders Peirce's doctrine of synechism to the study of cultural signs, emphasizing the continuity and progression of this comparison throughout the waxing days of the British Empire. The progression is both dialectical and cumulative. This first transition from origin legends to antiquarianism will be explored in chapters 1 and 2. Chapter 3 explores racial and Romantic comparisons that developed alongside burgeoning theories of race in the early nineteenth century, which, as many studies have shown, had direct imperial inspirations and colonial consequences. Just as the Celt's origins in West Asia lack material and linguistic proof, the Celtic history of Ireland has little archaeological proof. Racial comparisons emerged as philologists gradually disproved Celtic-Oriental origin theories in the mid-nineteenth century. Making such comparisons without any reference to empirical evidence became more popular, and many writers began to embrace comparisons along Romanticist lines: through exoticism to idealism and decadence. Chapter 4 focuses on Irish complicity with imperialism and the involvement of Irish Orientalism in that enterprise, which unlike most Anglo-French Orientalism often asserted East-West affinities. Later, in part 2, chapter 5, political comparisons between Ireland and Asian colonies are again discussed, concurrent with the rise of Irish cultural nationalism. Even before they were a leitmotif of Irish culture (alternately mythical, legendary, historical, linguistic, racial, romantic, and political), Celtic-Oriental comparisons existed in narratives of an ancient and remote land.

1 Origin Legends and Pseudohistories

They seized the ships of (Pharaoh), / They deserted their country; /
And in the night time over the track / Of the Red Sea they passed
// They passed by India, by Asia. / The way they knew; / To
Scithia, with noble might, / Their own country.
　—Maelmura of Fathain (Mael Muru Othna's "Can a mBunadas na
nGaedel"), translated by James H. Todd

[T]heir going to battle without armor on their bodies or heads, but
trusting to the thicknes of their glibbs [that is, locks], the which
(they say) will sometimes beare off a good stroke, is meere Scythian.
　—Edmund Spenser, *A View of the Present State of Ireland*

FOR EIGHT CENTURIES—from the twelfth to the twentieth—Irish histories opened with passages about the ancient origins of the Irish in the East, particularly in Scythia on the Asian steppes.[1] This written link between Irish culture and Asian and West Asian cultures has its roots in ancient Greek and Roman depictions of borderlands: in Ireland, Asia, and Africa where outlanders with magical and barbaric traits lived. This link developed in Ireland amid continent-wide suppositions throughout the Middle Ages about an original human language, an Adamic tongue, that was believed to predate the confusion of languages—God's punishment for humanity's attempt to rival the divine by constructing the Tower of Babel in the Hebrew Bible or Tanakh.[2] Theologians and scholars understood the world's languages to be partial or corrupted versions of this original language, all except ancient Hebrew, whose speakers had not taken part in the building of the tower. Hebrew, therefore, had stood apart from the confusion of the tongues, and theologians thus assumed it remained the same as that undivided first tongue. (The Bible, mostly written in Hebrew, was later translated into Aramaic.) The early church fathers, from Origen to Augustine, working in Greek and Latin, did not consider the separation of languages much of a problem because, as they understood it, Greek

5

and Latin had inherited those portions of the original language that corresponded with reason, whereas the barbarians (those with no language)[3] had received humanity's baser linguistic elements and communicated in babbles and grunts.[4]

Later, in the fifth, sixth, and seventh centuries, when scholars had to confront the existence of the vulgate languages of Europe, elaborate discussions of Babel's tower proliferated; genealogical frameworks designed the searches for a perfect language across the continent, either backward to ancient Hebrew and the language of Adam or forward to a universal language of reason.[5] The monumental studies of Arno Borst and Daniel Droixhe examine the history of the study of language (including early etymology, philology, grammar, morphology, and comparative linguistics, as well as theological and philosophic concerns) in medieval Europe. Borst's eight-volume *Der Turmbau von Babel* (1957) carefully traces discussions of the origins of Indo-European languages and the various European arguments about the confusion of tongues throughout medieval times, whereas Droixhe's *La Linguistique et l'appel de l'histoire (1600–1800)* (1978) focuses on the rationalist developments in philology in the seventeenth and eighteenth centuries—and what led to them. As both of their studies reveal, pre-Enlightenment language scholars explored grammar, etymology, and morphology alongside theology and genealogy in searching out the origins of languages and peoples. When medieval and early modern language scholars discovered linguistic similarities among European languages, they treated them as indisputable evidence of Europe's ancestral Semitic origins and of their connections to Noah's son, Japheth, father of European and West Asian languages. They saw it as a unity that demonstrated the confusion of the tongues at Babel and labeled the related languages "Japhetic." Language study and etymology seemed to offer these scholars the keys to understanding the character and history of these peoples and, more important, the origins of humanity and its ragged progression toward a perfect union with God.

In early language studies, two trends emerged: on one hand, scholars and theologians grouped languages together into families and histories, all tethered to biblical events; on the other hand, they also focused on the virtues of particular languages (usually their own) linking them to Hebrew, Latin, or Greek. Early modern scholars tracked similarities to supposed original tongues of the Gauls and the Germans, which they termed *Celtic, Scythian,* or *Celto-Scythian.* In so doing, they encouraged legends of Scythian and Celtic migrations—carrying connotations of ancient barbarisms—that would find enduring manifestations in Irish origin legends. They surmised that humanity's perfect language could be pieced together through studying its supposed constituent fragments. Across Europe, vigorous debates around which language most resembled this perfect language abounded, and efforts to demonstrate linguistic venerability and virtues were pervasive.

Ireland's own particular version of linguistic history became central to its origin legends and, as with many nations, contributed to its later cultural and national development. Many contemporary historians have discussed this "nationalizing" effect of medieval histories and origin legends. Medievalist scholar Maurice Olender has cogently argued in his essay "From the Language of Adam to the Pluralism of Babel" that "the impassioned quest for origins, the desire to know and speak the language of Paradise, gave rise to various forms of nationalism [French, Flemish, German, Spanish, English, and so on]—over the centuries—in Europe" (1997, 52). Walter Goffart similarly asserted in *The Narrators of Barbarian History (A.D. 550–800)* that this phenomenon was not a mere carryover from classical histories: "The advent of the Germanic barbarians, a weighty event in our estimation, is deemed to be directly mirrored in the history of historiography and to result in the emergence of 'national' history, a type of writing about the past not practiced until then" (1988, 4). Emerging after the initial "barbarian histories" in the early medieval period, Ireland's origin legends served a similar function, helping develop a collective cultural identity that later motivated national aspirations.

Irish monastic schools, from at least the seventh century, wove biblical narratives from sources such as Isidore of Seville (d. 636) into the beginnings of their historical genealogies, which were assiduously kept throughout the medieval period. The principal genealogical manuscripts for Ireland's pre-1200 material record the names and families of roughly twenty thousand actual people, their family connections, dynasties, and communities—a record more detailed than any other European society at the time.[6] Each genealogy was rooted in ancient biblical accounts, linking Irish families to Japheth and Noah's. Within this medieval paradigm, Irish origin legends became recorded as the first ancient histories (or pseudohistories) of Ireland. The legends appear most fully in an Irish-language work that has come to be known as *Lebor Gabála Érenn,* translated literally as "The Book of the Taking of Ireland" but often called "The Book of Invasions" or "The Book of Settlements." Although the versions of this text vary, all share similar narratives, having been synthesized from the same corpus: classical texts, the Hebrew Bible, early medieval works, genealogies, and native Irish legends—the last being the most difficult to trace. Like many histories written across medieval Europe, these synthetic Irish histories[7] placed their ancestors on the dais of antiquity beside Egypt, Israel, Greece, and Rome.

But even more than this fact, one of the early legends, first recorded in an eighth-century Irish grammar text, *Auracepit na n-Éces* (The scholar's primer), concerns how a Scythian ancestor of the Irish, Féinius Farsaid or Fenius Fein, oversaw seventy-two scholars in the construction of a single language from the best of the linguistic fragments at Babel; this reconstructed language became Irish.[8] No other language of Europe claimed to fully embody the original language from ancient times, although Hebrew, Egyptian, and Chinese were all often posited as original languages. This Irish legend developed more fully in the later redactions of the origin legends, where the legendary Scythian character Nel, son of Féinius, traveled to Egypt at the invitation of the pharaoh, who had heard of his linguistic abilities and knowledge of the Tower of Nimrod at Babel; from there Nel's progeny eventually made their way to Ireland's shores. For a variety of reasons, these Irish origin legends outlived their original context and retained their cultural currency longer than most other European origin legends and linguistic accounts, through the Renaissance into the eighteenth century, leaving a lasting impression on Irish national culture and seeding the discourse of Irish Orientalism.

Outside of Irish texts, a connection between Ireland and Asia was also established in ancient Greco-Roman texts (amid connections between Ireland and all borderlands) and repeatedly reinforced over the centuries in English texts. As references to Scythian and Japhetic origins subsided in other European histories during the Reformation and the Renaissance, many British works on Ireland increasingly focused on Ireland's Scythian roots as a way to confirm the "barbaric" natures of the Irish. Classical geographies, topographies, chorographies,[9] and histories, in addition to medieval commentaries, annals, and etymologies, all gave evidence that confirmed their arguments. This process of barbarization, in turn, further spurred Irish pseudohistorians to valorize both the legends and their heritage, and they sifted ancient texts for support. Further encouraged by protolinguistic speculations about Scytho-Celtic languages in the seventeenth century, Irish pseudohistorians confidently explicated Ireland's venerable genealogy, still based on biblical figures. In the eighteenth century, the semiotic connection deepened in philological, archaeological, pseudohistorical, and antiquarian studies, supported by broad, popular enthusiasms, literary trends, and generalized ideas about Celtic and Oriental cultures. In the first half of the nineteenth century, amid paradigmatic European developments in philology, enthusiastic (if often reckless) theories about the origins of the Irish began to be discredited—and not only in British circles but also in Irish ones. Yet even as speculations based on medieval origin legends became untenable, Irish satirists, Romantics, popular cultural nationalist historians, and pseudo-Oriental letter writers increasingly capitalized on the centuries-old semiotic pairing of Ireland and Asia, which through Orientalism and Celticism had become associated with cultural nationalism in the literary and popular imagination. Even as late as the twentieth century, and particularly during the Celtic Revival, Celticists, historians, and literary writers soberly referenced these enduring origin legends, often in cross-colony sympathies, offering them as possible clues to understanding the elusive and resolutely non-Victorian nature of the Gaelic Celt, the Western cousin of the distant, inscrutable Asian Oriental. The roots of these origin legends are as extensive as their influences.

Early Origin Legends

Before the eighteenth century, the Irish were rarely seen as Celts. Yet, by the dawn of the nineteenth century, the Gaelic Irish had come to signify the most authentic remains of a Celtic culture in existence, particularly in Celticist novels such as *The Wild Irish Girl* (1806), by Sydney Owenson (Lady Morgan). And even though it was widely understood in the eighteenth century that Ireland shared a linguistic heritage with Scotland, Wales, Cornwall, the Isle of Man, and Brittany, cultural nationalists in Ireland rarely recognized pan-Celticist cultural or political connections.[10] Nineteenth-century writers claimed Celticity as proof for Ireland's antiquity, but for many Anglocentric authors, including the Reverend Edward Ledwich writing around the turn of the century, a Celtic heritage confirmed Ireland's ancient Scythian barbarity.[11] European scholars long understood the ancient Celts to be Scythian, descended from Magog, son of Japheth, and related to the Gauls, descendants of another of his sons, Gomer.[12] Only gradually did Ireland and other contemporary Celtic cultures become seen as such.

In describing the ancestry of northwestern Europeans, the terms *Scythian* and *Celtic* cast a much wider net more than the specific terms *Gaelic, Hibernian,* and *Milesian,* which generally refer to people in Ireland and their connections with Scotland and Spain. But such identifications accumulated over time, so much so that when Morgan writes of the Gaelic Irish, she interchangeably labels people, dress, custom, and landscapes as Hibernian, Scythian, Milesian, Celtic, and Gaelic (and notes their supposed Phoenician and Egyptian heritages). Daniel Droixhe discusses the early connections between the terms *Scythian* and *Celtic:* "Germans were often called Celts or Scythians by classical authors. . . . Strabo was most responsible for the concept of an ethnic unity with the Germans: the family was labelled Celto-Scythian. The inflationist use of the term Celtic corresponded to a proportional non-recognition of its specificity" (1996, 23). At least since Strabo, this non-recognition of distinctive cultures allowed blanket understandings of Celts to thrive; nevertheless, eventually it became more specific and claimed political, linguistic, and ethnic identities in Great Britain, France, and, particularly, Ireland. A similar process seems to have been at work much earlier in the specification of Ireland as distinctively Scythian. Just as nineteenth-century Celticists discovered ancient continental Celtic attributes in Irish culture, fifteenth- and sixteenth-century pseudohistorians treated the Irish as the truest retainers of ancient Scythian traits. Although Irish culture was not alone in being given Scythian origins, its Scythian ties were more commonly used to both denigrate and distinguish it.

Except for the reference to Féinius Farsaid in Babel in a seventh-century grammar, the earliest existing Irish impressions[13] of what came to be regarded as the Orient occur in a ninth-century geographical and travel survey written by an Irish monk named Dicuil living in Frankish Gaul (under Charlemagne).[14] This, his only surviving work, *Liber de Mensura Orbis Terrae* (Book on the dimensions of the earth) (ca. 825) is based upon another work, a 435 C.E. survey originally commissioned by the Roman emperor Theodosius II. Dicuil's ninth-century text has an amazing sweep, providing details and measurements of Europe, Asia, and Africa, most of which were borrowed from Theodosius's survey and other texts. But a number of details appear to be from firsthand accounts by at least one peripatetic Irish monk.

As with nearly all ancient and medieval historians, Dicuil borrows liberally from established texts in addition to Theodosius, particularly from Pliny the Elder, Solinus, Isidore of Seville,[15] and Aethicus Ister. But *Liber de Mensura Orbis Terrae* also contains records of travels by Irish monks to Egypt and Iceland, and the Icelandic sections are among the first extensive impressions that we have of that land. Dicuil specifically records the travels of one monk, "brother Fidelis," whose name though common ("one to be trusted" in Latin) suggests he may have been Dicuil's own invention or possibly his pseudonym. Although much of Dicuil's survey unremarkably covers the territory laid out by previous historians and geographers, the original parts provide valuable descriptions. In the following passage, translated by J. J. Tierney, Dicuil describes the pyramids at Gîza from Fidelis's point of view:

> Although we read in no authority that a branch of the Nile flows into the Red Sea, yet brother Fidelis asserted this and related it, in my presence, to my teacher Suibne (to whom, under God, I owe any progress that I may have made). . . . [A]fter a long sail on the Nile, they saw, like mountains, and admired from a distance, the seven barns built by holy Joseph, according to the number of years of abundance, four in one place and three in another. . . . After this he carefully examined the three barns and again was filled with amazement that they were entirely made of stone from their very base to the summit. The barns were square at the base, but rounded at the top at the very apex they have, as it were, a slender point. . . . Next, embarking on their boats, they sailed along the Nile as far as the entrance to the Red Sea. From this harbour it is a small distance eastwards to the passage of Moses across the Red Sea. He who measured the side of the barn wished to go as far as the harbour where Moses with his people entered the sea, not only to enter the harbour, but in order to see in it the tracks of the chariots and the ruts of the Pharaoh's wheels; but the sailors would not oblige. (1967, 63)

Biblical stories established the baseline of both the text and the curiosity of the characters in it. Seeking the tracks of the chariots on the floor of the Red Sea neatly demonstrates how this Irish monk sought to ground biblical history in his contemporary world. But in this biblical reference, brother Fidelis also may have been referencing Irish origin legends.

In his and later texts, the ruts of the pharaoh's wheels as he chased Moses served as an important image for God's support for the righteous cause of the Israelites, but for Irish *filid* (historian poets) and their audiences, it also signified the moment when the Scythian Irish ancestors departed Egypt and wound up, eventually, in a land analogous to the Jewish "promised land": Ireland. Medieval Irish origin legends dated their ancestors' flight from Egypt from this shared moment of exile, catastrophe, and divine will. *Lebor Gabála,* the most famous written versions of these legends, appeared centuries after Dicuil's work. In the first part of the middle Irish origin legend, Gaedel Glass, son of Nel and Scota (the pharaoh's daughter), and his people flee Egypt. They had been the guests of the pharaoh because he admired Nel's knowledge of the world's diverse languages, learned from Féinius Farsaid and embodied in Irish. If these figures were silently complicit in the persecution of the Israelites, they clearly did not endorse the pharaoh's pursuit of them out of Egypt. Instead, they also hurriedly left after the violent miracle of the parting of the Red Sea and the pharaoh's drowning. They returned to Scythia (where Nel's brother Nenual had inherited the rule from his father, Féinius Fein), and over successive generations, they traveled, via Africa and Spain, to their own new prophesied home of Ireland.

A poem "Can a mBunadas na nGaedel," attributed to another ninth-century Irish writer, the poet Mael Muru Othna (d. 887), also references the drowning of the Egyptian pharaoh in the Red Sea, highlighting the same image as Dicuil. James H. Todd provides the following translation in his nineteenth-century edition of Gilla-Coemáin's (d. 1072) eleventh-century Irish version of Nennius's ninth-century *Historia Britonum* (1848), which records the story. Todd seems to have given the poem its name: "Duan Eireannach":

> Forann (Pharaoh) was drowned with all his multitude
> Of mighty chariots;
> The people of God reached their own country,
> The sea did not drown them.
>
> The children of Nel raised Foran's ire,
> So that they were sorrowful,
> Because they joined not in revenge
> Along with the champion [against Moses].
>
> But when Forann returned not
> From his onward journey [through the Red Sea]
> The people of Egypt were dreaded by the sons of Nel
> Lest they should enslave them.

> They seized the ships of Forann,
> They deserted their country;
> And in the night time over the track
> Of the Red Sea they passed
>
> They passed by India, by Asia.
> *The way* they knew;
> To Scithia, with noble might,
> Their own country.
>
> (233)

Although Dicuil did not retell the legends, he points to the resonant tracks on the floor of the Red Sea. In both voyages, the Irish sailors are depicted as passing over the pharoah's drowned army, imagistically floating above "actual" history. Here, in the first textual record of the Irish legend, Ireland's history is given its heroic origin by being embedded within the larger biblical discourse and Jewish exile story. The tracks on the ocean floor operate as a nod and a recognition of the broader Jewish narrative over which they pass crossways. The Irish story, existing in a discursive penumbra, gains authority within the setting and frame of the established history.

Dicuil also relays other fabulous stories, incorporating mythological figures and magical tropes from Roman, Greek, and medieval geographies and travel narratives: unicorns, the phoenix, the deadly and entrancing power of hyenas, as well as the troglodytes of Ethiopia. He generally accepts the validity of these texts, no matter how fantastic. Only occasionally does he doubt the veracity of the established sources, as when he treats Fidelis's oral account of India as more valid than Isidore's (85). Such doubt suggests a familiarity with texts such as Orosisus's fifth-century account (*Historiae Contra Paganos)* of Alexander in India—an Irish-language version of which (*Scela Alaxandair)* was written not long after Dicuil's text, probably in the tenth century.[16] But Dicuil's sympathy with Fidelis's account of India may have also extended beyond written sources. The experiences of "Fidelis" ("one to be trusted") may have been shorthand for Dicuil's own experience traveling to Egypt and India, or perhaps signified other native Irish accounts, written or oral, that are now lost.

Ireland, Thule, Scythia,[17] India (particularly Sri Lanka), and Libya (metonymic for Africa) border the habitable world as Dicuil maps it. However dissimilar in actuality, these "border cultures" became identified with one another because of their displacement from the center of the map and the great empires of the Mediterranean. Thule, generally understood today to refer to Iceland, was inhabited by Irish anchorites in the ninth century and, not long after, became a settlement of the

North Atlantic Viking world. This frame of the known world certainly did not originate with Dicuil; it was developed nine centuries earlier in the texts of Greek and Roman historians and geographers. This understanding of the world had little immediate impact on cultures in central Africa, eastern Asia, northern Europe, or any part of the Americas, but it significantly impacted Ireland's geohistorical identity. As Irish monks and scribes looked to these works, they found that their homeland was considered to be a borderland by all authorities. Even when Ireland emerged as a center of learning in the early medieval period, and Irish monks traveled throughout Europe helping establish monasteries and early universities,[18] Ireland's remoteness had been accepted for centuries.

Borderlands

The earliest Greek and Roman writers sketched European cultures vaguely, tending to conflate them under the term *Keltoi,* or Celts, as numerous scholars have noted in the past twenty years.[19] How the various groups designated Keltoi actually saw themselves, and even if they ever self-identified as a people, has been a matter of recent scholarly speculation and debate. We can read how Greeks and Romans recorded some of their perceptions of these peoples and, also, how the preserved texts influenced medieval and early modern Europe as authoritative histories of the ancient world. Scholar Timothy Champion describes the early Greek sense of Europe in his essay "The Celt in Archaeology":

> [T]he Greek use of the term Celts signified in a very general spatial or geographical sense the non-Greek inhabitants of western Europe (in contrast to the Scythians to the north, the Indians to the east and the Ethiopians to the south) or, in a more specific military context, invaders from the west; it had no significance at all for the ethnic, linguistic, or cultural homogeneity of these people. Their impact on Greek consciousness was as non-Greek barbarians and as warriors, whether invaders or mercenaries. (1996, 63)

Although the ancient Greeks certainly distinguished the Scythians from the Celts, the contrast was more geographical than cultural—they were all barbarians. Perhaps because cultural *others* are always imagined together in opposition to the familiar cultural "constant" of the writer's own culture, border cultures often seem to share traits and, to varing degrees, resemble one another in their strangeness. Later northern European cultures, Ireland included, traced their Scytho-Celtic ancestries to both groups, and they adopted Greek (and Roman) impressions of ancient European barbarity as true accounts of their own ancient, preliterate culture.

When Greeks and Romans specifically mentioned Ireland in their texts, they placed it at the very edge of the great northern barbaric wilderness. Places such as Ireland, Scythia, India, and Ethiopia occupied the utmost edges of the habitable world, outside civilization, and its peoples exhibited fantastic customs. Representations of Ireland in the eleventh and twelfth centuries remained remarkably consonant with such impressions. Having existed only at the fringe of Roman influence and under intermittent Viking power, Ireland had remained decentralized longer than other western European cultures, and Greco-Roman impressions of barbarians may have seemed to better suit the Irish, but, certainly, they held purchase up to the Renaissance for historians representing Ireland. Moreover, holding on to its origin legends as true history, Ireland passed through no major break with the established Church as much of northern Europe did in the wake of Martin Luther in the fourteenth and fifteenth centuries. Along with their long allegiance to the medieval Church in France and Italy, Irish scholars did not question the Christian explanations of linguistic differentiation, nor the predominance of Hebrew as the original tongue by which the Irish language claimed its venerability.

To Rome before the fifth century, however, Ireland largely seemed a country without culture or history, a blank space at the edge of the map. Romans generally referred to the continental Celts and Gauls as Keltoi (borrowed from Greek) and Galli; people in the British Isles were regularly referred to as Brittani, or Britons, not as Celts; and Ireland was referred to as Ierne, Hibernia, or Hierni. The west coast of Europe seems to have first become known to the Greeks and Romans through Phoenician traders who brought tin to the Greeks. Details of culture in Ireland are scant, however, in surviving Greek and early Roman sources. Most all of the Phoenician knowledge of the European Celts unfortunately disappeared along with their texts in the razing of Carthage by Rome, and few Greek and Roman fragments of Phoenician texts survive. Ireland had become known as the "Sacred Isle" (perhaps through a mistranslation of a Greek word) but also as the homeland of cannibals. The few accounts of Celts (and fewer of the Irish) that exist in the work of early authors—Hecatateus of Miletus (ca. 540–475 B.C.E.), Pytheas (ca. 330–300 B.C.E.), Timaeus (ca. 350–260 B.C.E.), Polybius (ca. 198–120 B.C.E.), and Posidonius (ca. 135–45 B.C.E.)—have survived solely in fragmented form through borrowings and references of later writers. Although many archaeologists have argued that the ancient Celts of Greco-Roman description never actually inhabited Ireland, such Celtic representations clearly influenced how later British and Irish writers perceived Irish culture. Also, little information exists from the texts of early tin-trading Phoenicians, who had established colonies in a number of places on the west coast of Europe. Only one Phoenician text that mentions Ireland, *The Periplus of Himilco,* survives and only in adulterated form. Himilco, a sixth-century B.C.E. Carthaginian, sailed up the Atlantic coast of Europe and wrote an account of his travels, including a reference to the "Hierni" (either the people

inhabiting all of Ireland or, possibly, a tribe of Munster). Himilco eventually became a source for at least one Roman writer, Rufius Festus Avienus, who references it in his *Ora Maritime* (Kenny 1993, 121).[20] Unfortunately, all but the
adulterated version of Himilco and all but one version of Avienus have been lost for
at least five hundred years. The last version of Avienus was printed in Vienna in
1488 and contains 4,015 lines attributed to Himilco (but paraphrased by Avienus)
about Atlantic Europe and its islands.[21]

Fuller geographical accounts of the Celts, Ireland, and the habitable world,
based in part or all on the texts of these earlier writers, can be found in Diodorus
Siculus (ca. 60–20 B.C.E.), Strabo (ca. 63 B.C.E.–23 C.E.), Pliny the Elder (23–79
C.E.), Pomponius Mela (ca. 20–50 C.E.), Ptolemy (ca. 130–180 C.E.), and Caius
Julius Solinus (wrote ca. 240–270 C.E.), among others. Here, images of a savage
Irish culture appear amid extensive discussions of Britons, Celts, Gauls, Phoeni-
cians, and Celtiberians. Diodorus Siculus (wrote ca. 60–30 B.C.E.) in his *Historical
Library* describes the ancient Gauls and "Galatae" (or Galatians) as including Celts
and living near Scythia: "Those tribes that live inland from Massalia [Marseille], as
well as those around the Alps and on the eastern side of the Pyrenees are called Celts.
But those tribes in the northern area near the ocean, those near the Hercynian
mountain [probably today in the Czech Republic], and those beyond as far as
Scythia [present-day Ukraine and South Russia], are called Galatae. The Romans,
however, group all these tribes together as Galatae" (Koch and Carey 2000, 14;
brackets, except first, in original). He also references the inhabitants of "Iris" and
links them specifically with the Scythians (a group that endlessly fascinated the
Greeks) on the eastern edge of the Galatian and Celtic lands: "The most savage tribes
are those in the north and those which are near Scythia. Some say they eat human
flesh, just like the *Prettani* [Britons] inhabiting the land called *Iris*" (14; brackets in
original). Emphasizing the uncivilized elements of this culture, Diodorus Siculus
further describes how men of the Gauls "prefer unnatural intercourse with other
men" over "natural" relations with women.[22] Equating the "savage" peoples near
Scythia and the cannibalistic inhabitants of Ireland became a somewhat common
move for the ancients when describing Ireland. The supposed unnaturalness of the
Gauls (who had long been seen as closely related to the Irish)[23] and the reinforced
Irish-Scythian connection became fodder to later British historians of Ireland.

According to the work of another Greek, Strabo's *Geography*, Scythia occupied
the most northern portion of the world, above India and all of Asia. But the most
northeasterly piece of land was the island of "Ierne" (see fig. 2). Romans and
Greeks in the first century C.E. continued to place Ireland at the northwestern border of the world, pitted, like the other borders of the habitable world, against the
civilized center of the map where the Roman Empire thrived. Strabo, who notes
that Herodotus and other Greeks conflated all northern tribes as Scythian, extends

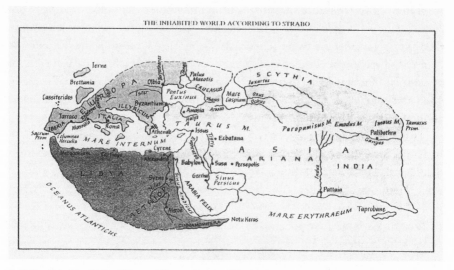

2. "The Inhabited World According to Strabo." Published in *The Geography of Strabo,* translated by Horace Leonard Jones and John Robert Sitlington Sterrett (1923).

the narrative of cannibalism and savagery for the Irish beyond Diodorus Siculus's speculations. He isolates the Irish in the degree of their savagery and distinguishes them from the Britons, who would in less than fifty years become subjects of the Pax Romana: "[T]hey are man-eaters as well as heavy eaters, and since, further, they count it an honorable thing, when their fathers die, to devour them, and openly to have intercourse, not only with the other women, but also with their mothers and sisters" (1997, 259). Such tales were common; incestuous and loose sexual mores also typified the Roman and Greek representations of Scythians, Africans, and Indians.

Although Rome's empire spread through Iberia and Gaul, absorbing local Celtic culture within itself, and further into Britain in the years A.D. 43–85, Ireland remained a land (like Scythia to Greece) that existed outside the borders of civilization and imperial ambition. Both represented lands beyond the semibarbaric edge of habitable lands and common humanity. Strabo takes as his purpose in *Geography* to depict the size, shape, and cultures of the "habitable world," which he described as stretching from India to Iberia (western Spain), from Ethiopia (Africa) to Ierne (Ireland); he dismisses Thule (Iceland) from his mapping, because, as he asserts, it is either uninhabitable or wholly imagined and nonexistent.[24] Although Greek by birth, Strabo was Roman in orientation and represented the world as it mattered to Rome: "The geographer takes into his purview only this our inhabited world; and its limits are marked off on the south by the parallel through the Cinnamon-producing Country [India] and on the north by the parallel through Irene" (505).

He calculated that the latitude of the inhabitable world, or *oikoumene,* was twice its longitude (for the ancients, the inhabitable world was only part of the Northern Hemisphere of the entire spherical, oval-shaped world): "[From] the extremities of India to the extremities of Iberia [(i.e. Spain) is] double that from Ethiopia up to the parallel that runs by Ierne" (237). For centuries, Ireland consistently represented the northernmost borderland in these influential Greco-Roman texts. If lands northwest of Ireland (such as Thule) existed, they were irrelevant: "For the modern scientific writers are not able to speak of any country north of Ierne, which lies to the north of Britain and near thereto, and is the home of men who are complete savages and lead a miserable existence because of the cold; and therefore, in my opinion, the northern limit of our inhabited world is to be placed there" (443). Such a border placement drew from both the cartographic and the fantastic.

Strabo's *Geography* contributes to the larger imperial Roman discourse, intended to aid trade and "governmental purposes" of Rome (both political and military). Strabo even weighs, amid a description of Britain, the advantages of "taking and holding" Britain, Ireland, and other lands.[25] Later, Claudius successfully invaded Britain but never ventured to Ireland, although invasions may have been planned. Strabo had argued against Rome taking Britain, arguing that more profit could be gained from trade tariffs than from taxes, which would also need to support a standing army there and, therefore, outspend any additional income through taxation (446–47). This argument is rehashed later in eighteenth-century Britain about the East India Company, with, remarkably, the same result: further colonization. But even more than with Britain, Strabo had emphasized that "taking and holding" Ireland was not at all advisable: "[T]he unprofitableness of an occupation would be still greater in the case of the other islands about Britain" (447), and Ireland remained an almost unrecognized hinterland for Rome and its writers—with the notable exception of Ptolemy, who charted the rivers and recorded the early tribes of Ireland. Long after the fall of Rome, during the Renaissance, the English eventually took the task the Romans avoided—that of "civilizing" Ireland.

For Strabo, Ireland resembled other borderlands because of their shared remoteness; his discussion links them as inhospitable climes: "[T]he remotest voyage to the north . . . the voyage to Ierne, which island not only lies beyond Britain but is such a wretched place to live in on account of the cold that the regions on beyond are regarded as uninhabitable" (271). His next passage turns to the "Cinnamon-producing Countr[ies]" of Sri Lanka and India. Later in the text, he describes these lands as "the limit and the beginning of our inhabited world" (439). These passages frame Rome's reach and the supposed boundaries of human civilization. Above India live another strange people, "the Roxolanians, the most remote of the known Scythians" (441). These people, however distant, live "farther south than the most remote peoples of whom we have knowledge north of Britain," which was where he placed Ireland. The Irish, the "most remote of peoples," continue to be seen as such throughout most of the texts of the Roman Empire. These border comparisons continued to be roughly the same in Pomponius Mela's *De Chorographia*[26] (44 C.E.), the oldest extant geographical work written (originally) in Latin. Such characterizations would later be picked up in Britain.

Mela's *De Chorographia* picks out and surveys areas of the world that he finds significant or interesting. Astonishing in its sweeping inexactitudes, peppered with occasional and surprising accuracies, this text continued to be read into the fifteenth century by Portuguese explorers and sailors, who consulted it on voyages (Romer 2001, 28).[27] Certainly, Mela's world and orientation, however, were merely the same as imperial Rome's. As Mela's most recent editor, F. E. Romer, has noted, the famous map of Agrippa was painted on a giant scale above the Porticus Vipsania in the Campus Martius, the Field of Mars, which was a former military drilling ground that Augustus had turned into a mall of imperial monuments. This map most likely figured prominently in Mela's mind as he began his written description of the known world. The world map, which Agrippa began, was finished by Augustus, who had it painted triumphantly above Rome's gates as the modern and imperial view of the world.[28] As a nineteenth-century reconstruction of the public map shows, Iuverna (Ireland) continued to exist in the northwestern corner, but Thule was then presented as the most northerly piece of habitable land, and the Cassiterides (Greek: Tin Islands and Isles of Scilly) had been made as the most westerly. Iuverna still remained remote, if it had moved east a little, appearing closer to northern Scythia.

Although Roman coins have been found in Ireland, the only real Roman knowledge of Ireland seems to have come through merchants who traded with the Irish, probably through Britain, and through earlier histories. As in the works of Strabo and Diodorus Siculus, Mela's *De Chorographia* offers little detail of Iuverna. Despite this lack (or perhaps because of it), the supposed barbarity of the Irish became an article of faith: "[Iuverna's] climate is hideous for ripening seeds, but the island is so luxuriant with grass—not only abundant but sweet—that sheep stuff themselves in a fraction of the day, and unless they are kept from the pasture, they burst from feeding too long. Its inhabitants are undisciplined and ignorant of all virtue, to a greater degree than any other nation, and they are very much inexperienced in piety" (116–17).[29] Later Irish writers would have to account for such aspersions,[30] just as later British colonizers and their apologists (such as Giraldus of Wales) would use them to justify their conquests.

Mela also describes other little-known peoples outside the purview of Rome: "We are told that the first humans in Asia, starting from the east, are the Indians, the Seres (Lat., Silk People) [the Chinese], and the Scyths. The Seres inhabit more or less the middle of the eastern part. The Indians and the Scyths inhabit the ex-

tremities, both peoples covering a broad expanse and spreading to the ocean"
(36–37). In addition to these Scyths and Indians, another distinct group of Scyths,
occupying a region closer to Ireland, inhabited northeastern Europe. Elsewhere,
Mela asserts the degree of Scythian antiquity:"The first human beings are Scyths"
(68). Such assertions provided the fundaments of a medieval European understanding of the Scythians, ones that medieval writers worked to synchronize with the
Hebrew biblical histories, which include origin stories of humanity. In building a
specific Irish history from these broader European conceptions of Scythian antiquity—and retelling various origin stories—Irish writers also had to reckon with
British, Roman, and Greek representations of the Irish, as Geoffrey Keating (Seithrún Céitinn) famously did in the early seventeenth century in the introduction to
his history, *Foras Feasa ar Éirinn,* in which he contests the many assertions about
Irish barbarity.

Distant Asia also signified the birth of humanity to Rome, West Asia, and Europe. Indeed, before the earth was recognized as a sphere, ancient cartographers
usually oriented maps with the East at the top, with the most ancient people living
there. Why Romans assumed the origins of the world to be in the East might have
arisen from the hoary assumption about the sunrise and human origins; it also may
have been reinforced from a passage suggesting the location of Eden in the Old
Latin Bible:"God planted a garden in Eden, in the east *(ad orientem)*" (Gen. 2:8).
Moreover, medieval origin legends, usually written down by monks or the learned
religious men of the time, often linked European ancestors with the most eastern
peoples in Asia, not with the Scythians. Similarly, Irish and Chinese were both argued at various points to be original languages,[31] and many early Christian pseudohistorians, including the Irish, treated the Chinese, again the Silk People—*Seres* in
Isidore's Latin and *Serdae* in the Irish of Airbertach mac Cosse (ca. 1016)—as the
"first of men" who, like the first migrants to Ireland, also survived the Flood. This
understanding of the Seres as the first humans may also have been based on a translation error, as John Carey has argued.[32]

As the first humans and the oldest culture, the remotest cultures of Asia became,
for the weavers of Irish legend, excellent candidates to become ancestors of the
Irish. Early Irish writing avers that if the Irish did not have a powerful place in the
world of Rome or medieval Europe, they might have had a remarkable one in a previous age. John Carey traces references to the origin of the world through medieval
texts and asserts in his essay "The Irish Vision of the Chinese":"That a 'prelapsarian'
race, living remote from all other men in the immediate vicinity of Eden, should
have survived the Flood is accordingly a concept with a natural place in the medieval
system of belief" (1987, 76). The "Seres," or the Chinese, might have been this people. "Seres" refers to both the land and the people at the far eastern *(orientis)* edge of
the world; this metonym underscores the idea that the people did not just inhabit

the land, but were directly derived from it, just as Jehovah formed Adam from the clay of Eden. Connoting emergence, the etymological root of the East or the "Orient" in the Latin verb *"orior"* means "to arise, to spring from, proceed from" (Simpson 1960, 416). The discourse of Irish Orientalism is grounded in such ideas and legends of origins, with their ready images of border peoples.

This supposed land at the eastern edge of the world, the antediluvian place from which humanity emerged, remained untouched by the sins of humanity and the purging waters of heaven, as Carey explains: "[I]t was also widely held that [Seres, the region,] had not been affected by the Flood, whether because situated on a mountain of unimaginable height or through simple remoteness from the haunts of sinful men" (1987, 76). In the origin legends, Ireland also remained above water during the Flood, and antediluvian figures also occur repeatedly there; Cessair, for example, was Noah's granddaughter and, according to Irish origin legends, led the first settlement of Ireland before the Flood, having escaped destruction by sailing to Ireland, which the waters never covered. Spanish sailors also supposedly visited Ireland before the Flood, perhaps, the implication goes, establishing Ireland's first community. John Carey traces the idea of an Oriental origin of the world through Bede and finds references to antediluvians and prelapsarians in early tales of Irish poets as far back as the eighth century.

> These were not the only Irish speculations concerning an unfallen, antediluvian people: similar claims were made on behalf of the Tuatha Dé, the old divinities of paganism. A passage claiming the authority of the lost eighth-century compilation Cín Dromma Snechta describes an encounter between the poet Amargen and the tutelary goddess Banba . . . : "The Book of Druimm Snechta says that Amargen inquired concerning her race. 'I am descended from Adam,' said she. 'To which lineage of Noah's sons do you belong?' said he. 'I am older than Noah,' said she. 'I was on the peak of a mountain in the Flood. As far as this peak,' said she, 'did the Flood's waves come; therefore it is called Peak of the Wave *(Tél Tuinne).*' " Still more apposite is Manannán's description of life in the Otherworld to Bran mac Febail: "We are, since the beginning of the world, without age, without a covering of earth; hence we do not expect a time of weakness (?)—the Fall *(int immormuss)* has not touched us." (76)

The figures, all untouched by biblical history, are distant from the centers of civilization; they predate the imperium of the Roman Church. Carey further argues that the Seres became models for other important pre-Christian figures in medieval Irish written texts.

The medieval stories of the first historian of Ireland, the shape-shifting Tuán, as well as Suibne (Sweeney), the mad king and protagonist of *Buile Shuibhne,* partly evolved from representations of the Seres in passages of Pliny the Elder, Julius Solinus, and Isidore. Carey refers to a passage from Solinus that describes the Seres gathering silk threads from trees, which closely resembles depictions of the wild man figure(s) of Tuán and Suibne, who lived in remote cliff haunts and trees: "The Seres themselves are gentle (*mites*), and very peaceful (*quietissimi*) among themselves, but flee the gatherings of other mortals." Tuán, having survived since the second settlement of Ireland, is presented in *Scél Tuáin Meic Chairill* as the first historian of Ireland, having knowledge of Ireland before the Flood. God lets him survive for hundreds of years by transmogrifying him into a variety of animals: a stag, a boar, a hawk, a salmon. Eventually, he is reborn a man. Reports of the Seres may have provided a basis for descriptions of Tuán as well as Suibne, the famous poet figure, who, cursed by a Christian cleric, was transformed into a bird, fled humanity, and perched in trees all over Ireland, singing his verses.[33] Carey finds sufficient textual evidence to draw a conclusion that "the association of [Irish] wild men with the days of the Flood is to be understood in terms of the Irish vision of the Chinese" (76). Although determining the details of influence may not be possible today, the association between the pagan Irish and the Seres points to an early semiotic bond between images of the ancient Irish and the antediluvian Seres at the other northern edge of the world in the Orient.

Cultural comparisons between peoples on the edges of the world carried on through Roman times in influential Roman texts. Pliny the Elder formulates an explicit cultural axiom for understanding border peoples in his *Natural History.* He compares specific magical beliefs and rituals of the Druids of Gaul and Britain (often conflated with the Irish by Romans) with those of the Persians. Pliny explains their belief in the protective powers of a "sort of egg," purportedly produced by a snake that coils around its own hardening saliva. This solidified egg-shaped object supposedly protected anyone who held it at court, during formal litigation. Pliny seems to entertain this magical possibility but then reveals his disbelief, which, he relays, arose after he watched a man be sentenced to death in a Roman court while he held such an egg. (The Romans themselves, it should be noted, were very superstitious by modern standards.) Moreover, the sentence, Pliny implies, resulted in part because the judge saw him grasping a "magic" egg. The egg, revealed as an ineffective charm in a court at Rome, and serving as a synecdoche for barbarian magic, provokes a larger, more significant question for Pliny: "Why do I comment on this craft that has spread beyond the ocean to the far reaches of the earth? Nowadays, Britain continues to be held spellbound by magic and conducts so much ritual that it would seem that it was Britain that had given magic to the Persians. *People of the whole world are alike in this way, though they are wholly ignorant of one another. Thus the debt to the Romans cannot be overestimated, for abolishing this abomination*" (Koch and Carey 2000, 33; italics added). To Rome (and later to Enlightenment Britain), disparate cultures were alike because of their different traditions and superstitions; the rational centers disclaimed any connection to strangeness, despite their own superstitions and taboos. To Rome, the "Hiberni," living even more so in "the far reaches of the earth" than the Gauls and Britons, as well as the peoples on other distant borders in India, Asia, and Africa, appeared both "alike in this way" and "wholly ignorant of one another." They were united only through the gaze of Rome, which made the Roman world coherent and assumed that these distinct cultures existed in distinct states of isolation. This coherence fallacy presumes that only the process of imperial "civilizing" could connect them. That such disparate and distant peoples were ignorant of one another gave Pax Romana the enviable position in the world as the hub of knowledge and power, one possessed of the ability to "abolish" savage "abominations" and to civilize and, even, humanize humanity. This idea reflects an assumption still current today: knowledge of one border culture by another, when it appears, is channeled, mitigated, delivered, and known only through the powerful hubs of globalized commerce and diplomacy. Unmitigated or circumventing knowledge—always subversive—is never wholly intelligible to, or welcomed by, metropolitan logic. Moreover, within a border culture, such knowledge is often coded—as allegorical, symbolic, parodic, mystical, allusive, obscure, or speculative.

Even as first-century Britain was brought into the imperial world of Rome, Ireland continued to be viewed by Rome as a remote place even more superstition-laden than Britain. Precise knowledge of Ireland was not recorded in Rome until Ptolemy's second-century *Geographical Guide,* based on reports from merchants, travelers, and sailors gathered mostly by Marinus of Tyre, a geographical writer of whom little is known. Because of its abundant lists of place-names, Ptolemy's book has always been of importance to Irish historians, as it was to early international traders. It also has a surprising lack of spurious conclusions about Irish culture, which may explain why so few English histories of Ireland reference it. Despite the mildness of this practical guide to ports, rivers, and tribes in Ireland, later writers such as Caius Julius Solinus mostly continued to focus on Ireland's supposed strangeness, wondrous elements, and lack of common humanity. Solinus's *Collectanea Rerum Memorabilium* (ca. 253–268 C.E.) borrows much from Pliny and Mela but seems to take little if anything from Ptolemy. As Joep Leerssen notes in his groundbreaking study of early modern representations of the Irish, *Mere Irish and Fíor-Ghael,* Solinus's work demonstrates the "fluid border between the genres of geography and fantasy." Solinus also reveals much of his strategy for representing the Irish in his conclusions about Ireland: *"Fas ac nefas eodem loco ducunt,"* which Leerssen translates idiomatically as "custom and aberration amount to the same thing" (1996b, 33).[34] Solinus seems to suggest that in Ireland, *fas* (divine law, religious custom, revered customs, or immutable or natural laws) becomes the same as its opposite, *nefas* (the denial or lack of observance of the aforementioned):

the Irish do not hold sacred the bases of human bonds—a mother's love or the sanctity of spilled blood. They exist outside common humanity.

Isidore and other medieval and early modern writers repeat many of Solinus's details and only occasionally the words of Ptolemy. Solinus's famous descriptions include references to Ireland's legendary lack of serpents and bees, the magical qualities of its soil, and the warlike propensities of the inhabitants. Even through the seventeenth century, historians of Ireland such as William Camden continued to repeat Solinus's third-century erroneous assertions about Ireland's absence of bees. This image of Ireland as a border of the habitable and civilized world continued during the decline of Rome in the fourth century and through medieval texts, both English and Irish, which relied upon the histories and geographies preserved from Rome and disseminated through the Church. As late as the early fifth century, Irish cannibalism was reported to exist—Saint Jerome (ca. 370–420 C.E.) wrote about the *Scotti,* or Scots, as the Irish were then known, in his tract *Adversus Jovinianum* (ca. 393 C.E.): "I myself as a young man saw in Gaul the Scots, a British race, feeding on human flesh" (qtd. in Kenny 1993, 138). Similar reports of other cannibalistic cultures bordering civilized places persisted into the twentieth century.

Saint Jerome reports another common tale of the noncivilized in the following quotation; the appellation Scots (Scotti) referred to the Irish from the fourth through the eleventh century: "The Scots have no separate wives, but, as if they read Plato's Republic and were following Cato's example, no woman among them is the wife of one particular man. According to the desires of each, they take their pleasures like the beasts of the field" (ibid.). Irish sexuality and polygamy clearly do not signify Platonic idealism here, only inhuman bestiality. Pomponius Mela describes the Garamantes, in Africa, in similar terms: "No one has one specific wife. Out of the children, who are born here randomly from such indiscriminate sexuality on their parents' part, and who are not clearly identified, the adults recognize by their similar looks those whom they are to raise as their own" (Romer 2001, 48). Such resemblances may seem idiosyncratic on their own but together appear systemic, and, over time, they encouraged affinities between borderland identities.

Milesians

What little the ancient Greeks knew of Ireland probably came through Phoenician sources and traveling Celts or Galatians in Greece and Turkey. The Greeks knew more about the Scythians, who eventually served as rough models for the barbarism attributed to Ireland and other border cultures. The Scythians traveled and marauded in Greece and Turkey and eventually traded with Greek Milesians (inhabitants of the city Miletus).[35] As with depictions of border cultures, sexual amorality also characterized *Milesian Tales,* an influential group of short erotic tales first collected or written by the Greek writer Aristedes of Miletus (ca. 100 B.C.E.). Miletus lay at the eastern border of Hellenistic culture adjacent to both the lands of the ancient Scythians and the actual Celtic Galatians' settlement. In Ireland, the name Milesian generally signifies a different set of people: the Gaelic Irish, or, more specifically, the descendants of the last wave of "invaders" of Ireland in *Lebor Gabála*—the sons of a leader descended from Míl Espáne, a legendary Scythian who traveled from Greece through Africa to Spain and whose sons colonized Ireland. The name appears to be taken from Nennius's Latin ninth-century references to the "soldier from Spain," or *"miles Hispaniae,"* in the oldest pseudohistorical tract to survive, the *Historia Britonum*. The same character is written as "Míl Espáne" in the first surviving eleventh-century Irish redactions of *Lebor Gabála*.[36] Despite such convincing textual evidence of the Irish origins of the word *Milesian,* some twentieth-century writers equated the ancient Milesians of Irish legend with the Greco-Anatolian Milesians of ancient history, based on the similarities of both Milesian groups: their Scythian connections, their Eastern geographical base, and their reputations as ancient sailors and colonizers. The lack of a textual trail in medieval texts, in addition to the dearth of archaeological, material, and linguistic evidence, however, has hardly dampened the enthusiasms of antiquarians, Internet Celticists, biblical speculators, and lost-tribes-of-Israel theorists from surmising that this nominal link was an actual genealogical one.[37]

The speculative reasons given for arriving at this conclusion, and for conflating legend and history, merit further note. Both the Irish Milesians and the Greek Milesians supposedly came from the same area—present-day Turkey, or what, in 1685, Roderic O'Flaherty termed "Græco-Scythia" (9). Both groups were intermediaries with the Scythians. Also, the history of the Celtic Galatae (Galatians), who lived in Anatolia (central Turkey) from the third century B.C.E. to the second century C.E., suggests that other groups may have traversed between Miletus and Europe, and perhaps even Ireland.[38] Although such claims have some material and textual support,[39] scholars generally agree that no uniform Celtic culture spanned Europe, let alone stretched to Anatolia.[40] The Galatians probably had little or no contact with or knowledge of the inhabitants of Ireland. Other ostensible reasons for the link include the following: both groups (one legendary, one historical) traveled through Greece, Turkey, Scythia, Egypt, and North Africa as sailing, colonizing peoples. Miletus was the colonial hub of Greece's eastern settlements on the Black Sea, and the ruins of the city are in western Anatolia, south of the city of Izmir, on the Aegean at the mouth of the Maeander (Büyükmenderes) River. Before the year 500 B.C.E., Miletus was the greatest Greek city in the East, famed for its cartography, mercantilism, and cosmopolitan nature, and it is still known for its pre-Socratic school of "natural" philosophy.[41] (It is also known as the city from which Julius Caesar was kidnapped by pirates and from which he raised a navy to

avenge and crucify his captors.) Milesian colonies existed throughout the Mediterranean, with more than sixty settlements on or near the Black Sea. Its colonizing
reputation, compounded by evidence that the Milesians had planted a colony
specifically in Egypt, a place where the legendary ancestors of Ireland also dwelled,
lends weight to the speculative supposition that these eastern Milesians seeded a
colony in Ireland.

When the initial pairing of the Milesians and the Irish legendary descendants of
Míl Espáne began is uncertain. Actually, the question of who came first—Míl or
the Milesians—is interesting. After all, many Irish legend makers created ancestors
in order to account for the various names of a people (for example, Gaedel Glass
for the Gaels and Scota for the Scots) through the practice known as eponymy.[42] In
other words, despite the fact that Irish annals and origin legends claim Míl as the
ancestor of the last settlement of Ireland, the word *Milesian* might have existed first,
borrowed from Greek histories, especially where the Scythians were discussed.
The great problem with this conclusion is that few references to "Milesians" exist
in Irish legends, and, as Irish-language scholar John Carey has noted, references to
Milesians from Miletus are not found in Irish-language origin legends.[43] Even in
the last redacted version, *Leabhar Sheáin Í Chonaill,* the Irish-speaking informant
uses only a Hibernicized loan word, "Na Milésian," to reference the Iberian invaders (Ó Duilearga 1948, 267–68). Indeed, no Irish-language cognate of the
word exists. Furthermore, no link exists among Míl, Milesians, and Miletus in the
early origin legends, that is, the word *Milesian* is not used to refer to the Irish with
any regularity until the eighteenth century, and Miletus is not referenced until even
later. Two possible explanations (at least) exist: the use of the word *Milesian* was
dropped in the retellings of the legends, or the word *Milesian,* with its Miletus references, began to be used only later.

Because no record of an Irish cognate exists, the word probably did not emerge
from an indigenous Irish tradition. Rather, it probably developed as a loan word
through English-language versions of the legend, most likely the ones developed in
the eighteenth-century antiquarian and philological practice of tracing ethnic genealogies through etymological resemblances (as Isidore of Seville had). In the earliest known uses of the word *Milesian* (or its Latin equivalent), in the
twelfth-century *Topography of Ireland,* Gerald of Wales uses *Milesius* as an adjectival
form of Míl Espáne (he describes Míl's descendants as *"stirps Milesia"* (Cambrensis
1982, 90). But no reference to Miletus is made. Also, although Roderic O'Flaherty
uses *Milesii* as a collective noun and mentions the word *Græco-Scythia* in his *Ogygia*
(1685, 9), he makes no reference to the ancient city of Miletus when it could have
strengthened his argument. O'Flaherty's use of *Milesii* is consistent with his tendency to "classicize" Irish names (as when he writes "Achaius" for "Eochaid," "Ae-
neas" for "Oengus," "Darius" for "Dáire") in his discussions of the migrations of the

Gaels. Charles Vallancey uses *Milesian* often, as in the 1781 preface to volume 2, number 5, of *Collectanea De Rebus Hibernicus* when he equates Milesians with "Phenians" (1770–1804, unnumbered 21), and traces its etymology in *A Vindication of the Ancient History of Ireland* to various Chaldean and Hebrew sources that mean "hero of the ship"; he also surprisingly treats it as a cognate for the Arabic word *mullah* (1786, 294). Around the same time, another antiquarian, Joseph C. Walker, uses the term in his *Historical Essay on the Dress of the Ancient and Modern Irish* (1788), referring to Míl's progeny in the origin legends found in the *Book of Lecan,* or *Leabhar Leacán,* a source for *Lebor Gabála.* In James MacGeoghegan's *History of Ireland, Ancient and Modern* (French version, 1758–1762; English translation, 1831–1832), the author calls the ancient Irish "Scoto-Milesians" and surveys Milesian culture without making any Miletus reference. After its influential translation in the 1830s, usage of the term became so ensured that in a review of John O'Donovan's (1809–1861) *Annals of the Kingdom of Ireland, by the Four Masters, from the Earliest Period to the Year 1616,* English historian Algernon Herbert (1792–1855) is able to reference in the *London Quarterly Review* "the Milesian creed" as if it were a philosophic stance (1853, 2). Fifteen years later, a popular historian, Mary Francis Cusack, referenced the Irish Milesians as both legendary and historical figures in her *Illustrated History of Ireland: From the Earliest Period* (1868), a work that is referenced for evidence by contemporary pseudoscholarly arguments about the Milesian and Miletus connection. The arguments develop by tracing out the logic of references in ancient texts according to the Bible and confirming the semiotic Eastern origins for the Celts. Clearly, most evidence for this connection emerges without textual evidence but in interpretations of legends, linguistic resemblances, and supposed cultural similarities. Nevertheless, such assumed connections have existed in Irish culture for centuries, in both the spotlight and in the penumbra.

Early Pseudohistories

The first prominent surviving written account of the Scythians voyaging to Ireland came three centuries after Saint Jerome, penned by the Venerable Bede, a Saxon monk and scholar living during the seventh and eighth centuries in Britain (ca. 672–735). Bede restates the magical qualities of Ireland found in Roman texts, yet he does not rehearse the familiar saws and sketches of barbarism, although later British writers returned to them. Neither does he relay the Scythian origins of the Irish, but he does note the arrival of Scythians in the British Isles. He may have borrowed this information, through Irish scholars who had traveled to Spain, from Isidore of Seville's *History of the Goths,* in which he derived *Scot(t)i* (the medieval name for the Irish) from *Scythae,* the Scythians.[44] Bede reports that three groups of peoples (*gentem*) live in the British Isles: the Scotti (Irish), the Britons, and the Picts.

The Picts, according to his unnamed sources, descended from the Scythians. In Bede's account, the Scythians arrived in Ireland after a long sea voyage; Ireland's inhabitants met them and politely directed the eastern sailors to Scotland, then unpeopled, where they were told they could settle with a gift of new Irish wives (1994, 16–21). No clear written connection exists between this first account and later written versions, in which the Scythians settle in Ireland, except that these accounts refer to Irish sources and were based on biblical extrapolations. Although the Irish sources cannot be clearly traced before the eighth century,[45] a glimpse of one origin legend is given in an early poem, "Moen Oen," which references, as John Carey has discovered, a son of Míl Espáne, in the line "the slopes of the lands of Éremón" (1994, 9). Éremón had helped lead the last "invasion" of Ireland, as is detailed in *Lebor Gabála Érenn*.[46] Interestingly, his brother Éber seems to be based on the biblical character Heber, revealing the syncretism of these legends, as Old Irish scholar Mark Scowcroft has discussed (1988, 20). A variety of late Roman and early medieval sources, from Flavius Josephus's *Jewish Antiquities* to the later-seventh-century *Etymologies* of Isidore of Seville, laid out the genealogical accounts of Japheth's progeny stemming from the Bible, with Magog as the progenitor of the Scythians (and, as in Isidore, as the father of the Irish).

After the breakup of the Roman Empire, theologians and scholars began to write pseudohistories of Rome's "successors": the Goths, Visigoths, Lombards, Franks, Britons, Vandals, Sueves, and others. These "barbarian" histories often began with ancient events from legends or the Bible but also recalled events leading from the early days of Roman expansion to contemporary times. Complementing Roman accounts of these "barbarians," these and other works produced origin legends that combined Greco-Roman legends with ancient histories and native origin legends. The written Latin accounts of these various peoples on the continent contributed to their collective identity, as scholars such as Walter Goffart in his *Narrators of Barbarian History (A.D. 550–800)* (1988) have argued. The most significant group of the barbarian historians include Jordanes (d. 554?), who wrote *Origin and Deeds of the Getae* based on a lost history of the Goths by Cassiodorus, his elder contemporary; Gregory, bishop of Tours (d. 593 or 594), who traced the Franks' origins to Troy in the so-called *Chronicles of Fredegarius;* Isidore of Seville (d. 636), who wrote tomes of lasting influence such as *History of the Goths, Vandals, and Sueves* and *Etymologies;* Bede (d. 735), who wrote *Ecclesiastical History of the English People* in which he touched on the origins of the English and (to a much lesser extent) the Irish; and Paul the Deacon (d. 799), who wrote *History of the Langobards* (or *Lombards*) (Goffart 1988, 3; Carey 1994, 4–5). These early historians clearly borrowed from Roman histories, but perhaps the influence of works such as Josephus's, which focused on the history of a particular people, had more significance. Goffart expands this point: "In the cosmopolitan Roman Empire of the Flavians

(A.D. 69–96), the resident Jews were deemed to be aliens, that is, 'barbarians' in the neutral sense of the word. Josephus wrote on the recent *Jewish Wars* and, at greater length, on *Jewish Antiquities* with a view to making his fellow Jews better known and more acceptable to the Greco-Roman public. Unintentionally, he provided the Christians of the third and later centuries with some of their most cherished reading" (1988, 5). For Roman writers, Goffart lists Eusebius (and Jerome, his translator) as well as Ammianus Marcellinus, Eutropius, and Aurelius Victor as early pagan Roman models for the later Christian historians.[47] Instead of treating their subjects as barbarians, these early medieval authors placed them on par with the Romans, as "equivalent entities," no matter how distinct their histories (6). Amid these more historical accounts, other scribes and pseudohistorians recorded annals, heroic legends, origin legends, and other material from native sources.

Outside of Bede's limited discussion of Scythians landing in Ireland, no surviving Latin works concerning Ireland exist from the early medieval period. Not until the late medieval period did Irish writers attempt to critique Greco-Roman impressions (and their subsequent uses by British writers) of the early Irish. In contrast to other groups such as the Franks, the Irish had been less integrated into medieval historiography, in part because they had remained outside of direct Roman control, if not influence. The collective identity of the Franks had been partly formed already by ideas of historiography and their depictions in Roman histories, but the "barbarian" histories significantly developed this process, painting them as the successors to Rome, through the reign of Charlemagne and afterward. Yet, because of the lack of early revised histories about the Irish, ancient barbaric images in Greco-Roman texts continued to carry influence in the early modern pseudohistories of Ireland and even in eighteenth-century works. Without medieval Latin histories, the Irish annals, poems, and origin legends served as the definitive native accounts of the past and contributed significantly to an emerging collective Irish identity. Moreover, as if to corroborate the evidence of Irish barbarism, the semiotic and genealogical linking of the Irish with the Scythians (most concretely seen in Isidore) greatly encouraged the transference of Greco-Roman impressions of Scythian barbarity to the Irish.

In the eighth and ninth centuries, Irish writers began to synchronize their native annals with the established continental views of history and the world, translating native Irish histories and legends into Latin and transposing them onto a biblical framework. Following Bede, the next surviving discussion of Scythian origins appears not in an Irish text, but in the ninth-century *Historia Britonum* of Nennius, written in England. Earlier Irish annals were probably first written down in the late seventh century, although these versions no longer exist.[48] Later synthetic histories elaborately developed Irish characters, stories, and themes within a biblical setting and context. As R. Mark Scowcroft notes in a key essay on the main written repository of Irish Oriental origin legends, *Lebor Gabála* or (as spelled in contemporary Irish) *Leabhar Gabhála,*[49] these histories were written

> not to collect native traditions as such but to find a place for Ireland in the biblical history of the world, for her inhabitants among the descendants of Noah, and for her many nations and dynasties in an immense genealogical scheme that subsumed their pedigrees and claims under those of the Tara kingship. Essential to these efforts were the standard authorities on chronology, geography, history, ethnography, and language, who had already brought the Old Testament, classical scholarship, and early medieval thought into some sort of harmony. The Irish *literati* read carefully, solving the riddle step by step; thus did *LG* [*Leabhar Gabhála*] germinate and take root in Irish traditions. (1988, 13–14)

The degree to which these stories borrowed from native Irish legends has been debated for centuries, as Carey, Scowcroft, McCone, and others have attested. What is clear is how sophisticated and intricate are the overlaying, weaving, and (possibly) generating of Irish origin legends in a biblical frame by these "literati." These have had a lasting impact, in part, because of the synthetic or syncretic narrative strategies these writers initiated. They overlaid and inserted the stories of Féinius Fein and Nel, and their supposed knowledge of all the world's languages, into the widely established pseudohistorical narrative of the Tower of Babel. In a continent-wide context where language scholars consented that Hebrew most resembled the original Adamic language, these literati daringly situated their own language beside Hebrew, arguing it had been created from pieces of all the world's tongues, as a reformed original language. This point is significant for future developments for two reasons: it did not refute the dominant biblical episteme, and it gave the Irish language, and the linguistic skills of the Irish, a venerable and esteemed position in the world.

Throughout the Middle Ages, church fathers and language scholars agreed (with few exceptions)[50] that Hebrew was the primordial language of humanity. Paralleling this, early language scholars, particularly in Germany and France, theorized several proto-European language branches following the sons of Japheth (see the works of Guillaume Postel [1510–1581], discussed in Borst 1957–1963 and Eco 1997). Medieval works had relied upon Josephus and Isidore and other accounts of the children of Japheth in tracing the Goths and northern European peoples to Magog and his progeny, the first Scythians and the Goths. All the peoples of northern Europe were seen as descendants of Japheth's sons; the French descended from Gomer, the Spaniards from Tubal, and the Germans, Britons, and Irish from Magog (and from Gomer, by some accounts). In the sixteenth and seventeenth centuries, as the understanding of Hebrew as the primordial language came into question, the Irish became known as the only clear descendants of Magog and the proper, most direct, inheritors of the Scythian bloodline in Europe. This acceptance owed a great deal to the legendary settlements recorded in *Lebor Gabála Érenn* of a distinct group of Scythians who had directly sailed from Scythia to Ireland and not migrated for centuries across northern Europe as previously argued. The first extant appearance of Scythians in Irish origin legends, in Nennius's ninth-century *Historia Britonum,* was probably the result of borrowings from Irish sources, Bede, and Isidore's etymological speculation in his *History of the Goths.* But its fuller development came only later in the Irish *Lebor Gabála Érenn,* which details the successive invasions of Ireland and the fates of its settlers.

Lebor Gabála Érenn

The fundamentals of standard literary scholarship transmute into uncertainties when discussing *Lebor Gabála Érenn,* making detailed conclusions about its construction difficult. Indeed, John Carey calls the work "a bewildering textual labyrinth, a tangle of variants and inconsistencies" (1994, 23). Scholars agree that multiple versions of the text, written during the rise of Latin literacy in Ireland, circulated and were copied and recopied over centuries, worn originals at times being discarded in favor of new copies. The copies still existing were constructed, therefore, over centuries by various hands following varied accounts. Indeed, referencing the work known as *Lebor Gabála* as a unified text is somewhat misleading. No two versions—even copies or recensions of the same source text—are identical, and no single authoritative text exists, yet many elements of the work remain consonant.[51]

As noted previously, the work relied heavily upon continental church and classical literature as well as (to an unknown degree) native histories in prose and poetry. The earliest extant verse versions, preserved in one or more recensions of the text, record the bare outline of the story—the outline that *filid* (poet historians) may have used as the base from which they would elaborate. Old Irish scholar John Carey has explored the possible and probable sources of the Irish origin legends in *Lebor Gabála* and elsewhere in two essays, "A New Introduction to *Lebor Gabála Érenn:* The Book of the Taking of Ireland" (1993) and "The Irish National Origin-Legend: Synthetic Pseudohistory" (1994). In the latter, he comments on the "process of hybridisation and invention whose results have been labelled 'synthetic history' or 'pseudohistory' by Irish scholars" (3–4).[52] Later sources for *Lebor Gabála* expanded the original stories and created further details, either by adding to the previously written copies, which are now lost, supplanted by *Lebor Gabála* itself, or by filling in details from other sources. Indeed, as Carey notes, "Traces of such writings can be found within the textual tradition of *Lebar* [sic] *Gabála* itself, however: portions survive as passages inserted in the text at various points in its evolution; and the organization of one of the poems indicates that its author had available to him in the first half of the eleventh century a version of what became in *Lebar Gabála* the section dealing with the Tuatha Dé" (17).[53] Two main branches (of redactions) of the text exist, sharing similar story progressions and characters, but neither of them was consistently copied faithfully, and many versions blossomed in subsequent recensions (copies made from written versions). Within the various works, generally, six distinct "invasion" stories can be made out with consistent characters (albeit with numerous variations) and shared plots and significant details; for instance, all of the earliest versions of the stories relay Scythian origins, independent of other supposed Scythian migrations to Europe.

The history of the written text begins not in Ireland but in England, where apparently the first full redaction was made. Around 830, Nennius recorded the first written summary of the invasions from oral sources in his *Historia Britonum*. Roughly two hundred years later, an Irish translation of Nennius, attributed to Gilla-Coemáin (d. 1072), appeared and included a fuller elaboration on the Milesian invasions of Ireland. Also, sometime in the late eleventh century, Tigernach hua Braein recorded his *Annals,* synchronizing Irish genealogical persons, events, and dates with Church histories as well as the works of Isidore, Josephus, and, possibly, Julius Africanus. His text, like other Irish annals,[54] alternates between Old Irish and Latin in its entries and combines the time lines of historical and legendary figures from Egypt to Ireland in its chronology. Figures as culturally distinct as Cleopatra and Cú Chulainn are presented beside one another as contemporaries.[55] Scholars of medieval Ireland have asserted that such texts eventually merged with existent verses of Irish origin legends to form *Lebor Gabála* over the next century. Other early contributions to the text have been attributed to the verse of Mael Muru Othna (d. 887), Eochaid Ua Floinn (d. 1004), Flann Mainistrech (d. 1056), and Gilla Colmáin; early Leinster genealogies may also have provided source material (Scowcroft 1987, 96–97; Welch 1996, 304). But whatever its various sources, clearly *Lebor Gabála* recorded these Irish origin stories in a much fuller fashion than Nennius's British history,[56] probably as an effort to affirm the veracity of the legends.

A much fuller version of the origin legends took form in the twelfth century, around 1168, and versions continued to be redacted until the last recension was given by Mícheál Ó Cléirigh in 1631 (Scowcroft 1987, 84). Much has been written about the relationship between Nennius's *Historia Britonum* and these next Irish versions of the legends, which borrowed considerably from Nennius[57] and from the reworkings of eleventh-century Irish poets, particularly Eochaid ua Flainn, Flann Mainistrech, Tanaide Eólach, and Gilla Coemáin. The text eventually acquired the name *Lebor Gabála Érenn,* translated as "The Book of the Taking of Ireland" or "The Book of Invasions."[58] R. A. Stewart Macalister compiled the most complete collection of the various redactions, copies, and recensions in 1938. But, as Old Irish scholar Mark Scowcroft has noted, this collated edition of the most significant versions is difficult to read. Apparently, Macalister brought great erudition and enthusiasm to the project, but also "a Byzantine *apparatus criticus,*" making it difficult to navigate (82).[59] Nevertheless, this edition synthesizes the versions of this already synthesized text and provides the first extended translations of these accounts of the Irish Oriental origin legends.

A number of perspectives on these origins of the work have arisen over the years. Some scholars have seen the legends as mere compilations of foreign sources with a sprinkling of Irish names and themes.[60] In contrast, in the late nineteenth and early twentieth centuries, fervent Celticists, such as Henri d'Arbois de Jubainville, argued that the work is a purely native one, being taken down verbatim from oral sources. That the story existed independently of the written sources is suggested by references to details of it in earlier written Irish texts by Mael Muru Othna, Dicuil, and others. "The Story of Tuán" (redacted in the ninth century), for instance, records the story of Tuán, son of Cairell, who is depicted as Ireland's first historian. Surviving for centuries, he transmogrifies into various animal forms, eventually being reborn as a human, and his various incarnations seem to signify the successive invasions later elaborated in *Lebor Gabála.*[61] But this view is too one-sided. Another more recent revisionist view is that oral origin legends, if they existed, are unknown and not that significant. Kim McCone explains in *Progress in Medieval Irish Studies:* "If the ancient Celts had a myth expressing their common ethnic identity similar to the one ascribed to their Germanic neighbors by Tacitus (*Germania* 2), this has disappeared without trace and the earliest origin tales of Celtic peoples that have come to us emanate from medieval Welsh and Irish pens imbued with clerical learning" (1996, 7).

John Carey, however, repeatedly emphasizes that *Lebor Gabála Érenn* is a blend of sources and recognizes that lost oral accounts may have genuinely shaped the work. He convincingly argues in his 1995 essay "Native Elements in Irish Pseudo-history" that "[t]he blending of pagan and Christian lore which confronts us in Ireland's legendary history bears witness to a commitment to both traditions: it is because they were convinced that both were true, and both important, that the Irish sought so persistently to reconcile them with one another" (48). Carey treats the book much as its originators may have: as a synthetic text that blends both native Irish stories and written sources provided by the Church:

> *Lebor Gabála* is both an inward-looking and an outward-looking book, in a way which typifies the intellectual culture of early medieval Ireland. Inward-looking, in that it reflects a deep and for its time remarkable reverence for, and interest in, native traditions concerning bygone times—a confidence that such traditions had a place in the evolving literature of Christian Ireland, and a determination to find

room for them side by side with the tenets of the new religion. Outward-looking, in that the full range of biblical and classical learning available to scholars of the day is drawn upon to create a niche, and a significance, for Ireland in the wider world. (48–49)

Such a blend of sources grows in significance for an Irish tradition, as Irish writers admit Ireland's "remoteness" as an aspect of its antiquity, a move that concomitantly aligns Ireland with border cultures and carries syncretism to the heart of the enduring semiotic identification of Ireland with Asia.

Lebor Gabála delineates six successive invasions, establishing each in relation to a biblical context, as well as king lists and histories that continue up to the writers' contemporaries. Scowcroft explains the overall construction of many different stories and histories "on a common narrative level":"The whole text, finally, comes to be attached, episode by episode, to the medieval framework for world history as set forth by the *Chronicle* of Eusebius (tract IV). This fusion of fact and fiction, of native and Latin (pagan and Christian) tradition furnishes the Irish *literati* with their own history—a history and re-enactment of the order of things—and with a historical framework for the sagas, the annals and the chronicles" (1987, 79). Although stories such as Tuán's had been written since the seventh century, the written text (though not stable or uniform) attempted to codify them into one account, classifying the stories into six distinct waves of settlement. These waves may, in fact, represent the redactors' attempts to account for numerous oral accounts in Irish of origin legends, yet we have no earlier and substantive written evidence to confirm this theory. The six stories concern the successive arrivals of Cessair, Partholón, Nemed, the Fir Bolg, the Tuatha Dé Danann, and the sons of Míl Espáne.

The various scribes and monks redacted *Lebor Gabála* from oral sources and referenced the earlier account by Nennius in the ninth century. Discussing the "rich interplay of native and imported ideas which went into the making of the pseudohistorical schema," Carey comments that "Partolón [*sic*] and Míl Espáne look like scholarly constructs, the figments of men steeped in Jerome and Isidore; but Nemed and the Fir Bolg cannot be so easily accounted for, and they appear to reflect—at whatever remove—indigenous memories and speculations about the peopling of Ireland" (1994, 8, 9). In the later elaboration processes, they or their sources (probably *filid*) altered and expanded the tale from its briefer mnemonic and poetic form that aided the *filid* in their recitation. The great bibliographer of Irish ecclesiastical sources, James F. Kenny, comments on the probable forces behind these versions in *The Sources for the Early History of Ireland: Ecclesiastical* (1929):

When Christianity arrived in Ireland, bringing in its train the Bible, Eusebius, Orosius, Isidore, etc., Irishmen began to learn world history as taught by the early mediaeval Church. There inevitably followed the impulse to fit their own Irish past into this scheme of history, and to pour their myths, traditions, sagas, genealogies, into an orderly historical mould. Apparently as early as the seventh century church-men, such as Mo-Sinu moccu Mín, and *filid,* such as Cenn-Faelad, were attempting to elucidate with the help of the Old Testament and Orosius, the origins of the Irish people, and, with the help of Eusebius and other chroniclers, to set up a chronological scheme of their later history. But it was not until the ninth, and especially the tenth, eleventh, and twelfth centuries, that this historical impulse acquired full momentum. Then many of the *filid* seem to have turned their energies almost entirely to the task of transmuting the national folk-lore into a harmonized history. A twelfth-century text declares that "he is no *fili* who does not synchronise and harmonise all the sagas." (1993, 13)

In this respect, *Lebor Gabála* legitimates the rule of Irish kings by providing them with a history equivalent to the Hebrews, and much of the story of the forefathers of the Gaels parallels the Exodus of the Jewish people from Egypt in the Bible, thereby synchronizing and harmonizing Irish and Church histories. Moreover, the writers of these accounts of Ireland's ancient past also worked to fit the Irish into the historical framework of the "barbarians" and late Roman histories. Carey notes that the "Irish scholar who invented the story of the Scythian nobleman was trying to do what Cassiodorus and Iordanes and 'Fredegarius' and Isidore and the rest had done—but he achieved it in his own way. The context is that which we find in other barbarian historiographers, but the story itself appears to be an independent invention" (1994, 9). Indeed, the complexities of the text itself, although pseudo-historical, seem to rival those complexities of actual historiography.

Most of the migrations described in *Lebor Gabála* are led by descendants of the previous migration, except, most prominently, the first migration and the migration of the euhemeristic Tuatha Dé Danann, the old gods who are reasserted in new form in Christian texts. Before their arrival, however, at the end of a deadly battle between the otherworldly Fomoiri and the descendants of Partholón and Nemed's people, a second flood covers Ireland, killing most of the population. The survivors flee into exile in Greece and Egypt and become the descendants of the Fir Bolg, or "Men of Bags," who eventually return and recolonize Ireland. In Greece, these Scythian Fir Bolg were made to carry earth in bags to mountaintops to create fields; after 320 years they escaped, using their bags as ships for their return voyage. The next invasion of Ireland is the euhemeristic reinvasion of the old gods, the Tuatha Dé, sometimes represented as fallen angels, or what "men of learning" call in the story of Tuán "the exiles who came from Heaven" (Carey 1994, 54). This work of the scribes reflects, among other things, the ways that *Lebor Gabála* preserved non-Christian elements of tradition. These prelapsarian figures, as the

Seres or the Scyths, also circumvent the standardizing influences of Rome and the Church. In the last, most extensive, invasion story, the sons of Míl Espáne arrive in Ireland, seeking revenge for their brother who visited Ireland and was killed by the Tuatha Dé, then rulers of Ireland. The "Milesians" soon subdue the otherworldly Tuatha Dé, however, and recolonize the island. They become the personifications of the most recent and identifiable Gaelic ancestors of the medieval Irish.

This last invasion story, the two-part story of Gaedil (the progenitor of Míl Es-páne), is the centerpiece of *Lebor Gabála*[62] and focuses much on the origins of the Celtic Gaels (Milesians) in Spain and, earlier, in Egypt. The author of one of the early recensions probably brought two distinct versions of the origin story together in one narrative strand, the result being a two-part story, each section concerning an "invasion" of Ireland.[63] Based on several versions of the text, R. A. Stewart Macalis-ter provides a reconstruction of the two tracts of the Gaedil story. Mark Scowcraft offers some background and then cites Macalister's summary in the following:

> The text begins with the division of the world by the three sons of Noah, and the pedigree of Féinius Farsaid, the Scythian ancestor of the Gaedil and descendant of Gomer son of Japheth, who witnessed the building and abandonment of Nimrod's tower [of Babel]. Féinius had two sons, Noenual (variously spelled), who succeeded him as king of Scythia, and Nél, who was invited to Egypt because of his great learning and given Pharaoh's daughter Scotta in marriage. Ninus son of Belus took the kingship of the world at that time. 42 (μ) or 62 (b)[64] years after Babel.
>
> "Nél's son, Gaedel Glass, is the ancestor of the Gaedil. They dwell in Egypt until the drowning of Pharaoh in the Red Sea, then fled to Scythia in four ships with 24 couples in each. They struggled with the descendants of Noenual for a long time over the Scythian kingship until finally, having slain Reflóir, they were sent into exile. From the singing of the sirens on the Caspian Sea Caicher the druid res-cued them by stuffing wax into their ears; at the Riphaean Mountains, he prophe-sied their advent to Ireland. They settled for a while on the sea of Azov, then sailed into the Mediterranean, past Crete and Sicily to Spain, which they took by force. On the way, they fought 54 battles and defeated the Frisians (b) or Tuscans (μ), Lan-gobards, and 'Bachra.' Bregon(d), the son of Bráth, founded Brigantia (Bragança) and built a tower, from which Ireland was seen one winter's night.
>
> (Here follows a summary of tract II).
>
> The Milesians invaded Ireland to avenge Íth, the son of Bregon and uncle (in b great-uncle) of Míl Espáine; 36 (in b 40) named chieftains and 24 named servitors led the invasion, which landed at Inber Scéne (the Shannon estuary). Éremón mac Miled sailed to the north-east of Ireland, landing at Inber Colptha (the Boyne estu-ary), and his brother Éber remained in the south. The population-groups de-scended from them, from their brother Ír, and from Lugaid mac Ítha are variously

listed. Éremón and Éber quarreled over the kingship of Ireland, which was therefore divided between them. Some credit them with twelve chieftains." (1988, 7–8)

Scholars have long discussed the connection here between Spain and Ireland, many
tracing the origin of the story to a similarity in names—in Latin, Spain is *Hiberia*
and Ireland is *Hibernia*. The story accounts for this similarity by treating it as the result of the Irish-Spanish Milesian connection. Much earlier, Isidore of Seville, citing Orosius, in his early medieval study *Etymologies* (14.6.3), traced the name
connection between Spain and Ireland and believed their proximity to be the
cause. Much was made of this connection in the sixteenth century, when Spain and
Ireland formed a number of anti-English alliances, but an African-Spanish-Irish
connection fueled speculations about the origins of the Irish through the nineteenth century. Though linguistic evidence does suggest some Spanish-Irish Celtic
connection, many contemporary scholars tend to attribute the Iberian-Hibernian
connection to the aforementioned practice of eponymy,[65] where the writer develops legends, names, and possible ancestors from existing group names. For example, several versions of *Lebor Gabála* assert that a man named Féinius Farsaid gave
what became the Irish language to Gaedil, for whom the language was supposedly
named, but more probably the ancestor was created to account for the name of the
language.[66] Likewise, the names of ancestors provide heritage stories for many Irish
and Gaelic names: Féinius Farsaid for Fenian; Scota, daughter of the pharaoh, for
Scotti and Scotland; Gaedil for Gaelic and Gael, to name a few. Although this practice follows a certain logic, the names seem to have been entirely created. Nevertheless, such etymological techniques had been long established on the logic of
patrimonial naming practices, and for us they spotlight the historical process of
how a collective past was used to secure a present identity. Nevertheless, excluding
that of the first ill-fated invasion led by Noah's granddaughter, Cessair, *Lebor
Gabála* links all of the successive invasions of Ireland to Féinius Farsaid, the supposed father of Scythia.

Later pseudohistorians generally treat Japheth as the last common ancestor of
the British and the Irish. But in works of later British historians, the genealogical
split between Britons and Scythian Irish occurs in other generations. Wherever it
occurs in these British texts, however, it generally creates a consanguineous fault
line that divides the wild Scythian Irishry from the more distinguished descendants
of Rome's Brutus, the Britons.

Early British Accounts of Irish Origins

The earliest written accounts in Latin of Irish origins in the several varying editions
of Nennius's *Historia Britonum* are slight, suggesting that Nennius (a Briton pseudo-

historian or possibly a group of such) worked from oral, or possibly written, Irish sources sometime in the mid–ninth century.[67] Nennius claims to have gotten his evidence from a variety of sources: "the annals of the Romans as from the chronicles of the sacred Fathers, Hieronymus [Jerome], Eusebius, Isidorus [Isidore of Seville], Prosper, and from the annals of the Scots [Irish] and the Saxons, and our ancient traditions" (1848, 385). Nennius notes that his Irish information came orally from respected sources: "Sic mihi peritissimi Scottorum nunciaverunt" (53)—"the wisest men of the Irish told me" (Kenny 1993, 154). *Historia Britonum* provides summaries of five of the six "conquests" later given in detail in *Lebor Gabála,* but he does not mention the first "invasion," Noah's granddaughter Cessair's, nor her unsuccessful antediluvian settlement,[68] which was supposedly almost entirely gone before the next settlement arrived, Partholón's (Bartholomew). But these origin legends of Ireland are subsumed within the larger historical framework of Britain.

Nennius distinguishes the Britons as the children of Rome and Greece (1848, 387), who descended from an early Roman leader, Brutus. After delineating the pedigree of the Britons, he explains why Brutus was exiled from Rome: "[I]t happened that the mother of the child [died] at its birth, he was named Brutus; and after a certain interval, . . .whilst he was playing with some others he shot his father with an arrow, not intentionally but by accident" (388). This image of patricide establishes an independence for the Britons (not unlike the hopes of latter-day fictitious father-murderer in Irish literature, Christy Mahon, in J. M. Synge's *Playboy of the Western World*). Nennius establishes Britain's link to Rome and repeatedly claims the right of the Britons to all of the islands. After the Britons settled in Britain and the Picts took Scotland, he asserts: "Long after this, the Scots arrived in Ireland from Spain" (389). "The Britons came to Britain in the third age of the world, and in the fourth, the Scots took possession of Ireland. The Britons who, suspecting no hostilities, were unprovided with the means of defence, were unanimously and incessantly attacked, both by the Scots from the west, and the Picts from the north. A long interval after this, the Romans obtained the empire of the world" (390). The Britons, after rebuffing Julius Caesar a number of times, eventually succumbed to Roman armies and, soon after, even embraced their imperial tutelage.

About Ireland, Nennius mostly repeats Rome's depictions of a barbaric land without change, as if the relevance of the passages had not diminished a day in the intervening centuries. He reserves criticism only for Ptolemy and Tacitus, presumably because of their more favorable and detailed accounts of Ireland.[69] Despite his earlier reports of Irish origin legends, he also suggests a British migration to Ireland, using the similarities in the Celtic languages (Welsh, Scots-Gaelic, Manx, and so on, although he does not use the term *Celtic*), to support this British claim for Ireland. This argument established the rhetorical route for subsequent British writers:

[Ireland] is the true country of the Scots, who emigrating from hence added a third nation to the Britons and Picts in Albion. But I cannot agree with Bede, who affirms that the Scots were foreigners. For, according to the testimony from other authors, I conceive they derived their origin from Britain, situated at no considerable distance, passed over from thence, and obtained a settlement in this island. It is certain that the Damnii, Voluntii, Brigantes, Cangi, and other nations [inhabiting Ireland], were descended from the Britons, and passed over thither after Divitiacus, or Claudius, or Ostorius, or other victorious [Roman] generals had invaded their original countries. Lastly the ancient [Irish] language which resembles the old British and Gallic tongues, affords another argument, as is well known to persons skilled in both languages. (459)

Nennius depicts the Irish as British refugees, but more significantly, in this first significant British report of Irish origin legends, they are disputed. Ireland's founders, he argues, fled before Rome and its civilizing imperative; the Irish did not defend against Rome and colonization. Rather, "[Hibernia] was reduced under the Roman power, not by arms, but by fear" (461). Through such arguments, Nennius establishes enduring strategies for British and Anglo-Irish historiography: (1) the British have a rightful claim to Ireland; (2) imperialism's civilizing force had not yet reached Ireland because of its remoteness; (3) Ireland's ancient inhabitants were, at once, cowardly and barbaric; and (4) Ireland's ancient heritage and legends of origins are phony. Not because of their syncretism or fabulousness were Irish legends regarded as false; rather, they contradicted the equally fantastic British origin legends. In the legends' translocation from native Irish culture to British literate culture, Nennius questions their veracity—after all, his authoritative Roman sources do not mention these origins for the Irish.

In subsequent years, pseudohistorians, particularly Geoffrey of Monmouth in the twelfth century, built on Nennius's text, arguing that an earlier British incursion into Ireland (for Geoffrey, that of Arthur) gave Britain a rightful claim to the island, which, in medieval British representations, had long since grown into a wild Irish wasteland.[70] Shortly after Geoffrey wrote his *Historia Regum Brittaniae* (ca. 1138), his readers took the work as a patriotic legend of the Britons more than an actual history.[71] Nevertheless, British historians until the sixteenth century often cited it for historical evidence of British prowess, especially in order to "prove" that King Arthur conquered Ireland—as well as Iceland, Norway, Denmark, Gaul, and parts of the "New World." The importance of such heritages of prowess in national narratives has long been recognized, as has the tendency of medieval writers to turn legends into history, giving rise to subsequent discussions about the authority of such legends. Clearly, both British and Irish pseudohistorians used their legends to help establish a national identity; Irish writers only held on to theirs longer.

Repeatedly over generations, British pseudohistorians and writers—including Nennius, Giraldus, Camden, Stanyhurst, Spenser, and others—discredit the origins of the Irish. Instead of merely dismissing the legends, however, these writers convey Ireland's fantastic origin legends as evidence of the wild nature of the Irish. Such a rhetorical move allows them to illustrate the barbaric character of the Irish before they, though contradictory, discredit Ireland's claims to antiquity—both activities gird the British interest of bringing Ireland into the kingdom. In addition to often demonstrating the ancient consanguinity of the Irish and British, these writers also, in the tradition of Roman historians, manufacture and strengthen resemblances between Ireland and other "uncivilized" cultures, from the Chinese to the African to the Native American. The logic runs as follows: because barbarous cultures resemble one another, imperial intervention needs uniform practices, and the supposed ease and righteousness of creating such civilizing programs convinced many staunch anti-expansionists of the importance of the imperial imperative.

Irish origin legends also persisted in British and Irish texts for other reasons, discursive continuity perhaps being a root cause. Once something is textually established and successfully received by an interpretive community (as these legends were), it serves as an element of a collective identity and continues as an established truth as long as a rhetorical value exists for it in that community. Moreover, in this case, the continuity of an Irish-British conflict sustained the Oriental-Celtic connection for both Irish and British writers, even after the origin legends lost their credibility, as with Arthurian and origin legends, which continue still to inform a vital element of British culture.

After the first recording of the Irish origin legends in Britain was simultaneously disputed, so each subsequent version refuted them. Moreover, not long after the principal Irish redactions of *Lebor Gabála* in the eleventh century, other British texts questioned their validity. Giraldus Cambrensis's *Topographia Hibernica,* written in the 1180s, undermines the Scythian origin legends while retelling them. As in his *Expugnatio Hibernica,* English-Irish politics serve as the backdrop for representations of Ireland. Giraldus, whose actual name was Gerald de Barri, served as the archdeacon of St. David's and accompanied Henry II's son, John, to Ireland to initiate a series of supposed reforms of Irish morality. A papal bull issued by Adrian IV in 1155, *Laudabiliter,* had given control of the Irish church to Henry II, specifying: "That you should enter that island [Ireland] for the purpose of enlarging the boundaries of the church, checking the descent into wickedness, correcting morals and implanting virtues, and encouraging the growth of the faith of Christ" (Leerssen 1996b, 34). Giraldus's representations of Ireland helped fuel this course of English action, depicting a fertile land in need of a civilizing force. Borrowing from oral Irish sources and Bede, but also from earlier Romans, especially Solinus's fabulous depictions, Giraldus presents the Irish as an uncouth and treacherous people living in a land redolent with wonders and miracles. What is most relevant here, however, is Giral-dus's development of an Irish connection to Asia beyond the origin legends.

In the third part of his polemical study, Giraldus repeats the Irish invasion stories, which were still being redacted from oral sources in versions of *Lebor Gabála*. He relays them carefully but with an air of speculation, especially the first story of Cesara's (his spelling) unsuccessful settlement, which was often left out: "[I]n spite of her cleverness, and for a woman, commendable astuteness in seeking to avoid evil, she did not succeed in putting off the general, not to say universal, disaster." Giraldus reserves some pointed skepticism for this story of Noah's granddaughter (particularly because she was a woman), but he treats all of the origin stories as suspect. "But since almost all things were destroyed in the Flood, one may reasonably have doubts as to the value of these arrivals and events that has been handed down after the Flood. Let those, however, who first wrote these accounts be responsible. My function is to outline, not to attack, such stories" (Cambrensis 1982, 93). This last disingenuous statement discredits the legends though entertains them as possible on the surface. Arguing for the "reasonab[ility]" of the invasion legends seems odd in an author who readily relays information about the magical properties of the soil and the miraculous wonders of the land, but his point of view was based not in Enlightenment empiricism but in territorial expansion. His refutation, like Nennius's, remains simple: the Irish legends are false because the English ones are true. Like the work of Solinus, Giraldus Cambrensis's work on Ireland might be understood as a geography of the fantastic in addition to being a prolegomenon for the imperial; indeed, it is difficult for contemporary readers not to read it as anticipating Strongbow's invasion. Except for many of the inhabitants, he explains, Ireland is splendid. He denies Ireland a sense of antiquity by undercutting its invasion legends, thereby removing Ireland from the then established historical framework. Even without this link, however, the semiotic discourse of Ireland's relation to the barbarous East indelibly persists.

The majority of *Topographia Hibernica* focuses on the benefits of Ireland for prospective settlers. The first part advertises the fertility and bounty of the land, provides a brief topographical overview of its rivers and bodies of water, and lists some fauna of Ireland: swans, kingfishers, cranes, barnacles, eagles, foxes, hares, stags, and badgers, making special note of the danger of mice—to production, that is: "Mice are infinite in number and consume much more grain than anywhere else, as well as eating garments though they be locked up carefully. Bede says that there are only two kinds of harmful beasts in Ireland, namely wolves and foxes. I would add the mouse as a third, and say it was very harmful indeed" (49–50). Apparently, Ireland was not as wild and dangerous as rumor had it, but certainly it needed some good housekeeping, husbandry, and, perhaps, some English cats. His comments on reptiles illustrate how he pitches a safe if exotic vision of Ireland to his readers: "Of all kinds of reptiles only those that are not harmful are found in Ireland. It has no poisonous reptiles. It has no serpents or snakes, toads or frogs, tortoises or scorpions. It has no dragons. It has, however, spiders, leeches and lizards—but they are entirely harmless" (50). Clear of snakes and dragons, Ireland appears as more than merely harmless. As in many ancient Greco-Roman texts, Ireland represents an antithesis to poison; its very soil repulses poison-bearing creatures: "[T]he soil of this land is so inimical to poison that, if gardens or any other places of other countries are sprinkled with it, it drives all poisonous reptiles far away" (51). Giraldus paints Ireland as an inviting land, with only a bit of infestation to be handled, and with a certain prosperous future. The Norman invasion had begun in 1169, more than a decade before Giraldus wrote his *Topographia*,[72] which lays the groundwork for further colonization and future English control. In a section of part 1, "A Frog Discovered in Ireland," he relays the augury of an Irish leader, Robert Poer, who understands a living frog in Ireland to be "an indication of what was to be, he said that it was a sure sign of the coming of the English, and the imminent conquest and defeat of his people" (52). Following this prediction at the end of part 1, the author paints Ireland as the Orient's twelfth-century opposite, both locked in a dialogic process of definition, in which they both share opposition to England.

The following list is of the section headings from Giraldus's text that outline his arguments that link Ireland with "the East." In a move that may seem initially strange, he carefully distinguishes Ireland from "the East." Within such a distinction lies the suggestion that opportunities for British expansion (mercantile or colonial) might be better sought in wild Ireland than in the pestiferous East:

The many good points of the island and the natural qualities of the country;
The advantages of the West are to be preferred to those of the East;
All the elements of the East are pestiferous;
The venom of poisons there;
The incomparable mildness of our climate;
Certain deficiencies here that are in fact praiseworthy;
The well of poisons is in the East. (53–56)

Why would Giraldus insert into this topography of Ireland (then understood to be the most westerly habitable island of the West) a lengthy and considered contrast with the East? Many answers may be posited, but Giraldus apparently discerned some rhetorical value in making these distinctions. Although the Irish may be true Scythians, which he asserts, fertile Ireland itself has nothing in common with the "well of poisons" in the East.

All the elements in the East, even though they were created for the help of man, threaten his wretched life, deprive him of health, and finally kill him. If you put your naked foot upon the ground, death is upon you; if you sit upon marble without taking care, death is upon you; if you drink unmixed water, or merely smell dirty water with your nostrils, death is upon you; if you uncover your head to feel the breeze the better, it may affect you by either its heat or coldness—but in any case, death is upon you. . . . The poisoned hand is to be feared there too: that of his step-mother by the step-son, of the enraged wife by her husband, and that of his wicked cook by the master. And not only food and drink, but also clothes, chairs and seats of all kinds. Poisons attack you from all sides, as also do poisonous animals. . . . Let the East, then, have its riches—tainted and poisoned as they are. The mildness of our climate alone makes up to us for all the wealth of the East, in as much as we possess the golden mean in all things, giving us enough for our uses and what is demanded by nature. (54)

The settlement of Ireland would supplant British imperial ambitions in the East. As with its miraculous soil, Ireland offers an alternative and an antidote to the "tainted and poisoned" East. Thus distinguished, Ireland's shared geographical place in the British Isles makes it in Giraldus's text part of "our climate," fertile and ready for English domestication, a special "gift from God, on this earth incomparable" (54), ready-made for English use.

Long before the "discovery" of the American continents, most geographers since Ptolemy[73] understood the earth to be somewhat spherical—if shaped more like an oblong American football; this fueled speculation about geographic and semiotic connections between the people living in the most easterly and the people in the most westerly lands of the world. Although the *Topographia* distinguishes Ireland from uncivilized and barbaric lands, Irish culture's connection with the East remains speculative and elusive. In the second part, Giraldus describes islands near Ireland, commenting on Iceland and later mentioning Thule (another name for Iceland) as if it were a distinct and perhaps fictitious land. A comment by Giraldus reveals the geographical false logic of a west-east connection; because Thule exists far to the west, he implies, it seemed to have a real connection with the East: "A remarkable thing about Thule, which is said to be the farthest of the western islands, is that *it is very well known among the eastern people* both in name and for its nature, although it is entirely unknown to the people in the West" (68; italics added). In his geographical perspective, a great ocean separated eastern Asia from these western islands. These western islands supposedly existed in the ocean that covered the other half of the world opposite the great Eurasian and African continents. In this sense, Thule and Ireland were imagined as geographic meeting places between the East and West; off the western edge of Europe, they approached the eastern edge of Asia.

But, despite its Scythian origins, Giraldus does not treat Ireland's strange culture as Eastern; he merely suggests that in their opposition, they touch and, in their remoteness, share extremities. He contrasts the two and occasionally links Ireland with another outlying land, Africa: "There was in ancient times in Ireland a remarkable pile of stones which was called the Giant's Dance, because giants brought it from the farthest limits of Africa to Ireland" (69). Although such stories of African-Irish connections occasionally crop up in later Irish histories and antiquarian documents, Europe's lack of knowledge and its romanticization about Africa, which continued in the twentieth century, seems to have limited such connections. This African connection appears amid a litany of tales about the bizarre events and misfits in Ireland (the second part opens with "The Wonders and Miracles of Ireland"), which Giraldus lists like a catalog of nature's "errors": descriptions of bestiality, a hermaphrodite, a wolf that spoke to a priest, and "a man that was half an ox and an ox who was half a man" (73). He follows with descriptions of miracles, holy objects, and supernatural stories. They provide the prologue for part 3, in which he tells the Irish origin legends (with reservations) and dispatches Ireland's history up to Henry II's advances into Ireland.

Similar to Nennius's approach, Giraldus summarizes the successive waves of invasion, foregrounding the Scythian connection. Immediately afterward, he cites the other origin legend that Nennius also mentions: borrowing from Geoffrey of Monmouth, he tells how the king of the Britons, Gurguintius, gave Ireland, then uninhabited, to the Basclenses. Giraldus shelves the native Irish legends and lays out the conclusions to be drawn from the second legend: "From this it is clear that Ireland can with some right be claimed by the kings of Britain, even though the claim be from olden times" (99). He then explicitly couples this conclusion with the recent papal bull *Laudabiliter* that placed Ireland under Henry II's authority, referring to them as "the twofold claim" of Britain (100). The book then proceeds with a picture of the "shameful" Irish: "[A]lthough they are fully endowed with natural gifts, their external characteristics of beard and dress, and internal cultivation of the mind, are so barbarous that they cannot be said to have any culture. . . . [They are] a wild and inhospitable people. They live on beasts only, and live like beasts. They have not progressed at all from the primitive habits of pastoral living" (101). The entire work concludes with praise for Henry II, pairing him with Roman emperors, the earlier conquerors of Britain. Henry will, he assumes, do for Ireland what the Romans did for Britain. Giraldus closes with advice given to the emperor Augustus, which seems partly intended to assuage the Irish in his audience: "A brave man regards those as enemies who are fighting for victory, but those who have been conquered he treats as men" (125). Whereas British historians accepted his conclusions for centuries, Irish historians over the next five centuries addressed and critiqued this text perhaps more than any other early British text. Notably, none contradicts (or even acknowledges) the contrast with the East.

Later British Commentators

Although William of Newburgh and William of Malmesbury wrote significant descriptions of Irish history, they did not venture into the origin legends, and few writers on Ireland borrow, respond, or comment on their works; Giraldus, outside Ireland, became and remained the touchstone authority on Ireland and the Irish until the sixteenth century. Ranulf (Ralph) Higden (d. 1364) continued the line of representation of Irish origin legends of Giraldus without much change, demonstrating the continuing relevance of its assertions; his *Polychronicon* was published in English in 1387, 1482, and 1495 (Leerssen 1996b, 36). Higden borrows extensively from Giraldus's and Solinus's comments on the nature of the Irish (as if the intervening thousand years between the two did not matter), detailing their culture as barbarous, incestuous, and fantastic, noting their use of witchcraft, their strange Scythian origins, as well as the story of Tuán ("Ruan" in his text). After a discussion of "wycchecrafte" and selections from Giraldus, he comments on "the Disposicion of the Inhabitatours of that Londe," likening them to the people of the Barbary Coast in North Africa: "Solinus, the grete clerke, rehersethe that the people of that londe be like to the peple of Barbre, bellicose, accomptenge ryghte and wronge as for oon thynge, a peple simple in habite, scarse and litelle in fyndenge, cruelle in herte, scharpe in speche, vsenge furtes for flesche, mylke for drynke, a peple that giffethe more attendaunce to ydelnesse and to disportes than to labour" (1865, 352–53). Higden's conclusions echo Pliny's here in that he sees the Irish sharing similarities with cultures at the borders of the world: "[T]he extremites of the worlde schyne in newe wonders and meruailes, as if that nature scholde schyne and play more in priuate places and remouede them in open places" (361). The Irish and other cultures at the extremities of the world all seem to Higden uncivilized, cruel, drunken, idle, and, perhaps most shocking to him, resentful.

Later British works complemented these impressions. John Derricke's contemporaneous portrait of the Irish wood kerns (1581) promoted images of an uncouth, immoral, and violent Irishry, seeming less civil than the ancient cultures in the East. Earlier, Andrew Borde's *Fyrst Boke of the Introduction of Knowledge* (1542) described the Irish outside the Pale around Dublin, the "wyld Irysh," as slothful, rude, and ignorant, and he again restates the ancient belief in the antipoison properties of Irish soil, among other things (132–33). Robert Payne's *Briefe Description of Ireland, Made in this Yeare 1589* continues such descriptions of Ireland, as does William Camden's *Britain* (1581, Latin; 1610, English). The English Catholic Edmund Campion wrote his *Historie of Ireland* in 1569 and revised it in 1571. The work circulated in manuscript until its publication in 1633 by James Ware. Before that publication, however, a former pupil and friend, Richard Stanyhurst, based his "Description of Ireland" on Campion's text and published it in Raphael Holinshed's *Chronicles* in 1586. Perhaps the most influential work that drew from Campion's manuscript, however, was Edmund Spenser's *View of the Present State of Ireland* (1598).[74] All of these works from this period comment on the barbarity of the native Irish, generally referred to then as the "meere Irish" (meaning pure but also limited). The proliferation of works commenting on Irish origin legends in the late Tudor period paralleled the increasing attention that English writers gave to classical Greek and Roman connections. Some British writers, such as John Dee and Humphrey Gilbert, drew from Geoffrey of Monmouth's *Historia Regum Brittaniae* (ca. 1138) and averred that they were recovering King Arthur's empire, rather than establishing a new one (Hadfield 1993, 390–91). But most British historians increasingly distrusted the use of Arthurian origin legends for the British, however, even though most historians of the time supported early British versions of Irish origin legends (as Nennius had) that support a British claim for Ireland. Such searches for connections to antiquity had spread across Europe during the Renaissance, and Irish-Oriental connections were treated as fitting into this enthusiasm. But even amid the rise of source criticism (in which the accuracy of the sources and the implications of the social contexts of ancient texts were considered), historians and writers increasingly used origin texts to explain political situations rather than historical truths, nevertheless continuing, in many ways, the rhetorical project established by Giraldus Cambrensis.

In the sixteenth and seventeenth centuries, English depictions of Ireland particularly corresponded with ideas about English governance in Ireland. In Ireland, Irish origin legends also continued to serve political aims and cultural functions, distinct from British aims. These origin legends carried no historical weight outside of Ireland—generally such legends had been abandoned across the continent by the seventeenth century—but images of the barbaric Scythian ancestry haunted representations of the contemporary Irish (more so than anywhere else in western Europe). Despite the prevalence of such images, however, we must be aware that British observers had no uniform vision of Ireland and often split over questions such as whether it was part of the kingdom or a British colony, as Andrew Hadfield explains in his essay "Briton and Scythian: Tudor Representations of Irish Origins": "To some, moving to Ireland might have seemed like migrating to any other part of mainland Britain; to others, Ireland resembled one of the nastier parts of the new world" (1993, 406). The writers who painted the island as belonging to these "nastier parts" emphasized Ireland's difference and employed the Scythian narratives, generally attempting to convince the Crown administration of the need for English governance in Ireland.[75] English representations of Ireland that employed the Scythian origin legends tended to promote England's civilizing mission there, and throughout the "Age of Discovery" (or the age of European colonial expansion) the semiotic connection over Ireland's ancient heritage developed in a push-and-pull battle between barbarization and veneration.

Remarkably, procolonial English writers tended to use the origin legends to confirm Irish barbarity even as they disputed the veracity of the legends. English claims to Ireland, based in similar pseudohistories, however, continued to be referenced in discussions of Ireland through the seventeenth century. Even in the late-sixteenth-century work of Edmund Campion—a Catholic convert who had some sympathy for Irish culture, writing his *Historie* (1571) in Ireland at the home of Richard Stanyhurst—the most ancient claim to Ireland is England's. Nevertheless, Campion still borrows from the Irish origin legends to praise the Irish for their Eastern learning and language skills, qualities that he links to their "Ægyptian" origins:

> The remnant [Gathelus (or Gaedel Glass) and his people][76] passed with him into Ireland, where the Barbarians highly honoured him, for his cunning in all languages, who also greatly perfected and beautified the Irish tongue, taught them letters, sought up their antiquities, practiced their youth in martially feates, after his Greek and Ægyptian manner. . . . A brute there is in Ireland but uncertainelie fathered, that in remembrance of *Pharo,* their good lord, the Kerne pitching his Dart, cryeth of courage *faro, faro;* but the learned thinke that to bee taken from the Spaniard, who in his *Ioco dicano* exclaymeth *fabo, fabo.* (1940, 27–28)

Although this cry certainly had no Egyptian etymology, Campion assumes this warning cry to be an ancient Egyptian tribute.[77] Not knowing Irish, Campion clearly misunderstands details and presents them as exotic aspects of Irish culture (but not as illustrations of an ancient Irish independence from Britain). That his conclusions went in this direction is significant; his guess reveals his assumptions about Ireland's ancient connections. On the most fundamental level, the Irish connection with the East seems to have persisted because the semiotic connection had been firmly established at the base of an Irish cultural identity, and it provided an amenable explanation of Irish difference. Moreover, granting that the Irish were Eastern did not mean Ireland could not belong to Britain.

Campion wrote during the buildup of Spanish-English conflicts over control in the Americas and ocean dominance in the late sixteenth century, which lessened after the destruction of the Spanish Armada off the coast of Ireland in 1588 and Spain's defeat in France in the early 1590s. Campion uses the origins of the Irish to explain Ireland's growing political alliance with Spain. Indeed, his reading of the legends seems to answer a question on people's minds about the origins of the Irish: "[to] give a light to the assoyling of a controversie, that is, whether the Irish came from Ægypt, or from Spaine. It shall appeare they came from both" (26). Campion recognizes, but downplays, the burgeoning Spanish-Irish connection in the mid- to late sixteenth century and gives credit to Ireland's ancient allegiance with Egypt. A decade after Campion's *Historie* appeared in 1569, this Iberian-Hibernian alliance came to a head when English forces routed and massacred a Spanish garrison based in Smerwick, and became embodied in Irish folklore after the Spanish Armada shipwrecked off the shores of Ireland and Spanish sailors supposedly swam ashore, married, settled, and (in one version) gave birth to the "Black Irish." Significantly, Campion sees the Irish Milesian migration story from Spain as valid and revelatory, but he treats it as only confirming Britain's right to Ireland. Andrew Hadfield further explains how Campion posits Irish Milesian history as one of continual subjection. In British pseudohistory, Spain had once belonged to the Britons: "[Campion's] story envelops an origin of the Irish as a subject people, a movement from freedom to slavery, disguising any act of colonial aggression or conquest, as they are said to come from a land already part of a British empire and simply to move to another part. When the lands in Spain became subject to Gurguntius we are not told" (1993, 396). Such accounts allowed Campion to textually deliver ancient Spain to ancient Britain, without controverting the Irish invasion stories, which seemed the most plausible explanation for the difference of Irish culture. Moreover, Oriental origins do not grant the Irish a history of political independence in British texts as they generally do in Irish texts.

With the exception of Campion, most other Tudor histories of Ireland retold versions of the origin legends but doubted their truthfulness. William Camden's *Britain; or, A Chorographicall Description of the Most Flourishing Kingdomes, England, Scotland, and Ireland* (1581, Latin; 1610, English) borrowed heavily from Strabo and Giraldus and extended many of their anti-Irish biases. Instead of relying upon contemporary accounts, his "descriptions" emerge *"out of the depth of Antiqvitie,"* as the long title notes. Significantly, Camden's respected history engages in source criticism, but only selectively, critiquing the construction of texts that contradict the conclusions he wished to reach. As Giraldus had done centuries before, Camden's chorography unquestioningly borrows incredible characterizations of Ireland from Greek and Roman texts. He also included accounts of the origin legends, somewhat undermining their impact: "My purpose is not either to averre these reports for true, nor yet to refute them: In such things as these let Antiquity bee pardonable, and enjoie a prerogative. . . . Surely, as I doubt not but that this Island became inhabited even of old time, when as man-kinde was spred over all quarters of the world: so it is evident, that the first inhabitants thereof passed thither out of our Britaine" (1610, 64). Through his discussions on the etymology of *Hibernia,* Camden seems most impressed by Ireland's reported antiquity, the wonder increased because of its apparent state of barbarity in the present.[78] In restating the most plausible history of the settlement of Ireland, Camden also reassures his readership of Britain's claim to Ireland—"it is evident, that the first inhabitants thereof passed thither out of our Britaine"—but he uses the Irish origin legends to lend an air of antiquity to the land. Such a move was common in the Renaissance, when readers valued things classical and ancient, and the best-regarded histories stood on the shoulders of ancient texts: "If that be true which the Irish Historiographers record, this Island was not without cause by *Plutarch* termed *Ogygia,* that is, *very ancient.* For, they fetch the beginning of their histories from the most profound and remote records of antiquity; so that in comparison of them, the Antientnesse of all other nations is but novelty, and, as it were, a matter of yesterday" (64). Ireland as Ogygia (the island of Calypso in Homer's *Odyssey* and once thought to be part of the mythical Atlantean island chain) made it the most ancient land in Europe, as later texts argued (perhaps most notably Roderic O'Flaherty's fabulous reworking of the Irish origin legends in *Ogygia* [1685]). Despite the far-fetched details of the legends, and the borrowings from ancient texts, suppositions about Ireland's Eastern ancestry developed in even more pointed ways.

Spenser's Dim View

The ancient, barbarous, and Eastern nature of the Irish finds its most damning expression of the period in Edmund Spenser's *View of the Present State of Ireland* (1633). This prose dialogue on Irish culture supplanted Giraldus as the primary authoritative text for the British on Ireland. For the Irish, it became and remained for centuries the prime textual example of imperial propaganda. Written between 1596 and 1598, the text, like Campion's, circulated for years in manuscript form, and, probably due to its graphic descriptions and extreme recommendations, it remained unpublished until after Spenser's death when antiquarian James Ware (1594–1666) in 1633 made it the centerpiece of his compilation *The Historie of Ireland.* Ware, an early Trinity graduate, served as the auditor general of Ireland, as an Irish MP, and privy councillor in 1639. Working with Dubhaltach Mac Fhir Bhisigh, whom Ware had commissioned to redact, copy, write, and collect Irish manuscripts, Ware assembled a large collection, which today forms the largest part of the Clarendon Collection in the Bodleian Library. Ware brought together three non-Irish works on Ireland: Edmund Campion's history, Meredith Hanmer's *Chronicle of Ireland,* and Spenser's *View,* all of which relayed some version of the origin legends. Campion's sympathies to Irish culture were well known at the time, as was the manner of his death (he had been martyred for his Catholicism), and his work attracted much of Ware's readership. But, clearly, Spenser's text was the main draw. In the four versions of Ware's publication, it was the only one to be included in every binding and the only one to be bound and sold separately.

A *View* consists of a dialogue between two English characters: the interlocutor, Eudoxus, poses rational questions about Ireland that the respondent, Irenius, answers in often lengthy digressions based upon his experience in Ireland and his knowledge of Irish culture (although occasionally Irenius asks questions).[79] Spenser developed fantastic images of the Irish from book 5 of *The Faerie Queene,* which allegorizes Ireland in the wilds of Faeryland.[80] Rather than connecting Ireland to an exotic Faery otherworld here, he emphasizes Ireland's Eastern connection with Scythia. Unlike any previous text, *A View* explicitly analyzes ancient Scythian influences on present-day Irish culture. Although the discussants retain a civil tone throughout the work, much of the commentary excoriates the contemporary Irish. In one explanation, Irenius repeats four of the Irish origin legends, treating them as fabulous histories that reveal only cultural truths: "[The stories] being made by unlearned men . . . doe erre in the circumstances, not in the matter" (1633, 48). Moreover, the "matter" that Spenser uncovers entirely supports the expansion of England's "civilizing" efforts in Ireland. The most infamous passage in the work is Irenius's disturbing and dispassionate description of the 1579 Munster famine during the Desmond Rebellion, which Spenser's narrator claims to have witnessed firsthand (as Spenser may have):

> Out of every corner of the woods and glynnes they came creeping forth upon their hands, for their legges could not beare them, they looked like anatomies of death, they spake like ghosts crying out of their graves, they did eate the dead carrions, happy were they could finde them, yea, and one another soon after, insomuch as the very carcasses they spared not to scrape out of their graves. . . . [I]n that warre, there perished not many by the Sword, but all by the extremitie of famine, which they themselves had wrought. (101–2)

The narrator concludes that the Irish brought this "folly" upon themselves and marvels at how little time it took before they began to "devoure one another." In addition to his inhumane distaste in witnessing these famine victims, Spenser subtly points to an act of cannibalism, which, as he noted earlier in the text (along with blood drinking), is Scythian in origin.[81] Irish barbarity was not treated as a degeneration from a past civil culture; rather, in Spenser's narrative, these horrors emerge as atavisms from a sinister Scythian past.

Significantly, origin legends arise, as in Campion, from a discussion of contemporary politics. Irenius retells the origin legends in an answer about the Spanish origins of the Irish. Indeed, both sides invoked Milesian history in the 1580s and 1590s during the Spanish-British (and Catholic-Anglican) conflicts. Irenius, on the Anglican side, treats the legends as "a forged history . . . deliver[ed] to fooles" and asserts Ireland's Scythian origins over Spanish ones:

> [The writers of Irish and Roman chronicles supposed] all that came out of Spaine . . . to be Spaniards, and so called them; but the ground-work thereof is nevertheless true and certain, however they through ignorance disguise the same, or through vanity, whilst they would not seem to be ignorant, doe thereupon build and enlarge many forged histories of their owne antiquity, which they deliver to fooles, and

make them believe for true; as for example, That first of one Gathelus the sonne of Cecropos or Argos, who having married the King of Egypt his daughter, thence sailed with her into Spaine, and there inhabited: Then that of Nemedus and his sonnes, who coming out of Scythia, peopled Ireland, and inhabited it with his sonnes 250 yeares, until he was overcome of the Giants dwelling then in Ireland, and at the last quite banished and rooted out, after whom 200 yeares, the sonnes of one Dela, being Scythians, arrived there againe, and possessed the whole land, of which the youngest called Slanius, in the end made himselfe Monarch. Lastly, of the 4 sonnes of Milesius King of Spaine, which conquered the land from the Scythians, and inhabited it with Spaniards, and called it of the name of the youngest Hiberus, Hibernia. (49)

Immediately following the end of this brief overview of the four principal "invasion" stories, Spenser has Irenius reduce all Irish-Spanish connections by highlighting the Scythian. The Scythian connection here becomes more than a way of differentiating the Irish and English; he emphasizes how the Irish, as Asiatic Scythians, differ from all Europe: "all . . . are in truth fables, and very Milesian lyes, as the later proverbe is: for never was there such a King of Spaine, called Milesius, nor any such colonie seated with his sonnes, as they faine, that can ever be proved; but yet under these tales you may in a manner see the truth lurke. For Scythians here inhabiting, they name and put Spaniards, whereby appeareth that both these nations here inhabited, but whether very Spaniards, as the Irish greatly affect, is no wayes to be proved" (49). Spenser's Irenius argues that, although a King Milesius never existed, the Irish pretend, in their "very Milesian lyes," to be related to the Spaniards for political convenience. As in the origin legends, Spanish Milesians are actually Scythians. The cultural base of the Irish, for Irenius, is Scythian, which in English texts was a metaphor for savagery (Hadfield 1997, 102–3; Cullingford 2001, 102–5).[82] Instead of entirely dismissing the legends—these "forged histories of their owne antiquity"—Spenser claims their falsity contains a grain of truth, revealing Irish culture to be Scythian.

Spenser's text rails against the Old English settlers and their adopting the hybrid customs and language of the Irish, but his overarching message is clear: Ireland must be reorganized along the lines of English culture and morality. Origin legends provided a clear model for affirming this mission, as Hadfield has argued.

English writers under the Tudors looked back to their own British origins and claimed that these validated a right to the possession of the Irish crown either through an ancestral conquest or the inhabitation of a common territory. At the same time the savage, alien nature of the Irish inhabitants was asserted. In other words, land and people were firmly separated, Irish land forming part of an ancient British unity and Irish people cast in the role of the intractable "otherness" which must be removed, voices which must be silenced, if that unity is to be recovered. (1993, 405)

Spenser works to identify the "otherness" of the Irish with Scythian origins, arguing that it predominates the mixed races of Ireland and will continue to do so (and possibly spread) unless extirpated. Only a complete reformation of Irish culture will make it civil. *A View* targets hybrid Irish-English customs, asserting that the only cultural practices to be encouraged should be British, based on English ideals and custom. Significantly, at the core of Spenser's use of the origin legends is an attack not merely upon the Irish that he demonizes, but on the entire process of cultural syncretism.

Although Spenser identifies four distinct groups in contemporary Ireland—Scythians (or Scottes) in the North; Spaniards in the West; Gaules (or Celts) in the South; and Brittaines in the East—he argues that Scythian customs, or "Scythian abuses" (1633, 59), underlay them all, their traits having tenaciously corrupted every group. Spenser's rational Englishman, Eudoxus, notes how Romans never integrated with the local population or "went native," and they therefore find the Roman imperial model the appropriate one for British and Irish relations. He is shocked that earlier English settlers from the twelfth century now speak Irish: "It seemeth strange to me that the English should take more delight to speake that language, then their owne, whereas they should (mee thinks) rather take scorne to acquaint their tongues thereto. For it hath ever beene the use of the conqueror, to despise the language of the conquered, and to force him by all meanes to learne his. So did the Romans always use, insomuch that there is almost no nation in the world, but is sprinckled with their language" (70). Such borrowing from Rome is acceptable, but no mingling of English and Irish language and custom is supported.

In Irenius's reply to Eudoxus, he feminizes the Irish threat and peril, identifying the contaminating link between Irish and English culture in three sources: Irish nurses, Irish wives, and the Irish language—all feminine seductions that corrupt the rational pillar of English masculine culture (71–72). Spenser not only identifies the agents that spread Irish cultural effeminate degeneracy (or just effeminacy?) to the English settlers but also enumerates Irish culture's connections to its Scythian roots based on observations and Greco-Roman texts—cattle herding, cooking, diet, manners of dress and hairstyle, weaponry, battle tactics, funeral customs, oaths, religion, superstitions, and other peculiar traits. Afterward, he admits he might have provided further examples: "Many such customes I could recount unto you, as of their old manner of marrying, of burying, of dancing, of singing, of feasting, of cursing, though Christians have wiped out the most part of them, by resemblance, whereof it might plainly appeare to you, that the nations are the same . . . the Irish are anciently deduced from the Scythians" (64).[83] To remove these "evills," Irenius proposes a draconian solution: stamp out pervasive and native Irish customs (especially Scythian ones) and "restrayne" the Irish language (71). Spenser hints that these traditions may spread if allowed to continue, playing on Tudor fears of the possible Gaelicization of England.

Origin legends provide the foundation for Irenius's assertions—"under these tales you may in a manner see the truth lurke" (49). His rhetorical strategy is not complex; it consists of simply tagging recognizable Irish customs as barbaric and, hence, Scythian. Cattle "boolying" or herding (55–56) and the wearing of mantles or cloaks and long curled, knotted locks of hair or "long glibbes" (56–59) become "Scythian abuses" (59): "[T]heir short bowes, and little quivers with short bearded arrows, are very Scythian. . . . Moreover their long broad shields, made but with wicker roddes, . . .are brought from the Scythians. . . . [L]ikewise their going to battle without armor on their bodies or heads, but trusting to the thicknes of their glibbs, the which (they say) will sometimes beare off a good stroke, is meere Scythian" (62). Assertions repeatedly constitute his argument—and anything offensive and non-English becomes Scythian. But he also describes the Catholic (or unreformed) Irish in more occult terms. After noting that the Irish and Scythians shared "certain religious ceremonies," Irenius conveys the most startling revelation about the beastly Scythian-Irish: "Also the Scythians said, That they were once a yeare turned into wolves, and so it is written of the Irish: Though Master Camden in a better sense doth suppose it was a disease, called Lycanthropia, so named of the wolfe. And yet some of the Irish doe use to make the wolfe their gossip" (64). Spenser may have found such stories in Irish folklore, and he certainly knew Giraldus's reference to a wolf speaking to a priest in his *Topographia Hibernica* (Cambrensis 1982, 73). But Spenser suggests more than a casual bestial affinity here. The trope helps humanize Queen Elizabeth's forces and their activities in Ireland by dehumanizing the Irish, pitting them and their Scythian forebears as werewolves waging war against humanity.

Despite its absurdly negative spin, Spenser's focus reinforced the reliability of Irish sources in which Scythian references abounded. Arguing that Spenser was familiar with the Irish language, Irish studies scholar Clare Carroll (building on the work of Roland M. Smith in the 1940s) explains how Spenser relied upon *Lebor Gabála* and other Irish sources for his retelling.[84] Significantly, Spenser not only advanced the discussion of Nennius, Giraldus, Higden, Campion, Camden, and Stanyhurst and Holinshed but also created a cross-cultural argument based on the supposed similarities between contemporary Ireland and ancient Scythia, a rhetorical move that prefigures many later Irish comparisons between the Celtic and the Oriental. Indeed, although his argument is more assertion than analysis, he delivered the most nuanced and detailed comparison up to that date. He also gave the most spurious invective against Irish culture yet written. Spenser advanced the case for English colonization in Ireland, a part of the larger discursive project that Giraldus had begun four hundred years earlier. In deepening Irish culture's link to ancient Scythia, however, he also encouraged a mode of distinguishing Irish culture from British culture through asserting its supposed ancient seat in the East.

Early Imperial Comparisons

In addition to Spenser's deeper cultural analysis/invective, comparisons between Ireland and other borderlands emerged during the early seventeenth century in British writing, following the establishment of the East India Company in 1600 and Britain's increasing supremacy on the ocean trade routes. Spenser asserted with a new authority (but reliant upon Greek and Roman sources) that the Irish and Scythian "nations are the same" (1633, 64), but he saw other barbaric traditions existing in Ireland, including the African, stemming from the Barbary Coast.[85] Spenser may have gotten such hints from Irish sources, a number of which claimed African origins for some of Ireland's early inhabitants, particularly the Fomorians.[86]

During the age of European discovery and expansion, many similar comparisons between the Irish and other cultures on the edges of the "civilized world" developed in ways similar to Spenser's cultural analysis.[87] For instance, William Camden, in his *Annales: The True and Royall History of the Famous Empresse Elizabeth, Queene of England, France and Ireland* (1625), describes how the Irish were often perceived by the English. He describes "Shan O-Neale's" visit to Elizabeth's court in 1563:

> At the same time, *Shan O-Neale* came out of *Ireland,* to performe that which he had promised the yeere before, having for his Guard, a troupe of *Galloglassorum,* who had their heads naked, and curled haire hanging on their shoulders, yellow shirts, as if they had beene died with Saffron, or steeped in Urine, wide sleeves, short Cassockes, and rough hairy Clokes. The *English* admired them no lesse, than they should doe at this day to see those of *China,* or *America.* Having been received with all courtesie, hee cast himselfe at the Queenes feete, and with teares acknowledged his crime, asked pardon, and obtained it. (1:90)[88]

In Camden's account, the great Irish leader arouses wonder in the English as if they were Chinese or Native American. The strangeness of Ireland's cultural difference fosters the ready comparison with other cultures at the distant ends of the earth.

This universalizing ideological perspective lumped those peoples on the edges of civilization together; such a perspective pervaded English imagination and encouraged Irish identification with cultures in Asia, North America, and the Caribbean.[89] Sir Philip Sidney in *Apology for Poetry; or, The Defense of Poesy* (written

1579–1580; published 1595) explains how poetry is foundational to all peoples, even barbarous and uncivil ones:

> In Turkey, besides their law-giving divines, they have no other writers but poets. In our neighbour country Ireland, where truly learning goeth very bare, yet are their poets held in a devout reverence. Even among the most barbarous and simple Indians where no writing is, yet have they their poets who make and sing songs, which they call *areytos,* both of their ancestors' deeds and praises of their gods—a sufficient probability that, if ever learning come among them, it must be by having their hard dull wits softened and sharpened with the sweet delights of Poetry; for until they find a pleasure in the exercises of the mind, great promises of much knowledge will little persuade them that know not the fruits of knowledge. In Wales, the true remnant of the ancient Britons, as there are good authorities to show the long time they had poets, which they called *bards,* so through all the conquests of Romans, Saxons, Danes, and Normans, some of whom did seek to ruin all memory of learning from among them, yet do their poets even to this day last; so as it is not more notable in soon beginning than in long continuing. (1989, 83)

Aside from the humanistic argument about the importance of poetry in disparate cultures, what is notable in this passage is Sidney's easy comparisons of the cultures of Turkey, Ireland, Native America, and Wales with "ancient Britons." The first four all signified Britain's ancestral culture; moreover, to Sidney they resembled one another just as the word *Indian* signified peoples native to both the Americas and the subcontinent. This origin could not have continued based solely on the story of Columbus's accidental misrecognition. Such comparisons, imperial in outlook, conflate disparate cultures based on scant evidence. The justification is initially based on the need to make sense of difference and create a coherent worldview in which disparate groups may appear the same. These comparisons, as with Pliny's argument about barbaric peoples who are both alike and "wholly ignorant of one another," make them cohere under the imperial gaze. But even after the comparison is shown to be incorrect, it may continue for reasons that are culturally and politically determined. As with the pathetic fallacy, in which a poet's emotions correspond with the natural world, the coherence fallacy makes a certain emotional sense because of its privileged and imperial outlook. Its rhetoric materializes out of limited anecdotal and casual comparisons into more purposeful imperial analyses, as in the texts comparing Oriental and Celtic cultures that developed throughout the span of the British Empire. Three centuries after Sidney, Matthew Arnold used this same line of reasoning in arguing for the value of literature in *On the Study of Celtic Literature,* freely pairing more "primitive" cultures while lamenting the decline of the place of literature in philistine Britain. Following the Greco-Roman uniting of barbarians, Sidney even notes the classical link directly following the passage quoted above: "But since the authors of most of our sciences were the Romans, and before them the Greeks, let us a little stand upon their authorities" (83). In borrowing authority, however, he also adopts much of their framing of the world.

Instances of such comparisons exist in English travel literature of the time, as might be expected. Fynes Moryson (1566–1617) explores Irish cannibalism and treats the Irish and the Turks together as the least-civilized peoples in *Itinerary Containing His Ten Yeeres Travell* (1617, 2:328).[90] One of the most acidic travel writers of the time, the Scottish writer William Lithgow traveled through Ireland in 1619 on a grand tour of much of Europe, West Asia, and Africa and described his travels in *The Totall Discourse, of the Rare Adventures of Nineteene Yeares Travayles* (1632). Lithgow, who had been held captive during the Spanish Inquisition, was fiercely anti-Catholic, as his work amply demonstrates.[91] Lithgow's work is full of unflattering portrayals,[92] and he notes how other Europeans (especially the Hungarians) were descended from the Scythians (414). His comments on the Irish signal for him that they can be best understood through comparisons with cultures outside civilized western Europe. Prefiguring the sources for Jonathan Swift's eighteenth-century satire of discovery narratives, *Gulliver's Travels,* Lithgow's narrator makes a number of voyages to and from Britain.[93] On his voyage to Ireland, he finds, like nearly every British writer before him, the land excellent but the inhabitants otherwise: "I found the goodnesse of the Soyle, more than answerable to mine expectation, the defect only remaining (not speaking of our Collonies) in the people, and from them, in the bosome of two gracelesse sisters, Ignorance and Sluggishnesse" (428). Lithgow also finds comparisons between the Irish and the Turks to resonate more deeply than a reader today might expect:

> But now to come to my punctuall Discourse of *Ireland;* true it is, to make a fit comparison, the *Barbarian Moore,* the *Moorish Spaniard,* the *Turke,* and the *Irish man,* are the least industrious, and most sluggish livers under the Sunne, for the vulgar *Irish* I protest, live more miserably in their brutish fashion, then the undaunted, or untamed *Arabian,* the Divelish-idolatrous *Turcoman,* or the Moone-worshipping *Caramines:* showing thereby a greater necessity they have to live, then any pleasure they have, or can have in their living. . . . And if sicke, scabbed, or sore, they solicit her mayden-fac'd Maiesty [that is, the moon] to restore them to their health, in which absurdity, they far surmount the silly *Sabuncks,* and *Garolinean Moores* of *Lybia.* (429–30)

In the emerging discourse of the Orient, the Irish serve as a touchstone for Lithgow, but he builds on the coherence fallacy to paint the Irish as more barbaric and absurd than these Oriental cultures. The Orient works here as a measuring stick for *otherness.* But for Lithgow, these words were not mere rhetorical posturing; after witnessing these North African and West Asian cultures, Lithgow could fit Irish culture into a more coherent worldview. The superstitious Irish resembled the "Divelish-idolatrous" Turk and the "undaunted, or untamed *Arabian*" much more so than the English or other Europeans. Moreover, such comparisons gave purpose to the destined English colonial efforts in "untamed" Ireland and elsewhere.

The comparisons to the Orient remain instructive to Lithgow's British readers. The strangest comparison that he makes is meant to elucidate an image of "Northern Irish women giving sucke to their Babes behind their shoulders": "The other as goodly sight I saw, was women travayling the way, or toyling at home, carry their Infants about their neckes, and laying the dugges over their shoulders, would give sucke to the Babes behinde their backes, without taking them in their armes: Such kind of breasts, me thinketh, were very fit, to be made money bags for East or West *Indian* merchants, being more than halfe a yarde long, and as wel wrought, as any *Tanner,* in the like charge, could ever mollifie such Leather" (433). In a typical move for writers who sought to denigrate the Irish, *otherness* and barbarism override human interaction; as in Solinus's third-century image of mothers feeding their children milk off sword blades,[94] maternity is removed from nursing and feeding. These women could also be credited with a monstrous practicality in keeping their hands free by not holding their nursing children "in their armes." These Irish women's elastic, leather breasts are objectified to an inhuman degree. They are emptied imagistically of maternal purpose but not sexualized; rather, Lithgow compares them to leather "money bags for East or West *Indian* merchants." The women become mere receptacles "as wel wrought, as any *Tanner . . .* could ever mollifie such Leather." The meanness within the traveler's exoticizing gaze here may overshadow his comparison and coherence fallacy: it seems the barbaric Irish may be understood only through comparison with the cruel Orient. Debates over whether the Irish had a noble or barbaric ancestry continued to be a question, but as these texts make clear, it seems that Ireland's status as an ancient culture had been established as a fact alongside Ireland's geographic remoteness.

Dehumanizing representations of the cultures of Ireland and the Orient (as well as unflattering comparisons of the Irish with apes)[95] became common to proimperial and jingoistic texts in Britain through the beginning of the twentieth century. Less spurious comparisons continued in less extreme texts, and much scholarship over the past forty years has mapped this textual terrain.[96] Few of these texts comment on the cultural continuity of such comparisons, however. The texts themselves at times admit their sources (as in Spenser's heavily referenced work), but other texts such as Lithgow's and Camden's rely mostly upon either hearsay, observation, or undocumented sources. To reference earlier similar comparisons, in Irish or British texts, would lessen the immediacy and verisimilitude of their claims, which are supposed to be based generally on empirical observation, as in Lithgow's text. Such comparisons, when read today, tend to foreground the gaze of the speaker more so than the object of study; much of the evidence presented (for example, of werewolves or elastic breasts) appears, in lieu of credible physical evidence, to be based on other cultural evidence, that is, oral, written, or even unspoken assumptions about the similarity of cultures in Ireland, the Orient, Africa, and the New World. The optics of cultural lenses, after all, rarely are perceived by the ones who gaze through them.

2 Ogygia

Europe's Backyard Orient and the Rise of Antiquarianism

> Ireland is justly called Ogygia, i.e. very antient, according to
> Plutarch, for the Irish date their history from the first æras of the
> world; so that in comparison with them, the antiquity of all other
> countries is modern, and almost in its infancy!
> —Roderic O'Flaherty, quoting William Camden citing Plutarch

> This enigmatical mode of philosophizing, so prevalent among the
> oriental, [the Irish] learned from the ancient Phœnicians, who had
> it from the Jews.
> —Charles Vallancey, preface to *Collectanea De Rebus Hibernicus*

DESPITE DISMISSALS by British Tudor historians of Ireland, Irish origin legends continued to inform the works of Irish writers and historians. In the first half of the seventeenth century, two masterful retellings were compiled in Irish, *Foras Feasa ar Éirinn* (Groundwork of knowledge of Ireland) (1618–1634) by Geoffrey Keating (Seathrún Céitinn;[1] ca. 1580-ca. 1644) and *Annála Ríoghachta Eireann* (1632–1636) by Mícheál Ó Cléirigh (Michael O'Clery; ?1590–1643), commonly called *The Annals of the Four Masters* (but properly translated as *Annals of the Kingdom of Ireland*). Other histories of this period, such as Philip O'Sullevan Beare's (?1594–?1634) *Compendium* (1621), attacked British denigrations of Irish culture and used the legends to both bolster a positive image of the Gaelic Catholic Irish and promote the Iberno-Hibernian-Milesian connection. Still other histories of the period, such as Peter Lombard's (?1560–1625) *De Regno Hiberniae Commentarius* (completed in 1600; Louvain publication, 1632), lauded Hugh O'Neill as a champion of the Counter-Reformation and presented an anti-English view of the events in Ireland under Elizabeth's forces, stirring support for Gaelic Catholic Ireland on the Continent and refuting Strabo, Solinus, and Giraldus Cambrensis. Other straightforward defenses of Irish Gaelic culture, such as the one by a Limerick attorney, Luke Gernaon, entitled *Discourse in Ireland* (1620), overtly sought to recuperate the image of Gaelic culture from tropes of Irish barbarization.[2] Keating's and Ó Cléirigh's works relayed the most comprehensive versions of the synthesized origin legends to date and became foundational sources for later cultural nationalists, antiquarians, and philologists. Moreover, Keating's elegant Irish prose distinguishes his work as a valuable piece of literature, not merely a collection of legends or repository of cultural myths.

Amid political turmoil in the mid-sixteenth century, particularly the events surrounding the Irish rebellion of 1641, Irish writing worked to address and refit the resistant and embattled cultural identity of the Gaelic Irish. In the wake of Giraldus, Camden, and Spenser, Irish writers used the legends as a basis for evoking allegiances of an ancient collective identity for Gaelic Ireland, prompted by scholarly work in Celtic languages on the Continent. When philologists and antiquarians—both Anglo-Irish and Gaelic—followed by historians, took on the mantle of retelling (and reinventing) the story of the ancient Irish in the eighteenth century, the Asian element became still more prominent, encouraged by both the emerging discipline of Orientalism and a lack of understanding of Celtic languages. Eighteenth-century antiquarians, in particular, latched onto this connection, extrapolating conclusions from many sources, ancient, medieval, and contemporary. The work of one of the last scholars educated in traditional bardic learning, Roderic O'Flaherty, had particular influence on the following generations of antiquarians. In 1685, O'Flaherty had written a new commentary on the legends in his *Ogygia*, which explicitly connected the Irish to the Phoenicians, expanding the work of Samuel Bochart. In the manner of O'Flaherty, later antiquarians treated the origin legends less as actual history and more as legends encoded with historical truths about the ancient Irish. Not doubting the validity of the Oriental model, they ran with etymological strategies and ballooned whatever insights they generated into fantastic conclusions about Ireland's roots in West Asia. Foremost among these antiquarians, General Charles Vallancey inspired many writers in Ireland through his position at the Royal Irish Academy (RIA), asserting Irish links to border peoples around the world with evidence marshaled from archaeology, historiography, language studies, literature, and cultural discussions.

The fantastic nature of these pseudoinductive studies swayed thinkers beyond Irish antiquarian circles. At its most influential, Irish antiquarianism spurred writers to make connections that had never been carefully considered. Two influential men in particular made use of ideas spawned in antiquarian speculations: the Welsh Orientalist Sir William Jones (1746–1794) (also known as "Persian" or "Oriental" Jones) and, later, the Irish Romantic and cultural nationalist Thomas Moore. Other less concrete yet more pervasive effects resulted from these arguments about Ireland's Eastern origins. Particular moments in the legends were read as indicators of ancient values. One key example from the legends illustrates: the king of Scythia, Féinius Fein, assembled a group of scholars after the confusion of the tongues to construct the Irish language from the world's seventy-two languages and then sent his son, Nel, to teach writing to the pharaoh of Egypt. The values attributed to Ireland's ancestors here include linguistic sophistication, cultural syncretism, and ancient nobility. The Oriental origin legends connect ancient Ireland to glorious and venerable events of the classical world; this remote island in the western ocean becomes—what O'Flaherty called *Ogygia,* the island where Calypso detained Ulysses for seven years—a last outpost of living antiquity.

Scholars often credit historians, writers, and artists with the initial impulses of cultural nationalism, focusing on nationalist commentaries and their attempts to forge new cultural identities through reworked myths and legends. John Hutchinson, author of *The Dynamics of Cultural Nationalism,* treats such writers as "moral innovators, constructing new matrices of collective identity at times of social crises" (1987, 9). Writers such as O'Flaherty certainly deserve credit for their work (as does Hutchinson), but it is important to emphasize that such innovators cannot construct "matrices of collective identity" on their own. Rather, moral and cultural innovators may articulate ideas, values, positions, arguments, tropes, narratives, images, and comparisons from various sources—popular, canonical, marginal, scholarly—that resonate with a group's collective identity, possibly even expressing the zeitgeist of a particular moment in time. In most cases, however, historical scholars and artists do something similar to what the *filid* did in harmonizing origin legends with other dominant narratives; whether they are geographies, annals, biblical accounts, histories, linguistic studies, or archaeological dissertations, updating the cultural story is the task at hand. In the texts of Irish Orientalism, this seems particularly true. Moreover, within this communal story of collective identity, the weights of values, legends, and myths are cumulative. They resonate more fully through repetition and reinvention, as Anthony D. Smith has argued in *The Ethnic Origin of Nations:*

> Myths and symbols, values and memories *shape* the nation-to-be. They are not simply "instruments" of leaders and elites of the day, not even of whole communities. They are potent signs and explanations, they have capacities for generating emotion in successive generations, they possess explosive power that goes far beyond the "rational" uses which elites and social scientists deem appropriate. Evoking an heroic past is like playing with fire, as the history of all too many *ethnie* and nations in conflict today can tell. The fires generated by these mythical pasts burn for several generations, long after the events that first stimulated their acceptance. (1986, 201)

In Ireland, Eastern origin legends burned throughout the seventeenth and eighteenth centuries, informing the cultural mythology and shaping the values within a nascent national narrative. Successive generations of writers relied upon this heat and stoked it with their own reinventions—and from such developed the modern semiotic connection between the Oriental and the Celt.

Most western European cultures abandoned their medieval origin legends by the thirteenth century and, certainly, by the sixteenth. The reasons for the persistence of Irish origin legends have had little scholarly treatment and deserve more space than can be afforded here. One basic reason may stem from Irish culture's collective need—from the thirteenth to the twentieth centuries—for a certain and noble past in light of its uncertain present and future. For Irish writers, "old books" seem to have held particular authority in part because they became both artifacts and repositories of this past, especially during the decline in traditional bardic learning in the sixteenth and seventeenth centuries. The origin legends and their texts, in some ways, became metonyms for the history of a besieged Gaelic culture, and to some degree, they survived because they still had cultural relevance; they continued to help explain Ireland to itself, affirming an identity through a representation of the past. Scholarly investigations did not entirely negate the historicity of origin legends until the nineteenth century, when academic and university disciplines became more established and the legends were read more mythopoetically and allegorically. Although Irish monks had helped found scholarly institutions on the Continent since the early Middle Ages, Ireland's first university, Trinity College, Dublin (TCD), was founded in only 1593. Universities had spread across Europe earlier in the fourteenth, fifteenth, and sixteenth centuries. Scholars there gradually confronted the veracity of their pseudohistories and began to treat ancient texts as a product of their times rather than ancient embodiments of truth.

The religious Reformation that spread across Europe in the early sixteenth century (and the subsequent Catholic Counter-Reformation) changed how much of Europe viewed religious and historical authority. Around this time, new investigations emerged concerning Greco-Roman antiquity, as can be seen in the interests of many Renaissance works. In scholarship, source criticism gradually became prevalent in European biblical, antiquarian, historical, and philological studies.[3] As far as a technique may transform any discipline, this one changed historical and textual scholarship across western Europe. Scholars in Ireland, however, continued to ply origin legends as pseudohistory into the eighteenth century, periodically translating them into a contemporary idiom—updating them without doubting their fundamental historical accuracy.

These seventeenth-century advancements in philology share little with eighteenth-century antiquarian philology and more with the rigorous analyses of the mid-nineteenth century, when German philology advanced and established Celtic linguistics. In particular, Johann Kaspar Zeuss's *Grammatica Celtica* in 1853 established the foundations of twentieth-century Celtic linguistics. The 150 years of Celtic research between Edward Lhuyd and Zeuss are generally understood in the

manner Stuart Piggott treated them in 1975: "On Celtic philology an almost unre-
lieved lunatic darkness had fallen for the century and a half between Edward Lhwyd
and the *Grammatica Celtica* of the German scholar Zeuss" (qtd. in Davis 2000, vi).
Daniel Davis, the editor of the eight-volume collection *Celtic Linguistics,
1700–1850,* claims the works of this period had value, however: "The conclusions
drawn in these texts had the effect of provoking reactions from later scholars. Ultimately this produced a general sense of dissatisfaction within the field, which may
have led to a more open reception of the new paradigm and its accompanying comparative method and, later on, a clearer definition of the subject of Celtic linguistics" (2000, vii). Instead of treating Celtic linguistics in this period as "absent, insane,
or plunged into darkness," Davis argues, we should recognize it as a period of discursive "adolescence," where the ideas serve as "necessary precursor[s]" to subsequent developments (viii). But beyond "a general sense of dissatisfaction," what did
the works of this period accomplish? One contribution was their speculative tracing
of Irish and Celtic connections to non-European languages, a process that encouraged other European philologists to seek and identify similarities within other
Indo-European languages. Other accomplishments of these speculative works include the development of a centuries-old discourse of Irish ties with the Orient.

This chapter charts the seventeenth- and eighteenth-century progression of the
origin legends and the treatment of an Irish-Asian connection in pseudohistorical,
antiquarian, and philological texts, particularly those of Geoffrey Keating, Mícheál
Ó Cléirigh, Roderic O'Flaherty, Charles Vallancey, and amateur antiquarians in
Ireland. The next chapter picks up there and follows the development of Irish Orientalist literature during the nineteenth century, particularly the movement of origin legends into Romantic, popular, and political literature.

Oriental and Celtic in the Seventeenth Century

Orientalism in Ireland undeniably influenced the coemergence of Celticism, and
vice versa. In Ireland, the crossovers between the two have particular significance,
but the work of Oriental and Celtic scholars in Germany, France, Wales, England,
and elsewhere also greatly influenced the formation and future of this discursive
network in Ireland and throughout the networks of European empires. The roots
of these discourses, both textual and contextual, however, can be found in European philological studies, especially in the sixteenth and seventeenth centuries,
when translations from both Irish and Asian texts began appearing more frequently
in western Europe. Even after antiquarianism split into philological, historical, and
cultural investigations of the Celtic and the Oriental, numerous exchanges tran-
spired among scholars, ideas, theories, funding, and institutions across these disciplinary divisions, particularly in Ireland but also in England, France, and Germany.

Generally, the discourses of Orientalism and Celticism have been assumed to be distinct, resembling one another solely in that Oriental and Celtic cultures bordered enlightened European society and its progressive modernity. Vast differences exist in geography, population, culture, religion, language, and history (and nearly every anthropological category) between Irish and Asian societies, and the colonial management of these places differed in many respects (as is discussed in chapters 4 and 5). But actual differences did not preclude later strategic comparisons on imperial or anticolonial levels and in Celticism and Orientalism. To countless writers and historians, representations of the Celt and the Oriental have seemed twins separated at birth. Their similarities have been debated in contemporary scholarship,[4] and though differences are irrefutable, similarities have been long imagined. The philological roots of Orientalism and Celticism can help us understand how such comparisons have so long endured. These discourses grew from seventeenth-century language studies in the period when European imperialism grew as an ideological center, which greatly influenced the arc of their progression. The Celt and the Oriental also developed in relation to one another, along similar paths, often promoted and inspired by the same individuals and institutions.

A particularly salient connection between these two discourses in Ireland can be seen in the fact that many early Orientalists in seventeenth-century Ireland (particularly at Trinity College, Dublin) studied the Irish language alongside Oriental languages as contemporary embodiments of distant, ancient cultures. But they also did crucial preservation work. By the midcentury, during Cromwell's brutal Irish campaign, the Orientalist James Ussher (1581–1656), Protestant archbishop of Armagh, collected a library of more than ten thousand volumes, rivaled in size by the later collection of James Ware, Ussher's younger contemporary whom Ussher had encouraged (Ware also published Spenser's *View of the Present State of Ireland* in 1633). Ussher's collection included medieval European manuscripts alongside contemporary ones from Persia and Ireland; Oliver Cromwell had appropriated the collection from Ussher, but Charles II later returned it to Trinity College after Ussher's death (and his Westminster burial under Cromwell).[5] Although long reputed to be bigoted against the Gaelic Irish, Ussher made significant contributions to the preservation and study of Irish manuscripts, as he also did with Hebrew, Arabic, and other "Oriental" languages. Mícheál Ó Cléirigh, when compiling and transcribing his genealogical work *Réim Ríoghraidhe* (Succession of the kings), borrowed the *Book of Lecan* or *Leabhar Leacáin* from Ussher via Connell Mac Geoghegan (or Mac Eochagáin [fl. 1620–1640]). And, in 1627, at the request of Ussher, Mac Geoghegan had translated into English an "old book," the *Annals of Clonmacnoise*—a version that Ussher preserved for posterity even after the last Irish version disappeared.

Since the founding of Trinity College, Dublin, in 1593, the Ussher family had close relations with the Protestant institution as students, administrators, and supporters. The Ussher collection in the library greatly aided the study and preservation of medieval, Irish, and Oriental manuscripts. James Ussher had been one of the first enrolled at TCD, and his brother, Ambrose (1582–1629), also studied there before settling at Cambridge where he translated Hebrew and Arabic before dying early (Mansoor 1944, 24). Robert Ussher, James's nephew, served as provost of Trinity in the early 1600s and vigorously promoted the study of Irish and Irish texts and encouraged prominent Irish-language lectures (Leerssen 1996b, 284–85). This youngest of the three Usshers followed the lead of one of his uncle's contemporaries, William Bedell (1571–1642), a Church of Ireland bishop who also served as provost at Trinity College, in promoting the study and use of Irish (particularly in order to facilitate Catholic conversions to Protestantism). Bedell, who had also been encouraged by James Ussher, oversaw the translation of the complete Hebrew Bible into Irish, Bedell being a scholar of both languages. The Bible was completed in 1640, but did not appear until 1685, long after Bedell's death, resulting from his imprisonment after harboring Catholic fugitives from the rebellion of 1641 (Welch 1996, 39). Though a Protestant, Bedell was buried with full honors by a Catholic group. Narcissus Marsh (1638–1713), another provost of Trinity College, continued to promote the study of Irish and other languages for divinity students in the early eighteenth century and saw Bedell's Irish-language Bible through to publication. He is perhaps best remembered, however, for assembling an impressive collection of Arabic, Syriac, Hebrew, Armenian, Coptic, Turkish, Russian, Persian, and Irish manuscripts housed at the library he built: Marsh Library, Ireland's first public library, constructed in 1701. Other Orientalists living in seventeenth-century Dublin include Dudley Loftus, "the greatest Orientalist of these [sixteenth and seventeenth] centuries" (Mansoor 1944, 24), and Robert Huntingdon, another provost of Trinity, best known for his correspondence with Samaritan scholars and gathering of manuscripts.[6] Roderic O'Flaherty credits Loftus with pointing to connections among the Irish and Coptic languages (1685, 35–36). Another of this circle, Anthony Raymond (1675–1726), a fellow of Trinity College, strongly encouraged Gaelic scholarship in Dublin in the early eighteenth century, and his strong adherence to the idea that Hebrew and Irish were closely related influenced later scholars such as antiquarian Charles Vallancey and historian Charles O'Conor the Elder (Welch 1996, 490). Such men established Orientalism in Ireland alongside Celticism and Irish-language projects. After this initial established scholarly overlap between Orientalists and Celticists, semiotic and cultural connections continued through the nineteenth century, particularly in Anglo-Irish circles, but also beyond the boundaries of Ireland. Many of the most famous continental Celticists—Johann Kaspar Zeuss (1806–1856), Ernest Renan (1823–1892), and Heinrich Zimmer (1851–1910)—began as students, professors, and scholars of Oriental languages.

The twin germinations of these scholarly discourses in Ireland on academic and institutional levels had expansive conceptual roots in continent-wide discussions of philology. Language studies during the middle of the seventeenth century both furthered and altered Ireland's origin legends, reborn in the seventeenth and eighteenth centuries thanks to scholars such as Keating and O'Flaherty. The reinterpreted legends inspired a new enthusiasm for Irish culture and for etymology, which, more than comparative grammatical analyses, fueled the philological arguments of the eighteenth century. To treat the work of writers in this period merely as pseudohistorical errors or cultural dead ends would be as wrongheaded as to believe that it was based on sound linguistics. Their ideas emerged from continent-wide developments in philology, in which the languages that would come to be known as Celtic grew to occupy a significant place in European cultures, in that Ireland became a link between Europe and Asia.

In the first chapter of Daniel Droixhe's *La Linguistique et l'appel de l'histoire*, "L'Origine historique: Avatars du premier comparatisme," the author explores the intellectual forces that led to the dissolution of the "la monogenèse hébraïque," the previously unshakable myth of a Hebrew mother language (1978, 34–35). The hypothesis of a monogenetic origin of language, based in Hebrew, gained credence in the early medieval period. Drawing from Aarsleff, Borst, and a number of earlier historians of linguistics, Droixhe explores the context that led to Gottfried Wilhelm Leibniz's (1646–1716) critique of the "inébranable" (unshakeable) monogenetic Hebrew hypothesis in his *Brevis Designatio* of 1710. Leibniz synthesized and popularized ideas that had been afoot for half a century. The first critiques of Hebrew as the mother language, however, accompanied the rise of the monogenetic Hebrew hypothesis in the early medieval period when Arabic scholars dissented from its preeminent assignation. The scholars of Moorish Spain posited Arabic as a rival first language, but ideas about Hebrew as the mother tongue became orthodox Church opinion, held by most medieval church fathers and scholars, including Jerome, John Chrysostome, and Augustine. For the most part, Hebrew maintained its position until the seventeenth century, when the revived rivalry led to research into the unity of the Semitic languages, now known to include Hebrew, Phoenician, Aramaic, Arabic, Punic, Syriac, Ethiopian, and others.[7] Moreover, increased knowledge of other world languages, including Chinese and Algonquin, pressed the entire monogenetic hypothesis into question.

Ideas about Hebrew being one of a group of languages instead of the original language eventually came to prominence in the early and mid-seventeenth century, as is demonstrated in the title of a 1648–1650 publication of Christian Raue, *Generall Grammer for the Ready Attaining of the Ebrew, Samaritan, Calde, Syriac, Arabic and the Ethiopic Languages, with a Pertinent Discourse of the Orientall Tongues.* By this point in time, the Semitic languages stood in relation to one another, constituting a family of languages, within which Hebrew did not stand as the monogenetic parent, let alone the keeper of the primordial, pre-Babel language. Along with Phoenician, Arabic, Aramaic, and others, Hebrew was treated as one of the "Orientall Tongues," as Raue's title indicates. Such conclusions owe something to a work published a decade previously, Ιστορούμενα *Linguae Punicae, Errori Populari Arabicam et Punicam esse Eandem Opposita* (1637) by Thomas Reinesius (1587–1667) (Droixhe 1978, 38). Leibniz later called his work "remarquablement en lumière" because, in part, it had posited a mother tongue for both Hebrew and Phoenico-Punic languages, thus destabilizing monogenetic ideas about Hebrew. Another result of such valid conclusions was a somewhat less verifiable "culte de phénicien" (qtd. in Droixhe 38), inspired by the very influential work of Samuel Bochart (1599–1667).

Bochart's *Geographia Sacra* (1646) relied on ancient sources to trace Phoenician from the confusion of the tongues to the actual settlement of Phoenician colonies along the coast of Europe (39). The second section of the work, *Chanaan, seu de Coloniis et Sermone Phoenicum,* follows the fortunes of this ancient maritime people, particularly discussing the actual Phoenician colonies on the Iberian peninsula. Although many of the arguments about Phoenician settlements are defensible, Bochart concluded that Phoenician place-names had been named after the ancient god Baal, using specious etymological similarities for evidence and setting an unfortunate trend. Most important for this discussion, however, he claimed that the Phoenicians had colonies in Ireland. One hundred and twenty years later, antiquarian Charles Vallancey embraced many of Bochart's ideas.[8] In the mid-seventeenth century, Bochart's theories provoked new ideas that displaced earlier medieval models for tracing European languages to Hebrew and, hence, easily to Adam and God. A more modern development because of their more historiographic basis, Phoenician theories offered new approaches to prove Europe's ties to antiquity, based in visions of ancient mercantile Phoenicians settling the coasts of western Europe. Ireland (and what would become known as the Celtic fringe) stood out because it had not been recolonized since the Phoenicians—if one does not count various English and Danish incursions.

Seventeenth-century scholars also made progress in studying Ethiopian, Syriac, and Chaldean languages, especially Hiob Ludolf (1624–1704), whose work *Grammatica Aethiopica* (1661) built on scholarship done a century earlier in Rome (Droixhe 1978, 39). The culmination of the work of Reinesius (1637), Bochart (1646), Raue (1648–1650), and Ludolf (1698) allowed what Droixhe describes as "la reconnaissance, vers le milieu du XVIIe siècle, d'une unité sémitique suffisamment étoffée permit ainsi d'envisager l'hébreu dans un cadre comparative plus réaliste, peu favorable à ses attributes mythiques" (1978, 40).[9] The resultant desacralization and relativism accompanying the end of Hebrew's predominance further encouraged the study of modern languages, as did the Reformation.

Motivated by the spirit of Protestantism (and, to a lesser degree, Catholic reformation), language scholars worked to establish uncorrupted versions of the Old and New Testaments and renewed efforts to translate the Bible into other languages. Concomitantly, scholars increasingly viewed the world as being occupied by various distinct peoples. New language studies less often sought ancient unities and instead categorized divisions. The split between European languages (descended supposedly from Japheth) and the languages of Asia, West Asia, and Africa (of Ham and Shem) became particularly pronounced. Early in the century, works such as Christoph Crinesius's (1584–1629) *Discursus de Confusione Linguarum* (1629; first version, 1610) had begun to pit Oriental languages (Hebrew, Chaldean, Syriac, Samaritan, Arabic, Persian, and Ethiopian) as fundamentally different from the Occidental group (Greek, Latin, Italian, French, and Spanish) (Droixhe 1978, 46). Such a global split, as later centuries would confirm, became one of the foundations of Orientalism. Significantly, the place of Irish, Welsh, and Celtic languages in general continued to be seen as anomalous, and they were generally left out of the European category.[10]

Scholars had long traced the influence and connections of European languages to Hebrew and Babel, but, increasingly, such arguments were replaced by modern categorizations and new explanations of Europe's connections to antiquity (47). Many scholars argued for the Greek origins of Germanic languages, particularly Anglo-Saxon, as demonstrated by Méric Casaubon's (1599–1671) treatise *About Old English, or Saxon, and its Relationship to Greek* (1650, 106–7). Others, such as Abraham Mylius (1563–1637), asserted that Belgic was an ancient transplanted root language for Persian, Phrygian, Scythian, Celtic, Cimbri, Flemish, and German (Borst 1957, 1:1223). Many new arguments connected northern European languages to ancient Scythian migrations, particularly the influential works of Marcus Boxhorn (1612–1653) and the great Germanic scholar Franciscus Junius (1545–1602). Early in the century, a number of Flemish and Dutch scholars, most associated with the University of Leyden, developed the model of the "Scytho-Celtic" family of languages. They endorsed a Scythian genesis for the northern European languages, particularly the Scandinavian, Germanic, and Gaulish (later called Celtic) languages (Leerssen 1996b, 288). Although usually the "Celtic" in Scytho-Celtic generally referred to ancient Germanic languages at the time, this approach included Irish and other Celtic languages in a European category. Justus George Schottel's (1612–1672) *Ausführliche Arbeit von der Teutschen Haubt-Sprache* (1643), in fact, explicitly linked Germanic and Gaulish or Celtic languages. Not everyone agreed with the overarching idea, however, particularly Matthäus Heller, in his *De Origine Gentium Celticarum Dissertatio* (1707), who called the Scytho-Celtic hypothesis imbecilic (Droixhe 1978, 131). Nevertheless, the Scytho-Celtic concept developed widespread application throughout the century. One of the more significant and erroneous arguments involved a conflation of ancient Scythian languages with present-day languages, as in Paul-Yves Pezron's (1636–1706) work, which synchronically compared ancient Scythian and Gaulish with modern Celtic languages, specifically Breton. This conflation signals yet another similarity between Celticism and Orientalism, both of which assumed that "ancient" languages and cultures had not changed over time as had the languages of England, France, Germany, Italy, Spain, and other European nations.

By midcentury most scholars either grouped the languages now known as Celtic within the Scythian family of northern languages or treated them as problematic, isolated entities. John Davies's 1632 dictionary, *Antique Linguae Britannicae, Nunc Vulgo Dictae Cambro-Britannicae, Dictionarium Duplex,* noted the links between Gaulish (Breton) and British (particularly Welsh) languages, helping form the basis of a Celtic family of languages. Accounting for the differences between Irish and Germanic languages (which supposedly had some similar "Scythic" roots), Samuel Bochart's Phoenician-origin thesis in 1646 settled the matter for many at the time. Moreover, Bochart's argument seemed to confirm the basic pattern of the multiple "invasions" described in the Irish origin legends. Perhaps most significant to this present study, however, is that Bochart's arguments placed Irish and Goidelic, as well as Brythonic, languages squarely within the Oriental language family.

The then living Celtic languages—Welsh, Irish, Manx, Scots-Gaelic, Cornish, and Breton (sometimes confused with Gaulish)—were rarely studied as such. The most significant study came at the beginning of the eighteenth century, when the Welsh-born scholar Edward Lhuyd (?1660–1709) wrote the first serious comparative work of Celtic philology in his *Archaeologia Britannica* (1707). He compares the etymology and grammars of the Brythonic and Goidelic branches, treating them as modern Celtic languages, and provides an Irish grammar and a grammar and dictionary of Breton. Lhuyd's main contribution to Celtic philology rests primarily in his detailed work and his comparative grammatical methodology. The relationship among languages such as Breton, Welsh, and Irish had long been guessed at. As a speaker of Welsh and Irish, Lhuyd certainly saw similarities between them before setting out on a series of trips to gather information through Scotland, Cornwall, Brittany, and Ireland, where he met Dubhaltach Mac Fhir Bhisigh, Roderic O'Flaherty, and other Irish-language scholars. At Oxford in 1694 and 1695, Lhuyd met John Toland, a native Irish speaker, and Toland noted that Lhuyd had already "perceived the affinity" between Welsh and Irish at that point in time (qtd. in Welch 1996, 310). Nevertheless, for Irish antiquarians and historians in the eighteenth century, the work of Bochart seems to have sparked more interest; in many respects, the enthusiasm and European need for a Celtic-Oriental link outweighed the desire for careful comparative studies of the Celtic languages. Both Bochart's and Lhuyd's works promoted the gathering Celtomania across Europe in the eighteenth century, but only Bochart's work encouraged the idea of the Celt as an Oriental latecomer to Europe.

The term *Celtic,* made much more prominent by the work of Lhuyd, quickly acquired connotations that had little to do with Lhuyd's work. By assigning this term to the Irish, Scots, Welsh, Cornish, and Bretons, the semiotic mantles of the Scytho-Celtic and Phoenico-Celtic theories (initially used to connect Europe with antiquity) transferred to these "ancient Celtic" cultures. They became regarded as living relics of ancient cultures. Works such as Paul-Yves Pezron's greatly encouraged this synchronic understanding. Because the term *Celt* had had little usage since ancient times, it carried connotations of antiquity. The word has its first usage in Greek texts, but for the ancient Greeks, and most Romans, the term had little specific application. Malcolm Chapman argues in *The Celts:The Construction of a Myth* that these Greeks and Romans used the term *Keltoi* not as a defined ethnic group, but rather as a catchall category somewhat similar to Scythian or, the most general, barbarian. Many commentators have pointed out that Greeks and Romans often seemed to have confused the various ancient groups of northern and western Europe. But Chapman asserts that this opinion might misunderstand their discussions:"It makes much more sense, from an anthropological point of view, to accord to the Greek category its own systematic success: it did not fail to account for the difference between Celts and Germans; rather, it expressed a truth about Greek perception, which was that northern and western Europe were, as far as Greece was concerned, full of the same kind of barbarians, that is, who shared the essential characteristics of being uncivilized, and unable to speak Greek" (1992, 39). The early labels of ancient European peoples as Celts or Scythians, therefore, had little initial ethnological significance but great barbaric resonance.

Based on such vague ancient sources, medieval barbarian histories, and pseudo-historical origin legends, eighteenth-century philological arguments about the Celts gradually came to fuel cultural nationalism in Ireland. Celtic scholar Hildegard L. C. Tristam explains:"As for the *achievements* of the philological model with relation to the Celtic languages—besides its value as an important step in the progress of linguistic thought in the nineteenth century—, its greatest effect lay within cultural and political history, because the linguistic construct *created* cultural and political realities. Celticism is a very obvious example of observers' categories bringing about the observer effect" (1996, 58). Tristam acknowledges that the term had not entirely disappeared in medieval Europe, however:

It is true that the Irishman Cormac mac Cuilleannáin (ob. AFM 903 AD), the Scot George Buchanan (1506–1582), and the Welshman Edward Lhuyd (1660?–1709; *Archaeologia Brttannica,* 1707) had to varying degrees already recognized that the P- and Q- isoglosses (as in Irish *mac* and Welsh *mab*) divided the Celtic languages into two groups with respect to corresponding sets of lexemes and that these isoglosses thereby lent each of these languages a separate identity. But such observations were isolated, unsystematized and generally not taken notice of by other linguistic thinkers of the time. (58–59)

Although Tristam's qualification here is helpful, writers generally treated Ireland as a repository of Scytho-Celtic culture, relying on ancient Greco-Roman texts. William Camden's *Britain; or, A Chorographical Description of the Most flourishing King-domes, England, Scotland, and Ireland, and the Ilands adioyning, out of the depth of Antiqvitie* (Latin version, 1586; translated, 1610) treats Ireland as such: "[W]hen the Roman Empire beganne now to decay, the nation of the Scots or Scythians (for, *in times past, as Strabo* writeth, *al people Westward were termed Celto-Scytæ)* grew mighty in Ireland, and beganne to bee renowned" (1610, 66). Edmund Spenser developed such ideas at the end of the sixteenth century in *A View of the Present State of Ireland* (written in 1596; published 1633); here, Spenser's Irenius responds to Eudoxus's questions about whether any signs of "Gaules" remain in Scythian Ireland:

[T]he *Gaulish* speech, is the very *British,* the which was very generally used here in all *Brittaine,* before the comming of the *Saxons:* and yet is retained of the *Welshmen, Cornishmen,* and the *Brittaines* of *France,* through time working the alteration of all things, and the trading and interdeale with other nations round about, have changed and greatly altered the dialect thereof, but yet the originall words appeare to be the same, as who hath list to read in *Camden* and *Buchanan,* may see at large. Besides there be many places, as havens, hills, townes and Castles, which yet beare the names from the *Gaules,* of the which, *Buchanan* rehearseth above in *Scotland,* and I can (I thinke) recount neere as many in *Ireland* which retaine the old denom-ination of the *Gaules,* as the *Menapii, Cauci, Venti,* and others; by all which and many other resonable probabilities (which this short course will not suffer to be laide forth) it appeareth that the chiefe Inhabitants in *Ireland* were *Gaules,* comming thither first out of *Spaine,* and after . . . *Gallia* itselfe, from all the Sea-coast of *Belgia* and *Celtica* into al the southerne coasts of *Ireland,* which they possessed and inhab-ited, whereupon it is at this day, amongst the *Irish* a common use, to call any stranger Inhabitant there amonst them *Gald,* that is descended from the *Gaules.* (1633, 32–33)

Spenser assigns the Irish-language roots in Scythian and Gaulish languages from "Belgia and Celtica," and he recognizes that Irish belongs to a family of languages that included "*Brittaine,* before the comming of the *Saxons:* and yet is retained of the *Welshmen, Cornishmen,* and the *Brittaines* of *France.*" Seemingly in consort with the origin legends, Spenser's Irenius argues for a late Celtic "invasion" of Ireland and an earlier Scythian settlement. The ancient barbaric resonances associated with

Celts and Scythians partly explain the transference of the terms to Ireland by British historians and help explain their sticking.

Early Irish Historiography: Keating and Ó Cléirigh

Reportedly written during years in hiding from British forces, Geoffrey Keating's *Foras Feasa ar Éirinn* (ca. 1634) begins with a critical review of the standard British histories of Ireland and significant descriptions of Ireland by classical authors. Although the work existed only in manuscript, hundreds of handwritten copies circulated through Gaelic Ireland and had a considerable impact; as Leerssen notes, scholars have argued that "this was probably the last important book in European literature whose influence and dissemination owed nothing to the printing press" (1996b, 274). In contrast to the limited review in the works of Camden, Stanyhurst, and others, Keating provides the longest, most thoroughly researched, and most cohesive retelling of the Irish origin legends to date. He demonstrates not only a close familiarity with Greek and Roman representations of Ireland and the Irish in his work, but also a thorough understanding of the major texts of British historiography. As the poet and scholar Eiléan Ní Chuilleanáin noted in "'Forged and Fabulous Chronicles': Reading Spenser as an Irish Writer": "Keating's prose is fluent modern Irish, quoting Camden and the classics as well as Cambrensis. Like his contemporary John Lynch whose major work is entitled *Cambrensis Eversus,* he is engaging in battle with the ignorant foreigners who have written about Ireland and Irish history over centuries, among them Spenser. The preface . . . declares the cultural independence of Gaelic society" (1996, 247). To be more specific, Keating's preface compares British historians of Ireland to dung beetles because of their attraction to the more unseemly elements of Irish culture (1902, 5). After refuting points in earlier histories and commentaries, particularly the works of Spenser and Cambrensis, Keating retells the origin legends.

He based his extended retelling upon Irish manuscripts. Unlike the more tribal and religiously focused defenses of Gaelic culture (for example, Philip O'Sullevan Beare's *Compendium*), Keating focuses on the successive waves of invasions and the resultant narratives of cultural hybridity. As in the earlier legends, the Asian and Scythian origins play significant roles. Keating begins by relaying a standard biblical history: "Noah divides the three parts of the world among his three sons, as the antiquary says: Sem took his place in Asia; / Cham with his children in Africa; / The noble Japheth and his sons / It is they who obtained Europe" (1:137). Highlighting the Magogian link between Europe and Asia, Keating notes how some sons of Japheth also occupied Asia: "Many of the people of Asia, and the people of all Europe descended from Japheth. The people of Scythia are of the posterity of Magog, son of Japheth, and especially the tribes who occupied Ireland after the deluge, before the sons of Mileadh" (139). Unlike Spenser's text, Scythian origins distinguish, rather than degrade, the Irish, treating them as the Europeans who have concourse with Asia. Readers outside of Gaelic circles, however, dismissed *Foras Feasa* as too fabulous.

Close details of the origin legends constitute most of Keating's history, but he distinguishes them at the outset from actual or "genuine" history (147). After Ceasair's story, as he is about to begin the other invasion stories, he addresses his reader:

> Know, O reader, that it is not as genuine history I set down this occupation, nor any occupation of which we have treated up to this; but because I have found them written in old books. And, moreover, I do not understand how the antiquaries obtained tidings of the people whom they assert to have come into Ireland before the deluge, except it be the aerial demons gave them to them, who were their fairy lovers during the time of their being pagans; or unless it be on flags of stones they found them graven after the subsiding of the deluge, if the story be true. (147)

His caveat here does not imply the same disingenuousness and disbelief as in the texts of Giraldus, Campion, Higden, or Spenser. Instead of dismissing the stories as Irish inventions, he remarks that he includes them because they have some worth, being from "old books." Nor does he speculate about his sources, treating them as originating from ancient sources. He does note, however, that "there is nothing but a poetical romance in the history which would relate Fionntain to have lived before the deluge and after it. Also Tuan son of Caireall, or Roanus, Caoilte son of Rónán" (151). He faithfully recounts the legends, generally treating them more as literature than spurious history.

Referencing the story of Nel (or "Niul"), whom the pharaoh invited to Egypt because of his learning, Keating refers to Herodotus, Josephus, and Polydorus (none of whom mentions Nel) in order to flesh out Ireland's Scythian ancestry. Before telling the origin legend, he argues that the Scythians predated the Egyptians and Greeks and introduced letters and writing to them. In the legend, Niul's father, Féinius Farsaid, understood all of the languages of the world, and educated Niul. In Keating's retelling, the son studied in Babylon at "the first school [that is, Féinius's] after the confusion of the languages of the world," and later "the Pharao Cincris, king of Egypt, hears of Niul 'conducting the public schools in Scythia' " and invites him to Egypt (2:15). His story becomes both the confirmation and the illustration of Scythian learning, which, necessarily, gives Irish learning and linguistic skills a much longer pedigree.

The other major Irish historical project of the age originated in the Franciscan College of St. Anthony of Padua, founded in 1606, at Louvain University in present-day Belgium, where many exiled Irish leaders and scholars stayed, after the

"Flight of the Earls" in the first decades of the seventeenth century. Some of the more well-known Irish leaders and exiles of the period who stayed there include Hugh O'Neill and Rory O'Donnell, who wintered there before heading south to Rome. One of the Irish scholars living there, Aodh Mac an Bhaird, began the important work of compiling comprehensive versions of all available Irish hagiographical, ecclesiastical, annal, and political records, which were gradually disappearing. Mícheál Ó Cléirigh took on the annal aspect of this project and traveled to Ireland to gather materials and compile an authoritative edition of Irish dates and events, dated on the calendar derived from the Bible.[11] Once much of the material was gathered, Ó Cléirigh with the help of three other Irish scholars[12] wrote the *Annals of the Four Masters* in a Franciscan friary at Bundrowse, County Donegal. The resultant text draws upon as many manuscripts and annals as Ó Cléirigh and his associates could locate, many of which no longer exist. As with other texts in the early seventeenth century, the *Annals* seeks to overturn British characterizations of Ireland. Like the *Annals* of Tigernach and other earlier ones, Ó Cléirigh's *Annals* synchronizes the Irish origin legends with biblical stories and classical histories in a genealogical time line that stretches from 1616 back to the Flood. Linking ancient Ireland to the Egyptians and the Scythians served as more than a base for family histories; it had become an integral element in asserting Ireland's right to independent sovereignty. These annals and Keating's history, more so than any earlier works, helped later writers imagine a modern Irish nation, with a vivid and ancient history and an independent future.

In less monumental works of the time, particularly historical and praise poems, Irish poets often alluded to the Gaels' ancestors listed in the *Annals* and *Foras Feasa,* primarily to the sons of Míl Espáne, *"Macaibh Míleadh Easbáin."* For these *filid,* origin references predominantly existed for their genealogical resonance. A number of poems, written in response to the new English settlements in Ireland, however, recount the "invasions" from the fourteenth to the seventeenth centuries, lamenting the Viking incursions in Ireland from the eighth to the twelfth centuries as well as the encroachments by the Normans and the English in Leinster during the period of Tudor expansion. In earlier texts, references to Oriental origin legends functioned as a means of differentiating the ancestry of the Irish from the Hiberno-Normans or, as they eventually became known, the Old English, Old Foreigners, or the *Sean-Ghall* (*Gael* and *Gall* originally differentiated the Irish from the Normans, but as *Gall* eventually came to mean any foreigner, *Sean-Ghall* [Old Foreigner] was used to distinguish the earlier settlers from the new Tudor settlers, the *Nua-Ghall).*[13] As the Gaelic order came under attack by the New English settlers, origin legends were used to unite the *Gael* and the *Sean-Ghall* into a hybrid *Éireannach* culture.

Moreover, the syncretic mode of these histories supported the cultural hybridization in Ireland, where earlier English Catholic settlers had integrated into Irish Gaelic culture. Spenser hotly attacked these "Old English" settlers and the process that had integrated them into Irish society, targeting Irish women in particular and perhaps the Irish recognition of matrilineal lines. References to ancient ancestry helped Gaelic *filid* textually integrate Hiberno-Norman families by emphasizing the heritage of the Irish women who had married the descendants of Hiberno-Norman settlers. A poem by Tadhg Óg hUiginn[14] mourns the death of a Norman lord by recounting an ancestry based in Irish origin legend. Although in such poems French and Greek ancestry was often referenced for the patrilineal side of the family, the Gaelic poets just as often relied upon Milesian lineages that many Normans (with Gaelic grandmothers, mothers, and wives) could also claim through matrilineal lines (Leerssen 1996b, 173). The poets also integrated Normans into Irish history by comparing their attributes and hospitality with ancient Irish heroes. Moreover, Oriental and Spanish origins emphasized the hybrid element of ancient Irish culture, emphasizing that Ireland's inhabitants were all migrants, ancient or otherwise. Ulster poets Eochaidh Ó hEodhusa and Fearghal Óg Mac an Bhaird incorporated James I into the Milesian clan (Cunningham 1986, 156). Geoffrey Keating, himself a descendant of the *Sean-Ghall,* also used the term *Éireannach* (in which he grouped himself) to unite the Irish in his *Foras Feasa ar Éirinn* (Ní Chuilleanáin 1996, 247). The Tudor settlers, unlike the *Sean-Ghall,* did not embrace such hybridity. Inspired by the Reformation, integration with Catholics was anathema. Indeed, Spenser and others treated hybridization as the abandonment of civility for mongrelized barbarity.

Roderic O'Flaherty: Reconstructing Ogygia

In the late sixteenth and early seventeenth centuries, British comparisons of the Irish with Europe's *others* evinced a perspective consonant with Britain's emerging mercantile empire; they also supported the increasing suppression of Irish Catholic and Gaelic culture (as well as non-European cultures). As British texts increasingly debunked Catholic and Gaelic Irish culture, Counter-Reformation and Irish responses, unsurprisingly, defended it with a sense of urgency. As the previous chapter has shown, Irish origin legends were one contested area. British writers critiqued and dismantled the legends to paint the Irish as barbaric. For Irish writers, such British revisions of Irish legend and culture suggested more than just their antagonism; they suggested the mutable nature of representation. Increasingly, Irish commentators (including Anglo-Irish antiquarians and native Gaelic historians) treated cultural representation as a realm for advancing agendas rather than recording truths. This application suggests that the strength of ancient histories and origin legends resided in their usage, whether bolstering or condemning cultural practices, denigrating or upholding a society. Irish writers often highlighted the constructed nature of their own arguments and encouraged speculative arguments when discussing culture, legend, and ancient history.

In particular, this development can be noted in the major work of one of the last scholars trained in traditional bardic learning, Roderic O'Flaherty's[15] *Ogygia* (1685). O'Flaherty (1629–1718) argues for a fuller place of Irish ancestors in the ancient Mediterranean world, particularly in Carthage and other Phoenician cities. He was also responding (if indirectly) to the research of Flemish and Dutch scholars who had developed ideas about a Nordic language group, the "Scytho-Celtic" family.[16] Such ideas had fueled Samuel Bochart, who was also a friend of the seventeenth-century Irish antiquarian James Ware[17] and had argued for the Phoenician or Carthaginian origins of many European languages and described Phoenician voyages and settlements along the European coast. O'Flaherty's work, an achievement less in historiography than in cultural mythologizing, matched Irish origin stories to some of these antiquarian and early linguistic theories and asserted the Phoenician origin of at least one settlement wave of Ireland's ancestors. By doing so, he delivered part of Ireland's ancestry to the Phoenicians and rescued the Irish from a pure Scythian ancestry, with its overtones of barbarism and its links to Germanic culture. Even more so than Keating, O'Flaherty treated the origin legends as fictions, highlighting the process of how such legends and cultural myths have been created over time. Nevertheless, he believed these fictions held some truth. Below is a translation of part of his Latin text from a popular 1793 edition by the Reverend James Hely of Trinity College, Dublin:

> [T]he Egyptians, not to seem inferior to the Chaldæns in point of antiquity, have fabricated a catalogue of kings prior to the deluge. Hence we may plainly see, that the origin of nations, since the restoration of mankind, is no more than a confused *chaos* of fables, blended together, if we put them in competition with the undoubted authority and touch-stone of the sacred writings. But much veneration is due to antiquity; all whose productions are most strictly attended to by the curious; and very often truths, when divested of their poetical colouring and dress, are discovered in *her* writings as fire in cinders. Lactantius properly says, "these things, that poets write, are founded in truth; but so chequered and fraught with poetical imagery, that the truth is disguised; nevertheless it does not derogate from public conviction." (O'Flaherty 1793, 4)

Overall, O'Flaherty set out to reassure Irish public conviction about the merits of Irish culture; he also saved these Irish legends—at least eight centuries old when he wrote—from the dustbin of history. His work attracted much attention, both approbation and scorn. Sir George Mackenzie, the lord advocate of Scotland, leveled an attack at O'Flaherty, seeking to claim Irish saints for Scotland. This prompted O'Flaherty's reply. In 1695 he wrote *Ogygia Vindiciae,* which was circulated in manuscript but not published until Charles O'Conor the Elder translated it from Latin in 1775, reprinting it in 1785, as *The Ogygia Vindicated.* Here, he lays out how his approach differed from the retellings of the legends: "[S]ome thought it glorious to their country to have their ancestors derived by a mother from the *Egyptian* PHAROES, and to have had familiar conversations with MOSES and the *Israelites;* which passage of our antiquities I took upon me to refute, as incompatible with the accuracy of our exact chronology and genealogy" (1775, 25). Like Spenser, O'Flaherty sought historical realities within the stories of ancient migrations and settlements—O'Flaherty's approach differed in that he set out to prove the antiquity of Irish culture, not its ancient barbarity; hence, he treats the legends more as allegorical shorthand histories than as invented "Milesian lyes" (Spenser 1633, 49).

After the turbulent years leading up to the Restoration of Charles II in 1660, including the 1641 rebellion and Cromwell's brutal campaign in Ireland in the early 1650s, Irish culture had been assaulted on many fronts, and only remnants of bardic learning remained. From 1540 to 1700, Irish landowners, both Gaelic and Old English, lost most of their land in Ireland through various settlement projects and confiscations. O'Flaherty's family lost considerable landholdings during the mid-seventeenth century, even though they lived in Connaught, where Irish landowners held on to more land than in the north and east. They continued to lose property over the next decades, and O'Flaherty died in poverty with only little of his library remaining; his English friend Samuel Molyneux, on a tour of Connaught in 1709, wrote that O'Flaherty had "nothing left but some pieces of his own writing and a few old rummish books of history, printed" (qtd. in Welch 1996, 431). Cromwell's policies aimed at dismantling the Gaelic social order, paying English soldiers with Irish land and vigorously pushing Gaelic culture "to Hell or Connaught." Before losing all of his property, however, in a period of relative calm following the Cromwellian incursion, O'Flaherty wrote *Ogygia;* soon after, James II landed at Kinsale in 1689, and the Williamite War commenced. Two years later, James's and Ireland's Catholic forces were defeated at the Battle of the Boyne, and, in 1695, Britain's Parliament passed the first anti-Catholic penal laws for Ireland. O'Flaherty's work reflects this turbulent atmosphere, adjuring for a place for ancient Ireland, attempting to rescue cultural narratives and ancient sources. He sought not merely to retell fabulous origin legends or to concoct fantastic histories but to reignite interest in the value and culture of Gaelic Ireland—truths being like "fire in cinders" waiting to be blown into flames (1793, 4). *Ogygia,* published in English, sparked enormous enthusiasm throughout the eighteenth century, much of it in Anglo-Irish antiquarian and patriot circles.

Exploring the distant past, O'Flaherty seized upon the semiotic relationship between Ireland and other remote border cultures. The exoticism of his work was a clarion call to Irish sympathizers in that time of upheaval; it also encouraged the emerging field of Celticism. Even the detractors of the speculations of eighteenth-century antiquarians rarely questioned the supposed similarities between the Gaelic Irish and other "primitive" and Oriental peoples. This process correlated with other contemporaneous investigations at the dawn of the Enlightenment in British culture, where reasoning about other cultures often meant viewing their social differences as either deficiencies or aberrations from the enlightened cultural norms of western Europe. Perhaps the new interactions with diverse cultures created a need in British and European cultures to find credible reasons to account for the crosshatch of cultural differences around the globe. In Britain, such reasoning coalesced tightly under the aegis of the Enlightenment—its cardinal principles embodied in reason, science, and modernity—and within concomitant cultural narratives that asserted the superiority of English civilization, Christianity, and, eventually, the "white" race (and Aryan culture). Significantly, many writers of the Irish Enlightenment, Edmund Burke being one example,[18] valued cultural difference and encouraged cross-cultural connections instead of the classifications of cultures through racial and cultural hierarchies.

O'Flaherty builds upon earlier pseudohistories of Ireland in order to juxtapose Irish culture against the increasing trend of a newfangled and rootless modernity in Britain. Asserting a new, ancient name for Ireland—Ogygia—O'Flaherty quotes Camden citing Plutarch, "Ireland is justly called Ogygia, i.e. very antient, according to Plutarch, for the Irish date their history from the first æras of the world; so that in comparison with them, the antiquity of all other countries is modern, and almost in its infancy!" (1793, 34). It is important to note that O'Flaherty does not cite all of Camden's sentence; he leaves out the introductory modifying phrase: "If that be true which the Irish Historiographers record" (Camden 1610, 64), a phrase that certainly qualifies the "just[ness]" of Irish antiquity in Camden's eyes. Instead of refuting Camden, O'Flaherty co-opts him, borrowing British authority, in order to underline Irish antiquity. Moreover, the renaming of Ireland as Ogygia leads O'Flaherty to establish Irish ties with another ancient land: Egypt.

Likewise it appears, that Egypt was called Ogygia for this reason: for the Egyptians are said to be the most antient people in the world. . . . Nor I am of opinion, that we should give some degree of belief and credit to the investigations of our antiquarians, which prove that Æria and Ogygia were given in common to Egypt and Ireland, and to that other most antient and universally allowed tradition of our historians, of the marriage of Scota, the daughter of Pharaoh, with a predecessor of the Scots: which evidently convinces us that there had been a commerce and an alliance of a very antient date carried on, and mutually maintained, between the Egyptians and our ancestors; and which, if they have not subsisted when Pharaoh was immersed in the Red-Sea, or when Moses flourished, at least might have been commenced with some one or other of the succeeding Pharaohs. Dudley Loftus, L.L.D. . . . assured me, that the word, *Agus,* which, with us, signifies, And, has the same force and meaning in the Coptic or Egyptian language. (1793, 34–36)

Building bridges to antiquity could be done by building bridges to the Orient. The eastern part of the globe was presumed to be saturated in ancient greatness, lolling in immutability as the antithesis of modernity, removed from the pace of the world, much like Ogygia in Homer, the island home of Calypso, where Ulysses spent seven years, and was tempted by Calypso to remain there for the rest of his life. Perhaps in order to demonstrate his modern approach, O'Flaherty relied on contemporary scholarship in exploring antiquity, following the developments of Bochart and Flemish and Dutch scholars into the realm of Phoenician or, more specifically, Punic language study. His arguments rest upon classical texts, origin legends, and contemporary history. This more philological and "enlightened" historical approach, to a degree, prepared *Ogygia* and the Phoenician model for antiquarians and Irish cultural nationalists.

Scholars have long dismissed his text because of its speculative nature, but as a piece of culture, his work is significant for the very leaps he makes. O'Flaherty values the ancient stories not as historical truths but as allegories about cultural beliefs; once "unravel[ed]," however, a clear Irish-Asian link remains.

[N]or can we contradict received opinions of matters that happened since the flood, until more circumstantial and authentic instances can be quoted. But I totally reject and disbelieve all these monstrous and fabulous accounts that have been penned by poets—such as that Fintan, the son of Bocrat, one of Cæsarea's triumvirs, [who] . . . was resuscitated, after the deluge, and lived to the time of St. *Patrick.* . . . The allegory of this fable may be unraveled, by considering, that those fantastical notions of the Phythagorean and Platonic systems concerning the metymsichosis [*sic*], or transmigration of souls, pervaded our Druids in the times of ignorance and idolatry. . . . [T]he Bonzii of the Japanese (for by this name they call the priest of their worship) are impressed even now with such ideas [of transmigration of souls]; so that it is admirable how this fanatical notion had been adopted and believed from east to west! (1775, 5–7)

Grounding legend in culture and belief, he imagines an avenue of representation that escapes the familiar saws of barbarity and fabulousness. This same connection crops up centuries later during the Celtic Revival when Irish cultural nationalists imagined a spiritual base beneath Occident-Orient divisions. Although he is careful not to credit reincarnation as a spiritual truth, he grants that Irish pagans once subscribed to an Oriental belief, and marvels at how it spanned East and West. The exoticism of the idea to his readers distracts from the important point he seeks to establish: like ancient Thule for Giraldus, Ireland is the meeting place of East and West. Relying on ancient accounts, he grants that Ireland may have been first settled by people crossing over from Britain, but if the ancient British accounts are correct, he implies, so probably are the stories of other waves of immigrants: Scythian, African, and Phoenician.

O'Flaherty also focuses on the potent linguistic elements of the origin legends. As one of the oldest cultures on the globe, according to O'Flaherty, ancient Ireland had its own system of writing, from which the Greeks derived their alphabet. Synthesizing origin legends and classical accounts of Phoenicians, O'Flaherty argues that "Fenius"—Féinius Farsaid, the eponymous Scythian ancestor of the Fenians, and father of Nél, who both understood all the languages after the fall of the Tower of Babel—appeared in Greek texts as "Phoenix" (to wit, the Phoenician), the one who "delivered letters to the Phœnicians" (1793, 2:80).[19] (Clear insurrection and resurrection connotations exist for this Irish hero of language and letters amid a threatened Gaelic culture.) Apparently, Fenius's fame did not end with the Phoenicians, however. Europe and China were also "indebted" to the same man for the same reasons. Indeed, presaging Charles Vallancey's later antiquarian speculations, O'Flaherty pairs the ancient Irish language alongside other ancient cultures with letters, mostly in the Orient: Egyptian, Hebrew, Chaldean, Chinese, Japanese, Indian, Arabian, Greek, and Persian (82–86). Along with the work of James Ware, Bochart, and others, O'Flaherty's writings on ancient Ireland set the trend for many antiquarian explorations in the eighteenth century into the Irish language and ogham writing, which in its cut strokes and limited alphabet was seen to resemble ancient northern European runic writing and Phoenician characters.

The crux of O'Flaherty's argument is that Ireland's ancient culture predates Britain and its imperial forebear, Rome. In *Ogygia Vindicated,* O'Flaherty explicitly states: "[T]he Irish were a settled nation in *Ireland* before *Rome* was founded. They came from a most antient, populous and renowned nation; and were so observant of their extraction, that, of all nations come from *Scythians,* they only, in the word SCOTS (a la Isidore, Bede, etc.), preserved the name of *Scythians.* They had a literature and uncorrupted primitive language and written records; their remote antiquities were of the colonies before them first planting *Ireland*" (1775, 25). For O'Flaherty, only because of (relatively) recent British advances has Ireland's ancient glory been reduced. Its "remote antiquities" linger, the strength of the past coupled with the hopes of its future. But O'Flaherty did not merely repeat origin legends in order to prove Irish antiquity, and he opens the door for later studies that build on classical texts, etymology, and archaeology (the primary tools of antiquarianism); the legends remain the salient starting points for such investigations at the dawn of the Enlightenment.

The textual root of Irish identity for O'Flaherty was in its various names.

Building on Bochart's theories, he also furthers the characterization of Ireland as a remote, peripheral land, referencing the earliest characterizations of the Greeks, who had learned of Ireland from the Phoenicians: "Bochart . . . derives Hibernia from the Phœnician word Ibernæ, which in that language, means the most remote, or extreme habitation; because the antients could never discover any place beyond Ireland, to the west, but a vast extensive sea, from which he infers, that Ireland was not unknown to the Phœnicians, formerly a people renowned in history for their discoveries and voyages to the most distant countries of the known world" (1793, 27–28). Remoteness, thus, remains a central trait of Irish identity for O'Flaherty and subsequent writers—one that repeatedly carries an Oriental signification with it. Ireland, in this Phoenician discovery narrative, becomes an ancient home of cultural remoteness, its very name proving it to be both a distant homeland and a borderland. By extension, Irish culture appears, particularly in texts concerning British-Irish or imperial relations, to embody an edgy doubleness, being both close (as home) and distant (as a remote land). Cultural proximity and distance, expressed through the doubleness of such narratives, become inherent traits of Ireland throughout the rise of the British Empire. The geocultural reinforcement and evidence for such a narrative of doubleness were Ireland's own emerging liminality in the growing British Empire, being both geographically close and culturally distant from London.

Antiquarianism

Antiquarianism concerns ancient cultures; philology concerns the study of languages. In the eighteenth century, however, these areas of inquiry often overlapped in both technique and purpose. Most Irish antiquarians and Celtic philologists of the eighteenth century worked to demonstrate the similarities between the contemporary Celtic languages and ancient ones. At times, the antiquarians extended their research beyond language, however, into investigations of ancient structures, ruins, and material artifacts, processes that later became the work of archaeology, the root, *archaios,* meaning "ancient" in Greek. Most eighteenth-century language studies focused on etymology and less on comparative grammar, which was the focus for Lhuyd and later philologers and linguists. Etymology afforded greater flexibility for "proving" an ancient connection based on similar phonetics and for imagining an Irish connection to the Orient. Through this pseudoscience, antiquarians traced the Celtic languages to various groups: Scythians, Titans, Phoenicians, Egyptians, Persians, Chinese, Indians, Mohawks, and others, depending on their purpose, audience, and position. Eighteenth-century philology and antiquarianism often seem to resemble the work of Isidore of Seville more than other period advancements in philosophy, natural science, and geography by Newton,

Locke, and Leibniz (who also wrote on philology). But Irish antiquarianism was not alone in its paradigmatic belief in a biblical time line; most European philologists, scientists, and historians, including Leibniz, subscribed to this framework well into the nineteenth century; their work just did not depend as directly on it as antiquarianism did. Nevertheless, the social, political, and cultural commentaries of these antiquarian and philological studies belong fully to the Age of Reason, when representations of distant and remote peoples had groundings in the supposedly universal ideals of history and science.

Perhaps the most telling error of philology at the time was the idea of linguistic purity. Eighteenth-century philologists believed that unconquered and uncolonized cultures retained a linguistic purity because their languages had not been forced to change through conquest. Without the process of colonization or permanent conquest, a language, and by extension its culture, remained relatively untouched since its first settlements. Daniel R. Davis, who edited the 2000 republication of the work of prominent eighteenth-century French Celticist Paul-Yves Pezron, as well as the work of many Celticists, discusses how this assumption played out: "[I]f there is not any mechanism for change other than borrowing and mixing [of vocabulary and syntax], both the processes undertaken by human agents in a social context of conquest, then a language which does not show the effects of borrowing and mixing, because its speakers have not been conquered, cannot have changed. Thus it is possible for Pezron to speak of the Bretons as inheritors of the Gaulish language" (xiii). Remarkably, Pezron argued that contemporary Breton language was actually the language of Greece's Titans, the forebears of the gods of Olympus. He read ancient Greek descriptions of the Titans as disguised descriptions of early Celts and gleaned his information accordingly. Instead of undertaking further comparative and pan-Celtic studies in the manner of Lhuyd, the peculiarly ancient and supposedly Oriental origins of modern Celts attracted scholars across the continent. In Ireland, investigations of Ireland's ancient Oriental connections seemed more immediately important than understanding its place in modern Europe.

For most scholars of the time, human history extended back only five or six thousand years, according to the reckoning of biblical scholars—James Ussher famously estimated the date of the earth's creation to be October 23, 4004, B.C. The paradigm and the idea of linguistic purity made the task of tracing human origins back to the earliest times seem achievable. The supposedly barbaric or premodern traits of the Irish appeared to confirm their Scythian, Celtic, and Phoenician heritages. The chronological belief was unshakable, even when evidence to the contrary presented itself: Charles Vallancey, for instance, dismissed Herodotus's "heathen" point of view of the history of the world: "Scripture, is certainly the only standard of all ancient history, and the touchstone by which the truth of it may be tried. Heathen writers, who, unassisted by this, attempt to search into antiquity have no stay whereon to rest.

Herodotus on all occasions talks familiarly of a *myriad* of years before his time" (1770–1804, vol. 4, no. 8, ii). Significantly, the other "never failing touchstone" that Vallancey mentions is language (iv). Finding the origins of all language, therefore, could begin with the most linguistically pure of languages, for which Irish was an excellent candidate, Ireland having never been colonized by Rome and Irish culture never having been fully displaced by Vikings or English culture.

Questions about linguistic purity and the origin of language were widely discussed in the latter half of the eighteenth century. In 1759 and 1771, the Berlin Academy posed philological and philosophical problems for a prominent essay contest (Aarsleff 1983, 143–55). Johann Gottfried Herder (1744–1803) won the second contest, with his *Ueber den Ursprung der Sprache* (1772), which answered the question: "En supposant les hommes abandonnés à leurs facultés naturelles, sont-ils en état d'inventer le langage?" (144). Herder's answer addressed the question's implication that language may be both natural and a product of human invention, arguing that language was intrinsically bound up in human nature and circumstance, much like his later arguments that historicized human and cultural development. In *The Study of Language in England, 1780–1860,* Hans Aarsleff paraphrases Herder as such: "Man in nature had cooperated with nature in man to create language, which in its continuous development left traces of the history of early man and the folk" (1983, 152). Along with a new appreciation for vernacular languages that surfaced with Romanticism, comparative philology developed from Herder's work, and German philologists would eventually develop Celtic philology in the nineteenth century. What perhaps is more significant, in relation to Celticism and Orientalism, is that after Herder's work, language began to be treated more as an independent entity, with its own organic life, able to be studied as having an independent existence that developed according to natural laws, without the creation of logical categories of syntax. Because languages had their own histories, they could be studied in terms of development and life span; older languages could be compared to younger languages, original ones to synthesized and derived ones. Ideas of a linguistic purity informed how so-called original and ancient languages operated. Again, Aarsleff explains the understanding of the time: "The older and more original a language is, for instance, the more clearly will the emotions dominate in the roots of words, and the fewer abstractions. Thus the study of language became a branch of natural history" (152). Languages that were seen as older and original—those languages related to Sanskrit and to the Celtic languages, for instance—could be studied for ancient wisdom and their proximity to original and primal language. The ramifications of this observation were manifold as it was applied and misapplied: so-called ancient languages would be understood as more sensual, more immediate, and more emotional, and less abstract, less refined, less advanced, and less intellectual than the modern languages of Europe. Although they had developed, their fundamental structure and sensibility mirrored their ancient origins.

Celtic languages, like the languages of India, were seen as immutably ancient, and various scholars searched them for evidence of antiquity and primordial tongues and extended their conclusions into culture. In addition to Paul-Yves Pezron's equating contemporary Bretons with ancient Gauls and Titans in *The Antiquity of Nations* (1706), John Cleland (1709–1789) treated a proto-Celtic language as the parent language for all European languages; James Parsons's (1705–1770) *Remains of Japhet* (1767) treated the Irish language as a nearly unchanged original language, variously tagged Japhetic, Pelasgian, Gomerian, Magogian, and Scythian;[20] Rowland Jones (1722–1774) in *The Origin of Language and Nations* (1764) went beyond looking for Japhetic origins and sought a language of primeval sounds descended from Adam in the tradition of medieval original language hunts;[21] Charles Vallancey (1721–1812) worked to reconcile the supposed Scythian aspects of Irish with the Phoenician origin posited by Bochart and O'Flaherty in his *Essay on the Antiquity of the Irish Language* (1772); Edward Davies's (1756–1831) approach in *Celtic Researches* (1804) expanded Pezron's biblical reckoning of Breton and other Celtic tongues, adding suppositions about the origin of the Druids; William Betham (1779–1853) in *The Gael and the Cymbri* (1834) extended Vallancey's ideas about the Phoenician origins of Ireland; and, last, the Scotsman Lachlan Maclean (1798–1848) in *The History of the Celtic Language* (1840) affirmed that Scots-Gaelic was indeed the original language descended from Adam via Japheth, as many before him had suspected.[22] The biblical schemata eventually played themselves out in the nineteenth century, and Orientalist philologists and Celticists in the 1830s and 1840s, particularly James Cowles Prichard, Adolphe Pictet, and Franz Bopp, moved away from this framework. In part because very similar etymological evidence had been used to support opposing arguments, nineteenth-century philologists eventually returned to the comparative-grammar approach that Edward Lhuyd had pioneered in 1707.

For most Irish eighteenth-century antiquarians, Irish culture existed at the edge of a classical frame of the world, never having belonged to the Roman Empire and always having been represented along the boundaries of the habitable or civilized or enlightened world. Because of the Irish's relative lack of Romanization, many northern European philologists in the seventeenth century had often grouped it with the Germanic languages. But to group Irish alongside English and German no longer seemed as preferable as placing it with other border languages of the Greco-Roman world: Phoenician, Coptic, Hindi, Persian, and Ethiopian. Irish and Celtic languages, along with Basque, were perceived as the most disconnected and remote languages (and cultures) of western Europe, especially after German connections to the Latin world had been established by Johann Herder in the mid-eighteenth century. By the time of Carl Wilhelm Friedrich von Schlegel (1772–1829), Celtic languages had been relegated to the sidelines of linguistic relevance, unassociated with the major languages: Germanic, Latin, Greek, Persian, and Indian.[23] But Celtic languages were not alone in being dismissed as a language family; Schlegel was much harsher toward Chinese and the native languages of America.[24] Only later in the nineteenth century did Celtic languages clearly take their place as a distinct branch of the Indo-European family.

In the early eighteenth century, two main schools of thought had developed on the origin of the Celts: on the one hand, the "Scytho-Celtic model" propounded that the Celts, descended from the wild Scyths, had migrated across Europe over a long period of time; on the other hand, the "Phoenician model" argued that the Celts (Scythian or not) had migrated more directly from the East, that is, either as Phoenicians or via the Phoenician tin trade route by sea from the Middle East to Carthage and around the southern edge of Europe to pre-Roman Spain and the British Isles. The differences on this matter usually corresponded with the cultural and political divide in Ireland over the English presence and influence in Ireland. Anglo-Irish antiquarians and native Irish intellectuals and writers, such as O'Flaherty, generally promoted the Phoenician model to argue for the ancient pedigree and civilization of the Irish, brought to their poor present condition by successive foreign invasions. More Anglocentric authors and scholars generally focused on Scythian origins, which had been long used rhetorically to assert the barbarity of the Gaels, Spenser's *View of the Present State of Ireland* (1596) being perhaps the most vicious instance. Joep Leerssen in *Remembrance and Imagination* elaborates on the nature and implications of this split later in the eighteenth century:

> Those who took a positive interest in Irish antiquity, who relied on native amanuenses and were willing to envisage a prestigious, highly civilized origin for the country's native inhabitants, tended to favour the Phoenician model. . . . More conservative, anglocentric scholars who preferred to believe that Ireland was primordially a barbaric country where all traces of culture were introduced by outside influences such as the Vikings or the English, naturally rejected the Phoenician model and endorsed the Scytho-Celtic one. . . . In the opposition between civility and barbarism, the Anglocentric view saw the Irish as savages and the English presence as a force of civility; the Phoenician hypothesis turned the tables, and predicated civility on the native Gaels. (1997, 73–74)

The Phoenician model definitely enjoyed prominence in the work of early Irish cultural nationalists, but, later in the century, most Irish antiquarians reconciled such differences by arguing that Ireland had been populated through multiple "invasions," as suggested in *Lebor Gabála*. Nevertheless, Oriental origin theories achieved such cachet in the eighteenth and early-nineteenth centuries that nearly every native history of Ireland included a section on, or at least a reference to, the Eastern origins of the Celts. Artifacts and ruins, particularly the round towers,[25] were drawn alongside contemporaneous structures in the Orient (particularly in India) to visually confirm the Oriental origins (via the Phoenicians) of the contemporary Irish.

Irish antiquarians furthered the tradition of the origin legends by developing O'Flaherty's work in pseudoscientific directions, treating Irish sources more as artifacts of a near-dead culture than as elements of a living culture. Nevertheless, many of the legends were preserved; indeed, without the efforts of these scholars many manuscripts and much Irish-language material might have been lost. Significantly, the ancient history that interested these readers and researchers was neither Catholic nor Protestant; such an ancestry, if proved, would validate Gaelic culture and help revive it, but it would also downplay sectarian divisions and broaden Irish identity to better include the Protestant Anglo-Irish. Predominantly, these researchers were Anglo-Irish, but, as opposed to the representations of earlier British newcomers to Ireland (such as Spenser and other *Nua-Ghall*), these representations tended not to vilify Irish culture. Nevertheless, they exoticized it, and as stories of barbarism and cannibalism lessened, images of premodern, mystical pagans increased. Significantly, after the attacks on the structure of Gaelic culture in the seventeenth century, Anglo-Irish attraction to Gaelic Irish culture was welcomed. Interest in Irish-language and Gaelic materials increased in the early years of the century as the descendants of bardic scholars worked to preserve both the language and old manuscripts. Irish-language poets, scribes, and scholars had somewhat of a Gaelic revival, centered somewhat around the father-son literary figures Seán Ó Neachtain (?1650–1729) and Tadhg Ó Neachtain (1670–1749). Both men wrote verse and prose works, and the son compiled an Irish-language dictionary. Together with new Gaelic historians such as Charles O'Conor (1710–1791), who translated O'Flaherty's *Ogygia Vindicated* in 1775, and Dermod O'Connor (fl. 1720), who translated Keating's *Foras Feasa ar Éirinn* into English as *The General History of Ireland* (1723), they represented the transfer and continuity of bardic learning to Dublin. Although some of these Irish-language writers demonstrated interest in Irish antiquities and Oriental origins, many more focused on contemporary culture, and Irish and Celtic antiquities were often dominated by Anglo-Irish antiquarians.

Despite the exoticism and autoexoticism of the period, most writers in Ireland during this period used the origin legends to firmly assert the dignity of Irish culture, as the works of Charles Vallancey, Charles O'Conor the Elder, Sylvester O'Halloran (1728–1807), Joseph C. Walker (1761–1810), and Charlotte Brooke (?1740–1793) demonstrate. O'Halloran had written *Ierne Defended* (1774), reviving Strabo's name for Ireland, in response to Thomas Leland's more conservative antiquarian *History of Ireland* (1773).[26] Walker, a prominent member of the Royal Irish Academy with antiquarian ties to Australia and Italy, did not focus specifically on the linguistic origins of the Gaelic Irish, but the fact that Walker endorsed James MacPherson's supposed translations signals his exuberant interest in Celticism. His *Historical Memoirs of the Irish Bards* (1786) traces the developments of poetry and music in Ireland and relies on the work of Theophilus O'Flanagan (1764–1814); it also provides translations of Carolan, the Welsh poet, by the esteemed translator of the day, Charlotte Brooke. Besides contributing to Charles Vallancey's antiquarian journal, *Collectanea De Rebus Hibernicus* (1770–1804), Walker also wrote on Irish drama and published his less literary antiquarian study, *An Historical Essay on the Dress of the Ancient and Modern Irish: Addressed to the right honourable the Earl of Charlemont to which is subjoined, a memoir on the Armour and Weapons of the Irish* (1788). In it, his comments on Irish links to Oriental cultures go beyond etymological similarities and origin legends: "Amongst the early Irish, the BEARD was cherished with as much solicitude, as formerly amongst the Orientals" (11). For eighteenth-century antiquarians, the Eastern antiquity of Celtic cultures revealed more than clues about Celtic languages.

The Oriental link distinguished Irish culture as an exotic culture amid its more modern and enlightened neighbors so that Ireland could provide a necessary antithesis to modernity. For a time, Celticism provided one of the most prominent intellectual links between the European and Asian continents while providing a focus for Anglo-Irish supporters of Gaelic culture. Many of these supporters considered themselves "patriots" of Ireland, arguing for cultural respect for Ireland and greater commercial freedom for Anglo-Irish merchants. They bucked against the various trade restrictions imposed that had begun in the second half of the seventeenth century (the Cattle Acts of 1663 and 1671 and the Woolen Act of 1699) and their inability to call an Irish Parliament because of the Poynings Act of 1493. Their positions as antiquarians and Celticists also allowed them to interpret and comment on Gaelic culture for English readers, who had developed a great appetite for the wild fashions and dreamy aesthetics of Celticism.

Tony Ballantyne has distanced Vallancey and other antiquarians from any Irish tradition in his important work, *Orientalism and Race:* "In this sense we can understand the work of Celticists such as Vallancey as part of a project of settler self-fashioning, where antiquarianism and ethnology were central in the attempts of local settler elites to mark themselves off from their metropolitan counterparts through an engagement with 'indigenous' tradition: an engagement, however, that was profoundly embedded in the structures of inequality engendered by colonial domination" (2002, 37). Beyond the fact that Vallancey often argued that the Irish were not Celts, and did not call himself a Celticist, Ballantyne's summation of these relations unfairly puts the significance of Vallancey's representations solely on his imperial vision. Though certainly significant, this imperial perspective did not invent or merely have "an engagement with 'indigenous' tradition" for the purpose of "settler self-fashioning"; Vallancey's work directly borrowed from Gaelic scholars, attempting to translate and modernize a centuries-old Irish tradition. Unfortunately, Ballantyne only discusses his links to English and continental philology.

Between 1770 and 1845, the Royal Irish Academy and *Collectanea De Rebus Hibernicus* published many tracts and essays on the similarities between the Irish language and Eastern languages. Two prominent studies roughly mark the beginning and end of this period in which linguistic and antiquarian proof for Ireland's Eastern origins was sought: Vallancey's *Essay on the Antiquity of the Irish Language, Being a Collation of the Irish with the Punic Language* (1772) and William Betham's *Etruria Celtica: Etruscan Literature and Antiquities Investigated; or, The Language of that Ancient and Illustrious People Compared and Identified with the Iberno-Celtic, and Both*

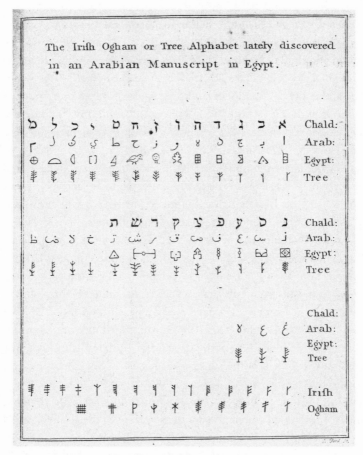

3. "The Irish Ogham or Tree Alphabet Lately Discovered in an Arabian Manuscript in Egypt," 1781. Published in Charles Vallancey's antiquarian journal *Collectanea De Rebus Hibernicus* 2, no. 7 (1781–1804). This chart followed William Beauford's essay "Of the Origin and Language of the Irish; and of the Learning of the Druids."

Shown to Be Phœnician (1842). Vallancey's work initiated a renewed interest in a distinctly Oriental heritage for Ireland from an Anglo-Irish patriot perspective, and it rejected English representations of Irish barbarity. Much of the Irish antiquarian work produced in this seventy-year period stemmed from Vallancey's speculations. Furthermore, more than only borrowing from English philology, Vallancey prompted other philologists and readers to reconsider a connection between European and "Oriental" languages via Ireland (see fig. 3).

General Charles Vallancey

Charles Vallancey, born to a French Huguenot family in either Flanders or Windsor, first came to Ireland from the newly acquired British colony of Gibraltar, where he had served as a British officer in the Army Engineers; afterwards, he became chief surveyor of Ireland. In Gibraltar since 1750, he had become interested in antiquities and studied Hebrew and Chaldean and ancient history there. Classical Greek texts repute Gibraltar to be the Phoenician landmark *Calpe,* where stood the Pillars of Hercules, a prominent landmark in classical texts and a strategic crossroads for modern naval powers. Though never a Phoenician city, Phoenician artifacts have been found there, and the Phoenician cities of Gades (now Cadiz) and Lixus (now only Roman ruins in northwest Morocco) were not far away. After spending years familiarizing himself with the antiquities of Gibraltar and the rudiments of "Oriental" languages, Vallancey transferred to Ireland in 1762 as a lieutenant colonel of the British Army Engineers, bringing with him an imperial vision of antiquity. Significantly, his passionate speculations about Ireland's ancient kinship with the Phoenicians mirror his own experience as an imperial officer in these British-controlled lands. As he once noted, his ideas connecting Ireland with ancient sailors from the Orient began in personal observation: "I had not been a week landed in Ireland from Gibraltar, where I had studied Hebrew and Chaldaic under Jews of various countries, when I heard a peasant girl say to [a] boor standing by her 'Teach an Maddin Nag' (Behold the morning star), pointing to the planet Venus, the Maddena Nag of the Chaldeans" (qtd. in Blavatsky 1882, 2:759). But this vision is only half of the impetus for his work. Soon after his arrival, Vallancey began study of the Irish language and was drawn to the ancient histories and "old books" of Ireland, encountering O'Flaherty's Phoenician-origin theories. By 1770, his writing exuded conviction about the extent of the connection: "The antiquities of this island bear uncommon and indelible marks of very remote times. Phœnician monuments are scattered over the surface of it, and what is more extraordinary, Phœnician names of things and places are retained even at this day" (1781, vol. 1, no. 1, ix). In little time, he developed the dizzying applications of etymology for Irish antiquarian arguments.[27]

In 1770, along with Anglo-Irish supporters, he established an antiquarian journal on Irish culture, *Collectanea De Rebus Hibernicis,* which ran until 1804 and included essays on Irish law, architecture, literature, religion, history, and language, among other topics. Within these pages, he would make some of his most pointed pronouncements about what he saw as an Irish-Oriental affinity. In "The Editor's Preface," dated 1786, to vol. 1, no. 1 of the six-volume bound edition (1809?), he comments on the enigmatic nature of the Irish: "This enigmatical mode of philosophizing, so prevalent among the oriental, they [that is, the Irish] learned from the ancient Phœnicians, who had it from the Jews" (1770–1804, 1:xi). In 1782 he helped found the culturally patriotic Royal Irish Academy, dedicated to "the cultivation of Science, Polite Literature, and Antiquities." He studied Ireland as an ancient culture and promoted a venerable heritage for it with great passion. Overall, Vallancey's arguments met a mixed response: favorable, if sometimes skeptical, in Dublin and generally dismissive, if somewhat inquisitive, in England.

Basing his ideas on O'Flaherty's (and Bochart's) Phoenician-origin thesis, and drawing on the Persian translations of Sir William Jones, the Asian histories of William Marsden and J. Z. Holwell, and eventually geographical work of Sanskritist Francis Wilford,[28] Vallancey extended his research over three decades into many areas but retained a pseudophilological approach. It is noteworthy that he never became fluent in the Irish language or developed lasting methods for Orientalism or Celticism. But the fact that most of his theories were dead wrong did not prevent his work from having impact, much like the pseudo-Ossianic translations of James MacPherson. His work later moved beyond proving Ireland's Eastern heritage into the mapping of an original Scythian language and culture across Asia and Europe (see fig. 4), a work that had its own degree of influence. Most of his essays, however, were corollaries to his best-known theories asserting Ireland's Phoenician origins. For instance, in the 1786 preface to "Fragments of the Brehon Laws of Ireland," published in *Collectanea De Rebus Hibernicis,* Vallancey discusses the Brehon laws of Gaelic Ireland, but mostly to refute ideas about Scytho-Celtic influence and claim Phoenician relevance (after referencing "the great luminary of eastern learning, Mr. William Jones"):

> Had the Irish received their feudal system from the northern nations, they would most certainly have adopted the technical terms of the people from whom they received them. On the contrary we find every term flies up to the fountain head, viz. the Arabic or Persic, which seems to indicate that some colonies from the east, have settled in Ireland, at a remote period; the ancient language of the people differing from all their neighbors [for instance, the Welsh], and having so great an affinity with the Persic and Arabic, strengthens this conjecture. (vol. 3, no. 1, xii–xiii)[29]

As this passage indicates, his linguistic acumen never expanded beyond locating apparent cognates in distant languages to confirm his theories. But his main goal was

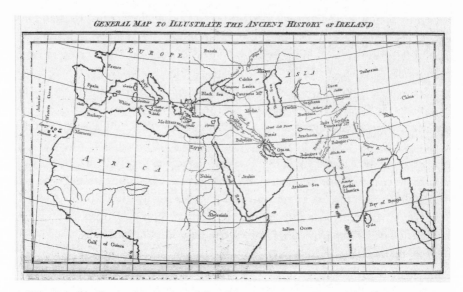

4. "The Schytho-Iberian Nation in Asia" or "General Map to Illustrate the Ancient History of Ireland." Published in Charles Vallancey's antiquarian journal *Collectanea De Rebus Hibernicus* 1, no. 3 (1770–1804) following a discussion by Vallancey. The map included the following caption: "Taken from de la Rochette's Indiæ Veteris. Georgr: Londini 1493 apud G. Faden, and from Sr. W. Ouseleys Map in the Geogr. of Ebn Haukal 1800."

less the advancement of philology and more the recognition of the ancient heritage and dignity of Irish culture, overturning British conceptions. In this preface, he praises Orientalists for "the pains they have taken to free the eastern nations from *barbarism* and *despotism,* by proving these people to have had a written law, time immemorial, reflects honour on their humanity," but he laments that such work had not been done for Ireland and its Brehon laws (xii).

Vallancey's linguistic oversights have most damned his legacy. Occasionally, he dismisses actual cognates that signaled real advancements in understanding, most famously the illustration of the p-q split of Celtic languages, advanced by Lhuyd, illustrating the link between Welsh and Irish, where the word for *son* is *map* in Welsh and *mac* (*maq*) in Irish. "In the progress of this work I have dissented from the common opinion, that the Irish language is of *Celtic* origin; and I have shewn, from extensive collations, its great connexion and affinity with the *Sanscrit, Hindoostanee,* and old *Egyptian*" (vol. 6, no. 1, xiii). Vallancey's later work incorporates other speculative work in the study of Indian languages and culture, for example *The Ancient History of Ireland, Proved from the Sanscrit Books of the Bramins of India* (1797). But Vallancey's arguments gained an audience for reasons other than his philological scholarship. His work confirmed a vision of Ireland as an independent, ancient, remote, and non-European culture. Moreover, it corresponded with the politics of Anglo-Irish patriots, who resented Ireland's trade restrictions and tariffs, especially to North America and other places within the British Empire. Anglo-Irish patriot antiquarians such as Sylvester O'Halloran worked with Catholic scholars and antiquarians to assert the dignity and heritage of Irish culture against representations of Irish barbarism. They encouraged a discursive realm through which observers could theorize, explore, and confirm Irish cultural differences by recognizing a distinct tradition.

In 1772, Vallancey published in *Collectanea De Rebus Hibernicus* an overview of the invasion legends, written by Charles O'Conor the Elder, for O'Conor's own never-completed history.[30] Vallancey also explicitly references how the origin legends were used by O'Flaherty, Keating, Mac Ferbis, Ware, Lhuyd, Davies, Barclay, Ussher, O'Conor, and how Caesar, Strabo, Pliny, Mela, Plutarch, and Virgil described the Irish to others. Toward the end of his career, Vallancey summarizes his ideas in "Proem." Clearly written after Charles O'Conor's death, Vallancey critiques his former guide, using arguments as unfounded as the ones he sought to overturn. Even this late in his career, however, he points to the enduring importance of the origin legends and the "mythology of the ancient Irish," which he calls "one of the strongest proofs of the history." But the origin legends alone, he argues, could not fully explain Ireland's ancient history: "*Keating,* and his translator *O'Connor* [*sic*], were unequal to the task of historians. They were ignorant of oriental history; making *Eirin* the name of *Iran* or Persia, in its largest extent *Ireland;* Casar the niece, instead of the grandson, of Noah; writing *Sothiana* for *Soghdiana;* and passing over in silence the mythology of the ancient Irish, one of the strongest proofs of the history" (1781, vol. 6, no. 1, xi). For Vallancey and other antiquarians, ancient Irish history could be best understood in the light of "oriental history," which was generally written by British and French Orientalists. Vallancey rebukes critics of the Phoenician arguments who ask for material evidence: "I am asked, with a tone of triumph, where are the ruins of the fine places, mentioned in the history of Ireland?—the ruins of the palace of Tara, of Emania, &c.&c.?—I answer these ignorant pretenders to historical knowledge, that they were all built of mud walls and timber (except the round towers, the sacred temples of the perpetual fire). . . . Where are the ruins of the buildings erected by the Phœnicians in Majorca, Minorca, Malta, Spain, &c.? Not a vestige of them remains" (xi-xii). Vallancey neglects to point out that other Phoenician ruins and artifacts had been discovered elsewhere. But in another work, he supposedly uncovers some material evidence: "In traveling through Ireland we frequently meet with mounts or raths, the repositories of the illustrious dead. In two very remarkable passages of the Iliad the poet intimates, that this was the practice both of the antient Greeks and Phœnicians, and their manner of burying their dead, particularly of their heroes and eminent men" (vol. 2, no. 8, unnumbered 11–12). But physical evidence was always secondary to that from language in these arguments.

Vallancey's main tool was etymology, through which he speculatively and confidently hunted phonetic similarities, usually in unrelated languages, and then resituated Irish cultural activities into a new heritage. In a new preface to the reprinted *Essay on the Antiquity of the Irish Language* in the bound *Collectanea De Rebus Hibernicus,* Vallancey admits the limits of etymology, but pins it on the "arbitrary liberties" of others, who lose sight of the "radical word and its primitive sense" (vol. 2, no. 8, unnumbered 13–14).[31] An excerpt from "Of the Kiss of Saluatation; of Curses, &c." illustrates his method. Etymologizing the Irish word *pòg* (kiss), he sets out to prove that the "kiss of salutation is universally practiced in Ireland, except in the metropolis: it is of Oriental origin, and at one time, was common to all polite nations" (vol. 3, no. 12, 543).

> The modern Irish have but one word to express a kiss, viz. *pòg* [*sic*]; those of the middle age had three, viz. *pòg, meam, falùt:* the first implies the kiss of salutation, given on the *poc, puc, pòg,* that is, the cheek; a word derived from the Syriac *pacca,* the maxilla or cheek bone; or from the Chaldee *pag,* the cheek, from whence *Bethphage,* i.e. domus *buccæ,* the temple of the *cheek,* or of the *trumpet,* because the cheeks are puffed out in the action of blowing. See *Bernhardus* in sermone ad milites templi. Perficè *pej,* the cheek.
>
> The *meam* of the Irish, was the *osculum lascivum* or the Jews (the Irish *suamb* or Latin *suafium* did not express the meaning of *meam;*) it was the obsece *memra* or *mumass* of the libidinous Arabians.
>
> The *faluth* or *foluth* was the *osculum salutationis,* made by kissing the tips of the fingers to every person they met; from whence *lùt* now implies respect; *dean do lùt,* make your bow or courtesy. (547)

Even if most readers did not investigate his specious and amusing cognates, or believe the entirety of his conclusions, the Oriental connection was often not disbelieved, in part because of the power of the semiotic resonance that had developed in representations and understandings of Ireland.

Vallancey's 1786 preface to *A Vindication of the Ancient History of Ireland* began the work of reconciling the two main theoretical camps on Irish antiquity: the Scytho-Celtic hypothesis and the Phoenician hypothesis. His main points seek to mediate English and Irish representations and include his speculations on the existence of an early dynamic people, the Scytho-Celts, who supposedly roamed from Ireland to Japan. This concept of these people stemmed from his trust in Greco-Roman descriptions of Celts and Scythians. Although he acknowledges how categories of peoples in ancient Scythia elided differences—"Men totally dissimilar are grouped together under one indiscriminate character, merely because they are known in Europe by one general name" (1786, 12), he fails to apply this principle (and source criticism) any further. In order to account for the wide influence of this ancient people, he simply notes that they moved around a lot, much like the nomadic Scythian horsemen were supposed to have lived.[32] Within the broad category of Scythian-Celts (termed variously "Celto-Scythians," the "Schytho-Iberian nation in Asia," the "antient Celto-Schythian nation"), the main distinction that he makes is between "the Nomade or Northern Scythian, and the civilized or Southern [Magogian] Scythian of Armenia" (11). He complains that many Anglocentric and continental studies have conflated these southern Magogian Scythians with the northern wilder Scythians, arguing that only the Northern Scytho-Celts fit the barbaric model.

> [T]he body of [Southern] Mogogian [*sic*] Scythians . . . were a polished people before they left Asia; the first astronomers, navigators, and traders, after the flood, and courted by the Arabs, the Canaanites, the Jews, and Egyptians, to settle amongst them. That, from their first settlement in Armenia, they soon passed down the Euphrates to the Persian Gulph, round the Indian Ocean, to the Red Sea, up the coast of the Mediterranean almost to Tyre. The Greeks knew them by the names of the Phoenicians of the Red Sea, by Icthyophagi and Troglodytae:[33] in Scripture they are called *Am Siim* or Ship people, and *Naphuth Dori* or Maritime folks.
>
> These soon mixed with the Dadanites and Canaanites, allied with them, and were absorbed under the general name of Phoenicians. . . . To a common reader, it must appear the reveries of an etymologist to compare the language and deities of the Brahmans with those of the ancient Irish; but to the philosopher . . . there will appear solid reason for so doing: the Brahmans and Guebres were originally a mixture of Dedanites and Persians, or Scythians. Fohi, the civiliser of the Chinese, was a Scythian. The Japanese were Scythians. . . . Zoroaster, if not a Scythian, at least studied Astronomy in Scythia. (13–14)

Emphasizing the mutable genius and great mobility of the southern Scythians, Vallancey ties Indian Brahmins to the Gaelic Irish via Phoenician sailors, prefiguring the work of later nineteenth-century anthropologists.

Vallancey's clearest articulation of his theories of the origins of the Irish can be found in his late 1812 pamphlet, *Ancient Stone Amphitheatre Lately Discovered in the County of Kerry with Fragments of Ancient History:* "[T]he ancient inhabitants of Ireland, who were all *Scuthæ,* as stiled by the Greeks, but of very different stocks. One, rude, ignorant, and unlettered; the other, a polished and lettered people since the invention of letters. These are the Aiteach Coti, or Scuthæ of the line of Cush, who came here under the name of Milesians; yet these, in their peregrinations through the East, were so blended with Chaldæan, Persian, and Arabic, as to form a dialect of mixed languages, hard to be discerned, but by an Oriental scholar" (2).

He continues to cite just such an Orientalist, Lord Moira, who explains the cultural influence and genealogical mixture of "Hindoo," Phoenician, Persic, and Arabic in the ancient Milesians. Vallancey then underscores the important point that these two tribes, although both bearing the name "Scuthi or Scythæ" (Scythian and Scotti conflated as in Isidore), were of different sons of Noah (at the time being used to distinguish the races of the earth)—"one deriving their origin from Cush, the son of Ham [Asian]; the other from Magog, son of Japhet [European]" (4). This clear ancestral conflation of the Asian and the European in the Irish probably coincided with the development of race theories that Vallancey had encountered, which were growing in popularity in the early nineteenth century.

Earlier Vallancey had made other attempts at reconciling this Irish Eurasian hybridity. In the preface to *Essay on the Antiquity of the Irish Language* in the second volume of *Collectanea De Rebus Hibernicus,* Vallancey had sought to merge the competing models of Irish antiquity. Opening the possibilities for the ancient Irish, he claims that Thule, the ancient name for Iceland, truly signified Ireland, as a number of classical writers had supposed. This ancient geographic marker of the farthest land in the West, that which "is very well known among the eastern people," reaffirmed Ireland's remote East–West borderliness (Giraldus 1982, 68).[34] He also updates his argument to more clearly and further differentiate between "the Asiatic Scythians and the European Scythians" (1770–1804, vol. 2, no. 5, unnumbered 18–19):

> If an affinity of the Irish language with the Punic be allowed, this discovery will throw great lights on the darker periods of the Heathen Irish history. It will show, that though the details be fabulous, the foundation is laid in truth. It will demonstrate the early use of letters in this island because nothing but *that use* could preserve the least affinity from the flourishing era of Carthage to the present, a space of more than 2300 years. It will account for the Irish assuming to themselves the names of Feni or Fenicians, which they have retained through all ages. It will with the same certainty account for their giving the name of Berla Feni (the Phœnician tongue) to one of their native dialects. In fine, it will show, that when they adopted the Phœnician Syntax, they confined their language to oriental orthography, while it harmonized itself out of its primitive consonantal Celtic harshness, by the suppression of many radical letters in the pronunciation of words. (unnumbered 20)

Based on details that are fabulous and impossible to prove, Vallancey argues that the Oriental Fenians harmonized, tamed, and suppressed elements of the more barbaric Celtic tongue. Returning to pseudohistory, he offers a last astounding piece of evidence from legend, which seems intended to cinch the claim: "Or are we to be surprised at the assertions of the Irish Seanachies, of the Milesians or Phenians finding themselves understood by the natives at the time of their landing; for the antient Gauls, who also colonized this country as well as Britain, spoke the same Phenian dialect" (unnumbered 21). These two Scythian "invaders" from the East—one northern Celtic and one southern Oriental—unsurprisingly speak the same language. The linguistic "foundation of truth" and reconciliation here is that the Oriental and the Celtic literally merged in Ireland as the ancestors of the modern Irish.

Over the course of Vallancey's career, his work extended beyond the history of Ireland into speculations about the Eurasian Scythians and their original language. Seeking root words, he included a foldout chart in *Collectanea De Rebus Hibernicus* that compares the "Names of Numbers in all the Languages that could be collected," including Hebrew, Chaldean, Arabian, Persian, Chinese, Japonian, Æthiopian, Sclavonian, Bengalian, Turkish, Annamitica, Mallays, Hindustan, Punico-Maltese, Irish, Welsh, Mohawk, New Guinea, and Shawanese (Vallancey's spellings) (vol. 3, no. 12). Such work, as well as many of Vallancey's methods, was in line with the approaches of many British philologists in the eighteenth century. But Vallancey ultimately lost his audience, particularly after the rebellion of 1798, when starry-eyed Irish antiquarianism suddenly seemed more ominous to many unionist Anglo-Irish and British readers and scholars.

Vallancey, Discovery, and the New Philology

Since medieval times, European origins had been traced back—spuriously—to the supposed fountainhead of language, Hebrew, as chapter 1 discusses. After the desacralization of Hebrew as the monogenetic language, scholars scrambled to find other origins for European languages in other "ancient" languages, still subscribing to a biblical time frame. Gradually, speculations about European links to Asia and West Asia, as in Irish antiquarianism, supplanted Hebraic-origin investigations. This process did not occur at once, however, despite a number of intellectual leaps, separated by decades, in that direction, and biblical frameworks for history were only gradually discredited in the second half of the nineteenth century (although such theories can still be found on the Internet and elsewhere, written by religious, amateur, and fringe scholars). In the eighteenth century, however, such biblical paradigms remained dominant for philologists, historians, and Orientalists.

Ranging through law, philology, literature, archaeology, and other areas, Orientalism in the late eighteenth and nineteenth centuries had two major and mutually informing branches: Anglo-French and German. Developing in the shadows of these two major branches of Orientalism, Irish Orientalism borrowed and contributed to the field according to its own agendas, which will be further explored in the next chapters. The underpinnings of these distinctions are not merely geographical but also philological and colonial and stem from the dissimilar relationships each branch had with the cultures of Asia and West Asia. The Anglo-French nexus had clear overlaps with imperial activities, but European Orientalists did not universally disparage Indian culture despite their imperial status. Sir William Jones (also "Persian" or "Oriental" Jones), who became one of England's most influential Orientalists, was the first to accurately discuss the relationship between the languages that would come to be labeled Indo-European. Jones also served as a judge of the Bengal Supreme Court at Fort William in Calcutta and worked on sympathetic translations of Sanskrit and Persian literature. His appreciative approach to Indian culture differed considerably from the later deprecating perspective that dominated British imperialism in the nineteenth century. Nevertheless, his writings simplified Hinduism, leading Orientalists to view it as a monotheistic religion that had devolved into polytheism. Also, his work, especially in law and translation, clearly operated within the British imperial discourse, what Tony Ballantyne astutely calls "[East India] Company Orientalism" (2002, 20).

Without clear disciplinary divisions between philology and philosophy, philology hosted a range of philosophic questions about the origin and development of humanity, thought, culture, art, and language in tandem with discussions of translation, etymology, grammar, phonetics, and language families (Aarsleff 1983, 4). Despite the emergence of Company Orientalism, philology in eighteenth-century England tended to focus on philosophical questions about a universal grammar and the origins of language. Scholars such as John Horne Tooke (1736–1812), author of a philosophical study of language and mind, *The Diversions of Purley* (1786), addressed broader questions, relying mostly on etymology for methodology and evidence, unlike Jones's more grammatical studies. Tooke held more prominence in England until Jones became more widely appreciated in the middle of the next century, thanks in great part to his contributions as a Company Orientalist. Significantly, Jones's work in the eighteenth century had greater influence in Germany and India than in England.

German Orientalism had less direct political impact in Asia in that no German state held any Asian colonies, but it had tremendous intellectual influence in Europe and North America, primarily through its ties to German idealism and Romanticism. The most influential German Orientalist of the period, Carl Wilhelm Friedrich von Schlegel (1772–1829), built on the work of William Jones (as Schlegel acknowledged).[35] Schlegel considerably advanced the study of Indian languages and culture, developed the use of comparative grammar in philology, and further demonstrated the relations between Germanic, Latin, Greek, Persian, and many Indic languages (Franklin 2001, xii).[36] In the late eighteenth and early nineteenth centuries, Indian culture and literature particularly enthused German thinkers and spurred an Oriental renaissance. After Jones, German Orientalists argued that Sanskrit could reveal the roots of Germanic languages—Schlegel wrote in a September 15, 1803, letter that "alles, ja alles ohne Ausnahme seinen Ursprung in Indien hat" ("all, yes, all without exception has its origin in India") (qtd. in Aarsleff 1983, 155). Some of this "Indological" interest in Germany can be attributed to the fact that Sanskrit helped demonstrate a clear connection between Germany and

Greco-Latin Europe. Germany's European identity was a dominant concern of German thinkers of the day, and issues of national identity complicated theories of the Orient, fueling concepts of an ancient Aryan culture that stretched to India.[37]

The late-eighteenth-century work of Jones and Schlegel demonstrates one of the most significant crossovers between Anglo-French and German philology and Orientalism; combined, their work tremendously influenced intellectual life in Europe, and scholars have documented how their translations of Indian literature and their philological discussions influenced a number of ideas and discourses.[38] Jones's translation and comparative work inspired Schlegel's, which, in turn, greatly affected many discourses, as scholars have shown for more than a century.[39] The influence of the speculative philology of Irish antiquarians such as Vallancey, linking Celtic and Asian languages, has had much less scholarly attention, normally being dismissed for serious consideration, as Irish Orientalism has also been overlooked. But these eighteenth-century antiquarians shaped the intellectual climate in which Jones famously recognized the connection between European languages, Persian, and Sanskrit. Scholars generally trace Jones's influence on Vallancey (see Ballantyne 2002, 36), but, significantly, Jones also read Vallancey and corresponded with him.

In general, scholars of intellectual history often point to the thinkers who cogently articulated the hypotheses and gleanings of a generation, such as Jones, Isaac Newton, or Charles Darwin, but rarely do we credit the more speculative thinkers who pointed to the doors that others unlocked. Because William Jones's methodology differed so considerably from Vallancey's and Tooke's, he is often regarded by linguistic historians as the lone thinker in an age of gripping ignorance. In a correspondence to the second earl of Spencer, dated September 10, 1787, Jones wrote a private, disparaging review of Vallancey's *Vindication of the Ancient History of Ireland* (1786). In the following passage, Jones admits but does not much elaborate on the "visionary" element of Vallancey's Orientalism:

> Have you met with a book lately published with the title of *A Vindication of the Ancient History of Ireland?* It was written by a friend of mine, Colonel Vallancey; but a word in your ear—it is very stupid. . . . [H]e insists with great warmth, that . . . the ancient Irish were Persians, who having emigrated from the Caspian settled in Ierne or Iran, and brought with them the old Persian history, which he finds in the Irish manuscripts. I conceive all this to be visionary; & am certain, that his derivations from the Persian, Arabick, & Sanscrit languages, are erroneous. According to him, when silly people gave me the surname of Persian, they in fact called me Irishman. Do you wish to laugh? Skim the book over. Do you wish to sleep? Read it regularly! (1970, 2:768–69)

Jones imputes Vallancey's work as "visionary" (that is, impractical or fanciful), but his word choice also hints at Vallancey's possible influence.[40] Reviving arguments from Irish pseudohistory, Vallancey's work points toward linguistic connections between European and "Oriental" languages—connections that Jones would prove.

Jones had also questioned the established divide between European and Asian and West Asian languages as early as 1779. In a letter of that year to Prince Adam Czartoryski, Jones commented on the work of scholars such as Vallancey, Bochart, and others:"Many learned investigators of antiquity are fully persuaded, that a very old and almost primæval language was in use among these northern nations, from which not only the Celtic dialects, but even the Greek and Latin, are derived. . . . We must confess that these researches are very obscure and uncertain; and you will allow, not so agreeable as an ode of Hafez" (1:285–86). Not long afterward, however, Jones became much more certain about the links between Sanskrit and European languages.

Already fluent in Greek, Latin, and Persian, in 1785 Jones set out to learn Sanskrit in order to better understand the Indic languages and Hindu law, as well as to enable translations of East India Company regulations. Soon he realized the similarities of Latin, Greek, Persian, and Sanskrit for himself; instead of focusing on their morphological differences, he saw the grammatical overlaps. In Calcutta on February 2, 1786, for the "Third Anniversary Discourse" of the Bengal Asiatic Society, Jones as president gave his famous address "On the Hindus" and first convincingly demonstrated a linguistic connection between India and Europe:

> The Sanscrit language, whatever be its antiquity, is of a wonderful structure; more perfect than the *Greek,* more copious than the *Latin,* and more exquisitely refined than either, yet bearing to both of them a stronger affinity, both in the roots of verbs and in the forms of grammar, than could possibly have been produced by accident; so strong indeed, that no philologer could examine them all three, without believing them to have sprung from some common source, which, perhaps, no longer exists: there is a similar reason, through not quite so forcible, for supposing that both the *Gothick* and the *Celtick,* though blended with a very different idiom, had the same origin with the *Sanscrit;* and the old *Persian* might be added to the same family, if this were the place for discussing any question concerning the antiquities of *Persia.* (qtd. in Aarsleff 1983, 133)

Jones challenged the common division between Oriental and Occidental languages, revolutionized the methodology of philology, and, some argue, founded Orientalism as a modern, imperial discourse. For the first time, an established Company Orientalist had clearly and accurately articulated these linguistic relationships. But, as his letters suggest, Jones had known of earlier "visionary" claims between European and "Oriental" languages in the speculative philological work of the period. Significantly, Jones's work emphasizes the Greek, Latin, and Persian connections with Sanskrit; he only mentions the Celtic and "Gothick," or Germanic, connections—moreover, Schlegel further distanced the Celtic languages from the discussion while emphasizing the Germanic connections to Sanskrit and the others. The result was that early formations of the Indo-European family of languages generally grouped Germanic (including English) and Latinate (including the Romance languages) with Greek, Persian, and Sanskrit languages (including Bengali, Hindi, and others) and excluded Celtic languages entirely. Irish and Welsh philologists and antiquarians worked for the next sixty years to prove that Celtic languages belonged in this Indo-European family until, eventually, the connection was confirmed by other German Celtic scholars.

Postcolonial critics Bill Ashcroft and Pal Ahluwalia, in a discussion of the origins of Orientalism, cite Jones's address to the Asiatic Society as one of the foundational texts. They assert that Jones's address changed "the face of European intellectual life":

> Jones's pronouncement initiated a kind of "Indomania" throughout Europe as scholars looked to Sanskrit for an origin to European languages that went even deeper than Latin and Greek. What remained in the aftermath of Indomania was the entrenchment of Orientalism and the vast expansion of philology. For the next century European ethnologists, philologers and historians were to be obsessed with the Orient and the Indo-European group of languages because these seemed to offer an explanation of the roots of European civilization itself. (1999, 58)

Jones "initiated" (not "invented") these intellectual changes by comparing the grammars of European languages and Sanskrit, unlike Vallancey, who had relied on pseudohistory and pseudoetymology in his speculations.

Why Vallancey's work might have prompted Jones is suggested in his aforementioned letter to the second earl of Spencer, written seven months after he had given his historic address. He notes: " *Vallancey* begins with stating a fact (which is the only curious part of the book) that the *Irish* have histories of their country, from the first population of it, *in their own language;* one of which histories he is translating. Then he insists with great warmth, that those histories could not be invented by modern priests: perhaps not; but what is his reason? Because those priests did not understand *Persian,* (which he calls *Southern Scythian*) and the ancient Irish were *Persians*" (1970, 2:769). Jones rightly doubts Vallancey's excesses, but his curiosity here about Vallancey's pseudohistorical sources is significant. Jones's method distinguishes itself from Tooke's, to a great extent, because Jones referred to history. His more historical, and less philosophical, approach brought the disapproval of James Mill and the Utilitarians of the late eighteenth and early nineteenth centuries and was later disparaged by scholars such as Thomas Babington Macauley. James Mill and others rather admired Tooke's work because of his rational, ahistorical, philosophical approach, which set out a general theory and then clearly and deductively reasoned it a priori through his evidence, not relying on any ancient texts (except the Bible). Jones's work, in contrast, used an inductive a posteriori approach, gathering evidence from language and ancient texts about histories before arriving at a general conclusion. By making philology "strictly historical, comparative, and structural" and jettisoning philosophical propositions and etymology, Jones's methodology led to the development of linguistics as a discipline (Aarsleff 1983, 134).[41]

As indicated by the title, Hans Aarsleff's *Study of Language in England, 1780–1860* lays out the intellectual development of philology in England and its contributions to German and continental philology. Although he does not explore Vallancey's work, Aarsleff's discussion helps to contextualize his "visionary" work, which has found no significant place in the history of philology, linguistics, or Irish culture:

> It is universally agreed that the decisive turn in language study occurred when the philosophical, a priori method of the eighteenth century was abandoned in favor of the historical, a posteriori method of the nineteenth. The former began with the mental categories and sought their exemplification in language, as in universal grammar, and based etymology on conjectures about the origin of language. The latter sought only facts, evidence, and demonstration; it divorced the study of language from the study of mind. This method was first introduced, clearly explained, and fully argued by Sir William Jones. To him there were two ways of knowing: history and science or philosophy. (1983, 127)

Tooke and Jones clearly exemplify these different approaches. Tooke's *Diversions of Purley* opens with a discussion of a theory of language and mind, which the second larger half sets out to prove through careful deductive reasoning, using etymological analyses of two thousand words for evidence. Tooke's approach has some scientific rigor, but his deductive method did not yield the same conclusions as Jones's inductive method.

Aarsleff treats 1786 as a crucial year in the development of linguistics, pointing to two major publications: the first volume of Tooke's *Diversions of Purley* in London and William Jones's address "On the Hindus" (3). Unsurprisingly, Aarsleff does not also note that Charles Vallancey's *Vindication of the Ancient History of Ireland* also came out in 1786. The work had great influence on Irish historians and writers, and both Jones and Schlegel reference it.[42] His unscientific and nonphilosophic approach resembles neither Tooke's nor Jones's—although he relies upon both etymology (like Tooke) and history (like Jones). If the categorical binarism of Jones's "two ways of knowing: history and science or philosophy" corresponds to inductive and deductive reasoning, Vallancey's work, viewed in conjunction with them, changes the binary into a triadic structure. Vallancey's rhetoric is based on another type of reasoning—speculative, visionary, and "obscure" (to quote both Jones 1970, 1:285–86; and Schlegel 2001, 464)—what pragmatist philosopher and semiotician Charles Saunders Peirce later termed *abductive reasoning*, which might best be summarized as the logic of discovery, which in accord with the doctrine of synechism seeks continuity over discontinuity.[43]

Bridging the collapse of the monogenetic Hebrew hypothesis and the Indo-European chart of languages, Vallancey continued a European-Asian connection by hypothesizing relationships among the languages somewhat familiar to him. Relying on Irish origin myths claiming a legendary cultural connection between Ireland and the East, Vallancey and others hypothesized a number of European-Asian theories, including a combined Phoenician-Scythian origin for the Irish language. Aware of such speculations Jones, the empirical lawyer, developed such hypotheses into more accurate linguistic understandings about the Orient and the Occident. Instead of understanding the Celtic philological scholarship of the eighteenth century as being "absent, insane, or plunged into darkness"—particularly Vallancey's—we might understand its significance to changes in Irish culture and as belonging to the progression of language studies from the monogenetic Hebrew paradigm to the recognition of the complex ties between world languages—how the work of O'Flaherty and Lhuyd led to the work of Vallancey, Jones, and Schlegel, and, eventually, the work of Johann Kaspar Zeuss. By the mid-nineteenth century, Zeuss, a German student of Oriental languages turned Germanic and Celtic philologist, further developed Lhuyd's comparative approach in the most extensive study of the Celtic languages to date, *Grammatica Celtica* (1853). In this formulation, Zeuss is at the end of a series of innovations, not at the beginning, as Matthew Arnold viewed him in *On the Study of Celtic Literature* (1867) and as most contemporary Celtic linguists treat Zeuss's monumental contribution.

It is not surprising that Jones read Vallancey's work and did not chafe at its glorification of Irish culture. Jones is also remembered for his admiration of Indian literature and culture, particularly in how he refused to dismiss contemporary Indian culture and Hinduism as a degraded falling-away from an ancient culture as did many other Orientalists (Franklin 2001, xix). Three years after his address to the Asiatic Society, Jones made the first widely influential translations of Indian literature in his translation of Kālidāsa's Sanskrit play, *Śakuntulā*, based on the *Mahābhārata*. The translation of the play had great lasting influence in European culture, perhaps more than his philological work. Jones's translation of the play, like his translations of the poems of Jayadeva, were built on a sensual blend of the divine and the erotic, which would draw writers to Orientalist representations for generations. Although English philology continued to be under the sway of the less linguistically sophisticated philosophical arguments of Tooke, Jones's literary translations had great impact on Romantic writers across Europe (Aarsleff 1983, 3–11). Notwithstanding, in Victorian times, his Indian translations, particularly his *Sacontalá* (Jones's spelling) had begun to scandalize the genteel English readers, as Michael Franklin (borrowing from Gauri Viswanathan's *Masks of Conquest* [1990]) notes: "Jones's ultimate failure was marked by the triumph of Anglicist forces in the subcontinent, a triumph so complete that in the Raj of 1853, *Sakuntulā* was condemned as a work of 'the greatest immorality and impurity,' unfit for use as a text for study in Indian schools and colleges" (2001, xxxii–xxxiii). But Jones's translation work had other successes; it influenced many nineteenth-century writers, including J. W. von Goethe, Robert Southey, Walter Savage Landor, Lord Byron, and Percy Bysshe Shelley. In Ireland, Jones's work directly affected the writings of Thomas Moore, Sydney Owenson (Lady Morgan), and, later, William Butler Yeats, as did the abductive speculations of antiquarians such as the Anglo-Irish Vallancey, who built upon the foundations of the legendary histories of Ireland.

Amateur Antiquarianism

A closer look within eighteenth-century Irish antiquarianism reveals how ancient Irish-Orient connections represented distinct Irish allegiances and purposes. Two amateur Anglo-Irish tracts published in this period illustrate contrasting Anglo-Irish responses to the Oriental origin theories. The first text, an amateur archaeologist's pamphlet, was printed in Dublin in 1790 and wholly embraced Oriental origin theories, and the second tract, published in London in 1821, was written by a collector of Irish topographical manuscripts and partially accepted the general theory of Oriental origins, refuting its application to the debate around the origins of Ireland's round towers. Both base their conclusions, and their reasoning to varying degrees, upon the flood of speculations about Irish-Oriental connections (especially Vallancey's own pool of philological correspondences, which both works reference).

The earlier pamphlet conveys the author's sense of revelation about Ireland's Oriental-Celtic antiquity. Their findings seem to come as the confirmation of suspicions about a mysterious Gaelic culture. In order to convey the tone of John Whittley Boswell's *Syllegomena of the Antiquities of Killmackumpshaugh, in the County of Roscommon, and Kingdom of Ireland, in which It Is Clearly Proved that Ireland Was Originally Peopled by Egyptians,* the entirety of his dedication is quoted below:

> To the members of the Royal Irish Academy. To You Gentlemen, permit me to dedicate the important discoveries in this little Tract. You alone are adequate to comprehend their utility in its full force, to whom the night of antiquity is entirely illuminated, and the dark parts of nature clearly revealed.
>
> To you we are indebted for a distinct view, and clear conception of those secrets

of nature, which we must otherwise have been in the dark about for ever; you have drawn aside the veil, which the absurdity and ignorance of the world have cast over those things: and nobly dared to descend to the bottom, the abysses, the penetralia of nature: and *monstra horrenda in lucem ducere,* and this even in the infancy of your society: what then may we not expect from your maturity, when such noble deeds are performed in the cradle.

To you we are also indebted for the little magic, which is as yet known in this ignorant land. The virtues of the talisman, of the great Valancy [*sic*], but for you must have ever been buried in obscurity; but for you must the wonderful properties of its mysterious characters been lost to mankind; and itself (shameful to be spoken) have ever appeared to the world a common Bombay coin.

Pardon my presumption in confessing, that I once had thoughts of soliciting a place for this work in your yearly volume; but I soon gave over such vain thoughts, when I reflected how it would be lost in the splendour of the surrounding publications. P. Haslter [Boswell's pseudonym]. (1790, iii-vi)

The obsequious gratitude of this Anglo-Irish author to the RIA is palpable and excessive. He credits their organization, and Vallancey in particular, for providing a "distinct view, and clear conception" of the ancient origins of the Irish. Through this view the *monstra horrenda* ("horrible wonder" or perhaps "terrible beauty") of Ireland can be brought to light, and the "penetralia [inner sanctum] of nature" can be plumbed, mapped, and published.

Before understanding Ireland's Oriental origins, the author apparently indicates that he had not previously appreciated Irish culture or his relationship with it—it was dark, obscure, and ignorant, only fit to be tossed away like a "common Bombay coin." But after realizing the exoticism and antiquity of the Celt (and his own necessary place as discoverer and interpreter), the rural Irish have become deep, mysterious, and magical. He sees Vallancey, the popularizer of Oriental origin theories, as the "talisman" who has wrought this change in his perception, who has made secret understandings accessible and, as his metaphor notes, helped spread light (through "reason"). Significantly, in this opening we see an extreme of the Irish-Orient semiotic relationship: disconnected, Ireland and the Orient seem worthless, ignorant, heathenish cultures. But connected, their bygone realms of ancient, veiled mystery and splendor become apparent. Under the gaze of the curious eighteenth-century European, various cultures in Asia and West Asia became increasingly unified as a generalized "Orient" through scholarship, literary representation, and imperial knowledge, as Edward Said has cogently argued in *Orientalism.* The Celtic fringe, unified as the periphery along with the Orient, presented an enormous civilizing task to the Empire—the periphery's lack of civil culture, enlightenment, and reason justified imperial control and tutelage. Celtic and Oriental cultures, without the unifying gaze situating them on the periphery, however, presented a myriad of disparate problems for imperialists. The power of seeing these cultures as connected could hit with the force of revelation, as Boswell notes in the first few pages. Unfortunately, cultural differences and distinct histories are erased through this coherence fallacy—if the artifacts are Egyptian, Celtic history requires less inquiry. Such "discoveries" in perception may have greatly eased British, French, and Anglo-Irish anxiety about cultural differences, but they also devalued actual and specific cultural distinctiveness.

Boswell's physical "discovery" was actually an ancient souterrain and cave, probably an Iron Age Celtic burial chamber, in Roscommon, south of Rath-croghan, mainly known today as the Cave of Cruachú.[44] Apparently, before Boswell it was known only to locals and then forgotten until 1864 when Sir Samuel Ferguson also visited the site and wrote up an account, which was published by the Royal Irish Academy. Boswell's first-person account walks the reader through the steps of his evidence and his half-tedious and half-ludicrous reasoning; not surprisingly, a number of his pieces of evidence could not be confirmed by anyone else. He begins by discussing his most crucial piece of evidence, the skeletal remains of an Egyptian body, which he claims to have found in the souterrain. Supposedly, Egyptian bones last for millennia under the right conditions, much longer than the bones of other peoples,[45] and this particular disinterred set, by Boswell's figuring (supposedly accurate within two or three years), was twenty-six hundred years old (1790, 18). After spending pages elliptically explaining the strange mathematical methodology of dating the Swiss-cheese perforations of the bones, he reveals—on the very last page of the pamphlet, no less—that the bones are gone: "[T]he old woman who lights my fire, not knowing their value, threw them out of the window with the sweepings of the room, but fortunately I had first made very sufficient experiments on them with my micrometer" (53). He assumes the reader will trust his micrometer as well.

Fortunately, however, his argument, which largely turns on how one should view the materials, also depends on several additional points. The first arguments reveal his reliance upon an Orientalist perspective, specifically a description of Egypt. His frame of reference and perspective are essential to his argument. After he has been led by a "native" Irish guide through the entrance of the souterrain and into the cave (see fig. 5), Boswell realizes what he is seeing:

> It was here that the near resemblance of this to an Egyptian burying-place struck me so forcibly, that I could not help crying out with the great philosopher [Archimedes] Ευρηχα [Eureka]. The difficulty and manner of the entrance, the situation and direction of the cavity for the dead body, all conspired strongly to confirm this opinion; and in the minds of those who had been conversant in the histories of the catacombs and pyramids, left an impression of the fact little short of certainty. . . . Anyone who has read the elaborate account* [his footnote reads:

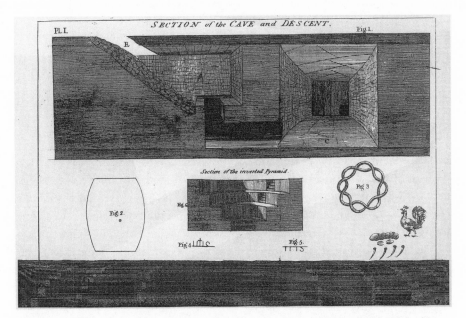

5. "Section of the Cave and Descent and Section of the Inverted Pyramid." Published in John Whittley Boswell's *Syllegomena of the Antiquities of Killmackumpshaugh, in the County of Roscommon, and Kingdom of Ireland, in which It Is Clearly Proved that Ireland Was Originally Peopled by Egyptians* (1790).

"*★Vid.* Letters from Egypt, published in 1784."] of the manner in which the passages of the pyramids were filled up by the workmen, can easily conceive how this was closed up. (8–9)

His reading, however cursory, of eighteenth-century Orientalist literature allows him to see the souterrain as an Egyptian catacomb. Without this Orientalist knowledge of Egypt, he would not have seen the souterrain as an Egyptian catacomb. But, without knowledge of the Oriental origin theory, he would not have believed the resemblance was a significant connection. He references specific Celticist sources, specifically the *Transactions of the Royal Irish Academy* (32), noting how their notions have guided his observations.

Later in the text, he reveals that he has discovered another Egyptian structure nearby, this one incontrovertibly revealing its Egyptian origins. Significantly, he (coyly or earnestly?) notes that his readers must have already accepted his conclusions.

Though the fact of the Egyptians having settled here, is established sufficiently; yet as I would not wish to leave a doubt on the subject, I will here mention some corroborating circumstances. The love of the Egyptians for pyramids, is too well known to need proof. Those Egyptians who settled here, have accordingly left be-

hind them a curious monument of that kind, about a mile from the temple and cat-
acombs: The only thing in which it differs from those in Egypt, is in its being
smaller, and that instead of being prominent, it is inverted and hollow, *vid.* fig. 6, pl.
1st. It descends about 20 feet in the perpendicular, is of a circular figure, and consists of 4 regular steps about 5 feet high each, and 4 feet broad. . . . The area at the
bottom, I suppose, was used for sacrifices, though I could find no traces of any altar
there. (39–40)

As in the ninth-century writings of Dicuil, the pyramids of Gîza serve as a clear
shorthand for and resonant image of the Orient (as do images of Red Sea crossings,
which Boswell also references), but here the pyramid image works as material proof
of the Celts' Oriental heritage. This vision of an "inverted pyramid" (as he tags it;
see fig. 5) buried in western Ireland demonstrates a cardinal dynamic of the Oriental-Celtic connection from an imperial point of view: Ireland is the Orient inverted. In disrepair, this abandoned, pagan, and possibly nefarious ("for [*human?*]
sacrifices") structure is both an ancient mystery and a pagan folly, but it becomes
significant only through its connection to Egypt. Celticism and Orientalism not
only share the same lenses, methods, and approaches but, in this case, also the same
objects of study.

In Gaelic Ireland, Boswell finds the Orient, upside down and belowground, a
European image, negative and recessed, of a remote land's ancient prominence.
This discovery is convenient, in a manner of speaking, rural Ireland being more accessible than Egypt (a place, as his tract reveals, he has never visited); in short, the
Orient has come to him. He explains how these Egyptians came to be in Ireland
via a variation of O'Flaherty's (via Vallancey) Phoenician origin story: "We have
now been able to trace up the Irish language, through the Carthaginians, to the
Phœnicians, and through them to the banks of the Red Sea, where the Phœnicians
did first dwell; from thence it is easy to trace it to its original source Egypt; for as the
Phœnicians were not Aborigines, they must have been derived from some other
nation, and that nation must have been Egypt" (25). Boswell either gets the theory
wrong or ignores the old legends, which assert a Scythian origin for the Irish (and
explain that they resided in Egypt for some time). But this quibble is truly moot;
the point here is that the foundation of Boswell's supposition is both Celticist and
Orientalist. The Scythian origins become conflated with Egyptian, signifying an
interchangeable nature of Oriental cultures in the European discourse of Orientalism. He depends, however, upon both Celticist and Orientalist arguments to find
this backyard Orient in Ireland.

Boswell's other "proofs" confirm his suppositions in lengthy discussions of the
history of the Phoenicians and of ogham and supposed hieroglyphic writing in the
"catacomb": "My joy was very great at perceiving even these hieroglyphics, as they

so well confirmed my former opinion, that this place had been built by Egyptians" (31). Upon fallacious observations and shaky points such as that the Hebrew and Egyptian languages are sister tongues (44), Boswell builds a philological argument, the heart of any antiquarian argument of the day. He may have referenced tables similar to Vallancey's comparative table in the *Collectanea De Rebus Hibernicis,* which provided a key for comparing ogham, hieroglyphics, Arabic, and Chaldean (see figs. 3 and 6) because he works with a nearly accurate Roman letter key to ogham script. But somehow his translation comes out as "The shrine of Belus, who is an eternal oracle, sacrifice to him" (33), whereas other later visitors, including Ferguson, read the ogham writing as "VRAICCI MAQI MEDVVI," probably signifying something like "(The stone of) Fraic son of Medf" or possibly "son of Medbh" (Ferguson 1867, 168). Clearly, Boswell's antiquarian and Celticist readings have dominated his conclusions.

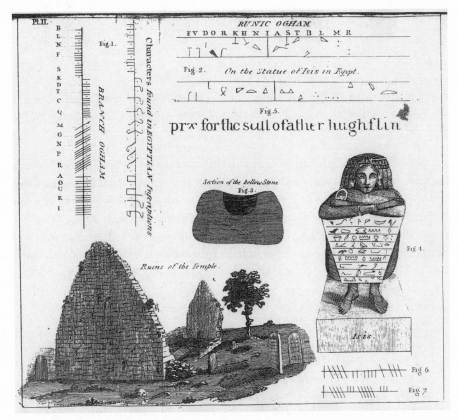

6. "The Irish Isis and Temple Ruins." Published in John Whittley Boswell's *Syllegomena of the Antiquities of Killmackumpshaugh, in the County of Roscommon, and Kingdom of Ireland, in which It Is Clearly Proved that Ireland Was Originally Peopled by Egyptians* (1790).

7. "Pillar-Towers from Kildare, Ardmore, Cairo, and Alexandria." Published in Hervey Montmorency-Morres's *Historical and Critical Inquiry into the Origin and Primitive Use of the Irish Pillar-Tower* (1821).

Boswell does not limit his speculations to antiquities; he also makes comparative cultural analyses. In addition to discussing some of the benefits of modernity over antiquities (18), the value of ogham as modern shorthand (34), and the benefits of vegetable eating (29), he describes these Egyptian-Phoenician Celts as "the first East India Company," noting that "East-India trade has always brought every nation, which carried it on, to the greatest splendour and opulence" (29). Such comparisons between the ancient and the modern explain the relevance and ramifications of his conclusions. Near the end of the tract, he presents his final argument, his specious observations about shared Egyptian-Irish customs:

I must beg leave to mention some Egyptian customs which are still prevalent among the common people of this kingdom. The first I shall mention, is the posture in which they sit round the fires in their huts. . . . In this posture numbers of antique statues are found in Egypt, particularly the two famous one of Isis and Osiris; the first of which I have copied in fig. 4 [see fig. 6], from a print in the learned Doctor Pocock's travels through Egypt; and the same learned author informs us, that the Egyptians make use of the same posture even unto this day. Another custom which the Irish have in common with the Egyptians is that of living in the same houses with their cattle. Herodotus in recounting the extraordinary customs of the Egyptians, says, . . . in Egypt men and beasts live together. . . . The Irish also resemble the Egyptians in their food, living chiefly on vegetables, as did the Egyptians of old. . . . Wheat, or barley is scarce used as food [in Ireland], but by the descendants of the English, the natives universally preferring potatoes to them. However, great quantities of both are raised in Ireland for the purpose of commerce, as was formerly the case in Egypt; and from the great increase in the exportation of them in those last years, we are safe in saying, that Ireland bids fair to be the granary of Europe, as Egypt was formerly of the Roman Empire. (46–50)

Pairing ancient Egypt and modern Ireland projects Boswell's contemporary Irish neighbors into the distant past and divorces them from modernity. The future, however, seems preordained; Ireland will serve Europe (via Britain) as Egypt did imperial Rome, as a granary. Viewed with hindsight of the successive famines, resulting in part from a monocultural crop and governmental mismanagement, which devastated Gaelic Irish culture in the decades that followed, Boswell's prediction reads ominously.

Another later tract, *A Historical and Critical Inquiry into the Origin and Primitive Use of the Irish Pillar-Tower* (1821), by Hervey Montmorency-Morres (1767–1839), rejects most of Vallancey's argument about the Phoenician origins of the round towers. Unlike Boswell, who was a newcomer to Ireland, Montmorency-Morres is a member of a large Anglo-Norman Irish (*Sean-Ghall*) family that traces itself back to Strongbow (17), and refers to himself as Irish and a "descendant of the Milesian" (preface, unnumbered 1). Although he argues against the notion that the round towers were built by colonizing Oriental Phoenicians, he seems to have Irish nationalist sympathies and does not dispute an Oriental existence in Ireland. Instead he argues, correctly but all too predictably because of his Anglo-Norman Irish identity, that the round towers owe their origin to Norman "Strongbonian" influence. "History, and our records assure us, that those great Towers, Keeps, or *Dungeons,* such as the Round Towers . . . were erected in the reigns of King John and King Henry III. by the Strongbonian Barons" (25). Significantly, his argument predates (by ten years) the point of view of George Petrie, who is generally credited with convincingly establishing the Norman origins of some of the towers (most had an early medieval origin).

Montmorency-Morres's tract opens with an obligatory reference to that common image of the Orient: "Much has been said and written, on no other grounds than those of conjecture and supposititious evidence, concerning the Origin and intended use of the Pillar-towers of Ireland. Yet we might repeat with Pliny, when speaking of the Egyptian pyramids—'That the Gods, to punish so much vanity and presumption, had consigned to everlasting oblivion the founders' names, dates, periods, and all records relating to them' " (1). He refutes the arguments of the Reverend Edward Ledwich (an Anglo-Irish historian who argued the towers were

Danish in origin) and the "chimerical and fabulous" arguments of Vallancey, to whom he nevertheless offers a "passing tribute of veneration and gratitude" for praising "the virtues of [Ireland's] ancestors" (10). Nevertheless, he takes Vallancey to task: "The late General Vallancey, who, on the romantic topic of aboriginal Ireland, outstrips in extravagance the Author of Ogygia [footnote: "Roderic O'Flaherty"], insists, very positively, on those mysterious buildings owing their origin to our Heathen ancestors; by whom they were erected, he says, for receptacles to preserve the sacred fire of Beal, Ball, or the Sun" (2–3). Montmorency-Morres does not dispute the Phoenician-origin theory in totality, only that such "heathens" could have achieved such feats.

For proof, he turns, like Camden and Spenser before him, to assert the ancient barbarism of the Irish: "Moreover,—to pass in silence what has been recorded by Strabo, Pomponious-Mela, Solinus, Diodorus-Siculus, and other writers of antiquity, respecting the barbarous condition of Ireland and its inhabitants, in their days, in common with their neighbours the Britons, Gauls, and Germans, to whom the art, systematically to manufacture stone, had been unknown" (5). The discourse of Irish barbarism, vanquished almost entirely in eighteenth-century discourse concerning contemporary Ireland (until 1798), still existed in works on ancient Ireland. Instead of ancient pillars, Montmorency-Morres notes, the ancient Milesians had other sites of worship:

> In remote ages, the *cave* was an indispensable appendage on the mysterious rites of pagan superstition. The worship of Zoroaster's deity (Baal), having been introduced by a Phœnician colony, the formation of caves became a serious, civil, and religious concern. The Druids, no doubt, took an active lead in promoting the dreary science, which had at the same time in contemplation to furnish the poor Troglodite inhabitant a wretched dwelling. Hence, it came to pass that, in process of time, the most frequented portions of the island acquired the gloomy character of a region of catacombs: differing, however, as widely from the Indian caves of Carli and the grottoes of Elora, . . . nothing in the imagination of man surpassing in dreariness an Irish cave. (6–7)

Apparently, ancient Ireland, although partly Oriental in origin, was more "dreary" than the Orient. As with earlier poets who blended ancestries for newcomers, Ireland is represented as a meeting ground where Oriental, Celtic, and Norman origins all blend into a composite Irish identity.

Montmorency-Morres's argument is significant because it reveals the multiplicity of Irish-Oriental comparisons, and the pervasiveness of their impact. Citing "the sour testimony" of Giraldus Cambrensis (20), as well as Irish historians such as Sylvester O'Halloran, Abbé McGeoghegan, O'Flaherty, and Keating, he grounds his argument in multiple Irish traditions. Through such a position, after the Act of

Union of 1800, he even asserts the value of imperialism:"the geographic and polit-ical condition of primitive Ireland, her untutored population, and the avowed tardy progress towards civilization and an acquaintance with the fine arts, then common to those nations not conveniently placed within the enlightened and enlivening pale of Attic and Roman instruction" (10). Ireland is hybrid, he argues, if some-what primitive, as the round towers demonstrate; the influence of the architectural style of the towers is Greek and Roman, yet "it wears a certain Gothic air" (57). Nevertheless, he admits that the "pyramidal shape" and structure of the towers re-semble other towers in the Orient—the minarets in Constantinople, Cairo, and Alexandria (58–59) and the "Towers, (two) situated near the river Ganges, in the province of Bahar, adjoining that of Bengal, India" (59) (see figs. 7 and 8).

In order to address this Irish-Orient resemblance, he notes:"[W]e may only call conjecture to our aid" (62), and "there is certainly no kind of analogy between their primitive use and destination. Still, in the architecture and style both [the Irish towers and those in the East], will the antiquary recognize the offspring of one original parent" (64–65). To account for this similarity, he argues that in early-fourth-century Syria, similar towers were built to protect early Christian Cœno-bite monks from marauding Arabs, and both European and Egyptian monks stayed there, concluding:"A community of sufferings appears, in an equal degree, to have

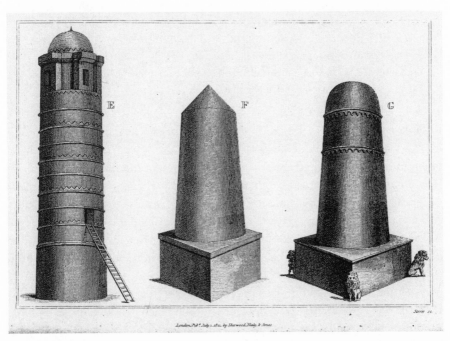

8. "Pillar-Towers India." Published in Hervey Montmorency-Morres's *Historical and Critical Inquiry into the Origin and Primitive Use of the Irish Pillar-Tower* (1821).

afflicted both those religious societies: the Irish, groaning under the tyranny of the Danes; the Cophtes [and Egyptian monks], a prey to the inroads of the wild Arabs; the system of defence resorted to by the one and the other class of monks, was likewise established upon a corresponding principle and plan" (71). A significant phrase here is "community of sufferings"—an idea that over the next century increasingly linked Ireland and places in the Orient, particularly Egypt and India.

William Betham's later and much less accepted antiquarian work on the Oriental origins of the Irish language, *Etruria Celtica: Etruscan Literature and Antiquities Investigated; or, The language of that Ancient and Illustrious People Compared and Identified with the Iberno-Celtic, and Both Shown to Be Phœnician* (1842; the Royal Irish Academy rejected his *Etruria Celtica* for publication in 1838[46]), extended even further the logic of the Irish antiquarian supposition about the origins of the Celts. Relying on etymology and ideas such as Montmorency-Morres's, Betham compared his rudimentary knowledge of Irish to ancient Etruscan. He not only predated Celtic civility and learning to pre-British times, but also set it before pre-Roman times:

> It is repugnant to common sense to suppose that these remote [Celtic] islands were the means by which civilization was communicated to the countries surrounding the Mediterranean and the East. . . . [B]ut if we are able to show that [the Irish] language is the same as that spoken by the people who occupied Italy and the countries bordering on that sea, the absurdity vanishes and the fact ceases to surprise. A man will laugh in your face if you assert that Latin is mostly derived from the Irish, but if you are able to show that the Etruscan inhabitants of Italy spoke the same, or a kindred language, with what is now called Irish, if he be not convinced, his sarcasm and ridicule will certainly be deprived of all its point. (11)

Elaborating on Vallancey's ideas, Betham's antiquarian Celticism provides origin legends for the settlement of the British Isles as well as for Latin learning, which, by implication, would make Celtic languages and thought foundational not only to Rome but to Roman Catholicism and European learning as well. Such a move imaginatively alters the dynamics of Irish colonial discourse by giving the Celts a dominant place in the early classical world, while offering Betham, and perhaps the Anglo-Irish in general, a place of legitimacy and discursive power in Ireland—that is, one of "supplementarity"[47] as the interpreters of the Celtic Irish for civilized British society. Such a position could give the Anglo-Irish significance as mediators between the metropole and the periphery. Little serious attention was given to Betham's work outside his circle of believers—who included, for a time, Thomas Moore, the Irish Romantic writer who never took a strong stance in the public debate over the origin of the round towers in his history of Ireland, supporting the theories of the Celtic past while admitting some Phoenician influences. Earlier in his career, Moore had somewhat supported the more Gael-centered theories and had many Irish antiquarian works in his library, including Betham's *Gael and the Cymbri,* which is signed, "To Thomas Moore, Esq. With the Author's respects." Betham's work, which did not employ the au courant techniques of scientific scholarship and rigor, was soon refuted by more rigorous scholarship. Moore and others distanced themselves from him. Few but devout believers were convinced by this ascientific process of piecing together roughly translated linguistic fragments.[48] Betham's narrative was a desperate attempt to validate through scholarship the connection between Ireland and the Orient and retain the Celt's non-European exotic origins. Such a strategy, however, could not coexist in nineteenth-century intellectual circles, where antiquarian arguments had lost respect and where ethnology, philology, and archaeology were emerging alongside history as respected disciplines.

George Petrie's methodical and long-awaited work on the round towers, originally written for an essay contest in 1833 but published in 1845, convincingly argued for early medieval and Norman origins of the round towers. Petrie was not the first to argue this; Montmorency-Morres had asserted a similar argument in 1821, partly to give his family a more prestigious ancestry. Until Petrie's published essay, claims of the Oriental origins of the ancient Irish enjoyed a prominent place in Irish intellectual circles, and such Oriental origins had continuing influence for cultural nationalists, Romantic writers, and Theosophists, long after being discredited. More significantly, Celtic philologists such as James Cowles Prichard (an English ethnologist) found the antiquarian work useful and built linguistic arguments for the inclusion of Celtic languages in the Indo-European family of languages based on work Vallancey began (see Prichard's *Eastern Origin of the Celtic Nations Proved in a Comparison of Their Dialects with the Sanskrit, Greek, Latin, and Teutonic Languages* [1857]). After many permutations, the legacy of the Oriental Celt continued through the nineteenth and into the twentieth centuries in more representational and allegorical forms.

Because the Irish antiquarian claim to an Oriental heritage parallels the development of Anglo-French Orientalism, the Celtic-Oriental connection has often been seen as part of the larger European Orientalist search for origins in Asia and West Asia. But the chief ideological motive (for Celticists, Irish antiquarians, and Irish cultural nationalists) to argue for Ireland's Oriental origins was to establish a pedigree for Irish culture—they used the Orient, primarily, to validate Gaelic culture or to justify Anglo-Irish supplementarity or both. This can be understood within the context of Orientalism in general, which argued that the Orient had devolved into a state of collapse and decadence from former grandeur. In imperially focused Anglo-French Orientalism, Europe appeared as a redeemer and modernizer. Within Irish Orientalism, the Orient's former state paralleled Ireland's past.

In the seventeenth and eighteenth centuries Irish philologers and antiquarians sought historical truths in Ireland's origin legends. The details of ancient migrations, however, never found scholarly accord, and the impressions of ancient Ireland frequently vacillated between Oriental and Celtic origin theories, an ambivalence that helped furnish semiotic ties between both of these antitheses of enlightened, modern Europe. The debates over Ireland's ancestry, either in the physically distant East or the temporally distant Celtic past, also frequently raised underlying disputes about whether Ireland's was a venerable or a barbaric heritage. While such quarrels burned steadily in historiography and antiquarian circles— Irish ancestors alternating between Scythian, Phoenician, Egyptian, Milesian, Indian, Celtic, and others—philologers elsewhere established, for the first time, clear linguistic connections between Western Europe and West Asia. The fact that these Orient-Occident parallels most prominently existed in Irish antiquarianism just prior to the pronouncements of William Jones suggests that the abductive reasoning of antiquarians such as Charles Vallancey helped lay the groundwork for the burgeoning understanding of a shared Indo-European linguistic heritage. Enlightenment thinkers, especially in England and France, had almost entirely divorced their work from historiography, especially histories written in "barbaric" cultures. All of these language scholars had been working in the theoretical vacuum left after the discrediting of the monogenetic Hebrew theory, and the enduring Irish origin theories helped point them back to ancient texts and suggest new possibilities for shared linguistic and cultural origins between Europe and West Asia.

At the end of the eighteenth century, as Oriental origin theories were disproved, Irish orientalism became more peripheral—speculative, allegorical, cultural, circumspect, connective—as both Gaelic historiography and Anglo-Irish antiquarianism became mainly sources for Irish writers interested in a glorious heritage. In the nineteenth and twentieth centuries, the semiotic connection between the Oriental and the Celt also became less a puzzle to philologers and historiographers and more an inspiration for pseudoscientific discussions, nationalist histories, and allegorical literary texts, all of which addressed Ireland's standing in the world. Significantly, the discourse of Irish Orientalism slipped into the shadows of more prominent discourses of the day, many of which it was used to bolster—imperialism, anti-colonialism, nationalism, unionism, religion, language, race. At the same time, Gaelic culture came to increasingly emblemize a pre-classical European antiquity, a Western Ogygia, Europe's forgotten, backyard Orient. In such a position, Orientalist texts in Ireland retained many of the characteristics that had emerged over the previous centuries including a respect for cultural hybridity and antiquity as well as an identification with diverse "communit[ies] of suffering" across the globe.

3 Allegory and Critique

Irish Orientalism in Eighteenth- and Nineteenth-Century Literature

[T]he melodies of Ireland soon found itself at home in the East.
—Thomas Moore, preface to *Lalla Rookh*

Thou vagabond varlet! / Thou swiller of sack! / If our heads be all
scarlet / Thy heart is all black! / Go on to revile / IRAN's nation and
race, / In thy fish-faggish style!
—J. C. Mangan, "To the Ingleezee Khafir,
Calling Himself Djaun Bool Djenkinzun"

THE DEVELOPMENT OF THE ORIENT as a realm of critique in Irish literature and
culture has a number of distinct strands emerging from literature, philology, history, and legend. The impression of Irish difference from English culture long
compelled Irish attention to its own legendary history, itself rooted in a sensibility
of Irish geocultural remoteness and peripherality. As English impressions became
more influential in Irish culture, a number of Irish writers interrogated the exoticizing lenses of imperial culture, some seeking to expose the Oriental and the
Celtic as constructions, some hoping to challenge the negative tropes, some working to reverse the tropes and perform more positive images of Irishness through a
process of autoexoticism.[1] By the late eighteenth century, the age of sensibility,
tropes of the Oriental and the Celtic had taken root in various genres of English literature: imperial romances, Gothic literature, Romantic poetry, Celtic Revival
works, and Orientalist translations.

One flourishing subgenre, accompanying the eighteenth-century rise of the
novel of letters, was the pseudo-Oriental letter collection, popularized by Charles
Montesquieu's *Les Lettres Persanes* (1721). Similarly, a number of Celticist works,
loosely based on Irish, Scots, and Welsh works, posed as actual translations. James
MacPherson's Ossianic tales in *Fragments of Ancient Poetry, Collected in the Highlands
of Scotland, and Translated from the Galic or Erse Language* (1760), *Fingal, an Ancient Epic*

115

Poem, in Six Books (1762), and *Temora* (1763) mostly expanded and augmented the Fionn cycle of Gaelic legend, forming a wilder, dreamier, and gloomier Celtic aesthetic that the English poet Thomas Gray (1716–1771) had helped pioneer in "The Bard" (1757), which is set in Wales. Spanning the eighteenth-century rise of modernity—and its ideals of newness, innovation, science, reason, and imperialism—and Europe's nineteenth century's industrial revolutions, both the Celtic and the Oriental developed as semiotic lifelines to supposedly ancient, sensual, mystical, and poetic realms. These widely popular worlds of the past, however, existed synchronically alongside Enlightenment Europe. At the same time, images of the despotic Orient and the barbaric Gael signaled the antitheses of imperial Enlightenment culture, that is, an absence of liberty, rationality, progress, and autonomy. In Ireland (as later in India, Egypt, and elsewhere), Celticism and Orientalism resonated on more immediate levels and often expressed cultural, racial, and political issues, if often through idealizations and allegories.

Irish connections with the Orient, as the discussion of the origin legends has shown, were used to both distinguish and denigrate Ireland. In both cases, the Oriental connection gave Ireland a more certain antiquity, and the tenor of the past, barbaric or not, depended on the writers and their contexts. Influenced by discussions of the various Eastern origins of the ancient Irish in antiquarianism and history in Ireland, references to Oriental origins cropped up in texts throughout Irish culture: political tracts, occasional poetry, Celticist works, pseudoletter collections, Oriental romances, novels, newspaper articles, children's literature, British and Anglo-Irish novels, and Irish-language stories. For example, in a footnote to one of W. Smith's *Historical Explanations of Emblematic Cards: For the Use of Young Persons* (1801; card 80, King Henry VII, or the Union of the Roses), the following explanation is given, "[T]he Iberno Celtic (or Irish) somewhat resembles the primitive language of the Hebrews; and is very like that of the old Phoenicians" (57). Similar references occur in overtly unionist Anglo-Irish pamphlets, such as the anonymously written *Hiberniæ Lachrymæ; or, The Tears of Ireland, a Poem* (1799). The author of this poem relied upon the Phoenician model of Celtic origins, despite being Anglocentric, connecting the ancient Irish to the "Philistines" (who sounded more like the contemporary people of Palestine), also referring to them as both "Milesians" and "Phœnecians" (4–5).[2] As Anglo-Irish patriots had in the late eighteenth century, nationalist political pamphleteers began to increasingly invoke the Oriental origins of the Celt, as Julius Vindex (a pseudonym) does in *Vindication of the Irish Nation, and Particularly of the Roman Catholics, Against the Calumnies of Libellers, Part IV* (1802), turning the lens of "savageness" and barbarity onto British imperialists and invoking Oriental-Celtic pseudohistory to bolster Ireland's pedigree. The cumulative, lasting cultural effect of this widespread supposition cannot be easily tallied, but it certainly influenced a number of Irish writers, including

Sydney Owenson (Lady Morgan), Thomas Moore, and James Clarence Mangan. Moreover, even as the understanding of the Eastern Celt, the Phoenician Irishry, or the Scythian Gael continued to spread in popular culture, it diminished as a valid argument in philology.

During this early nineteenth century, as the previous chapter notes, the Irish language gradually became less associated with Asian languages in European philology, even though suppositions about Ireland's Phoenician origins continued in less acceptable scholarship. Also, as discussions about origin legends—focalized in the early nineteenth century on the origin of the round towers—gradually began to treat the legends not as embodiments of historical truths but as ancient literature, Ireland's Oriental link moved into more allegorical and literary realms. Often, the link carried encoded critiques of imperialism, nationalism, or often the very discourse it participated within: Orientalism. The Oriental heritage of the Irish carried over into literary and popular culture, at first through direct references that aimed to ground Irish traditions in Celtic and Oriental antiquity. The Oriental origin legends, as employed by antiquarians such as Charles Vallancey and Joseph Cooper Walker and historians such as Charles O'Conor and Sylvester O'Halloran, directly influenced many of the best-known Irish writers of the early nineteenth century, particularly Thomas Moore and Sydney Owenson (Lady Morgan), both of whom credit antiquarian and Orientalist sources in their copious footnotes.

Irish Orientalist literature also cultivated Oriental themes, genres, and devices from the literary and scholarly representations of France, England, and Germany. From across Europe, two popular and influential genres that led to the rise of the novel had Orientalist dimensions: discovery or travel narratives and pseudo-Oriental letter collections. The former often concerned European voyages to Asia (among other places), and the latter concerned Asians coming to Europe. These imagined interchanges between Europe and the emerging concept of the Orient were also central to the rise of the novel. Both early-eighteenth-century genres enabled sustained critiques of both Asian and European cultures and imperial politics through the vehicle of the distant Orient—either under the guise of an Oriental persona or through a comparison of Europe with distant lands. Many Irish writers (including Jonathan Swift, Oliver Goldsmith, and James Clarence Mangan) used these genres to encode political critiques in the Orient. The allegorical dimensions and allusive qualities of this literature allowed variant readings by different audiences in England, Ireland, and elsewhere and contributed to the rhetorical doubleness that became a hallmark of much Irish literature.

The Celt occupied an ambiguous position in early-nineteenth-century Europe, being both an exotic construction of urban intellectuals and a centerpiece for collective identities. French leaders often used images of France's Gaulish and

Celtic past for various imperial and nationalistic ends, as Annie Jourdan has noted.[3] In late-eighteenth-century France, leaders recuperated the French enthusiasm for Gaulish and Celtic origins that had been widespread in the fifteenth and sixteenth centuries, and later Napoleon again reconstructed Celtic imagery to fit his imperial plans (Jourdan 1996, 183). Following Napoleon's interest: "The nineteenth century had brought with it [in France] the arrival of a modern history-writing and archeology; and it was in these new, modernized disciplines that the glory of the Gaulish ancestors was to shine forth in its true splendour" (204). International Celticism likewise had many overlaps in England, France, Germany, Wales, Scotland, and Ireland—as demonstrated by the earlier widespread enthusiasm and controversy over James MacPherson's Ossianic pseudotranslations across Europe in the early to mid-eighteenth century.[4] Much of this enthusiasm emerged from a communal longing for an ancient heritage with which contemporary Europe, including Ireland, could identify. In Ireland, the ancient Celtic past gradually supplanted the Oriental origin legends in the nineteenth century, and the pseudohistorical and philological arguments turned from exploring Oriental origins to finding Celtic ones by comparing actual archaeological artifacts and evidence that pointed to similarities among Gaelic and Gaulish and other Celtic cultures. Moreover, because of the long history of Irish peripherality, the Celt found a ready semiotic position in early-nineteenth-century Ireland. This transference from the Oriental to the Celtic in Irish historiography manifested itself in a number of ways: scholars and historians increasingly argued for multiple waves of settlement—Scythian, Phoenician, and Celtic, referencing the "invasions" of the origin legends. Scholars also transferred the supposed bardic authorship of Ireland's Oriental origin legends to early Celtic settlers. In this respect, Celts became understood as the spokespeople and authors of Ireland's Oriental heritage.

Discovery Narratives: Home and Away

Claiming the Phoenicians as the greatest discoverers and colonists of the ancient world, Roderic O'Flaherty treated Irish origin legends as discovery narratives, a genre that enjoyed popular interest in the late seventeenth and early eighteenth centuries, also known (in Europe) as the Age of Discovery. O'Flaherty's rhetorical appeal to these narratives made good rhetorical sense, if slippery historiography, and it is significant to recall that his work was the first work of Gaelic history to be printed in London. Also, being published (in Latin) during the rise of discovery narratives, his ancient discovery narratives drew much attention. Discovery narratives reached their apex of popularity in 1719, when Daniel Defoe had his *Life and Strange and Surprising Adventures of Robinson Crusoe* published. Not long afterward, discovery narratives received their greatest parody when the Anglo-Irish writer Jonathan

Swift incisively satirized them in *Gulliver's Travels* (1726); its original title was *Travels into Several Remote Nations of the World,* the word *remote* certainly resonated with impressions of Ireland. Swift, as a young man writing in the Orientalist library of his English patron and employer, William Temple, found sufficient textual sources for his later parody, which included a brief stay in Japan and many fictional lands. Beyond Orientalism, English relations with remote lands, especially Ireland, find representation in *Gulliver's Travels* and exploit the image of Ireland as a remote homeland. As Frank Boyle has argued in his monograph *Swift as Nemesis: Modernity and Its Satirist,* Swift's narrative critiques the genre of discovery narratives by employing one: "'What if,' [Georges] Van Den Abbeele asks in [the introduction to] *Travel as Metaphor,* 'the critique of a system were itself encoded as an institutionalized part of the system?' " (2000, 53). The widely popular travel narratives could provide such an "encoded critique" of the discourse (53–54). Irish writers made particular use of this mode of critique, especially within the broader discourse of Orientalism.

At the end of *Gulliver's Travels,* Lemuel Gulliver confides that it had been "whispered" to him that he was "bound in duty, as a subject of England" to report the location of the lands he visited because "whatever lands are discovered by a subject belong to the crown" (Swift 2001, 269). But Gulliver excuses himself for not conveying their locations for a number of reasons, not the least of which is: "as those Countries which I have described, do not appear to have any Desire of being conquered, and enslaved, murdered or driven out by Colonies, nor abound either in Gold, Silver, Sugar, or Tobacco; I did humbly conceive they were by no means proper Objects of our Zeal, our Valour, or our Interest" (270). After considering the impracticality of a British colonization of floating islands and Lilliputians, he offers a critique of the process of setting up a "modern colony":

> But I had another Reason, which made me less forward to enlarge his Majesty's Dominions by my Discoveries. To say the truth, I had conceived a few Scruples with relation to the Distributive Justice of Princes upon those Occasions. For instance, a Crew of Pirates are driven by a Storm they know not whither; at length a Boy discovers Land from the Topmast; they go on Shore to Rob and Plunder; they see an harmless People, are entertained with Kindness, they give the Country a new Name, they take formal Possession of it for their King, they set up a rotten Plank or a Stone for a Memorial, they murder two or three Dozen of the Natives, bring away a Couple more by Force for a Sample, return home, and get their pardon. Here commences a new Dominion acquired with a Title by *Divine Right.* Ships are sent with the first Opportunity, the Natives driven out or destroyed, their Princes tortured to discover their Gold; a free License given to all Acts of Inhumanity and Lust, the Earth reeking with the Blood of its Inhabitants: And this execrable Crew of Butchers employed in so pious an Expedition, is a *modern colony* sent to convert and civilize an idolatrous and barbarous People. (269)

Directly after unfolding these horrors, Gulliver quickly defends the justice of British colonialism in a Swiftian parody of a tradition that Claude Rawson has recently traced in his *God, Gulliver, and Genocide* (2001)—the "tradition of celebrating British imperial achievements as superior to those of other countries, whose many spokesmen include Hakluyt, Gibbon, Darwin, and Conrad" (XXX). Through Gulliver's earnestness, we hear Swift's sarcasm:

> But this Description, I confess, doth by no means affect the *British* Nation, who may be an Example to the whole World for their Wisdom, Care, and Justice in Planting Colonies; their liberal Endowments for the Advancement of Religion and Learning; their Choice of devout and able Pastors to propagate *Christianity,* their Caution in stocking their Provinces with People of sober Lives and Conversations from this the Mother Kingdom; their strict regard to the Distribution of Justice, in supplying the Civil Administration through all their Colonies with Officers of the greatest Abilities, utter strangers to Corruption; and to crown all, by sending the most Vigilant and Virtuous Governors, who have no other Views than the Happiness of the People over whom they preside, and the Honour of the King their Master. (269–70)

This instance of an ironic critique embedded within a discourse is one of the more overtly coded instances of Irish critiques of colonialism. Although Swift's parody is not restricted to Oriental voyages—much of what he targets is Spanish colonialism, as Rawson notes—the doubleness of his satire became a common response for Irish writers depicting the Orient. As Heinz Kosok has pointed out in his essay "Charles Robert Maturin and Colonialism," Maturin's (1780–1824) "Tale of the Indians" in *Melmoth the Wanderer* continues this same explicit critique of imperialism, focusing on a European "discovery" of an island in the Indian Ocean:

> There came on the European vessels full of the passions and crimes of another world—of its sateless cupidity, remorseless cruelty, its intelligence, all awake and ministrant in the cause of its evil passions, and its very refinement operating as a stimulant to more inventive indulgence, and more systematized vice. He saw them approach to traffic for "gold, silver and the souls of men" [a quotation from Rev. 18]—to grasp, with breathless rapacity, the gems and precious produce of those luxuriant climates, and deny the inhabitants the rice that supported their inoffensive existence;—to discharge the load of their crimes, their lust and their avarice, and after ravaging the land, and plundering the natives, depart, leaving behind them famine, despair, and execration; and bearing with them back to Europe, blasted constitutions, inflamed passions, ulcerated hearts, and consciences that could not endure the extinction of a light in their sleeping apartment. (qtd. in Kosok 1996, 228)

One significant difference in Maturin's damning critique is that it is not satiric but straightforward, although it is a fictionalized account that does not link Irish colonization with Indian. Nevertheless, such explicit critiques coming from Irish authors fostered the development of cross-colonial comparisons among Ireland, India, Egypt, and other British colonies.

Irish Orientalism as an Analyzable Formation

The unacknowledged discourse of Irish Orientalism developed in conjunction with British and French Orientalisms and as an imaginative riposte to colonialism in Ireland and elsewhere. Anglo-French Orientalism had much purchase in Ireland, as did many Anglo-French narratives, but it cannot fully account for the place of Orientalism in Irish culture, particularly in the texts of Irish cultural nationalists and anticolonial intellectuals and writers. Orientalism (academic, literary, and popular) in Ireland often differs in audience and purpose from British and French Orientalisms. It often remains rhetorically similar, however, as a parody is similar to an original.[5] One area of similarity concerns how Orientalist texts comment and build upon one another in a highly intertextual fashion. Edward Said provides some useful terms to discuss the intertextual and author-audience relationships inherent to Orientalism: "Every writer on the Orient . . . assumes some Oriental precedent, some previous knowledge of the Orient, to which he refers and on which he relies. Additionally, each work on the Orient *affiliates* itself with other works, with audiences, with institutions, with the Orient itself [and with specific colonial events and places]. The ensemble of relationships between works, audiences, and some particular aspects of the Orient therefore constitute an analyzable formation" (1995, 20). The precedents for Irish writers in the eighteenth and nineteenth centuries were most often English, French, and German.

Their affiliation with these established centers of Orientalism lent authority to their texts, which they could then compound, extenuate, or subvert, according to their own *strategic locations* (to borrow again from Said). Analyzing Orientalist philology and literature, Said maps the distinct positions of British and French Orientalists, which, en masse, he argues constitute different *analyzable formations.* In identifying these "ensembles" as *analyzable formations,* Said admits the possibility of other analyzable formations outside the Anglo-French nexus, most obviously in Germany, but also in Ireland, America, and the Hispanic world. Such formations differ in that they affiliate with audiences, institutions, and events other than English and French Orientalists and imperialists. Despite such differences, however, many techniques and discursive strategies of Irish writers, such as the common tendency of *affiliation* itself, do not differ from most Anglo-French writers on the Orient. Irish Orientalists frequently and at times excessively ground their ideas and strategies—even anticolonial ones—on literary and Orientalist precedents, which tend to be British, French, and German. Jonathan Swift, as discussed, parodied early Orientalist travel accounts to Japan and elsewhere in a fictional discovery narrative in *Gulliver's Travels*. Also, the copious Orientalist notes in Owenson's *Missionary*, Moore's *Lalla Rookh,* and Mangan's "Literae Orientales" repeatedly refer to, build upon, and parody the works of widely respected Orientalists, including d'Herbelot and Goethe, often wavering between ironic earnestness and overt parody.

The train of affiliations and borrowings in Irish Orientalism can be seen in the anonymously published *Letters from an Armenian in Ireland to His Friends at Trebisond* (1757) (alternately attributed to the Anglo-Irishmen Viscount Edmund Sexton Pery and Judge Robert Hellen),[6] which borrowed characters from, and purported to be the successor of, Baron George Lyttleton's *Letters from a Persian in England to His Friend at Ispahan* (1735) (the first collection of pseudoletters written originally in English), which had itself borrowed characters from, and purported to be the successor of, Charles Montesquieu's anonymously published *Les Lettres Persanes* (1721; John Ozell's English translation, *Persian Letters,* appeared in 1722), which in turn had popularized the genre that was made well known by Giovanni Marana's internationally popular *Letters writ by a Turkish Spy . . . at Paris* (translated 1687–1693).[7] Another Irishman, Oliver Goldsmith, wrote a later prominent work of this epistolary genre, *The Citizen of the World* (1762), which critiqued English and European culture through a Chinese narrator. Irish Orientalist literature fully operates within the Orientalist process of borrowing and building upon earlier texts, but one difference is that it often parodies the discourse in which it participates. Intertextual affiliation and parody, in a sense, became fundamental strategies of Orientalist literature in eighteenth- and nineteenth-century Ireland. Building on Oriental-Celtic connections, authors reimagined Ireland through Oriental allegories, attempting to rhetorically alter the parameters of the discourse of Empire.

Lisa Lowe, in her comments on Anglo-French Orientalism, addresses the heterogeneity of that discourse, exploring how it was "bound up with" other discursive formations:

> There is, of course, a very important political statement contained in the thesis that orientalism is an expression of European imperialism. Yet, when one proposes polemically that the discourse of orientalism is both discrete and monolithic, this polemic falsely isolates the notion of discourse, simplifies the power of this isolated discourse as belonging exclusively to Europe, and ignores the condition that discursive formations are never singular. Discourses operate in conflict; they overlap and collude; they do not produce fixed or unified objects. Orientalism is bound up with—indeed it reanimates some of the structuring themes of—other formations that emerge at different historical moments: the medical and anthropological classifications of race, psychoanalytic versions of sexuality, or capitalist and Marxist constructions of class. (1991, 8)

European historicism also greatly contributed to the emergence of Orientalism, and for Irish writers, the search for the origin of the Irish—Celtic, Scythian, Milesian, Phoenician, or otherwise—led into Irish Orientalism. Furthermore, anticolonialism, unionism, and nationalism inflected Orientalism in Ireland.

Much of Edward Said's analysis of Anglo-French Orientalism in *Orientalism* accounts for many modern impressions of the Orient in Ireland, but it does not account for the long tradition of Oriental representations in Irish culture. Indeed, Said's work is based upon the premise that "knowledge of any kind is always *situated* and given force by political reality" (Ashcroft and Ahluwalia 1999, 67). The relationship between topic (the Orient) and author (the Orientalist) is crucial in the analyzable formation of any Orientalist text. As Said notes, "Everyone who writes about the Orient must locate himself vis-à-vis the Orient." These Irish writers tended to locate themselves differently vis-à-vis imperialism and the Orient than either British or French writers, which is not to say that Irish writers uniformly wrote against the British Empire. On the contrary, no uniform response to imperialism existed in Irish culture, particularly within a discourse such as Irish Orientalism, which embodies both collusive and subversive representations of Empire.

Irish Orientalism developed both imperial and anticolonial strains, mirroring the Irish population in their participation in and resistance to the British Empire. Literary scholarship has only just begun to trace such complex cultural strains, but some important understandings have been reached. Elizabeth Butler Cullingford maps a related connection in her 1996 essay (reprinted 2001), "British Romans and Irish Carthaginians: Anticolonial Metaphors in Heaney, Friel, and McGuinness," noting, "The Rome-Carthage motif operates in complex and variable ways: as origin legend, colonial parable, and site of intersection between nationalism and sexuality." Cullingford traces the imaginative resistance fostered by the link between Ireland and Carthage back to the eighteenth century, crediting it with what she calls the development of an "oppositional identity for the colonized Irish" (222). Later Irish writers—from Romantics to Celtic Revivalists to late-twentieth-century Ulster writers—inherited this oppositional identity and employed both colonial parables and Oriental origin legends in their representations of Irish culture, and even in their discussions of more equitable East-West relationships. But, in addition, in the mid-nineteenth century, many Irish Orientalists were concerned with establishing and then furthering Ireland's share in the British Empire. Surprisingly, their works also employed Irish-Oriental affinities but for very different rhetorical ends, as the next chapter discusses.

Irish Pseudo-Oriental Letters

Irish writers encode critiques within representations of the Orient for divergent ends, depending upon each writer's particular strategic location. Within the genre of pseudo-Oriental letters, these locations differ widely, from Edmund Pery's pseudo-Oriental letters to the letters of Oliver Goldsmith, John Wilson Croker, and William Sampson. Sampson used an Oriental voice in his "Chinese Journals" to advance radical patriotic issues of the United Irishmen in the 1790s.[8] Croker's Chinese correspondent in *An Intercepted Letter from J— T—, Esq., Writer at Canton, to His Friend in Dublin, Ireland* (1804) discusses the Quang-tongese, an allegorical Oriental group representing the Dublin Irish, in mixed tones of condemnation and appreciation.[9] Goldsmith's narrator describes London and, in vivid contrast, Edmund Pery, the more Anglocentric author of *Letters from an Armenian in Ireland* (1757), discusses both the Anglo-Irish and the "old Native" Gaelic-Irish (78). Before examining the textual dynamic in these and other texts, a definition of this genre is needed.

In 1926, Hamilton Jewett Smith coined the clunky but precise term *pseudo-Oriental letters,* and describes them as such: "Works in which a foreigner is pictured satirizing the country he visits in a series of letters, made public in alleged translation from the original tongue" (39). Smith also comments on the pervasiveness of this genre in mid-eighteenth-century England:

> [To the Londoner of 1760], if the true East was still unknown, a pseudo-Orient was no undiscovered land. Newspaper and magazines with Oriental tales, pseudo-Oriental letters, accounts of Eastern countries, innumerable works of history, travel, and fiction, brought him report of it. Few of the writers of the age neglected to tell him of it. The magical stories of the *Arabian Nights,* which had been first translated into English in the reign of Queen Anne, still held their fascination in the mid-century. Dr. Samuel Johnson contributed numerous Oriental tales to the *Rambler* and the *Idler,* and in 1759 published *Rasselas,* the best known of the writings on Oriental subjects which flooded England. (1–2)

Stepping rhetorically into the Orient allowed writers a distant and usually humorous vantage point.

Most representations of the Orient in the British Isles were Chinese at this time, followed in popularity by Persian, Arabian, and later Indian. Europeans copiously described, copied, staged, and discussed China as the most advanced culture of the Orient, yet also imagined it as a strange, upside-down culture on the other side of the world. Pamphlets and letter collections flourished in London, and many came out of Dublin also, as with John Wilson Croker's *Intercepted Letter,* supposedly written by a Chinese visitor, and an anonymous pamphlet parodying the memoirs of England's ambassador to China, Lord MacCartney (an Irishman), *The Imperial Epistle from Kien Long, Emperor of China, to George the Third, King of Great Britain, &c. &c. &c. in the Year 1794* (1799). A host of popular British and French works informed the works of Irish authors on the Orient. Some of the more prominent eighteenth-century Orientalist works (prior to works by Sir William Jones and James Mills) include the English translations of the Jesuit histories of Louis Le Comte and Jean-Baptiste Du Halde and translations of other French works on the Orient by Giovanni Marana, Thomas Gueullette, and the Marquis D'Argens (Jean Baptiste de Boyer); the English literary and theatrical works of Joseph Addison, George Lyttleton, William Collins, Horace Walpole, Arthur Murphy, John Hawkesworth, Samuel Johnson, and Thomas Percy; and hundreds of essays on China, Japan, India, or Persia in *Gentleman's Magazine,* the *British Magazine,* and the *Monthly Review.*[10]

Whereas pseudoletters from a foreign correspondent (Oriental or otherwise) had existed for some time, Charles de Secondat, Baron de Montesquieu (1689–1755), developed the genre with his *Lettres Persanes* by merging aspects of other genres, namely, the philosophical essay and the emerging epistolary novel, with the romance of exotic Oriental tales (such as *The Arabian Nights,* first appearing in French in 1704). His pointed and philosophic critiques of contemporary European culture, particularly France's, transformed the genre into an attractive rhetorical mode for social critics, such as Johnson, Addison, and Goldsmith.[11] In this respect, it prefigured alien critiques of humanity in twentieth-century science fiction. Oliver Goldsmith provides some insights into the rhetoric of the genre in an article in the *Monthly Review* (Aug. 1757).

> Charles Montesquieu, President of the Parliament of Bourdeaux, born in 1689, published at the age of thirty-two, his *Persian Letters,* a work of humour, abounding with strokes which testify a genius above the performance. It is written in imitation of the *Siamese Letters* of Du Freny, and of the *Turkish Spy;* but it is an imitation which shews what the originals should have been. The success their works met with was, for the most part, owing to the foreign air of their performances; the success of the *Persian Letters* arose from the delicacy of their satire. That satire which in the mouth of an Asiatic is poignant, would lose all its force when coming from an European. (1966, 1:104)

This last line restates Voltaire's famous statement about the success of the *Persian Letters,* but what is also relevant is that it highlights Goldsmith's interest in the "foreign air" and exoticism of the letters—and its satirical possibilities.

Goldsmith's aperçu demonstrates not only the appeal of the exotic to European audiences but also his awareness of how the exotic may enable satire with poignancy and rhetorical force. In other words, the exotic could enable critique because it masked the author in the guise of the *other.* The voice of this *other* character is always already (in the burgeoning discourse of Empire and Orientalism) inferior in power, intelligence, and knowledge to the European, and therefore the critique never overtly threatens the power dynamics of the discourse. Indeed, its humor arises out of the absurdity of an exotic foreigner finding the familiar and standard to be strange. The popular comic element arises partly out of the imagined reversal of power. Indeed, the popularity of these Oriental critiques of European society had much to do with the fact that the critiques were satirical but rarely taken as subversive.

At this early historical juncture in European colonial expansion, such rhetorical "writing back" did not represent mutiny or insubordination; it was merely comic. Perhaps this explains why this particular genre, with its poignant Oriental critiques and its imagined reversals of power, fell out of popularity as the colonizing project of Empire expanded in the nineteenth century. Such letters were based on the entertainable premise that an Oriental traveler could naively criticize civilization better than an Englishman or a Frenchman—his or her distance and naïveté functioned like the occasionally profound yet innocent words of children who observe and comment without understanding ramifications and contingencies.

If the social critiques were taken seriously to any extent—as, originally, Montesquieu's critiques were—the validity of the criticism was beside the Oriental voice, which was understood as a device. Certainly, an Oriental *character* could critique the obvious paradoxes of civilization, and even some of the more inhumane elements of European society, but few imagined the Orient offered a better civilization.[12] Later, as the pseudoscience of race developed and the discourse of Orientalism was more fully established, Ernest Renan could state the superiority of the European in no uncertain terms: "Every person, however slightly he may be acquainted with the affairs of our time, sees clearly the actual inferiority of Mohammedan countries" (1896, 85). The crux of the Anglo-French discourse is based on the premise that the East and West are absolutely distinct. Orientalism in Ireland, however, did not foster such absolutes. In a very real sense, the most westerly part of the British Isles had long cherished its fantastic Eastern credentials, which grew into semiotic affinities. Moreover, these affinities had as much to do with the colonial situation in Ireland as they did with any antiquarian ideas.

The attraction of the Orient as a rhetorical realm of critique, especially in the form of the pseudo-Oriental letter, was widespread in Europe at the end of the eighteenth century. George Lyttleton's *Letters from a Persian in England to His Friend at Ispahan* (1735) was the first collection of pseudoletters written originally in English and published in England (H. J. Smith 1926, 52). As noted, Lyttleton's English *Letters from a Persian* purports to be the successor of Montesquieu's *Persian Letters.* Lyttleton even has his principal correspondent, Selim (a supposed friend of Montesquieu's central character, Usbek),[13] address his letters to another of Montesquieu's Persian characters, Mirza. Significantly, Selim continues Usbek's analysis of European culture and his philosophic tale of despotic troglodytes. The first letter explains the purpose of his correspondence: "The relations we received from our friend Usbec [sic], of those parts of Europe which he had seen, raised in us an ardent desire to know the rest, and particularly *this famous island,* of which, not having been there himself, he could give us but imperfect accounts" (5). Thus, the British work purports to be an extension of the earlier French ones, illustrating the similar French and English impressions of Persia.

If the extension of the characters from France to England does not greatly alter the strategic location of the author and the narrators vis-à-vis the Orient and Europe, Edmund Pery's Anglo-Irish collection of pseudo-Oriental letters does. It extends and redirects the strategy of Montesquieu and Lyttleton, in part, by discussing Ireland. As Lyttleton moved Montesquieu's Persians to England from France, Pery transports them to Ireland in his *Letters from an Armenian in Ireland to His Friends at Trebisond.*[14] The correspondence begins with a letter from "Aza" to "Abdallah," a correspondent of Lyttleton's Selim: "Learned Abdallah, Thou hast seen in the Letters of *Selim* to *Mirza,* a just Representation of the People of *England,* their Genius, their Manners, the Frame of their Government, and the Dangers to which it is subject. But I will not engage thy Minutes by Remarks upon that Island; I will endeavour to give thee some Account of a People a little more remote, but subject to the same King, among whom I have lived since my Departure from *London*" (1757, 7–8). Leaving the European metropole, journeying to the fringes of the continent (to "remote" Ireland), Pery's Persian becomes more than an Oriental visitor to Europe. He becomes an Oriental explorer in the Occident, mapping cultural and political issues in the Gaelic periphery, representing native rural Irish culture to readers of English. On the whole, Pery's letters conform to the genre of the pseudo-Oriental letters, but the dynamic of an Oriental traveler commenting on the strangeness of his host European country takes on a new significance when the host country is itself not entirely "civilized." When Aza perceives exotic natives within this country of Ireland, he is shocked by the precivilized "vassals."

Pery's Oriental narrator finds two populations in this "remote" place, and like Lyttleton's and Montesquieu's letter-writing characters, Mirza and Selim, Aza draws philosophical, moral, and cultural conclusions from his observations. For the most part, the correspondence is an analysis of Anglo-Irish politics and society, as well as the economic dominance of England,[15] as a review by Goldsmith indicates.[16] Aza positions the Anglo-Irish as a supplementary community of colonial settlers, existing on the edge of Empire as the translators of the frontier.[17] Pery's Oriental narrator recommends both further colonial trade in the Orient and continued English dominance, hoping to strengthen the position of the Anglo-Irish in Ireland, functioning as England's intermediaries with the "barbarous" Irish. Significantly, the Orient is depicted as more civil and modern than Ireland.

Asserting Irish ties to England and to the Orient, Aza notes that both populations in Ireland share some traits with the Orient: "These People call us Easterns
Voluptuous, *Abdallah,* yet there is no Sense ungratified by them" (85).[18] The Irish
exhibit traits normally attributed to "Easterns"; the "Voluptuous" Irish begin to become the Oriental's Oriental. The letter in the volume that most exoticizes the
Gaelic Irish actually purports to elucidate their customs. Aza describes an excur-
sion through the "wild and varied beauty" of the Irish countryside, marred only by
its "dismal" and primitive Milesian inhabitants (83). The rural Gaelic Irish, once
glorious but presently rude, become the rhetorical counterparts of Montesquieu's
troglodytes. Aza witnesses a funeral procession and the *caoineadh* (keening) of the
women,[19] and treats the Gaelic Irish as superstitious and custom-laden, the antithesis of modern Enlightenment Europe. He records his Gaelic driver as saying, "Custom is with us more powerful than Laws" (84). This Gael is, in a sense, Orientalized
by an Anglo-Irish representation of the Orient.

Ireland as a place "possessed of peculiarities" increasingly fascinated the British
reading public in the late eighteenth century, and interpreters of Irish, Celtic, and
Gaelic cultures were sought after, as illustrated by the increasing number of travel
narratives (and pseudo ones) to Killarney and Clare around the end of the eighteenth century. One pseudoletter and travel account featured a British narrator recounting his tour to a wild and scenic Ireland. Attributed to Goldsmith, the piece
appeared in the *Weekly Magazine* in November 1759 under the title "A Description
of the Manners and Customs of the Native *Irish.* In a Letter from an *English* Gentleman." It appeared the month before Goldsmith's series of "Chinese Letters" (collected as *The Citizen of the World* in 1762) began to run in the *Public Ledger* on
December 29, 1759. Like the "Chinese Letters" that he continued the following
year, this "Letter from an *English* Gentleman" is a travel journal, similar to the genre
of pseudo-Oriental letters. Notably, Goldsmith also uses an English persona in this
letter to critique his home country and the English manner of comprehending it.
The letter opens by arguing the need for increased study of England's "peculiar"
backyard—"our conquered kingdom of Ireland"—contending that interest in the
Orient has wrongly superseded such local studies: "While our travellers are busied
in studying the manners, the soil, and produce of distant countries, there are several
which are at our very doors possessed of peculiarities hitherto unknown, and yet
quite neglected; like conquerors who have been too eagerly employed in foreign
conquests, we leave our native dominions without notice or regard" (24).[20] Rationalizing his journey to Ireland, the narrator argues the need for Orientalist or
Celticist studies of "the manners, the soil, and produce" of Ireland.

The Oriental origin legends also find a place in the piece. In the fourth paragraph, the narrator references the Oriental origins: "Their women have exquisite
complexions, though their features are a little broad somewhat approaching that

turn of visage which we are told of the Tartars, from whom they pretend to be originally descended." The "original Irish" make this Oriental connection, but the narrator adds: "The manners of the original inhabitants, which they to this day preserve unvaried, are entirely different from those of the English, and partake somewhat of the ancient Scythian, and modern Spanish customs, as described by travellers and historians, for by these two nations the country was at different times inhabited. Their burials, pattons, and cakes, their houses, furniture and dress, all partake somewhat of these two different nations, and sufficiently mark the original from whence they sprung" (25). The narrator then proceeds to relay his adventures with the "original inhabitants" (26); not surprisingly, like Pery's Aza, Goldsmith's narrator highlights Irish funeral customs and the *caoineadh:* "This custom of rejoicing instead of sorrow upon the death of a relation, is still preserved among the Tartars, and I fancy from them it is that the native Irish have taken it. When they have thus watched one night for they never keep the body two, it is next day carried upon men's shoulders to the churchyard, and the women continue howling all the way" (29). Goldsmith's "English Gentleman" narrator, like Pery's Aza, discovers the living Irish Orient that pseudohistorians and antiquarians had also historicized in other works.

The fact that Goldsmith used an English narrator in his letters on Irish culture and a Chinese narrator to comment on English culture begs the following questions: Why did Goldsmith not write his pseudo-Oriental letters with an exotic Gaelic narrator, or write them about Ireland with an Oriental narrator? Little is known for certain about why Goldsmith chose the narrator he did, but Sir James Prior reports in his 1837 biography: "[H]is first design . . . was to make his hero a native of Morocco or Fez; but reflecting on the rude nature of the people of Barbary, this idea was dropped. A Chinese was then chosen as offering more novelty of character than a Turk or Persian; and being equally advanced in the scale of civilisation, could pass an opinion on all he saw better than the native of a more barbarous country" (qtd. in Goldsmith 1966, 2:x). Perhaps Goldsmith chose a Chinese narrator over an Irish narrator for similar reasons, or perhaps not. But we must also consider the position that Goldsmith found himself in as a celebrated (and often chaffed) Irishman in England. In the preface to *The Citizen of the World,* he writes powerfully about his place as an Irish author in a "class" of his own in London, as an exile living under the lens of another culture:

[A]t present I belong to no particular class. I resemble one of those solitary animals, that has been forced from its forest to gratify human curiosity. My earliest wish was to escape unheeded through life: but I have been set up for half-pence, to fret and scamper at the end of my chain. Though none are injured by my rage, I am naturally too savage to court any friends by fawning; too obstinate to be taught new tricks; and too improvident to mind what may happen: I am appeased, though not contented: too indolent for intrigue, and too timid to push for favour: I am—but what signifies what I am. (1840, n.p.)

This last line not only speaks volumes of Goldsmith's position in the established literary circle in London but also suggests his emotions and his awareness of his forced identification with a representation:"I am—but what signifies what I am." Goldsmith's "Letters from a Chinese Philosopher," and his Oriental persona, enabled him to "write back" to England while avoiding the uncomfortable persona of the barbarous Irishman. The exotic but civilized Chinese guise enabled his satire, and the Oriental stood in for the Irish author as a spokesman to satirize English culture.

Much of Anglo-French Orientalism depicted Europeans making pilgrimages or traveling to the Orient to discover it, map it, control it, or resuscitate it to the civilized state from which it had supposedly fallen—in short, to "recivilize" it.[21] In contrast, much of Irish Orientalism either depicted "civilized" Orientals visiting Ireland and Britain (or, in the case of Irish antiquarianism, "Orientals" coming as the first colonizers of the British Isles) or gave voice to Oriental individuals or nations as they struggled against the British or another imperial force (such as the Ottoman Empire). For example, an "Irish Officer's" anonymous Dublin pamphlet, *The History of Mirza Abul Hassan Khan . . . with Some Account of the Fair Circassian* (1819), depicts the Persian ambassador to England on a visit to Ireland[22]—which he admires and compares to Persia:"Mirza Abul Hassan Khan . . . is a great admirer of Hafiz, the last and best of the Persian poets, whose sonnets can be compared to nothing but the effusions of our countryman, Moore. On hearing some of the productions of the Irish poet, which were read to him at Bilton's Hotel, he immediately observed the similarity" (18). The author perhaps conflated the Persian ambassador to England, Mirza Abul Hassan Khan, who did not visit Ireland but was well known in England, thanks to James Morier's works and the British press, with Mirza Abu Talib Khan, who was one of the first Indians to visit Ireland (see fig. 9). The link between the Irish and the Persian echoes the centuries-old Irish link to the Orient. Significantly, it is not merely a projection of Irish desires onto the Orient; it is reported as a mutually imagined link similar to later cross-colony identifications between Irish and Asian writers and nationalists.

Continuity and Oriental Origins in Irish Historiography

Throughout the nineteenth century, stories of Ireland's Oriental origins opened Irish nationalist histories, despite being increasingly dismissed by archaeologists, philologists, and ancient historians. For instance, a history primer on *Pre-Christian Ireland* (1887), written by Canon Ulick Bourke as an examiner in "Keltic" and Irish

9. "Mirza Abul Hassan Khan [by] T. C. Clifford, Stephens Green." Frontispiece from an anonymous pamphlet by "An Irish Officer in the Service of Persia," *The History of Mirza Abul Hassan Khan, the Persian Ambassador, with Some Account of the Fair Circassian* (1819).

history at the then Royal University of Ireland, opens with a section in catechistic format on the "Certainty of Early Keltic Settlements in Eire": "Q. 1. Where did the earliest races who first reached Ireland come from? A. From the East; from the high table-lands reaching from Mount Ararat in Armenia, by the Caspian Sea, south and east; from the present Persia and the country stretching eastwards to the Hindu Kush Mountains, and to the River Hindus. Q. 2. What proofs exist to show that

the first settlers in Ireland came from this eastern land?" (1). Even though it is purported to be "Keltic" history, it begins in the Orient and confirms a dual Oriental
and Japhetic ancestry of the Irish, similar to Vallancey's syncretic theory a century
before. Alongside such transmuted pseudohistorical accounts, Orient-Celtic correspondences developed in relation to nineteenth-century conceptions of history,
progress, and race.

For jingoistic British historians such as Thomas Babington Macaulay, writing in
a May 1828 review essay,[23] the distinction between modern and ancient historiography was easily evaluated: "[T]he writers of modern times have far surpassed those of
antiquity. The historians of our own country are unequalled in depth and precision
of reason; and even in the works of our mere compilers, we often meet with speculations beyond the reach of Thucydides or Tacitus" (1897, 151–52). For Macaulay, ancient histories (much valued in eighteenth-century antiquarianism) had misled the
moderns, encouraging wild speculations, such as associating Europe with Asia and
giving "currency to many very erroneous opinions with respect to ancient history.
They have heated the imaginations of boys. They have misled the judgment and corrupted the taste of some men of letters, such as Akenside and Sir William Jones"
(138). Although the work of "Oriental" Jones eventually proved accurate and
achieved recognition in England, Macaulay's ideas about the untrustworthiness of
ancient sources dominated English historiography in the early nineteenth century.
Just the opposite was true for most Irish historians of this period, who relied on the
"old books" of early modern Ireland for clues about their past. In general, the distinction between ancient and modern texts developed as a product of European
source criticism and ideas about sociocultural progress. Orientalism transferred this
temporal division between the ancient and modern, however, into geography,
where physical distance between modern Europe and the Orient matched supposed
temporal distance; even the Celtic fringe (along with African, Native American, and
other cultures) continued to be viewed as mired in antiquity. Both the Oriental and
the Celtic, however, continued to contribute to aesthetic trends in Europe in the
nineteenth century, as primitivism would later inspire new looks at Africa.

Writers and thinkers in nineteenth-century Ireland also widely subscribed to
this geotemporal division but often understood its relevance differently. In a speech
delivered in Mayo on July 16, 1826, an amateur Irish historian, Eneas MacDonnell,
discussed the gap between antiquity and modern times:

> [If] any traveler over the countries which formed the states of ancient Greece, or
> Rome, were to write, that within forty miles of some place where he had rested,
> there stood more than forty ruins of religious and literary establishments, many, nay,
> most of which bore marks of ancient splendour and magnificence; would not his
> reader hesitate in his confidence, and the caution be considered not more than rea-

sonable? But, let the doubting reader come here; let him visit our tottering walls of Mayo and any one, the very youngest amongst us, will point out to him how he can realize the story; yes, here in *uncivilized* Ireland!! (1826, 19–20)

MacDonnell and many cultural nationalists encouraged Irish culture to "realize the story" of its antiquity in terms other than it was posed by standard British historiography and fashion. Irish writers saw Ireland like the Orient: *"uncivilized"* in modern times but "[bearing] marks of ancient splendour." This historical gap was not understood in terms of neglect or misdirection, nor as an atavistic slide back to barbarism: "Those who upraid us, at the present day, should recollect, that if our People are uneducated, the fault is not with that People, but with those who demolished their institutions, plundered their libraries, burned their books, and persecuted their teachers" (20). British colonial forces were understood to be the clear impetus for Ireland's regression, in marked opposition to the supposed progressive forces of imperialism. Nationalist historians argued that *"uncivilized* Ireland" could be returned to its former "magnificence" only through a cultural rebirth—not through any modernizing, progressive forces. Writers in the nineteenth century also began to suspect that the Orient's cultural regression might have similar causes.

Heartened by antiquarian and pseudohistorical arguments about actual Irish links to ancient Eastern cultures, eighteenth- and nineteenth-century historians began their otherwise modern histories with Eastern origin legends. Eighteenth-century historians, both Gaelic and Anglo-Irish in heritage, such as Charles O'-Conor and Sylvester O'Halloran, accepted O'Flaherty's speculations as plausible early on. Eventually, antiquity became even more politicized, and cultural sympathies divided at the end of the eighteenth century, but throughout the century the main historiographic debate between Anglocentric and Hibernocentric historians concerned the representations of the Rebellion of 1641, a dispute broiling since the second half of the seventeenth century. Following Sir John Temple's (1600–1677) anti-Catholic work, *History of the Irish Rebellion, Together with the Barbarous Cruelties and Bloody Massacres which Ensued Thereupon* (1644), Thomas Leland's (1722–1785) *History of Ireland from the Invasion of Henry II* (1773) depicted the rebellion as a Catholic massacre of innocent Protestants. Responding in the subsequent years and fueling the controversy, Sylvester O'Halloran, John Curry (1710–1780), and others worked to refute Leland. Despite such sectarian wrangling, Irish antiquity had less historiographic dispute in these years, and scholarly accord and exchanges existed about antiquity for a time during which Vallancey emerged as an influential persona (for example, Charles O'Conor shared translations of Irish annals with Leland) (Welch 1996, 306).

The first substantial politicized attack on Irish antiquarianism came in 1790 in Edward Ledwich's (1738–1823) *Antiquities of Ireland*. Ledwich's stated purpose is to dispel the fabulous stories of Irish ancient history, but his critiques are leveled at the origin legends and the Phoenician origin theories and support the Scythian and Celtic origin theories, much in the tradition of British historiography. But he does not frame his attack as supporting one interpretation over another; he argues that "Bardic fictions and unfounded traditions are the oral records of every barbarous nation" (1804, 1) and relies on Greek, Roman, and British texts.[24] With some accuracy, he pairs "bardic fictions" and popular antiquarian theories with the "oriental fabling" of medieval times (2), but also labels them as "sure mark[s] of an oriental fancy" (3). Such comments signal the development of shared similarities among imagined Celtic and Oriental sensibilities (for instance, inscrutable, imaginative, unrealistic) that were developing in the wider European imagination. Ledwich's stated purpose has also been seen by scholars as representing a shift in Irish historiography. Oliver MacDonagh in *States of Mind: A Study of Anglo-Irish Conflict, 1780–1980* gives Ledwich's history the distinction of beginning modern Irish historiography for its Enlightenment metaphors and rhetoric, its sectarian arguments, and its politicization of antiquity. Though claiming impartiality, Ledwich's work is less accurate historiography than careful polemics; his targets are contemporary works by prominent Catholic historians, "rising papists like Charles O'Connor [*sic*] and Thomas Wyse, founders of the Catholic Committee in 1760, who had combined agitation for Catholic relief with attempts to preserve the traditional Gaelic culture" (1983, 1). In his attack, he dismisses Vallancey and O'Flaherty and their sources, particularly *Lebor Gabála* ("leaver Gabbhala") (7), yet relies on Tigernach's annals, which are seen as more reliable. The section titled "Of the Colonization of Ireland" concludes with an "enlightened" dismissal: "Let others enjoy the gibberish of oriental etymologies, and the company of Milesians, Phœnicians and Magicains in that gloomy cave [of Plato's allegory]" (31). In place of these fabulations, Ledwich supposedly walks the reader into the clear light of day. In actuality, he presented the Scytho-Celtic model, borrowing from the fabulous accounts of Camden, Spenser, and classical authors. Partly because of Ledwich's work, ancient Celts became more accepted later in the century as Ireland's ancestors than ancient Phoenicians, particularly by Irish cultural nationalists. But these latter-day Celts differed considerably from Ledwich's barbaric Celts, who resembled Spenser's savage Scythians or the "savages of America," "destitute of mental and civil cultivation" (Ledwich 1804, 15).

MacDonagh notes that a greater historical perspective was also at stake in the debate that Ledwich initiated: "The nationalist-Catholic saw the course of Irish history in terms of degeneration from an initial purity whereas the unionist-Protestants presented it in terms of a triumphant, if lengthy and incomplete, emergence from barbarism." In the nineteenth century, Anglo-Irish historians generally worked to undermine the romantic representations of ancient Ireland while cultural nationalist historians sought to flesh out such images and narratives. But doing so was not new; such a polarization retraced the fault line that had existed between Anglocentric and Hibernocentric historiography from the twelfth century.[25] Treating "antiquity as a touchstone of the present" (1983, 2) was, in many ways, an old tradition, and Irish antiquity has long inspired political debates.

Eighteenth-century collaboration was, in many respects, anomalous for modern Irish historiography and more closely resembled the days of cultural hybridity with the Old English or *Sean-Ghall* settlers. But after the open rebellion of the United Irishmen in 1798 and the 1800 Act of Union, as well as the divisive years leading up to these political shifts, representations of ancient Ireland's cultural hybridity dropped away, and religious differences in the past intensified and racialized, reflecting the increasing distrust among Anglo-Irish Protestants and Gaelic Catholics in Ireland.[26] Oriental-Celtic comparisons of the period reflected these divisions, though often indirectly. Cultural nationalist historians continued to entertain Oriental origin theories as Anglocentric writers disputed them, reserving their comparisons of Ireland and the Orient to discussions of the degrees and types of barbarity.

Historical investigations of Irish antiquity rarely adopted the historiographic rigor that Macaulay seemed to call for, and, despite careful work by scholars such as Petrie, much of nineteenth-century historiography of ancient Ireland remained dependent on fabulous classical and early modern accounts. Historian Ann Rigney comments on a related phenomenon in her essay "Immemorial Routines: The Celts and Their Resistance to History," asking why the Celts have generally been treated as immured in the past and rarely as historical subjects: "That the Celts and the 'past' go together seems self-evident. . . . But what about the Celts and 'history'?" (1996, 159–60). Although Rigney focuses on French historiography, this question is also applicable to Irish historiography of that period. Most representations of the Celts were dissociated from historical time (and many were fictional); in brief, the line between the ancient past and the legendary past was imprecisely drawn. The shift from legendary Phoenician and Oriental origins to suppositions about Scythian and Celtic origins does not seem to have contributed to any real historical accuracy, nor did it alter the sense of Ireland's pastness. Moreover, this shift did not negate the supposed Oriental history or sensibility of the Irish; it merely pushed Oriental-Celtic connections into more legendary, literary, and racial realms. Ancient legends, for Romantic writers in particular, became attractive subject matter and resonated as an ancient "traditional" history of the folk of Ireland. But this general shift does not signify that a consensus was ever reached among historians about ancient Ireland. As pseudohistorians and antiquarians had done for centuries, historians merely reattributed the legendary waves of "invasions" to multiple migrant peoples: Scythian, Phoenician, Celt, British, Egyptian, Gallic, Spanish, Moorish, or others.

Despite the surge in the number of published histories of Ireland in the nineteenth century, few new theories of Irish antiquity emerged after the Celtic theories took hold. Following the controversies in the late eighteenth century, most historians of Ireland made room for the various competing theories, as the editors of Ireland's *Mirror* note in their 1804 pamphlet, *A New and Impartial History of Ireland from the Landing of Partholan to the Present Times, Faithfully Extracted from the Most Received Authorities*. In 1826, another attempt at an impartial history, *Ireland in Past Times: An Historical Retrospect, Ecclesiastical and Civil* by an anonymous author, published in both London and Dublin, also sought a middle ground. The author's aim was to "give a plain and simple narrative of the progress of the Christian religion in Ireland" (v), devoid of "superstition" and "perversions" but recognizing that "the Irish certainly have not all been, (what too many deem them,) buried in barbarism and ignorance from the beginning of time" (vi). A noble Celtic past gradually became the most conciliatory path for Irish history, as the first section heading demonstrates: "Ireland first peopled by Celtic tribes from Gaul" (1). John O'-Driscol's 1827 *History of Ireland* returned to discuss Thomas Leland's Protestant history, which he treats as Ireland's best history, though unnecessarily divisive. Instead of renewing the differences over Irish antiquity, he skips lightly over them. Thomas Moore's (1779–1852) four-volume *History of Ireland* (1835–1846) likewise took a middle path, emphasizing a Celtic origin with some "Phoenician intercourse with the Irish" (1843, 2:iii), also highlighting the Eastern origins of the Milesians (32–44) and comparing the ancient Irish with "Greeks, Asiatics, and Egyptians" (42).

The outstanding exception to the transmutations of the origin legends into Irish history is the careful scholarship of George Petrie (1789–1866), who wrote and edited with Caesar Otway the *Dublin Penny Journal* (1832–1833) and inductively developed ideas from other speculative sources such as Montmorency-Morres. Most famously, Petrie refuted ideas about the Phoenician origins of the round towers in an essay that won a gold medal from the Royal Dublin Society in 1833, later published in *Ecclesiastical Architecture in Ireland* (1845). After Petrie, Irish historians were much more cautious about their reliance on antiquarian theories of the eighteenth century. Nevertheless, ancient Irish history and origin theories continued to attract readers. Another significant work that had been written eighty years earlier came out in translation in 1831–1832. Abbé James MacGeoghegan's (1702–1764) *History of Ireland, Ancient and Modern, Taken from the Most Authentic Records* (French version, 1758–1762) adopted a complex origin scheme for what he calls the "Scoto-Milesians" who originally had Scythian origins. His work was very influential on later cultural nationalists. Following these works of the early 1830s, arguments for a Phoenician settlement of Ireland subsided, but Phoenician influences continued to be guessed about, as in George Lewis Smyth's *Ireland: Historical and Statistical* (1844, 49–50). The origin legends remained in circulation but disappeared from serious scholarship, persisting in the more glorified nationalist histories intended for North American readers, such as Thomas Mooney's (1815–1888) two-volume *History of Ireland from Its First Settlement to the Present Time* (1845) published in Boston, which treats the Irish as hybrid descendants of Egyptians, Phoenicians, Scythians, and Celts (1:3). Later in the century, Irish history began to be read through racial theories, in which the Celts occupied a nebulous position on the outer edge of Europe with a society that apparently resembled Oriental ones, even in sympathetic histories such as *The Irish Race in the Past and Present* (1883) by Augustus J. Thébaud, S.J.

Other nineteenth-century Irish works copied and translated the origin legends into English from their textual sources for a new audience of readers, in both Ireland and England. By this point in time, Irish historiography and pseudohistory had been pegged in England as an unreliable quagmire of dubious books and, in Ireland, as a discipline that mirrored Ireland's besieged history. Perhaps the most prominent translation of the period was John O'Donovan's (1809–1861) translation of Mícheál Ó Cléirigh's *Annála Ríoghachta Eireann* (1632–1636), published in English as *Annals of the Four Masters* (1848–1851). The work inspired a new generation of Irish cultural nationalists in the second half of the century and was generally read as a collection of venerable legends, not as ancient history. O'Donovan's earlier *Grammar of the Irish Language* (1845) had given a précis of the legends, calling their authors "the writers of the traditional history of Ireland" (xxviii)—traditional history apparently contrasted with modern historiography. The popular interest in the translated legends prompted his fuller and influential work.

The review of O'Donovan's translation in the *London Quarterly Review* (July 1853) points to the wide gap between English and Irish audiences. The anonymous reviewer was, in actuality, the English antiquarian and historian Algernon Herbert, who also had written a history of Ireland in 1848. Herbert found O'-Donovan's work to be less significant than touted and gave it a mixed response, treating it as a readable translation of "a book of rapine, vengeance, and bloodshed; the annals of a race of disunited warriors and nomadic cattle-lifters, preying upon each other" (11). Herbert also considers Irish historiography burdensome if sometimes curious, noting at the outset that "Erin has, in truth, too much ancient history" (2). Significantly, after comparing O'Donovan's work to earlier histories of Ireland, he relegates all of Gaelic culture to the past: "Now all is past and gone, and the Gael are at an end. They belong to history; their neglected, unpublished, and perishing history" (13). Although they supposedly have a place in history, it apparently is not a recorded one; for this Anglocentric reviewer, theirs was an unknowable history, best forgotten and left to the past. Herbert's ungenerous dismissal must have had particular resonance for readers sensitive to the traumas in Ireland at the time, being written only a few years after Ireland's Great Famine of 1845–1849 in which approximately one million people died.

This review essay reveals how, after centuries of social and political intercourse, the Irish continued to be viewed as backward and beholden to the civilizing light of the English. Significantly, the cultures of Asia were understood similarly, and the Irish continued to offer an example of how a rude and barbarous people might be transformed. The faint praise that Herbert reserves for the Irish subtly reveals how this imperial dynamic endured through historical impressions:"If the [Irish] boys of our time could behold the days of Surley Boys and Shan O'Neill, and the long-haired gallo-glasses who followed Tirone and Hugh Roe O'Donnell to Athboy and Kinsale, they would be utterly astonished, and overjoyed to come out of that." In the footnote to this passage, the author quotes a sanitized Victorian version of William Camden's 1625 passage about these Gaelic visitors to London:"'Now was Shan O'Neal come out of Ireland to perform what he had promised a yeere before, with a guard of ax-bearing Galloglasses, bareheaded, with curled haire hanging downe, yellow suprlises dyed with saffron or man's stale, long sleeves, short coates, and hairy mantles; whom the English people gazed at with no less admiration than nowe a dayes they doe them of China or America.' Camden's Elizabeth, p. 48" (13). Highlighting the difference between ungrateful contemporary Irish "boys" and seventeenth-century Gaels worked to prove the barbaric tradition of Ireland as well as the civilizing force of the British Empire.[27]

In vivid contrast to this divide in understandings of Irish antiquity, another trend was emerging in Irish writing as illustrated by the works of Richard Madden, who focused on contemporary histories, seeking to amplify Irish and Asian voices in English-language texts. A historian of the relatively recent United Irishmen In-surrection of 1798, Madden also wrote about his years spent in the Turkish Empire, and much of his work supports nationalist and emancipation movements in Ireland and elsewhere. For instance, he documented both Cuban slavery (1840) and the story of Egyptian nationalist Mohammed Ali (1841). Madden's work followed in the footsteps of other Irish political critiques of British imperialism. In the 1790s, direct critiques brought persecution by British authorities, as in the cases of the poet and politician William Drennan, who was tried for sedition for a speech to the United Irishmen in 1794, and the 1798 hanging of a satirist and Presbyterian min-ister, the Reverend James Porter, who wrote pseudoletters satirizing local landlords in the periodical the Northern Star, reprinted as Billy Bluff and Squire Firebrand in 1796.

Discussing other aspects of the British Empire seems to have been safer. In the 1780s, Irish MPs in the British Parliament had delivered critiques of British mis-conduct in India; most famously, Edmund Burke criticized the East India Company's mismanagement of India (1782–1783) and led the efforts to impeach Warren Hastings, the governor general of the East India Company.[28] Also, Richard Brinsley Sheridan's maiden speech as an MP on the Begum of Oude defended wronged Indians against British misconduct and supported Burke's 1787 impeachment of Warren Hastings. Although these speeches had their own contexts, they clearly established a distinct Irish perspective that could be critical of British imperial activities in Asia—critiquing imperial policies was politically and socially safer (and it gained a wider audience in Britain) than attacking specific English policies in Ireland. Such speeches stand as clear articulations of a perspective of the Irish Enlightenment, which contemporary scholars such as Seamus Deane and Luke Gibbons discuss in greater detail than can be afforded here.

Orientalism and Celticism in the Nineteenth Century

English and French Orientalists increasingly represented Asian and West Asian cultures as sensual, exotic, and primitive in the nineteenth century, often discussing their lack of skills for self-governance as cultures and as races—categories that elided into one another. The concept of race emerged in the eighteenth century through the pseudoscientific work of a number of early anthropologists, including Louis Morea de Maupertuis (1698–1759); Carolus Linnaeus (1707–1778); Louis LeClerc, Count de Bufon (1707–1788); and, most famously, Johann Friedrich Blumenbach (1752–1840). Developing from the biblical classifications based on the sons of Noah: Japhetic (European), Shemitic (Asian and American), and Hamitic (African), Linnaeus delineated four groups of humanity, making American its own category, and LeClerc brought the concept of race into the natural sciences. Immanuel Kant (1724–1804) further expounded on the concept of race in a number of essays beginning in 1775. Later, Blumenbach broke the four categories of humanity into five, differentiating the Asian from the Malay, and labeled them according to color and race in the third edition of his *De Generis Humani Varietate Nativa* (1795).[29] Ideas of race were soon brought into English-language discussions by writers such as Samuel Stanhope (1750–1819) and Charles White (1728–1813), particularly into British imperial evaluations of the cultures of the Orient. Such portrayals of colonized peoples undergirded colonial administrators and imperial sympathizers in justifying and administering colonial rule.

As Orientalists pigeonholed the increasingly racialized Oriental in the early nineteenth century, English pundits, imperial administrators, and French and English Celticists began to further subdivide ideas of race, applying them to Ireland and characterizing "the Celtic races" in general as feminine, unintellectual, natural, and premodern. The nineteenth-century Irish grew to be seen as the modern manifestation of an ancient people, a leftover of a remote, premodern East-West culture, especially in the decades around the Irish Famine. Two seminal works from the nineteenth century on the Celtic races—an essay by historian, philologist, Orientalist, and Celticist Ernest Renan (1823–1892), "The Poetry of the Celtic Races" (1854; first English translation, 1893), and a critical study by the critic and poet Matthew Arnold (1822–1888), *On the Study of Celtic Literature* (1867)—treat the "Celt" as essentially feminine and, therefore, complementary to the more masculine Germanic or Teutonic races (emphasizing the Saxon influence in English society). For Arnold, the Anglo-Saxon and the Celt formed a sort of family—with the Anglo-Saxon as the stern, unimaginative parent and the Celt as the ineffectual, intractable, and dreamy child—*"always ready to react against the despotism of fact"* (1973a, 343; emphasis in original). Significantly, both works refer to the Orient while defining Celticity.

The contemporary Irish inherited the ancient and classical characterizations of the "Keltoi" and many other "barbarians" of Europe and Asia as in *The Irish Race in the Past and the Present* (1883) by the Jesuit Augustus J. Thébaud (1807–1885). Thébaud treats the Irish in a patronizingly sympathetic light as immutably ancient Celts, similar to the peoples of the immutably ancient and "apathetic races of Asia" (41).[30] Other writers less sympathetic to the Gaelic Irish, especially conservative Anglocentric intellectuals, compared the Celt and the Oriental in a more damning manner. As British colonialism took hold in Asia and West Asia, these Irish intellectuals, most of whom had long opposed theories of the Oriental origins of the Celts, asserted and highlighted their lack of civilization and promoted the racial "primitive" similarities of the colonized peoples. In an 1833 article, the Reverend Samuel O'Sullivan compared Irish Ribbonism to the Thuggee in India, "if the Thugs are their superiors in the article of safe and expeditious murder, they are immeasurably beyond the Thugs in the article of skilful perjury" (qtd. in Gibbons 1996b, 143). Such comparisons became more racialized with colonial expansion. For instance, John Pentland Mahaffy's (1839–1919) severely racist *Twelve Lectures on Primitive Civilizations and Their Physical Conditions* (1869) repeatedly compares the Celts with Orientals, Africans, and Native Americans, as well as with Neolithic hunter-gatherers (243).

Mahaffy, a Trinity professor and well-known Dublin intellectual, cites ancient Greek and Roman texts as well as Renan and other Orientalists in drawing his conclusions that the Celtic Irish represent a "perpetually" primitive people, semiotically linking the Drunken Irishman to the Red Indian and the Black Sambo and directly applying Roman representations of continental Gauls and Celts to the contemporary Irish:

> Celts have shown indubitable and marked peculiarities from the days of Julius Caesar to the present; so much so, that a brilliant description of the Gauls, by a great living German historian, might pass for an account of the present Irish peasantry. . . .
> "[T]he laziness in the culture of the fields; the delight in tippling and brawling; the ostentation; the language full of comparisons and hyperboles, of allusions and quaint turns; the droll humour; the hearty delight in singing and reciting the deeds

of past ages, and the most decided talent for rhetoric and poetry; the curiosity—no trader was allowed to pass before he had told in the open street what he knew, or did not know, in the shape of news—and the extravagant credulity which acted on such accounts." (8–9)

Mahaffy's essentialist argument, overtly disdainful of the working class and rural Irish culture and ignorant of sociopolitical factors, was not uncommon in Anglo-Irish intellectual circles. Nor were depictions of the rural Irish as a primitive people uncommon in conservative English culture, as numerous studies over the past two decades have demonstrated. Although the political perspective of Anglocentric scholars like Mahaffy differed enormously from the point of view of cultural nationalists, they drew on similar Celtic-Oriental affinities. These pseudoscientific categorizations of Celts, Orientals, and other "primitives" strengthened an East-West semiotic connection and treated Irish culture as the inheritor of Europe's barbarian past.

Irish Romantic Orientalism: Sydney Owenson's Celtic and Oriental Tales

Before Victorian writers treated Celtic and Oriental sensibilities as unproductive and uncivilized, many British Romantics, including Samuel Taylor Coleridge, Walter Savage Landor, Robert Southey, Percy Bysshe Shelley, and Lord Byron, esteemed Celtic and Oriental realms, treating them as wild and sensual and occasionally as similar. They based much poetry and many novels on the scholarly work and sympathetic translations of Orientalists such as Schlegel and Jones. Irish Romantic writers, particularly Sydney Owenson (Lady Morgan) (1776–1859) and Thomas Moore (1779–1852), likewise celebrated the Celtic and the Oriental and relied on German, English, French, and Irish Orientalist scholarship. Both writers linked the two types, relying on Irish origin legends and antiquarian works, and created a dialogue between them in their allegorical and allusive works. Near mid-century, the Irish nationalist poet James Clarence Mangan (1803–1849) exposed the politics of Orientalist representation in his translation parodies. Later in the century, other Irish literary Orientalists, such as Aubery de Vere (1814–1902), continued a tradition of an idealized Orient but also recognized Ireland's Oriental affinity and imperial participation. These Irish authors have rarely been discussed as part of a tradition of Irish Orientalism, but their Oriental and Celtic tropes comment on Ireland and carry what John O'Donovan called the "traditional history" of Ireland through nineteenth-century literature (1845, xxviii).

Into the beginning of the twentieth century, Irish writers continued to discuss the processes of Orientalist representations and encouraged Irish cross-colonial affinities with nationalists in India, Egypt, China, Africa, and elsewhere in the Empire. Based in part on ancient Irish consanguinities with the Orient, Irish writers discovered the malleability and cultural power of representations of both the Oriental and the Celtic. The constructed nature of the Orient, and its supposed lure of sensuality, had been thematic tropes for Irish authors since the eighteenth-century rise to prominence of the East India Company. In *The History of Nourjahad* (1767), an Oriental romance by Frances Sheridan (1724–1766) (née Chamberlaine and mother of Richard Brinsley Sheridan), the protagonist learns how to govern his desires over the course of the story. As with Johnson's *Rasselas,* this is a fablelike tale of moral education, but in Sheridan's work, the Oriental realm of opulence and unlimited sensuality is revealed as a construction and an illusion, unlike the Xanadu of Johnson's *Rasselas,* which exists, although it cannot be found. In Sheridan's tale, the just king (though he at times appears despotic) constructs a complex illusion of a false Orient in order to satiate the youthful prince Nourjahad and dispel his fascination with opulence and ease. Although the story relies upon standard Oriental tropes—seraglios, despotic rulers, sensuality, superstition, untrustworthy Orientals—these tropes are shown to be fabrications that have little to do with the business of actual life in Persia. In the end, Sheridan exposes the Orient to be a construct and rhetorically de-Orientalizes Persia. This awareness of the constructed nature of the Orient pervades Irish literary Orientalism, and occasionally exposes the Irish Celt.

Ireland's first professional woman writer, Sydney Owenson (later Lady Morgan), published seventy volumes over the course of her career and received an annual literary pension of three hundred pounds from the British government beginning in 1837. Her most popular novel, *The Wild Irish Girl: A National Tale* (1806), went through seven editions between 1811 and 1834 (Wright 2002, 40) and established her as an Irish literary figure across Europe. Another novel, *The Missionary: An Indian Tale* (1811), also found a wide audience. Both influenced many writers of the day, and Percy Bysshe Shelley repeatedly read and prompted others to read *The Missionary.* The earlier work also influenced many Romantic novels and nineteenth-century romances, and critics of the day used the term *Owensonian school* to describe sentimental novels. Charles Robert Maturin's (1780–1824) novel *The Wild Irish Boy* pays tribute to Owenson's work in its title, but Owenson's work also shaped the vision of writers outside Ireland. As Ina Ferris argued in 1991, the first of Sir Walter Scott's Waverley Novels owes much to Owenson's national tale.[31] The narrative form of *The Wild Irish Girl* principally resembles the English epistolary novel of the eighteenth century, but ideologically, historically, and culturally, the novel has other sources. Owenson highlighted these sources in her footnotes, which function as the paratext to the text, offering a historical commentary, and grounding the plot within antiquarian and cultural nationalist historiography.

The popularity of this novel in England, Ireland, and across Europe owes much to the manner in which Owenson introduced a "wild Irish" culture to the readers. Her lens, as in the earlier pseudoletters of Oliver Goldsmith, was that of an English protagonist visiting Ireland. Most of the novel is composed of the letters of Horatio, the son of a landlord, and concerns his forays into the wild culture of western Ireland. There he meets the local fading Gaelic aristocracy, still vibrant and redolent with the past and an Oriental heritage. Horatio falls in love with Glorvina (from *glór bhinn,* "sweet voice" in Irish), a forceful woman, daughter of the prince of Inismore. He also spends time conversing about Irish antiquities with Father John, a Catholic priest steeped in Irish antiquarianism. These letters from a sympathetic English witness to Gaelic culture create a sentimental bridge from the modern world to an idealized Gaelic, Celtic realm. Although the characters in the novel clearly belong to distinct groups and cultures, the novel's happy ending suggests hybridity and tolerance.

Owenson's own family and identity were mixed. Her mother, Protestant and English-born, married an Irish-speaking Catholic actor, who Anglicized his name from MacOwen to avoid prejudice when he began his stage career. Owenson grew up in a cross-cultural atmosphere, "bilingual, binational, and bireligious" (Wright 2002, 17). Owenson's own hybrid identity allowed her to mingle in various circles—political, literary, musical, aristocratic, Protestant, and Catholic in Ireland and England—that are reflected in her writings about religious and cultural differences. When abroad in England as a young novelist (as Julia M. Wright, Kathryn Kirkpatrick, and other Owenson scholars have pointed out), she often performed her "Irishness," becoming an exotic lass from wild Gaelic country, similar to the less successful performative personalities of Oliver Goldsmith ("I am—but what signifies what I am") and W. B. Yeats's dreamy and masked London Celticism in the 1890s. She answered socially to the name Glorvina, wore a Gaelic mantle to society parties, and played the harp for her hosts, displaying what she called her "flimsy, fussy, flirty Celtic temperament" (qtd. in Campbell 1988, 100).

Many of Owenson's novels, particularly *The Wild Irish Girl* and *The Missionary* (later republished as *Luxima, the Prophetess: An Indian Tale* [1859]), are striking in their use of an iconographic feminine figure at the center of the novel. In *The Missionary,* Owenson explicitly has Hilarion, the missionary, see Luxima as "the emblem of that lovely region" (2002, 202). Such use has a long tradition in Irish literature, perhaps most famously in the *aisling* tradition of Irish poetry, in which a woman stands as an emblem of the nation that the male narrator fights to liberate or recover.[32] Owenson's female protagonists in these novels do not merely wait for rescue from a nationalist hero, however. Nor do they merely represent in their independence the embodiment of the imperial feminization of both the Celt and the Oriental. Both of these novels, this "national tale" and this "Indian tale," rhetorically defy the discourses they operate within, illustrating typical rhetorical moves within the unacknowledged discourse of Irish Orientalism.

In *The Wild Irish Girl,* the most salient allusions to the Orient occur as references to the origins of the Irish, which also serve as refutations of British depictions of Irish barbarism. Applying antiquarian scholarship to her fictional Gaelic, Celtic, and Milesian aristocracy, Owenson fanned the enthusiasm for Celtic tropes in European literature, glowing since MacPherson's Ossianic tales. But this Celticism also borrowed heavily from its twin discourse of Orientalism, then increasingly appearing in Romantic writing. As ethnographic representations of Oriental cultures increased, Irish pseudohistorians pursued similar studies, using Orientalist generalizations to bolster their impressions of an ancient Celtic Irish culture, which supposedly lingered around the fringes of the British Isles.

Owenson built her idealized western Ireland on explanations such as the ones discussed in chapter 2 but also used her own family for evidence. A footnote to an observation of Horatio, the Saxon admirer of the Celts in the novel, demonstrates the train of affiliation that Owenson uses. Her footnote to the following quote demonstrates how Owenson validates and fictionalizes antiquarian theories. She backs up the apparently accurate observations of Horatio, the rational English observer, with antiquarian pseudoscholarship, both validating Ireland's Oriental heritage and fleshing out the exotic Celtic-Oriental vision:"I observed that round the heads of the elderly dames were folded several wreaths of white or coloured linen." The note to the line cites and paraphrases Joseph Walker's 1788 antiquarian text: "'The women's ancient headdress so perfectly resembles that of the Egyptian Isis, that it cannot be doubted but that the modes of Egypt were preserved among the Irish.'—*Walker on the Ancient Irish Dress,* page 62." Following this evidence, we are given additional proof, which uses the author's voice to support the fictional and scholarly evidence given by the narrator and Walker: "The Author's father, who lived in the early part of his life in a remote skirt of the Province of Connaught, remembers to have seen the heads of the female peasantry encircled with folds of linen in form of a turban" (45). Another footnote a few pages later further discusses the veil "termed fillag, or scarf" by Irish women in the fifteenth century, and cites "a quaint and ancient author" for reference. The note compares the Irish to the Greeks (one of many such comparisons throughout the novel) but ends by noting that the real "origin was probably merely oriental" (48).[33] The appellation "mere" echoes an English classification of the Irish—differentiating them from their Norman and *Sean-Ghall* neighbors in the fifteenth, sixteenth, and seventeenth centuries[34]—but here it is used to distinguish the Celtic origin of the Irish from their other supposed origins: from Phoenicia. This network of references—fictional, scholarly, personal, traditional, English, and Irish—sustains the plausibility of Oriental origins, at least in the world of the novel. But such origins are not ends in themselves in the novel; they correlate actions in the present to antiquity with the goal of distinguishing Irish culture.[35]

Two types of Irish-Oriental comparisons are presented, reflecting the Irish origin legends and the history of Irish-Oriental comparisons. Through Horatio's reeducation, Owenson provides the reader further details of Ireland's Oriental origins, mostly when Horatio studies Irish (predictably using "Vallancey's grammar") (162). Both the prince and Glorvina agree to help him, and Horatio writes to his friend back in England about the blurring of the past and the present, making antiquity familial:

> Behold me then, buried amidst the monuments of past ages!—deep in the study of the language, history, and antiquities of this ancient nation—talking of the invasion of Henry II as a recent circumstance—of the Phœnician migration hither from Spain, as though my grandfather had been delegated by Firbalgs [*sic*] to receive the Milesians on their landing. . . . In short, infected by my antiquarian conversation with the Prince, and having fallen in with some of those monkish histories which, on the strength of Druidical tradition, trace a series of wise and learned Irish monarchs before the Flood, I am beginning to have . . . much faith in antediluvian records. (88)

Having agreed to entertain the validity of Irish antiquarian studies, Horatio's point of view and cultural allegiances shift, and the references to Irish origins move from the footnotes into the main story.

In support of Oriental origin legends, Owenson cites Irish authors Keating, Ledwich, Walker, Brook, O'Hallaran, and Vallancey, moving their theories into this new "novel" genre. But she also develops Irish-Orient similarities, which include comparisons with the ancient Greeks. The Gaels in the novel carefully distinguish themselves from the Greek culture; nevertheless, they give both ancient groups a common origin. Horatio writes:

> When I remarked the coincidence of style which existed between the early Greek writers and the bards of Erin, Glorvina replied, with a smile, "In drawing the analogy, you think, perhaps, to flatter my national vanity; but the truth is, we trace the spirit of Milesian poetry to a higher source than the spring of Grecian genius; for many figures in Irish song are of oriental origin; and the bards who ennobled the train of our Milesian founders, and who awakend the soul of song here, seem, in common with the Greek poets, 'to have kindled their poetic fires at those unextinguished lamps which burn within the tomb of oriental genius.' " (92)

Such an analogy points to how a casual English visitor may see all peripheral cultures similarly. As Pliny saw barbarians as culturally alike (if "wholly ignorant of one another" [Koch and Carey 2000, 33]), so Horatio often sees the Irish Celts as Oriental. Horatio later compares the local "devotees" at a Catholic mass to Muslims praying: "[A] crowd of *devotees* were prostrated on the earth, praying over their beads with as much fervour as though they were offering up their orisons in the golden-roofed temple of Solyman" (Owenson 1999, 134). Horatio's suspicions of both religions inspire this comparison of Catholicism to Islam. His wonder of the mystical men leading the mass, one of whom is Father John, inspires another Orientalist comparison: "The sermon was delivered by a little old mendicant, in the Irish language. Beside him stood the parish priest in pontificalibus, and with as much self-invested dignity as the *dalai lama* of Little Thibet could assume before his votarists." A little further on, another side of his imperial vision becomes manifest when describing Glorvina's dancing: "Her little form, pliant as that of an Egyptian *alma,* floats before the eye in all the swimming languor of the most graceful motion, or all the gay exility of soul-inspired animation" (146). Horatio's comparisons between Irish culture and the Orient reveal an exoticizing vision, in which the Oriental Celt is painted variously as fanatical, mystical, and sensual, with Father John as an exotic Tibetan lama and Glorvina as a languorous Egyptian dancing girl.

Through Horatio's education, Owenson co-opts such comparisons within the "traditional history" of Ireland, which is gradually revealed to the Englishman by the Irish characters, particularly Glorvina, the prince, and Father John. The priest explains, for instance, how Ireland, "owing to its being colonized from Phœnicia, and consequent early introduction of letters there, it was at that period esteemed the most enlightened country in Europe" (107) and how customs were carried "from Greece by our Phœnician progenitors" (143). Father John also offers reasons based in English colonialism to explain the disappearance of further records of Ireland's Oriental heritage: "'Manuscripts, annals, and records, are not the treasures of a colonized or a conquered country,' said the priest; 'it is always the policy of the conqueror, (or the invader) to destroy those memento of ancient national splendour which keep alive the spirit of the conquered or the invaded' " (174–75). This leads to a discussion in which Horatio asks: "'[H]ow is the barbarity of the present to be reconciled with the civilization of the enlightened past?' " Father John carefully addresses the process of barbarization, and the formation of Horatio's belief in Irish barbarity, which leads Horatio to admit his prejudice in his letters: "'When you talk of our *barbarity,*' said the Priest, 'you do not speak as you *feel,* but as you *hear.*' I blushed at this mild reproof, and said, 'what I *now* feel for this country, it would not be easy to express, but I have always been taught to look upon the *inferior* Irish as beings forming an humbler link than humanity in the chain of nature' " (176). After this discussion are some of the lengthiest footnotes in the book—on colonialism in Ireland and elsewhere.

The imperial comparisons of Horatio contrast vividly with the arguments and views of Glorvina and Father John, which are based in Irish origin legends and pseudohistory—arguments that are painted, like Glorvina herself, as "at once both *natural* and *national*" (120). Inevitably, the visions collide, as when Irish characters criticize the arguments of Spenser or Sir Philip Sidney (205) or seek to ground all Irish-Oriental comparisons in evidence (scholarly or personal), as when Glorvina asserts that the yellow dye of Gaelic clothing is indeed Oriental but is derived from local plants—not from urine as Camden suggested.[36] As Horatio's education proceeds, he admits the change in his perspective: "What a dream was the last three weeks of my life! But it was a dream from which I wished not to be awakened. It seemed to me as if I had lived in an age of primeval simplicity and primeval virtue. My senses at rest, my passions soothed to philosophic repose, my prejudices vanquished, all the powers of my mind gently breathed into motion, yet calm and unagitated" (123).[37] Understanding Irish antiquity and learning from Ireland's primeval sensibility prepare Horatio to overcome his anti-Gaelic prejudice. But the main result of his reeducation is his cross-cultural and antisectarian love for Glorvina. Out of tolerance, Owenson suggests, develop understanding and love.

Owenson later wrote explicitly about tolerance and bigotry in *Patriotic Sketches of Ireland* (1807), condemning its manifestations:

> The odiom of bigotry is generally thrown upon the subordinate sect of every country. Bigotry, however, is in fact the cosmopolite of religion, and adheres with more or less influence to every mode of faith. Of the countless sects into which the Christian church is divided, it appears that each, "dark with excessive light," arrogates to itself an infallible spirit, which shuts the gates of mercy on the rest of mankind, while it condemns or opposes to the utmost stretch of its ability, all whose faith is not measured by the standard of its own peculiar creed. All perhaps are alike zealots; the difference is, that the zeal of some is their privilege, and of others their crime. (qtd. in Owenson 2002, 284)

The perception of such religious and sectarian conflict accompanies Owenson's representations of the Orient and the Celt, perhaps because she was aware of the presence and history of the tropes. Julia M. Wright discusses Owenson's interest in religious (in)tolerance: "[P]erhaps because religion was so thoroughly politicized in Ireland, she makes her strongest statements against religious intolerance in her non-Irish novels" (43–44), particularly in *The Missionary: An Indian Tale*.

In response to cultural and religious difference, both of these novels promote tolerance, a dominant theme in much of the literature of Irish Orientalism. Unlike the Anglo-French discourse of the Orient, predicated on binaries such as civilized and savage, religious and superstitious, reason and feeling, these Irish Oriental differences are predicated on more triadic structures, in which a hybridity is immediately foregrounded. Such synthesis emerges after characters wrestle with imperial and anticolonial forces, vacillating between modernity and tradition. In *The Missionary* the protagonists struggle tragically toward consensus, caught between opposing cultural and religious forces. The novel's encoded critique of imperialism and missionary activities fosters its theme of tolerance and provides a number of hybrid East-West images, rooted in a Celticist aesthetic. Such affects made the novel influential both outside and inside Ireland.

Percy Bysshe Shelley's passion for *The Missionary* has been documented in Dennis R. Dean's 1981 introduction to the republished novel, and the entire Romanticist context, particularly the interest and praise of second-generation Romantics (Byron, Moore, and the Shelleys), has been explored elsewhere.[38] Clearly a novel of sensibility, *The Missionary* is also arguably one of the first historical novels and one of the first imperial romances. Set against the backdrop of the Spanish Inquisition as played out in India and imperial Spain's domination of Portugal—demonstrated in the tensions between "partisan" Spanish Jesuits and "patriot" Portuguese Franciscans (Owenson 2002, 71)—the plot of the novel concerns the mutual love of Hilarion, a Portuguese missionary, and Luxima, a Hindu Brahmin priestess.[39] A goal of any novel of sensibility was to refine readers' emotions and foster their moral feelings, prompting a change of action in the world; Owenson wrote also to encourage anti-imperial and antisectarian sentiments. As Julia M. Wright notes in her masterful introduction to the 2002 republication of *The Missionary:* "[Within Owenson's novel] colonial activity is not moderated by sensibility, but is the very sign of a faulty sensibility: as Hilarion falls in love with Luxima and rediscovers human feeling, he qualifies, then halts, and finally argues against the missionary project" (36). Critics have often pointed out[40] that this novel is less about a Portuguese priest's vacillating feelings for his beloved and his God than it is a debate about the ethics of missionary activity and colonialism. The novel traces the failed conversion of an Indian Brahmin priestess to Christianity. She struggles against her own designated place in Hindu culture and her unwitting embodiment as an Indian emblem of passionate resistance to European colonialism. The novel also offers a thinly veiled commentary on Ireland's internal and external conflicts. As with Owenson's later Italian travel narrative, which was more than once banned and burned, Irish politics can often be read in her discussions of other places (13).

The opening of the novel presents clear parallels between Portugal under Spanish domination in the early seventeenth century and Ireland in the years around the Act of Union and the 1798 uprising:

> [T]he national independence of a brave people faded gradually away, and Portugal, wholly losing its rank in the scale of nations, sunk into a Spanish province. From the

torpid dream of slavish dependence, the victims of mild oppression were suddenly awakened, by the rapacious cruelties of Olivarez, the gloomy minister of Philip the Fourth; and the spring of national liberty, receiving its impulse from the very pressure of the tyranny which crushed it. . . . It was at this period, that Portugal became divided into two powerful factions, and the Spanish partisans, and Portuguese patriots, openly expressed their mutual abhorrence, and secretly planned their respective destruction. Even Religion forfeited her dove-like character of peace, and enrolled herself beneath the banners of civil discord and factious commotion. (Owenson 2002, 71)

Complementing this allegorical political dimension, Portugal's antiquity suggests Ireland; as in *The Wild Irish Girl: A National Tale,* pastness is highlighted from the outset: "[T]he view seemed extended to infinitude by the mightier ocean, beyond whose horizon fancy sought the coast of Carthage; and memory, awakening to her magic, dwelt on the altar of Hannibal or hovered round the victor standard of Scipio Africanus." As in her "national tale," remnants of Portugal's ancient Oriental past survive alongside its contemporary Christianity: "the fragments of a Moorish castle, whose mouldering turrets mingle, in the haze of distance, with the lofty spires of the Christian sanctuary," providing "a magnificent assemblage of great and discordant images . . . harmonize[d] in one great picture!" (72). The overall imagery of the Portuguese landscape conveys "wildness," "solemnity," "grandeur," "gloom," and "genius and melancholy"—descriptions similar to the ones of Celtic locales.

Although Ireland is not mentioned in the text, Irish issues—political, historical, and cultural—are addressed at one remove. Many of the restrictions on Catholic civil liberties in the penal laws were still in effect, and the recent Act of Union (1800) had disbanded the Irish Parliament, bringing Ireland under British parliamentarian rule. The religious discrimination against Catholics is represented in the Spanish Jesuit persecution of the Portuguese Franciscans. The main lessons of the novel concern tolerance among religions, cultures, casts, and sects, lessons that are hard-won by the long-suffering protagonists. The cruelty of religious zeal is not limited to either Christianity or Hinduism, and both of the main characters are eventually excommunicated: Hilarion by Catholic Inquisitors and Luxima by Brahmin traditionalists, headed by her grandfather. Julia M. Wright describes the context of Ireland at the time: "In 1800, the Act of Union took away 'savage' Ireland's Parliament, and then gave 'sister' Ireland some seats in the British Parliament—one of the many signs of uncertainty over how to fit Ireland into the British Empire, as the outer rim of the imperial centre, or as the inner rim of the colonial periphery. Throughout the nineteenth century, Ireland teeters on the brink of both" (2002, 22). This liminality or doubleness, belonging to Europe and not, existing on the rim of the metropole and the periphery, however, had emerged before the rise of the East India Company. Ireland's position may have become clearer in the nineteenth century, but this liminality stretches back to Ireland's origin legends and Greco-Roman imaginings of Ireland, the barbaric Celts and the wild Asian Scythians. British imperialism did not create Ireland's border identity, but it certainly reified and strengthened it. In response to this doubleness in culture, many in Ireland had long embraced a hybridized culture, as portrayed in the origin legends. The dualism of the Anglo-Irish conflict fitted within this heritage.

Owenson's choice of India was strategic; it built upon existing semiotic ties between Ireland and India, and, as Wright suggests, at the time India focalized the debate on imperial ethics:

> In the context of an ongoing debate about religious tolerance and colonial policy in India, Owenson's choice of location is particularly apt: in 1810, a decade after the Act of Union, and before O'Connell re-energized the fight for Catholic Emancipation, Ireland was largely considered a settled matter by the British. India, however, was the new field of imperial debate: economic ethics, administrative policies, official toleration, and the advisability of allowing missionaries unfettered access were all being hotly debated. (29)

Following on the tremendous success of her autoexoticist "national tale," *The Missionary* shows another element of Irish cultural identity. Instead of continuing to wax about Ireland's antiquity and its "oriental nature," Owenson wrote allegory and discussed issues relevant to Ireland in an imagined Oriental realm.

Nevertheless, the novel had some grounding in Indian politics. The first edition was written after a revolt by Indian soldiers in 1806, known in Britain as the "Vellore Mutiny." The title of the later edition—*Luxima, the Prophetess* (1859)—released shortly after the Indian revolt of 1857,[41] reveals Owenson's, then Lady Morgan's, shifting concerns. In a sense, the novel has two central characters, both of whom Owenson/Morgan gave titular status. As Gauri Viswanathan has noted: "Luxima's displacement of the missionary as the plot's main figure [in the 1859 edition] is Owenson's concession to the progressive irrelevance of missionaries in the confrontational atmosphere immediately preceding and following the 1857 rebellion" (1998, 27). The climax of the novel arrives as a crowd of Indians spontaneously revolts as they watch the Spanish Inquisitors begin to execute (by burning) unnamed Indians along with Hilarion, the male protagonist and former missionary. Luxima, in a trancelike state, provokes the revolt when she attempts to throw herself into the fire:

> A sudden impulse was given to feelings long suppressed:—the timid spirits of the Hindoos rallied to an event which touched their hearts, and roused them from their

lethargy of despair;—the sufferings, the oppression they had so long endured, seemed now epitomized before their eyes, in the person of their celebrated and distinguished Prophetess—they believed it was their god who addressed them from her lips—they rushed forward with a hideous cry, to rescue his priestess—and to avenge the long slighted cause of their religion, and their freedom. (Owenson 2002, 249–50)

The transport of Luxima from a priestess to a "prophetess" and "avatar" (249), an embodiment of the divine, signifies how she, even more than Glorvina, becomes an emblem of resistance.

This work is not a straightforward anticolonial text, however. It clearly operates within the discourse of Irish Orientalism, both strategically deploying Anglo-French narratives and complicitly repeating tropes that served imperial aims. For instance, because Owenson's knowledge of India was limited to Anglo-French representations (and her suspicions of them), she presented Hinduism as more or less monotheistic, dominated by a sensual spirituality. The inner struggle—what Owenson calls the "complexional springs of passion" (100) of Hilarion, or the "Nuncio," between physical and divine love—signifies the broader European preoccupation and misapprehension of the Orient, which based its understanding of India on Vedanta and Bengali Vaishnavism. They, in turn, were based to a large degree on the translations of William Jones and others in the Asiatic Society at the time, and treated Hinduism as a sensual religion that mingled the erotic with the divine, basing their understandings of Hinduism primarily on Sanskrit texts (consonant with the Protestant tradition of locating religion in its texts).[42] Luxima describes her understanding of the distinction between European Christianity and the sensual religion of the Orient in terms of sensibility and emotion: "Father, with us the divine wisdom is not personified, as cold, severe, and rigid; but as the infant twin of love, floating in gay simplicity in the perfumed dews which fill the crimson buds of young camala-flowers" (149). Such "gay simplicity" developed as an aspect of the mystical stereotype of Oriental religion in the Orientalist literature of the nineteenth century, as Richard King, Edward Said, and other postcolonial scholars have noted.[43]

Owenson originally wrote her novel during a period when the question of whether European missionaries should be allowed in India was debated. The East India Company, founded in 1600 under the leadership of General Robert Clive (1724–1775), had enmeshed itself with local Indian governments in the eighteenth century, principally in Bengal in northwest India. But Britain did not have a civilizing mission there at the time. The critic and Romanticist Siraj Ahmed treats *The Missionary* as complicit in the development of such a mission within the British Empire, referencing the 1805 publication of Claudius Buchanan, *Memoir of the Expediency of an Ecclesiastical Establishment for British India*. Buchanan served as the Calcutta chaplain for the East India Company and called for "civilizing the natives": "Although the East India Company had established the colonial government in Calcutta four decades earlier in 1765, it prohibited missionary activity, and the *Memoir* was the *first* statement by a Company official calling for the evangelism of the native population" (n.d., 3). Following a lengthy public debate about civic and religious principles and imperial policy, Parliament renewed the EIC's charter in 1813 but with significantly different terms, as Ahmed notes: "Parliament in effect transformed the public rationale behind British imperialism in India fundamentally: while the eighteenth-century merchant empire justified itself merely in terms of the revenue it provided the British state, 1813 in effect finally inaugurated the civilizing mission in British India" (8). Irish missionaries later played significant roles in these missions well through the twentieth century, particularly in humanitarian and educational work. Such missions demonstrated Irish complicity with British imperial projects, even though within missionary ranks and often in Ireland these efforts were treated in opposition to the British Empire, their "Christian" activities, they believed, composing an alternate empire—of God, not man. These modernizing missionary programs, nevertheless, often sought to dismantle the religions of the cultures they worked to aid.

Dramatizing both imperial complicity and anticolonialism, *The Missionary* is a cornerstone of the unacknowledged discourse of Irish Orientalism. Owenson brings binary tropes of the East and West together in her novel, as imagined in Irish pseudohistory; for instance, when Luxima and Hilarion meet, Owenson writes: "Silently gazing, in wonder, upon each other, they stood finely opposed, the noblest specimens of the human species, as it appears in the most opposite regions of the earth; she, like the East, lovely and luxuriant; he, like the West, lofty and commanding" (2002, 109). Although Julia M. Wright does not acknowledge an Irish tradition of Orientalism, her discussion reveals some of its characteristics:

> Owenson's text is ideologically and representationally hybrid. It uses orientalist clichés that align the East with the passive, emotional and feminine, and the West with the active, rational and masculine. It uses sentimental clichés that posit a universal sensibility that cuts across cultural difference, and privileges emotion over reason. And it has a heroine who thinks and acts on her own, retaining her commitment to her religion and arguing with the man she loves instead of submitting to his strong desire for her conversion. (2002, 38)

We witness the Western "lofty and commanding" perspective of Hilarion begin to soften, however, just as Horatio's had after spending three dreamy weeks in the west of Ireland.

In volume 2 of the novel, Hilarion's severity begins to crack as he recognizes the similarity of his and Luxima's points of view: "The Missionary remained motionless. The result of this interview convinced him, that in the same light as the infidel appeared to him, in such had he appeared to her; alike beyond the pale of salvation, alike dark in error" (Owenson 2002, 113–14). Temporarily returning to his dogmatism, Hilarion presents an absolutist, imperial argument about conversion in an either/or proposition:

> "Luxima," said the Missionary, sternly, "there is no medium; either thou art a Pagan or a Christian; either I give thee up to thy idols and behold thee no more, or thou wilt believe and follow me."
>
> "Then I will believe and follow thee," she replied quickly, yet trembling as she spoke.
>
> "O Luxima! would I could confide in that promise! for, through thee alone, I count upon the redemption of thy nation." (150–51)

Believing in her conversion (as the emblem of India) and denying his own feelings for Luxima, he seeks "pertinaciously to deceive himself" (159) and uphold the East-West, pagan-Christian binarism, but his feelings for Luxima do not fit the duality: "Love was not only opposed to religion, to reason—in his belief, it was at that moment opposed to his eternal salvation! . . . The voice of Luxima came between him and his God" (163). By the third volume, we see Hilarion speak "with the circumspect reserve of one who feared to trust his feelings" (214), but his allegiance to Luxima clarifies during moments of crisis and revolt.

In volume 3, Owenson presents Hilarion as a failed missionary, unable to drive a snake away from his beloved embodiment of the Orient: "Close to the brow of the innocent slumberer lay, in many a mazy fold, a serpent of immense size: his head, crested and high, rose erect; his scales of verdant gold glittered to the moonlight, and his eyes bright and fierce were fixed on the victim, whose first motion might prove the signal of her death. . . . Twice he raised his crosier to hurl it at the serpent's head; and twice his arm fell nerveless back, while his shuddering heart doubted the certain aim of his trembling hand" (213). Here Owenson nods to the apocryphal story of Saint Patrick, whose symbols include a crosier, when he drove the snakes out of Ireland and established Christianity, supposedly through a nonviolent conversion "nurtured by the same mild principle of toleration" and not "at the sword's point" (284).[44] Reading allegorically, with contemporary India and the Orient paired with early medieval Celtic Ireland, a significant difference arises. In Owenson's narrative, Christianity does not take hold; the snake avoids the missionary's crosier, being led away instead by the flute of an untouchable snake charmer. The scene reveals Owenson's critique of zealous missionaries as well as Hilarion's slippage from priest to lover, as he later realizes: "[H]e felt it was the heart of the woman he had seduced, and not the mind of the heathen he had converted" (220). Instead of conversion and Christian salvation, Owenson posits a sort of intercultural unity, symbolized by the caravan at the center of the novel.

The caravan poses a culturally diverse image of India: including the many Hindus of various castes, two Europeans, and others, "[t]he caravan was composed of five hundred persons of various nations and religions;—Mogul pilgrims, going from India to visit the tomb of their prophet at Mecca; merchants from Thibet and China, carrying the produce of their native climes, the Western coasts of Hindostan; Seiks, the Swiss of the East, going to join the forces of rebelling Rajahs, and faquirs and dervises, who rendered religion profitable by carrying for sale in their girdles, spices, gold-dust, and musk" (223). Amid this diversity, in an interview with the two Europeans in the caravan (who turn out to be Hilarion's Spanish Jesuit enemies), the missionary becomes "[o]ccupied by feelings of a doubtful and conflicting nature" (223–24) and launches into a critique of the "zeal of Christianity [that] should never forsake the mild spirit of its fundamental principles"—"hands stained with the blood of those, to whom they had been sent to preach the religion of peace, of love, and of salvation; for even the zeal of religion, when animated by human passions, may become fatal in its excess, and that daring fanaticism which gives force and activity to the courage of the man, may render merciless and atrocious, the zeal of the bigot" (225). The caravan is depicted as the syncretic model for the novel, offering the most inclusive vision of India, where violence comes only at the hands of colonizing Europeans.

As Luxima lays mortally wounded toward the end of the novel, Hilarion is struck with an image that suggests the tragic admixture of the religions of East and West: "[H]e turned his eyes on the Indian, he perceived that hers were ardently fixed on the rosary of her idolatrous creed, to which she pressed with devotion her cold and quivering lips, while the crucifix which lay on her bosom was steeped in the blood she had shed to preserve him." Owenson describes the pairing of Luxima's Hindu rosary and her bloody Catholic crucifix as an "affecting combination of images so opposite and so eloquent in their singular but natural association." This sight strikes Hilarion and overpowers his reason and zeal: "and the words which religion, awakened to its duty, sent to his lips, died away in sounds inarticulate, from the mingled emotions of horror and compassion, of gratitude and love" (256). Here the juxtaposition of these religious objects seems meant to assert the irrelevance of religious doctrine and the similarity of practices across cultures.

The most positive and hopeful image of East-West unity centers on nature and appears both early on and at the end of the novel. In volume 1, Hilarion finds Luxima's private place, the "secluded retreat of the vestal Priestess of Cashmire":

> He wandered through its illuminated shades, till he suddenly found himself in a little valley, almost surrounded by hills, and opening, by a rocky defile, towards the

mountains of Sirinagur, which formed a termination to the vista. In the centre of the valley, a stream, dividing into two branches, nearly surrounded a sloping mound, which swelled from their banks. The mound was covered with flowering shrubs, through whose entwining branches the shafts of a Verandah were partially seen, while the Pavillion to which it belonged, was wholly concealed. The eye of the Missionary was fascinated by the romantic beauty of this fairy scene, softened in all its lovely features by the declining light, which was throwing its last red beams upon the face of the waters. All breathed the mystery of a consecrated spot, and every tree seemed sacred to religious rites. (111)

This sacred spot, the "fairy scene," was also the place where Luxima often prayed. A few pages later, this "consecrated grove of the Priestess" sets the scene for where Hilarion finds "a young fawn in the fangs of a wolf." Hilarion spears the wolf with his crosier, then "rushes the animal" and strangles it, saving the fawn, which turns out to be a pet of Luxima's. The fawn's "moan of suffering," which had initially drawn him to the area, foreshadows Hilarion's later grief (115). This place, where the streams meet, later becomes the place of Hilarion's mourning for Luxima and his hermit's retreat. In the conclusion of the novel, twenty years after the revolt, local people tell of Hilarion's last years as a recluse—supposedly referenced by "an European *Philosopher*" (275) (Owenson drew on an account of Kashmir by François de Bernier):"'[H]e was,' they said, 'a wild and melancholy man! whose religion was unknown, but who prayed at the confluence of rivers, at the rising and setting of the sun; living on the produce of the soil, he needed no assistance, nor sought any intercourse; and his life, thus slowly wearing away, gradually faded into death'" (260). This place of confluence, rescue, and grief where once both protagonists prayed represents the symbolic juncture of East and West, a "fairy" place that pre-dates their religions. Notably, Hilarion prays at the rising and the setting of the sun—the same crepuscular hours, when day meets night, that inspired the "Celtic Twilight" writers at the end of the century.

Doubleness of Application: Moore, Mangan, and de Vere

Irish references to origin legends diminished in literature for much of the later nineteenth century, although Thomas Moore references various pseudohistorical arguments in his *History of Ireland* (1843), crediting arguments about Ireland's mixed Celtic-Phoenician origins.[45] But his most significant Orientalist work, *Lalla Rookh* (1817), does not mention Ireland's Oriental origin legends.

Later, another nineteenth-century Irish poet, Samuel Ferguson (1810–1886), did reference the origin legends in his poem "The Origin of the Scythians" in his *Lays of the Western Gael* (1865) and in his epic *Congal* (1872). Also, based on the format of *The Arabian Nights Entertainment,* he wrote a series of historical and legendary fictions, *The Hibernian Nights Entertainments* (first collected in 1857), but his references generally resist Irish-Oriental pairings and emphasize Ireland's "Western" status. Colin Graham in *Ideologies of Empire: Nation, Empire and Victorian Epic Poetry* offers valuable commentary on the works of this unionist and cultural nationalist poet of Ireland: "Ferguson was certainly aware that Ireland and the Irish were often understood in terms similar to those used of non-white races in the empire. To counter this he places Ireland in this 'descending' (or rather ascending) line of European civilization when he compares cultural practices in the Ireland of *Congal* with current practices in India" (1998, 116–17). In his footnotes to *Congal,* Ferguson compares bardic practices in India, citing the *Calcutta Review* (Aug. 1944) and "a similar tale preserved by Keating." He argues that the similarities in these tales demonstrate only that Ireland preserved ancient traditions that spanned East and West in primeval days; for Ferguson, Ireland's only distinction in this matter is that it sustained these legends longer than other European cultures. Graham continues: "According to Ferguson, India is now at the stage of development that Ireland (and the rest of Europe) was at centuries ago; therefore, Ireland is not like India, it is instead a European nation, involved in the development narrative of European culture, sharing a classical heritage with the rest of Europe (including, and especially, England)" (117). Ferguson, in short, emphasizes Ireland's place alongside England in the Western world; in order to do so, however, he had to address Ireland's Oriental heritage.

Outside philology and history, the Celtic-Oriental link developed more on allegorical levels, as seen in one of the most popular works of the early nineteenth century, Thomas Moore's *Lalla Rookh*. This Oriental romance received one of the largest advances of its day from the English publisher, Longman and Company.[46] The book became an incredibly popular success in both England and Ireland, as well as in other European countries and even in Persia. In some British magazines, favorable reviews made overt Celtic-Oriental comparisons between the subject (the Orient) and the author (an Irishman) of the text, discussing the similarity in Irish and Arab temperaments and natures. For example, Francis Jeffrey (a friend of Moore and fellow Whig) makes a particularly pointed comparison in the *Edinburgh Review:* "The beauteous forms, the dazzling splendour, the breathing odours of the East, seem at last to have found a kindred poet in that Green Isle of the West, whose genius has long been suspected to be derived from a warm clime, and now wantons and luxuriates in these voluptious [*sic*] regions, as if it felt that it had at length required its native element" (qtd. in Brown 1988, 22). Moore, the celebrated author of the *Irish Melodies* (and later author of *The Epicurean* [1827], set in Egypt), is rhetorically "suspected" of belonging to the Orient because of both the Celt's supposed Eastern origins and the nationalist affinities the work propounded.[47] But even before its much anticipated publication, *Lalla Rookh* was linked to the cause of

Irish nationalism; Lord Byron, for instance, referred to both the justness of the Irish "cause" and the brilliance of the forthcoming *Lalla Rookh* in his 1814 prefatory epistle to *The Corsair,* which was dedicated to Moore.

Moore tailored his Oriental romance to fit with the tenor of Oriental interests in Europe at the beginning of the nineteenth century, especially to fit with the enthusiasm for the luxurious East that English writers, such as his friends Byron and Samuel Rogers, had raised.[48] But he also appropriated Orientalism to suit Irish issues, particularly Irish nationalism, as we see in "The Fire-Worshippers" section, a point that has often been missed in recent criticism. The splash that *Lalla Rookh* made in England and Ireland—some critics hailed it as the pinnacle of Orientalist poetry—strengthened the link between the geniuses of the Celt and the Oriental while subverting British Orientalism.

Thomas Moore explained in the 1820 preface to *Lalla Rookh* that, following the tremendous success of his early *Irish Melodies,* he was in a sort of postfame hangover and had difficulty beginning *Lalla Rookh.* The task of writing something for an Irish nationalist and Catholic audience as well as an audience of Oriental Romanticism must have seemed difficult. But once he found an allegorical path in which he could represent the tensions of Ireland, he launched into the work: "But, at last, fortunately, as it proved, the thought occurred to me of founding a story on the fierce struggle so long maintained between the Ghebers, or ancient Fire-worshippers of Persia, and their haughty Moslem masters. From that moment a new and deep interest in my whole task took possession of me. The cause of tolerance was again my inspiring theme; and the spirit that had spoken in the melodies of Ireland soon found itself at home in the East" (1850, x). Reading allegorically, the Ghebers in "The Fire-Worshippers" represent the rebellious Irish, hounded by the invading Muslim and British forces. As Howard Mumford Jones noted in 1937, "The overtones are unmistakably those of Irish rebellion, particularly the Robert Emmet episode. Moore hymns the doomed patriots and goes out of his way to excoriate the wretch who betrayed their cause. . . . Hafed is a Persian Robert Emmet, Hinda the unfortunate Sarah Curan, and the traitor a composite portrait of government spies" (181). In addition, Daniel O'Connell is allegorically lambasted in "The Veiled Prophet of Khorassan" as the satanic demagogue, Mokanna, who manipulates the religious faith of the masses. In *British Romantic Writers and the East: Anxieties of Empire,* Nigel Leask contextualizes Moore's Oriental tale within British Romanticism and Whig Orientalism but notes:

> The political message of Moore's oriental revolution seems to be most fully intelligible in his native Irish context. . . . The ["Fire-Worshippers"] poem reworks the love story . . . in Byron's *Bride of Abydos* in a context allegorical of the predicament of Irish nationalists under the yoke of British domination. As Moore writes of the

Fire-worshippers (followers of a more ancient religion—Zoroastrianism/Catholi-cism—than that of their conquerors—Protestantism/Islam), "I should not be sur-prised if this story of the Fire-worshippers were found capable of *a doubleness of application*." (1992, 113, quoting Moore 1875, 90; emphasis added)[49]

Moore's use of allegory—"a doubleness of application"—seems to be a more reg-ulated and considered, but no less integral, version of what Luke Gibbons has de-scribed as allegory in other works and performances in Irish literature, culture, and politics.[50] In discussing the use of allegory by the agrarian protestors, the White-boys, Gibbons astutely notes how allegory had become, to some extent, a cultural condition: "It is not simply, therefore, that allegory [is] . . . a mask that can be re-moved at will: it is part of consciousness itself under certain conditions of colonial rule" (1996b, 142). Moore's Orient allegorizes the liminality of Ireland, which Gibbons describes as embodying a "double struggle"—"the anti-imperial struggle, on the one hand, and, on the other hand, an internal struggle . . . between consti-tutional nationalism and a dissident, insurrectionary tradition" (146).[51] Moore does not treat the Orient as an escape or pilgrimage for curious Europeans; rather, he seeks a symbolic "home" in the Orient to illustrate this double struggle of nation-ality in Ireland—both anti-imperial and an "internal struggle" over divergent modes of decolonization.

In *Lalla Rookh,* Moore constructs what he terms "the cause of tolerance," un-doubtedly an underdiscussed cause in Irish literature. This deliberately Irish cause, however, is not easily noticed when reading his work in the light of British Orien-talism. For instance, Terence Brown has argued that the immensely popular *Lalla Rookh* merely "confirms prejudices about Ireland and the Orient" without check: "So the Irish are oriental exiles who find their 'native element' in 'voluptious [*sic*] regions' east of the Bosphorus. In writing an Oriental romance, therefore, Moore confirmed British stereotypes of Ireland. But, he also wrote of the Orient in ways that made quite certain that any politically suspect potential in his material would have no opportunity to inhibit his critical and commercial success" (1988, 22). Al-though Brown is correct in concluding that Moore used the discourse of British Orientalism to guarantee financial success and even to cloak his politics, *Lalla Rookh* does more than merely echo British and French Orientalisms. In Moore's numerous and voluminous footnotes, we can discern a subversive difference and discover how the author straddles the divide between the center and periphery of Empire. One particular footnote demonstrates Moore's liminal position through his redefinition of the Enlightenment view of liberty. The footnote refers to these lines from "Paradise and the Peri":

> Downward the Peri turns her gaze,
> And, through the war-field's bloody haze

Beholds a youthful warrior stand,
Alone beside his native river,—
The red blade broken in his hand,
And the last arrow in his quiver.
"Live," said the Conqueror, "live to share
"The trophies and the crowns I bear!"
Silent that youthful warrior stood—
Silent he pointed to the flood
All crimson with his country's blood,
Then sent his last remaining dart,
For answer, to the' [*sic*] Invader's heart.

False flew the shaft, though pointed well;
The Tyrant liv'd, the Hero fell!—
Yet mark'd the Peri where he lay,
And, when the rush of war was past,
Swiftly descending on a ray
Of morning light, she caught the last—
Last glorious drop his heart had shed,
Before its free-born spirit fled!

"Be this," she cried, as she wing'd her flight,
"My welcome gift at the Gates of Light.
"Though foul are the drops that oft distil
"On the field of warfare, blood like this
"For Liberty shed, so holy is."
(1850, 117–18)[52]

This fallen hero may seem to indicate a sense of resignation and acceptance of
earthly defeat at the hands of the invading forces in exchange for eternal rewards in
heaven. But Moore's sentimental heroism also challenges the discourse from which
it emerges. The last line of this quote is interrupted on the page with the following
footnote, which has a marked change of tone. This note begins by implicating the
trope of the despotic Orient, highlighting its place in the readers' sense of the Orient—but then it turns to another agenda:

Objections may be made to my use of liberty in this, and more especially in the
story that follows it, as totally inapplicable to any state of things that has ever existed
in the East; but though I cannot, of course, mean to employ it in that enlarged and
noble sense which is so well understood at the present day, and I grieve to say, so little acted upon, yet it is no disparagement to the word to apply it to that national independence, that freedom from the interference and dictation of foreigners,
without which, indeed no liberty of any kind can exist; and for which both Hin-

doos and Persians fought against their Mussulman invaders with, in many cases, a bravery that deserved much better success. (118)

Here is the divided heart of Irish Orientalism—complicit and subversive, imperial and native. Although the text may seem supportive of Empire, the footnote actually undercuts ideas of imperial expansion. Although Moore mingled in an Anglocentric (though Whiggish) world when he wrote *Lalla Rookh,* he nevertheless wove strong anticolonial sentiments into a melodramatic Oriental romance, offering nationalist rhetoric and allegory amid the tropes and language of British Orientalism. Whereas Moore refers to "Mussulman invaders" instead of English colonizers, the allegory clearly implicates English imperialism. Moore's footnote— the paratext to the text—instead of justifying Orientalist conclusions offers a redefinition of Eastern liberty, one clearly amenable to Irish nationalism, one in which liberty itself depends upon "national independence."

James Clarence Mangan also picked up on the associations between the Oriental and the Celt, incorporating them into his "Literae Orientales," a series of pseudotranslations of West Asian poetry and prose (along with Mangan's invented Oriental poems), which appeared in *Dublin University Magazine* from 1837 to 1846. As David Lloyd has argued, these versions of Oriental translations are best understood as "parodic translations" of Persian, Turkish, and Arabic literature (1987, 115). What is relevant to note here is that Mangan did not merely reproduce the standard Orientalist techniques of translation; instead, he revealed (and thus subverted) the process of translation itself, as Lloyd explains in his intricate study of Mangan's cultural nationalism, *Nationalism and Minor Literature:* "What [parodic translation] refuses to do is to supersede the anterior [or original] texts on which it depends, a relationship which is itself parodied [by Mangan's footnotes]. . . . By holding open that relationship, the parodic text invokes reflection upon the appropriative or refractory nature of translation precisely by refusing to exonerate itself from the same processes" (1987, 115). Lloyd treats Mangan's translation strategy as both a subversion of contemporaneous translation theories and an element of his cultural nationalism. But Mangan's strategy had even wider ramifications. By encouraging the reader's consideration of the translation process by "refusing to exonerate" the traitorous work of the translator,[53] Mangan's translations and accompanying texts also challenge the very process of supplanting an "original" Oriental text with a civilized Orientalist version. In other words, by pointing out the incommensurability of Orientalist translations and their original West Asian texts, Mangan rhetorically undermines a fundamental goal of British and French Orientalism: to revive, supplant, and govern the Orient with European knowledge and capital.

Furthermore, while Lloyd does not discuss Mangan's sense of the semiotic link between the Oriental and the Celt in detail, he does point out that Mangan dryly noted that "according to Vallancey every Irishman is an Arab" in his preface to "Literae Orientales" (123). Many of his pseudotranslations also evince anticolonial, anti-British, and cross-colony sentiments; for example, "To the Ingleezee Khafir, Calling Himself Djaun Bool Djenkinzun" (1846) addresses John Bull:

> *Thus writeth Meer Djafrit—*
> I hate thee, Djaun Bool,
> Worse than Márid or Afrit,
> Or corpse-eating Ghool.
> I hate thee like Sin,
> For thy mop-head of hair,
> Thy snub nose and bald chin,
> And thy turkeycock air.
> Thou vile Ferindjee!
> That thou thus shouldst disturb an
> Old Moslim like me,
> With my Khizzilbash turban!
> . . . .
> Thou vagabond varlet!
> Thou swiller of sack!
> If our heads be all scarlet
> Thy heart is all black!
> Go on to revile
> IRAN's nation and race,
> In thy fish-faggish style!
> (1997, 3:158–59)[54]

While the voice of the "Old Moslim" Meer Djafrit rehearses stereotypes about the Orient, the allegorical connection between Erin and Iran cannot be overlooked. This image of the Oriental, and the Celt by allegory, is not uncritically put forward; rather, it is presented in order to be exposed as a production. Mangan was attentive to the constructed natures of what Lloyd calls "the parallel fashions of Orientalism and Celticism":

> The exoticism of both, which is sustained in the popular imagination by the comparative remoteness of their location from the centers of empire, is involved in the notion of an "original people" in the sense of one that is less removed from untamed natural origins than the civilized European. . . . The "originality" of the Oriental poet—or the Celtic—lies in his closeness to the "origins" of humankind and human feeling [which, it was supposed, had begun in the Orient]. Mangan's re-

sponse to such theories, particularly with regard to Oriental poetry, is simply to deny and even invert the premises on which they are based. (1987, 123–24)

This strategy of inversion, and even obviation, is prevalent in many Orientalist texts of Irish writers, particularly the works of cultural nationalists. Like the earlier intertextual Orientalism of eighteenth-century Irish writers, Mangan's inversions of Anglo-French Orientalist poetry succeeded, at least in part, because his inversions or translations did not immediately appear to be parodies. Unlike burlesques or travesties, they do not openly satirize an "original"; rather, they satirize translations of originals as well as the enterprise of Orientalist translations. The subtlety of his parodies is enhanced by the Orientalist tradition of literary repetition and affiliation, within which they purportedly operate. His "translations" thus seem, on one level, to contribute to the field of Anglo-French Orientalism, even as they subvert it. Mangan's "parodic translations" furthered such subversive uses of Orientalism in Ireland by disrupting both the process and the conclusions of many Orientalists and, by extension, many Celticists.

The allegorical dimension of Irish Orientalism continued to appear in the works of Irish writers throughout the century, particularly texts by writers who were concerned with Irish cultural nationalism, whether constitutional, insurrectionary, or unionist. Perhaps one of the most revealing examples of this Irish Oriental narrative in the second half of the nineteenth century is Aubrey (Thomas) de Vere's lyrical narrative, "Antar and Zara or 'The Only True Lovers,'" an Eastern Romance." De Vere began writing the romance in 1855 in the wake of the Irish Famine and during a swell of public sympathy for the reported persecution of Lebanese Christians by Muslims. He explains in the poem's preface that he began writing it during his Eastern travels in the 1850s but did not complete it until 1877. When it appeared in book form, it was paired with reprints of many of his "poems meditative and lyrical," which often promoted a vision of "Irish nationality" (as opposed to Irish nationalism)[55]—for example, "Roisin Dubh," "The Irish Slave in Barbadoes," and "Inisfail: A Lyrical Chronicle of Ireland." "Inisfail" (1861), in particular, is dedicated to "the sons of Ireland who, during the ages of her affliction, sustained a just cause in the spirit of loyalty and liberty" (1877, 49). This dedication illustrates de Vere's political sympathies, which belonged to many apparently conflicting camps: Anglo-Irish, Catholic, unionist, and Irish cultural nationalist. Moreover, tolerance, as in Moore and Owenson, became an important theme for him as he straddled several communities.

De Vere was the son of a prominent Romantic writer and friend of Wordsworth, Aubrey Hunt de Vere; the work of father and son was very similar and sometimes appeared in the same issues of magazines, such as the *National Magazine* in September 1830. Following his father's death in 1846 and throughout the

Famine years, de Vere's Irish sympathies became more politicized and outspoken. His *English Misrule and Irish Misdeeds: Four Letters from Ireland, Addressed to an English Member of Parliament* (1848), written during the first two years of the Famine, clearly outlines his critique of English-Irish relations, which he states perhaps most succinctly in "Letter III": "I believe England to have been and to be on the whole the justest, the wisest, and the strongest nation in the world: I believe also that the miserable state of Ireland proceeds mainly from [England's] injustice, folly, and weakness" (1970, 146). These "letters" resist clear-cut lines of blame yet promote an Irish national identity. Furthermore, they both subvert and enhance stereotypes of the rural Irish in discussions of England's misgovernance of its closest colony. Most relevant to this study are the numerous cross-colony and intra-imperial comparisons that de Vere makes between Ireland and other British holdings, particularly India. Although de Vere asserts that the "Irish are a race more dissimilar from the English than from most other European races, and they have reached a very different period of social progress" (147), he goes to lengths to portray the *ethnie,* nation, or "kingdom" (248) of Ireland as a willing, essential, and even consanguine member of the British Empire: "[W]hen the most warlike of the eastern nations precipitated itself upon your path, and all asked to whom India was to belong, two men rode, side by side, into the battle: one governed that empire, the other commanded her hosts; one was an Englishman, the other an Irishman. On those great occasions the soldiers who fought in common ranks were of no exclusive race: death was there impartial; and if Saxon and Celtic blood had never met before, it mingled on the . . . banks of the Sutlej" (261). Such admiring attention to Irish complicity with the British Empire did not preclude discussions of Ireland's position as a colony of England; indeed, for de Vere both are related. Though he distinguishes Ireland from India and other colonies, he still groups them in discussions of poverty, wealth, and Empire, concluding, "There is a direct connection between the wealth of your nation and the poverty of the obscure millions who produce that wealth" (206). Colonialism, first and foremost, is what links Ireland to India and other colonies. Although de Vere does not invoke the origin legends of the Celt, or make any explicit claims of racial affinity between the Celt and the Oriental, a connection between the two groups nevertheless persists.

Having converted to Catholicism in 1851, de Vere conspicuously resented English and Anglo-Irish religious discrimination and intolerance in Ireland. In *English Misrule and Irish Misdeeds* he compares England's strategies of addressing religious differences in its present and former colonies, contrasting England's policies and actions in America, India, and Ireland. Unlike America, which "was your colony [but] you did not plant your church in her soil," and unlike India, which "is yours; but its hundred millions belong not to your Master" (203), de Vere argues that Ireland had suffered immensely because of England's religious intolerance of Irish

Catholicism. Like Owenson and Moore, de Vere found the romantic Orient to be an apt vehicle for expressing religious intolerance. De Vere's "Antar and Zara," however, does not allegorize Irish tensions to the extent of Moore's *Lalla Rookh,* in part because it is a much shorter poem with a lesser scope. But de Vere also seems to have been more aware of Ireland's unique experience of colonial exploitation.

"Antar and Zara" is not an anticolonial narrative, nor is it anti-English, yet it argues for the cultural autonomy of a beleaguered people who define themselves in the face of a more powerful invader through their ethnic (or "racial"), geographical, and religious unity. The poem is meant to be a narrative in the form of songs. The lyrics, sung by the lovers, are set in Lebanon; both lovers belong to a "race" of Arab Christians who have lived "hundreds of years" resisting "the crescent flags of Saladin." Antar's description of their history signals that of Irish Catholics; indeed, this entire section could be accused of the same "doubleness of application" that Moore noted of his own Oriental romance:

> Seldom for us the unequal strife hath ceased:
> Age after age that martyr-crown we bear,
> Here in our old, untamed, inviolate East.
> (1877, 22)

In terms of scenery, setting, and tone, "Antar and Zara" resembles *Lalla Rookh,* but such similarities are only enough to make the plot differences more apparent. For instance, one particular passage of Antar's song addressed to Zara seems to build upon the passage from Moore's "Fire-Worshippers" previously quoted in which a "youthful warrior" fights a Muslim "Invader." In Moore's version, the "Invader" wins an advantage over the youth and asks him not to sacrifice himself needlessly but instead to "'live to share / 'The trophies and the crowns I bear!' " Spurning the offer to join forces, the youth continues to fight and is killed. In de Vere's poem, however, the role is reversed, and the defender has the upper hand:

> In single fight we met: the Invader fell;
> Two hosts stood mute, one gloomy, both amazed;
> His eyes, the eyes of one that hears his knell,
> On me, and not my lifted sword, were raised.
>
> Forth from that shivered helm outstreamed afar
> His locks dust-stained. From out those eyes there shone,
> Baleful in death, Hate's never-setting star:
> He hoped no mercy, and he asked for none.
>
> Then cried my heart, "A sister's hands have twined,
> How oft! those locks; a Mother's lips have pressed:

Perhaps this morn the cassia-shaking wind
Waved them, rich-scented, o'er his true love's breast."

"Foe of my Race," I said, "arise; live free
But lift no more against the Faith thy sword!"
Was it thy prayer, or but the thought of thee,
Rescued that sentenced warrior and restored?

(23)

Although the endings of the two poems differ enormously, they share the use of allegory and set tolerance as a dominant theme for these beleaguered Easterners. As an allegory for Ireland, de Vere's Orient not only posits a triumphant and enduring culture for Ireland, but also imagines a new tolerant relationship between the "Invader" and the "old, untamed, inviolate East." De Vere stresses the connection between the East and Ireland in both the preface to the poem and by publishing the Oriental romance beside the culturally nationalist poem "Inisfail."

As Owenson, Moore, Mangan, and de Vere explored issues of religious tension, advocating tolerance and unionism, in allegorical constructs of the Orient, later Irish writers envisioned a mystical and cultural unity for the Oriental and the Celtic. Such ties developed in a variety of ways during the Revival and differed from writer to writer, but by the twentieth century the use of the Orient as a realm in which to work through Irish cultural issues had been firmly established in Irish literature. Furthermore, in the mode of Swift Revivalists and Irish critics of colonialism and Irish culture often focused their attention on the *construct* of the Orient in order to foster an awareness of the processes of representation and, in general, Irish cultural decolonization. For many Revivalists, the analogical process that had historically linked the Celt and the Oriental (racially, culturally, politically) could be employed in the creation of a new Irish identity, one distinct from Britain. At the close of the nineteenth and the beginning of the twentieth centuries, as the Oriental and the Celtic became increasingly fashionable in Europe, Irish writers delved again into Asian and West Asian sources, renewing Celtic-Oriental connections and creating neo-Oriental-Celtic forms, images, and representations. Whereas some repeated the essential and stereotypical nature of images of the Orient and endorsed imperial ventures, as will be discussed in chapter 4, others focused on the constructed nature of the Orient and the Celt. Nevertheless, their various representations of the Orient—the various Celtic Orients of the Revival—thrived at the heart of literary production in late-nineteenth- and early-twentieth-century Ireland. Moreover, Irish Orientalism increasingly informed Irish anticolonialism and cosmopolitanism through cross-colony identification, which is explored in chapter 5. In chapters 6, 7, and 8, I explore how a quartet of Celtic

Orientalists, W. B. Yeats, George Russell (AE), James Stephens, and James Cousins, all inspired to varying degrees by Theosophy and Indian philosophy, consciously identified the Irish Celt with the Occident's cultural other as a means of cultural decolonization and Irish literary production. Almost to the same extent that they rhetorically identified with the Celt, they identified with the Oriental.

4 Empire, Ireland, and India

> Those Englishmen who know something about India, are even now those who understand Ireland best.
> — John Stuart Mill, *England and Ireland*

> [I]f Saxon and Celtic blood had never met before, it mingled on the . . . banks of the Sutlej.
> — Aubrey de Vere, *English Misrule and Irish Misdeeds*

A MAP OF IRISH INVOLVEMENT in the British Empire in the nineteenth and twentieth centuries would not divide neatly along sectarian borders. Even the political issue of Irish independence did not break evenly along sectarian lines. Too often, however, discussions of Irish participation in imperial projects devolve into nationalist, religious, or sectarian arguments. Indeed, polemicism is a hallmark of such discussions, which rarely do more than confirm convictions. Many Irish representations of the Orient expressed sympathies, particularly in the second half of the nineteenth century, with both British imperialism and Irish nationalism. Irish socialists, nationalists, and Republicans who worked for Irish independence did not always oppose British imperialism in Asian or African colonies, and Irish unionists did not unanimously support British imperialism in Asia and Africa. In actuality, a crosshatch of divided loyalties permeated Irish culture and its representations of the Orient; in the words of S. B. Cook, "a spectrum of responses . . . resulted from the complexity of the imperial relationship with Britain" (1987, 507).[1] Cross-colony ties did develop for many Irish writers, but such sympathies were nowhere near universal. Irish unionists, conservatives, popular writers, and missionaries tended to side with European imperialism in general, yet occasionally they wrote surprising critiques of imperialism and expressed an affinity with Asian anticolonialists and their cultures. Moreover, this complex blend of ideologies, representations, and experiences existed throughout the Irish diaspora.

Although Catholic nationalists did not always oppose imperialism and Protes-

167

tant unionists did not always embrace it, anticolonial arguments more often accompanied nationalist arguments than unionist ones, yet detailed criticisms of imperial day-to-day operations (in the tradition of Edmund Burke) often came from unionist camps, particularly prior to the twentieth century. Reading Irish culture as a network of influences and ideologies may contradict arguments based on Catholic and Protestant allegiances, but it certainly facilitates the recognition of a back-and-forth exchange among traditional Irish texts, modern British ones, and political actions.

Because of Ireland's increasing involvement in and resistance to British colonialism in the nineteenth century, the Irish-Oriental connection developed in myriad forms. Two recognizable elements continued throughout these various narratives, however: Ireland's perceived affinity with the Orient and the presentation of Ireland as a liminal culture, having a "both/and" quality that reflected Ireland's anomalous position in the British Empire.[2] Technically part of the United Kingdom, nineteenth-century Ireland embraced aspects of both imperial and anti-colonial politics. In the imagined geography of Empire, Ireland belonged somewhere between the backward periphery and the civilized metropole, and it unevenly assimilated (to borrow from Lloyd 1993) aspects of British culture. Yet, Irish culture had strong ties to its own ancient traditions, often unacknowledged as Irish, as in the case of Irish Orientalism. This liminal position recurs in many texts of Irish writers depicting the colonized Orient. Moreover, because Irish individuals involved in Empire often assume an intermediary role—as the interpreters of the colonized and as the representative of the colonizer—their texts promote a similar role in which Ireland is both peripheral and metropolitan. Understanding this anomalous position helps clarify the distinctive representations of Irish Orientalists in popular, academic, political, and literary texts, which have long been read through maladjusted and borrowed lenses.

Irish representations of the Orient shifted in the nineteenth century because of the increase in Orientalist knowledge in general. Texts from the eighteenth century and first half of the nineteenth century tended to depict a romantic Orient as a distant and allegorical realm. Individuals from the Orient, when represented, often appeared as fantastic figures on par with the remote Gaels and Celts of Ireland. As more Irish people traveled to Asia and Africa, mostly through the East India Company, other British concerns, or missionary organizations, more Irish texts, unsurprisingly, depicted Irish travelers in the East and began to more regularly depict Asian and West Asian cultures as backward and heathen. Nevertheless, an extraordinary number of texts continued to represent an Irish affinity (or even an ancient consanguinity) with the Orient, and this affinity took many forms, inspiring both resistance and submission. British comparisons of Irish and Oriental cultures also developed within specific analogies made by British imperialists, what have been termed "intra-imperial analogies" (Cook 1993, 17). Such imperial comparisons grew out of the practices of British administrators and out of the semiotic history between the Celt and the Oriental.

The history of the Irish in India and other territories of the British Empire deserves much discussion and study, but the emphasis of the present study is Irish Orientalism and not Ireland's role in India per se—both imperial and nationalist. Such work has been begun, and a number of historians, social scientists, and cultural critics are presently engaged in such studies. Some of the many existing studies are listed in the bibliography, including texts by Thomas Bartlett, Christopher Bayly, H. V. Brasted, S. B. Cook, T. G. Fraser, Michael Holmes and Denis Holmes, Narinder Kapur, Keith Jeffrey, Anne Maher, Hiram Morgan, Kavita Philip, and Michael Silvestri. Two of the most significant works are essay collections that address the diversity of Irish-Indian connections—military, political, literary, imperialist, nationalist, and missionary— *"An Irish Empire"? Aspects of Ireland and the British Empire,* edited by Keith Jeffrey (1996), and *Ireland and India: Connections, Comparisons, Contrasts,* edited by Michael Holmes and Denis Holmes (1997). Also, the fine work by the notable historian Christopher Bayly and the less academic history by Narinder Kapur, *The Irish Raj: Illustrated Stories about Irish in India and Indians in Ireland* (1997), present solid overviews of Irish involvement in India, as well as (in Kapur's work) the Indian involvement in Ireland. Thomas Bartlett, Michael Holmes, and others have argued that discussions of Irish nationalist affinities with India ignore the large numbers of Irish soldiers, civil servants, administrators, and missionaries who helped build and run the British Empire. H. V. Brasted and Michael Silvestri examine how Indian nationalists borrowed and learned from Irish nationalists, Brasted looking at the late nineteenth century and Silvestri at the 1920s. Christopher Bayly has explored the quadrilateral history of Britain, Ireland, India, and Egypt, discussing both nationalist identification and imperial analogies that have been drawn from the days of Wolfe Tone to the twentieth century. Not aiming to reproduce these important historical works, the ensuing discussion examines various nineteenth-century representations of Irish-Indian and Celtic-Oriental relations, mostly written by Irish Orientalists. Chapter 5 explores cross-colonial representations of the Orient, often rebounded off various "intra-imperial analogies," themselves often drawn from Celtic-Oriental comparisons.

A Story of Irish Orientalism

In the "General Survey" that opens *The Story of Irish Orientalism,* M. Mansoor (Menahem Mansūr)[3] notes that a group of "dauntless" Irish Orientalists "have gone out to convert and have ended in themselves being converted." Mansoor argues that this tendency toward conversion is due, essentially, to an Irish affinity with the

Orient: "[A]n affinity with the East had long been part of the Irish temperament." More so than their English counterparts, he asserts, "those [Irish] who went forth for other reasons soon succumbed to the fascination of their new environment and loved it for its own sake." For Mansoor, the Irish traveler's fascination and love of the Orient distinguishes them because the "Irish temperament" has always had "an affinity with the Orient" (1944, 13). Although this idea has a long tradition, Irish connections with the East often came through the British Empire throughout the eighteenth and nineteenth centuries. Indicative of a different quality in this connection, however, Mansoor employs collegial and familial language in describing how "indefatigable Irish Orientalists together with their British colleagues" (12) worked as the joint "builders of the Empire" (26).

The dozens of Irish Orientalists that Mansoor describes generally worked within the imperial realm of Irish Orientalism, being employed by Trinity College, Dublin, or one of the English universities in Oxford or Cambridge, yet even for such scholars Mansoor assigns independent, if less tangible, affinities with Oriental cultures. This assignment in part may have to do with the fact that many of these men studied not only cultures in the Orient but also Irish culture. As discussed in chapter 2, a number of Orientalists also doubled as Celticists, including, perhaps most famously, Ernest Renan, the French scholar. In Ireland, Whitley Stokes (1830–1909) serves as another example; he is primarily regarded as a Celtic philologist, but he spent much of his career working in the legal administration of British India. He drafted much of the Code of Civil and Criminal Procedure, published in the two-volume *Anglo-Indian Codes* in 1887 and earned the Most Exalted Order of the Star of India in 1879 (Welch 1996, 541). Along with the semiotic link between Ireland and India, the number of Irish soldiers, missionaries, and administrators going to India grew tremendously in the nineteenth century. The introduction to *Ireland and India: Connections, Comparisons, Contrasts* comments on Irish participation in British India: "In 1853, entry into the Indian Civil Service, the main administrative arm of British rule in India, was altered to a system of competitive examinations, and a number of Irish schools and colleges geared themselves towards the ICS entry exam. The ICS constituted the third main path through which Irishmen were attracted to India, alongside the military and missionary channels" (Holmes and Holmes 1997, 5). A difference often existed for Irish Orientalists based on the age-old semiotic comparison, and at times Irish writers seemed to go to lengths to overcome this supposed Oriental affinity, and other times they seemed to embrace it. The language used in Irish Orientalism repeatedly reflects this doubleness.

Even when critical of imperialism, many Irish writers (including nationalists) remained supportive of the British Empire, especially those writers whose identities had overlapping allegiances. Aubrey de Vere, for instance, straddled various camps as a unionist Catholic and Irish cultural nationalist critical of the British Empire (see chap. 3), writing to a British audience in 1848: "There is a direct connection between the wealth of your nation and the poverty of the obscure millions who produce that wealth" (1970, 206). Nevertheless, the Orient seemed the realm that could unite the British and the Irish. In 1848—the start of the worst Famine years—de Vere described Ireland as a willing and destined part of the British Empire: "[W]hen the most warlike of the eastern nations precipitated itself upon your path, and all asked to whom India was to belong, two men rode, side by side, into the battle: one governed that empire, the other commanded her hosts; one was an Englishman, the other an Irishman. On those great occasions the soldiers who fought in common ranks were of no exclusive race: death was there impartial; and if Saxon and Celtic blood had never met before, it mingled on the . . . banks of the Sutlej" (261). This mingling of Saxon and Celtic blood, a consanguinity achieved through violence, signals how Irish-English parity could be achieved within Empire. Ireland, though subjugated at home, could gain a privileged position in the imagined geography of Empire—often subjugating others. To this end, many Irish texts asserted the importance of Irish involvement in the soldiering as well as the subjugation and governance of Asian colonies. Normally, the role of the Irish abroad was in the development and maintenance of the Empire; generally, similar ideals, curiosities, and lusts motivated both the Irish and the British. As Mansoor asserts, "To a certain extent [Irish Orientalists] were influenced by the same motives as British Orientalists," that is, trade, power, the "responsibility of administration," and a "keen" linguistic and cultural interest—what amounts to the blend of historical specificity, knowledge, and power that unifies the discourse of Orientalism (1944, 13). Like the Irish literary Orientalist, the Irish academic Orientalist had recourse to the narratives of both colonizer and colonized, working with British colleagues and identifying with colonized cultures.

Spoils of Empire

Early in the period of imperial expansion, the Irish began to participate in the Empire as soldiers, low-level civil servants, merchant marines, missionaries, and Orientalists. Michael Holmes summarizes the history of Irish military participation:

> The East India Company was first allowed to raise a small number of troops in Ireland in the 1680s, but the numbers recruited were initially very low. It wasn't until the Seven Years War of 1756–63 that Irish recruitment began to take off. Between 1757 and 1763, almost 17 percent of recruits were from Ireland—825 out of a total of 4911. Between 1778 and 1793, almost 1,500 Irish soldiers were recruited. In the

early nineteenth century, as official reservations about enlisting Irish soldiers ended and demand increased, Irish recruitment rose dramatically. (2000, 236)

At the height of Irish involvement, Irish soldiers accounted for 40 percent of the East India Company's troops. Moreover, prominent Anglo-Irish aristocrats, such as Lord Mayo and Lord Dufferin, served as viceroys, and two men with Irish heritages, Frederick Roberts and Claude Auchinledck, held the position of commander in chief; furthermore, one-quarter of those employees in the Indian Civil Service were Irish (Silvestri 2000a, 40; Holmes 2000, 236). Holmes also reports that Indians generally held Irish soldiers to be somewhat more brutish than their English counterparts (237). Although the origin of such reputations raises many questions, the brutal acts of a number of Irish leaders abroad are well documented, including those of John Nicholsan, who orchestrated horrible mass executions in the Punjab after the Revolt of 1857; Sir Michael O'Dwyer, lieutenant governor of the Punjab, who assented to the use of force at the massacre in Amristrar in 1919; and Sir Charles Tegart, the police commissioner of Calcutta who headed the antiterrorism campaign in Bengal that suppressed Bengali nationalist activities. As Thomas Bartlett has argued, "[T]he archetypal Irishman on the sub-continent was neither missionary nor merchant, neither doctor nor administrator, but soldier" (1997, 12); moreover, the old adage about the British Empire that "the Irish fought for it, the Scottish and Welsh ran it, and the English profited from it" has some per capita truth. All the same, images of the Irish in Empire commonly accentuate the role of Irish nationalism over imperialism, as in the famous example of the mutiny of the Connaught Rangers, stationed in Solon, India, who refused to fight in 1920[4] after hearing of unrest in Ireland. This example is often used to point to the unified sympathies of the Irish abroad and at home and of their cross-colony identification—something that Thomas Bartlett and Michael Holmes flatly refute: "The mutineers of the Connaught Rangers 'made no attempt to make common cause with the Indians who surrounded them,' [argues Bartlett] and if anything sought to avoid any suggestion that there was a connection [argues Holmes]" (Holmes 2000, 237). Nevertheless, the memory (imagined or not) of this cross-colony identification in 1920 inspired generations of nationalists in both Ireland and India.

Despite Ireland's enormous imperial participation, Ireland's place in the British Empire has been infrequently acknowledged in Britain and Ireland, both now and then. Back in the 1840s, Irish MPs and leaders argued for greater recognition of Irish participation in British India while also lamenting the horrific results of British relief policies in Ireland in the 1840s. A reprint of an 1848 speech in the *Irish Quarterly Review,* "Government Patronage at Home and Abroad," by William Keogh, a leader of the Independent Irish Party in the British Parliament, mainly discusses the famine but begins by criticizing British discrimination against Irish officers in the

Indian Civil Service. As we will later see, this moment was significant in the development of Irish Orientalism. Attacking the "ruthless spirit of British domination," Keogh argues that Ireland is a neglected but reliable part of the British Empire:

> The inherent claims of this country—as an integral part of the empire—to a due participation in the honors and emoluments of the public service, have over and over again, for a long series of years, been recognized and acknowledged—verbally, of course, we mean—by every successive leader of the great contending English parties. . . . We have for ages, owing to our credulous confidence in plausible professions, been the poor and pitiful sport of every English faction in turn, which has used us to and for its own selfish purposes when, and where, and as it happened to require our aid, and then gratefully treated us in return with the grossest injustice, or the most galling contempt. That ruthless spirit of British domination, which for centuries of our early and mournful history marked its devastating progress through our island, in wholesale and undiscriminating confiscation, is still busily, though insidiously, at work in the piecemeal spoliation of our few remaining institutions, and in the stern and studied exclusion of Irishmen from the service of the Sovereign. (1851, 490)

With an urgent tone, Keogh attacks England's gross neglect and inhumane mismanagement of Ireland in the 1840s, but his main supporting point is that Ireland needs more responsibility within the British Empire and more recognition of its present activities within it. Ireland, he asserts, has not received the benefits it deserves as "an integral part of the empire."[5]

Keogh discusses discrimination against the Irish in tandem with the Famine in Ireland in 1848, yet he draws no connection between this "spoliation" of Ireland and other ruinous operations in other colonies. His arguments are clearly imperial. The benefits that Keogh lobbies for in this first section include more powerful governing positions for Irishmen, not for any fundamental change in the dynamics of the Empire—an argument that had real cultural force at the time. Keogh complains that "the ban of the Milesian brogue is upon" the "Hibernian Celt" when an Irishman wishes "official promotion." Indeed, only 13 out of 217 appointments in law or to the bench in India between the years 1832 and 1848 were given to Irishmen. This small percentage of ranking appointments particularly galled because of the high percentage of Irish soldiers enlisted.

A century later in an essay that manages to be both nationalist and imperialist at once, "Irish Soldiers in India," Sir Patrick Cadell cites the Bengal register of recruits in the India Office, noting that out of the 7,620 recruits "from 1825 to 1850 . . . 2,844, or 37.3 per cent, were English" and "830, or 10.9 percent [were] Scots," while "3,639, or 47.9 per cent, [were] Irish," and only "307, or 4 per cent, were born elsewhere" (such as Asia), a majority of whom had Irish surnames

(1950–1951, 78). Cadell also goes on to report that during the late 1840s there was a notable surge in the numbers of Irish recruits who sought relief from famine, totaling around 40,000 troops out of 100,000.[6] These numbers had a significant impact on Irish impressions and representations of India and the Orient, as historian Christopher Bayly notes: "The city of Cork may have had a more direct personal contact with India than any other place in the British Isles, including Dundee, during the nineteenth century" (2000, 389). Most Irish rarely had a proprietary relationship with the Orient (as Keogh's essay implies), particularly in the first half of the century, for the simple reason that the Irish dominated only the lower ranks; they had few positions of authority, a discrepancy that would change for a time in the second half of the nineteenth century.

Unlike other Irish Orientalist texts, no affinities are made in Keogh's text; no notions of sameness between the Irish and Indian (or the Celt and Oriental) are drawn in sensibility, race, temperament, culture, history, or situation. Indeed, they seem rather carefully avoided, and Indians are not discussed in his essay, nor are racial differences between the European and the Oriental explored. Nevertheless, as in de Vere's previously cited account of the Irish and British soldiers riding side by side, published in 1848, the same year of Keogh's speech, Irish and English racial and "blood" issues are specifically evoked in order to be reconciled and mingled. Indeed, the Empire and the Orient are what makes consanguinity and bring the blood of the Irish and English together: "[I]f Saxon and Celtic blood had never met before, it mingled on the plain of Waterloo, and the banks of the Sutlej" (1970, 261). Similarly, a main rhetorical goal of Keogh's essay seems to be to bring together the Saxon and the Celt through Empire, particularly by undermining the narrative of "Saxon" racial privilege.

> A proscribed Irishman, to be sure, may ambitiously dream of, or wistfully pine for, the "opima spolia" of the Indian bench, but then he must not seriously aspire to the proud distinction of an Oriental judgeship. Oh, no, no! "The established course of practice" forbids any such presumptuous Celtic pretension. There must be no mere Hirish interlopers in the quarter. For prescription and precedent have now clearly established an exclusive vested right to the Indian bench—which must be maintained—in their Saxon betters. (1851, 492)

Keogh asserts that the Celt should serve alongside the Saxon, but an assumption lies behind the argument: the Irish deserve a place on the Indian bench in 1850 because the Irish are European and, therefore, are as effective as the English and more so than native Indians.

Keogh does not pretend, however, that the Empire is greatly benefiting the Indians. A position on the Indian bench, for Keogh here, does not represent "civilizing" work; rather, it is a fruit of conquest. In the previously quoted paragraph, through his use of an appropriate phrase, *"opima spolia"* (more commonly *spolia opima*—literally, abundant spoils), he reveals his motives clearly. Roman historian Livius (59 B.C.E.–C.E.17), defined this idiomatic Latin phrase more precisely as "the spoils taken from the enemy's general when slain by the commander of the army himself" (Simpson 1960, 413). Such spoils signal not merely the death of an enemy general but also the transfer of authority and the end of official resistance. Another important distinction needs to be made concerning the implications of this term: these spoils belong to the general, not to the common soldier. These are the spoils of the master, not of the servant. The *spolia opima,* in a colonial sense, indicates the privilege of power and control over Indian society, something the English general acquires, not the Irish foot soldier—"there must be no mere Hirish interlopers in the quarter" (Keogh 1851, 492). The privileged positions of authority that Keogh seeks are the *spolia opima* precisely because they are not a one-time gain. Rather, they signify the "established course of practice," the owned system of imperial power that belongs to the colonial government, whose main business was to protect English interests.

Seven years later in 1855, however, the established Civil Service of India and the army began accepting more loyal Irish appointments into its ranks (despite a continued ban on Catholics). Trinity College, Dublin, began to tailor its curriculum for the Civil Service exams, building its language courses from the ones created by eighteenth-century Irish Orientalists; Queen's College, Belfast, developed language programs teaching Sanskrit and Arabic; and Cork created courses in Indian geography and history as well as Hindu and Muslim law (Holmes 2000, 238).[7] Ninety years later, Mansoor comments in *The Story of Irish Orientalism* on the significance of this change, which Keogh inspired. Perhaps most pertinent to the present study is that this change encouraged the growth of Oriental studies at Trinity College, Dublin, and it furthered Ireland's place in the entire project of Empire, particularly in terms of careers for Irish Orientalists and civil servants.

> [W]hen in 1855 appointments to the Civil Service of India and to the Army were thrown open to public competition and Trinity College was chosen as a centre, a new career was offered to men of talent, and the range of the Academic curriculum was widened. Among other chairs, the chairs of Arabic, Persian, Hindustani, and soon after of Sanskrit were founded. The results were gratifying both to the College and to the British Government. By the end of the century over 200 graduates of T.C.D. had passed into the Civil Service of India, and held important military and administrative posts, and had greatly contributed to the welfare of the British Empire. . . . [Such men] will always be remembered in the annals of British history as the builders of Empire. (1944, 26)

For Mansoor, there is no doubt that these Irish Orientalists and "builders of Empire" played significant roles in the colonial enterprise. Repeating a common assertion that the British Empire owes itself more "to men than to policy," Mansoor also argues that "no one can ignore the share of Irish travellers, administrators, soldiers and last but not least, the band of Orientalists" (26). Neither Mansoor nor Keogh identifies inequity as the natural product of colonialism—the system to which they sought access—and they do not link the "established course of practice" with imperial mistreatment. Because colonialism itself is never critiqued and rather praised in both writer's texts, Ireland's imperial service—from that of soldiers to Orientalists—is painted as self-sacrificing, courageous, nationalistic, morally righteous, adventurous, and in need of greater recognition.

Around this time of increased contact in the mid-nineteenth century, shifts in relations between Irish and Indian nationalists also occurred, as Christopher Bayly notes in a recent essay, "Ireland, India and the Empire: 1780–1914": "[In India] the writers of the 'Young Bengal' movement of the 1840s and '50s began to cite writings on Ireland and Germany as proof of the evils of a rigid system of free trade. By 1857 the beginning of a change of tone in Ireland was also apparent. Assumed racial difference began to be supplanted by a sense of common grievance under the yoke of imperialism. Irish Catholic patriots began to discover a bond with India" (2000, 387–88). For the most part, India and Egypt still represented to the Irish public a distant, exotic land, in which they might find work opportunities as well as adventure. Moreover, as Bayly notes, the Irish had actual investments of time, energy, money, and people in the East: "[T]he Irish were not only the victims of the imperial state, but also some [of] its greatest beneficiaries, a position which hardly changed until the 1930s. These benefits flowed both to Protestants and to Catholics, both to North and to South, although unevenly" (17). Bayly's assertion that the Irish were beneficiaries of the British Empire, as well as its victims, especially in the late nineteenth and early twentieth centuries, highlights the liminal position of Irish culture, which in many respects it had textually occupied since the earliest representations of Iuverna and Hibernia.

Popular Irish Orientalism

The popular literature of Irish Orientalism in the late nineteenth and early twentieth centuries celebrated the lure and exoticism of the Orient. In such Orientalist narratives, the Orient was seen as a ticket to adventure and romance as well as a place to prove one's mettle. James Coleman's 1908 article, "A Tipperary Adventurer in India," succinctly illustrates several typical motifs. Coleman recounts the real exploits of George Thomas (1756–1802) in India in the late eighteenth century, emphasizing this "Adventurer's" relationship with "the faithless Begum" of "Sumroo" in India. Although Thomas was an actual soldier who deserted the

British navy,[8] this brief account reads more like a summary of Irish Oriental romances and adventure stories than a biography. But it is also a story about the illusory nature of the Orient, and the familiar reliability of the British Empire. Resembling British Orientalists' accounts reminiscent of Kipling, the article focuses on how the "Tipperary Adventurer" repeatedly acts honorably and bravely toward the despotic Indian Begum, who repeatedly betrays him because of her unquenchable and despotic (Oriental) thirst for power. But just as in Kipling's *Kim* and Rabindranath Tagore's *Gora*—both eponymous characters are the orphan sons of Irish soldiers and "pass" as Indians—the Irish subject straddles the divide between the East and the West. As an independent Irish agent in the Orient, Thomas begins his career en route to India as a sailor but jumps ship in Madras and becomes the commander in chief of the Begum's forces. After some treachery on her part, he escapes and joins "a cosmopolitan corps of desperadoes" and not long after establishes himself as the sovereign of "Harianna." After more battles, he eventually seeks asylum in "British territory," where he dies a natural, if early, death in 1802. Coleman's condensed account of Thomas's story emphasizes a number of themes and motifs common to Irish popular narratives, namely, the mutability and independence of the Irish abroad, the exceptional level of their successes in the Orient, their survival in strange lands filled with treachery and danger, and their special ability to comprehend the exotic nature of the "Orientals," which often meant a propensity toward "going native," or even becoming a native.

Another striking example of a popular account of the Irish in the Orient, "The Bishop's Cash-Chest: A True Story," by J. J. L. Ratton, develops these same themes, demonstrating the close ties of consanguinity of the Irish Orientalist to Empire and endorsing the reliability of the Irish in the imperial project. This story brings the themes together in what might be described as a churchman-turned-colonial-detective story. The piece appeared in the *Irish Monthly* in 1911 and was meant to serve as a tribute to the recently deceased Archbishop Colgan of Madras. The first few lines paint the man to be a dutiful and staunch supporter of the Empire:

> There died in India, in the month of February, 1911, one of Ireland's great men, the Most Rev. Dr. Colgan, Archbishop of Madras. He belonged to that famous band of Irishmen who have ruled in Church or State, with conspicuous ability, vast provinces of the British Empire. . . . He went out to Madras as a young man of twenty years of age, and . . . remained at work in his diocese until he died at the age of eighty-eight years, beloved by his flock and honoured of all men of every religious persuasion in the Madras Presidency. The following anecdote shows how well he knew the Tamuls (natives of Madras) and their language. (80)

Following this introduction, the narrator unfolds the story of a crime solved by the bishop. A group of "natives" steal the bishop's "cash-chest," and he suggests to the narrator that they "look into the business ourselves" (81). As opposed to driving to a distant colonial and British police station, they assume the colonial intermediary role. Colgan then sets out to discover the culprits, leading the narrator—who plays Watson to the bishop's Holmes—around the remote compound, inspecting the buildings and grounds, interrogating the servants and their families.

Leaving the colonial authorities out of the matter for the moment, the bishop's first order of business is interrogation: "He shouted out 'Boy!' and quickly a venerable grey-haired servitor appeared, his turban all awry" (81). This hoary "boy" assembles "every man in [the bishop's] service" out in the open for "inspection and interrogation." The bishop then questions them in Tamil, but, as far as the author can see, "there was not a pin's choice between them. They were all in a great state of fright and all looked equally guilty" (82). To the narrator, the natives all appear guilty merely because they have been lined up for questioning and because they seem Orientals. He does not recognize how he and the bishop contribute to the situation, even assigning an appearance of universal guilt in the natives.[9]

In Anglo-French Orientalist representations, Oriental characters are often presented as guilty of something; in *Orientalism,* Edward Said draws the conclusion that in the discourse of Orientalism, "Orientals are inveterate liars, they are 'lethargic and suspicious,' and in everything oppose the clarity, directness, and nobility of the Anglo-Saxon race" (1995, 39). The Irish, when abroad, often had to prove that they were closer in mentality and sensibility to the Anglo-Saxon than to the Celtic or the Oriental, in many ways by outdoing the Anglo-Saxon in clarity, directness, and percipience. Ratton's emphasis on the bishop's insights into the Oriental character might be seen as a manifestation of such compensation. After the interrogation, the bishop and the narrator tour the grounds and search the servants' huts. The whereabouts of the great chest mystifies the narrator, but the bishop soon understands the crime. While leisurely smoking a cheroot, he explains it to the author before unearthing the buried chest. The coachman and his horseman had sweated during the interrogation, and he asks, "'Did you notice that in one room the women and children were sleeping close together near the centre of the room? . . . The natives sleep well apart in the hot weather, so as to get what little ventilation they can. . . . Could it be that they did so to conceal the floor?' " (1911, 83). In the end, the bishop's perspicuity wins out over the conniving and lying natives.

Ratton highlights this incident to indicate the Irish bishop's success in the Orient. Such is the intermediary role of the Anglo-Irish in the British Empire, as an interpreter of exotic others both in Ireland and in the Orient. A difference in accounts between the supplementary place of an Anglo-Irishman in Ireland interpreting the Gaels and Celts (for instance, Edmund Pery, Aubrey de Vere, and J. M. Synge) and that of an Anglocentric Anglo-Irishman in India interpreting the Orientals is that in the latter accounts, the "natives" are portrayed as enthusiastically admiring the Anglo-Irish—about 80 percent of the Irish in the Indian Civil Service were from middle-class Protestant backgrounds, much like their British counterparts (Holmes 2000, 238). According to the narrator, the locals seem to admire the "great man," even the suspected ones who had been lined up in the middle of the night, had been interrogated, and had their homes searched: "[The cash-chest] was soon excavated and removed by willing hands to its rightful pedestal in the office, amidst murmurs of applause. Every native face, but those of the culprits, beamed with delight. . . . Next day I went up country, and heard no more about the burglary, except that the men were duly tried and condemned to prison" (Ratton 1911, 83). Written seventy years after Keogh's essay on discrimination against the Irish in the empire, Ratton presents an Irishman in much fuller possession of the *spolia opima* of Empire and making use of an Irish-Oriental affinity.

Other popular accounts of the Irish in Asia during the early twentieth century often include tributes to Irish soldiers and Irish colonial administrators, such as Conlans of Allahabad[10] and the Lawrence family from Ulster, who held several important posts within the Indian Civil Service, Henry Lawrence being appointed provisional governor general (but dying from wounds received at the siege of Lucknow before learning of the appointment) and John being appointed to the position that Warren Hastings had once held, as the viceroy and governor general of India (1864) (Harlow and Carter 1999, 168). Most of these accounts tend to emphatically claim these men of Empire as Irish, often highlighting their mutability, righteousness, and adventurous natures. The Irish identity of Sir Charles Tegart, police commissioner of Calcutta in the early twentieth century, was a topic of discussion in Anglo-Indian circles at the time, as Michael Silvestri notes: "Calcutta's Anglo-Indian community typically linked Tegart's unorthodox policing methods and the obvious thrill he took in opposing terrorism to his Irishness; few failed to comment on what one fellow officer called his 'characteristically Irish make-up.' . . . [Nevertheless, i]n spite of comments by English observers that his 'Irishness' gave him a natural understanding of Bengali nationalists, Tegart had little sympathy for Bengali revolutionaries" (2000a, 43–44). Irishness, it was assumed, like Celticity, gave imperial access to the Oriental mind—the Irish being familiar with both sides of the imperial milieu.

Irish Missionaries

The rise of Irish nationalism in the first decades of the twentieth century, as well as the Anglo-Irish War and the establishment of the Irish Free State in 1921, greatly influenced other cross-colony comparisons and Irish representations of the Orient and colonized lands, particularly the increasingly common representations of Irish missionary movements. Although missionaries had been allowed in India since the early nineteenth century—Protestants were allowed entry in the late 1820s and Catholics in the 1830s—the missionary activity was primarily directed toward the "spiritual needs" of the Irish soldiers in the British army (Maher 1997, 33). For most of the nineteenth century, Irish missionaries ran schools, orphanages, hospitals, and mission churches in India; it was only late in the century that they began taking Indian novitiates and making serious conversion efforts, which met with little success. Such is not the case in other colonized societies, particularly in Africa, where European missionary activity (including Irish) vigorously undermined traditional cultures. Most nineteenth-century Irish missionary activity, however, was in Australia and North America, where millions of Irish had emigrated. In the twentieth century, however, Irish Catholic missionaries increasingly established themselves in Africa and China (see fig. 10). The Maynooth Mission to China, in

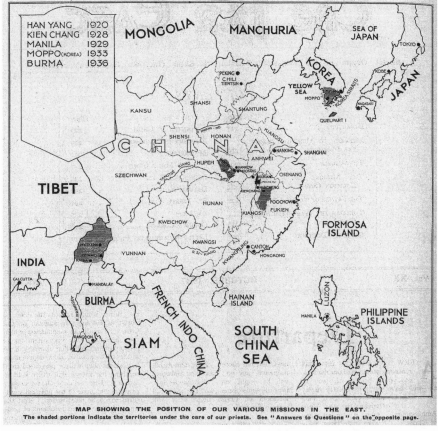

10. "Map Showing the Position of Our Various Missions in the East." Published in the *Far East* 20, no. 10 (Oct. 1937).

fact, became a well-known institution in Ireland, publishing its own magazine, the *Far East,* for much of the twentieth century.

In addition to being a fund-raising effort, the *Far East* promoted the civilizing ideology of European imperialism, filling its pages with stories of Irish priestly endurance and pagan conversions, mostly set in China and Korea. The discussions of the Chinese differ from many jingoistic representations of the Chinese in that they appear within an Irish framework. A typical article might discuss Chinese farming, poetry, or "national characteristics" of the Chinese in order to stir the sympathy and camaraderie of the Irish readership. One piece from 1936, "Some Types in a Chinese Congregation," signed anonymously by "A Missionary," describes a typical parish in China as if it were only the next county over: "I'm often asked what the Chinese are like. Is there any link between them and us? For answer let me describe some types in the congregation as I see them each Sunday when I turn around to say a few words. Right up near the top is Mrs. Shu. 'They tell me I am proud because I sit near the front,' she says, 'but I tell them I'm humble because I sit with the little children.' She is certainly a pious woman" (184). The essay goes on to describe a host of parish personalities: old John, gentle Mrs. G., Philip ("a good man, but a bit of a pessimist"), Paul ("our representative on all local 'boards' "), and Teresa ("my stand-by in all matters that concern the womenfolk") (184–85). The goal of the magazine was to familiarize the Chinese, and to do so, the magazine generally played up similarities between China and rural premodern Ireland—between the Oriental and the Celtic. In "Answers to Questions about the Missions," the anonymous author answers questions about Chinese cows, missionary activities, and paganism. For instance, one reader wrote: "Has their belief in the existence of evil spirits much effect on everyday life of the Chinese?"; after gleefully discussing some of the "superstitions," the author concludes:

> With the passage of time, however, most of these superstitions will probably be relegated to the realms of our fairy tales. It is quite possible, indeed, that many Chinese cling to them today, not because they believe in them, but because they have come down to them from their ancestors. With a people so tenacious of tradition one can understand how hard they would find it to give up traditions and legends that have been consecrated by the passage of perhaps thousands of years. Christianity, of course, deals a death-blow to superstition wherever it is propagated. So, too, do the new schools with their modern curricula. (1938, 75)

Similar discussions of Irish superstitions had long been a part of rural Irish culture. In another article by the same name, one year later, the author claims that the process of learning to speak Chinese is similar to learning to speak Irish, but admits the writing is harder to learn (1937, 123). Such discussions and representations had enormous impact on twentieth-century Irish impressions of the Orient, which endured as an attractive place much in need of Christianizing forces. One piece directly linked the mysticism of rural Ireland and China, "A Mystic Journey: How a School-Mistress Went to China," by Enid Dinnis. The story, as with so many in the *Far East,* is a conversion narrative, and concerns the mystical powers of an old rural Irish woman, "Martha Brigson" (as she was described to the narrator, "[D]on't expect anything more modern than the year one. That's about Martha's date" [1936, 16]). In the course of the narrative, this *Sean Bhean Bhocht,* Mother Ireland figure, mystically travels to China to help convert a Chinese family patriarch on his deathbed (hence allowing others in the family to follow suit). She goes and returns in one night, where she dies pious and exhausted a few days later.

Influential sympathetic representations of the East rose in consort with nationalist power, as the Reverend T. Gavan Duffy notes in a 1921 account of Irish missionaries:

> It is no mere coincidence that, alongside (or, more accurately, within) the present revival of national consciousness in Ireland there should have arisen a proportionately powerful missionary movement. For it has only been during those periods of depression, when we have lost confidence in our destiny, that, simultaneously, we have forgotten our missionary vocation; but whenever the nation's call has rung more urgently in the ears of Irish youth, the apostolic spirit seems also to have revivified Irish missionary effort. (464)

This "missionary zeal" of the Irish, in many cases, worked in tandem with the civilizing mission of English imperialists. Very often, Irish missions offered complementary cultural work to colonialism, replacing indigenous belief structures with European Christian morals and strictures. Duffy links this missionary movement, which often had strong imperial ties, directly with Irish nationalism, noting its history in nationalist narratives: "In the very first number of the Nation, when Young Ireland came to birth, there was a column of world-wide missionary news" (464). It remained linked with Irish nationalism throughout much of the twentieth century. Occasionally, however, criticisms were voiced, especially in cross-colonial arguments, such as the ones often published in *An Phoblacht* (Republic) in the 1920s and 1930s. One article, written by a Chinese anticolonialist, has some sharp words for missionaries: "That the Christian Missionary activities are the opening wedge for Western Imperialism is a matter beyond dispute. The Opium War of 1840 was merely one aspect of the foreign invasion of China. The Missionary War of 1856 was its logical complement" (Jan. 28, 1927, 3). Other cross-colonial voices also blamed missionaries for their imperial complicity (as chapter 5 discusses).

Not all pro-missionary essays in the popular magazines of the day, however, uniformly promoted colonial projects. Whereas the increasing missionary movement tended toward colonialist-style expansion of the Catholic or Protestant Church, debates about the validity of such projects occasionally raged in the popular press. For instance, one serious debate in several issues of the *Irish Monthly* in the mid-1920s concerned where Irish missionaries should go, that is, should they follow Irish immigrants to England, Australia, and America and help them lead moral lives, or go to Asia and Africa to set up missions (see L. D. Murphy's "Indian Vignettes," Oct. 1925, which responds to an earlier 1925 essay, author and date unnamed)? Writers who favored the expansion of Irish missions in Asia and Africa needed to assert the great need for their missions in these distant lands. They painted the East in a desperate light: perpetually destitute and famine-ridden, resembling Ireland of the previous century. L. D. Murphy also argues in "Indian Vignettes" that the Irish missionary must go to the "Heathen" because Catholicism is underrepresented in India (being under English control) and that heretical Protestant missions will convert them (528). The Irish have a certain responsibility to "save" the Indians from the Protestant "soupers": "Paganism is not a thing of yesterday, nor has it become effete with the progress of civilisation. Vishna, Siva, and the belly-god Ganesha have reigned too long easily to be ousted" (530); good, earnest Catholics were needed. The chauvinistic side of the Irish missionary movement often appeared alongside such nationalist arguments, in which Catholicism competed against the British Empire. Unfortunately, the lessons of cultural tolerance, expressed so emphatically in earlier works such as Sydney Owenson's *Missionary*, were easily lost amid such rhetoric.

Academic Irish Orientalism

Still other Orientalist texts outside missionary arguments and tales of Irish exploits existed in Irish culture. In particular, numerous Irish Orientalists, mostly from Trinity College, Dublin, over two centuries produced hundreds (if not thousands) of histories, travel books, linguistic studies, and primers, as well as surveys of Oriental languages, cultures, coins, architecture, religions, and other items and traditions. Mansoor's *Story of Irish Orientalism* opens by noting: "The contribution of Irishmen to Oriental studies has rarely received adequate recognition even in their own land. It is a mistake to suppose, as it is commonly done, that this enthusiasm for things Eastern first makes its appearance in the sixteenth and seventeenth centuries" (1944, 11). He then proceeds to discuss the travels of medieval Irish monks and specifically mentions Dicuil's measurements of the pyramids of Gîza. Most of the study, however, is devoted to providing an overview of more than fifty Irish Orientalists, including Lafcadio Hearn, Stanley Lane-Poole, Vincent Arthur Smith, George Grierson, Whitley Stokes, Rowan Hamilton, Edward Hincks, T. W. Haig, Edward Fitzgerald (of *The Rubáiyát of Omar Khayyám* fame, whom Mansoor claims as Irish by descent), and many other academic Irish Orientalists. Generally, these Irish Orientalists wrote within the context of Anglo-French Orientalism, unlike many more literary and political Irish Orientalist writings, which made more of Ireland's history as a colony itself. In contrast, such colonial parallels are rarities in academic Irish Orientalism, partly because of genre restrictions but also because such European-Asian parallels disrupted the geographically absurd maxim of Anglo-French Orientalism, popularized by Kipling: "East is East and West is West, and never the twain shall meet."

Most of these academic Orientalists charted Asian and West Asian cultures, religions, literatures, and histories, contributing to the knowledge base of imperial Europe. Nevertheless, a number also sought to use this knowledge to strengthen the parallels between Ireland and the Orient or to assert nonimperial and antisectarian agendas. For instance, Mansoor himself, like other Irish Orientalists, referenced Irish-Oriental origin legends, writing in his first major publication on Irish Orientalism, "Oriental Studies in Ireland," in *Hermathena*: "Perhaps there is some truth in the legends that assign an Eastern origin to some of the earliest settlers in Ireland, and that is why so many Irishmen have felt the fascination of the Orient, or perhaps it is merely the Celtic temperament, with its peculiar blend of restlessness and veneration for the past that has turned the gaze of so many Irish scholars towards the ancient sources of civilisation and religion in the lands of the sun-rising" (1943, 60). Positing the sameness of the Celt and the Oriental, as we have seen, often was an anticolonial strategy, but in this case it clearly means to establish Irish complicity with the colonial enterprise. The Oriental origin legends were clearly employed for various ideological ends, even if their most forceful deployments in the twentieth century supported cross-colony ties.

The life and works of Lafcadio Hearn (1850–1904), who was known as "the Japanese Irishman," illustrate another distinctive parallel drawn between Ireland and the Orient, one that echoes the themes that pervaded Irish and Celtic cultures (Mansoor 1944, 37). The geographical and cultural parallels between Ireland and Japan (and between England and Japan) had been asserted by others before Hearn (and would later be by W. B. Yeats in his Irish-Japanese Celtic Noh dramas), but his comparisons focused on the stereotypical strangeness of atmosphere in both Celtic and Japanese lands. Hearn, whose childhood had been spent in Ireland and Wales, left Europe for America and later resettled in Japan as an adult, marrying a Japanese woman. During his Japan years he wrote prolifically on Japan, the Orient, and Buddhism. His father had been Anglo-Irish (although rumors of Romany descent existed) and his mother Greek, from the Ionian islands, which the English army held at the time his parents met. Their union was opposed violently by her family, but they married anyhow, and she gave birth to Lafcadio on the island of Lefcada, for which he was named. The family moved to Dublin, but at the age of seven, his parents separated painfully, and he and his younger brother moved to rural Wales to be raised by a Catholic aunt of his father.

An early Hearn biographer, Elisabeth Bisland, notes that Ireland, Wales, and Celtic lands, in general, occupied a magical place in his mind, indicating what she calls his "nascent interest in the ghostly and the weird" (Hearn 1923, 14).[11] He carried visions and memories of Ireland and Wales with him throughout his life, referring in letters and autobiographical fragments to the tales of fairies and his childhood days of seeking out fairy forts, which he and his brother loved as a boy. He often projected such idealized visions onto Japanese culture, as in the record of his first day's impressions of Japan in *Glimpses of Unfamiliar Japan:* "Elfish everything seems; for everything as well as everybody is small, and queer, and mysterious: the little houses under their blue roofs, the little shop-fronts hung with blue, and the smiling little people in their blue costumes. . . . Everybody describing the sensations of his first Japanese day talks of the land as fairy-land, and of its people as fairy folk" (1894, 2, 7). This perspective never disappeared from Hearn's writings on Japan, even as his explorations of Japanese history, religions, literature, and culture grew more extensive than any other Western studies. The depth of his work is attested to by continuing Japanese interest in his works, which are still considered important texts for the contemporary reader interested in traditional Japanese culture, and his memory as the Japanese Irishman is generally respected.[12]

Hearn recorded, as his biographers have described it, a significant period of change in Japanese culture, as it became more Westernized in the late nineteenth century. Hearn's work of recording the religions, traditions, "the daily lives, the songs, the dances, the names, the legends, the humble lore of plants, birds and insects" was often regarded as the invaluable work of an Occidental chronicling the life of the East before it vanished into modernization (1923, 100). Such work resembles the process of recording the disappearing life on the Blasket Islands as in Tomás Ó Criomhthain's *An tOilenach* or, perhaps more appropriately, the work of the Englishman Robin Flowers or the life on the Aran Islands in J. M. Synge's *Aran Islands,* for Synge was not Aran born. Like Synge's, Hearn's supplementarity and attitude to the Japanese are conveyed in his minute details, which are both patronizing and full of wonder. For Hearn, these island people were of another world:

> For in no little time these fairy folk can give you all the softness of sleep. But sooner or later, if you dwell long with them, your contentment will prove to have much in common with the happiness of dreams. You will never forget the dream—never; but it will lift at last, like those vapours of spring which lend preternatural loveliness to a Japanese landscape in the forenoon of radiant days. Really you are happy because you have entered bodily into Fairyland, into a world that is not, and never could be your own. (101–2)

The Orient is often represented as a land outside of contemporary time. Hearn is the interpreter and the explorer in both geography and history. Lured by strange-

ness, the Orientalist paints himself as a journeyman in the study of ancient or traditional life, discovering the elusive secrets of the ancient East, ones that, particularly
for the Irish Orientalist, resonate with Celtic lands. "You have been transported
out of your own century, over space enormous of perished time, into an era forgotten, into a vanished age, back to something ancient as Egypt or Nineveh. That
is the secret of the strangeness and beauty of things, the secret of the thrill they give,
the secret of the elfish charm of the people and their ways" (102). Hearn also drew
comparisons between the Orientals and the Celt in more direct ways, in addition
to his usual comments on the fairy nature and "elfish charm[s]" of the Japanese that
(as he records) he had first encountered in his childhood in Wales.

Like so many before him, he discovers for himself the popular legends of the
Oriental origins for the Celt. For instance, in an 1878 letter to H. E. Krehbiel,
Hearn comments on the similarities of these peripheral cultures, drawing clear
Celtic–Oriental connections through music and physiognomy:

> L'Orient is in Brittany, and the chant is that of a Breton fisher village. . . . Your crit-
> icism about the resemblance of the melody to the Irish keening wail does not sur-
> prise me, although it disappointed me; for I believe the Breton peasantry are of
> Celtic origin. Your last letter strengthened a strange fancy that has come to me at
> intervals since my familiarity with the Chinese physiognomy—namely, that there
> are such strong similarities between the Mongolian and certain types of the Irish
> face that one is inclined to suspect a far-distant origin of the Celts in the East. (179)

If "L'Orient" could be located in Brittany, then another Orient could be found in
the Celtic borders of the British Isles: Scotland, Wales, and Ireland, particularly the
west of Ireland. In a sense, these cultures continued to constitute an Orient in the
backyard of England long after antiquarianism had lost its scholarly reputation.
Moreover, because Celticism and Orientalism developed simultaneously, Celtic–
Oriental stereotypes originated in both representations of the Orient in Asia and
West Asia as well as in the one beyond the (figurative and literal) Pale in Ireland. At
the end of the nineteenth century, when Hearn wrote the above passage, ideas
about the qualities of an international modern society were emerging alongside
colonialism and in opposition to images of ancient civilizations.

Other Irish Orientalists, such as Stanley Lane-Poole, Vincent Arthur Smith, Sir
George Grierson, and Watson Pasha (Sir Charles Moore Watson) also felt a powerful pull to the Orient. M. Mansoor comments, for instance, that "[Watson Pasha]
displayed a great interest and zeal, almost amounting to fanaticism, in travel and geographical works in connection with the Near East" (1944, 46–47). But intense interest, in itself, does not greatly distinguish Irish Orientalists from English, French,
or German ones, though Mansoor does emphasize it in regard to Irish Orientalists.

Mansoor also goes to lengths to stress that Irish Orientalists contributed to the welfare of both their "second home" (the Orient) and the British Empire. For instance, in addition to pointing to Hearn and referring to him as "the Japanese Irishman," he notes that Grierson's role as superintendent of the *Linguistic Survey of India* had a considerable impact on the academic Orientalist world and that it encouraged Indian scholarship and cultural pride. "This work is not only an inexhaustible mine for all those who study the languages of India, but beyond any other it has stimulated in the Indians themselves a just pride in their own vernaculars and a deep interest in the long history that lies behind them." Yet he also asserts that projects such as Grierson's are complementary to the often touted, if infrequently attempted or achieved, humanistic goals of imperialism, restating that the survey is "one of the most unquestioned glories of British Rule" (35).

George Grierson (1851–1941) came from Dublin and studied under Robert Atkinson, the editor of *Ancient Laws of Ireland* (1865–1901), and won university prizes for Sanskrit (1872) and Hindustani (1873). Inspired by Atkinson, Grierson began a career in the Indian Civil Service in 1873 and continued his linguistic studies. His *Bhär Peasant Life, Being a Discursive Catalogue of the Surroundings of the People of that Province, with Many Illustrations from Photographs Taken by the Author* (1885) may be his best-known work outside of the *Linguistic Survey*. He also published translations in *Curiosities of Indian Literature* (1895), which included "The Result of Good and Evil Company" in which he emphasized the value of taking care in choosing one's associations, citing the "Irish proverb, 'Tell me whom you're with and I'll tell you who you are' " (1). If we apply Grierson's logic to himself, we would conclude that he was a staunch imperialist. His allegiance is clearest in his *Report on Colonial Emigration from the Bengal Presidency* (1883), a report on the state of emigration from India to the Caribbean colonies.[13] This treatise is a fascinating and brutal look at how to encourage emigration. The emigrants are looked at only in terms of their labor, discussing how the Indian "cooly" is essential for British operations because the Caribs did not work the plantations as effectively: "The difference therefore between the tropical indogen of the colonies, and the cooly imported from India is that the former has developed, in the course of centuries, into an animal incapable of protracted labour, and the latter into an animal naturally industrious, and skilled in the arts of agriculture."[14] The Indian in the tropics, moreover, is depicted as having a yield and profit "such as he had never even dreamed of before," and, therefore, no downsides to his or her emigration are given or, apparently, imagined (36).

In the nineteenth century, the process of creating knowledge about the Orient always interacted with the European colonial enterprise. The cohesion and intertextuality of the entire enterprise were fundamental to the study of the Orient. Edward Said notes in *Orientalism:*

The result for Orientalism has been a sort of consensus: certain things, certain types of statement, certain types of work have seemed for the Orientalist correct. He has built his work and research upon them, and they in turn have pressed hard upon new writers and scholars. Orientalism can thus be regarded as a manner of regularized (or Orientalized) writing, vision, and study, dominated by imperatives, perspectives, and ideological biases ostensibly suited to the Orient. The Orient is taught, researched, administered, and pronounced upon in certain discrete ways. (1995, 202)

Irish academic Orientalists such as Grierson certainly participated in this discourse. The goal of many Irish Orientalists was to reach a position of equivalency with their British counterparts. Mansoor argues that Oxford was not the only center of Orientalism in the British Isles: "[I]f Oxford was the chief home of Orientalism in the British Isles, Dublin was not far behind, and a lively intercourse was maintained between both centres" (1944, 25–26). Clearly, little that academic Irish Orientalists wrote or researched contradicted the general idioms and doctrines of Anglo-French Orientalism, or the tendencies of European colonialism.

Most of these academics and scholars treated colonialism as progress and a globally unifying process that rarely encourages injustice and domination. When they did compare colonialism abroad to colonialism in Ireland, the comparisons usually supported imperialism and the need for European governance abroad as it had been done in Ireland. Nevertheless, Irish Orientalists often wrote against imperial cruelties, albeit often indirectly. The history of Irish academic Orientalism has much to do with the fact that most students of the Orient in Ireland studied in the Oriental Studies Department of Trinity College, Dublin, and their participation offered them a way to rise in wealth and status and increase Ireland's (Anglo-Irish or otherwise) share of the spoils of the Empire. Orientalism apparently offered some sense of compensation for the denigrations of Irish history, guaranteeing the successful student a place in the Empire as a British citizen—a category that, for many, embraces the diversity of Saxon, Celt, Norman, Cambrian, Anglo, and Gael. Few of these men would then critique the system that then employed them, and Orientalism and imperial service became seen as moral paths to uplift the denigrated lives of people across the world.

In contrast to many popular and literary writers, Irish Orientalists, civil servants, and soldiers in India often did not represent themselves as belonging to a specific nationality. And, more often than not, when they did so it was British. As the Irish soldier in Henry's army in Shakespeare's *Henry V* exclaims, "Of my nation! What ish my nation? What ish my nation? Who talks of my nation ish a villain, and a basterd, and a knave, and a rascal" (3.1), an Irish identity was only ambiguously national. Being involved in the British forces, and being seen abroad as white (after the rise of racial theories), often superceded but did not replace Irishness, but exceptions are numerous, particularly during moments of strong Fenian action in Ireland. Nevertheless, there is much truth to the idea of the Irish as nonnational when in British employment and sharing Kipling's "white man's burden." [15] Whereas many Irish individuals went to the East, such as the later Revivalists James and Margaret Cousins, explicitly in opposition to the jingoism of imperialists, many other Irish often felt a strong desire to be the "White Man" and receive a more powerful position in the imagined geography of Empire.

Many, however, embraced a more liminal position. The notable Irish Orientalist Stanley Lane-Poole once commented on Jonathan Swift's response to the "wretched condition of Ireland" in the eighteenth century, which he notes "still oppress[es] the Irish people." Lane-Poole might have been describing his own politics in his further comments on Swift's Irish politics: "His remedies are, it may be noticed, less legislative than moral. He would raise the spirit and rouse the energy of the Irish to counteract the oppression of England, rather than attempt to cure the evils they laboured under by new enactments" (1896, 283). Knowledge, not political or economic reform, would uplift the colonized. Lane-Poole, like many academic Orientalists, tended to assert the same recipe for the improvement of conditions throughout Asia, West Asia, and Africa.

A disproportionate number of Irish Orientalists pointedly defined themselves in opposition to imperial jingoism, advocating a sort of cross-cultural cosmopolitanism that resisted the divide between East and West and between Asian and European cultures. Bryan Turner, in his essay "Outline of a Theory of Orientalism," builds upon Said's concern to "identify a number of scholars whose work attempted to transcend the narrow limitations of the Orientalist tradition of which they were members" (2000, 24). Louis Massignon was one such cosmopolitan critic, whose principal work was *The Passion of al-Hallaj* (1962–1963); he analyzes the political and religious significance of this Islamic and Christian mystic, who died as a martyr in 922. Like many Irish Orientalist writers outside the academy, Massignon advocates the mystical traditions of both European and Asian cultures, in order to emphasize tolerance and recognize "a common experience of man's alienation and humanity's need for reconciliation." Turner elaborates:

> One can suggest that the components of cosmopolitan virtue are as follows: irony both as a method and as a mentality; emotional distance and reflexivity with respect to our own cultural values; scepticism towards grand narratives of modern ideologies; transcultural sympathies and interests; care for other cultures arising from an awareness of their precarious condition and acceptance of cultural hybridisation; support for positive programmes of multiculturalism; and an ecumenical appreciation of other religions. Intercultural sensitivities and the need to interact constantly

with strangers and to promote irony as the most prized norm of wit and principle of taste. For Said (1984a: 29 [*The World, the Text, and the Critic*]), irony is a useful word to use alongside "oppositional" and "critical." (26)

This sort of oppositional or critical irony resembles the parodic translations of James Clarence Mangan, Thomas Moore's "doubleness of application" and para-textual allegory, and Jonathan Swift's encoded critiques—common values and techniques for many Irish writers on the Orient. Such encoded critiques are most prominent in political and literary writings, but such manifestations also exist in Irish academic Orientalism.

An identifiable tendency of Irish Orientalism (outside of missionary texts) is the theme of tolerance, either through the ecumenical appreciation of other religions or through the promotion of a religious syncretism. The ecumenical Islamic mystic and Mogul emperor Akbar (1542–1605), whose story James Cousins later dramatized in his syncretistic play *The King's Wife,* had also been the subject of scholar Vincent Arthur Smith, who wrote the first full-length European account of Akbar. Smith, as Cousins would, paid particular attention to Akbar's syncretistic energies devoted toward "the evolution of a new religion," which "would, he hoped, prove to be a synthesis of all the warring creeds and capable of uniting the discordant elements of his vast empire in one harmonious whole" (1966, 115–16). Smith's choice of subject matter is significant. Although traces of liberal imperialist affinities exist in the quote above, this strategy is remarkably similar to the ones used by Celtic-Orientalist Revivalists. Reminiscent of Sidney Owenson's *Missionary,* Smith contrasts Akbar's religious syncretism to the bigotry of European missionaries who visited his court in 1580. "The attitude of the missionaries was so uncompromising and fanatical that nothing but the strong protection of the emperor could have preserved their lives. They made no pretence of sharing the sympathetic feeling for the religion of the Prophet of Arabia" (125). Quoting missionaries' comments from a missionary's letters, Smith proves his point: "In a word, Mahomet is everything here. Antichrist reigns. In honour of this infernal monster they bend the knee, prostrate, lift up their hands, give alms, and do all they do" (126). Akbar, in contrast, is welcoming and open to other cultures and religions. Smith explores Akbar's religious syncretism and paints the emperor in a somewhat cosmopolitan light, noting his brief correspondence with Queen Elizabeth, emphasizing his generous welcomes and his curiosity about other cultures and religions, and pointing out that Akbar worked to prevent suttee. Smith's account of Akbar, however, is not entirely sympathetic and unattached from Orientalist tropes and representational idioms.[16]

But Smith's critique also demonstrates what Thomas Moore alludes to as a "doubleness of application." After noting that Akbar's rule was not "more tortuous than that of the European princes at the time" (248–49), Smith differentiates Akbar from modern imperialists:

> The ruling passion of Akbar was ambition. His whole reign was dedicated to conquest. His aggressions, made without the slightest regard to moral considerations, were not determined in any instance by desire to better the condition of the people in the kingdom attacked. He would have laughed at the canting apology for his action tendered by a modern, uncritical panegyrist, who was rash enough to write: "Akbar did not conquer in Rajputana to rule in Rajputana. He conquered that all the Rajput princes, each in his own dominions, might enjoy that peace and prosperity which his predominance, never felt aggressively, secured for the whole empire." (251)

In other words, Akbar did not conquer the Rajput princes for their own good, as many modern imperial apologists claim. He conquered them for material gain and power. Smith's critical irony of the "uncritical panegyrist" resembles anticolonial criticism of the British Empire in India, without being overt. In a more overt instance, the Irish anticolonialist writer Frederick Ryan also rebuked imperial justifications in an issue of *Dana:* "The unvarnished truth is that no nation interferes from motives of philanthropy in the affairs of other nations, and the ideal of world-rule is itself fundamentally vicious, since the rule of communities by themselves is infinitely better in the long run than the most wise and benevolent outside despotism" (qtd. in Eagleton 1998, 266). Smith's critique is not as forceful, but it certainly aimed to deflate grandiose humanistic pretensions of British rule in India.

Like Smith and other Irish writers, Stanley Lane-Poole (perhaps the most famous Irish Orientalist) was also known for his tolerance, antisectarianism, and criticism of religious bigotry. Mansoor discusses and quotes from a relevant account of Lane-Poole in Egypt.

> "Nothing can be more absurd or misleading"—announced Lane-Poole in one of his lectures—"than the popular way of confounding all creeds that are not Christian under the opprobrious name of 'heathen.' A sergeant-major of the British Army of occupation in Egypt"—continued Lane-Poole—"at Church parade on Sunday morning used to give the word of command in something like these terms: 'Church of England—one pace to the front, Roman Catholics stand fast, and miscellaneous religions one pace to the rear!' Islam is not a miscellaneous religion. It is one of the three great missionary faiths of history. Allah is Arabic for 'the God,' the One Almighty Creator and Eternal Ruler of the Universe and there cannot be two such Gods." (1944, 45)

This attempt to bridge religious prejudice in disparate cultures is perhaps the most striking and distinguishing strategy of Irish Orientalism, and it resonates clearly with the syncretistic tradition stemming from the Irish Oriental origin legends and continuing in the later Theosophical, Orientalist, and cross-colonial interests of Revivalists.

Reviewers of Mansoor's *Story of Irish Orientalism,* which is primarily concerned with academic Orientalists, uniformly praised the book for "its pioneering spirit" and for its "inspiring reading" (Luce 1945, 113). As a contribution to Ireland's claim for an international presence, the reviewers in 1944 seemed surprised that so many Irishmen did such significant things outside Ireland. They have some complaints, however. Luce, for instance, notes that Mansoor includes only a "short chapter on the Eastern Influence on English Literature" (113). Also, the anonymous reviewer H. F. N. of *Dublin Magazine* gives much fuller and more direct criticism of the prominent influence of Oriental and Indian texts on Irish literature:

> [W]e miss one aspect of classical Oriental study, translations from the Indian sacred books. Is there nothing to note relevant to the *Upanishads,* the *Bhagavad Gita* (of which an Irishman, W.Q. Judge, made the recension AE loved best), the *Vedas?* We are told, indeed that Prof. Atkinson had a fine record in many languages "in Sauskrit [sic] having confined himself to the language of the Vedas"; and it is good to know that "there is now an increasing interest in Sauskrit," seeing its primacy, but save for this reference and an account of J.V.S. Pope's fine Pali scholarship, the most interesting aspects of Orientalism perhaps unavoidably are not discussed. And, I have one small regret—not a complaint—that that picturesque figure of our youth Mir Aulad Ali is given so little space. It was our pleasant experience in those days when his turban adorned the streets of Dublin to hear him discuss the affinities of Kismet and Karman [sic], to whose ethical marriage he would have offered no impediment. (1945, 60)

Mir Aulad Ali was a significant figure to many, including Yeats and AE, and he offered one of the only learned counterpoints to the perspective of self-proclaimed gurus such as Mohini Chatterjee and the Theosophists. Such, indeed, is a limitation of Mansoor's volume. Nevertheless, this "native Arabic speaker," as R. M. Gwynn refers to Mansoor in the foreword to *The Story of Irish Orientalism* (1944, 5), made Irish cultural critics more self-aware of the long history of Orientalism in Ireland. But Luce, although appreciative of the work, seems to not know exactly what to make of this foreign-born scholar who writes about the Irish writing about his own country; Luce ends his review with a sentence that seems a backhanded compliment for a doctoral graduate of Trinity College: "The author is to be congratulated on his mastery of English" (1945, 114). In Ireland, an "Oriental" remained so.

Intra-Imperial Analogies

A comment from a letter to the *Times* in London in 1871 points to how Irish-Indian analogies were used to reach conclusions about imperial policy:"We cannot suppress the freedom of thought or conscience in India any more than we can in Ireland. Still less can we propose to exterminate large bodies of people, even though their religious or political opinions are dangerous to the peace of our Empire. They will exist in the East as they do in the West" (Lees 1871, 10).[17] The dangers posed by India and Ireland stemmed also from anticolonial resistance. Behind some fears also lay impressions of Celtic and Oriental races and cultures as essentially wayward. Their resistance, real or imagined, further confirmed the increased need for British imperial guidance. Analogies made between the Indian and the Irish situations signify a turning point in English representations of an uncivilized Ireland. No longer perceived as barbaric or wild (to the same degree) as in previous centuries, to many Victorian eyes the Irish Celt signified rebellious and loutish behavior, and Fenian nationalism verified the moral inferiority of the Celtic Gael. But Irish-Indian analogies were not merely incidental or rhetorical; they pointed to both widespread public conceptions and systemic imperial policies.

Such comparisons became increasingly common in political discussions in the second half of the nineteenth century, as a number of recent studies have demonstrated, the most prominent being Scott B. Cook's tightly reasoned *Imperial Affinities: Nineteenth Century Analogies and Exchanges between India and Ireland.* Within a larger discussion about the cohesiveness of the British Empire, Cook argues against the larger notion that culture is primarily shaped by the "immutable laws" of history, as historians of the time argued (1993, 131). Instead, cultural understandings, in this case, "the well-formed habit of analogy and exchange" between Ireland and India, directly affected land policies in India, as well as policing, censorship, and other imperial activities (31–33), particularly leading up to the creation of the Bengal Tenancy Act of 1885.

Examining the legislative and administrative practices of Ireland and British India, Cook asserts that policy makers viewed the colonial situations of Ireland and India as similar. Because of the advent of the telegraph and increased global communication, along with the fact that many administrators had experience in both Ireland and India, legislators and officials began to see political parallels between these disparate cultures:"The apparent similarities in certain Irish and Indian circumstances combined with a relatively small and homogeneous officialdom which prided itself on pragmatism, experience and adaptability, produced a limited but significant period in which Irish ways were refashioned to fit Indian environs. As a result, the historical development of modern India bears some surprising traces of influences from Ireland, a place with an awkward and ambiguous identity" (136).[18]

Although the subject of Cook's work is not Irish Orientalism or cross-colonial sympathies, he may too readily assume that this connection was entirely originated by imperial analogies. As previous chapters have demonstrated, intra-imperial analogies have a long history, as do Irish-Asian comparisons. Furthermore, Irish nationalists regularly referred to Ireland as a colony during the nineteenth century, increasingly comparing it with India, Egypt, China, and elsewhere. Especially following the 1800 Act of Union, British officials refrained from calling Ireland a colony, however, just as many conservative historians today refuse consideration of Ireland as a postcolonial state.[19] Their own comparisons, however, belie their denials.

Ireland certainly had a colonial history with England, considering the waves of British colonizers who "planted" Ireland, particularly in the East and North, over centuries. Moreover, because Irish culture existed outside the English metropolitan core of the Empire, it was often treated as a peripheral, colonial outpost. In any case, Ireland's status as a colony is only partly relevant. Whether British policy makers and officials considered Ireland a colony or not, they, along with commentators as diverse as General Charles Vallancey, John Stuart Mill, and Karl Marx, compared it to colonial India. The applicability of the Irish situation to the Indian one was too helpful to be ignored, as Cook notes:

> The British were inveterate gatherers of ideas, models and techniques regardless of where they had been developed. Indeed, the imperial habit of borrowing and adapting practically became institutionalized. . . . Because Ireland and India were thought to be similar in certain respects, politicians, officials, journalists and writers started to construct Indo-Irish analogies that were used as justifications for importing and adapting administrative policies from one imperial unit to another. The landmark reassessment of tenurial legislation that occurred in each dependency between the late 1860s and the late 1880s involved the use of exogenous examples, particularly in the cases of the Irish Land Act of 1870 and the Bengal Tenancy Act of 1885. (134)

The concrete application of Irish-Indian analogies (rooted in Celtic-Oriental semiotics) to imperial policies demonstrates a close relationship between semiotics and history. Imperial analogies of peripheral cultures are at the core of an imperial worldview, and, as such, they have a history as old as empires.

Celtic-Oriental comparisons—stemming from both imperial influences and a native heritage of origin myths—developed within collective Irish identities as a matter of both pride and resistance. Cook identifies intra-imperial analogies with British ideologies, practices, policies, and events, showing how the experiences of British policy makers and colonial administrators were "at once interactive and mutually referential" (132). He also argues for the significance of historicist thought at the time: "Central to historicist inquiry . . . was the apprehension of laws that engineered and explained the evolutionary development of society." The linking of "undeveloped" cultures, in this case, Ireland with India, received new justifications from nineteenth-century historicist explanations of global inequities, as well as through the pseudoscience of racial discourse and developments in linguistics, which contrasted modern, ancient, and primitive languages. Moreover, a semiofficial recognition "of a link between famine and peasant indebtedness" and specific parallels between the Indian Revolt of 1857 and Irish agrarian violence in the 1860s further cemented the rationale for the intra-imperial analogy. Further proof came through legal, sociological, and anthropological publications in the 1860s and 1870s. Significantly, these influential studies were based both on Orientalist arguments and on Celticist translations, as Cook notes: "[T]he pertinent documents were the Brehon Law Tracts [of Ireland], various Indian official reports and surveys and studies of comparative philology" (131). This crossover between respected British ethnology and traditional Irish texts reintroduced Celtic-Oriental comparisons into valid scholarship, something that had existed only in nationalist histories, literature, and fringe antiquarianism since eighteenth-century philology. To some degree, Romantic imaginings in the first half of the century became in the second half the substance of Victorian pseudoscience, imperial policy, and nationalist aspirations. The reintroduction of Celtic-Oriental comparisons to accepted scholarship, paralleling advancements in Celtic and Oriental linguistics, also brought the comparison into new political territories.

Ethnographic and anthropological arguments connecting the Oriental and the Celtic also emerged in the late nineteenth century and have been explored recently by Kavita Philip in "Race, Class, and the Imperial Politics of Ethnography in India, Ireland, and London, 1850–1910" (2002). Philip points to the connection between ethnography and nationalism and examines similar racialized and gendered representations of the Irish and the Indian, relying on works such as James Mill's *History of British India* and those by numerous European Orientalists, as well as representations of poor Irish immigrants in England by Karl Marx, Friedrich Engels, and Henry Mayhew. Building on the work of L. Perry Curtis (particularly his *Apes and Angels: The Irishman in Victorian Caricature* [1971]), Philip explores how Irish and Indian nationalists addressed scientific stereotypes of the Oriental Indian and the Celtic Irish, finding a significant difference: Indian nationalists embraced elements of British materialism, whereas Irish nationalists generally resisted materialist and scientific rhetoric, and instead embraced cultural and religious rhetoric, which resonated more with a redemptive Celticism.

Brigadier General F. P. Crozier's *Word to Gandhi: The Lesson of Ireland* saw differences between Irish and Indian nationalism as inherent and constitutional, however: "The denial of self-expression in the constitutional manner by England led both countries into the paths of resistance, Ireland eventually finding her soul at the pistol's mouth, while India resorted to the weapon of non-co-operation and non-violence" (1931, 17–18). Michael Silvestri points out how perceived racial differences also created another potent difference in the tactics of Indian and Irish nationalists:

> One obstacle to Indian emulation of Irish tactics was the perceived racial difference between the Irish and the Indians. While the racialist beliefs of some Victorians branded Celtic races such as the Irish as inferior, and some Irish revolutionaries claimed that Indians shared a common Aryan heritage, for most Indian nationalists, the position of the Irish as a white, Christian race placed limits on their desire to imitate Irish tactics. Indian nationalists feared that because of racial similarity between the Irish and English, revolutionary activity by the Irish would be treated much more leniently than would such action by Indians. (2000b, 459)

The shared imperial experiences of soldiers and civil servants in India also dissipated perceived racial differences between Anglo-Saxon and Celt, as discussed previously, and increased it between Indian and Irish. Despite these divisions, intra-imperial and cross-colonial comparisons continued throughout the Empire.

The movement of Irish-Indian and Celtic-Oriental comparisons from ethnographic scholarship to cultural nationalism and to political action took varied and, at times, circuitous paths. One of the most striking instances arises from the lectures and writings of Sir Henry Maine (1822–1888), an ethnologist and jurisprudence scholar widely respected in the second half of the century. Maine traced English and modern law back to Roman jurisprudence and also did comparative analyses of "ancient societies"—often comparing them with sketches of "primitive" cultures around the world—in order to theorize the evolution of modern law and society. Although he made many solid advancements, his imperial biases often prevented accurate conclusions. Having served in India and studied Indian law and languages, Maine began with Indian and British comparisons. Following the gradual publication of translations by Irish scholars from *Senchas Már* (Great tradition) and other seventh- and eighth-century law texts in *Ancient Irish Law* (six volumes, 1865–1901), Maine also began to find similarities between Ireland's Brehon laws and India's ancient laws of Menu (what Maine repeatedly refers to as "Brahmin" law, capitalizing on the alliterative comparison to Brehon).

Maine's lengthiest comparison also became, unwittingly, his most historically potent. His comparative discussion of the practices of "fasting" in Ireland and India sparked discussions in Ireland and elsewhere that ultimately led to the cross-colonial practice of hunger striking. Throughout the next century, Irish and Indian nationalists "revived" this supposedly ancient practice, focusing the world's attention on the causes of Terence MacSwiney, Mohandas Gandhi, Bobby Sands, and others. Yet decades before the first hunger strikes, Maine had dismissed the power and viability of this form of protest, treating it as an ineffective, premodern, and barbaric practice, employed only in lieu of viable legal sanctions. Partly because his work carried the mantle of British imperialist authority, Maine's conclusions met with interest mingled with resistance by Irish cultural nationalists. They perceived his dismissal of this barbaric practice of "fasting" with resistant eyes, but saw his Celtic-Oriental comparison as accurate. Reading Maine's sense of British superiority as a slight on Irish and Indian traditions, they inverted what he considered implausible, making the practice of fasting public and powerful because of the fierce determination of the strikers.

Maine had established his reputation through imperial service and the publication *Ancient Law* (1861), a work still referenced today by historians of law. He served as the law member of the Council of Governor General of India until 1869, a position similar to the one held by Sir William Jones nearly a century before (G. Carey 1976, 15). In that capacity, he worked to reform and codify law in British India, based on traditional Indian law, allowing him to institute concepts from *Ancient Law*. His imperial post also influenced his perception of an ancient Irish-Indian connection. Following his return to England, Oxford University appointed him the first professor of comparative jurisprudence, and shortly thereafter, in 1871, he was named knight commander of the Star of India.

At Oxford, he published three works based on his lectures, all of which compare Irish and Indian cultures: *Village Communities in the East and West* (1871), *Lectures on the Early History of Institutions* (1875), and *Dissertations on Early Law and Custom* (1883). In *Ancient Law*, Maine frequently referenced the relatively recent establishment of modern law in the Orient, dismissing the practicality of ancient codifications (such as the laws of Menu) as wishful thinking on the part of Brahmins (1864, 17). In *Village Communities*, Maine notes the influence of Indian culture on European culture, in "The Effects of Observation of India on Modern European Thought" (a chapter that opens with the section "Dulness of Indian Topics") (1889, 205). In this volume, he first references the recent government-sponsored publication of *Ancient Laws of Ireland* (itself borrowing from Maine's famous *Ancient Law*), headed by John O'Donovan, Eugene O'Curry, and later by the Celticist-Orientalist Robert Atkinson, who oversaw the publication of five of the six volumes over the next thirty-six years (186–87).[20]

Maine's most significant comparisons between the Brehon and Brahmin appeared in *Lectures on the Early History of Institutions*, shortly after the publication of the third volume of *Ancient Laws of Ireland*. His ultimate conflation of the ancient Brehons and Brahmins, which I will signify as "Br_h_n," is based on questionable arguments about an ancient and cohesive Aryan culture. These arguments were developed in the nineteenth century by British and German Orientalists, most prominently Max Müller (1823–1900). Maine argues: "[Irish] Brehon law, growing together without legislation upon an original body of Aryan custom, and formed beyond the limit of that cloud of Roman juridical ideas which for many centuries overspread the whole Continent, and even at its extremity extended to England, should present some very strong analogies to another set of derivative Aryan usages, the Hindoo, law, which was similarly developed." Ancient Irish culture, again, was used to demonstrate the link between the Occident and the Orient—here not through language but through the "archaic peculiarities" of ancient Aryan legal codes (1966, 11).

Maine treats the legal "sanctions" (or the consequences for lawbreaking) within both societies as based in religious or supernatural fears of retribution: "[W]ant of a sanction is occasionally one of the greatest difficulties in understanding the Brehon law. Suppose a man disobeyed the rule or resisted its application, what would happen?" (38). Maine supplies several possibilities: first, he could have his property seized; second, he could be excommunicated by the Druids (an answer that "Cæsar supplies");[21] or third, "If you have a legal claim against a man of a certain rank and you are desirous of compelling him to discharge it, the Senchus Mor tells you to 'fast upon him.' . . . ('Ancient Laws of Ireland,' vol. i. p. 113)" (39). Having identified this recourse as being prominent (if ineffective), Maine, in no uncertain terms, links it with the Orient: "The institution [of "fasting"] is unquestionably identical with one widely diffused throughout the East, which is called by the Hindoos 'sitting *dharna*.' It consists in sitting at your debtor's door and starving yourself till he pays" (39–40). This speculative comparison between Irish "fasting" and Indian "sitting *dharna*" soon entered cultural nationalist circles in both Ireland and India, as the publication of Laurence Ginnell's (1854–1923) *Brehon Laws: A Legal Handbook* in 1894 testifies. The prestige increased for this "ancient practice" because of its supposed connection to India, making it "verifiably" ancient. Not long after, the practice extended into nationalist (and suffragist) praxis in the political act of hunger striking in Ireland and India.

Maine's perspective on this "fasting" practice deserves further examination because it reveals the dynamic of the unifying imperial gaze at disparate colonies. Fueled by justifications of modernity and progress, this discourse reaches backward to draw from the traditions of the colonized (the "old books") in order to justify future reforms. Toward this end, the intra-imperial analogies are instrumental. Because of its needed reliance on Irish and Indian traditions (which it aims to correct), the modernizing discourse carries seeds of its own undoing, germinated through the resistant practices of nationalists—in their reversals and reclamations, cultivated particularly in moments of cultural revival. Unwittingly, Maine dismisses the curious practice of "fasting" as superstitious and ineffectual. But he is not entirely unsympathetic to Ireland and its sense of lingering antiquity—as an aficionado of antiquity, he nods to these ancient laws, asserting that the English colonialization of Ireland interrupted the development of the Brehon laws into a modern system. If England had never colonized Ireland or if English governors had translated and enforced Brehon law (as in India),[22] much cultural misunderstanding might have been averted, or, as Maine puts it, "the gap between the alleged civilization of England and the alleged barbarism of Ireland during much of their history, which was in reality narrower than is commonly supposed, would have almost wholly disappeared" (55). All the same, when discussing the particulars of "fasting" and other laws, Maine uses modern English jurisprudence as his yardstick, treating the "ancient" practices as either abominable or frivolous:

> From the English point of view the practice has always been considered barbarous and immoral, and the Indian Penal Code expressly forbids it. It suggests, however, the question—what would follow if the debtor simply allowed the creditor to starve? Undoubtedly the Hindoo supposes that some supernatural penalty would follow; indeed, he generally gives definiteness to it by retaining a Brahmin to starve himself vicariously, and no Hindoo doubts what would come of causing a Brahmin's death. We cannot but suppose that the Brehon rule of fasting was once thought to have been enforced in some similar way. Cæsar states that the Druids believed in the immortality and transmigration of the soul, and considered it the key to their system. A Druid may thus very well have taught that penal consequences in another world would follow the creditor's death by starvation. . . . But an Irish Brehon could scarcely make any distinct assertion on the subject, since fasting had now become a specific ordinance of the Christian Church, and its conditions and spiritual effects were expressly defined by the Christian priesthood. (39–41)

The practice of "fasting" receives Maine's particular censure because of its very supposed necessity in those ancient societies, which existed "at a period when Courts of Justice [were] not as yet armed with resistless powers of compelling attendance and submission" (41). Such compelling and resistless powers came, however, with the advent of British imperialism. Until then, these preimperial societies had to rely on barbaric practices, in accordance with "supernatural sanctions," in order to enforce the Br_h_n law: "Both the Brahmins and the Brehons assume that Kings and Judges will enforce their law, and emphatically enjoin on them its enforcement; but, while the Brahmin could declare that neglect or disobedience would be followed by endless degradation and torment, the Brehon could only assert that the unlearned brother who pronounced a false judgment would find blotches come on his cheeks, and that the Chief who allowed sound usage to be departed from would bring bad weather on his country" (41–42). Prior to colonial and penal law, Br_h_n society relied on a higher authority, "Kings and Judges" backed by supernatural forces. Reminiscent of Cambrensis, Maine's picture of Irish and Indian culture presents cultures ripe for imperial intervention and civil guidance. Maine's primary discrimination between the latter development of the Oriental and the Celtic from a shared Aryan source seems to be the distinction between the Indians' servile fears of "endless degradation" and the Irish's credulous worries of "blotches [on] cheeks" and "bad weather"; the Oriental sensibility is based in supernatural cruelty and the Celtic in silly superstition.

Although in other instances Maine claims that the ancient Celtic laws hinted of modern jurisprudence, he also sees them as inherently frivolous: "[T]he Brehon law pays heavily for this apparent anticipation of the modern legal spirit. It must be confessed that most of it has a strong air of fancifulness and unreality" (45).[23] Because Br_h_n law, Maine argues, was not created through legislation, the "classes" that devised the laws, the Brehon and Brahmin, stand as the seminal cross-hemisphere figures—and, thus, become of imperial and cross-colonial interest.[24] For Maine, the similarity of the laws bolsters the appearance of a shared ancient Aryan heritage. Moreover, Maine clearly does not anticipate how noting this similarity would encourage nationalists to "revive" hunger strikes.

Following the publication of *Ancient Laws of Ireland* and Maine's Indo-Irish comparisons, Laurence Ginnell and James P. Kerr helped transform "fasting" into a modern volatile political practice. Kerr's introduction to Ginnell's *Brehon Laws: A Legal Handbook* (1894; third edition, 1917)[25] argues that the practice embodies and enacts a number of forces that Maine misses:

> Force of an overwhelming public opinion, force of an inherent ethical superiority, force of an interior dread of disobedience. . . . To "fast" upon a wrong-doer as a means of forcing him to do justice was a legal process as common and as recognized in ancient Ireland as the distraint of a tenant's furniture by a landlord is to-day in British Law. The object of the "Fasting" was to make the alleged wrong-doer give a "Pledge" to submit the matter in dispute to the award of a Brehon or Judge.[26] In its efficacy and practicability, because backed by public opinion, it was a great advance on the much more drastic process of arrest for debt known to both Roman Law and English Law. . . . To "Fast" was therefore to make a two-fold appeal for justice—first, a direct appeal to the humanity of the defendant, and, secondly, an appeal at large to the spirit of justice of the community. (1917, ii-iii)

Kerr treats this apparently ancient practice as an ethical force, rather than as a barbaric last resort. In Kerr's formulation, "fasting" is a tactic to be employed by the wronged powerless in order to publicly disgrace the unjust powerful. Despite disagreeing with Maine's dismissal of "fasting," Kerr acknowledges Maine's achievement: "Sir Henry Sumner Maine, LL.D., . . .has done much to make clearer to a possibly unsympathetic English public the fact that this 'Fasting' was a practice common among other ancient peoples beside the Irish" (iii). Kerr then cites Maine's Irish-Indian comparisons, juxtaposing both the Irish and the Indian as "ancient peoples" apparently against the modern English.

Laurence Ginnell (later an Irish MP) summarizes the Brehon law in "Distraint by Fasting," first explaining the workings of the law and then noting:

> Sir Henry Maine thought that fasting was regarded with a superstitious awe. I rather think the law, without superstition at all was calculated to inspire a good deal of awe, and that the distinguished defendant if he possibly could, paid the debt or gave a pledge in order to get the faster, as a dangerous nuisance, away from his door. Distress by way of fasting, now so strange to us because so long obsolete, was clearly designed in the interests of honesty and of the poor as against the mighty. How or why it assumed this particular form is not known, and shall probably never be known. It was not peculiar to Ireland, however. A system precisely similar has existed in India from time immemorial, and exists in some parts of that country at the present day. It is called "sitting *dharna*." (1917, 93–94)

The law, though "calculated to inspire a good deal of awe," was "long obsolete" in the 1890s. Significantly, the model of Indian fasting is presented as a model of current use in India—once again the ancient and absent Celtic is paired with the distant and present Oriental, as in Vallancey's round-tower woodcut. In chapter 9, "Native, Not Roman," Ginnell adds to the idea that Ireland has long been anti-colonial by refuting the idea that the Brehon laws were based in Roman law: "[T]he fact is, that in the Brehon Laws such coincidences with Roman Law are really fewer than might be expected without derivation at all. The coincidences with Hindoo Law are actually more numerous; yet no one suggests that the Brehon laws are derived from the Hindoo" (130). Here "native" correlates with "Hindoo" in opposition to imperial Rome and Britain.

Although this train of comparisons—Brehon and Brahmin, Celtic and Oriental—is generally not acknowledged as constituting a tradition or discourse, the comparisons between Irish and Indian were ready-made for Maine, Kerr, and Ginnell. Even though this cross-cultural comparison remarkably resembles eighteenth-century antiquarian and philological arguments, Ginnell's publication differs in several respects. Foremost among these differences is that Ginnell's book claims in the subtitle to be "a legal handbook"—something to be used to guide practice—in addition to being scholarly and historical: unlike much antiquarianism, it was intended to have actual political application.

Although the first modern hunger strikers were suffragists, the first recorded death of a hunger striker—nationalist Thomas Ashe (on September 25, 1917)—resulted from an attempted force-feeding by his British jailers after five days of striking. Dan Breen, the famous physical-force nationalist and later Fianna Fáil T.D. (representative) for Tipperary, notes in his autobiography, *My Fight for Irish Freedom* (1924):"The tragedy enfuriated the whole Irish nation, and two days afterwards the British gave in and accorded prisoners in Mountjoy the conditions for which they had campaigned. Forcible feeding of political prisoners on hunger-strike was never again attempted" (1991, 18–19).[27] Such a report contrasts vividly with Maine's questions about the ineffectual "sanctions" of "fasting," and demonstrates the success of what Ginnell posits as the "force of an overwhelming public opinion."

At the center of the most renowned hunger strike of the period was the Sinn Féin lord mayor of Cork, Terence MacSwiney (1879–1920). He died along with two other strikers in a Brixton prison following their arrest for possessing a name list (supposed targets) of the Royal Irish Constabulary, part of the British force during the War for Independence. MacSwiney had also served as the head of the local Cork Brigade of the Irish Republican Army (IRA) and wrote plays, poems, and essays from a cultural nationalist perspective. His death focused worldwide attention on the Irish struggle for independence and made hunger strikes a powerful strategy for Irish political prisoners. The sacrifice was clearly understood in America, but in India it stood as an exemplum for action, particularly in Bengal, where MacSwiney became a cross-colonial icon for nationalists and a particular model for an Indian nationalist, Jatindranath Das. Michael Silvestri discusses the valorization of hunger strikes in Bengal in his cogent article, "'The Sinn Féin of India': Irish Nationalism and the Policing of Revolutionary Terrorism in Bengal, 1905–1939":

> Bengalis believed that the experiences of Irish nationalists provided a blueprint for liberation from British rule. The Irish republicans offered to Bengal a tradition of heroic martyrdom to add to the ranks of Bengali revolutionaries who had already died in the campaign against the British. A famous revolutionary leaflet seized by the Bengal police in 1929 quoted Patrick Pearse ["the gem of young Ireland"] and urged Bengalis to imitate his sacrifice. . . . [28] A more direct link was the imitation of Terence MacSwiney, the Lord Mayor of Cork who fasted to death in 1920, by the Bengali revolutionary Jatindranath Das, who died while on a hunger strike in Lahore Jail in 1929. According to Nirad C. Chaudhuri,[29] "MacSwiney was almost worshipped by politically conscious Bengali's and the mayor of Calcutta sent a message to MacSwiney's widow in which he stated that 'Terence MacSwiney showed the way to Ireland's freedom. Jatin Das has followed him.'" (2000b, 469; reprinted in *An Phoblacht,* Sept. 29, 1929)

The enactment of this parallel by Irish and Indian nationalists demonstrates how an intra-imperial analogy became cross-colonial. In moving from a tradition of imagined affinities to scholarship to praxis, the Celtic–Oriental comparison no longer was only ancient, remote, and peripheral; it entered the future as an ideal and shaped the present for nationalists in Ireland and India.

The semiotic relationship between the twin discourses of the Oriental and the Celtic developed through such political actions, lending a resistant and subversive force for anticolonialists around the world. On the fifth anniversary of Terence MacSwiney's death, Frank Gallagher, a writer for the Republican newspaper *An Phoblacht,* wrote: "Terence MacSwiney had ceased to be an individual when the sentence of the court martial was pronounced upon him in Cork Military barracks. He became a nation, *the* nation. . . . Speaking through him Ireland sent such a message to the world as will live and live, echoed back from the Andes to the Alps, from the Himalayas to the last hill of the two hemispheres, it will be heard . . . and bring liberty to little peoples, men of all nations and of his own" (Oct. 23, 1925, 3). In literary and cultural comparisons, both nationalist and unionist, from Republican leaflets to ethnographic studies, the Celtic–Oriental comparison was pervasive. Because doubly peripheral, however, it was rarely recognized as having an independent history, emerging from Irish imaginings of the Orient, but the semiotic and textual continuity is evident. Celtic–Oriental comparisons increasingly inspired cross-colonial politics in the early twentieth century, encouraging resistant practices such as the hunger strike. This practice in particular has had great force in nationalist and anticolonial circles and made known the struggles of figures such as Mohandas Gandhi and Bobby Sands. Less well-known figures, such as the Irish-Indian woman's rights advocate and anticolonialist Margaret Cousins, also found hunger strikes to advance issues, local and international as chapter 8 notes.

Part Two ☉ The Oriental and the Celt

The Syncretism of the Revival

> Dr. Kenealy quotes, in his "Book of God," Vallancey, who says "I
> had not been a week landed in Ireland from Gibraltar, where I had
> studied Hebrew and Chaldaic under Jews of various countries,
> when I heard a peasant girl say to a boor standing by her 'Teach an
> Maddin Nag' (Behold the morning star), pointing to the planet
> Venus, the Maddena Nag of the Chaldeans."
> —Madame Helene Petrovna Blavatsky, citing Edward Kenealy,
> citing Charles Vallancey, *The Secret Doctrine*

THE YEAR that James Connolly organized the Citizen's Army to protect striking workers during the General Strike, or the Dublin Lock-Out, 1913, Ireland entered a period of intermittent violence that continued for nearly a decade. The Celtic Twilight period of the Celtic Revival had faded, and the Abbey Theatre was producing realistic dramas under the leadership of Lennox Robinson. This same year, three very different texts were published, Ellis H. Minns's *Scythians and Greeks: A Survey of Ancient History and Archaeology on the North Coast of the Euxine from the Danube to the Caucasus* (1913), Sophie Bryant's *Genius of the Gael: A Study in Celtic Psychology and Its Manifestations* (1913), and A. Schwarz's pamphlet *Man: Whence, How and Whither* (1913). The first two works demonstrate that the Irish-Oriental connection no longer existed in the ways it had in previous centuries. Minn's *Scythians and Greeks* discusses the Scythians and their connections to other peoples using archaeological evidence; Bryant's *Genius of the Gael,* a psychological study of the Irish character, bases its conclusions on stereotypes of racial traits and ethnological assertions about the people living in Ireland, a place she tags "the Zion of the Celtic race." Schwarz's pamphlet, however, reinvents the Irish-Oriental origin legends in a discussion of how mystical beings on the astral plane fostered the "Keltic" race, bringing them from the Orient into Ireland. Such texts point to how, at the turn of the twentieth century, Irish interest in the Orient had moved from the romantic and literary to the mystical (and political); the occult fervor of the late nineteenth century had fostered the movement of the Oriental and Celtic into the penumbra of rational Victorian sensibility as fearful and strange peripheral possibilities.

Bryant explores how various races make up the Irish genius, as *filid* had done in the sixteenth century, yet, instead of relying on Irish texts directly, her ideas are extensions of the ideas of Matthew Arnold and other Celticists. She comments on the influence of the Saxon, Norman, Iberian, Celtic, Fir Bolgian, Norse, and Teutonic, but does not mention any Scythian, Phoenician, or Oriental ties, although she does discuss the "well-purposed, though partly fictitious Milesian history" and the character of these pagan Milesians (1913, 26). Bryant, not herself of "the ancient Gaelic stock" (287), develops her conclusions based on stereotypes about the sociable, mystical, imaginative, and hospitable Irish: "This is the key to the Irishman's social nature: he is *other-conscious as a matter of course*. . . . [T]he other-conscious man is naturally loyal because the other man's hurt hurts him. We think of loyalty more especially in relation to friends, but it applies to strangers and even enemies as well. Its psychological cause is the consciousness of the other man's mind" (88–89). Such an argument must have seemed to account for Irish culture's sympathy and hospitality and its cross-colonial sympathies. Bryant also reductively explains that the Irishman's "danger is that he will follow his idea with too much eagerness. Fanaticism is near him" (73). Pop ethnology had supplanted other narratives about the nature and origins of the Irish.[1]

Minns's work on the ancient Scythians remains a bit more palatable than Bryant's by today's standards. In tracing the history of the Scyths, he outlines the different genealogies that were attributed to them in the previous centuries, first noting: "So many different views as to the affinities of the Scythians have been propounded that their enumeration seemed too much of a burden for the text" (1965, 97). For the most part, the Scythians had been seen as early Slavs (98), although in the eighteenth century, they were commonly believed to have become Tartars and Mongols. He cites Johann Kaspar Zeuss, the groundbreaking Celticist, who treats the Scyths as Iranians (98) and E. Bonnell, who "seem[s] to waver between assigning Germans, Lithuanians, Slavs, and Kelts as descendants of the Scythians, whom yet he calls Iranian" (99). He also notes that a number of archaeologists and linguists have argued that there may be Scythian-Indian connections; for instance, M. Nagy argued that the Scyths made it to the "Panjáb" based on etymologies (99). Minns comments, "The upshot of all this is to prove from the other side that no one etymological key will open all the locks that bar the way to a full understanding of the Scythian problem" (100). On the once dominant explanation of the Celto-Scyths, Minns's explanation demonstrates how scholars generally received that theory in the early twentieth century:

On the mountainous south coast of the Crimea lived the Tauri, some have called them Kelts, comparing the name of the Taurisci: but some theorists find Kelts everywhere. We have no data whatsoever for giving relations to the Tauri. They probably represent the earliest inhabitants of S. Russia, perhaps akin to the aborigines of the Caucasus; possibly they would be Iranians. . . . Then we could understand their later mixing with the Scythians, when in the latter the Iranian element had again come to the top. Otherwise we must take the Scytho-Tauri to be like the Celto-Scythae and the Celtiberians, products of the Greek belief that a race of which little was known was best named by combining the names of its neighbors. (101)

No viable archaeological or historical reason existed to argue that the Celts had Scythian origins, or Phoenician, Egyptian, Indian, Persian, Chinese, or Oriental origins. Notwithstanding, many writers still commented on such connections, from James Joyce to journalists in the nationalist newspaper *An Phoblacht.* In addition to frequent cross-colonial comparisons, old and new variations on Oriental origin theories appeared occasionally in *An Phoblacht,* as in the article "Prehistoric Inhabitants." Dr. Pokorny, a German Celticist, asserted that the Irish were linked to North Africans, Eskimos, and peoples on the Baltic shores. "Dr. Pokorny based his Eskimo theory largely on the evidence of Cuchulaun's mysterious weapon, the *Gae Bolga,* which he believed to be simply the Eskimo 'bag-spear.' . . . Dr. Pokorny also drew support for his theory from a comparison between New Grange and the snow huts of the Eskimos, showing that both were built on the same plan" (Nov. 6, 1925, 5). Significantly, Pokorny's theories are presented as tenuous, and arguments by other philologists and archaeologists, such as R. A. Stewart Macalister, counter his points. For the most part, archaeology had disproved most of the Oriental origin theories.

Macalister and other archaeologists often wrote for Irish newspapers and gave lectures on ancient Ireland, the study of which had developed enormously. They exposed and dismissed earlier theories:

It was supposed that the Mediterranean peoples, especially the Phoenicians, traded directly with the tin owners of Cornwall. From this it was but a step to suppose that it was the Phoenicians who brought their civilization and their religious beliefs and cultus to these islands. Happily for the theorists, nobody even yet knows very much about the Phoenicians, their religion and their civilization, so there was and there still is free scope for speculation—of which Vallancey and his modern imitators have fully availed themselves. (Macalister 1970, 134)

Overall, by the Celtic Revival, most rational scholarly arguments—linguistic, archaeological, ethnographic, and psychological—had dismissed connections between the Irish and any group in the Orient. The primary areas where this semiotic connection still existed were in nationalist politics, mystical treatises, and Celticist literature.

A number of Irish writers such as Oliver St. John Gogarty, James Joyce, and Samuel Beckett poked fun at the Irish-Asian connections in Celticist and Orientalist writings. Although Joyce gave a lecture in Trieste, "Ireland, Island of Saints and Sages," in which he reasserted the theories of Vallancey, his use seems more strategic than sincere.[2] Joyce perceived the elements of the discourse clearly, opening his lecture: "Nations hate their egos, just like individuals. The case of a people who like to attribute to themselves qualities and glories foreign to other people has not been entirely unknown in history" (1959, 154). Irish remoteness and antiquity remained foundations of the discourse. In Joyce's short story "Araby," a young boy becomes disillusioned with romance at an exotic Oriental carnival; the story's setting links the Orient with illusion and fancy. Joyce was not alone in such a perspective.[3] Gogarty and Beckett also lampooned misty images of the Celt and the Orient, dismissing them as romance and indulgent fancy. And the Celtic-Oriental connection was not the only subject for ridicule.

In *As I Was Going Down Sackville Street* (1937), Gogarty's narrator notes: "[W]e are suffering from a nightmare culture of imaginary Gaels" (1994, 200). Along with deflating Celticism and Hibernophilia, the book abounds with references to India and China; when two characters discuss how to represent Dublin, one concludes: "The only way to treat this town is the way the Chinese [*sic*] treat their pictures; eschew perspective" (58). Only outside the realism of Europe could the peripheral nature of Dublin be evoked. Later, just after commenting on a queue outside the cinema house—described as "Dubliners willing to buy a dream that will let them escape for an hour from their surroundings"—the narrator meets Tim Healy, the "First Governor-General of the Irish Free State," and they briefly discuss the book of another governor, "a translation of the Chinese of Po-Chu-I when he was Governor-General of Chung-Chou" (92–93). China (and, by extension, the Orient) is seen as not only unrealistic and nonpragmatic, but the various comparisons enacted by characters in the book are presented as spurious. Strikingly, however, political comparisons remain apt, partly because of common colonial histories with Britain but also because of the supposed traits and similar imperial justifications that made these cultures supposedly susceptible to outside rule. The lure of the exotic—if not the primitive—in general had faded for modernists and scholars. In Samuel Beckett's *Murphy* (1938), Miss Counihan, an Irish exile in London, becomes entranced by an "Oriental" atmosphere in a hotel, just as she and other characters are bedazzled by a "Celtic" atmosphere: "Here she cowered, as happy as the night was short, in the midst of Indians, Egyptians, Cyprians, Japanese, Chinese, Siamese and clergymen. Little by little she sucked up to a Hindu polyhistor of dubious caste. He had been writing for many years, still was and trusted he would be granted Prana to finish, a monograph provisionally entitled: The Pathetic Fallacy from Avercamp to Kampendonck" (1957, 195–96). The Celtic-Oriental connection, in the Irish case, is burlesqued, in part because it could not reconcile present-day Irish culture with the increasing demands of rationalist modernity; it appeared to only offer modes of slipping the march of progress through speculations about antiquity or about a bold new age for Ireland and the world.

General European literary Orientalism had also changed. Moving away from earlier Romantic uses, the Orient had developed as a subject of fantasy and adventure writing (Rider Haggard), as an exotic realm for jingoistic writers (Rudyard Kipling), and as an alternate, premodern, and emotional world for disillusioned modernists (E. M. Forster). Anglocentric Irish works such as Lord Dunsany's Gods of Pegana (1905), written in a biblical style and encouraged by George Russell (AE), also depicted the Orient, but in a fashion more consonant with such Anglo-French Orientalism, devoid of any cross-colonial allegorical resonances (Welch 1996, 162). As Dunsany's short story "A Tale of London" demonstrates, the binary of the glorious metropole and the envious periphery was deeply rooted within his vision of the Orient. The story opens: "'Come,' said the Sultan to his hasheesh-eater in the very furthest lands that know Bagdad, 'dream to me now of London' " (1996, 54). The hasheesh eater tells him of the glories of London, which is "without a peer for beauty or excellence of its ways among the town of the earth or cities of song" (56). At the end of the story, the sultan lightly applauds, and the narrator notes, "there was envy in that palace, in lands beyond Bagdad, of all that dwell in London" (56–57). Although the story could be discussed for the dynamics that it exposes within Orientalism, this representation clearly does not depict an Orient in the same manner as most of Dunsany's contemporary Celtic Revivalists, which the following chapters discuss.

Most of the literary Irish Orientalism in this period generated a mode that merged the Asian and the Irish in a sort of discursive syncretism building on tropes of the Oriental and the Celtic. By the early twentieth century, W. B. Yeats abandoned his youthful attempts at writing plays and poetry based in an Orient resembling Dunsany's; in his new works, he combined Irish and Japanese forms and Irish and Indian themes, seeking a hybrid fertilization. James Stephens, who helped form the new genre of magical realism, most evident in The Crock of Gold (1912), certainly relied on Orientalist and Celticist images within his folklore and legend-laden work; he also mingled Irish and Chinese characters and steeped his Irish stories and poems with classical Indian philosophy. James Cousins in 1913 was preparing to leave Ireland for India and was immersed in Indian and neo-Celtic mysticism and poetry while writing a geography textbook. The unacknowledged discourse of Irish Orientalism also grew through intra-imperial comparisons (as in the previous discussion in chapter 4 on hunger strikes). But independent of British commentaries, other "sympathetic" Irish political and cross-colonial commentaries on "Oriental" figures and politics emerged, as in the essays of Augusta Gregory, Frederick Ryan, James Connolly, Roger Casement, and others. George Bernard Shaw, in his 1907 and the 1929 prefaces to *John Bull's Other Island,* explicitly compared the violence of British Black and Tans in Ireland with British violence in Egypt at Denshawai and in India at Amritsar. Indeed, such comparisons became common for the nationalist press, most notably for the Republican newspaper *An Phoblacht* during the 1920s and '30s.

Intra-imperial analogies between Ireland and other colonies continued in the twentieth century, as fears of the disintegration of the Empire and the unification of the periphery grew. The very idea of borderlands uniting became anathema to imperialists in the nineteenth and twentieth centuries, when European and American empires promoted universalist discourses that stressed an absence of cultural boundaries. Indeed, the case can be made that contemporary American globalization has in many regards supplanted European imperialism; today, in the discourse of Americanization, to be everyman, to be fully human, is to appreciate and absorb American ideals, culture, and hegemony. During the Celtic Revival, however, universalist discourses were not always synonymous with imperialism, and border cultures could imagine connections across the frontiers of Empire. Imperial fears about the joining of Irish and various nefarious forces from other colonies, although not well founded, clearly existed. An instance exists in the recently published memoirs of an English officer, W. A. Tilney, or "Colonel Standfast," who after serving in India and fighting in the Boer War was stationed in the west of Ireland during the Anglo-Irish war with the Black and Tans[4] (in a move that typified intra-imperial exchange). In the chapter "A Confrontation with Sinn Fein," "Standfast" writes: "It was a common rumour at this time that the rebels were importing foreigners—Chinese, Tartars and Russians—to carry out their nefarious assassinations, as on many occasions the Irishman had declined to perpetrate some of the worst crimes. About 9 a.m., as I was approaching Nenagh, I met a body forty to fifty strong of the worst-looking ruffians imaginable, consisting of Mongolians and other foreigners, the only Irishman being the man in command" (2001, 147–48). Significantly, the fact that the Irishman is the commander signifies how this British imagination kept the Irish as an intermediary to the nefarious Orient. But this time the intermediary had switched sides and commanded and represented the Oriental to the European instead of the other way around. The absurd "facts" of the case are almost irrelevant, except that such stories existed. The affinity of the Irish and the Asian feared by the imperialist representative becomes embodied in this fictitious band of Mongolians in rural Ireland.

Another equally fantastic connection can be found in an essay by an early-twentieth-century Theosophist, Celticist, and amateur archaeologist, Pierce Leslie Pielou, who was a friend of the Cousinses and traced his ancestors in Kerry back to Norman settlers.[5] Before the much broader cultural acceptance of "New Age" ideas, mystics such as Pielou, the Welsh writer Evan Evans, and others propounded a fringe connection between Ireland and Asian cultures, particularly India and Egypt. As late as 1955, Pielou was writing articles such as "Ireland's Link with Egypt, Crete, and the Middle East" for the journal *Theosophy.* In a pamphlet, *Megalithic Remains in Ireland, Particularly Those of the Valley of the Boyne,* Pielou gives a number of extraordinary recountings of Irish-Oriental origins that resemble Vallancey's. In order to back up his mystical arguments, he often refers to and cites bona fide archaeologists, including Macalister. After citing Walter Fitzgerald, a South African professor in Manchester, on "the De Danaan of Irish traditions," he adds, "At this point let us consider what the occultists have said about these people" (1937, 15) and turns to A. Schwarz's *Man: Whence, How and Whither,* which discusses the intentions of beings on the astral plane, the "Manu," who are, supposedly, the breeders of humanity, both racially and spiritually.

Schwarz develops the Oriental origin legends into a strange mystical treatise, but Pielou's comments reveal even more. Pielou comments in a footnote: "The Manu selected the most refined people for the nucleus of the fourth sub-race, striving to awaken imagination and artistic sensibility, to encourage poetry, music, painting. The valley was practically managed as a separate state and artistic characteristics remained the special mark of the Kelt." Pielou continues commenting on Schwarz and other mystics, discussing a complex metaphysical system that approaches the breathless aspirations of Yeats's *Vision* through a fantastic genealogy.

[T]he waves of emigration [came] from this cradle of the fourth sub-race into Europe, . . . the first was that of the Ancient Greeks, sometimes called the Pelasgians. From them sprang the Trojans who fought with the modern Greeks. Then the Albanians, the Italian race, the "Keltic" wave which spread over north Italy, France, Belgium and the British Isles, western Switzerland and Germany, west of the Danube. The fifth wave practically lost itself in the north of Africa, and traces of it are to be found among the Berbers, the Moors, the Kabyles and the Guanches of the Canary Islands. It is said that the Milesian invaders of Ireland about the fourth century B.C., those who defeated the Tuatha De Danann, were the result of a mixture of the third and fourth wave. Then it is said that a far more splendid element of the Irish population had come into it before from the sixth wave of the Keltic people, which had left Asia Minor in a totally different direction, pushing north-west as far as Scandinavia where they mingled to some extent with the Fifth Sub-race, the Teutonic, and descended into Ireland from the north. They are celebrated in its history as the Tuatha de Danann. The Tuatha-de-Danann were not only so much handsomer, but also intellectually and spiritually so very much in advance of the mixed race which they found in Ireland that they were regarded by the latter as of celestial lineage, and to this day tradition speaks of them as a race of gods who ruled Ireland during a golden age, which is by no means entirely legendary as historians generally suppose. Ireland was unquestionably the seat of a high civilisation and a centre of philosophy and learning while the neighboring island of England was largely covered by dense forests and peopled by naked savages who painted themselves blue. The Tuatha De Danann were also described as fine horsemen. (15)

In clear opposition to rational and modern studies that rely upon source criticism and verifiable facts, this narrative builds upon phantasm and tradition. It borrows antiquated methodologies from racial theories, antiquarianism, philology, archaeology, linguistics, historiography, origin legends, and Theosophy to construct a narrative-grounded mysticism. For a number of reasons, this nonrational approach appealed to many writers in early-twentieth-century Ireland.

Such nonrational approaches to aesthetics and spirituality inform a great deal of the thought, writings, and program development of the Celtic Revival. Most scholars and critics of postcolonization literatures dismiss writings that have nonrational arguments. But much may be missed in such a categorical elision, particularly in the work of W. B. Yeats, AE, James Stephens, and James Cousins. David Matless has written on the value of mystical writings in his essay "Nature, the Modern, and the Mystic: Tales from Early Twentieth Century Geography" (1991). Building on his work, Catherine Nash has discussed James Cousins and his geographical and Theosophical writings:

> Recent reflection on geographical epistemology has been critical of the discipline's foundation in masculinist and exclusionary ideas of science and rationality. Less attention has been paid to forms of geographical knowledge based on the mystic or occult or the imaginative geographies of esoteric spirituality. Yet David Matless has suggested, a critical approach to the politics of geographical knowledge means taking the apparently fanciful seriously, rather than weeding out from a discerning historiography what seems most absurd and irrational. A critique of the dominance of rationalist epistemology is limited if the non-rational only features as a comic diversion. (1996, 401)

Although writings such as those by Pielou may not have been crafted according to any careful aesthetic, other writings by accomplished writers during the Revival were carefully crafted yet had similar Theosophical, Orientalist, and Celticist themes, subject matter, and even conclusions. Although writers such as Macalister and Minns might confidently assert the fictional nature of Irish-Oriental origin theories through historiography, archaeology, and ethnographic psychology, such irrational spiritualist works clearly retained some appeal for the Revivalists.

After describing "The Cave-Temples of New Grange and Dowth" (1937,

16–21), Pielou gives a clearer impression of the occult circles in Dublin at the time.[6]

> About thirty years ago a little group of students who were accustomed to meet in Dublin at the house of Mr. J. H. Cousins (now Kulapati James H. Cousins, D.Litt., of Madanapalle College, Madras Presidency), decided to combine with the Dublin branch of the Society for Psychical Research in inviting Mr. Vout Peters, the well-known medium, to come to Ireland. It was Mr. Peters' first visit to this country and the first private meeting took place in Mr. Cousin's house. Two members of the group went to New Grange the day before, and got a few chips off the basin-like stone on the floor of the central chamber of the mound, which they at once wrapped up carefully and placed, next day, on the tray on which lay a number of articles to be psychometrised. All the articles were on the tray before Mr. Peters entered the room, and he was told nothing about the chips of stone or about the persons who brought them. In due course he took up the little packet containing the chips and, after holding them in his hand and to his forehead for a short time, proceeded to describe the tumulus as it stands at the present, stating the number of upright stones standing in a circle around it. [T]he number was unknown to any one present but was afterwards found to be correct. He then said, "I am going back some hundreds of years in time" and then described the place as it was then, saying that the district was inhabited by a people who had no definite knowledge of the origin and purposes of the building, but that they had a superstitious reverence for it and buried their chieftains there. He continued, "I feel myself going back an immense distance in time and I see coming into Ireland a tall, fair race, clothed in white. They are coming into this country to preserve their ancient religion. It is they who built this mound, and I can see them gathering men and women around them in a circle and teaching them their ancient wisdom." I think Mr. Peters also said that they used this buried temple for initiation purposes. Mr. Peters was carefully questioned by Mr. Cousins and others but evidently had no knowledge of the antiquities of Ireland, and had never been here before. He knew nothing whatever about the chips of stone, where they came from or who brought them, before he gave the above psychometric reading. (21–22)

The writers who are the subjects of chapters 6, 7, and 8 all sought out and experienced occult or Theosophical moments such as this one. This tight-knit group of Celtic Revivalists inherited and embraced much of the unacknowledged discourse of Irish Orientalism. Other writers developed cross-colony ties, partly from intra-imperial analogies and partly because they had developed critiques based in their own experiences. The connections between the Oriental and the Celt had been rationally debunked on many fronts, but many Irish writers still embraced political, mystical, and exotic connections to the Orient, bringing with them a healthy mixture of credulity and skepticism.

Outside Theosophical circles, writers such as James Joyce also continued to reference Ireland's Oriental affinity as a way of signifying immutability, antiquity, and perpetuity. For instance, as Joyce's Leopold Bloom drifts about his own Dublin Ogygia in the "Lotus Eaters" episode of *Ulysses,* images of an outmoded Oriental-Celtic continuum drift through his mind as do thoughts of streets, houses, and bricks:

> Cityful passing away, other cityful coming, passing away too: other coming on, passing on. Houses, lines of houses, streets, miles of pavements, piledup bricks, stones. Changing hands. This owner, that. Landlord never dies they say. Other steps into his shoes when he gets his notice to quit. They buy the place up with gold and still they have all the gold. Swindle in it somewhere. Piled up in the cities, worn away age after age. Pyramids in sand. Built on bread and onions. Slaves Chinese wall. Babylon. Big stones left. Round towers. Rest rubble, sprawling suburbs, jerrybuilt. Kerwan's mushroom houses built of breeze. Shelter, for the night. (135)

Here, the round towers point to Ireland's link to antiquity, and even timelessness, in consort with a vision of the enduring Orient, but such references do not indicate the new syncretism of Irish Orientalism in the literature of the Celtic Revival.

The works of W. B. Yeats, George Russell, James Stephens, and James Cousins demonstrate a flowering of Irish literary Orientalism during the Celtic Revival. Their antimaterialist and anticolonial Celtic imaginings provoked Irish (and Indian, in the case of Cousins) culture into new directions of cultural decolonization. The most prominent mystic of the day, AE, introduced each of them to Theosophy and Indian philosophy, which he once claimed, in a letter to Sean O'Faolain, was his "aid to understanding" (qtd. in Kuch 1986, 18). One of the most significant similarities that these four authors share is the fact that they were not from Catholic traditions; all were born to Protestant families. Numerous critics—as ideologically disparate as John Wilson Foster, Terry Eagleton, Terence Brown, and Roy Foster—have explored these writers' sectarian inheritances and their cultural allegiances as non-Catholics, observing how their Protestantism manifests itself in their works and their occult curiosities. Also, many critics have argued that many of these writers' Oriental and Eastern spiritual interests arose in order to reconcile the differences they each perceived with the dominant religion of the emerging Irish nation. Although such arguments have a good deal of validity, such a perspective runs the risk of overshadowing other lines of inquiry and ignoring other Catholic uses of Orientalist themes and images. The deep influence of Indian philosophy and Theosophy had fueled AE's own influential brand of Celtic spiritualism,[7] which dominated his works and influenced the works of Yeats, Stephens, and Cousins, moving Irish Orientalism in new syncretic directions.

5   Uniting the Circumference

Cross-Colonialism

That some disorder prevails is likely enough, for the Affghans are
not yet thoroughly united; if they were they could make short work
with their invaders.
    —"The English Army in Affghanistan, and the 'Notions' of the
        English Press Thereupon," in the first issue of the *Nation*

Every man born in Ireland holds a "hereditary brief" for the
opponents of English sway, wherever they may be.
        —Roger Casement, *The Crime Against Europe*

ALTHOUGH IRELAND'S PARTICIPATION in the British Empire informed Irish
Orientalism, Celtic affinities with the Orient distinguished the discourse from
Anglo-French Orientalism. The popular and academic representations discussed in
chapter 4 focused on how Celtic-Oriental comparisons operated within Empire.
Moreover, as in the development of the idea of Br_h_n fasting to Irish and Indian
hunger striking, cross-colonial ties often developed in response to imperial representations, inverting and recovering traditional Irish references within pseudoscientific, ethnographic categorizations.

   This chapter examines Irish texts that imply or assert an affinity with the Orient and, very often, critique the dominant British modes of representing the Oriental and the Celtic. Many Irish authors, Catholic and Protestant—Lady Augusta
Gregory, George Bernard Shaw, Frederick Ryan, Roger Casement, and others—
critiqued the imperial mode of representing the Orient in a variety of genres, literary and political, throughout the Celtic Revival of the late nineteenth and early
twentieth centuries. Discussions of Irish relations with the Orient also emerged in
the anticolonial essays of Marxist labor leaders, particularly James Connolly. Anticolonial politics suffused these writers' representations of the Orient, as such politics informed their lives and, at times, their deaths. Namely, Casement and

Connolly were both executed by British authorities for their anticolonial activities, particularly their leadership in planning the Easter Rising.

While Lafcadio Hearn, W. B. Yeats, M. Mansoor, and James Joyce speculated as to the possible truth (genealogically or discursive) of the legend of the Oriental origins of the Irish, most Irish writers treated the legends as curious, erroneous historical speculations from an earlier time (as in "The Round Towers of Ireland," *Irish Builder* [Dec. 1899]). Nevertheless, narratives of Oriental-Celtic and Asian-Irish affinities continued to develop into the twentieth century, mostly through the literary inventions of Revivalists. Many political thinkers also construed and actualized cross-colonial ties. Irish references to India, Persia, China, Afghanistan, Egypt, and other cultures subsumed within the Orient increased in the nineteenth century and forged a modern expression of the Celtic-Oriental affinity: cross-colonialism.

Imperial Critique in the *Nation* and *An Phoblacht*

Irish nationalist discussions of other British colonies in the nineteenth century developed in both Orientalist literature and nationalist periodicals. Partly because most reports of activities in the colonies were received through British sources, nationalists began to suspect the discussions, the representations, and the very discourse of the Orient. Aware of the long textual history of British barbarizations of Ireland, Irish writers speculated about and often mistrusted the accuracy of British reports of other colonies, even if Irish soldiers numbered in the occupying forces. Such skepticism developed concurrently with the parodic translations of James Clarence Mangan, both building on a tradition of encoded critique at the heart of Irish Orientalism.

An early nationalist instance of Irish political discussion of British colonial activities appeared on October 15, 1842, in the first issue of the *Nation,* the prominent nationalist weekly newspaper of the midcentury, which would later publish much of Mangan's poetry. Founded by Thomas Davis (1814–1845), John Blake Dillon (1814–1866), and Charles Gavan Duffy (1816–1903), the paper espoused the views of Young Ireland, and supplied the words of Chief Baron Woulfe as its motto in the first issue:"To create and to foster public opinion in Ireland—to make it racy of the soil" (8). The paper sold an average of 10,000 copies per issue, which were then privately circulated within communities, raising the estimated readership of each issue to the neighborhood of 250,000 (Welch 1996, 390).[1] Suppressed by the British government in 1848, one of the worst years of the Famine, the paper soon reformed and continued from 1849 to 1896, with a somewhat different focus, reporting more on the land debates in Ireland.

Page 6 of the first issue, however, is packed with reports from the Empire (almost 10,000 words) about British activities in "India, Affghanistan, and China."

This section of the paper, "The Overland Mail," brought news of Irish soldiers to families and friends at home—often framed with a particular Irish angle: "Is it not a lamentable absurdity—a blunder almost too ludicrous for an English commander in Affghanistan to have officers of an army less resolute and courageous than the soldiers?" (8). These news stories are filled with accounts of troop movements, physical hardships, and bad weather. Letters from British officers provide the numbers of killed and wounded, and the size and "Strength of the Brigade," every category being subdivided into European and "Native." But relaying the news from English sources certainly did not distinguish the paper. Rather, that difference comes in the commentary on the news; page 8 offers a detailed analysis of the reported events, after a declaration—"the first article of our political creed"—that attempts to unify Irish political culture. The article opens: "With all the nicknames that serve to delude and divide us—with all their Orangemen and Ribbonmen, Torymen and Whigmen, Ultras and Moderados, and Heaven knows what rubbish besides, there are, in truth, but two parties in Ireland: those who suffer from her National degradation and those who profit by it. To a country like ours, all other distinctions are unimportant." Moving one's eyes two columns over, such a sentiment is echoed in the discussion of the anticolonial activities in Afghanistan: "That some disorder prevails is likely enough, for the Affghans are not yet thoroughly united; if they were they could make short work with their invaders." The topic of this essay is revealed in its title, "The English Army in Affghanistan, and the 'Notions' of the English Press Thereupon." Although criticisms of the press were valid and acceptable, the paper could not call for British defeat, especially with so many Irish soldiers in the "invad[ing]" army. Targeting the press was a somewhat safer approach that nevertheless implicated the imperial agenda. With a suggested comparison—encouraged by a culturally pervasive Celtic-Oriental link—the situations between Ireland and "Affghanistan" could seem parallel. The development toward an overt comparison was gradual, and many nineteenth-century statements with cross-colonial implications may not initially appear cross-colonial—but they seem to have been gauged for readers who would arrive at such a critique on their own.

As the title of the aforementioned section makes clear, the editors viewed the presentation of Afghanistan in the English press circumspectly. They first relayed the news from English sources and two pages later treat those very stories as "Notions" and not accurate records of real events. Such foregrounding of the process of representation became a significant anticolonial tool, and served as a partial deconstruction and revelation of the Anglo-French arguments. Such a method struck an intrinsic chord for Irish Orientalism, while the discourse itself remained unacknowledged. The section discussing "Affghanistan" begins by noting that Irish papers should decode the English news:

> The news brought by the last Overland Mail from Asia is, to our thinking, most important—nor is its import the less because the English press, and such portions of the Scotch and Irish periodicals as confine their sources of information to the writings of London editors have misrepresented it. According to *their* account—which our readers will see detailed in our news-columns—the army of General Pollock was in excellent health and spirits . . . and the whole force, backed by an army of warlike and disciplined Sikhs, was about to march on Cabul. . . . Now, what are the facts? Pollock's army is sick and dispirited, unable to move for want of commissariat cattle, "three months in arrear of pay," . . . ; the heat so intense in that prison plain, of Jellalabad, that the officers were obliged to dig holes four feet deep in the ground, within their tents, "to sit naked in" and the men were dying of dysentery. The Sikh troopers were disaffected, and an incumbrance. (8)

This description is not the image of the glorious British army to which readers of the British press were accustomed. In the article doubt also spreads to standard Orientalist representations of the Afghans.

Referencing earlier articles, the writer also discusses how the English press demonizes the anticolonial "murderer Akhbar Khan," who reportedly tried to gain control over a group of European or "Feringhee" prisoners (6). The critique on page 8 describes such English reports as "notorious" and attributes them "to design." The Irish commentator also accuses the British papers of novelizing the experiences of the English prisoners in "Cabul":

> As we are taking these statements, in local order, it is as well to notice that the prisoners really, and in truth, are in a large fortress, five miles from Cabul, and that they are, and ever have been, treated with the greatest attention as to their residences, food, and even amusements. The "heroine," Lady Sale, goes out every day, it seems, "botanizing" among the hills, attended by two Affghan guards. Is it come to this? Mark, reader, how the English press deals with these prisoners. One while [*sic*] they all swore, by all their gods, that these prisoners *must* be undergoing every misery— that the Affghans were brutes, and their Chief a lustful murderer. Advance, cried the Palmerston journals and rescue our unhappy brethren and sisters. Don't stir, cried the Peel press (believing advance impossible!). (8)

The manipulation of the readership through dramatic images of lustful and murderous Oriental despots is recognized as such. But this critique is not merely pointing to inaccurate reporting.

In the previous column, another criticism appears, this one targeting the distorting lenses of the colonized: "[N]o National feeling can co-exist with the mean and mendicant spirit which esteems everything English as greater and better than if it belonged to our own country, and which looks at all the rest of the world through the spectacles of Anglican prejudice" (8). Although these words partly target Irish "sycophancy," the larger circle of the mark implicates the domineering discourse of Empire. The metaphor is noteworthy; "spectacles of Anglican prejudice" highlights both perspective and ideology in the viewing of "all the rest of the world." The discussions of "Oriental" cultures here, however, engender critique instead of complicity.

The first issue of the *Nation* further illustrates the somewhat oblique tone of Irish-Asian affinities in nationalist rhetoric of the time, particularly in discussions of British colonialism elsewhere. The complicity of Ireland in Empire—particularly here of Irish soldiers in the British army—seems to have then discouraged overt attacks on imperial efforts. Such care was needed at the time, as the suppression of the paper in 1848 demonstrates. Overt comparisons among Ireland, Afghanistan, China, India, Egypt, and elsewhere, and overt imperial critiques, however, eventually became common for nationalist newspapers in Ireland.

A clearer example of such nationalist, cross-colonial reporting occurred seventy-five years later in the Republican newspaper *An Phoblacht* (Republic) (1925–1937), established after the founding of the Irish Free State in 1922. Until its suppression in 1931, Peadar O'Donnell (1893–1986) edited the paper, which was a mouthpiece for IRA views at the time (the new incarnation of the paper is fully a publication of Sinn Féin, the political wing of the contemporary IRA). From the early issues, news from across the British Empire filled columns of the paper; a cross-colonial view of the history of John Bull abroad is vividly represented in a cartoon by "Fionnbarr" from the third issue of *An Phoblacht* (July 31, 1925, 6) (see fig. 11). In this vein, for several years, the paper highlighted stories and opinions about the British conflicts in China—some articles as direct as this image: "Britain's Bloody Trail: Women and Children Murdered in China," and others more informational about nationalist politics in China, as in "Who's Who in China" (Oct. 1, 1926, 3), or in the center of the front page of the fourth issue: "China States Her Case" (July 10, 1925, 1). Information about the Orient—although at times wildly misrepresenting certain Asian cultures through romanticizations—in these cases was meant to undermine imperial efforts.

The first issue, emblazoned with an image of Wolfe Tone in the center, provided news on France's occupation of Morocco; above the fold, page 1 also had an obituary of C. R. Das, a former chair of the Indian National Congress and Swarajist leader, in "Death of a Great Indian Nationalist" (June 20, 1925, 1). Beside prominent coverage of China, Morocco, and India, the paper frequently reported on anticolonial activities in Syria, "Transjordania," Palestine, Lebanon, Egypt, Iraq, Turkey, and Afghanistan, as well as in eastern Europe and South America. At times, racial and cultural barriers limited affinities, but more often recognition of racism itself helped build cross-colony sympathies, as in the article "British Rule in India":

JOHN BULL'S DREAM OF EMPIRE.

11. "John Bull's Dream of Empire," by "Fionbarr." Published in *An Phoblacht,*
July 31, 1925.

"On the rare occasions on which a coloured man kills a white man in India justice
is speedy and swift, and the verdict a foregone conclusion. The verdict is also a
foregone conclusion when the positions are reversed" (Jan. 15, 1926, 4). More
commonly, the editors evoked parallels between nationalist movements, particularly in British colonies, girding the purview of the paper, invoking convictions
and heroes, as in comparative pieces such as "Pearse and Young India" (Mar. 18,
1927, 3) and "Indian Separatists and James Connolly" (Aug. 20, 1926, 3). Moreover, Indian and Chinese nationalist correspondents often had their own articles
printed.

In addition to Chinese "letters," *An Phoblacht* occasionally printed translated articles from Chinese papers. They offered a real version of the imagined critiques
that prospered nearly two hundred years previously in pseudo-Oriental letters.
One such (poorly) translated article provides a brief and sympathetic view of the

present state of Ireland: "The people of Ireland wish for self-Government. They often oppose the English Imperialists. They have often fought with the English. They have declared for the Independence of Ireland but in vain. At present they rise up and declare that they will be independent" (Dec. 31, 1926, 4). The dynamics of otherness and distance came full circle in such pieces, in which real voices occupied the same role that the imagined ones had centuries earlier. In other articles, Chinese, Indian, and other voices (albeit mainly nationalist ones) from the colonies found representation. For instance, on the same page as this translated article, an Indian correspondent lists mill-worker grievances from Bombay. Such a juxtaposition frequently appeared, encouraging a perception of a worldwide class struggle against colonialism. *An Phoblacht* gave space to anticolonial positions and stories from around the globe, a strategy expressly intended for counteracting the dominant British press. One article taken from a speech of a Chinese nationalist leader made the cross-colonial link overt. "The Sinn Feiners of China" included a speech of Chu Pu Sze, representing the Nationalist Party of China at an Irish convention: "Coming as I do from Canton, China, to address this great Irish Convention, I could not help feeling the strong likeness that exists between the two peoples. In the first place, my people, the Cantonese or Southern Chinese, because of their part in the battle for Republicanism, have been called the Irishmen of China. In the second place, the Irish and the Chinese great as they are, are still oppressed peoples, and oppressed more or less by the same enemy" (Aug. 28, 1925, 2).[2] Almost in tandem with British intra-imperial analogies, such cross-colonial analogies (from a Chinese voice in an Irish paper) promoted a united anticolonial periphery.

Complementing these peripheral voices, *An Phoblacht* also questioned, as a matter of course, representations of the East given by imperial British sources. For instance, a June 26, 1925, article, "Terrorists Again," takes on the well-worn image (even then) of the terrorist: "The Free State daily Press is busily engaged unloading on to the public every lie told about the insurgent Chinese by the British-controlled Reuter's news agency. The latest is that the whole national protest is simply the result of 'gangs' who are 'terrorizing' the peaceful rank and file into supporting them" (3). Discussions of the complicity of English press representations of the Orient no longer needed to be as guarded or encoded in the 1920s, even though conservatives frequently targeted *An Phoblacht,* and the editors were often turned away from printers who had been threatened, and more than once arrested for sedition. Declaring cross-colony sympathies was clearly a priority of the editors as an editorial, "England's Enemy" (probably written by Peadar O'Donnell), makes clear:

> Ireland to-day is pro-China. The sympathy of the Irish people is with the Chinese in their efforts to boot England out of the concessions. . . . The British press is

working to create an atmosphere. That may be under the influence of certain British interests in China or it may be a Government inspired measure. . . . All we know is that the moment China and England should happen to get in conflict this nation will spring to life.

Every ounce of Irish energy will be thrown into a campaign of sabotage against England's war interest in every corner of the world. . . . So far back as poppy day an old citizen army man summed up the Irish attitude towards the British intrigues in China.

"God bless you, John Chinaman," he prayed, "and send you lots of Russian rifles."

. . . The England that tried to represent the I.R.A. to the world as a crowd of murderers is attempting to portray the Chinese as savages attacking missionaries![3] As she is in Ireland for the good of the Irish people, so is she in China for the sole purpose of bringing the blessings of her civilization to the heathen Chinese! (Jan. 14, 1927, 4)

The editors did not limit their exposés of British propagandizing to discussions of Chinese nationalists. Articles such as " 'Ungrateful Egypt!' " quote and explicitly criticize the British and Anglocentric press, particularly images of bloodthirsty Orientals: "And there is all the talk of Egyptian murder gangs, assassins, etc., with which we were familiar during the best days of our fight here" (July 2, 1926, 1). Reporting the executions of seven nationalists in 1925, an *An Phoblacht* writer noted: "Egypt is to-day enduring the agony Ireland knows too well. As happened in Ireland, the doomed men were defamed as well as murdered; they were 'fanatics,' 'criminals,' 'cowards' " (Aug. 28, 1925, 6).

But discussing the tactics of the British press was not the only cross-colonial strategy of the nationalist press in Ireland. Other articles critiqued the broader, supposedly humanitarian process of "civilizing the East" (July 9, 1926, 1). On a page filled with inflammatory articles such as "'We Must Fight Now' " (signed by Peadar O'Donnell) and nationalist political analyses such as "Britain and China," a brief article, "Anglicising India," extends beyond strictly political discussion into the use of the arts as propaganda or as an ideology-building tool; the article discusses cultural colonialism, particularly "a scheme towards the anglicisation of India": "A chain of cinemas, all showing British films only, will be built across India, and the promoters hope that within twelve months, three hundred of these British cinemas will have been built. The motive of the enterprise is 'to save the native population of India from gaining a distorted conception of Western life and morals.' In other words, Indians are to be taught only such things as England wishes, and by England only" (Sept. 17, 1926, 1). The writer presents India less as a variation on an Oriental type and more as a distinct culture besieged by English values.

Alongside such arguments about English colonial programs, *An Phoblacht* continually worked to reverse the history of barbarizations, turning the lens of savageness onto imperial England: "Imperialism has kept England in a state of savagery. Her whole civilization is rooted in brutal appetites. Her interference in any corner of the world is for soulless commercial reasons. . . . Do we believe British machine guns mowed down defenceless Chinese? What of Croke Park? What of Amristrar? England to-today, caught in the control of Imperialism, is an armed savage. Hatred of England is hatred of evil. It is holy" ("Barbaric England," Jan. 21, 1927, 3). Whereas the editors promoted cross-colonial sympathies in order to spread a cosmopolitan cross-colonial awareness, such extreme invocations of a "holy" "hatred of England" seem intended to inflame the population into continued rebellion. But such calls may have alienated as many as they enthused.

Such hate-filled statements, playing on Ireland's troubled history, appeared regularly, if not frequently, in the pages of *An Phoblacht*. But articles and essays asserting similarities between Ireland and other struggling nationalities did not merely work toward such ends. The presence of Irish soldiers in the British army at times muddied the clarity of nationalist Irish rhetoric. Examples of Indian soldiers in the employ of the British army, however, sometimes enabled a broader understanding on this topic. In "Tired of Thuggery," the reporter writes exuberantly:

> Indian troops have become unreliable! This fact has been driven home to British militarists in China. Already detachments are being withdrawn from Shanghai. News of disaffection among Indian troops is a hopeful sign for India. British power to hold India in slavery rests on listlessness of the Indian masses and on the organisation of the thugs out of Indian workers. As in Ireland, so in India, Britain's desire is to have patriots killed by the "natives." . . . The enthusiasm of the Chinese masses has unsettled the Indian troops, and they are being transferred. But unsettled armies are a useful factor. (Feb. 25, 1927, 4)

In a similar article five months later, on the front page just below the fold, the writer explains the ideas and actions of the Indian nationalist Sailendra Ghose and the result in "Indian Soldiers Refuse to Shoot":

> We have received from Sailendra N. Ghose, the active New York secretary of the Friends of Freedom for India, copies of cablegrams he forwarded . . . to the native press of China and Sikh regiments in British "treaty ports," appealing to them not to shoot their Mongolian brothers in China. A reply cablegram from China reads:— "Representatives of the nationalist movement of India in China and Japan are in touch with Sikh regiments in Hongkong and Shanghai. In several cases Sikh soldiers refused to obey the order to fire on the Chinese, and, as a consequence, their whole regiment has been transferred to unknown destination and new regiments are replacing them."
>
> Mr. Ghose, who speaks frequently from Irish platforms on this side, is in favor

of a closer working alliance between all the revolutionary groups inside the noble Empire, contending that the Irish, Egyptians, Indian, and also the Chinese rebellions, should have all been timed simultaneously. (July 17, 1925, 1)

Ghose, indeed, spent time with Irish-American nationalists, as the forthcoming work of Michael Silvestri on Irish and Indian nationalist relations in America details. Victories such as the above case rarely materialized. More often, news of imperial victories appeared in the paper in the 1920s, as in the coverage of the French (and Spanish) victory in "The End of the Moroccon [sic] War": "The surrender of Abd-el-Krim is a tragedy of which Irishmen feel the poignancy. One other small nation has been broken under the juggernaut of Imperialism. But it is not for ever" (June 4, 1926, 1). The paper worked to create parallel nationalist heroes across the world bolstering cross-colonial and cosmopolitan sympathies, which, unfortunately, withered during Ireland's isolationist politics of the twentieth century.

The editors give, in an unsigned editorial, the purpose of such cross-colonial investigations in "The Army and Its Task": "The study of the striving of small nations struggling for freedom against Empire is useful to those on whom the duty of similar struggles falls" (Oct. 29, 1926, 3). This explication appeared beside another article explaining the "Senchus Mor" (Great Tradition) and its ancient laws for the public. Much less studied discussions of the Orient also appeared in the paper, as they did throughout Irish culture, but the lack of references in such pieces should not suggest a lack of sophistication. One of the most witty and sophisticated plays on the doubleness of the Oriental-Celtic connection came in the column of "Dan the Cobbler," this particular one being titled "Dan the Cobbler and the Chinaman." The first section heading in the article, "Sinn Finn," suggests the linguistic play and malapropisms common to the bumpkin speaker (distinct from the writer), whose ignorance is half-knowing and half-suggestive:

> "It's a bit like ould times," said Dan. "Not so very ould, maybe, but still ould enough to be forgotten by many that are goin' now. D'ye remember how, after Easter Week of Nineteen-Sixteen (nine whole years ago, an' it might be ninety-nine for all the people are thinkin' of it)—do ye remember, I ask you, the story of the English Tommy that done his bit to put down the rebellion? He cum over first an' foremost not knowin' whether 'twas East Africa or Armonteers he was in. They landed him at Kingstown. . . . Then they marched him up into Dublin, an' left him wonderin' if the people talkin' English to him in the streets were the same as them that were addressin' him in the universal language of bullets from the roofs. In this way he came to learn somethin' about our national aspirations, and after a fortnight's precarious existence, he was heard to tell a G-man that th' Irish people 'ud be all right if they weren't led asthray be that so-an'-son Chinaman, Sin Finn." (June 26, 1925, 4)

The Englishman's conflation of Ireland with other battles in "East Africa or Armonteers" is confirmed in his misunderstanding of the nationalist organization Sinn Féin (the emphatic "ourselves" in Irish) for a fictional Chinese leader. The soldier's ignorance of the Irish language and his general difficulty comprehending Hibernicized English prompt his general confusion, and he understands only the "universal" language of violence.

Dan explains why he mentioned this story, referring to the papers and a debate in Parliament, and eventually unwittingly exposing some of the roots of cross-colony sympathies:

> "It was just a bit on news in this mornin's paper that brought the whole thing back to me. . . . I read a piece in the paper about a debate in the British House o' Commons. . . . But this debate wasn't about Ireland. . . . It was about China. . . . It appears from the papers that people who have been in the bad habit of livin' in China for a hundred generations or so without the blessin's of British rule are, like everybody else outside th' Empire, not to be depended on. They are, in fact, liable to become Chinese. They get quare ideas in their heads. They dress themselves in outlandish ways that no thrue Britisher would tolerate in anything but a Cabaret or a golf tournament. . . . In other words, their uncivilized. And that isn't the worst about them. Be no manes. Over an' above all their other misbehavious, a considherable number o' them are addicted to Politics. . . . It's the curse of any country that indulges in it. Egypt has it bad. Injia has it bad. Ireland had it bad a long time and might still only that she's undher chloroform." (4)

The use of the word *Chinese* here reveals the slippage between the Orientalized meanings of the term, understood from the perspective of a "thrue Britisher," and the reality of the Chinese people who have had "the bad habit of livin' in China for a hundred generations." What is customary to the Chinese is seen as gamey or inappropriate to the "universal" Britisher. Moreover, "Politics" is what unites these several disreputable cultures across the world.

The second-to-last section, "On the Flure," brings up the other side of the cross-colonial connection, as Dan quotes a British perspective:

> "An that brings me back to the debate on the flure o' the House in Westminsther, when the statesmen of England met to discuss every way of dealin' with China except lavin' China alone. A Mister Trevelyan, overflowin' with love an' sympathy for the Chinese people, said the thruble was caused be the bad labour conditions in the facthories. Then Chamberlain stood up and says he, ''Tis not that. 'Tis the natural discontent an' unrest of the Chinese people that's bein' used be politicians.' . . . Then up Lloyd-George, the friend of small nations an' the man that won the Thruce, an'—I'm tellin' ye what I read in the paper—he med the whole thing as

simple as A.B.C. 'It's not,' says he, 'Bolshevism that's stirrin' up the Chinese. It's Sin Finn.' " (4)

Sin Finn returns as a provocative leader. The piece ends, "Good Old Sin Finn": "'I'm tellin' ye it warmed me heart to hear of poor ould Sin Finn afther all these years. I thought he was dead. An' even though he's badly wanted here again, I can't grudge him to be back with his own people, showin' them the way to Freedom' " (4). The doubleness of having this Irish organization returning to "his own people" in China evokes the history of much of Irish Orientalism—with an imagined origin in the Orient, intra-imperial comparisons, and cross-colony sympathies.

Imperial Disintegration

Stemming from the many intra-imperial governing analogies at work in the nineteenth century, significant comparisons between nationalists in Ireland were made by resolute supporters of Empire. As a case in point, Lord Salisbury (Robert Cecil, 1830–1903) popularized the political comparison between Irish and Indian nationalist movements in a speech to Parliament reprinted in 1883. Witnessing the rise of Indian nationalism, he describes Irish Land League advances (and Gladstone's government's slightly more conciliatory "Irish policy") as the emblematic catalysts and indicators of what he feared was the "disintegration" of the Empire. Of course, one person's sense of disintegration may be another's sense of unification and liberation, as was the case with Irish and Indian nationalists who looked to one another's countries for models. Salisbury argues that the land-reform movement and the "partial surrender of long-established [English] rights" (1883, 559) in Ireland could augur a similar case scenario for India: "Of course, when the word disintegration, as a possible peril of the present time, is mentioned, the mind naturally reverts to Ireland: and Ireland is, no doubt, the worst symptom of our malady" (563). While Salisbury's main focus is on what he sees as the foolhardy concessions the English government has given to the "ancient" "peasant" Irish, he also compares the Irish land agitation and nationalist movements to similar growing movements in India. His words on India are remarkably direct in their support of domination and resemble earlier debates (such as Keogh's) about Irish advancement in the Indian civil service.

> [Disintegration] menaces us in the most subtle and in the most glaring forms—in the loss of large branches and limbs of our Empire, and in the slow estrangement of the classes which make up the nation to whom that Empire belongs. . . . What a marvellous illustration of this spirit is being enacted before our eyes in India! The very maintenance of that empire—the stupendous achievement of thousands ruling

over millions to whom they are strange in colour and creed and race—depends on
the respect in which the superiority of the English race is held. To gratify some theorists at home who might have weight in Parliament, we are deliberately humiliat-
ing the English race in the eyes of the natives; and announcing the policy, which we
cannot fulfil without suicide, that race-distinctions in the bestowal of administrative
offices shall cease. (562)

Salisbury's interest in keeping Indians out of "administrative offices," like the "ban
of the Milesian brogue" that Keogh railed against, derived from an interest in preserving the (racial) unity of Empire. But by pointing to the similar weak links in
Empire, or to the growing areas of dissolving imperial control in India and Ireland,
Salisbury unintentionally reinforces the Irish-Indian affinities that nationalists and
(later) Theosophists developed.

From at least 1870 on, Indian nationalists often looked to Ireland for "models of
emancipation," as H. V. Brasted notes in his 1985 article, "Irish Models and the Indian National Congress, 1870–1922" (25). Indeed, as historian S. R. Mehrotra
comments in *The Emergence of the Indian National Congress,* "probably no other
country in the world has exercised greater influence on the course of Indian nationalism than Ireland" (1971, 324). Irish writers at the time increasingly noted the
similarities and anticolonial affinities between Ireland and India and Ireland and
Egypt. Even after the establishment of the Irish Free State, J. Chartres Molony
compared India and Ireland in *The Riddle of the Irish* (1927) in an attempt to define
the "Irish experience." In one chapter, he specifically explores cross-colony affinities between Ireland and India: "Diwan Bahadur N. Subramaniam, once a well-
known figure in South Indian life, remarked to me that Indian and Irishman
should understand each other. 'Each,' he said, 'is one of a conquered race, and the
conqueror is the same for both' " (1970, 158). These arguments of cross-colony influences, however, exist more as shared strategies and emblems of resistance to Empire. Although these connections in Indian and Irish nationalism existed and have
been more examined over the past two decades since Brasted's article, particularly
in the study of Indian history, Brasted's comment that "the Irish-Indian connection remains a presumed but unspecified association" (1985, 24) continues to be
accurate, particularly when one is thinking about Irish and Indian literature
and culture, where connections were often loose affinities, marked by imprecise
references.

H. V. Brasted, Christopher Bayly, and Michael Silvestri have traced specific historical links between Ireland and India, focusing on the developments of nationalism in both colonies. Brasted provides the most detailed argument on Indian
nationalism in the late nineteenth century, exploring how various Irish models
served Indian nationalists, particularly Isaac Butt, Charles Stuart Parnell, Arthur

Griffith, and Sinn Féin. He notes that Indian nationalists studied these nationalists and either employed or rejected various tactics of resistance as they worked or failed in Ireland. He does not explore, however, the reverse influence of Indian politics on Ireland. Although scholars of India have reconsidered emphasis on European models in arguments similar to Brasted's,[4] Irish-Indian affinities nevertheless continue to offer significant evidence of international nationalist and cross-colony movements. Brasted continues:

> Despite its special relationship with England, Ireland was symbolically cast in the role of rebellious colony, the very first in the nineteenth century to mount a separatist challenge on the basis of nationalist theory. As such it provided the prototype of national revolt within the British empire. . . . Ireland presented the obvious and most pertinent model for Indian nationalists to consult. For a start, it supplied the actual frame of reference in which political India was obliged to operate—within the orbit of an alerted British imperialism. (24)

For forty-two years, Indian nationalism often turned to Irish models, until many Indians returned to non-Irish Gandhian forms of nationalism, including nonviolent noncooperation, which later informed the civil-rights movement in Northern Ireland. Nevertheless, in Bengal, an area that gave much less support to Gandhi, as Silvestri has recently discussed (2000b), Irish models continued to inspire. But, certainly, cross-colonial links extended beyond India in what Bayly has called "the quadrilateral of Britain, India, Ireland, and then Egypt" (2000, 11).[5]

Augusta Gregory and Arabi

The Arabi Uprising in Egypt in 1881–1882 stirred cross-colonial resistance in Ireland, Egypt, and India. The very slogan of the Egyptian nationalists, "Egypt for the Egyptians," echoes numerous other anticolonial movements across the globe, including Ireland. Many supporters of Irish nationalism, such as Lady Augusta Gregory, Wilfred Scawen Blunt, Frederick Ryan, James Connolly, and Roger Casement, closely monitored and analyzed the Egyptian situation, and their writing about these movements influenced both Irish nationalism and the tenor of Irish representations of the Orient. Gregory, in particular, expressed her perspective on Britain's bombardment and seizing of control of Egypt by writing a profile on the Egyptian nationalist and former Egyptian minister of war Ahmed Arabi Pasha. In her long, one-page article in the *Times,* "Arabi and His Household" (Oct. 23, 1882, 4), she reveals not only her support of the man, but also her anger at the misrepresentation of him in the British press as a bloodthirsty despot—a representation that harks back a century and a half to Montesquieu's Usbek in *Les Lettres Persanes* and continues today. The very process of representing the Orient is a main target of her essay.

Gregory wrote her essay during Gladstone's occupation of Egypt after Arabi's arrest by British forces and the failed uprising. Barbara Harlow summarizes the context of the events in England in *Imperialism and Orientalism:*

> [I]f Britain was to assume control of Egypt, Arabi and his followers must first be dealt with. Arrested in fall 1882, the trial took place shortly thereafter. There were those in England and Egypt alike who clamored for Arabi's immediate and sum-mary execution. Others would argue just as adamantly for the imperative of a "fair trial" and due process. It was perhaps not just the man but his example that needed to be disposed of. For Lord Cromer (Sir Evelyn Baring), it was urgent to cancel the effects of such insubordination as Arabi's. (Harlow and Carter 1999, 139)

After the physical battle had ended in Egypt, another continued in the press and political literature of Britain, both sides needing to publicly justify their arguments. The image of Arabi was the prize fought over. But along with other supporters of Arabi, Gregory and Blunt (her friend and lover at the time, until 1883) had an up-hill fight and won to some degree (Arabi was not executed). They not only had to counteract specific negative representations of Arabi but also sought to expose and critique the broader processes of Oriental representation in the metropole and spe-cific Orientalist idioms, such as the one of the Oriental despot.[6] The image of the despot enabled colonial rule by offering an example of a cruel and inept method of governance that needed to be taken over (for the people's sake) by the enlightened colonial forces, who would then pave the way for democracy, constitutional gov-ernment, and free trade.

Edward Said begins his first chapter of *Orientalism* with an examination of how these forces took shape in occupied Egypt:

> Egypt was not just another colony: it was the vindication of Western imperialism; it was, until its annexation by England, an almost academic example of Oriental backwardness; it was to become the triumph of English knowledge and power. Be-tween 1882, the year in which England occupied Egypt and put an end to the na-tionalist rebellion of Colonel Arabi, and 1907, England's representative in Egypt, Egypt's master, was Evelyn Baring (also known as "Over-baring"), Lord Cromer. . . . British exports to Egypt equaled those to the whole of Africa; that certainly in-dicated a sort of financial prosperity, for Egypt and England (somewhat unevenly) together. But what really mattered was the unbroken, all-embracing Western tute-lage of an Oriental country, from the scholars, missionaries, businessmen, soldiers, and teachers. (1995, 35)

Cromer once gave a perspective on his imperial philosophy, "I am only a diploma-tist and an administrator, whose proper study is also man, but from the point of view of governing him," concluding that "I content myself with noting the fact that somehow or other the Oriental generally acts, speaks, and thinks in a manner ex-actly opposite to the European" (qtd. in Said 1995, 35). Cromer and other British administrators and politicians, such as Arthur James Balfour, treated the Egyptian and the Oriental as (to quote Said) "something one judges (as in a court of law), something one studies and depicts (as in a curriculum), something one disciplines (as in a school or prison), something one illustrates (as in a zoological manual)." Said's point here is that these forms of categorical knowledge represent the Orien-tal as a racial type, which is part of the larger discourse of Empire—"[in] each of these cases the Oriental is *contained* and *represented* by dominating frameworks" (40). This strategy, he argues, is typical for Orientalism. Gregory, in vivid contrast to these impersonal and categorical frameworks, works to evoke a more human image of Arabi. Although her representation does not escape the "dominating frame-works" of Orientalism, she writes to subvert what she sees as the dominant repre-sentation of the Oriental in support of anticolonialism. Emphasizing the humanistic and cosmopolitan traits of Arabi, she points to the personal, ordinary, and familiar traits of his life, rather than categorical ones that have positioned him "exactly opposite to the European."

While staying with Blunt in Egypt, Gregory had met Arabi and been impressed with his nationalist commitment. Although Blunt also had his arguments printed in the *Times,* Gregory's article stands as a focused attack on the representation of Arabi in Britain—an attack that Blunt later extended in his 1907 account of the events, *The Secret History of the English Occupation of Egypt,* which serves as a mani-festo of sorts for his radical "Nonconformism" and anticolonial political beliefs. Fif-teen years earlier, in her long article, Gregory counteracted the standard Oriental stereotypes of those individuals who resisted British rule, describing Arabi as "gen-tle," "humane," "earnest," "honest," and "truthful" and attacking common British representations of Oriental insurgent leaders—images that hark back to the Indian Rebellion of 1857–1858, which John Ruskin, among many others, described as a vicious betrayal. As in her play *The Image* (1909), representation of political dis-course differs tremendously from actual lived experience. Gregory relies upon her personal interactions with Arabi in her efforts to counter the impersonal and more overtly ideological British image of him. She quotes his family and friends, partic-ularly the women in the family, using personal anecdotes to displace and loosen the impersonal public depictions, which were infused with imperial ideology. She dis-misses outright the "ready belief" of the press and public that he is a violent mon-ster: "In appearance Arabi is a tall, strongly-built man; his face is grave, almost stern, but his smile is very pleasant. His photographs reproduce the sternness, but not the smile, and are, I believe, partly responsible for the ready belief which the absurd tales of his ferocity and bloodthirstiness have gained." She sets up a neat binary, arguing that the impersonal and technological media of photography and newspaper reporting are the propagandistic tools intended to cloak the human and real character of Arabi. Her own picture of him, however, is intended to appear simple, womanly (that is, as that was meant at the time), and without strategy or ideology.

> I believe him to be exceedingly gentle and humane. An English official, one of the fairest of his class, said to me, "He has too much of the gentleness of the fellah, and too little of the brute in him to succeed. If he would take lessons in brutality at 100 francs a week, he would have a much better chance of getting on." . . . I do not understand Arabic, the only language spoken by Arabi, so could not judge of his eloquence. It is said to be striking, and his words well chosen. . . . He speaks very earnestly, looking you straight in the face with honest eyes. I have an entire belief in his truthfulness; partly from his manner; partly because from everyone, without exception, who had known him long or watched his career—some of them members of the Viceregal family—I heard on this point the same report. "He is incapable of speaking untruth;" partly because it was many months ago—it was in November— that my husband first saw and spoke with him, and to every word he said then he has adhered ever since.

Writing against the trope of the lying Oriental despot, Gregory draws from several sources to formulate her conclusions. Personal observation is foremost, but she also draws from comments and testimonials made by others, both British and Egyptian.

Clearly, the British used negative accounts of Arabi, along with stock Orientalist idioms, to discredit and depose the popular Egyptian leader and gain control of Egypt and the Suez Canal. As with the Indian Revolt of 1857, the British press would generally not even acknowledge the validity of the rebellion, calling it "the third mutiny of the Egyptian army" (Cromer 1999, 146). Categorical images of the despot were crucial in justifying British actions in Egypt, including the July 11, 1882, bombardment of Alexandria and the brutal punishment of Egyptian peasants at Denshawai after the death of a single British officer. Wilfred Blunt comments on this process in "The Arabi Trial," highlighting the dynamics and implications of the close ties between colonial knowledge, representation, and power: "[Gladstone's] only excuse for all this military brutality was the fiction that he was dealing with a military desperado, a man outlawed by his crimes, and, as such, unentitled to any consideration either as a patriot or even the recognized General of a civilized army. I have reason to know that if Arabi had been captured on the field at Tel-el-Kebir, it was Wolseley's intention to give him the short benefit of a drum-head court martial, which means shooting on the spot" (1999, 149). This "fiction" of a "military desperado" and other stereotypes of Oriental leaders enabled the British actions in

Egypt. Other accounts of the uprising, particularly Lord Cromer's "Mutiny of the Egyptian Army: January–September 1881," devote much space to painting Arabi's character as a duplicitous and disrespectful Oriental who acted out of fear and thirst for power. Cromer writes: "Yet, whilst Arábi was heading a mutiny against his Sovereign, and employing language which could only lawfully proceed from the [English-backed aristocratic] Khedive or from one of his Ministers, there can be little doubt that his conduct was mainly guided by fear" (1999, 146). This purposeful image meant to establish Arabi as a cowardly military leader who acted desperately, fearing retribution for his earlier cowardly mutinous actions (which a smear campaign detailed), and attempted to seize control and inflict his despotism. We can thus understand why Gregory's essay explicitly seeks to disprove and counteract such an image of Arabi, which pervaded the British press.

Unlike her friends Yeats, George Russell (AE), and Stephens, Gregory visited Asia and West Asia and had genuine connections there. Her vision of the Orient, furthermore, did not emerge from Theosophical borrowings from India; they were less mystical and more actual. She drew upon firsthand knowledge and experience in counteracting the British representation of Arabi, which did not differ from numerous other stock images of Oriental despots. Even before visiting Egypt and Arabi's family, she had had relations in the East. Her husband, prior to marrying her, had been the governor of Ceylon. Also, after Arabi's trial, she visited India and Ceylon from November 1885 through April 1886. Her later involvement with Irish cultural nationalism had been greatly informed by the events in Egypt and her trips to India and Ceylon as well as by the power of colonial representations, which she sought to counteract. One cannot help wondering if her political involvement in Asian and West Asian politics kept her from overly romanticizing the mystical East the way so many of her fellow Revivalists did. Significantly, no Irish Orientalist (literary, popular, academic, or political) mingled the mystical and the political in an analysis to any great extent, even though the narratives of both were often similar. Cousins probably came closest, having gone through the Celtic Revival's mystical awe of India and then having lived in India. Nevertheless, Gregory's crucial experiences in Asia and West Asia before the Revival greatly informed her understanding of Orientalism. Moreover, it greatly differed from the first real connections that Yeats, AE, and Stephens had with Asia, meeting, for example, Mohini Chatterjee after a talk not about imperialism but about nondualism and the Upanishads. Nevertheless, many similarities exist among all of their representations of the Orient.

Gregory's representation also works against images of the unity of the British imperial family. She devotes considerable space to exploring Arabi's ties with his own family and people. Thus, in Gregory's text, Arabi is not disloyal to the Crown of Empire; instead, he is presented as loyal to his actual family and people, which, as

Gregory alludes, seems more admirable. She further presents Arabi as a religious man (but not a fanatic) in quoting his mother, who complains that Arabi has too much faith in fate and God and worries about her dutiful son. In particular, the mother worries about what his enemies will do to him. "I can do nothing but pray for him all the time. There are many who wish him evil, and they will try to destroy him. A few days ago he came home suffering a great pain, and I was sure then he had been poisoned; but I got him a hot bath and remedies and he grew better, and since then I keep even the water that he drinks locked up. But, say all I can, I cannot frighten him or make him take care of himself; he always says 'God will preserve me.'" When referring to Arabi's belief in God, Gregory shrewdly avoids using the words *Allah, Muslim,* or *Islam,* instead choosing the corresponding general terms of God and religion. Arabi's family members cannot understand why he is so beleaguered by British forces. To them, he is such a conciliatory and gentle man. Gregory uses these personalized images of him to counteract the publicity machine of the Empire. In this battle for the image of Arabi, she pits British reporters and dispatch writers against Arabi's mother and wife: "The words of a man who believes God has given him work to do and will support him while he does it—not the words of a coward. But those who wrote the published despatches say that cowardice is the mainspring of his character, and surely they know better than his old mother! . . . Poor old soul! she must have had sore and anxious days since then. I often think of her, and of the poor wife, puzzled and troubled, 'Why should the Christian Powers want to harm my husband?'" The sympathy that Gregory shows here for Arabi's mother and wife seems intended as an antidote to the way the English press was pillorying him. Her strategy of personal observation, making the political personal, appealed to the ideals of family and justice.

Arabi's own "Appeal to Gladstone," printed in the *Times,* July 2, 1882, which Gladstone received too late, after the bombardment of Alexandria, also helped his public image. Gregory reports in her article that Arabi continued to be concerned about how he was portrayed in the English press: "A little worried and troubled by false accusations made against him in English newspapers, he was still confident that some day his character would be cleared. 'They must know some day that it is the good of the people that we seek.'" Both he and Gregory recognize the importance of this image battle in colonial politics. Arabi's letter to Gladstone makes a nationalist stand against British aggression but also notes, "Egypt is ready still, nay desirous, to come to terms with England, to be fast friends with her, to protect her interests and keep her road to India, to be her ally. But she must keep within the limits of her jurisdiction" (Pasha 1999, 147). The letter in the *Times* did not help Egypt retain its independence; it only helped to contradict the prevailing image of Arabi and other Egyptian nationalists in the British press. Indeed, when Arabi went to trial, Gregory and Blunt continued to attack his negative public image. Blunt also organized legal counsel for Arabi, who, in the end, escaped the sentence of execution and was sentenced to exile in Ceylon, where he was later visited by Blunt and Gregory (Harlow and Carter 1999, 139). Though independent since 1922, Egypt remained under British occupation until 1956 and the Suez Canal War.

Cross-colony nationalist affinities among India, Egypt, and Ireland aided Gregory, Blunt, and others in attacking British Orientalist representations; these cross-colony connections helped them assert the appearance of a united front against Gladstone and Empire. Christopher Bayly comments that Blunt remarked that "the Gladstone cabinet which ordered repression in Ireland was also the one which crushed the Egyptian National Movement. 'The two causes, the Irish and the Egyptian' he wrote, 'the Catholic and the Mohammedan, seemed to me to stand on a common footing of enlightened humanity.'" Later Blunt was to become active in land agitation in Ireland and was even jailed for a period. From his point of view (to quote Bayly again), "Egyptian bondholders, Irish rentiers and Indian administrators merged into one terrifying incubus. He might have called them 'gentlemanly capitalists'" (2000, 393).

These writers made the direct connection between Egyptian and Irish nationalism; indeed, they were not alone in comparing nationalist movements in Egypt to Ireland. So did Gladstone, Balfour, C. G. Gordon, G. B. Shaw, Frederick Ryan, James Connolly, and many others (Blunt 1999, 149). Irish Land League organizers also made the comparisons, stressing cross-colony political and social affinities. For instance, one 1879 poster read in bold letters: "From the China towers of Pekin to the round towers of Ireland, from the cabins of Connemara to the kraals of Kaffirland, from the wattled homes of the isles of Polynesia to the wigwams of North America the cry is: 'Down with invaders! Down with tyrants!' Every man to have his own land—every man to have his own home."[7] These affinities and analogies were also made in more cosmopolitan circles. Internationalist Irish writers, such as George Bernard Shaw, compared Ireland with India and Egypt in his acidic prefaces (both 1906 and 1929) to *John Bull's Other Island* (1907). Irish socialist journalist and playwright Frederick Ryan, who edited the *Egyptian Standard* (1905–1907), the mouth of Egyptian nationalism established by Mustafa Kamil in Alexandria, also wrote particularly direct critiques of global colonialism while espousing a form of cosmopolitan Irish nationalism.

Frederick Ryan

In his essay "The Ryan Line," Terry Eagleton has begun the important work of recovering the significance of Frederick Ryan as an Irish thinker and international cultural and political critic. Ryan's most important works were essays published in a variety of journals, newspapers, and magazines in Ireland and elsewhere, including the *United Irishman, Irish Independent, Irish Nation, Irish Review, Harp, Dana,* and the *Egyptian Standard,* as well as Wilfred Blunt's anticolonialist paper, *Egypt,* and Ryan's own journal, the *New Democrat.* Eagleton argues that Ryan, principally a Social Democrat, combined "a whole range of identities: 'socialist, internationalist, anticolonialist, free-thinker, cultural critic, libertarian, social philosopher' " (1998, 249). Ryan had been drawn to both the literary circles of the Revival and the labor demonstrations of workers and socialists in Dublin. Ryan's materialist perspective primarily focused on the material conditions of people and asserted that spiritual fulfillment essentially required time off work and the freedom from worry about basic necessities. Eagleton expands this perspective:

> Like every orthodox materialist from Marx to Morris, Ryan held that the highest ends of human life were spiritual, but that most men and women were currently prevented from achieving them by material want and the excessive demands of labor. The point of political transformation was to create the material conditions in which they could cease to be so distracted by these needs, and be free instead to live predominantly by "culture." "The most spiritual work today," Ryan writes, "is material: what use is it to tell a man who has to work thirteen or fourteen hours a day for mere subsistence wages that he ought to cultivate his mind?" (263)

Such internationalist materialism enabled Ryan's critiques of Empire in both Egypt and Ireland and reinforced affinities between Ireland and the Orient, while confronting the apoliticism of many Celtic Revivalists.

Like Gregory and Cousins, Ryan was involved with the literary and dramatic Revival and with cultural and political movements in a country occupied by British forces, living in Egypt while working as an editor for the *Egyptian Standard* from 1905 to 1907. Ryan had acted and written plays for the Irish Literary Theatre with Cousins and the Fays and was later treasurer of the Abbey. As part of Revival lore, Ryan is also remembered as the man who first opened the doors of the Abbey Theatre and admitted its first patron. Today, Ryan, like Cousins, is mostly forgotten, and only one act of one of his plays survives. Nevertheless, a significant number of his journalistic essays, as I have noted, are extant, although not in collected form. Like many other Irish writers at the time, Ryan became interested in the Orient, but, unlike most Celticist Orientalists, he was not primarily interested in creating a new syncretic spirituality and mysticism. He saw other similarities. Unlike other writers critical of the spiritualism of the Revival, such as Joyce, Ryan did not lampoon the Revival's spiritual and rhetorical affinities with the Orient. Instead, he developed cross-colony comparisons and investigated the political affinities between Ireland and other colonies. As Gregory and many other Irish writers had done, he attacked the idioms of British Orientalism. In an editorial in the

Egyptian Standard, "A Question of Character," he focuses on the politics of representation, reformulating the standard stereotype of Oriental and colonized people, which paints them as being in need of European governance:

> [Imperial sympathizers] are always romancing about "developing character"—developing it, one may add, by playing the despot and encouraging subservience. But when real "character" presents itself, character which is not to be cajoled or browbeaten, which is not prepared to play the sycophant, and which demands its rights in no cringing tones, then a new note is struck. That is not the "character" the school-master wanted to develop at all, and so he turns round and denounces and misrepresents and belittles those who exhibit it. Yet its existence confutes his case. For the most striking proof that can be afforded of a subject person's capacity for freedom is that they strenuously demand it. . . . [The truth is that] there is no honest desire that there shall ever exist in Egypt the capacity for self rule, as long as the growth of such capacity can be hampered. (Jan. 23, 1908; qtd. in Eagleton 1998, 268)

Ryan's sympathies are clearly with subjected peoples, and his tone illustrates his affinity. The purpose of such discussions was, in part, to enable cross-colony understandings between Irish and Egyptian nationalists. Likewise, he sought to create bridges within Ireland, and like many Irish Orientalists, this goal became manifest as antisectarianism.

Eagleton discusses both Ryan's antisectarianism alongside his anticolonialist internationalism: "An essay by Ryan entitled 'Political and Intellectual Freedom' denounces the 'rival bigotries' of Orangeism and Catholicism, but sees the winning of national self-government as an essential first step beyond this sterile antagonism. His antisectarianism is of a radical rather than liberal brand, seeing political and intellectual independence as allies rather than opposites" (258). Ryan often criticized the chauvinism of much Irish nationalism, particularly when it did not support cross-colony sympathies, and, as a consequence, he made a few friendly enemies such as Sinn Féin nationalist Arthur Griffith. Ryan criticized such nationalism from an "international socialist republican" standpoint, which Eagleton positions in opposition to "the viewpoint of a middle-class liberalism," not being "complicit with the social and economic system of the colonialist" (262). Eagleton, a consummate defender of Irish nationalism, concludes that Ryan's "internationalism, in short, actually makes him a more fervent supporter of national independence than those in Ireland who are most vociferously patriotic" (261).

Ryan drew criticism from other nationalists, however, for putting other colonized struggles and cultures on the same par as Ireland and its nationalist struggle. Arthur Griffith offered a soft criticism of the late Ryan in an obituary of him in the journal *Sinn Féin* (Apr. 12, 1913), claiming that "the suffering Egyptian had not less claim on him than his own countrymen" (qtd. in Eagleton 1998, 262). But, as Eagleton concludes, such internationalist affinities are understandable from a materialist point of view: "Because he is an Irish anticolonialist, he regards himself as a citizen of the world" (271)—a statement that (as with Oliver Goldsmith) is indeed the rule rather than the exception.

Ryan's penchant for seeking out political and anticolonial affinities among Ireland, Egypt, India, and Persia gave him an educated perspective on the unity of the British Empire's actions, as well as the hypocrisy it exhibited. He sums up the supposedly humanistic aims of Empire in an editorial in the *Egyptian Standard,* arguing that Europe and America have erroneously assumed that "the whole non-European world is morally inferior to all Europe and is sunk in a barbarism from which it is the duty of Europe to rescue it. The methods of 'rescue' generally consist in shooting down the people with all the ingenuity which immense attention to the arts of destruction has begotten in Europe, and then introducing every vice that the more moral side of Europe denounces and deplores" (qtd. in Eagleton 1998, 268). Empire's double standards are the frequent targets of Ryan's critique. In his editorials, which usually center on colonialism and Egyptian and Irish politics, Ryan turns the standard Orientalist idioms of the East back on the colonizer:"The imperialists are quick to label as 'fanaticism' any resistance to their rule, but what is the whole Imperialist cult but a gross fanaticism? This egoistic feeling that the East is uncivilised and needs to be 'led forward,' if one can assume it to be sincere, which is a severe strain, what is it but a gross superstition?" ("Fanaticism," *Egyptian Standard,* Feb. 29, 1908). Like many other Irish anticolonial writers on the Orient, Ryan attacks the representations of the metropole concerning the periphery, of the Orientalist concerning the Orient, striking at the portrayal of the "Oriental" as a means of resistance. Such is one unifying hallmark of these narratives of affinity, from the mystical to the political.

Ryan often focused on the hypocrisy of the imperial governments and the imperial sympathizers in Europe. One particular target of his biting satire was the "moral Imperialist," who, he argues, will "perforce stick to the 'white man's burden'—and the swag—through an ineradicable sense of duty. . . . It is excellent for the subject races to know that 'for generations' they will be denied their liberty in their own interest—through the strict application of Christian principles" ("The 'Reasonable' Imperialist," qtd. in Eagleton 1998, 270). Ryan continues, discussing the British imperialist's hypocritical and damning representations of the Orient, "[A]ny people who do not delightedly welcome political slavery—when the brand is English—are . . . morally inferior beings, with a double dose of original sin. But if the slavery be other than English—Turkish, or Russian, or Austrian—then the people who resist it are patriots and heroes" (266). By highlighting England's strategy of using Orientalist idioms and representations to reinforce and justify its imperial projects, Ryan reveals the process of representation in the projects of Empire across the globe.

Moreover, Ryan traces English imperial hypocrisy and domination as one of the main unifying factors between Celtic Ireland and the Orient. Eagleton paraphrases and quotes the arguments of Ryan's 1908 editorials "The 'Reasonable' Imperialist" and "'True' Imperialism" in the *Egyptian Standard* as such:

> Nobody but the colonialists themselves recognise their own remarkable disinterestedness; in fact they don't believe in it themselves, reverting to the language of the bully after playing the philanthropist. Lord Curzon speaks of the empire as having wiped out misery and destitution, and was himself Viceroy of a country [India] where "the people die in myriads almost every year from famine, where freedom of speech and action are invaded at every turn by the Government of which he was the nominal head, and where 'prosperity' as a term to describe the state of the vast mass of the people is an odious perversion of the truth. . . . The nauseous hypocrisy of the whole business, the alteration of shoddy sentiment and brute threat, is disgusting to anyone not brought up to the business." (270–71)

Eagleton draws the broad conclusion that much of the "Ryan line" has to do with him being Irish, noting that "Ryan is writing in the era of Kipling, Henley and Conrad; what makes him sound like a precursor of Edward Said is among other things the fact that he is an Irishman" (268). Although, of course, not all Irish writers on the Orient could be classed as "precursor[s] of Edward Said," certainly there was a large school of Irish writers who saw that the logic of Irish nationalism and anticolonialism might be extended into the support of other anticolonial movements around the globe; but a number of Indian, Egyptian, and Persian nationalists also came to the same conclusions. Eagleton reports that Ryan used "a good few of his editorials for the *Egyptian Standard* to report on the political situation in Ireland" but that sometimes he gave "rather more detail than his Egyptian readers perhaps required" (268–69). But, as we have seen, such cross-colonial comparisons were often of great interest to activists and writers in India, as Ryan apparently believed they were in Egypt.

Before Ryan's untimely death in 1913 of a burst appendix while staying in the home of Wilfred Blunt, he applied his experience in Egypt and his knowledge of Orientalism toward understanding how knowledge and representation informed the colonial projects in Persia, Egypt, and elsewhere. For example, in a review of a book on Persian history, in a 1911 issue of the *Irish Review,* Frederick Ryan intelligently explores the "Persian Struggle" against foreign capital, concluding: "How entirely intelligible, one had almost written, how Irish, it all is." In examining nationalist struggles in Persia and British representations of Persian politics, Ryan also draws humanistic and cosmopolitan lessons for decolonizing Ireland. The model-ling process is two–way:

> In the case of Persia, also, we learn the essential unity of the human problem under all its different phases and the futility of the philosophy of Western despots who, anxious to dominate and exploit the East, set up the pleasant doctrine that the peo-ples of the East love despotism, and thus fundamentally differ from the peoples of the West. . . . It is in this realisation of human kinship, this shattering of the pride of race and the pride of power and the pride of religion . . . that there lies the greatest hope of moral advance. (286)

Ryan's focus on representation—like Gregory's focus on the depiction of Arabi in the *Times* and Mangan's on Orientalist translations—encourages political affinity between Ireland and Asian and West Asian colonies. By applying the stereotype of the despot to the West and attacking the "pleasant doctrine" that British Oriental-ists and imperialists set up, Ryan entirely avoids disputing the colonial doctrine of Oriental despotism. Rather, he exposes how the colonizers use this narrative of despotism to justify their domination, claiming what they do is for the betterment of the "natives."

James Connolly

James Connolly also exposed the contradictions between what imperial England promoted in the press and what its actions revealed. In his 1914 subtly pro-German *Irish Worker* essay "The Friends of Small Nationalities," Connolly contrasts Britain's talk of support for "small nationalities" with its actions against them. Like Gregory and Ryan, a main target of his blast is the process of representation, which he cri-tiques as "the lying press of Ireland and England" (1973, 249). He begins the essay by referring to a tag phrase of the time: "The 'war on behalf of small nationalities' is still going merrily on in the newspapers" and soon begins a critique of the Russian government's invasion of "small nationalities." After noting that English officials and publicists have criticized Russia as "a foul blot upon civilisation," Connolly notes that British officials flip-flopped in their public stance toward Russia; using irony, he then gets to his point: "But all that is forgotten now, and the Russian Gov-ernment and the British Government stand solidly together in favour of small na-tionalities everywhere except in countries now under Russian and British Rule." Nationalist movements and protests in Egypt, India, Persia, and Ireland are sup-pressed, while Germany is criticized for similar aggressions.

Yes, I seem to remember a small country called Egypt, a country that through ages of servitude has painfully evolved to a conception of national freedom, and under leaders of its own choosing essayed to make that conception a reality. And I think I remember how this British friend of small nationalities bombarded its chief seaport, invaded and laid waste its territory, slaughtered its armies, imprisoned its citizens, led its chosen leaders away in chains, and reduced the new-born Egyptian nation into a conquered, servile British province. (250)

Connolly points out that not only did England take Egypt as a province and arrest leaders such as Arabi, but its imperial aggression also took the form of bombing and executing "peasants": "And I think I remember how, having murdered this new-born soul of nationality amongst the Egyptian people, it signalized its victory by the ruthless hanging at Denshawai of a few helpless peasants who dared to think their pigeons were not made for the sport of British officers" (250). Such moments of a "small nationality" being ruthlessly subdued resonated for all of these Irish writers and emblematized English aggression.

Like his close friend Frederick Ryan, Connolly's cosmopolitanism was based in his nationalism and materialism. Ryan, along lines similar to Connolly, asks about aggressions against other nationalist groups outside Ireland in an earlier essay in *Dana*, "Are we to acquiesce . . . in base and ignoble wars against the liberty of small communities?" (qtd. in Eagleton 1998, 266). Significantly, like another Irish citizen of the world, Roger Casement, Connolly also had experience in the employ of the British Empire. He served in the British army as a young man, having been raised by working-class Irish emigrants in Scotland; he enlisted at the age of fourteen in 1882.[8] His regiment was Irish, and it has been argued that this period is when Connolly first developed his Irish nationalist consciousness (in addition to a pan-Celtic sensibility). The king's Liverpool Regiment had been infiltrated by Fenians to the extent that during the Fenian uprising of 1867 and again during the Land League unrest in 1881, their weapons were locked up in case they decided to defect and support the cause of the Irish insurgents (P. B. Ellis 1973, 9). After spending a number of years in Ireland, Connolly eventually deserted in 1889 and returned to Scotland to provide for his destitute family, miraculously escaping prosecution. In the intervening years, he had learned a good deal of the operations of the British military and of the place of the Irish in Empire. Shortly after leaving the army, he joined socialist circles and equated England's defense of Empire as primarily the defense of "the uninterrupted domination of the commerce of the world" with Britain as the financial hub (Connolly 1973, 248). Connolly's cross-colony ties were based on beliefs about international class solidarity, and he assumed an internationalist perspective based on his socialist principles. His critiques of English imperialism extended beyond Ireland, Scotland, and Egypt; he also criticized England's aggression and domination in South Africa, India, and Persia: "I remember reading of a large number of small nationalities in India, whose evolution towards a more perfect civilization in harmony with the genius of their race, was ruthlessly crushed in blood, whose lands were stolen, whose education was blighted, whose women were left to the brutal lusts of the degenerate soldiery of the British Raj" (250). Connolly, if less nimbly than Ryan, could resort to sarcasm to expose the duplicity and hypocrisy of imperial justifications: "Oh, yes, they are great fighters for small nationalities, great upholders of the sanctity of treaties!" (251).

Roger Casement

Roger Casement, while still working as an imperial administrator in the Congo in the late nineteenth century, had begun to become disillusioned with the "benevolent" projects of colonialism in Africa, seeing through the civilizing missions of European governments and trade organizations (Sawyer 1997, 29). He eventually vigorously promoted reforms in Africa, South America, and Ireland, before being executed, like James Connolly later was, by the English government for his part in the preparation for Ireland's Easter Rising of 1916. Casement, in line with Gregory, first criticized European colonialism outside of Ireland in European colonies and protectorates. Later, he argued, like Ryan (who died five years before the Easter Rising), that to support Britain's enemies is to support Irish nationalism: "Every man born in Ireland holds a 'hereditary brief' for the opponents of English sway, wherever they may be" (Casement 1958, 80). Although Casement wrote essays, poetry, and lengthy and critical reports of atrocities in the European colonies as a British consul, he is more widely known as a martyr and icon for the Irish nationalist cause, as W. B. Yeats's cross-colony poem "The Ghost of Roger Casement" indicates. The poem attacks John Bull's sanctimonious political and cultural command in England, India, Ireland, and throughout the Empire, in which

> . . . all must hang their trust
> Upon the British Empire,
> Upon the Church of Christ.
> (1973, 424)

Yeats's haunting anticolonial refrain, *"The ghost of Roger Casement / Is beating on the door,"* signals exactly what Lord Salisbury augured and feared about anticolonial forces.

Casement argues in his many essays, collected in *The Crime Against Europe* (1958), that Ireland is both an integral part of the British Empire and has a close tie and "hereditary brief" for other colonized peoples. In short, he acknowledges

Ireland's liminal place at the edge of Europe. Although he deplores the atrocities of colonization and the greed of imperialists in Ireland and elsewhere, he also acknowledges that Ireland has been instrumental for the imperial project. He describes Ireland's relationship to England as parasitic (see his essay "The Emerald Isle and Its Giant Parasite" [131–37]). He argues that "England's Empire at bottom rests upon Ireland to make good British deficiencies. . . . [It is upon Ireland's] rich mine of human fertility and wealth that the British Empire has been founded and maintained" (68). Whether discussing Irish soldiers, Irish wool, Irish beef, or capital raised in Ireland, Casement treats Empire as predominantly reliant on its backyard: "The British Empire is founded not upon the British Bible or the British dreadnought but upon Ireland" (22). This argument differs from the ones that posit Irish consanguinity with the British Empire, in part because Casement repeatedly asserts an essential racial difference between the Saxon and Celt, instead of asserting their brotherhood, collegiality, or dutiful unity. Ireland, he asserts, is an integral, but unwilling, partner in Empire. Unknowingly echoing Keogh's 1848 argument about the unacknowledged importance of Ireland, Casement writes in "The Keeper of the Seas": "Without Ireland there would be to-day no British Empire. The vital importance of Ireland to England is understood, but never proclaimed by every British statesman. . . . To them it has not been a European island, a vital and necessary element of European development, but an appanage of England, an island beyond an island, a mere geographical expression in the titles of conqueror" (18–19). As in the geocentric perspective of James Cousins, or as in James Stephens's early speech to Sinn Féin (both discussed in later chapters), one of the worst things Ireland could be is a "mere geographical expression" in the imagined geography of Empire. But because a "geographical expression" principally exists within the realm of representation, this point is where Ryan and others make their attacks. Furthermore, they need to establish Irish international ties beyond the ones designated by England, ones that would see Ireland as more than merely a name in "the titles of conqueror."

In Casement's essays, he frequently attacks the British Empire's tactics of subjugation and domination, linking Britain's colonial efforts in Ireland to its imperial doctrines and tactics around the world. By recognizing that other "races" are held down in the same ways as the Irish, Casement expands the logic of Irish nationalism to international anticolonialism: "The lands called the British Empire belong to many races, and it is only by the sword and not by the Book of Peace or any pact of peace that those races can be kept from the ownership of their own countries" (87). Casement had had extensive experience in other colonies, working as an administrator and consul in Africa and South America, and he began his critiques of colonialism by writing scathing reports of Dutch, English, and Spanish enterprises across the globe, which in turn unified and inspired his anticolonial vision, as his poetry reveals:

I hate oppression with a hate profound,
and wheresoever in the wide world round,
Beneath a traitor king, a cruel sky,
I hear a strangled people's cry—
("Translation from Victor Hugo's
Feuilles D'Automne," 176)

But not all of the international ties that Casement sought were in the colonies. Another prominent topic in his writings is the greatness of Germany, with whose government he worked to build Irish alliances. From his vantage point in history (he was executed in 1916), Germany seemed to have a better international record than Britain. "The wars that Germany has waged have been wars of defence, or wars to accomplish the unity of her people" (86). He links the future of Ireland with Germany's, not believing that Ireland could achieve its independence on its own and hoping to see both as free nations in a unified Europe: "As an Irishman I have no fear of the result to Ireland of a German triumph [in World War I]. I pray for it; for with the coming of that day the 'Irish question' so dear to British politicians, becomes a European, a world question" (52). By treating Ireland as the "oldest and youngest of the European peoples," Casement here hopes to win European support for the Irish nationalist cause and strengthen continental animosities toward England. In general, he hoped to recast the imagined geography of Empire by isolating England from Europe. Casement presented a vision in which England existed in a nether realm outside Europe, suspended by its international capital and colonialist greed. He repeatedly treated the British Empire as a unified set of lies, justifications, and discursive strategies, even asserting: "The British Empire is the great illusion" (64). What was attributed to English racial and cultural superiority in the press and in culture was, Casement argued, in reality merely colonialist exploitation, which began in Ireland and spread across the globe. Indeed, he saw Empire as the primary factor that separated Britain from its European neighbors. In one essay, Casement extends the idioms of English superiority in Asia into a European context, resembling in some ways contemporary arguments about England's place in the European Union. As Casement argues, the unjust and racist arguments that separate England from its colonies infect its relationship to the rest of Europe.

Nothing is clearer than that no Englishman can think of other nations save in terms of permanent inferiority. . . . Far from being indifferent, Sir R. Edgecumbe asserted these poor [Tamil, Japanese, Chinese, and Malaysian] workers nourished a reverence "bordering on veneration" for the Englishman. "This is shown in a curious way by their refusal to call any European 'a white man' save the Englishman alone. The German trader, the Italian and the Frenchman all are, in their speech coloured men." After this appreciation of themselves the English cannot object to the present writer's view that they are non-Europeans. (51)

Casement not only reacts to British representations, but also co-opts the narrative and attempts to write Britain out of its geographical place as the metropole. In this view of Europe, Ireland has a clearer place. Moreover, he argues that countries such as Germany should assist Ireland in "forcibly restor[ing itself] to Europe" (51).

Casement's tireless advocacy of Germany and his assertions of Irish-German ties have put off many critics, even though he was writing before the horrors of Adolf Hitler and the Third Reich. Significantly, although Casement's focus on the superiority of the German nation and people is disturbing, it parallels similar Irish nationalist arguments for the superiority of the Irish people, which were widely advocated at the time and are not entirely forgotten today. Casement's judgments certainly fitted the racial discourse of the day: "[T]he Irish race still presents a type, superior physically, intellectually and morally to the English" (32). Similarly, he argues that the Irish have a spotless international record and a morally just ethos: "Irish wars have been only against one enemy, and ending always in material disaster they have conferred always a moral gain. Their memory uplifts the Irish heart; for no nation, no people, can reproach Ireland with having wronged them. She has injured no man" (86). Although this is standard Irish nationalist propaganda, which still holds some sway today for many nationalist writers and critics, Casement elsewhere evenly articulates Ireland's more culpable participation in the British Empire, and does not always dismiss it as the work of a coerced people. In the following quote, he mourns that England's complex role in South Africa and the Boer War was enabled by Irish soldiers.

> It was on Irish soldiers that the English chiefly relied in the Boer War, and it is no exaggeration to say that could all the Irishmen in the ranks of the British army have been withdrawn, a purely British force would have failed to end the war and the Dutch would have remained masters of the field in South Africa.
>
> It was the inglorious part of Ireland to be linked with those "methods of barbarism" she herself knew only too well, in extinguishing the independence of a people who were attacked by the same enemy and sacrificed to the same greed that had destroyed her own freedom. (32–33)

This recognition of Irish culpability, though not that of Irish leaders, is significant, as are his other acknowledgments of Irish complicity in India. Despite acknowledging Ireland's part in the British Empire, Casement does not assert any narratives of Saxon-Celtic consanguinity but instead asserts a sort of "politics of otherness." As he notes in "Speech from the Dock," his own involvement in Empire never superceded his devotion to Ireland: "If charity begins at home, *Empire* begins in other men's homes, and both may cover a multitude of sins. I, for one, was determined that Ireland was much more to me than *Empire,* and that if charity begins at home, so must loyalty" (155).

Even outside of his German arguments, Casement repeatedly posits Ireland's need for other allies and direct foreign intervention. Casement was devoted to this thought; indeed, he was executed for treason after being caught in the west of Ireland, having just been dropped off by Germans on his way to warn the insurgent Irish forces in 1916 that German forces would not be landing in Kerry. While he was in prison, his homosexuality (still a crime at the time) was revealed through his infamous "Black Diaries," fortifying the British case against him. But he was arrested for his Irish nationalist activities and German ties.[9]

At the foundation of his critique of Empire are narratives that assert Irish affinities with other colonies. Casement argues presciently that the only real hope for the dissolution of the British Empire will come from "the great millions of mankind who make up the greatest realm of her empire," that is, India—in the end, Ireland's hope is in India: "Ireland *might* be bought or bribed, at any rate in this generation, to forfeit her national ideals and barter the aspiration that six centuries of contact with England have failed to kill; but the 350,000,000 of Indian mankind can never be, or bought, or bribed in the end" (82). Within Casement's cross-colony sympathies, however, some of the idioms of Anglo-French Orientalism remain,[10] but by basing Indian patriotism on Irish models, Casement hoped that India would be able to do what Ireland, at the time he was writing, had been unable to do: break the stranglehold of Empire.

The focus on human anticolonial affinities and a cross-colony cosmopolitanism in the texts of Irish newspapers and, even more so, by writers such as Gregory, Ryan, Connolly, and Casement helped refocus the representations of Asia and West Asia in Ireland away from essentialized differences between Orientals and Occidentals. These Irish representations of the Orient redirect the discourse of Orientalism in Irish texts and contexts, as Casement sought to rhetorically displace England as a European country. By seeing through the British discourse of Orientalism and Empire, by making cross-colony studies, these writers began to understand their own relationship with imperial England better. Such understanding and knowledge lent a global context to Irish nationalism and helped Irish cultural nationalists develop new political affinities besides the ones they had inherited. The fundamental point here is that these Irish anticolonialists need to be considered as both part of the Irish "school" of Orientalism, which W. B. Yeats sought to understand (as the next chapter explores), and part of the discourse of Irish Orientalism that M. Mansoor sought to map.

As a group of representations, Irish Orientalism is as ranging as, if less cohesive than, British Orientalism, primarily because of Ireland's liminal place in Empire. It housed narratives of imperial consanguinity and anticolonial Oriental affinities (whether materialist or antimaterialist). In this sense, Irish Orientalism both secured a better place for Ireland within Empire and encouraged (demanded at times) the dissolution of Empire. Certainly, English fears about the disintegration of Empire created, to some extent, a self-fulfilling prophecy. But the similarities and actualities of colonial rule in Ireland, India, Egypt, Persia, and elsewhere—spurred by a centuries-old cultural link between the Celt and the Oriental and their international "community of sufferings" (Montmorency-Morris 1821, 71)—inspired cross-colonial affinities and models, hastening global decolonization.

6   W. B. Yeats's Celtic Orient

> Tradition is always the same. The earliest poet of India and the Irish
> peasant in his hovel nod to each other across the ages, and are in
> perfect agreement.
> —W. B. Yeats, "Irish Wonders"

> Why has our school . . . been interested mainly in something in
> Irish life so old that one can no longer say this is Europe, that is
> Asia?
> —W. B. Yeats, preface to *The Cat and the Moon and Certain Poems*

IN THE INTRODUCTION to Rabindranath Tagore's *Gitanjali* (1912), Yeats comments that reading Tagore's verse was like recognizing a voice in a dream. Yeats's identification with Tagore points to the fascination that many Irish Revivalists had with the cultural and philosophical motifs subsumed within the rubric of the Orient. The Orientalism of these Irish cultural nationalists developed from earlier constructions of the Orient, especially nineteenth-century national and anticolonial narratives set in Asia and West Asia. Yeats's personal fascination with the Orient was varied and long-lived. His ardent interest in Indian literature and philosophy developed early and continued throughout his life, responding to the works and personae of three particular Indians: Mohini Chatterjee, Rabindranath Tagore, and Shri Purohit Swami. Other representations and seeming embodiments of the Orient also drew Yeats from his apprentice days to his old age: the mysticism of the Moors and Arabs, the continuous ancient culture of the Chinese, and the "aristocratic" art and tradition of the Japanese. He found in all of them remedies for modern ills; moreover, within them he discovered age-old parallels to what he saw as a vanishing Celtic Ireland.

Throughout his Orientalist works, Yeats represents Indians, Chinese, and Japanese in similar ways to his contemporaneous European Orientalists. In *Orientalism,* Edward Said discusses the "body of ideas, beliefs, clichés, or learning about the East" that were subsumed in the discipline of Orientalism. "[O]ne of the important developments in nineteenth-century Orientalism was the distillation of essential ideas about the Orient—its sensuality, its tendency to despotism, its aberrant mentality, its habits of inaccuracy, its backwardness—into a separate and unchallenged coherence" (1995, 205). Yeats often repeated similar stereotypes and tropes, but in contrast to English imperialists he usually treated such traits as positive. His late Romantic thinking on Celtic and Oriental sensibilities grew alongside his ideas on sensuality, spiritualism, tradition, and occult aesthetics, all meeting in the rich tapestry of his early poems. From the outset of his career, the Oriental and the Celtic shared the same deep source—not modern, not industrial, but imaginative and sensual.

Yeats's hybrid position as an Anglo-Irish poet allowed him access to the narratives of both the colonizer and the colonized. Because the goals of his narratives were generally anticolonial and decolonizing, and because such strategies contributed more to the cultural decolonization of Ireland and India than to their colonization, these narratives are best understood in a postcolonization and decolonizing context.[1] A great deal has been written on how Anglo-French Orientalism generally contributed to the colonizing and civilizing mission of Empire. But Irish cultural nationalists employed Orientalist narratives for other ends. Their strategic use of the Orient attempted to forge new national ideals and a new identity for Ireland in opposition to Empire—attempting to refashion what Homi Bhabha has termed a "national narrative"[2] or, to use a term George Russell (AE) coined in 1916, the "national being."[3]

Celtic enthusiasts at the end of the nineteenth century continued to exploit the Celtic-Oriental connections that had developed over the previous one hundred years, blending Celticist and Oriental aesthetics in opposition to the rational and utilitarian ideals of the times, in the mode of the aesthetes and the Pre-Raphaelites. Such a blend aimed to produce a supposed East-West aesthetic. Throughout his works that concern the East, Yeats highlighted positive, antimodernist elements of Oriental stereotypes and comparisons, as he did with Celtic tropes, believing he was uncovering an ancient sensibility by borrowing "directly" from Asian art and philosophy.[4] In "The Celtic Element in Literature" (1897), Yeats famously responded to Ernest Renan and Matthew Arnold, not by refuting Arnold's formulation of a dreamy and ineffectual Celt but by emphasizing the positive and heroic traits of the imaginative and nature-loving Celt. Significantly, Yeats does not drop the incidental comparisons between the Oriental and the Celt, but rather he adds a more specific comparison between Celtic tropes and "Mahomedan" literature (1961, 175).[5] Such a move reveals the central purpose of Yeats's Orientalism: borrow from the Orient to refurbish an ancient Celtic sensibility. Such a refurbished ancient sensibility, according to Renan, Arnold, Yeats, and many others, was needed to offset the mounting materialism of modern Europe.

In transvaluing the more imperial representations of the Celt and the Oriental, Yeats acts as an intermediary between the English and the Irish, a role familiar to Anglo-Irish writers. The centuries-old Irish interest in Asian and West Asian cultures and traditions, particularly of India, Persia, and Japan, enabled Yeats to refashion this central motif of Ireland's Celtic Revival and postcolonial moment. Yeats along with other Revivalists, such as James Stephens, James Cousins, George Russell, and Frederick Ryan, continued to rely upon notions of the Orient developed by Anglo-French Orientalists, but they did not merely project Irish issues onto the Orient. Combining their study of Celtic legends and myths with specific traditions of Asia and West Asia further enabled strategies of allegory or, as Moore put it, the "application of doubleness," which characterized the Oriental literary works of Owenson, Moore, Mangan, and de Vere. They furthered this tradition by digging deeper into the philosophy, literatures, and histories of Asia and West Asia and by identifying with spiritualists, artists, and cultural nationalists from Asia, whom they often took to be representative of the Orient.

As Irish cultural and literary nationalism increased (even came into vogue), their "application" often became more explicit in its criticism of English colonialism, linking colonialism with Arnoldian critiques of the "philistine" culture of the modern West. In fact, their literary productions worked against many Orientalist stereotypes, exposing them as such, but they simultaneously rehearsed other centuries-old tropes of the sensual, mystical East. Such a move transferred the seemingly positive anticolonial and antimodern values of the Orient to its European cultural cousin, the imaginative, mystical, and Celtic west of Ireland. But whatever the extent of the Revival's borrowings from Orientalism, they were rarely straightforward. The very acts of incorporating Orientalist tropes into neo-Celtic works helped transform the Celtic-Orient connection into anticolonial and decolonizing narratives, which, in turn, affected other decolonizing narratives in places such as India and Egypt.

As in the projects of earlier Irish writers, Revivalists not only created allegories for Ireland in the Orient but also imaginatively distanced Ireland from England and "de-Europeanized" the country with Orientalized images of a non-British, nonindustrial, nonurban Celtic, Gaelic Ireland. In Yeats's preface to *The Cat and the Moon and Certain Poems* (1924), addressed to Lady Gregory, the poet recounts how he invented verse for the Irish hero Cuchulain, based on "[verses] Indian poets have put into the mouth of Krishna," and how some plays of the Revival had "an odour, a breath, that suggests to me Indian or Japanese poems and legends" (1973, 854). He then asks the pointed and reflective question of the Irish literary Orientalist: "Why has our school . . . been interested mainly in something in Irish life so old that one can no longer say this is Europe, that is Asia?"[6] Although Yeats probably did not fully recognize the cultural tradition of a Celtic-Oriental "something in Irish life," he nevertheless recognized its subversive, antimodern, and (often) anticolonial resonances and saw how such motifs reverberated within Irish literature and culture. Indeed, his comments about this "something" signify how foundational to Irish culture the centuries-old links between the Celt and the Oriental had become. During the Revival when cultural nationalists reinvented this pairing by identifying with the Orient as both something new and something traditional, the Oriental element that they recognized "in Irish life" felt familiar because of both the long Oriental tradition in Irish culture and because of the fact that Oriental and Celtic mantles are so closely related as exotic *others* to the center of Empire. Significantly, what Yeats saw as a "something in Irish life so old that one can no longer say this is Europe, that is Asia" was categorically *neither* European *nor* Asian; rather, it was *both* European *and* Asian. This "school" sought to override the distinction between the East and the West through Ireland's cross-colony identification. Orientalism was their text, thesis, and field, but unlike many English Orientalists, their goals were not imperial.

This chapter moves through Yeats's Celtic Orientalism chronologically, beginning with an exploration of his early play *Mosada* and moving into a discussion of his relationship with Indian literature and thought. Early on, he wrote poems with Indian subject matter and borrowed characters and ideas from the classical Indian playwright Kālidāsa. Afterward, his interest in Theosophy and Indian philosophy led him toward more personal relationships with Indian mystics and writers, namely, Mohini Chatterjee, Shri Purohit Swami, and, most important, Rabindranath Tagore. After this extended discussion, an overview of his Japanese Noh dramas is given as well as a glimpse into Yeats's relationship with Japan. Interspersed throughout the chapter and in notes, I have summarized the most pertinent arguments of many critics who have also explored Yeats's relationship with the Orient and helped shape how we read Yeats's Celtic Orientalism, both to garner valuable insights and to note the limitations of the arguments.

More has been written on Yeats's interest in the Orient than on the interest of any other Irish writer. The reasons concern Yeats's prominence in the Irish, English, and modernist canons as well as his overt use of Oriental themes in his otherwise ostensibly "Irish" or neo-Celtic pieces. Studies approach Yeats's Oriental works from many angles, but, as of yet, no critical overview of his work as Irish Orientalism, paying close attention to Oriental-Celtic links and his place in the history of Irish Orientalism, has been written. Moreover, although many detailed studies exist on specific aspects of Yeats's Orientalism (most notably by Edward Larrissy and John Rickard), many critics who discuss the topic have not advanced our understanding of Orientalism in Yeats's work much beyond what prominent Theosophist and schoolfellow of Yeats Charles Johnston noted in his 1906[7] reflections on the poet's younger days:

In the work of the earliest days, there was nothing to reveal or even suggest the poet of mystical Ireland; no consciousness, even, of any special poetical material to be drawn from mystic Eire. One can realize this by turning over the leaves of the earlier book of verse, or better still, by noting the order of first publication in the rare folios of the *Dublin University Review*. There were Princesses of Sweden, there were Greek islands with a mystical people of statues; there were Moorish magicians, Spanish Inquisitors, and Indian Sages; nothing peculiarly Celtic or Irish; yet everywhere a largeness, a vague gloom, an imaginative and dreamy depth, a sense of cavernous things, of overhanging deeps, from which were presently to issue the more purely Celtic forms of vision and of dream. (1977, 11)

Johnston merely lists the Orient as a precursor setting for the Celtic in Yeats's poetic imagination, and this is the basis of the arguments of most Western critics. But this seemingly commonsensical approach to understanding Yeats's youthful fascination with the exotic and the Oriental—that his interest in the Orient fed his more mature "Celtic forms of vision and of dream"—misleads a study of Orientalism in Yeats's work and in the Revival. Such an argument is based on the not-self-evidently false assumption that Orientalism is a foreign (Anglo-French) discourse that has no immediate connection with Celticism, that is, a belief that the Celtic could be cleanly and essentially distinguished from the Oriental. Furthermore, the arguments that the Orient merely supplied models for Yeats's reinventions of a Celtic Ireland usually only isolate specific instances of Yeats's involvement with the Orient, addressing them as if they were tangential interests that Yeats soon dismissed, rarely taking into account his lifelong fascination with the Orient. Oriental representations developed throughout Yeats's life, and his use of them was in a distinctly Irish tradition and milieu. In short, his representations of the Orient and of the Celtic "mystical Eire" have more do with one another than a case of influence. Furthermore, to isolate the Celtic from the Oriental is to downplay their related semiotic history, ignoring how their narratives operate in tandem, particularly in Ireland.

The nativistic legacy of Irish literature, particularly prominent in the twentieth century, has been principally concerned with "things Irish" (comely maidens, Irish folklore, funerals and wakes, heroic historical events, and martyrdom on Irish soil, sea, or pavement). Such a perspective continues to haunt critical understandings of Irish literature, limiting the field with a narrow and narcissistic servant's looking glass that only reflects images of an Irish literature that is "Oirish." The fact that Yeats's Oriental themes are normally not considered an integral part of an Irish literary tradition is illustrated by a descriptive comment made one of the leading scholars in Irish studies today, Roy Foster, Yeats's most thoroughgoing biographer. He describes Yeats's early Oriental interests as such: "All this work was deeply conventional. It was also, as [Charles] Johnston noted, utterly *unIrish*, coming out of a

'vast murmurous gloom of dreams' " (1997, 37; emphasis added). Although Johnston never actually uses the word *unIrish*, Foster's gloss accurately characterizes
Johnston's perspective. Yet, this point is precisely where, I believe, the common
problem in our understanding of this material exists. Foster is only one of many
critics, scholars, and writers who have long treated such exotic and Oriental material as "unIrish," thus undermining its significance in the study of Irish literature
and culture. To avoid belaboring this point, I will allow a simple analogy to make
my point: to see this material as "unIrish" is akin to arguing that Johnson's *Rasselas*
is unEnglish or Montesquieu's *Lettres Persanes* unFrench.

Mosada

The Orient drew Yeats. He mingled Celtic and Oriental representations not
merely out of a youthful fascination, later discarded by the mature poet. Throughout his life he explored representations of the Oriental and the Celtic, paralleling
other lifelong ideas such as the mask of the artist. But Yeats's fascination with the
Orient was dynamic, developing and changing throughout his life. The fact that
the youthful Yeats began his career writing about a magician in central Asia and
soon after looked to western Irish folklore and the Sidhe (the race of fairy folk) reveals how this architect of the Revival found an easy bridge between the two.
While living in his father's house in Dublin, Yeats wrote his first dramatic poem,
Mosada (1883–1884), which both inaugurated his long-lasting literary fascination
with the Orient and presented the Orient as an allegorical realm in which to work
out Irish issues. Yeats had been reading James Clarence Mangan and Samuel Ferguson during his school days and was familiar with Ferguson's *Hibernian Nights Entertainments,* which told the Red Branch cycle within the frame of *Arabian Nights.*
The technique of weaving Irish or Celtic stories together through this Oriental
frame was thus familiar to the young Yeats, as were the Oriental works of Byron,
Moore, and other Romantics. According to Yeats's 1892 interview with Tynan in
Sketch, Mosada was the first real literary work he attempted: "The first attempt at serious poetry I made was when I was about seventeen and much under the influence of Shelley. It was a dramatic poem, about a magician who set up his throne in
Central Asia, and who expressed himself with Queen Mab–like heterodoxy" (qtd.
in Foster 1996, 37). Though Oriental themes were not the only ones that drew the
young poet's attention, they opened an avenue for exploring symbolism and mysticism in literature while expressing the Irish cultural and sectarian tensions that
troubled Yeats throughout his career. Early on, the Orient became an attractive
realm, at once exotically foreign and strangely familiar.

Mosada is the story of a young Moorish woman, persecuted by Catholics during the Spanish Inquisition. At the piece's opening, Mosada has been separated

from her lover, Gomez, and is seeking methods of finding him. Arabic astrology has informed her that she will see her lover again before she dies; moreover, she is told that if she burns some fragrant herbs and gazes into the "charméd depth of whirling smoke," she will learn of his whereabouts (1987, 55). Through dramatic irony, this prediction is precisely what happens. Her young, lame friend Cola warns her not to perform the magical ritual because of "the far reaching powers of the church," but she ignores him and prepares for the ritual. But before she can begin, Cola scatters the herbs, calling her (in Yeats's first draft) a "Moorish witch" (65). Two "Inquisitors" then burst in and seize her—having pried information about the "heretic" Mosada from the weak-willed Cola. As they lead her away to prison, Cola, Judas-like, begs forgiveness from her at the scene's close—her reply: "'Twas Allah's will" (67). In prison, anticipating being burned at the stake, Mosada swallows poison from a ring she wears and awaits death. Soon after, the feared head Inquisitor, a monk named Ebremar, bursts into her cell to force a confession from her. Immediately upon entering, however, he recognizes Mosada as his old lover. His passion reawakens, and the reader realizes that he is her Gomez. In a death trance, Mosada recognizes her lover and assumes she is meeting with him in a mystical interworld between life and death. She dies in his arms, never realizing his treacherous double identity.

The tensions in *Mosada* between Oriental magic and European Catholicism reveal Yeats's position as a young Anglo-Irish Protestant poet interested in a heretical mysticism and Celtic legend. Yeats's family, particularly his mother's brother, had distinct traditions of mysticism from Protestant Masonic connections, which existed in dire opposition to Catholicism. Many of Yeats's early mystical influences were certainly Anglo-Irish, and in many ways his Orientalism reflects this inheritance. It is not a new idea that Protestant Masonic rituals in Ireland worked as Anglo-Irish cultural parallels and substitutes for the more overtly ritualized and mystical Catholic Church. Understanding such as an Anglo-Irish "strategy for coping"[8] helps to contextualize Yeats's attraction to the occult and the Orient, but, significantly, such a strategy had a history prior to Yeats (Foster 1997, 50). Edward Larrissy in *Yeats the Poet* extends the point, asserting that Anglo-Irish mysticism and Yeats's Orientalism were more than the reactionary results of Protestant compensation and "search for psychic control," as many commentators have argued.[9] Larrissy explores Yeats's interest in the Orient as, in part, a continuation of his family's long interest in Protestant and Anglo-Irish mysticism: "I follow Elizabeth Cullingford and Roy Foster in finding far more than merely suggestive the following two facts: that Freemasonry was an all-pervading institution of Irish Protestantism; and that the Golden Dawn was a quasi-Masonic organisation" (1994, 9). Larrissy traces this path in Yeats's work,[10] finding places where Orientalism emerges in conjunction with this tradition. He also highlights Yeats's poetic role "as mediator and then instructor of the Celtic," a role not dissimilar to his role with the Orient (11).

The Orient, which often included Moorish Spain, offered a symbolic realm in which Yeats could work out his religious tensions, which happened to be similar to many in the Revival. In *Mosada* the Orient was not overtly political or consciously anticolonial like other pieces of Irish literary Orientalism, which is not to say it was not personally allegorical or resonant. The poetic figure of the dramatic poem was a persecuted Moorish magician, after all, with whom Yeats was clearly sympathetic. As in Owenson's *Missionary*, the conquering Catholic Church is clearly a target and operates in opposition to this more subversive mysticism. This is not to argue that Yeats's Orientalism was entirely distinct from Irish-Catholic Orientalism, only that it reflected his own cultural inheritance from Protestant Ireland.

The Orient in *Mosada* is a subversive and underground realm, associated with magic and longing—associations the Celtic also invoked, as contemporaneous and senior Irish writers such as Lafcadio Hearn often noted (as explored in chapter 4). Describing the revision of the piece, Yeats coupled the Orient with fairyland in a well-known letter to Katharine Tynan in 1886 (the year *Mosada: A Dramatic Poem* appeared as a booklet): "I have much improved Mosada by polishing the verse here and there. I have noticed some things about my poetry, I did not know before, in this process of correction, for instance that it is almost all a flight into fairy land from the real world, and a summons to that flight. The Chorus to the 'stollen [*sic*] child' sums it up—That it is not the poetry of insight and knowledge, but of longing and complaint—the cry of the heart against necessity" (1986, 54–55). Although Yeats is discussing his writing in general here, his use of the metaphor of fairyland is significant in that it parallels *Mosada*'s Oriental magic, both describing a flight from "necessity" and the real or quotidian world. Yeats along with most Celtic Revivalists wanted to develop the representations of this Celtic otherworld ("fairyland") in literature. They turned to the Orient for models: a realm that had been extensively studied and offered a similar semiotic meaning and emotional force. But, as we will see, the more they learned about the Orient through studying Asian religions and cultures, the more they focused on its possibilities for resisting modern culture, which, increasingly, meant resisting colonialism.

For Yeats, both narratives of the Orient and "fairyland" encouraged the "cry of the heart against necessity"—which is close to saying that both reacted "against the despotism of fact," to borrow from Arnold's famous formulation of Celticity (1973a, 343). As Yeats's career developed, the Oriental and the Celtic became more intertwined as distinct strands of the same rope. His attraction to the Orient grew because of its antimodern and mystical reputation and its semiotic opposition to Victorian conventionality. Just as he was drawn to the Oriental, he was drawn to the Celtic. In Larrissy's discussion of Yeats's Anglo-Irishness, he notes what many critics have observed: "Yeats considered himself fitted by birth—better fitted than his Catholic social inferiors—to be the purveyor and translator of an exotic Celtic quality and an ancient wisdom, through the medium of poetic norms of the English tradition" (1994, 1). This characteristically Anglo-Irish position as "purveyor and translator" allows the Anglo-Irish writer a valuable place in the cultures of both England and Ireland; it also grants these writers a degree of cross-cultural authority and mobility.

In *Decolonisation and Criticism,* Gerry Smyth describes this position as one of "supplementarity," that is, the Anglo-Irish, culturally speaking, could supplement the authenticity of Celtic culture by representing it, thereby securing a mediator role for the Anglo-Irish writer in Ireland and granting the Anglo-Irish writer a sense of deferred Celtic authority, difference, and authenticity in England. Smyth describes the term as follows: "In political terms this supplementarity is conceived as a necessary cosmopolitanism dimension which will avert the evils of provincialism and insularity" (1998, 75). Thus, in Ireland, Anglo-Irish supplementarity is at once both cosmopolitan and parochial, and promises to establish a balance between the modernism of the colonizer and the traditions of the colonized. Larrissy also comments on this role, "Yeats . . . thought that it was desirable to mediate between 'Celtic' and 'English' qualities. He saw himself as effecting this in his poetry. In *Autobiographies,* besides striking descriptions of the Anglo-Irish consciousness of internal division, one finds revealing suggestions of the Anglo-Irish capacity for mediation" (1994, 7–8). Similarly, Yeats as an Irish Orientalist drew on a literary and intellectual tradition of representing and translating the Orient and rhetorically mediating between Europe and Asia.

Indian Philosphy and Literature

Yeats's involvement with the East continued to develop before and during the 1880s when his interest in Theosophy and Indian philosophy grew. His friendships with Charles Johnston and George Russell prodded him into deeper investigations of mysticism, the occult, Theosophy, and Eastern philosophy. Foster notes that one of the most influential books of Yeats's early adult years was A. P. Sinnett's *Esoteric Buddhism,* "a founding text of the fashionable New Age religion, Theosophy, blending East and West in a spiritual synthesis" (1997, 45). Significantly, the book had been sent to Yeats by his "intellectually modish" aunt, Isabella Pollexfen Varley, who lived in London. Soon after, Yeats lent it to Charles Johnston, who went to London not long after to study Theosophy and, upon returning to Dublin, introduced it to Ireland.[11] Other important texts to Yeats included English translations of the Vedas and the Upanishads as well as the works on Eastern philosophy by Max Müller and Goethe, all of which combined to give Yeats a rigorous (if fantastical) education in not only Theosophy but also its version of Orientalism. By the mid-1880s, Yeats had also begun to read Indian literature; one text in particular would heighten his interests in India and in the literature of Asia and West Asia and foster his future identification with living Indian writers: Kālidāsa's *Śakuntulā*, the text that William Jones had influentially translated in the late eighteenth century. Significantly, before Yeats met Mohini Chatterjee, Rabindranath Tagore, and Shri Purohit Swami, he wrote in the style of the translated Kālidāsa and borrowed characters from his most well-known play. Both Sinnett's and Kālidāsa's texts were crucial in his development of a poetic persona. In a sense, they prepared him for his meeting in 1886 with Mohini Chatterjee, the Indian mystic and Theosophist, in many ways, a crucial moment of the Revival.

Yeats had met other Indians and West Asians; for instance, he had met Mir Alaud Ali, a professor of Persian, Arabic, and Hindustani in the Oriental Studies Department at Trinity, a local figure who reflected the intellectual and artistic attraction to Indian culture and philosophy in the 1880s.[12] But Chatterjee represented something different from Ali, whose principal task, whatever his erudition, was training TCD men to serve in the Indian Civil Service; as M. Mansoor reports in *The Story of Irish Orientalism,* in 1855 when "appointments to the Civil Service of India and to the Army were thrown open to public competition, Trinity College rose nobly to the opportunity and encouraged her more enterprising alumni to find scope for their native talents in this field" (1944, 59). In contrast to Ali's academic and intellectual persona, Chatterjee was a holy man, an expounder of mystical truths, and something of a poet. Yeats was deeply affected by what Chatterjee had to say but even more by whom he believed Chatterjee to be. Foster describes Yeats's first encounter with the ascetic:"[T]he exoticism, the simplicity, the gnomic utterance all appealed, and were recapitulated in a number of poems. Mohini Chatterjee in his youth was a genuinely impressive presence, preaching the Vedantic way of meditation, asceticism and renunciation—he was described by Blavatsky as 'a nutmeg Hindoo with buck eyes' " (1997, 47). But Chatterjee found the trials of asceticism too great in a land where he was the sensual exotic of the day, and he was called back to India where he continued his career. "[H]e shortly proved unable to resist the sexual opportunities offered by his English disciples. . . . By 1900 he had become, according to Russell, 'a very corpulent Brahmin who has a good practice as a lawyer at Bombay,' but he still produced a widely read book on Indian spirituality in 1907, as well as his translation of Sankaracharya into German" (47–48).[13] Yeats was drawn to this man for many reasons, and much had to do with the newness of Chatterjee's ideas to the young Yeats. Foster continues in describing what the philosophical attractions were to Yeats:

> To WBY (not yet exposed to Blake, Pater or the French Symbolists, and forty-odd
> years before his discovery of Berkeley's metaphysics), Theosophy could not have

been presented more attractively, although some of the other doctrines, such as the abjuration of all worldly ambition, were probably not so appealing. Mohini's visit was still vivid when he recalled it in an important essay fourteen years later ("The Way of Wisdom"; later becoming, "The Pathway"); and by then he was able to link the message with the esoteric reading from other sources. (48)

But Yeats was more than intellectually and philosophically drawn to Chatterjee, and this point is where many studies fall short in understanding the depth of Yeats's interest. He seems to have been drawn to Chatterjee's persona, which resonated with his own assumed identity and youthful mask as a poetic Celtic magus. Although there is no way to know for certain what Chatterjee meant to the young Yeats, Chatterjee must have appeared as a new type of poet-magus to Yeats, one that was not conventional in the English sense, nor derivative or stereotypical in any sense (at least for him at the time). In him, he saw not only an "Oriental wisdom" and Indian spirituality but also an ancient mystical sensibility, all of which is what he hoped to develop in his own writing. His identification with Chatterjee, however, pales in comparison with his later more explicit identification with Tagore, which the bulk of this chapter will address.

Before moving into a discussion of Yeats's relationship with Tagore, other elements of Yeats's attraction to Indian literature need to be discussed. In particular, his early Indian poems in *Crossways* (first published in *The Wanderings of Oisin and Other Poems* [1889]) reveal a crucial theme in the poet's involvement with the Orient. These early Indo-Irish poems illustrate a close association between spirituality and sensuality, between the independent passions of eros and agape, which are characterized by, on the one hand, physical sensuality and, on the other hand, mystical or spiritual wonder. Certain Vaishnava sects of Hinduism in Bengal articulated a blending of two similar sensibilities (which I will discuss in more detail in relation to Tagore) that later drew the young poet's attention. Although Yeats had been interested in Indian philosophy through Theosophy since his days at the High School, it was not until Yeats encountered Mohini Chatterjee in London that his interest became particularly literary. He then began to investigate Indian literature, being particularly impressed by Kālidāsa's *Śakuntulā,* which had been first translated by Sir William Jones in 1789 (Yeats read Monier Williams's translation, second edition, 1876). The close ties between the sensual world and the spiritual world—eros with agape—drew Yeats to Kālidāsa's play, so much so that he borrowed Oriental characters from it, in the tradition of pseudo-Oriental letters.

Drawing the character of Anushuya (Williams's spelling) from *Śakuntulā* in his "Anashuya and Vijaya," Yeats created a poetic dialogue. Anusuya (a contemporary spelling)—a close friend of the eponymous young female character Śakuntulā— prays and talks with her lover, Vijaya, who seems to have been Yeats's own creation. In the first four acts of Kālidāsa's play (out of seven acts), Anusuya always appears with her companion, Priyamvada. Both live with Śakuntulā and other ascetic hermits in the woods, under the protection of Śakuntulā's stepfather, the holy man Kanva. Anusuya contributes to the play's action by relaying important information to the audience regarding King Dushyanta and Śakuntulā's attraction and lovemaking. Her role as the go-between, however, does not resemble the self-serving lover-brokering of a Pandarus character; rather, she mediates and articulates the varieties of love, social code, and spiritual devotion, providing a basis for Yeats's character. Anusuya and her continual companion, Priyamvada, arrange a meeting between the king and Śakuntulā, and later, after they are secretly married, they worry about the king keeping his vow to their pregnant friend. Their dialogue is chiefly concerned with Śakuntulā; nevertheless, it explores many of the main themes of the play, the emotional nuances of love: desire, anxiety, compatibility, dejection, self-awareness, intimacy, faithfulness, trust, jealousy, forgiveness, and destiny. Likewise, they represent and explore issues of spiritual fulfillment and proper behavior.

Throughout the first half of Kālidāsa's play, Anusuya repeatedly voices what is not said by other characters: speaking their fears, hopes, desires, and curiosities. Her role as the outspoken one is crucial to the development of the action because she asks the most pointed questions that both speak their inner thoughts and propel the characters. K lid sa made Anusuya's role as this speaker of the unspoken explicit twice, saying words of truth that the lovers are too shy to utter.[14] Furthermore, it is Anusuya who first anticipates the king's later betrayal of Śakuntulā, which she correctly qualifies: "Perhaps it is not the good King's fault. It must be the curse of the Durvasas" (1959, 42). She also first suggests that the king's betrothal ring will be the vehicle that will reunite the lovers. The ring is soon lost in the Ganges and found in a fish gullet; when it is returned to him, it magically reminds him of his love and marriage with Śakuntulā. Furthermore, Śakuntulā's last line in the play highlights Anusuya's abilities of mystical premonition, especially in matters concerning love: "I suppose I did not hear the curse in my absent-minded state, for my friends warned me most earnestly to show my husband the ring" (92). Yeats furthers this character, but we see Anusuya's role as mediator in a different light in Yeats's dramatic poem, as she mediates her own love and mystical premonitions.

In his "Anashuya and Vijaya," which was first titled "Jealousy," Yeats seems to pick up Anashuya where Kālidāsa left off, that is, in the fourth act, when she is doubting the king's faithfulness and hoping to restore their union by sending Śakuntulā to the palace. Yeats's Anashuya is a young priestess and lover who senses that her lover loves another, as the initial title indicates. But, in this incomplete version, we do not find out if her suppositions are correct. As Yeats tells us in a 1925 note, he initially intended the poem to be the opening scene of a play about two women and their mutual lover or, as he puts it, "about a man loved by two women who had 'the one soul between them, the one woman waking when the other

slept, and knowing but daylight as the other only night' " (1973, 489).[15] Antino-
mies, oppositions, contraries: such dualism is typical of Yeats, as many critics (from
Robin Skelton to Edward Larrissy) have noted. Yeats blends opposites together in
this poem, specifically blending the spiritual with the physical. In Anashuya's opening prayer, we hear how close-knit spiritual and physical love is as desire, jealousy,
prayer, and curse mingle:

> Send peace on all the lands and flickering corn.—
> O may tranquility walk by his elbow
> When wandering in the forest, if he love
> No other.—Hear, and may the indolent flocks
> Be plentiful.—And if he love another,
> May panthers end him.—Hear, and load our king
> With wisdom hour by hour.—May we two stand,
> When we are dead, beyond the setting suns,
> A little from the other shades apart,
> With mingling hair, and play upon one lute.
>
> (44)

These lines reveal the main themes and movement of the dramatic poem, setting
their physical love within a spiritual and mystical context. The striking image of
the panther is accented by the break in the rhythm provided by the spondee "end
him," and both devices combine to signal the prescient jealousy of Yeats's devout
priestess and lover.

We might assume that Anashuya's other half or opposite in Yeats's scheme
would have been her constant companion in Kālidāsa's play, that is, the more playful Priyamvada. As Yeats indicates in the previously mentioned note, the two characters in his poem share "the one soul between them, the one . . . 'knowing but
daylight as the other only night' " (489). The opposite of Yeats's serious and prescient lover, Anashuya, therefore, would most likely be the playful and light-
spirited Priyamvada, to whom Śakuntulā once says in Kālidāsa's play: "I see why
they call you the flatterer" (1959, 9). Perhaps Yeats abandoned his projected play
because Anashuya already embodied the reconciliation of conventional opposites
and Priyamvada would have lessened it.

The dramatic poem that we do have, nevertheless, offers a movement similar to
Śakuntulā. But, instead of resolving the conflict, Yeats's "Anashuya and Vijaya" ends
with Anashuya sending Vijaya away to hunt (and perhaps, we might guess, meet
with his other wakening lover). She then gives another love prayer:

> O Brahma, guard in sleep
> The merry lambs and the complacent kine,

> The flies below the leaves, and the young mice
> In the tree roots, and all the sacred flocks
> Of red flamingoes; and my love, Vijaya;
> And may no restless fay with fidget finger
> Trouble his sleeping: give him dreams of me.
>
> (1973, 47–48)

By ending with this smooth and mostly regular iambic rhythm—Yeats even uses "fay" instead of "fairy" to make an iambic pentameter line—he brings the two sensibilities of eros and agape seamlessly and smoothly together. Even if the resolution of the dramatic piece is incomplete, there is a sense of victory in the character of Vijaya, whose name means just that.

The general point here is that early in his poetic career, Yeats internalized a blend of physical and spiritual passions, associating it with Oriental and Celtic sensibilities. As critics have noted, his burgeoning passion for Maud Gonne, which increased in the late 1880s, also encouraged his merging of the two passions as he tried to entice Gonne into a love affair. Foster reports: "In early 1889, as WBY was drawn into the world of Maud Gonne, he was simultaneously proceeding with his ventures into occult experimentation. The two obsessions became closely associated in his mind, and would remain so. Throughout his life, episodes of sexual energy and confusion would be closely paralleled by periods of magical experimentation" (1997, 101). Likewise, two other poems in Crossways written in 1886 signaled that these twined passions were emerging. Taken as a unit, both "The Indian to His Love" and "The Indian upon God" further the themes that Yeats had found in Orientalist representations and in Kālidāsa. Like "Anashuya and Vijaya," "The Indian upon God" is written from the perspective of another character from Śakuntulā, Kanva—the ascetic holy man and stepfather of Śakuntulā. In fact, the poem was originally published in The Wanderings of Oisin as "Kanva the Indian upon God."[16] Although Foster and others have argued that Yeats "turned Mohini's injunctions straight into poetic form" (Foster 1997, 80), I would argue that this conclusion is too easy. More than recasting Mohini's spiritual program, which tended to be as existential as Vedantic, these poems illustrate the close knit between sensuality and spirituality popular in both Theosophy and international Vaishnava sects of Hinduism at the time.

Interestingly, "The Indian upon God" reveals Yeats's understanding of what we might call spiritual projection. In the poem, the speaker examines how various supplicants project images of themselves onto the divine. The Indian speaker of the poem (based on Kanva) relays how various beings see God in their own image, moving from a "moorfowl" who sees God as he "Who holds the world between his bill" to a lotus, who reasons "He hangeth on a stalk, / For I am in His image made," to a roebuck, who sees God as

> . . . The Stamper of the Skies
> He is a gentle roebuck; for how else, I pray, could He
> Conceive a thing so sad and soft, a gentle thing like me?
> (1973, 48)

Yeats ends the poem with pontifications from the proud peacock: "He is a monstrous peacock, and He waveth all the night / His languid tail above us, lit with myriad spots of light" (48). Significantly, these lyrical projections reveal that the speaker is not only aware of these projections but also recognizes their beauty and sympathizes with their lack of scope. The very title of the poem, "The Indian upon God," underscores the fact that it is itself a projection of the poet onto an Indian spiritualist who emphasizes how all minds personalize the divine in ways they can understand. Significantly, the message is conveyed by an Indian and not by an Anglo-Irishman. It is more than Yeats repeating "Mohini's injunctions"; the subject matter and theme of the poem—spiritual projection—reinforce the idea that Yeats was self-consciously identifying with the Indian through a sort of cultural projection. By using the Indian narrator to voice his own lyrics—as the Indian uses the characters of moorfowl, lotus, roebuck, and peacock to relay his perception of God—Yeats reveals his own understanding through his speaker.

The last poem in this series, "The Indian to His Love," resembles the movement and setting of his first widely successful poem, "The Lake Isle of Innisfree," which he wrote two years later, in December 1888, a month before the publication of *The Wanderings of Oisin*.

> The island dreams under the dawn
> And great boughs drop tranquility; . . .
> Here we will moor our lonely ship
> And wander with woven hands. . . .
> Murmuring how far away are the unquiet lands:
>
> How we alone of mortals are
> Hid under quiet boughs apart
> While our love grows an Indian star.
> (49)

In a letter to Katharine Tynan, which included a draft of "The Lake Isle of Innisfree," we hear Yeats, in giving criticism to Tynan, explain his need to shift his settings from the distant and exotic Indian to the West of Ireland: "We should make poems on the familiar landscapes we love not the strange and rare and glittering scenes we wonder at—these latter are the landscape of Art, the rouge of nature" (1986, 119). In a sense, such a move is a revision of Yeats's landscape of the exotic, bringing his own personal memories—he was in London at the time—of Sligo into his poetry. But because his newer poetry in the 1890s and afterward emphasizes the Celtic and rural Irish does not mean that the Oriental disappeared from his poetic vocabulary.

Celtic Orientalism

Whether Sligo's landscape was familiar or exotic to Yeats, in a sense, does not matter. It was exotic to London readers, as was the persona of the Celtic poet of the west of Ireland, a persona that Yeats began to assume, just as many Indians visiting London, including Rabindranath Tagore, took on deliberate Oriental personae. Both Oriental and Celtic personae clearly differentiated the writers from the dominant ethics and aesthetics of conventional and imperial English society. Yeats's personal attraction to the blending of physical and spiritual passions became part of the new crepuscular aesthetic of the Celt, which was gaining popularity in literary London. This aesthetic also resembled the flamboyant and sensual aestheticism of Oscar Wilde, another Anglo-Irishman trading on his Irishness in London, whom Yeats met in 1886. Indeed, Yeats had gotten to know Wilde fairly well in London, so well as to be invited to the Wildes' home for a Christmas dinner.

> At least one of his aphorisms sounded ringingly in WBY's ear: "I think a man should invent his own myth." . . . Wilde fascinated him: not only as another middle-class Irish Protestant who had remade himself, but as a conscious phrase-maker who "always dismissed questions with epigrams." . . . He "perpetually performed a play which was in all things the opposite of all that he had known in his childhood and youth." But for all his delight in high life, WBY later stressed that Wilde was not a conventional snob; England was fairyland, the social ladder was a "pantomime beanstalk" and the English aristocracy like "the nobles of Baghdad." This too struck a personal echo. (Foster 1997, 81)

Significantly, Wilde also used Oriental themes in his work, particularly in *The Picture of Dorian Grey* (1891) and *Salome* (1893), in which Orientalism is equated with unbridled sensuality and lushness, as well as with cruelty, decadence, and released emotions. An antinomy of Victorian ethical culture, Wilde's unconventionality drew Yeats, as did his self-created and self-assured public persona.

Moreover, the exoticism of the Orient, as Oliver Goldsmith's "Chinese Letters" attested a century earlier, offered an alternative realm for an Irishman in London to explore the mantle of *otherness,* which gave a freedom and furthered a stereotype. But though Orientalism had long been an attractive topic for Irish authors in England, Celticism had mostly evoked images of uncouth Irishmen. As I have noted, Ernest Renan's and Matthew Arnold's essentialist formulations of the

Celt signified a shift in the public image of the Irish. A new appreciation of the dreamy, ineffectual, and mystical Celt grew, one that Yeats could easily co-opt and adopt. Even as he investigated the Orient, and in particular the literature and authors of India, Yeats began to cultivate the persona of a Celtic poet, using spiritual-sensual projections of the Oriental as a guide.

Unlike most critics of Yeats's Orientalism, Edward Larrissy recognizes the Orient's long tradition in Irish letters, which he refers to as "Anglo-Irish" letters. Apparently, this appellation signifies anything written in English by Irish authors, regardless of religion, nationality, or cultural inheritance. As I have noted, however, this theme was not limited to an Anglocentric perspective.

> That Ireland possessed oriental qualities, and even origins, is a notion of great date, but one that becomes prevalent from the late eighteenth century onwards. Yeats is not the first Anglo-Irish poet to be fascinated by or to exploit the Oriental: Moore, Darley, Ferguson and Mangan did so too. And Yeats's own interest has certainly not gone unrecorded. He could see himself as mediating oriental qualities and dispositions in a facilitative way, or, when readiest to identify with the "harsh geometry" of *A Vision,* as offering a codification and measure of an oriental wisdom best felt upon the pulses or "embodied." (1994, 11)

Larrissy continues to explore the similarities between Yeats's use of Oriental tropes and the use of the dominant Anglo-French Orientalism that Edward Said explores, paying particular attention to Orientalism's vague conflations of Asian and West Asian cultures, or what John Barrell terms Yeats's "miscellaneous oriental soup" (qtd. in ibid.). This confused amalgamation of various Asian and West Asian cultures into a unified Eastern world was a common strategy for Orientalists. But this "soup" did not boil down to broth; it retained a number of distinct and recognizable ingredients. As Edward Said notes in *Orientalism:* "It is as if, on the one hand, a bin called 'Oriental' existed into which all the authoritative, anonymous, and traditional Western attitudes to the East were dumped unthinkingly, while on the other, true to the anecdotal tradition of storytelling, one could nevertheless tell of experiences with or in the Orient that had little to do with the generally serviceable bin" (1995, 102). Said, Larrissy, Barrell, and others have made more efforts at illustrating the similarities between anticolonial and imperial Orientalisms, however, than in highlighting their differences.

For instance, Larrissy shows Yeats to further the aims of Romantic writers, such as Shelley and Byron, who also wrote on the Orient. "Yeats can be seen to repeat some of the discriminations made by previous Romantic writers, and, where he does not repeat them, to play a comparable game of oppositions within the broad field of the East." Not recognizing the anticolonial aspects of Yeats's and other Irish writers' identification with the East, Larrissy elaborates upon Barrell's position, much in the vein of Said:

> [Barrell explains] that oriental objects could serve as "blank screens on which could be projected whatever it was that the inhabitants of Europe, individually or collectively, wanted to displace, and to represent as other to themselves." In the case of Yeats, who moved in the freer atmosphere of *fin-de-siècle* syncretism and occultism, this could be rephrased to include sameness alongside otherness. And the displacements and representations are those of the Celtic and—what is often in various ways distinct in Yeats's mind—Irishness. (1994, 11)

Although I agree with most of Larrissy's argument, one particular point—concerning sameness alongside otherness—needs to be examined. Although numerous similarities exist between Yeats's use of the Orient and the usage of various Anglo-French Orientalist and Romantic writers, Yeats's representation remains within the tradition of Irish Orientalism.

We should keep in mind that no European projection onto the East can accurately represent the Asian and West Asian cultures; after all, projection, like allegory, requires a known base setting or narrative—a "blank screen"—for the projection to be read clearly, especially when the projection is allegorical. Furthermore, in a post-Saidean context, we always need to recognize the complicit relationship between Orientalism and Empire. Nevertheless, the act of using the colonizer's representations to subvert the ends of Empire needs to be recognized as something distinct from proimperial or protoimperial discourse. The significant theoretical question here can be posed as such: If some European projections onto the colonized Oriental *other* are *intended* to be anticolonial, will it differ from the numerous duplicitous and imperial narratives of Orientalism, which are often disguised as sympathetic representations of Asian cultures?

Anticolonial representations are often dismissed with the pat and leveling poststructural explanations of the futility of anticolonial responses, being reasoned away as extenuations for Empire. I suggest, however, that in order to understand the dynamics and history of Irish Orientalism, we must differentiate anticolonial Orientalism from imperial Orientalism. In the Irish case, one marker of anticolonial Orientalist narratives is the projection of "sameness"—rather than "otherness"—onto the "blank screen" of the Orient. Doing so entails more than a "rephras[ing]" of Orientalism "to *include* sameness alongside otherness," as Larrissy argues (emphasis added). If we read this type of projection (of sameness) as identification and not lump all projections together, we can recognize a common anticolonial aspect of Irish Orientalism.

Such anticolonial representations contributed to Ireland's amorphous decolonizing process, which at times seemed explicitly nationalist and other times merely anticonventional, peculiar, or disjointed. David Lloyd has written on a related point in "Discussion Outside History: Irish New Histories and the 'Subalternity Effect' ":

> [T]he *anti-colonial* nature of the Irish nationalist struggle is not expressed through any 'objective' decision as to the political status of Ireland within the United Kingdom or the British Empire. It is located rather in the peculiarity, within the Western European frame, or the typicality within the context of global anticolonial struggles, of Irish nationalism's appeal to its premodernity as the site of significant cultural differences on which to found a distinct but no less *modern* state formation, equivalent to if not identical with that of Britain. Or, to put it differently, Irish nationalism appealed to the very characteristics that were, to imperial eyes, the marks of the people's underdevelopment and inherent dependence to provide the very grounds of its claim to independence. (1996, 267)

Irish identification with the "underdevelop[ed]" Orient functions as a part of Irish nationalism and is integral to the process of Irish decolonization. Recognizing this aspect helps us to contextualize Yeats's (and other Irish writers') attraction to the Orient. Although the process of European projection may indeed further aspects of European colonialism, it also enabled nationalist, anticolonial imaginings in Ireland and elsewhere including Asia. Differentiating Yeats's Orientalist work from, say, Kipling's is easy: Yeats often identified with the Oriental; Kipling never did. We should also recognize, however, that Yeats had a similar sort of possessive relationship to the Celtic as Kipling did to the Oriental. But, in Yeats's case, as a supplementary translator and mediator, such a relationship valorized nationalism over imperialism.

Rabindranath Tagore

Yeats's representations of Irishness developed through the 1890s and into the twentieth century, but it was not until his sojourn with Ezra Pound at Stone Cottage in the second decade of the twentieth century that Yeats returned to the Orient for literary material in his Irish-Japanese Noh dramas, *Four Plays for Dancers: The Dreaming of the Bones, At the Hawk's Well, The Only Jealousy of Emer,* and *Calvary* (first performed between 1917–1920), which are discussed in more detail later. Yeats's interest in Indian writers was lifelong; John Rickard explores in detail Yeats's long relationship with the Indian philosophy and its espousers in his essay "Studying a New Science: Yeats, Irishness, and the East." Rickard traces Yeats's interest in the East over the course of his entire life, focusing on what he sees as Yeats's culminating relationship with the East in his friendship with Shri Purohit Swami, whom he met in 1931. Rickard discusses "Yeats's 'Indo-Irishness'—his conjunction of Irish and Indian ethnicity and culture," exploring how "'India' functioned as a construct for Yeats" within a broader historical and ideological context (1997, 97).

Much of Rickard's analysis is pertinent to this study, although Rickard does not recognize Yeats's participation in the discourse of Irish Orientalism. Also, though he notes Yeats's borrowings from ideas about Celticity that Renan and Arnold articulated, he does not acknowledge the long tradition of Celtic-Oriental links and the history of Celticism. Instead, Rickard credits Renan and Arnold with the "creat[ion of] a Celt who was essentially antiscientific, antimaterialist, highly sensitive, spiritual, pantheistic, and politically ineffectual" (97). Though these essayists had articulated and furthered ideas on the Celt, they certainly had not created them. Similarly, Rickard asserts that Yeats created "the germ of the idea of an ancient connection between Celtic and Indian cultures" based on his reading of Renan and Arnold. Although these points may seem niggling, they point to the pervasive lack of awareness of Irish Orientalism in otherwise excellent criticism. The semiotic connection between the Celt and the Oriental had existed for centuries, as section 1 details. Indeed, Charles Vallancey theorized in 1780 much of what Rickard notices in Yeats's thinking 150 years later:

> Central to Yeats's conception of Irishness or Celticity, then was the conviction that the Irish were the most "ancient" of races and Ireland by extension the most ancient of places in Europe. Yeats came to see Irishness as a repository (or as he later called it, an "ancient deposit" (*Essays and Introductions* 516) of pre-Christian, premodern beliefs that could be useful in what he hoped would be "a reaction against the materialism of the nineteenth century" (187), as if Ireland were a tidal pool washed up and then left on the western edge of Europe, where the original beliefs of Indo-European culture still survived intact, at least up until the end of the nineteenth century ("We are all Asiatic in our youth according to Hegelian philosophy," Yeats wrote to Olivia Shakespear in 1933. [*Letters* 813]). (97)

Most useful to this study, however, is Rickard's focus on Yeats's personal relationships with Indians, particularly Shri Purohit Swami.

Between his fascination with Mohini Chatterjee and Shri Purohit Swami, however, was perhaps Yeats's most significant identification with an Indian and a "representative" of this ancient Oriental sensibility: Rabindranath Tagore. When Tagore first arrived in London in the summer of 1912, W. B. Yeats told Ezra Pound, who was living with him as his secretary, that Tagore was "someone greater than any of us," and both poets lavished praise on Tagore and his writings (Longenbach 1988, 23). Only two weeks after meeting Tagore, Yeats hosted a dinner for the Bengali writer,[17] and soon helped Tagore publish a volume of his poetry in

Tagore's own translation, *Gitanjali* (1912). In *Stone Cottage: Pound, Yeats and Modernism,* the chronicle of Yeats and Pound's friendship and time living together at Stone Cottage, James Longenbach calls them "[Tagore's] two most devoted readers. . . . [T]hey put together what Pound would later call 'the cleverest boom of our day' in order to promote his work" (23). Although Yeats and Pound were not Tagore's only supporters, they, along with William Rothenstein, were his best advocates and promoters in Europe at the time. They created an impressive mantle for the Bengali poet and successfully drew international recognition to his writing—Tagore was awarded the Nobel Prize for Literature the following year, 1913, ten years before Yeats's own Nobel. Pound's interest in Tagore was sparked by Yeats. But Yeats was not merely interested in Tagore's works; he was deeply affected by Tagore's vision and persona. Just prior to moving into Stone Cottage, Yeats wrote an introduction to Tagore's prose translations of his poetry, *Gitanjali* (first published by the India Society, 1912).

Longenbach informs us that both Yeats and Pound admired Tagore's work, and that they compared his writings and persona to the works and personae of Theocritus, Boccacio, Dante, and Chaucer. After reading Tagore, both Yeats and Pound felt cultural ties between India and Europe and wanted to highlight the connections. But Longenbach reports that both Yeats and Pound had motives other than admiration for holding dinners in his honor, nominating him for awards, and generally promoting him. Pound was striving for a place in the "inner circle" of literati in London, which centered for a brief time around Tagore; by associating closely with Tagore and Yeats, he positioned himself near the hub of London's literary world (25). Yeats, who was already within "the inner circle," however, felt genuine ties to Tagore, even more so than with Chatterjee, partly because Yeats and Tagore were closer contemporaries and fellow poets.

Yeats had also discovered the symbolists' writing in the intervening years. Like the symbolists, he too turned to the Orient and Oriental literature to mine images and symbols to express the conflicts and degradation of modern Europe. The symbolists are notorious for their fantastic stereotypes of the Orient. Paul Valéry, in particular, popularized the use of Oriental symbols, translating them into anticonventional and antimaterialist European literature. Also, Pound's translated "ideograms" of Chinese characters represent an egregious, if creative, error in reading another culture. Other writers in Ireland beside Yeats, such as James Stephens and George Russell, also saw the Orient as a storehouse for traditions from which they could arbitrarily parody and borrow, as they sought remedies for Ireland's colonial and sectarian problems. For Yeats, however, Tagore's writings and his persona were more than a "blank screen"; Tagore helped Yeats define his idea of the place of the poet in Ireland's burgeoning national culture.

Yeats's enthusiasm for Tagore and his national and poetic voice seems to have been reciprocated. Tagore was fascinated with the persona of Yeats as the "national" voice of colonial Ireland, even writing that he found Yeats to be an exemplary poet, comparable to the Vedic poets. The reasons for this mutual admiration—identification even—are complex, however, and require some discussion. Although Yeats did not understand much of the actualities of colonial life in England's distant colony, he had a surprisingly personal connection, or cross-colony identification, with Tagore. As I noted in the introduction, by "cross-colony identification" I mean a strategy for decolonization that includes establishing cultural (and sometimes political) connections across both geographic distance and the colonized periphery. Connections such as Yeats's and Tagore's are imagined within the boundaries of Empire yet exist without the mediation of the imperial center. Such connections form when colonized individuals recognize an experience in a distant colony as familiar or notice that other colonized groups share circumstances or racial and cultural traits—even attributes that are constructed in reaction to Empire.

Yeats's and Tagore's connection cannot be limited to politics, ideas, or poetry, however. Both Yeats and Tagore had similar positions in their own societies, both assuming the persona of a "national" poet in a British colony, albeit one in the "East" and one in the "West." Indeed, their personal similarities are worth considering. Both writers emerged from artistic, influential families in British colonies to become figures on the world stage. Both grew up in liminal cultures, belonging to the culture of both the colonized and the colonizer—British and Bengali or Irish. Both had strong, intellectual, or artistic fathers and little contact with their mothers (as Mair Pitt notes in *The Maya-Yogi and the Mask: A Study of Rabindranath Tagore and W. B. Yeats* [1997]). Both had aristocratic leanings and sympathies,[18] and both emblematized the peasantry in their work. Both were nationalist poets but eschewed patriotic violence and racial hatred. At the time they met, both were writing and producing symbolic and mythical dramas.[19] And, in regarding one another, they both respected the persona of the other more than the work, even viewing one another as the embodiment of a culture and a poetic sensibility. Additionally, both felt the role of the poet in society to be enormous. Although their poetic visions had some similarities, perhaps their main difference concerned the range and scope of their politics, which varied considerably.

Perhaps most notably, both poets described one another as the embodiment of his own country, the spirit and voice of a people. Their perspectives on one another, therefore, also function as their commentary on each other's cultures. Their cross-colony relationship, however, was mitigated by Yeats's distorted (Orientalist) knowledge of Asia and his ties of consanguinity to a European empire. Nevertheless, because Yeats commented on India's culture and Tagore commented on Irish culture (especially while discussing one another), their relationship illustrates the complex macrorelations between a colony in the "Orient" and a colony in the "Occident."

By examining their own statements on one another, especially Yeats's introduction to Tagore's *Gitanjali* and Tagore's essay "Poet Yeats," the personal reasons for their mutual admiration become clearer. Tagore's prose translations of his Vaishnava-inspired poetry in *Gitanjali* greatly impressed Yeats. As he writes in his introduction, "I have carried the manuscript of these translations about with me for days, reading it in railway trains, or on the top of omnibuses and in restaurants, and I have often had to close it lest some stranger would see how much it moved me" (1916, xii). The blend in Tagore's "songs-offerings" of direct, sensual imagery with spiritual concepts seems to have struck a chord with Yeats, who had himself worked to create such a blend in his early poetry, particularly in his Indian poems of *Crossways* in the 1880s.

The Tagore family belonged to the European-influenced monotheistic Indian religious organization the Brahmo Samaj, which blended "modernized" elements of Hinduism with Christianity. In fact, Tagore's grandfather was one of its founders earlier in the nineteenth century. Nevertheless, much of Bengal's popular Hindu Vaishnavism found its way into Rabindranath's verses. Vaishnavism concerns the worship of Vishnu, particularly during Vishnu's incarnation as Krishna. In Bengal, the religion often focused on Krishna's passionate and physical love for Radha, especially as described in the *Gita Govinda*—often called the "Indian Song of Songs." This erotic Sanskrit verse, written by the Bengali poet Jayadeva, links physical and divine love in rich poetry, and is considered a "high point of Vaishnavism" (Dutta and Robinson 1996, 40). As noted by Tagore's biographers, Krishna Dutta and Andrew Robinson, Tagore was familiar with the *Gita Govinda* from a young age, despite his family's tacit disapproval of it. Similar to it, Tagore's *Gitanjali* incorporates spiritual concepts in richly sensual imagery. As Dutta and Robinson explain: "The combination of physical passion, sensuous imagery and verbal music in the best Vaishnava poetry is almost unrivalled in world literature. . . . Rabindranath was definitely influenced. There can be no doubt that Vaishnavism was a wellspring of the imagery in *Gitanjali* that would overwhelm W.B. Yeats in 1912" (41). Tagore almost acknowledges his use of such poetic Vaishnavism and its relationship to the enthusiastic European response to his work in his 1912 essay on Yeats: "[A] universal poet, while reflecting universal ideas, also belongs to his country, and his ideas are coloured by the special passions of his native land. The one who can express these well is considered blessed. In our country Vaishnava poetry, by virtue of it being genuinely Bengali, must be considered world poetry. It gives the world its due, but in doing so, it adds a particular flavour, it renders the universal in a particular form" (1997c, 217). Tagore's feeling that Vaishnavism had universal appeal (despite sounding like a precursor to the International Krishna Consciousness

Movement, which emerged from Vaishnava sects) demonstrates the importance of it in his early European translations. Moreover, by describing the "particular flavor" of Bengal's Vaishnavism as an aspect of "universal" poetry, Tagore makes an argument that resembles the universal aesthetic arguments made by Yeats and others about the Oriental and the Celtic.

Vaishnavism and its blend of the divine and the physical were often mistaken to be a dominant "Oriental" sensibility and a main component of Hinduism (see Vasudha Dalmia's essay "'The Only Real Religion of the Hindus': Vaisnava Self-Representation in the Late Nineteenth Century" [1996]). Whereas Bengali Vaishnavists encouraged such generalizations, as Dalmia notes, Orientalists ballooned such representations in Europe. The same dynamic seems to have replicated between Tagore and Yeats. Tagore encouraged his Oriental mantle as the mystical poet from the East, and Yeats comments on the subtlety, spontaneity, and passion of his poetry. If much of Yeats's praise of Tagore was actually a naive Occidental's praise for the Orient—or a confusion of Vaishnava poetry for all of Asia's "temperament"—Tagore did little or nothing early on to discourage such misunderstandings. The result of their combined efforts, as well as the efforts of Pound, William Rothenstein, and others, was that for much of artistic and intellectual Europe during 1913 (the year of massive strikes in Ireland), spiritual health was seen to be embodied by the artistic, spontaneous, and mystical Rabindranath Tagore.

In *Orientalism,* Edward Said notes that the "East" was understood to be spontaneous and "essentially mystical" (1995, 253). This essential mystery appealed especially to Yeats. "Mr. Tagore, like the Indian civilization itself, has been content to discover the soul and surrender himself to its spontaneity" (1916, xx). According to Yeats and many modernists, and often to Tagore himself, modern European society lacked this spontaneity. Yeats wanted his aristocratic aesthetic to rediscover and preserve such sensibilities by copying them from the Asian traditions. But in his introduction to *Gitanjali,* we see that Yeats treated these sensibilities as essential racial and cultural traits, not merely as concepts or traditions. For instance, in a passage that reminds us of Matthew Arnold's characterizations of the Celt (and Yeats's response to Arnold in "The Celtic Element in Literature"), Yeats suggests that the "childlike" or "saintly" traits of Tagore might be characteristic of a family or a people: "An innocence, a simplicity that one does not find elsewhere in literature makes the birds and the leaves seem as near to him as they are near to children. . . . At times I wonder if he has it from the literature of Bengal or from religion, and at other times, remembering the birds alighting on his brother's hands, I find pleasure in thinking it hereditary, a mystery that was growing through the centuries" (xxi). Yeats's ideas on the resuscitative quality of "Oriental" art were in vogue at the time.[20] Said notes that scholars and artists believed that the "Orient" was a force that "releases the spirit from sterile specialization, it eases the affliction of excessive parochial and nationalistic self-centeredness, it increases one's grasp of the really central issues in the study of culture" (1995, 257). As Yeats's dreamy Celtic poet had (like Sidney Owenson's), Tagore's "Oriental" mantle and persona in Europe at once extended and cinched the stereotype.

For Yeats, Tagore's poetry represented a fresh expression of representing the spiritual, one that conveniently avoided the claptrap of established European religions, especially the schisms between Catholicism and Protestantism. In other words, for Yeats, it provided neutral spiritual ground to discuss "universal," cultural, and national issues. Indeed, Yeats once commented (in an uncollected letter to Lady Gregory in April 1913) that "my last lecture [in Dublin]—that on Tagore—was to some extent an attempt to free myself from the need of religious diplomacy" (qtd. in Foster 1997, 483). Freeing himself from this "religious diplomacy" meant he did not have to choose his words to avoid offending or alienating either Catholics or Protestants; he was free to discuss more "universal" spiritual, philosophical, cultural, and national issues. With Indian philosophy and poetry as a subject, Yeats was free from that very Irish dilemma—sectarian politics.

For Yeats, these sectarian conflicts were especially difficult to reconcile—his own family being of the Anglo-Protestant minority in Catholic Ireland and his political sympathies aligned (to a large extent) with Catholic cultural nationalists. He often criticized both sects and found himself the target of criticism by both, just as he criticized both the English and the Irish middle classes. Yeats felt conflicting allegiances to the Irish and English cultures, for he identified, in a sense, with the cultures of both the colonized and the colonizer. We may recall that in 1910 Yeats accepted a pension from the prime minister of England that doubled his annual income. This acceptance earned him the condemnation of hard-line Sinn Féin nationalists, who for the rest of his life tagged him "Pensioner Yeats." As an important point of comparison, we might also recall that Tagore, the rich son of a large estate owner, or zamindar, had accepted the title of knighthood from the English king but later famously asked Lord Chelmsford to "relieve" him of it in response to the British government violence at Amristrar in 1919 (1997d, 164–65). Moreover, though Yeats had rejected an offer of knighthood in 1915, he did keep his pension until his death in 1939. As Roy Foster notes, "Sinn Fein journalists took to pillorying 'Pensioner Yeats' as a lackey of the British government" (1997, 428).

Reminiscent of Thomas Moore's ambivalent Catholic nationalism, Yeats's dual allegiance was subtly supportive of Empire, at times seeming to be the devotion of a subject. This Orientalist aspect of his view of Tagore is summed up in a statement he made to Edmund Gosse, urging him to make Tagore an honorary member of the Academic Committee of the Royal Society of Literature. Yeats wrote that his election would be "a piece of wise imperialism" and that "if we pay him honour, it will be understood that we honour India also" (qtd. in Longenbach 1988, 25).[21]

But despite his conflicting allegiances, Yeats still found Tagore's "message" to be akin to his own antimodern aesthetic and his national aspirations for Ireland. Tagore helped Yeats visualize a "supplementary" role for the Anglo-Irish in Ireland ("through which English colonialist discourse functioned" (Smyth 1998, 76), as an intermediary between the English and the Catholic "Irish-Irish."

In the following example from the Irish nationalist paper the *Leader,* the writer contrasts Yeats with another famous Protestant nationalist, Robert Emmet. "The Pensioner is, of course, a pure-souled patriot; in payment for his patriotism Emmet got the rope [in 1803] but Pollexfen Yeats, the author of 'Cathleen ni Houlihan', gets three pounds a week from the British Government" (Nov. 25, 1911; qtd. in Foster 1997, 428). "Pollexfen Yeats" refers to the poet's mother's family, the Pollexfens, who were landed Anglo-Irish gentry in County Sligo. This comment reveals more about Yeats's difficult position at the time; words such as "pure-souled patriot" implied that Yeats had aligned himself with Irish "patriots" in his "soul" without risking his privileged position in Irish and English society.

Yeats's interest in promoting Tagore also corresponded to his interest in the supposed ancient continuity of India's and the "Orient's" culture. Like many Europeans, he saw in India, and in all of Asia for that matter, a unified and "traditional" culture. Because he barely understood the fractious history and diverse traditions of Bengal, India, and Asia as a whole, he could easily unite diverse cultures in a universalized sensibility. In India, he saw many things: a culture that had not been overrun by "modernization" or completely subverted by English colonialism, a culture that valued the arts as much as religion and commerce, and a culture that had retained its "primeval" character. Unlike Ireland, which had a "disrupted" national tradition, he describes Bengal as having an "unbroken" culture in his introduction to *Gitanjali:* "The work of a supreme culture, [Tagore's lyrics] appear as much the growth of the common soil as the grass and the rushes. A tradition, where poetry and religion are the same thing, has passed through the centuries, gathering from the learned and unlearned metaphor and emotion, and carried back again to the multitude the thought of the scholar and of the noble" (1916, xiv). Yeats was often concerned with the relationship between the Anglo-Irish aristocracy—"the scholar and the noble"—and the "multitude," despising the interfering and philistine middle class. Ideally the aristocrat (namely, himself as the Anglo-Irish "Pollexfen Yeats") would communicate with the "multitude" (the Irish Catholic "peasantry") through poetry. Tagore seemed a living proof that such an example still existed in the world. Elsewhere, Yeats explicitly noted that he saw Tagore's work as a cultural exemplar, as he explained to William Rothenstein: "[Tagore] pointed a moral that would be valuable to me in Ireland." Moreover, as Foster notes, Yeats in arranging the Irish performance of *The Post Office,* "determined that [Tagore's] message should be spread to Ireland" (qtd. in Foster 1997,

472). This "moral" and "message" refer to the idealized relationship between the aristocrat and the multitude, with whom, he felt, Tagore had communicated, a point I will return to later. Yeats anticipated the play would be received enthusiastically in Ireland, where it made a sensation similar to the one Mohini Chatterjee had made in Dublin twenty-five years earlier.

Yeats's interest in Tagore's persona and work also had much to do with his interest in Irish cultural nationalism. In discussing the period directly following the two poets' introduction, Roy Foster notes, "Now completely devoted to Tagore's work, [Yeats] described the Indian poet's advent as 'one of the great events of my artistic life . . . I know no man in my time who has done anything in the English language to equal these lyrics.' . . . To connoisseurs of WBY's enthusiasms, the note was familiar, but it was more extreme that anything since his endorsement of [Lady] Gregory's *Cuchulain*" (469). The connection between Lady Gregory's work in Irish legend and Tagore's spiritual poetry in Foster's quote indirectly highlights this very important link for Yeats. Yeats viewed Tagore's works as an ancient and universal memory, which had spoken to him like a "voice in a dream" (Yeats 1916, xvii). For Yeats, this "voice" spoke not only of Bengal, India, or the Orient, but also of an ideal culture—one in which an intermediary or "supplementary" place existed for the Anglo-Irish (that is, between the English and the Catholic "Irish-Irish"). And, like Gregory's *Cuchulain of Muirthemne,* Yeats felt Tagore's spiritual songs and his poet-aristocrat persona could help to fill a void in Ireland's national narrative, one left by a lost Celtic tradition.

For many writers in Ireland's Celtic Revival and for Irish historians alike, British colonialism seemed to have erased most of Ireland's Celtic and Gaelic culture and history and, therefore, the roots of its national being. As scholars (from Norway, Germany, England, and Ireland) struggled to understand Ireland's precolonial history, Irish writers and artists created images and narratives of rural Ireland that echoed themes, images, moods, and ideas borrowed from stereotypical understandings of the Oriental, as well as the Celtic. In weaving together a Celtic past from Celticism and Orientalism, these Revivalists posited an independent and modern Irish future. But because of its often repeated colonial stereotypes while positing anticolonial ideas, that is, working both within Empire and against Empire, critics have often dismissed Irish Orientalism as a betrayal of anticolonialist aims or as an unthinking furtherance of traditional Anglo-French Orientalism. But, as David Lloyd has argued in his *Subaltern Studies* essay, we need to rethink Irish "popular culture not in terms of tradition or its 'betrayal', but in terms of its capacity to conjoin processes of adaptation and resistance" (1996, 269). Because the "Orient" was commonly thought of as a premodern, unified culture (stretching from Turkey to Japan), it could provide images and conceptions for a non-British, nonindustrial, nonurban Celtic and Gaelic Ireland. In a sense, Irish cultural nationalists assayed "Oriental" cultures for its cache of "primeval" or "premodern" spiritual and cultural ideals and semiotic artifacts.

Celticists and Irish cultural nationalists intended to rejuvenate an ancient Celtic sensibility and create a new Irish nation. As with Tagore's "song offerings," which appeared both intensely human and spiritual—incorporating the divine within the physical—Yeats felt the new Ireland needed a new spiritual sensibility, a nonsectarian one that would link the "multitude" with the "scholar and noble." As Roy Foster notes: "For [Yeats], Tagore's poetry not only reminded him of the Indian aesthetic fusion of sensuous and spiritual love [sic], so influential in his own early work; it seemed linked, like [John Millington] Synge's art, to a noble and ancient tradition binding together aristocrat, peasant and poet. Unity of being arose from unity of culture" (1997, 470). Tagore's work offered a pattern that fitted Anglo-Irish traditions into the new Irish nation.

In a work dedicated to Rabindranath Tagore, *New Ways in English Literature* (1920), James Cousins[22] discusses both Tagore and Yeats, telling of a time in France when he heard Yeats adoringly read Tagore aloud just after the Irish poet had "discovered" the Indian poet. The experience of hearing Tagore first through the mouth of the celebrated Irish national poet provides an apt symbol of Irish Orientalism: "At that time, Rabindranath was a name unknown in English letters, but . . . Yeats carried with him in Normandy a manuscript book containing the poems of Tagore which he was then prefacing for the India Society's edition of 'Gitanjali.' He read—or, rather, chanted as only he can—every one of the poems, adding to their inherent quality a glory of music and interpretation." Tagore, thus, seems an original, Yeats his discoverer. But this is not the standard colonial explorer in search of untainted cultural goods, for Cousins goes to pains to place both on equal footing, calling them "brother-poet[s]": "[There is] something stirring in the spectacle of a poet of transcendent genius standing on the house-top of enthusiasm, proclaiming, on the slightest provocation, the splendours of the genius of a brother-poet" (18–20).

All the same, cultural differences and misunderstandings between these two "brothers" were somewhat severe. At the time, Yeats argued simultaneously against the "debasement of modern politics" and "the lowering of artistic standards for a general audience" (Foster 1997. 483). And without realizing that Tagore may not have entirely agreed with his aristocratic aesthetic, Yeats praised Tagore in the *Irish Times* for "his determination to adhere to higher things":

> Do not think I am condemning politics. They are necessary for Ireland, and I have no doubt they are necessary for India; but my meaning is—different men for different tasks. For those whose business it is to express the soul in art, religion or philosophy, they must have no other preoccupation. I saw all this years ago, at the beginning of this movement, and I wrote the "Countess Cathleen" to express it. I

saw people selling their souls that they might save the souls of others. (Mar. 24, 1913, qtd. in Foster 1997, 483)[23]

But Tagore, at the time, did not seem to treat politics merely as a "preoccupation," even though he devoted most of his time to literature. Indeed, Tagore's awareness of international and colonial politics was much clearer than Yeats's. In 1922, when Tagore's essay "East and West" was published, he expressed his concerns with the enterprises of an overly nationalistic and imperialistic Europe, as well as the violent nationalistic factions in India—themselves a result of Indian decolonization. Though both poets hoped to bridge the perceived differences between the "Orient" and the "Occident" through their writing, Tagore also hoped to achieve it through political and social action.[24]

In "East and West," he argues that colonialism is damaging not only to Asia and Africa but also to Europe: "[T]he forcible parasitism [that Europe] has been practising upon the two large continents of the world—the two most unwieldy whales of humanity—must be causing to her moral nature a gradual atrophy and degeneration" (1997a, 210). For one antidote, he characteristically speaks to the European and American poet: "Earnestly I ask the poet of the western world to realize and sing to you with all the great power of music which he has, that the East and the West are ever in search of each other, and that they must meet not merely in the fullness of physical strength, but in the fullness of truth; that the right hand, which wields the sword, has need of the left, which holds the shield of safety" (213). Yeats saw the poet's role as no less significant, but he was much less concerned with international imperial politics. Rather, Yeats hoped to copy the "Orient's" "illustrious" continuous tradition—as he urges in the introductory essay to Ezra Pound and Ernest Fenollosa's "translations" of Japanese Noh dramas, "[I]t is now time to copy the East and live deliberately"—in creating both Ireland's national culture and a new modern European literature (1961, 228).

Echoing European Orientalist notions about a unified premodern Orient, Yeats writes in the *Gitanjali* introduction, "If the civilization of Bengal remains unbroken, if that common mind which—as one divines—runs through all, is not as with us, broken into a dozen minds that know nothing of each other, something even of what is most subtle in these verses will have come, in a few generations, to the beggar on the roads" (1916, xiv). This idea that the "East" embodied an "unbroken" "common mind" was central to Yeats's aesthetic and understanding of the "Orient." Because of this supposed "common mind," a poet's verse could infiltrate a culture, even to the cultural low of a "beggar on the road." Tagore's accomplishment and popularity in Bengal seemed admirable for a nationalist poet such as Yeats, who wanted to create a unified culture for a nation without actually mingling with the beggars on the roads.

Yeats's ideas about an Irish aristocracy and the supplementary place of the

Anglo-Irish in Ireland also suffused his projections onto the screen of the Orient and onto Japan in particular. For instance, in his introduction to *Certain Noble Plays of Japan* by Ezra Pound and Ernest Fenollosa, Yeats reveals his desire to recreate an upper-class elite aesthetic. "[W]ith the help of these [Japanese] plays . . . I have invented a form of drama, distinguished, indirect and symbolic, and having no need of mob or press to pay its way—an aristocratic form" (Pound and Fenollosa 1959, 151). Relaying a conversation he had had with an Indian man, Yeats quotes himself telling the man: "In the East you know how to keep a family illustrious. The other day the curator of a museum pointed out to me a little dark-skinned man who was arranging their Chinese prints and said, 'That is the hereditary connoisseur of the Mikado, he is the fourteenth of his family to hold the post" (1916, xi-xii).[25] But Yeats's growing interest in an aristocratic aesthetic did not involve only Japan and Japanese art.

Yeats believed that Tagore's Bengali verse lyrically avoided politics and propaganda while subtly furthering an ancient aristocratic and Brahmin tradition. It was aloof and "universal" (also read: unspecific) enough to preserve a social hierarchy but spontaneous enough to speak vitally to the whole of his society. Tagore's radical political thinking and his grandfather's reform-minded critiques of tradition and caste would probably have surprised Yeats. Indeed, Yeats's understanding of Bengal seems to have been limited to literature. Astoundingly, in Yeats's idealizations, he seemingly mistook Bengal to be a place of few political debates and critical arguments. In his introduction to *Gitanjali,* Yeats writes of an interchange he had with an Indian doctor about political writing: "I thought of the abundance and simplicity of the poems and said, 'In your country is there much propagandist writing?' " Yeats records the man as responding: "[W]e too have our propagandist writing. In the villages they recite long mythological poems adapted from the Middle Ages, and they often insert passages telling the people that they must do their duties" (xii-xiii). Despite some probable miscommunication, we can clearly see that Yeats envied this fictitious culture and its rich, unbroken, mythological tradition, where commentaries on poems were the only "propagandist" writing. Especially early on, he probably imagined Bengal as a land free of Sinn Féin nationalists and middle-class philistines.

Conversely, Tagore recognized Yeats's cultural nationalism in Ireland as something important for a colony, even as something to emulate in Bengal. In his essay on Yeats, he explains: "Yeats has made his poetry confluent with the ancient poetic tradition of Ireland. Because he has achieved this naturally, he has won extraordinary recognition. With all his vitality he has been in contact with this traditional world; his knowledge of it is not second-hand" (1997c, 218). What Tagore did not understand about Yeats or the Celtic Revival is that much of the imagery and sensibility had less to do with Yeats's confluence with ancient Ireland than with a tradition of Celticism and Orientalism. Nevertheless, Tagore understood much, and he reveals a clear understanding of what is now seen as the process of decolonization: "Everyone knows that for some time past Ireland has been undergoing a national awakening. As a result of the suppression of the Irish spirit by British rule, this movement has grown in strength. For a long time its chief expression was political, in the shape of rebellion. But in due course it acquired a new form. Ireland now understood that she need depend on no one and stood ready to give of herself. Her situation is reminiscent of our own country" (219). He later warns of the "arrogance" of a colony striving for independence, and describes the nativistic Celticism that Joyce and, later, Yeats came to despise:

> In Ireland, as in our country, there has been an earnest effort to achieve self-expression. The first products of any such mental churning are bound to be frothy, and for a fair while it is not worth attaching much importance to what is often ludicrous. . . . But notwithstanding, a few Irish writers of real genius did find their voices and by drawing upon the ancient stories and legends, gave new voice to the soul of Ireland. Yeats was one of them. He has won Ireland a place in world literature.
>
> When he raised Ireland's standard in the field of literature, it was even then showing signs of weakening. She had already wandered from the path of political rebellion and entered a period of political chicanery. (220)

Tagore was also familiar with the "political chicanery" in Bengal and India. But what Yeats achieved in Irish literature is remarkably similar to what Tagore achieved in Indian literature.

If Yeats saw India in Tagore, Tagore also saw Ireland in Yeats; even though he did not greatly admire Yeats's poetry, he could still write with a characteristic extended metaphor in 1912: "Like a cut diamond that needs the light of the sky to show itself, the human soul on its own cannot express its essence, and remains dark. Only when it reflects the light from something greater than itself, does it come into its own. In Yeats's poetry, the soul of Ireland is manifest" (216). Clearly, Yeats and Tagore served as models for each other. For Tagore, Ireland also resonated as an instance of "national awakening."

Tagore recognized that Yeats also worked against the inhuman machine of materialistic modernism, the "giant engine . . . propelled by the steam of hunger," as he described London upon arriving in 1912 (qtd. in Dutta and Robinson 1996, 163–64).[26] Indeed, Yeats may have benefited from reading some of Tagore's political critiques of the "West," which include a deft critique of colonialism. In Tagore's essay "East and West," which is at times very poetic, he comments that there is little human and harmonious interaction between Europe and India. This lack, he argues, will further divide Europe and Asia.

It is true that [the East and the West] are not yet showing any real sign of meeting. But the reason is because the West has not sent out its humanity to meet the man in the East, but only its machine. . . . You must know that red tape can never be a common human bond; that official sealing-wax can never provide means of mutual attachment; that it is a painful ordeal for human beings to have to receive favours from animated pigeon-holes, and condescensions from printed circulars that give notice but never speak. (1997c, 212)

Instead of Western bureaucracy and an inhuman imperialism, Tagore hoped to build an international community on the values that Yeats had articulated.[27] In creating his educational community Santiniketan, Tagore wanted to bridge the learning of Europe and India in an atmosphere that promoted "perfect sympathy" between people (253). Tagore writes:

In our highly complex modern conditions, mechanical forces are organized with such efficiency that the materials produced grow far in advance of man's capacity to select and assimilate them to suit his nature and needs. Such an overgrowth . . . creates confinement for man. The nest is simple. It has an easy relationship with the sky; the cage is complex and costly, it is too much itself, excommunicating whatever lies outside. And modern man is busy building his cage. He is always occupied in adapting himself to its dead angularities, limiting himself to its limitations, and so he becomes a part of it. (251)

Such a critique has clear parallels with the tradition of English Romanticism and the Celtic Revival. But Tagore also realized how his argument may have been perceived in the ensuing paragraph: "This talk may seem too oriental to some of my listeners. I am told that they believe in a constant high pressure of living produced by an artificially cultivated hunger for material objects" (251).[28] Tagore himself recognizes that such a critique of the modern may be viewed as "Oriental," which is indeed how many Europeans would have seen it, but they may have seen it also as too Celtic.

The last comparison I will draw between the two poets—that of poetic vision—is the one they may have considered the most significant in their mutual identification. The poetic visions and aesthetics of both men also shared some striking resemblances, yet differed in significant and telling ways. To illustrate in a succinct fashion the similar yet different foci of their poetic visions, I pair below two statements, the first written by Yeats in 1902, the second by Tagore in 1912:

Once every people in the world believed that trees were divine, and could take a human or grotesque shape and dance among the shadows; and that deer, and ravens and foxes, and wolves and bears, and clouds and pools, almost all things under the sun and moon, and the sun and moon, were not less divine and changeable. They saw in the rainbow the still bent bow of a god thrown down in his negligence; they heard in the thunder the sound of his beaten water-jar, or the tumult of his chariot wheels; and when a sudden flight of wild ducks, or of crows, passed over their heads, they thought they were gazing at the dead hastening to their rest. (from "The Celtic Element in Literature"; 1961, 174)

Yeats believed that the Celts had a direct relationship with the spiritual world, that is, within nature. Although this world was gone, the new Ireland could recover aspects of this world, at least through literature, spirituality, and the arts—in part by "copying the East."

Tagore, in comparing Yeats to the Vedic poets, describes poetic vision as a recognition of the divine in the physical.

[A]ll those who look candidly, see similarly. The Vedic poets too saw the life spirit in nature. The rivers and clouds, dawn, fire and storm were not scientific facts to them but manifestations of the working of the divine law. Their own experiences of joy and sorrow seemed to be re-enacted in the earth and heavens in wonderful disguise. As it is in our minds, so it is throughout nature. The whole drama of the human heart, with its laughter and tears, its desires, fulfillments and failures, is played out on the grandest scale in the light and shade and colour of the firmament. (1997c, 217)

Yeats's vision is of the disappeared sensibility of an entire people, whereas Tagore's is of the sensibility and vision of individual poets, both in the past and in the present. Small wonder that after reading and meeting Tagore, Yeats felt invigorated—in Tagore, he found a living, lost Celt, one who had not been effaced by Christianity, British imperialism, and modernization.

In sum, Yeats projected his personal connection to, and admiration for, India and the "Orient" onto Tagore. Yeats had had other contacts with Indian culture before Tagore, having been a pupil of Mohini Chatterjee two decades before and moved by his Vedantic philosophy, but most of Yeats's contact with India had been through Theosophy and Orientalized understandings of Indian philosophy. As for many Irish Orientalists before him, for Yeats, the East held the keys to understanding the seemingly lost culture and literature of Gaelic Ireland. He writes in "The Celtic Element in Literature": "All old literatures are full of these or of like imaginations, and all the poets of races who have not lost this way of looking at things could have said of themselves, as the poet of the Kalevala[29] said of himself, 'I have learned my songs from the music of many birds, and from the music of many waters' " (1961, 174). Tagore represented to some extent a poet of the "races who have not lost this way of looking at things," and, therefore, he was not only someone to study but also someone to promote, especially in Ireland.

But although Yeats felt some genuine ties to the vision and persona of Tagore, he soon admitted that he found his writings at times dull—perhaps he held Tagore's work to too high of a standard, that is, to the standard of his ideal Celtic poet. To modern readers who are able to read Tagore's verse only in poor translations, however, Yeats's admission will not be surprising; indeed, Tagore himself knew that his poetic songs had not translated well. He once commented to Edward Thompson, his first biographer, "I have come to the conclusion that translating a poem is doing it wrong, especially when the original belongs to a language which is wholly alien to the medium of its translation" (1997d, 353). Conversely, Dutta and Robinson report in their biography that Tagore also did not really like Yeats's poetry all that much (1996, 225). It was Yeats's presence, stature, and imagination that Tagore admired, as he writes in his 1912 tribute essay "Poet Yeats":"Though I have not yet had the opportunity to know him fully as a poet, by knowing him as a man I have come to feel that his is a soul in contact with life in all essentials" (1997c, 221). Seemingly, Tagore repaid Yeats a compliment by describing him as a poet in touch with the essence of life, as a poet who embodied Ireland. But they also saw something very familiar in one another.

Tagore's vision was one Yeats seemed to personally recognize and see as a model for Ireland: "A whole people, a whole civilization, immeasurably strange to us, seems to have been taken up into this imagination; and yet we are not moved because of its strangeness, but because we have met our own image, as though we . . . had heard, perhaps for the first time in literature, our voice as in a dream" (1916, xvi-xvii). Yeats encouraged comparisons between India and Ireland by helping to arrange the Irish Players' performance of *The Post Office*. As a blurb for the play taken from a review in the *Philadelphia Public Ledger* notes: "The play has been presented in England by the Irish Players, and fully adapts itself to the charming simplicity and charm which are their principal characteristics" (Tagore 1916, end advertisements). Yeats, along with Irish writers for more than one hundred years, knew of this type of comparison and encouraged it throughout his life.

Although Yeats and Tagore grew indifferent toward one another over the years, when they did meet again, Yeats told Tagore that he admired his novel *The Home and the World* (1915, first English translation 1919), claiming that he thought it also "very true of Irish society: had it not stirred up strong feelings in Bengal as it would have done in Ireland if written by an Irish writer?" (Dutta and Robinson 1996, 225). Years earlier, in writing about his contemporary India, Tagore found a symbolic role for an Irishman, as the titular character of his 1910 novel *Gora*. In the story, the character Gora (meaning white) is an Irish orphan—similar to Kim in Rudyard Kipling's novel—who, unaware of his Irishness, has assimilated into Indian culture. This position of the Irish orphan, adopted by Indian culture, is like an ion with a neutral charge—it depends upon another charged atom to determine its own charge. In a sense, an Irishman in India is a free-floating signifier that Kipling could use to bolster imperialism and Tagore could use to bolster Indian independence. But in both books, the Irish character functions as the meeting ground between the English and the Indian, between the colonizer and the colonized. Of course, Tagore was not ignorant of the roles the Irish had played in British expansionism in India (Gora's father served in the British army), but neither was he ignorant of Ireland's quarrel with England.

Yeats, in a sense, had a relationship with Tagore similar to the one he had with the "Orient." Yeats's admiration for, and promotion of, Tagore was tinged (or tainted) with the patronizing attitude of European imperialists. But their identification with one another and the cultural crossovers between Indian and Irish texts reflect some sense of a shared colonial identity, even though the sociopolitical realities of the two cultures differ enormously. Nevertheless, the imagined cross-colony connections that inspired these two writers furthered the cultural unity and independence of both nations. Both men admired what each other stood for: in Tagore, Yeats found a model for an Irish past; in Yeats, Tagore found a model that bolstered the hopes for an independent Indian future. Both were, in a sense, "voices in each other's dreams."

Japan and the Noh

In 1916 Yeats wrote an introduction for Ezra Pound's book based on Ernest Fenollosa's Japanese translations, *Certain Noble Plays of Japan*. He further developed his ideas of Oriental and Celtic aesthetics, which were national, antimaterialistic, and aristocratic. The Orient, particularly Japan, came to stand for an unadulterated traditional culture from which modern Ireland could learn. Around the same time, Yeats actualized this aesthetic in his Irish-Japanese Noh dramas, *Four Plays for Dancers: The Dreaming of the Bones, At the Hawk's Well, The Only Jealousy of Emer*, and *Calvary*. As Yeats states in his eponymous introduction to *Certain Noble Plays*, which in some ways functions as a commentary on *Four Plays for Dancers*, his "aristocratic form" of symbolic drama would play to a select audience; the dramas could "be played in a room for so little money that forty or fifty readers of poetry can pay the price" (Yeats 1961, 151). Yeats shunned the realistic and psychological drama of the popular theater, relying instead on a blend of painting, dance, music, and lyric poetry: "Realism is created for the common folk and was always their peculiar delight, and it is the delight today of all those whose minds educated alone by schoolmasters and newspapers are without the memory of beauty and emotional subtlety" (155). Significantly the indicators of "memory of beauty and emotional subtlety" functioned as characteristics of cultures that had not experienced the materialism of Europe, which for him included both the Orient and the Celts (or the rural Irish). Capitalizing on the semiotic link between Ireland and the Orient, his new form of drama borrowed heavily from the East, mainly imitating the ancient Japanese Noh drama, or rather the Orientalist imitations of Noh drama written by Pound and Ernest Fenollosa.

Yeats valued cultural continuity within literature, just as he valued the continuity of an educated elite that he wanted as his audience. As he noted in his introduction to *Certain Noble Plays,* "A poetical passage cannot be understood without a rich memory, . . . for the ear must notice slight variations upon old cadences and customary words, all that high breeding of poetical style where there is nothing ostentatious, nothing crude, no breath of parvenu or journalist" (156). For Yeats, Japan was a traditional culture par excellence, its arts filled with "that high breeding of poetical style"; a drama based on Japanese forms required an audience bred to appreciate art. In the notes to *At the Hawk's Well,* he refers to this audience of "learned people" (1969, 416). At its first performance, Yeats invited literati, dignitaries, cultural leaders, and European royalty; he wanted his new syncretic form performed initially for the Anglo-Irish elite.[30] The audience for this Celtic-Oriental drama had to be educated not only in poetic cadence, but also in dramatic form and mythological allusions. By avoiding the public spectacle of popular theater, he relied less upon patrons and the press, even claiming to have enjoyed turning newspaper photographers away from the opening of *At the Hawk's Well.* For Yeats, this aristocratic audience, like the Japanese Noh audience, had tradition and aesthetics as "part of their breeding" (Yeats 1961, 157).

In line with the Noh's rich tradition, Yeats imagined the entire "Orient" as a storehouse of primeval traditions. Later in the introduction to Pound's text, Yeats suggests that a new drama should mimic Asian tradition and forms. Echoing a common Romantic and Orientalist idea, he explained that the flower of European art had already fully opened: "Europe is very old and has seen many arts run through the circle and has learned the fruit of every flower and known what this fruit sends up, and it is now time to copy the East and live deliberately" (156). *At the Hawk's Well* loosely follows the form of the Japanese Noh play *Yoro* (The sustenance of age) by Seami Motokiyo, which Pound had adapted from Fenollosa's translations (S. C. Ellis 1995, 136). Yeats also incorporated other elements from the Japanese form, such as dance, masks (first used in *The Land of Heart's Desire* and *Deirdre*), a "patterned screen," a chorus, and a symbolic folding of a cloth (representing perhaps the raising and lowering of the theater curtain or the folding and unfolding of the drama); the style of all of them was meant to signify the Noh form of drama. This highly stylized play, however, owes as much debt in its plot to William Morris's *Well at the World's End* as it does to *Yoro* (137). What Yeats primarily copied was the intense focus on a moment; the play's overall structure most resembles the Japanese Noh, as Sylvia Ellis notes in *The Plays of W. B. Yeats:* "[The play] is simple and immediate and closely approaches Japanese Noh by being one episode of a passionate moment" (136).

Just as his Oriental borrowings provided a partial resolution for Yeats's colonial tensions, so his extraworldly and nonpolitical art sought to blend together opposing cultures. Positing the "East" as a neutral party enabled Yeats to work out cultural tensions without overtly staging them. As Edward Said comments in his essay "Yeats and Decolonization": "For Yeats the overlappings he knew existed between his Irish nationalism and the English cultural heritage that both dominated and empowered him as a writer were bound to cause an overheated tension, and it is the pressure of this urgently political and secular tension that one may speculate caused him to try to resolve it on a 'higher,' that is, nonpolitical level. Thus the deeply eccentric and aestheticized histories he produced . . . are elevations of the tension to an extraworldly level" (1990, 80). Significantly, the magical and the extraworldly play key roles in all of these Celtic-Oriental dramas. In particular, either the supernatural or the Sidhe controls most of the action in the plays. In *At the Hawk's Well,* the guardian of the well and the Hawk woman guard the most sacred and desired object of men's quests, the well of immortality. In *The Only Jealousy of Emer* (1919), the immortal "maker of discord among gods and men, / Called Bricriu of the Sidh," mediates between Emer, Eithne Inguba, and the ghost of Cuchulain (543). The other principal character, only named "Woman of the Sidhe," plays seductress and dream weaver to Cuchulain. In *Dreaming of the Bones* (1919), the two quasi-historical figures and legendary lovers Diarmuid and Dervorgilla, who betrayed Ireland to the conquering Normans, wander Ireland as ghosts unable to touch or kiss one another. To be released from their purgatorial penance as ethereals they must first be forgiven by a living Irishman. The focus of the play is the rejection of their apology by an Irishman they find fleeing through the fields at midnight, heading west, hiding from British soldiers after his participation in the Easter Rising of 1916. The last "Noh" drama in *Four Plays, Calvary* (1920), concerns Christ's walk to his crucifixion. On his way Christ is confronted by Lazarus, who berates him for raising him from the dead. Judas also appears and tells Christ that he had betrayed him in order to be free of his power, only to find out that his betrayal of Christ fulfilled his predestined role. By removing agency and culpability from the human world, Yeats took social and cultural action out of the hands of mortal characters, and out of the immediate consciousness of his audience, the cultural elite and artistic aristocracy. By placing agency in the hands of the Sidhe and the extraworldly, Yeats allows them to dramatize Ireland's cultural tensions.

Yeats's Irish Orientalism

The Orient continued to provide Yeats with ancient antimaterialistic images for his poems based upon his personal life, such as his 1918 poems "Solomon to Sheba" and "Solomon and the Witch," which posit Oriental symbols for Yeats and his wife, George. Yeats continued using Oriental symbols for himself and his wife in his 1923 poem "The Gift of Harun Al-Rashid," in which his wife's "automatic writing" is given an Oriental context. In these poems, the East does not so much represent the premodern realm of antiquarians and Celticists to which the poet longed to return as it represents a freedom to experience intense moments of passion, free from the materialism and grind of modern life. The main story of "The Gift of Harun Al-Rashid" is embedded within a letter and a conversation of Persian characters, and although the characters Kusta ben Luka and Harun Al-Rashid are based on actual historical figures, many phrases and images in the poem are drawn from English versions of the *Arabian Nights*. Nevertheless, this Oriental voice allows Yeats a context upon which the poet can project his mystical experiences with his wife.

> When the full moon swam to its greatest height
> She rose, and with her eyes shut fast in sleep
> Walked through the house. Unnoticed and unfelt
> I wrapped her in a hooded cloak, and she,
> Half running, dropped at the first ridge of the desert
> and there marked out those emblems on the sand
> That day by day I study and marvel at,
> With her white finger. I led her home asleep
> And once again she rose and swept the house
> In childish ignorance of all that passed.
>
> (1973, 340)

The mystical strangeness of the events seemed to fit better within the exotic Orient. Written in the first person, the central story is also given through dialogue—thus, the three voices in the poem all speak in the first person and seem to speak the poet's own concerns. Although Oriental personae are common to many European traditions of Orientalism, they are especially prominent in Irish literary Orientalism. Yeats takes it, however, to a very personal level in this poem—or at least he wants his readers to believe that he has.

We can see this fact most clearly in the Harun Al-Rashid's revelation of his secret fears to his "Vizir" Jaffer:

> What if she lose her ignorance and so
> Dream that I love her only for the voice,
> That every gift and every word of praise
> Is but a payment for that midnight voice
> That is to age what milk is to a child?

. . . .
And now my utmost mystery is out.

(340–41)

Reading the poem with knowledge of Georgie Yeats's mystical persona, Leo Africanus (ca. 1485-ca. 1554) (who was also a real historical figure—his given name being al-Hasan ibn Muhammad al-Wassan Al-Zayyati), seems to reveal the poet's deeply personal fears. But, as the first narrator, Kusta ben Luka, implies, Al-Rashid later executes his "Vizir" after telling him his secret in order to protect word of his hidden fear from getting out. The Oriental despot Al-Rashid guards the personal for the poet, while also revealing it through the poem.

Although during the 1920s Yeats did not have any momentous contact with the Orient or its "representatives," toward the end of the decade he returned to thoughts on Mohini Chatterjee in his poem by that name:

> I asked if I should pray,
> But the Brahmin said,
> "Pray for nothing, say
> Every night in bed,
> 'I have been a king,
> I have been a slave,
> Nor is there anything,
> Fool, rascal, knave,
> that I have not been,
> And yet upon my breast
> A myriad heads have lain.' "
>
> That he might set at rest
> A boy's turbulent days
> Mohini Chatterjee
> Spoke these, or words like these.
> I add in commentary,
> "Old lovers yet may have
> All that time denied—
> Grave is heaped on grave
> That they be satisfied—
> Over the blackened earth
> the old troops parade,
> Birth is heaped on birth
> That such cannonade
> May thunder time away,
> Birth-hour and death-hour meet,

Or, as great sages say,
Men dance on deathless feet."
(362–63)

The lessons that the touring Bengali gave to Yeats as a young man still resonated and served as a foundation on which Yeats could link his mature poetic persona with Chatterjee's.

In the 1930s Yeats became fascinated with the life and writings of Shri Purohit Swami, whom Yeats persuaded to write his autobiography. Although Swami was not a writer, he seems to have symbolized much of what Tagore and Chatterjee had meant to Yeats. Yeats not only prompted Swami's English-language autobiography, *An Indian Monk* (1932), for which he wrote the introduction, but he also encouraged Swami to write his mystical treatise *The Holy Mountain* (1934) and his translation of the *Ten Principal Upanishads* (1937), which Yeats coauthored.[31] In these writings, Yeats returns to the roots of Irish Orientalism, even relying on the unscientific "Phoenician model" of Celtic origins:

> I associated early Christian Ireland with India; Shri Purohit Swami . . . might have been that blessed Cellach who sang upon his deathbed of bird and beast; Bagwan Shri Hamsa's pilgrimage to Mount Kaílás, . . . suggested pilgrimages to Croagh Patrick and to Lough Derg. . . . Saint Patrick must have found in Ireland, for he was not its first missionary, men whose Christianity had come from Egypt, and retained characteristics of those older faiths that have become so important to our invention. (1973, 837)

But Yeats's introduction to *An Indian Monk* does more than restate old formulations of Irish Orientalism and the Oriental origins of the Celts. It recommended the supposed spiritual health and antimaterialism of the Orient for the increasingly isolationist Irish Free State. During a period of artistic disillusionment with the new conservative state, Yeats wrote that he expected "a counter-Renaissance" (1961, 526; qtd. in Rickard 1997, 94) and returned to his ideas of the Orient even more firmly than perhaps at any time in his life.

Rickard argues convincingly that "[t]he *Upanishads* and other Indian texts became essential tools in Yeats's counter-Renaissance, providing for young Western writers examples of an ancient literary and philosophical tradition that preserved in its strangeness the earliest distillations of Celticity" (106). Indeed, as Rickard points out, Yeats seems to have returned to the Orient toward the end of his life, in part to have his legacy bring together the traditions of India and Europe through Irish literature and in part as a way of turning away from the "political and cultural forces that [he] found obnoxious in the Ireland of the 1930s" (103).[32]

Rickard traces Yeats's references to the Orient throughout his later work, linking them to his general conceptualization of Irishness and Celticity, which, as antimodern narratives, could theoretically undermine the power of the middle class and restore an aristocratic sensibility to Ireland (and elsewhere). Yeats's return to the Upanishads resembled his passion for ancient Celtic Ireland.

> For Yeats, the *Upanishads* were an Asian source for something very close to an ideal Irishness or Celticity. They had the appeal of representing an ancient, traditional culture that he found simultaneously strange and familiar, like Ireland primarily agrarian, and also colonized by England. He sensed something pure and innocent about them, something untainted by the complexities of recent Irish and European history, so that Yeats could view them as representations of a deeply spiritual, mythical culture unblemished by the religious wars and philosophical errors of the West. An additional attraction of the *Upanishads* was their peasant origin; Yeats felt that— like his own poetry—they could embrace both peasant farmer and Brahmin while implicitly excluding any class in between. (108)

Although not very aware of the workings of global colonialism or of modern India and its anticolonial struggles,[33] Yeats sought to combat the "growing tide" of modernity in Ireland with a "new science" based in Orientalism and Celticism. But toward the end of Yeats's life, Rickard argues, Yeats's "old working notions of Irish ethnicity" no longer functioned, and he therefore earnestly turned to basing a new sense of Irishness and Celticity on the Orient (95).

Yeats's sense of this Oriental-Celtic connection was perspicacious, however. He acknowledges the roots of these twin discourses, which have a long tradition and undergird Irish culture, appearing in both imperial and anticolonial literature. Shri Purohit Swami, in many regards, was the last figure from India and the Orient with whom Yeats identified, finding an ancient and parallel voice in the Indian mystic.

In the last days of his life, Yeats was paid a visit by a Japanese translator of his work, Shotaro Oshima. Yeats had written poems that referenced China and Japan, "Lapis Lazuli" in 1936 and "Imitated from the Japanese" in 1937. Both poems stress Yeats's enduring sense of the importance of artistic expression: music, dance, sculpture. This crucial theme had also long been united in Yeats's mind with China and Japan. In a 1921 uncollected letter to the Japanese poet Yone Noguchi, Yeats discussed the prints of Hiroshige, which were published in London around that time.

> European painting of the last two or three hundred years, grows strange to me as I grow older, begins to speak as with a foreign tongue. When a Japanese, or Mogul, or Chinese painter seems to say "Have I not drawn a beautiful scene?" one agrees at

once, but when a modern European painter says so one does not agree so quickly, if at all. All of your painters are simple, like the writers of Scottish ballads or the inventors of Irish stories. . . . [About the lives of Japanese artists] their talks, their loves, their religion, their friends . . . I would like to know these things minutely. . . . It might make it more easy to understand their simplicity. A form of beauty scarcely lasts a generation with us, but it lasts with you for centuries. You no more want to change it than a pious man wants to change the Lord's Prayer, or the Crucifix on the wall. . . . I wish I had found my way to your country a year or so ago and were still there, for my own remains uncomfortable as I dreaded that it would. (Oshima 1965, 20–21)

Oshima, writing of his own visit with Yeats in 1938, likened the older Yeats to a Japanese Zen priest:

With almost reverent awe for the poet who had been untiringly writing poems in his old age, I asked, "Are you still writing poems?"

"Yes!" he answered positively with a clear voice.

I was shocked to hear this single word as if struck by a sudden thunder. This curt answer was enough to make me feel ashamed for having asked such a foolish question. His attitude at the moment reminded me of an old *Zen* priest who was asked, "Are you still pursuing enlightenment?" and answered, "Away with you! Never ask me a question only to throw dirt at me!"

Indeed, Yeats had never ceased to write poems and his poems had reached us in Japan in golden tones or in passionate silence. It was quite natural that the poet, who was full of great ideas and beautiful images, could not receive my question calmly. (106–7)

Identifying Yeats with a Japanese artist or priest would doubtlessly have been a great compliment to him. Yeats's identification with the East, though it had gone through varying stages, had a certain continuity in that it always linked the Celtic with the Oriental and modern times with ancient traditions. Just as the realities of Irish rural life often did not find their way into his verse, the realities of Asia and West Asia often remained obscure and romanticized. But such is the tenor of much of Yeats's verse.

Although Japan had been rapidly undergoing a process of modernization, Yeats continued to look for the traditional Japan in art. Other Asian cultures, however, attracted Yeats's interest for their modern situation and conflicts with colonialism. In his later years, India seemed the culture that shared the problems facing Ireland. His use of Indian themes and philosophy, though at times reflecting the stereotypes of Anglo-French Orientalism, continually remained in opposition to both English convention and Empire. Although he did not often concern himself with politics, he still aligned his work with anticolonial Irish-Indian narratives, as his poem about the legacy of a famous anticolonialist and Irish cultural nationalist reveals. I quote two stanzas from "The Ghost of Roger Casement" as a way of making the point and closing:

> John Bull has stood for Parliament,
> A dog must have his day,
> The country thinks no end of him,
> For he knows how to say,
> At a beanfeast or a banquet,
> That all must hang their trust
> Upon the British Empire,
> Upon the Church of Christ.
> *The ghost of Roger Casement*
> *Is beating on the door.*
>
> John Bull has gone to India
> And all must pay him heed,
> For histories are there to prove
> that none of another breed
> Has had a like inheritance,
> Or sucked such milk as he,
> And there's no luck about a house
> If it lacks honesty.
> *The ghost of Roger Casement*
> *Is beating on the door.*
>
> (1973, 424–25)

7   Theosophy and the Nation

George Russell (AE) and James Stephens

All the names [of the Mahābhārata], ten thousand, Bhisma, Drona,
Yudhishthira, & the Twins, are of my household.
—James Stephens, *Letters of James Stephens*

We are less children of this time / Than of some nation yet unborn
/ Or empire in the womb of time.
—George Russell (AE), "On Behalf of Some Untraditional
Irishmen"

CRITICS REGARD JAMES STEPHENS as one of the most whimsical of modernist
Irish writers. Consequently, his writings are rarely read for their social, national, or
Orientalist implications. But though whimsy certainly composes much of his poetry and prose writings, much of Stephens's work, particularly his later short stories
collected in *Etched in Moonlight* (1928), portrays social realities of early-twentieth-
century Ireland.[1] In these stories, Stephens's characters struggle against poverty, un-
employment, and class subjugation amid tropes of Indian and Irish legend and
myth. Throughout his writing career, Stephens wove folkloric elements into realistic stories, seeking to construct, like many writers of the time, narratives of the
emerging Irish nation. During the years of the Celtic Revival, Stephens also retold
old Irish legends, updating them for modern readers. Both of these sets of narratives borrow heavily not only from Revivalist versions of Irish legend, but also
from Orientalist versions of Eastern philosophy and mythology, with which
Stephens, like many other Revivalists, had become fascinated. In his works,
Stephens sought to represent what might be called Ireland's *national narrative,* to
borrow from Homi Bhabha, or, to use a similar term coined by George Russell
(AE), Ireland's *national being.* Attempting to reinvent a national narrative for Ireland, Stephens, like Yeats, relied upon tropes of the Orient and India in particular,
looking for ideas, images, and structures that predated English colonialism.

290

Writing the Nation

Stephens's stories of his nation's modernity were written on the threshold of the contemporary and the epochal, relying both upon Celticism and Orientalism. Homi Bhabha's term *national narrative* signifies a narrative in the broadest cultural sense, that is, a narrative that permeates a culture, embodying its collective identity and hegemony. Most nations have a *national narrative,* as well as literary attempts to represent, invoke, and indicate the nation, or *national analogies.* These national analogies are particularly evident in burgeoning nations that are breaking from colonial rule; they seek to guide the process of nation building. Rarely, however, do they pervade a national culture or embody its identity. In fact, they always exist, perforce, as failed attempts to capture the national being. Nevertheless, taken together they forcefully illustrate the varied impulses and strategies of nation building and cultural decolonization. AE's description of his term is similar to a description of a Neoplatonic ideal, a nation as a spiritual principle to which cultural nationalists contribute and from which an individual citizen receives meaning:

> The building up of a civilization is at once the noblest and the most practical of all enterprises, in which human faculties are exalted to their highest, and beauties and majesties are manifested in multitude as they are never by solitary man or by disunited peoples. In the highest civilizations the individual citizen is raised above himself and made part of a greater life, which we may call the National Being. He enters into it, and it becomes an oversoul to him, and gives to all his works a character and grandeur and a relation to the works of his fellow-citizens, so that all he does conspires with the labours of others for unity and magnificence of effect. So ancient Egypt, with its temples, sphinxes, pyramids, and symbolic decorations, seems to us as if it had been created by one grandiose imagination; for even the lesser craftsmen, working on the mummy case for the tomb, had much of the mystery and solemnity in their work which is manifest in temple and pyramid. (1930, 11)

Here, the ubiquitous pyramid of Orientalism stands as a symbol of possibility to the burgeoning nation. Although the Revival may not have achieved the same unity of work as was credited to the ancient Egyptians, their national analogies did share purposes and themes, including a reliance on Eastern themes and philosophies. As Irish writers redoubled their assertions of an ancient cultural heritage at variance from England, Stephens and other Irish writers felt this imperative to "write the nation." As Maurice Goldring notes in his study of the role of intellectuals in the Revival, "writers of all sorts—journalists, poets, novelists and playwrights—came forward to put their stamp, that is their word, on the nation. There was a kind of goldrush towards a true national culture. Like Yeats, they considered themselves to be guides, prophets and messiahs—flaming torches of the spirit. . . . They carried precedents in their heads—they felt themselves carried forward by the nation's history" (1993, 18–19). James Joyce's *Ulysses,* to take a paramount example, sought to represent a slice of the burgeoning nation on one June day in 1904, including the aspirations of young writers who also considered themselves "flaming torches of the spirit." But, although Joyce's is the most celebrated and accomplished example of this, it mainly drew upon an ancient Celtic-Oriental connection through the fantastic notions of characters in the library scene, as Elizabeth Butler Cullingford has detailed in her chapter on Joyce and Phoenician-origin theories in her *Ireland's Others* (2001).

Generally, the national analogies of Celtic Revivalists sought to embody more than the quotidian everyday; they also sought to represent an ancient past and a bright future. In a sense, the writers of the Revival asked themselves the same question that postcolonial critic Homi Bhabha poses in his important essay "Dissemi-Nation: Time, Narrative, and the Margins of the Modern Nation" in *Nation and Narration:* "How does one write the nation's modernity as the event of the everyday and the advent of the epochal?" (1990, 293). AE, whose ideas on Indian philosophy Stephens and others absorbed, saw national identity as something to hold sacred, claiming in 1916 that as long as the "spiritual atom of the [Irish] people" existed, the past and the future of an Irish nation were accessible and imaginable. "[W]hile that incorruptible spiritual atom still remains all things are possible if by some inspiration there could be revealed to us a way back or a forward to greatness, an Irish polity in accord with national character" (1930, 14). What the Revivalists wrote had a significant impact on Irish culture; indeed, many of their national analogies were later incorporated into the Irish Republic's programs of official nationalism. For example, Yeats's poetry and Lady Gregory's plays about the West of Ireland helped form the Republic's self-image; Padraic Pearse's stories became assigned reading for schoolchildren. Stephens's works, however, never achieved such lasting prominence. To consciously create the identity of a nation, its national being, or its spiritual atom is, of course, an impossibility. Both the identity and the hegemonic *narrative* of a nation emerge through the events and accidents of history, developing through the shared experiences of its members, not through the conscious constructions of a few individuals. Imagining the national being depends on perceiving its continuity.

Believing in the need for a unified national culture in Ireland, however, Stephens and other Irish writers tried to unify the nation by writing narratives that linked Ireland's antiquity to its present. Theorists of nationhood as far back as Ernest Renan in 1882 have noted the need for a coherent past in nation building: "A nation is a soul, a spiritual principle. Two things, which in truth are but one, constitute this soul or spiritual principle. One lies in the past, one in the present. One is the possession in common of a rich legacy of memories; the other is present-day consent, the desire to live together, the will to perpetuate the value of the heritage that one has received in an *undivided form*" (1990, 19; emphasis added). Prompted by AE and others, Stephens assembled and concocted ancient pasts as a way of positing a new direction for the nation. Many of his literary projects attempted to assert a vision of a past in an "undivided form," but they also sought to represent the gaps between such an undivided heritage and contemporary Ireland, and, in so doing, returned to one of Ireland's oldest semiotic pairings and largest (if unacknowledged) traditions. In fact, by the twentieth century, clear Celtic-Oriental ties had lasted for two centuries, and the Oriental origin legends had been in circulation for more than a millennium.

One of Stephens's fundamental literary strategies (particularly for his national analogies)—creating a literature of overlapping pasts and presents—also astutely points to the foundations of the process of nation building itself. Homi Bhabha discusses the spaces between, and the overlaps of, the past and the present in a national culture, or what he sees as the inherent *liminality* of a *national narrative:* "The language of culture and community is poised on the fissures of the present becoming the rhetorical figures of a national past" (294). Constructed in this "double narrative movement" between the past and the present—between an ancient racial or national memory and everyday reality—a nation tends to conceal contradictions behind its traditional authority. Normally, a nation's authority mysteriously embodies, and thus conceals, this opposition within its state formation (295). In contrast, Stephens's national analogies tend not to conceal these contradictory oppositions at all but, instead, to exploit them. Such explicit narrative oppositions may also signify a fractured cultural identity—a hybrid of the peripheral and nonmodern, on the one hand, and the metropolitan and modern, on the other. But, more ostensibly, they expose the overlapping continuity of the past and the present. Stephens's constructions are anything but mysterious; we need only notice the blend of the urban and modern with the folkloric and mystical in Stephens's work *The Crock of Gold* (1912)—where policemen brawl with leprechauns, and philosophers debate ancient Irish and Greek gods—to realize that Stephens paints the disparities of cultural hybridity and colonial and national traditions with gusto. Indeed, he tends to flout these disparities of form in the face of England's smoothly realistic novel, which had been the standard for Irish novels.[2] Because many of Stephens's liminal narratives are overt, however, does not mean that his narratives are simple to dissect.

Synthesizing the Nation: AE and Orientalism

In synthesis alone, AE argued, would a new Ireland emerge. The most prominent Dublin mystic of the day, AE introduced the major Irish Revival writers to Theosophy and Indian philosophy, which he once claimed, in a letter to Sean O'Faolain, was his "aid to understanding" (qtd. in Kuch 1986, 18). Theosophy also fueled AE's own Celtic spiritualism, which dominated his works and greatly influenced the works of Yeats, Stephens, and Cousins. Despite his knowledge and passion for Indian philosophy, he was primarily committed to this visionary neo-Celtic mysticism, and Russell even often denied that he borrowed from Indian philosophy in his mystical writings. For instance, Peter Kuch, citing an unpublished letter, reports that later in life, "Russell often asserted that he 'had never tried to put Eastern mysticism into poetry' because he had 'a natural mysticism of his own.' This contention is partly supported by *Song and Its Fountains* where he shows how a number of his poems came directly from his own visionary experiences" (18). But Kuch also cites several clear borrowings of AE's from the Upanishads (19).[3] AE's reluctance to identify his work with Indian or Eastern works seems to have stemmed from his intense desire to reestablish Irish culture from the remnants of its own antiquity, from organizing, and from mysticism. But he clearly saw Celtic and Oriental parallels.

Beside his passion for mystical experience, he worked to promote Ireland's birth as a cosmopolitan culture and modern nation. His diverse publications (editorials, criticism, essays, poems, novels, and drama) and varied experiences as an author, Theosophist, newspaperman, painter, diplomat, and agricultural cooperative organizer helped him promote Ireland's literary and cultural renaissance in a range of arenas during the Celtic Revival.[4] Through his advice and support, he aided an emerging generation of writers, including James Joyce, Padraic Colum, Liam O'Flaherty, Frank O'Connor, Patrick Kavanagh, and James Cousins. Moreover, he knew nearly every prominent person in early-twentieth-century Ireland: writers, thinkers, organizers, and nationalists, as well as heads of state in Great Britain and America. His influence is undeniable.

Following an early move to Dublin as a boy, Russell spent years training as a painter and writer while working as a clerk. Still a young man, he found employment with the Irish Agricultural Organization Society (IAOS), first as a cooperative organizer in rural Ireland and later as an editor, for the *Irish Homestead*. Around this time, he began to study Theosophy and mysticism. Later, he edited and wrote for Ireland's main cultural journal of the 1920s, the *Irish Statesman*. Over his career, he published seventeen books and pamphlets of poetry, seven books of prose, and countless commentaries, essays, letters, pamphlets, and reviews, also selling and donating many paintings. His most prominent works illustrate the many genres in which he wrote: *Collected Poems* (1913), *Imaginations and Reveries* (essays, 1915), *The National Being* (cultural and political critique, 1916), *The Candle of Vision* (mystical essays, 1918), *The Avatars* (mystical novel, 1933), *The House of Titans and Other Poems* (1934), and his posthumous collection of essays from the *Irish Statesman, The Living Torch* (1937). These key works carried great weight in early-twentieth-century Ireland, inspiring discussion and debate.

Outside of Theosophy, one of the greatest influences on AE was Standish James O'Grady's two volumes of *History of Ireland* (1878 and 1880), which also inspired Yeats and others in the Irish Literary Society (formed in 1895). This new history, like so many before it, retold many of Ireland's major legends, but instead of focusing on the origin legends, it showcased the Ulster cycle legends concerning the warrior hero Cuchulain. Perhaps more than any works at the time, O'Grady's work—through AE, Yeats, and Augusta Gregory—shaped a national mood, and AE based his later ideas about Celtic spirituality in these supposedly Celtic works. The myths hit AE with the force of revelation, as he relays in his essay on O'Grady (1915, 19–20). Unlike earlier translations, these materials did not appear barbaric; rather, they seemed heroic (if sanitized by today's standards). Based on such translations, AE proclaimed the need for a national recovery of a lost mythic and literary heritage that resembled the histories of Britain, Greece, and India.

Reading these myths through the lenses of Theosophy and Indian philosophy, AE developed his own influential, speculative, and syncretic mysticism. For instance, the essay "The Legends of Ancient Eire," published in the *Irish Theosophist* in 1895, argues the possibility and need to recover the wisdom of the druids. Moreover, it claims that the primeval giants of Celtic legend, the Firbolgs and Fomorians, hailed from Atlantis and posits that the legendary otherworld, *Tír na nÓg* (the Land of Youth), might be best understood as a mystical principle resembling the Tibetan "Devachan," or the "Abode of the Gods," where beings exist between incarnations. Also similar to Sydney Owenson, he draws on the apocryphal story of Saint Patrick's banishment of the snakes from Ireland. Instead of using it as a literary allusion, however, Russell treats it as mystical Celtic-Oriental allegory, arguing that it, in actuality, had to do with the Christian banning of ancient "Serpentine Power" from Europe and, therefore, was now only known in the East. This Theosophical argument identifies this "Power," represented by the snake, with the practice of kundalini yoga in India.

AE's best-known works, however, do not focus on Orientalist ideas. His volume *The Earth Breath and Other Poems* (1897), for instance, has few, if any references to the Orient. For AE, Irish rural life and Celtic visions helped reveal a land equivalent to the Orient in the West of Ireland, as it had for antiquarians and writers during the eighteenth century's Celtic Revival:

> Aureoles of joy encircle
> Every blade of grass
> Where the dew-fed creatures silent
> And enraptured pass.
> And the restless ploughman pauses,
> Turns and, wondering,

> Deep beneath his rustic habit
> Finds himself a king;
> For a fiery moment looking
> With the eyes of God
> Over fields.
>
> (1913, 39)

Two 1897 pamphlets—*The Future of Ireland and the Awakening of the Fires* and *Ideals in Ireland: Priest or Hero?*—proclaim the immanent rebirth of an ancient pre-Christian Ireland. The pamphlets brought some notoriety to AE, who had been known chiefly around Dublin as the poet of *Homeward: Songs by the Way* (1908). Both supposedly recover cultural forms predating outside influences by mystically visiting an ancient Aryan culture. As with Henry Sumner Maine, this ancient culture could be glimpsed through cultural remnants:"The genius of the Gael is awakening after a night of troubled dreams. It returns instinctively to the beliefs of its former day and finds again the old inspiration. It seeks the gods on the mountains still enfolded by their mantle of multitudinous traditions, or sees them flash by in the sunlit diamond airs. How strange, but how natural is all this!" (1988, 367). In actuality, AE and other writers interested in this ancient Aryan culture, revealed only in its premodern fringe cultures, drew less from cultural remnants than from the semiotic history of the Oriental and the Celtic in Ireland

In 1898, after being appointed assistant secretary of the IAOS, AE resigned from the Theosophical Society, disillusioned by its charlatanism and the political infighting over leadership in the wake of Blavatsky's death in 1891. Though AE adhered to many Theosophical doctrines throughout his life, he distanced himself from the organization that continued after her death. Instead, he resurrected the Hermetic Society, originally founded by Charles Johnston, and served as its president until 1933. At the end of 1903 and the beginning of 1904, with the publication of his third and fourth volumes of poems, AE was increasingly regarded as an important new poet of the aesthetic school, eventually referred to as the "Celtic Twilight" (a phrase that was initially meant as an unkind reference to Yeats's collection of the same name). In these volumes, AE's poems continue to focus on Ireland's mythical Celtic past, accessible to the poet through mystical vision and imagination. In 1904 Macmillan signed him on as an author, signifying his international stature as a poet, and after 1904 his poems found a wider audience in Europe and the United States.

Borrowing from Greek, Indian, and Jewish sources, and focusing on many mystical traditions that countered the practical materialism, realism, and naturalism of English literature, AE treated other traditions as partial revelations about a nearly vanished ancient Irish tradition, which could lead to a new Celtic culture, based on ideals of art and beauty. Such a change, he prophesied, would be ushered in by a new leader, an incarnation of the divine, an avatar, a term he borrowed from Indian philosophy via Theosophy. Though Russell never found this avatar, he later imagined two roaming the Irish countryside together in his novel *The Avatars*. Perhaps his most enduring and cogent mystical work is an account of his mystical experiences from boyhood to the present, *The Candle of Vision,* which outlines his conceptions of meditation, imagination, dreams, power, and Celtic myth, similar to many mystical Theosophical works. His overall argument concerns the importance of imagination and, by extension, mystical insight. The East remains a philosophic and traditional touchstone, as illustrated in a critique of modern science and psychology, which he sees as dismissive of the imagination and vision:"I think few of our psychologists have had imagination themselves. They have busy brains, and, as an Eastern proverb says, 'The broken water surface reflects only broken images.' . . . They discuss the mode of imagination as people might discuss art, who had never seen painting or sculpture" (1988, 102). Believing that imagination was integral to the wholeness of individuals and nations, AE argued that it and vision connected people to their nation and the divine. His mysticism, often antimodern, never led him away, however, from practical matters such as journalism, agricultural reform, and political mediation, through which he directly impacted Ireland's future nation.

Indian Philosophy: From AE to Stephens

To many eyes, AE was not an Orientalist; rather, he did not study the Orient but embodied it as a neo-Celt. Stephens, having been greatly influenced by the elder northern poet AE, remembered him, however, as not only a hub of the Revival but also as an authority on Indian spirituality and philosophy. Indeed, in 1942, long after the Revival, Stephens recalled his elder friend's devotion to Indian philosophy and spirituality, by way of asserting AE's Oriental qualifications and (deferred) authenticity:"It has also been said of him that outside of India he was the greatest living authority on the Advaita philosophy and the Vedas. With all this there was not one scrap of the pedant in him. . . . No day passed in which he did not tuck his long legs under him, squat in the Eastern meditation posture, centre his mind into one point and visualize beauty, or truth, or power, or God. He was a practising Yogi" (1964, 111). AE was the mystic upon whom Stephens relied; he was also an organizer upon whom many relied. The philosophies and Orientalist texts of Asia and West Asia from which he gleaned his mystical concepts, along with his study of popular Indian texts (in translation), contributed to his influential nation-building, anticolonial, and mystical agendas. As earlier chapters have indicated, an Oriental affinity was common for Irish writers, particularly Theosophists, most of whom were Irish Protestant spiritualists, and Stephens was no exception; he had been born to Protestant parents and educated at a Protestant school before being drawn to Catholic nationalist movements and Celtic Revivalism. This is not to say that thinkers and writers from a Catholic tradition (such as Stephen McKenna and Frederick Ryan) were not also drawn to Asian and West Asian cultures, only that the trend seems to have been more dominant in Protestant writers during the Celtic Revival.

Stephens's Orientalism emerged from his nativism. Stephens and other Revivalists, such as Yeats, felt they must look beyond what they often saw as foreign forces in Ireland—both Britain's and the Roman Catholic Church's—in resurrecting an authentic Irish culture. Stephens was particularly vehement in his attacks on the "Seoinini," or "west-Britons"—Irish who favored English culture over Irish.[5] Also, he routinely angered Catholic clergy in his attacks on the church and Christian history; indeed, some clergy had supposedly called him the "Anti-Christ," as he reported in 1930.[6] Furthermore, Stephens's adaptation of the Irish cycle of legends, the *Táin Bó Cuailnge* (Cattle raid of Cooley), portrayed a culture that far predated English colonialism. Although the narrative format that he used was clearly a product of English literature, he also used other techniques, such as the common Irish story-within-a-story technique, which helped him depict interwoven levels of reality and the cycles of reincarnation (both common to Irish and Indian legends) in *Etched in Moonlight* as well as *In the Land of Youth* (1924). He also shared with Yeats the tendency to use his ties to the Orient as a way to resolve Ireland's colonial and sectarian tensions on an "otherworldly" and nonpolitical level.

Orientalist versions of Hindu and Buddhist spirituality, often propounded in the Theosophical Society, carried a certain avant-garde, antimaterialist, and anticolonial cachet during the Celtic Revival. Outside of the context of this Irish literary Orientalism, Stephens's use of Asian tropes might seem strange, but his Indo-Irish works might be best understood in relation to Celtic Revivalism and cultural nationalism. Having been born into a working-class family in 1880 or 1882 and orphaned at a young age, Stephens was acquainted with poverty and despised a society primarily concerned with material prosperity and not with the responsibility for its most unfortunate. As a young man he was drawn to nationalist and labor politics, but he soon found them unsatisfying, particularly in the aftermath of the Easter Rising of 1916. Nevertheless, they had a lasting effect on him. He generated his Orientalism from an interest in spiritual and mystical expressions that differed from the dominant Christian ones in Ireland and England. His most successful and characteristic works superimpose a blend of (what he saw as) "primeval" spirituality—borrowed from Orientalist and nativist depictions of ancient Ireland and India, as well as from Greece—onto modern society.

In "Ireland Returning to Her Fountains" (1921), Stephens argues that modern

Ireland would have to "grow all over again," feeding on rediscovered ancient spiritual sensibilities. Irish culture could not be united through Catholic or Protestant religions, or through materialism. The present Catholic and Protestant varieties, as well as the independent visions of a Blakean religious impulse that he had long favored, had not—and could not—serve as the new models for Irish culture. Instead, he argues, a primeval sensibility must provide that model: "Behind her is an age-long inheritance of history and culture, almost unknown to the present generation, but containing in itself boundless possibilities of interest, inspiration and pride. The new psychology will grow out of the old one; the new religion may have much to do with the old mythology. We do not have such deep roots in the past for nothing, and we are bound to go back before we can dream of going forward again" (1983, 180). Stephens clearly recognized the new Republic's need for a new, accessible, and meaningful version of cultural history and Irish national identity, one in modern English, not in nineteenth-century prose or in the Irish language, and one that could reconcile ancient Ireland with modern Ireland.

"The Unity of National Culture in Ireland"

Literature, according to Stephens, is the perfect place to redress Ireland's cultural identity, or its *national narrative,* because it emerges from the continuity of culture, as he noted in his somewhat humorous interview with himself in 1923: "A book . . . is only to a limited extent the work of its titular author. It is really a communal effort, and, as such, it should be credited to the community it derives from. . . . The author is no more than a glorified amanuensis, or a listener-in to the section of people, actions or ideas, that he is sympathetically related to" (1983, 196). Stephens in many ways became a modern medium for the unacknowledged tradition of Irish Orientalism. After Ireland broke from England, he summed up the history of the two countries in "Ireland Returning to Her Fountains":

> It is one of the curiosities of national psychology that the gifts of one nation are not readily accepted by another. England had power and wealth and culture to give, and, although these could not be got elsewhere, Ireland refused them. Whatever good Ireland might have brought to the common stock England did not require, and did not get. The fact is that England and Ireland are self-sufficing nations, each containing within itself all that is required for national existence. England required nothing of us: She might then very easily have left us alone and it is true to say that naught but the English will-to-power is at the root of our shameful history.
>
> I am inclined to predict that Ireland will turn more and more completely from England, and will cultivate the human relations she requires in quite other directions. (179)

Recognizing certain parallels with English culture but remaining unsympathetic, Stephens looked to other cultures of the world for cultural, literary, and philosophical models that could help Irish culture return to its "fountains." In "The Outlook for Literature" (1922), Stephens further discusses Irish literature's relationship to the world:

> Literature is an ideal expression of the environment; that is, of the human society it is born from. As that society is noble, greedy, brutal, or artistic, so the literature it generates reveals this, that, or the other quality of the time. In my own country of Ireland man is now in the making, and in a very few years our national action will tell us what it is we may hope for culturally, or what it is that we may be tempted to emigrate from. But Irish national action and culture can no longer be regarded as a thing growing cleanly from its own root. We have entered the world. More, the world has entered us, and a double, an internal and external, evolution is our destiny, as it is the destiny of every other race in the world. (1983, 187–88)

Although Irish cosmopolitanism has a long history, Stephens meant to forge Ireland's "national action" through a new syncretic literature and culture. His sense of Ireland's "double . . . internal and external evolution" demonstrates his awareness of the double movement of the nation, which must move not only between the past and the present, but also between the world and Ireland and the "traditional" and the "modern."

In "The Unity of National Culture in Ireland," a previously unpublished typescript, Stephens argues that the popular Irish epic *Táin Bó Cuailnge* could contain "all Ireland" (59). In rewriting it, Stephens hoped he could re-create a national analogy or story for Ireland in a modern idiom. In her essay "The Route to the *Táin:* James Stephens' Preparation for His Unfinished Epic," Joyce Flynn notes, "Irish writers in the first quarter of this century were responding to a larger challenge to retell the events of the old epics, the sagas, and the court romances" (1981, 125). This larger challenge was, in a broader sense, to create literature that would help create a nation out of colonial Ireland. Stephens's response to this challenge was to write his self-declared magnum opus, a five-volume version of the *Táin,* as he confessed in a letter to historian Alice Stopford Green:

> I find I have only been playing at literature up to this, and I believe, egoist that I am, not alone that I can build big & deep stories, but that I can hit our country such thumps on the head as will awaken her from the artificial torpor that she is in. In short I want to write La Comedie [*sic*] Humaine of Ireland. Every writer should have some kind of literary ambition big enough to explain his failure if he is too little for the job. That may be my fate but I want to put it to the test. (1974, 150)

Unfortunately, Stephens only wrote two, *In the Land of Youth* and *Deirdre,* of the planned five volumes. Yet they are among his most read and appreciated works.

To resuscitate ancient stories, such as the *Táin,* Stephens tried to free them from Christian doctrine and sectarian conflicts, but because the Christian sources were often the only ones, the process was difficult. Discussing Ireland's premodern, pre-Christian culture, Stephens explores the cultural changes the Church influenced:

> [Like other countries] Ireland has been overrun by successive invasions. The new-comers brought their own religious experience with them, and would impose on the conquered people not only a political mastery, but in time a cultural one as well. Less than that is not conquest. The new gods would at last be universally accepted and the older ones, living only in the folk memory, would become the demons of a new race. . . . From the earliest historic time the rationalizing process had been at work in Ireland, and vast tracts of our history and story show the effort that was made to Christianize the older legends. (1983, 164)

Attempting to undo the cultural "mastery" of the colonizer—the "rationalizing process" that transformed traditional legends to fit with Christian theology—Stephens hoped to expose the fissures between the precolonial culture and the colonized culture of Ireland. In imagining this precolonial Ireland, Stephens both turned to Irish Orientalism and inverted the negative and stereotypical representations of the colonizers. In both cases he reproduced, to varying degrees, the imperial superstructures. Edward Said writes lucidly on the topic of nativism:

> Nativism, alas reinforces the distinction by revaluating the weaker or subservient partner. And it has often led to compelling but often demagogic assertions about a native past, history, or actuality that seems to stand free not only of the colonizer but of worldly time itself . . . to accept nativism is to accept the consequences of imperialism too willingly, to accept the very radical, religious, and political divisions imposed on places like Ireland, India, Lebanon, and Palestine by imperialism itself. To leave the historical world for the metaphysics of essences like negritude, Irishness, Islam, and Catholicism is, in a word, to abandon history. (1990, 82)

Of course, Stephens did not believe that he was abandoning history for a nativist impression of it in his attempts to reproduce an ancient Irish sensibility and tradition. Instead, he believed he was plunging headlong into history. Said's critique here of nativist projects as colonial productions is too simple to fully explain such decolonizing work. These inventions did more than reproduce the power structures of colonialism; they also expressed a history that was both colonial and insurrectionary, a hybrid culture that had long worked to reconcile a troubled history and imagine a future that was both international and local. Indeed, the same impulses and strategies of the medieval Irish *filid* existed for Stephens in seeking Irish roots in the Orient. The Revivalists' fierce debates over national culture may seem passé, irrelevant, narrow-minded, or sectarian to critics, scholars, and readers today. But such readings still open relevant and pertinent avenues of discussion, avoiding the schisms of a sectarian history while reconciling a postcolonization history in an international context. In short, nativist explorations did not merely propel the nation's culture into a distrustful isolationism. The reactionary traditionalism of later midcentury Irish nationalists and state leaders can also be understood as a reaction to the experimentalism, syncretism, and cultural universalism of Revivalism, to which Irish Orientalism provided continuity and focus.

Stephens's modernization of the *Táin* was intended to provide a meaningful rhetorical past that would rally and unify the emerging nation. But in writing it, Stephens did not simply rely upon Irish legend; he felt that "Irish national action and culture can no longer be regarded as a thing growing cleanly from its own root" (1983, 188). Hilary Pyle notes in her study *James Stephens* (1965) that in *In the Land of Youth* and *Deirdre,* Stephens also relied upon Indian philosophy and spirituality: "Yeats was sufficiently impressed to remark in his letters that Stephens had read the *Táin* in the light of the *Veda*. . . . during the 'twenties he read and re-read the *Upanishads* and the *Bhagavad-gita,* and the commentaries on them, and he went to great trouble to obtain the four huge volumes of *The Yoga-Vaishtha-Maharamayana of Valmiki* by Vihari-Lana Mitra. All were thoroughly read and marked or annotated, and some of his verses were drafted roughly in the fly pages" (128). Stephens partly based his national epic (containing "all Ireland") on Indian spiritual doctrine in order to incorporate his spiritualist notions of the Orient into Ireland's *national narrative.* Stephens seems to have considered the comparisons between ancient Ireland and the present Orient in more detail than Yeats. Unlike his impressions of ancient Ireland, Stephens saw the Orient as a mass of cultures that had not been fully "conquered" and, therefore, represented a repository of traditions similar to the traditions of precolonial and premodern Ireland. In part because Stephens did not have access to an undivided Irish heritage, he drew on the unacknowledged strategies of Irish Orientalism and looked to India's traditions: "Irish literature will be a part of world literature, drawing nourishment from the ends and ends of the earth" (1983, 192). Remote Ireland would seek other remote ends of the earth.

The Orient as a Unifying Force

Stephens mingled images of ancient and contemporaneous India, China, and Ireland, borrowing tropes from Anglo-French depictions of both Celtic and Oriental cultures as mired in the past, viewing them noncoevally. For Stephens and most Orientalists, the Orient was a place mired in the past, which might provide examples for a premodern, pre-Christian Celtic culture. Stephens's national analogies often rely upon classical Indian philosophy as if it were a native Irish philosophy and spirituality that he was merely recovering. In this way, Stephens allied the Celtic with the Oriental in a vision of a precolonial Indo-European past. But his notions of the Orient were not informed by any ensured ethnographic realities of India or Asia; instead, they relied heavily on an imagined European Orient, which he tailored in his writing for his reading public in contemporary Ireland, England, and the United States. Because Anglo-French Orientalists did not normally view the Orient (or western Ireland) coevally, Asian and West Asian (and Irish) cultures seemed to embody a more "traditional" world—one that offered a spiritual panacea for the ailments of modern Euro-American culture, and, for the Irish literary Orientalist, offered a recipe for the undoing of British materialism and cultural colonialism in Ireland. Reading Charles Johnston's Sanskrit translations in Dublin and applying them to images of Ireland, Stephens used exotic images as a means of wresting discursive control from dominant discourses of Orientalism and Celticism. His Orient, like his Celtic Ireland, stood as a rhetorical way of opposing English culture and the modernizing discourse of colonialism in Europe and the United States; if he repeated stereotypes from the discourse of Empire, he also gave them an evasive parodic twist that was often anticolonial.

As most Orientalists did, Stephens divided the world:"There is a European culture and there is an Asiatic one, the world has grown so small! One or other of these gigantic conceptions will emerge from the final struggle for supremacy as the world culture, and it is for that great struggle that the world is set prow on" (1983, 193). For Stephens, this "great struggle" for supremacy was between the modern (seen as European) and the traditional (Asiatic and Celtic). This dualistic worldview provided modern Europe (with its perceived ailments) with the panacea of an Oriental *other*. In *Orientalism*, Edward Said discusses European Orientalism during the years in which Stephens was writing:

> The ground had shifted. . . . No longer did it go without much controversy that Europe's domination over the Orient was almost a fact of nature; nor was it assumed that the Orient was in need of Western enlightenment. What mattered during the interwar years was a cultural self-definition that transcended the provincial and xenophobic. . . . [For many] the West [had] need of the Orient as something to be studied because it releases the spirit from sterile specialization, it eases the affliction of excessive parochial and nationalistic self-centeredness, it increases one's grasp of the really central issues in the study of culture. (1995, 257)

For Stephens the "really central issue" for Ireland was how to recover a nonmodern, noncolonial Celtic tradition. As with Swift, Goldsmith, Moore, Owenson, Mangan, de Vere, Yeats, Cousins, and other Irish writers, the Orient provided models for allegorizing a nonsectarian, nonfactional Irish tradition, as his parodic historical essay "For St. Patrick's Day" (1928) illustrates, drawing on the tradition of Oriental affinities.

Toward the end of Stephens's account of Saint Patrick, he relays a story of two groups of traveling Irishmen from rival townships in Leinster, Rush, and Lusk who happen upon each other in a teahouse in a Chinese port town.[7] Not long after they recognize one another, the men from Lusk taunt the men of Rush with a fourteen hundred-year-old story about how Saint Patrick's first dinner on his first day in Ireland was stolen by the people of Rush. The rival groups then brawl in the teahouse and are subsequently arrested for destroying the place. The next day they are brought before the "Chinese Justice," who is described as "an ancient man, clad all in silk, with a thin beard of the finest silken web, and with gentle, brown eyes that glowed as from delicately-carven ivory" (1983, 225). In a twist typical of Stephens, the justice lauds the men after hearing their story—instead of fining or jailing them for the mayhem they caused. The justice praises the Irishmen's tenacity in clinging to the "tradition" of what he calls that "so-honorable dinner." The justice himself is immured in tradition, and his address to the Chinese court that ends the story humorously reveals a value system in which a tradition, even a fractious one, may unite warring factions under the same cultural identity:

> He began by extolling the ancestors; he continued by glorifying Saint Patrick, and he concluded by praising the men of Rush and Lusk. He pointed out that, although of antagonistic parties, nine of the men concerned bore the very name of the ancestor himself. That the men of Lusk had fought to commemorate the pilfering of the ancestor's dinner. That the men of Rush had denied in the Court itself, and with the customary ceremonial oaths, that the honourable-dinner had ever been stolen by their pious forefathers, and they had each personally professed a boundless affection for the ancestor. That the story of these poor men faithfully reverencing the ancestor even after the lapse of nigh fifteen hundred years, was one that should be an example to the youth of China, where, when a paltry century or two had passed away, the very name of an ancestor was unremembered and unextolled. (226)

Despite the irony of this pseudohistorical essay, Stephens uses a standard trope of the Orient, as a place that both venerates and embodies tradition, to recast Irish sectarianism in a positive light. Oriental understandings here used to help the factional Irish parties recall a unified tradition. Reviewing their antagonism as togetherness, the Chinese justice ironically admires the Irish travelers for their remembrance of Saint Patrick, despite the fact that it has been fodder for a long history of fighting. Although not modern, the Chinese justice, a synecdoche of the Orient, offers a unifying antisectarian vision that counters the partitioning and divide-and-conquer logic of Empire, whose consequences are seen around the world today from Pakistan and and India to Israel and Palestine to Northern Ireland.

In such figures, Stephens saw something for both the past and the future of Ireland. His project of merging a rhetorical past and present also included many other essays and stories. In particular, his later short stories, seven of which were collected in the 1928 book *Etched in Moonlight,* reveal the liminality of his national analogies, that is, they reveal Stephens's unique amalgam of Celtic nativist legends, Orientalist representations, and modern Irish social depictions.

Oriental Turf

Stephens's project for Ireland's "national action" borrowed from Anglo-French Orientalism and used a view of the classical Indian caste system. For Stephens, an Orientalist view of caste could function as a metaphor for class stratification and status groups in early-twentieth-century Irish life, which, he felt, had become too influenced by British materialism. Particularly in his later fiction, class issues are treated as if they were Indian caste issues, modeled upon the classical *varna* caste stratification presented in the Bhagavad Gita. In so doing, he emphasizes the distinctness and autonomy of each class, positing a natural hierarchy for their social stratification.[8] Theosophical doctrine and Orientalist versions of Indian philosophy had greatly influenced Stephens, as they had AE and Yeats. But translations of the Mahābhārata, the Bhagavad Gita, and the Upanishads, which AE introduced to Stephens in 1913, were the bedrock of Stephens's inspiration and philosophy.[9]

Stephens felt strongly about the sacredness of these texts, as he frequently stated in his writings. In "Enter Mr. James Stephens," a letter to the editor of the *New Age,* Stephens gives a characteristically witty critique of "the worst poem ever written," publicly attacking a contemporary English poet for her "cliché[d]" rendition of a piece of classical Indian verse (1974, 102). Stephens criticizes "Beatrice Hastings's" (E. A. H. Thomson's) poem "Arjuna Kartavirya," which was based on a section of the Mahābhārata, ending with "I hold strongly that the person who bowdlerizes a Sacred Book should be strangled and stuffed and stuck in a wax-works" (103). In the subsequent exchanges, Stephens gets the best of his English critics, one of whom, "R. H. C." (A. R. Orage), borrowing from Nietzsche, refers to Stephens (as an Irishman) as "a hopeless slave" (104). Similarly, in "Beatrice Hastings's" reply to Stephens's letter, Hasting's resorts to attacking his "native" birth as a "buffoon," perhaps a lightly veiled attack on his Irishness: "Mr. Stephens was clearly born to be ridiculous. Another man, to whom buffoonery was not native, might have been shocked into respectable self-criticism after such a public guy as was made of Mr. Stephens when [his poem] 'Rhythm' strung all the names of the major poets to make a garland for his feet" (103). In his subsequent reply, Stephens mocks her gravity and parodies her criticisms before further attacking her defense of her "translation" poem as well as R. H. C.'s knowledge of (and way of knowing) the Orient:

> I do not mind when Mrs. Hastings calls me a ridiculous, a buffoonery, a guy, a skittish and an aesthetically disreputable—it is the penalty of greatness; but I protest when she charges me with wearing garlands on my feet. This is a cruel, a malicious invention, for everybody knows I wear them on my tall hat.
>
> But I have been grievously disappointed by Mrs. Hastings' reply to my last letter: she must be off her feed. She seeks to justify her villainous poem by stating that it is just as bad in the original, and that she only slung it into four-line stanzas because it takes that form in the Sanskrit, or is it Italian? (Ask "R.H.C." what is the Mahābhārata's native tongue. He reads all languages with his eyes shut, and he talks them all with his mouth shut. God bless him before he bursts of culture, but not after!). . . . Later, in a frenzy of culture, he quoted that Nietzsche had said I was a hopeless slave. Bad, bad man! Nietzsche never spoke of me except in terms of affection. Alas! "R.H.C." is a "quoter," and this is a malady from which one never recovers. He is of those who run about the world with another man's verb in his mouth. (104)

The literary turf that Stephens fights for is both Indian and Irish; he uses humor to deflate and criticize these English literary Orientalists who "run about the world with another['s] verb in [their] mouth[s]" as if he were defending his own turf, which, in a sense, he was. He once wrote in a letter to William Rothenstein, "All the names [of the Mahābhārata], ten thousand, Bhisma, Drona, Yudhishthira, & the Twins, are of my household" (398). Indeed, Indian philosophy became personally important to him, and, as we can see, he was particular in choosing his translations.[10] Indeed, it was Stephens who first gave a copy of the Upanishads to Yeats, which became vital to Yeats in the 1930s (well before he published his own translation, with Shri Purohit Swami, *Ten Principal Upanishads,* in 1937). Yeats commented in one of the typescripts of the revised version of *A Vision* (1937): "When I spoke to [Stephens] about [*In the Land of Youth*'s philosophical system] he gave me a little book of 'The Thirteen principal Upanishads' that I have studied, as the first paragraphs of my Fourth Book attest as well as my ignorance permitted" (qtd. in Finneran 1978, 19). Despite Stephens's passion for these Indian texts, they gave him little knowledge of contemporary India. But we can see he defended their value vigorously.

These works also provided him with, among other things, an understanding of the four or five main castes in the classical *varna* caste system—a model that greatly differs from the ethnographic realities of the actual caste system in India. Stephens's recommendation for the new Ireland propounded individual transcendence over "social views and actions." He often argued that the contemporary Irish "mind" had need "[for] a new psychology, for a new valuation of the values, for a new art, and for a new technic of human conduct, whether in art or morality" (1983, 192). The *varna* tradition represented this new psychology with its attendant values, art, and human relations—in short, for his national action. The *varna* caste system became a metaphor for Stephens and functioned in many of his works as both an ancient signifier and a critique of present-day Ireland. Several stories written during the late teens and early twenties portrayed a rigid class-caste hierarchy, namely, *Hunger: A Dublin Story* (first published in book form in 1918), "The Thieves," and "The Boss" (the latter two published in the *Dial,* 1920).[11] The actions and conflicts within these three stories derive from the differences among the upper, middle, and lower status groups, which Stephens ironically treats as caste stratifications.

Earlier, in the first fifteen years of the twentieth century, Stephens wrote numerous articles for nationalistic and labor journals, particularly *Sinn Fein* and *Irish Citizen.* By 1912 he had begun to advocate woman suffrage, labor, and the freedom of speech, as editor Patricia McFate points out in *Uncollected Prose of James Stephens.* Moreover, after the General Strike of 1913, Stephens wrote an article, "Come Off that Fence!" to Irish workers (as McFate notes), "urging them to fight capitalism, the newspapers, and the clergy" and praising James Larkin "for remaining true to his principles during the period of his incarceration in Mountjoy Prison" (1983, 93). Another target became "the populace mind," about which he wrote a series of articles (including one by that very title):

> There are two great and glorious helpers to life which, if they got anything like adequate scope, could make the world a place of beauty—they are Liberty and Justice. The populace mind has re-christened these friends and made them enemies; they name them now License and Law. In fact, this populace mind is incapable of statecraft or of religion or liberty or justice or anything that is unselfish. Its sole preoccupation is how to guard its property, and amongst its chattels women occupy a costly place. (100)

Later in the teens and twenties, Stephens's critique of Ireland's socioeconomic problems shifted. Before Irish independence, Stephens had admired the analyses by Irish labor leaders and anticolonialists James Connolly and James Larkin. After first witnessing and then writing about the confused politics of the Easter Rising in *The Insurrection in Dublin* (1916), however, Stephens lost his admiration for organized politics, as Hilary Pyle notes in her study, *James Stephens:* "[Stephens] had reached the point where he deliberately disassociated himself from his former enthusiastic support of James Connolly's labour movement and, though still in complete sympathy with the dilemma of the working classes and with the insurgents, he could evaluate Connolly's aims, and commend his intellect and the benefit of his practical thinking to the Volunteer force in Dublin, while stating that politics were not his concern" (1965, 84). His increasing interest in Eastern philosophy signaled this shift in his perspective—he no longer overtly promoted Marxist and labor analyses in his writings. He did continue to criticize capital and the upper class in his essays and stories, however. But his later stories subverted the conventions of labor's depictions by positing transcendence as the only relief from oppressive class structures.

Conversion

This move away from promoting labor politics and socialism toward Theosophy and Indian philosophy, on its own, may seem idiosyncratic for Stephens. But if we recognize that Stephens was not alone in this type of "conversion," we begin to discern the outlines of a broader cultural and social shift. Gauri Viswanathan explores specific instances of a related trend in her study, *Outside the Fold: Conversion, Modernity, and Belief* (1998). In particular, chapter 6, "Conversion, Theosophy, Race Theory," explores Annie Besant's similar move from the English political movements of British secularism and women's rights to Fabian socialism and then to the even less accepted Theosophical movement. Throughout the book, Viswanathan explores the overlapping interests of differing movements from which, and to which, individuals have converted—differing movements that seem in direct opposition to one another. She describes this work as studying the "crucial but largely covert historical connections. . . . [and] successive linkages between British secularism and Orientalism; between dissent from Christianity and imperialism; and between British support for Indian nationalism and race theory" (185). Because the connections between such movements and ideologies are not obvious, instances of individual "conversion" have typically been seen as idiosyncratic and have usually been explained away through the events of that individual's biography. But such a seemingly personal decision also signifies broader cultural issues. Viswanathan elaborates:

> I do not wish to appear as if I am restating a familiar and well-worn truism—that biography is a form of history. Rather, I want to suggest that individual conversions are an index of cultural change without themselves being subject to a crude form of historical determinism. . . . I have been tracing instances of conversion as forms of activity—often oppositional—that alternatively are triggered by and shape the tendencies accruing around sociopolitical developments. If the advance of culture influences (and is influenced by) a progressively differentiated consciousness, it is also the case that the culture(s) in which an individual conversion occurs lends its own

structural features to the content of this new consciousness. Crucial to this process is an elaboration of the full range of meanings of cultural forms and institutions to which the convert's sensibility subsequently gains unmediated access. What, therefore, appears to be a shift from one doctrinal affiliation to another may well reveal not continuity but rather points of overlap and convergence. (185)

Viswanathan explores James Cousins's Theosophy alongside Annie Besant's. Along with Cousins's conversion, the conversions of Stephens, AE, and Yeats represent a similar shift, motivated by "points of overlap and convergence" from anticolonial and labor politics, on the one hand, to Theosophy and Orientalism, on the other.

Stephens's movement, in particular, from socialism and political nationalism to Theosophy and Indian philosophy indicates a broader cultural movement; his "conversion" is not merely a case of Protestant avoidance of sectarian conflict, or a validation of non-Catholic mysticism to which some more dismissive critics have attributed similar conversions. The similar "structural features" of Larkin socialism, Sinn Féin nationalism, and Vedantic mysticism and Theosophy, as they were touted at the time, include both a form of ethical universalism and an anticolonialist and cross-colony agenda. Indeed, Stephens's narratives remained antistate and anticapitalist despite his "conversion." In his late 1916 essay "In the Interval," Stephens states only one firm hope for the Irish: "[that] our traditional policy of being against the government may preserve us from being proletarian as it has preserved us from being Englishmen" (1983, 139). The primary difference exists in the manner in which social conditions were to be improved. Instead of class war and political reform, spiritual solutions to social problems became Stephens's favored recommendation for Ireland's national action.

Stephens's evolution away from a strict Sinn Féin nationalistic agenda to a literary nationalism also highlights his belief in the power of art and beauty as well as in this version of Vedantic spiritualism. Widespread political disillusionment in modern artistic circles occurred during the interwar years in Europe and, more particularly in Ireland, during the years of the Easter Rising executions, the Irish War for Independence (or the Anglo-Irish War), and the Irish Civil War. In the midteens, Stephens began to comment more specifically on the permanency of the Irish class system, comparing class stratification to what he believed was a spiritually based system of stratifying society in India, the caste system. For example, in his essay "In the Interval," Stephens comments on the "die-hards" in Ireland who resisted any mobility between the classes, using the word *caste* instead of *class*: "Their antagonism to this country is so real, and has such twisted strands of interest and *caste* and power and historical recollection" (137; emphasis added). For Stephens, despite the shift from English to Irish governments, these "twisted strands" remained in post-colonization Ireland; the strands had merely changed hands.

Despite the fact that the caste system is a complex, functionalist system of social stratification composed of status groups, Stephens used it to represent the superimposed socioeconomic stratification of the class system in Ireland. Class is classically determined by peoples' relationship to ownership and capital; it often includes cultural and status segregation, but it is rarely (if ever) determined by such cultural markers.[12] In his writings, however, Stephens tended to conflate the natures of these two systems, substituting the cultural strata of the spiritually based *varna* caste system for the economic strata of the class system. The only similarities these ontologies share are based solely on their similar functions of social stratification. Furthermore, Stephens probably did not realize the complexity and the ethnographic realities of the caste system. Within each caste are subcastes, and each subcaste, or *jati,* has complex and varied interrelations depending on their local socioeconomic and historical dynamics. But Orientalist glosses on Indian society normally were not that detailed, and they often gave limited and Eurocentric explanations of traditional Indian society and Vedantic texts as the essence of modern Indian society.

Irish literary Orientalists often repeated many of the stereotypes of Anglo-French Orientalism, despite a tendency toward anticolonialism. Likewise, the repetition of colonial stereotypes in nativistic Indian culture often posited Hinduism, India, and the Orient as profoundly mystical, sensual, and spiritual. Such Irish representations of and attractions to the Orient correspond with what has been called *romantic Orientalism*. Ronald Inden coined this term in *Imagining India* (1990), explaining that this type of nativistic Orientalism reflects assumptions about the mystical East similar to the ones held by European Romantics. As Richard King points out in *Orientalism and Religion* (1999), these assumptions tended to be "motivated by an admiration for, and sometimes a firm belief in the superiority of Eastern cultures" (92). This notion corresponds somewhat to what other more culturally conservative critics have termed *affirmative Orientalism,* that is, an Orientalism that was a supposedly positive force in Indian culture, helping Indian society redefine and modernize itself. King, in line with Inden, offers a critique of this conception of India.

> This reflects the fact that "romantic Orientalism" agrees with the prevailing view that India is the mirror-opposite of Europe; it continues to postulate cultural "essences" and thus perpetuates the same (or at least similar) cultural stereotypes about the East. The romanticist view of the Orient, then, is still a distortion, even if motivated at times by a respect for the Orient. As such, it participates in the projection of stereotypical forms that allows for a domestication and control of the East.
>
> What is interesting about the "mystical" or "spiritual" emphasis that predominates in the romanticist conception of India is not just that it has become a prevalent theme in contemporary Western images of India, but also that it has exerted a great

deal of influence upon the self-awareness of the very Indians that it purports to describe. Some might argue, as David Kopf clearly does, that such endorsement by Indians themselves suggests the anti-imperial nature of such discourses, yet one cannot ignore the sense in which British and colonial ideology, through the various media of communication, education and institutional control, has made a substantial contribution to the construction of modern identity and self-awareness among contemporary Indians. (92–93)

One question that arises is how reasonable is it for one to argue the benefits of reversing or exposing a stereotype if the overarching discourse persists? A similarly pertinent question for this study concerns the degree to which Irish Orientalists perpetuated stereotypical understandings of India promoted by Indians and romantic Orientalists, believing such understandings to be part of an anticolonial and antimodernist aesthetic or philosophy. Irish cultural nationalists had embraced this particular image of the mystical Hindu during the Celtic Revival, correlating it with the dreamy, mystical Celt—yet both of these are at times exposed for their constructed nature.

Richard King discusses one of the main Indian figures of this universalist school of Hinduism, a man who promoted nativistic images of mystical India, Vivekānanda. He was also the founder of the Ramakrishna Mission, which promoted a contemporary form of Advaita Vedânta (nondualism) throughout the world. As the previously quoted comment of Stephens on AE implies, "Advaita philosophy and the Vedas" had a large following in Dublin—indeed, Stephens saw it as an area of expertise for the Irish mystic. King continues:

> [Vivekānanda] placed particular emphasis upon the spirituality of Indian culture as a curative for the nihilism and materialism of modern Western culture. In Vivekānanda's [sic] hands, Orientalist notions of India as "other worldly" and "mystical" were embraced and praised as India's special gift to humankind. Thus the very discourse that succeeded in alienating, subordinating and controlling India was used by Vivekānanda as a religious clarion call for the Indian people to untie under the banner of a universalistic and all-embracing Hinduism. (93).

AE had vigorously promoted this form of Hinduism in Ireland, introducing it as the essence of ancient Hindu thought to Yeats, Stephens, Cousins, McKenna, and other Revivalists. Their use of it extends beyond reactionary nativism and supports cross-colonial ties, which triangulate Empire in unexpected and unacknowledged ways. King quotes two particularly illustrative sections from Vivekānanda's collected works, the tenor of which reminds one of writings of these Celtic Revivalists, who were also seeking a new (ancient) spirituality to oppose English colonialism and unite Ireland: "Up India, and conquer the world with your spirituality. . . . Ours is a religion of which Buddhism, with all its greatness is a rebel child and of which Christianity is a very patchy imitation. The salvation of Europe depends on a rationalistic religion, and Advaita—non-duality, the Oneness, the idea of the Impersonal God,—is the only religion that can have any hold on intellectual people" (93). Such calls to "conquer the world with your spirituality" became familiar within the Irish diaspora throughout the twentieth century. This inversion and triangulation of colonial stereotypes simultaneously served as a clarion call to Irish writers to unearth the anticipated wonders of Celtic mysticism. Similarly, the call paralleled the inspiration of anti-British Irish Catholic nativists, who consolidated state and social power in Ireland after its independence.

Nativism and National Action

The role of this nativist repetition of colonial stereotypes, both Indian and Irish, in the programs of building national cultures is like the colonial stereotype itself: ambivalent. Stephens used tropes of the East to put forward his critiques of post-1916 Ireland, which may have, in turn, clarified his nativist Irish Orientalist impulse. A glimpse into an earlier essay of Stephens, "Irish Idiosyncrasies," reveals both how Stephens perceived Ireland's relationship with India and how nativism melded with colonialism. Stephens discusses Ireland's future role in the world while criticizing the self-importance of Irish cultural nationalists—"I have seen a whole room-full of young men and women [at a *ceilidhe* (or singsong and dance)] enjoying themselves with the most deplorable gravity" (1983, 71). He seems to be attacking a sense of duty to a sanctimonious Irish nationalism—duty and gravity, he argues, have no place at a supposedly festive atmosphere, national or otherwise. But it is not the cultural limitations of the Irish that he is hoping to change:"As long as we retain our discontent Ireland will continue to be something more than a geographical expression. She will still be a nation, an entity with a practical and impulsive existence and a future, with ambition and hope spreading out beyond the horizons and with all her possibilities of freedom and greatness and majesty intact—and impending" (74–75). With discontent, he hopes to retain an impulsive antimaterialism that he had once perceived in Irish nationalism. The "intact" and "impending" "possibilities of freedom and greatness and majesty" are what he argues made the Revival vital and helped Ireland realize its "national action."

Stephens's use of the very suggestive phrase "geographical expression" to describe the dawn of the Irish nation is significant. It shows what was at stake and points to an awareness of Ireland's place in Empire or, to use Edward Said's term, in the *imagined geography* of Empire, that is, it points to Ireland's postcolonization status. To see Ireland as "more than geographical expression" would be to treat it as more than a footnote to the history of global imperial "progress." A new Irish future, he argues, depends upon Ireland recovering "something in Irish life so old that one can no longer say this is Europe, that is Asia" (to borrow from W. B. Yeats's preface to *The Cat and the Moon and Certain Poems* [1924]). As was typical of Stephens, he refers to figures of speech for evidence and argument:

> There is some eastern nation has a saying to this effect. "If you have twopence buy some bread with one penny, and with the other buy a flower of the white narcissus." That is not only a proverb; it is also a philosophy—it ought to be a religion. It does not indicate only a love of and a camaraderie with beauty, it is also sanity and high-thinking and tense, abundant life. What have we to put beside this in the way of proverbs? A collection of ready made English flatulences, sordid, dirt-grubbing, materialisms, such as A stitch in time saves nine, or that ineffective and cowardly compromise—Half a loaf is better than no bread, or the equally futile Bird in the hand is worth two in the bush, and Silks and satins put out the kitchen fire—a proverb certainly to sneer at. All the proverbs we have are materialistic, canny and base, and have crawled laboriously from the grosser aspects of existence. . . . Of course I am aware that the proverbs I have quoted are not Gaelic; they are English, and they prophesy to me more insistently than German Dreadnoughts the degradation and downfall of that race. (73)

This unnamed "eastern nation" represents "a love of and a camaraderie with beauty" as well as "sanity and high-thinking and tense, abundant life" through a proverb and philosophy or what "ought to be a religion." This "eastern" proverb that Stephens has adopted suggests buying a "narcissus" (the original Persian phrase recommends a hyacinth)[13] with one's remaining penny. Significantly, the narcissus flower also signifies self-involvement or, more accurately, one's involvement with one's reflection or image. Stephen wanted to push beyond modern Ireland and noted that Ireland's national character required fresh models—hence Yeats's dictum for Revival writers: "Copy the East and live deliberately." Stephens used this quote in the hope of getting Irish cultural nationalists (this essay was first a lecture given at the Central Branch of Sinn Féin) to side with an "eastern" sensibility and be free from the ideological trappings of English culture. He linked, therefore, "English flatulences, sordid, dirt-grubbing, materialisms" with the ideology of imperial England; both were inseparable for him. The wisdom of England's capitalistic colonialism had emerged from English materialism, not from any spirituality, aesthetic, literature, or ethic. It had "crawled laboriously from the grosser aspects of existence" and was "ineffective and cowardly . . . materialistic, canny and base." In connecting English colonialism with modern materialism, Stephens helped focus the Revivalist project against both colonialism and materialism, refuting the projects of Empire when refuting the "grosser aspects" of modern materialism. The Orient appeared as the perfect ally.

The logic of his argument, however, meant that empires, in and of themselves, were not base. Other empires—of aesthetics, legend, religion, and culture—had existed before and, Stephens hoped, might again. The crux of the problem was that English colonialism had supplanted Ireland's original sensibility and social order (which included the supplanting of oral culture with print culture)[14] with English material culture.

Because Stephens dealt in cultural stereotypes, however, does not mean that he was not aware of the process of cultural stereotyping and its work in cultural colonialism. Earlier in his essay "Irish Idiosyncrasies," Stephens explored the colonial stereotypes of both the Irishman and the Celt, treating them as images of Irish "idiosyncrasies":

> We are all, of course, aware of those idiosyncrasies which have been put to our credit or discredit by other people, and which, even to the present time, are believed by the world at large to represent this country. The humorously careless vagabond, the humorously foolish vagabond, the humorously pugnacious and the humorously criminal vagabonds—vagabondia of all descriptions. . . . After this a careless and gay, wad-in-a-window kind of Irishman we have been introduced to a different type which is again held up to us as being the Irishman par excellence. He is a lackadaisical misanthrope who spends his time wandering on the shores by lonely waters thinking sad, sad thoughts about nothing in particular. Now I am not at all sure of the genesis of this individual, but I believe the idea of him took root in England, and was introduced into literature under the title of the Celtic Genius. (67–68)

He further comments on the destructiveness of the process of reinforcing such stereotypes through what would now be grouped under nativism. In addition to the cultural traumas caused by English colonization, embracing images provided by the colonizer weakens the national "vitality": "We are quite sufficiently devitalised by a condition of serfdom and a persistent and terrible emigration–drainage without further lessening our vitality by an endeavour to become Mist that Does Be on the Bog types of people who think shoddy poetical thoughts and act shoddy theatrical acts" (68). Stephens clearly saw how a Celtic type—the "Mist that Does Be on the Bog types of people"—could reinforce the postcolonization condition.

Stephens was not alone in rejecting this sort of mystical stereotype. Many writers at the time reproved Celticism for its romanticizations, foreshadowing more recent critiques that treat Celticism as a debilitating type of nativism; likewise, they criticized the similar and related enthusiasm for the Orient. As mentioned in the introduction to this section, James Joyce, Oliver St. John Gogarty, and, later, Samuel Beckett disparaged both the fancy of the "Celtic Twilight" and the popular fascination with Oriental images and themes. Nevertheless, Stephens was drawn to cultures beyond his own immediate ken, that is, beyond England, Ireland, and the

United States. Like other cosmopolitan Irish writers such as James Connolly and Roger Casement, he argues in several places that in order to find new models for an Irish national identity, Irish thinkers must look outside postcolonization Ireland: "We can visualise our country best by looking at other nations" (68). This often translated into cross-colonial aspirations. In his review of James Cousins's book-length survey of Irish legends and comparative study of Irish, Greek, and Indian cultures, *The Wisdom of the West* (1912), Stephens notes: "[I]t is particularly necessary that we should be familiar with our own national lore, and, concurrently, with our national psychology, whether we understand the Grecian or Indian myths or not—although perhaps it will be impossible to attain this local knowledge without the more extended survey, on the grounds that you cannot see Ireland until you are familiar with France" (102).

In part, this process of "looking at other nations" resembles a different form of internationalism familiar to Revivalists: British colonialism. Later in "Irish Idiosyncrasies" Stephens maps one possible future of Irish internationalism.

> All the diverse nationalities, the separate and jealous civilisations, the individual and stringent bigotries, all the groupings of art and stars, the clusters of crafts and suns will meet at some point and grow from thence to that consummating flower of life. The secret of each nation, of all national rivalries and bitternesses, is the unexpressed aspiration of each to be the branch to which all the others must converge, to impose on all other nations its own culture and take those other diverse nationalities into itself, absorb and merge them into one world growth and be itself the branch of attainment. . . . I look for the coming of the Gael to be that branch of the nations to preach our own doctrine of life and freedom and beauty. (1983, 75)

Although the universalism and internationalism that Stephens advocates here is not the exploitative mercantilism of British colonialism, its parallels to Britain's cultural colonialism are striking—"to impose on all other nations its own culture and take those other diverse nationalities into itself." While Stephens is ironic, the ideology of Empire is still suggested. The process of establishing independent international relations across the periphery (part of a cross-colonial strategy for cultural decolonization) also usually means traversing the metropole and acquiring some of the systems and ideology of the metropole.

Caste as Class in "The Thieves" and "The Boss"

In the early 1920s, Stephens offered little public comment on Irish politics; however, he continued to examine issues of materialism and economic determinism in his works. Instead of commenting on the civil war and partition politics, Stephens focused his attention on Ireland's national inheritance and the evils of materialism.

He felt much needed to be done to create Ireland's new identity, writing in May 1922, "It takes time . . . to attain to, or to recognize and organize, a national inheritance, and much water will flow before any change is apparent in existing conditions" (1983, 187). In organizing Ireland's national inheritance, Indian philosophy could dispel what Stephens saw as the *illusion* and Englishness of material struggle. In other words, he used Indian philosophy as a rhetorical tool of decolonization. In his stories of the teens and twenties, Stephens dismissed the ultimate goal of Larkinite class struggle—to create a society without class strata—and offered instead instances of spiritual transcendence.

In many stories Stephens imaginatively "cop[ied] the East" and paralleled Irish social stratification with the Vedantic *varna* caste system as follows: the wealthy, the capitalist owners, and the imaginative thinkers, including artists, poets, philosophers, and spiritualists (represented the Brahmin caste); the Anglo-Irish government, military, and professional class (Kshatriya caste); the shopkeepers and "gombeen-men" of the Catholic middle class (Vaisya caste); the laboring poor, including servants, charwomen, house painters, clerks, rural people, and so on (Sudra caste); and the traveling and destitute, or vagabond, "tinker" class (Adi-Dravidas or Untouchables). Stephens tended to portray these groups hierarchically, with the ones at the top having the most power, capital, and social prestige, excluding the imaginative thinkers and divine beings who usually transcended class, caste, and worldly ambition. This simplified view of the caste system represented Stephens's view of the status levels in Irish society and, in some ways, paralleled Yeats's nostalgia for an Irish aristocracy.

Similar to an aristocratic stratification, classical Indian philosophy presents its social stratification as a permanent fixture in maya, or the reality of the earth.[15] In the Bhagavad Gita, Krishna implores Arjuna to perform his "duty as a *kshatriya* [member of the warrior caste]" and to continue the "maintenance of the social order of this world" (1990, 8, 14), lines that reveal the permanent social stratification of classical Hindu society. In order to forge a precolonial and premodern past for Ireland, Stephens projected onto Irish society the four principal castes of Aryan Hindu society and the Adi-Dravidas or Untouchables (which actually included at least four aboriginal Indian groups). Furthermore, Stephens seems to have appropriated them because he knew little about ancient Ireland's social organization. Stephens's imposition of Orientalist images of India onto Dublin certainly stands out—one might have to go back to John Wilson Croker's *Intercepted Letter from J— T—, Esq., Writer at Canton, to His Friend in Dublin, Ireland* (1804) and his amalgam of the Cantonese and Dublin cultures of the early nineteenth century to find an earlier instance. Classical India and the Orient provided an allegorical structure for his critique, unknowingly using images promoted by the Empire in order to critique its materialistic mission.

The influence of Indian philosophy, both Hindu and Buddhist, on his later writings has been thoroughly noted by Hilary Pyle in her work *James Stephens*. Pyle traces the themes and devices of yoga, contemplation, reincarnation, love for animals, levels of reality, the laws of karma, and so on, throughout *The Demi-Gods* (1914), *Irish Fairy Tales* (1920), *Deirdre* (1923), *In the Land of Youth* (1924), *Etched in Moonlight* (1928), *Strict Joy* (1931), and other works. As noted earlier, Pyle comments that Stephens had been intently studying Indian philosophy throughout the teens, but that it was not until the twenties that he devoted "himself to Indian philosophy to the exclusion of all else . . . [when] he read and re-read the *Upanishads* and the *Bhagavad-Gita,* and the commentaries on them" (1965, 128). The stories published in *Etched in Moonlight* were, in part, the fruit of this interest. In the stories the resolutions of conflict often require transcendence on the part of one or more of the characters, and this became his main suggestion for social change.

In these stories, Stephens treated different classes as having not only varying amounts of capital, but also distinct inherited cultural roles, just as castes have in the *varna* stratification. His depictions of distinct status groups in society, therefore, have some surface parallels to classical divisions of Indian castes. Dipankar Gupta discusses caste and stratification in the introduction to *Social Stratification* (1992), "[Social stratification] must be socially amplified with respect to dress, or food, or occupation, or residence, or mobility, or a combination of these and more" (3). Stephens make some of these very distinctions between the different castes or classes in his stories. The main distinctions among classes in Stephens's works from his first novel, *The Charwoman's Daughter* (1912), to *The Demi-Gods* (1914) and *Etched in Moonlight* (1928) involve dress, appearance, morals, politics, diet, and wealth, all sociocultural differences and practical identities [16] that also divide Indian castes.

Stephens's disillusionment with the new Irish government and what he called the "parochial politics" of nationalism and labor fueled his writings, and an absence of class mobility marks his later stories. The lack of governmental support and aid for the poor can be seen most poignantly in "Hunger," first published in book form in 1918 (as *Hunger: A Dublin Story*) and later included in *Etched in Moonlight*. This story presents the grim social exigencies of a lower-class family; it concerns an unemployed house painter who cannot feed his family because of a lack of work. The bleak story begins with the lines: "On some people misery comes unrelentingly. It comes with such a continuous rage that one might say destruction had been sworn against them and that they were doomed beyond appeal, or hope" (1928, 23). In "Hunger," poverty becomes the ultimate destroyer of happiness, security, and, eventually, life—a realistic scenario at the time when no central aid office and few government relief programs existed at the time. The main character of the story is the mother of three children; the father leaves halfway through the story to find work at a munitions plant in Scotland. But as the first line foreshadows, he dies of exposure and starvation before he can begin working. The mother then begins begging in the streets. Stephens describes her difficulty with this degrading occupation: "[Passersby] recognized her at a distance as a beggar, and she could only whisper to the back of a head or to a cold shoulder." She becomes a type of untouchable in Dublin's society, functioning outside the social system: "Sometimes when she went towards a person that person instantly crossed the road and walked away hastily. Sometimes people fixed upon her a prohibitive eye and she drew back from them humbled" (42). After the death of a child, she learns of a relief kitchen and of a "gentleman who might assist her" (46). It is significant that Stephens does not reveal any tie between this man and the British or Dublin government. In fact, the government is absent throughout the story, and class and caste distinctions are nearly absolute. Stephens clearly recognized the problems of the lower class and recommended individual resourcefulness and transcendence, encouraging distrust in the state and industry as well as nationalist and class politics. The fundamental question of how to be free of class struggle was, for Stephens, an intellectual and spiritual question, not a socioeconomic one.

Stephens's uppermost caste comprised characters in ownership positions or wealthy status groups. Class divisions are represented as permanent in his later stories. The rich are portrayed as having too much freedom and too little morality. A view of the wealthy class can be found in "The Thieves" (1920). The main character's lack of morality destroys her position in society and her self-righteousness. Two similar actions begin and end the story: two thefts of silk stockings—one by a servant girl and the other by a wealthy lady. When held up for comparison, the servant's theft seems understandable, and, though not morally right, at least economically justifiable. The wealthy woman's theft is depicted as malicious, pompous, and unjustifiable, yet it is rationalized by her own form of justice. The story opens with the wealthy woman discovering that one of her servants has stolen a pair of her silk stockings. Because she does not know which servant stole it, she gives them all a day off so she can rummage through their possessions. Even after she finds the evidence, she reads all of her servants' personal letters.

> She would certainly read their letters . . . it was a duty which every right-minded person owed to her home and to the community in which she moved.
>
> Indeed some of the letters which she discovered she bore away within her blouse as keepsakes—no, as evidence; she would produce them later on when the domestic person concerned had become the culprit which all servants do eventually become. (1983, 171)

The rich woman rationalizes her invasive curiosity by telling herself that is not only her right, but also her *social* duty, "owed to her home and to the community in which she moved," to maintain the social hierarchy, to affirm her caste.

Stephens often depicts women of all classes as especially bound to property and materialism—both of the silk-stocking thieves are women. Rarely do his women characters overcome their materialism or transcend their social situations. We see this perspective in most of his female characters; from "Desire" to "The Thieves," women tend to function solely as victims and tools of the social order, not as individuals with agency—because for Stephens an individual's main agency was the ability to transcend caste. Stephens is remarkably consistent in not giving his female characters ability to change their circumstances—all of them rely upon the generosity or power of male characters. Significantly, the heroes are primarily male, whereas the victims are female. But it would be unfair to characterize Stephens as unsupportive of women's rights, as we can see from a series of articles advocating woman suffrage, which offers an insight into his perspective on women. "In this age especially there is an intense female activity in literature, painting and music: in every direction women are drawing abreast, and the reason they have not done so long ago is that they were subjected to most arbitrary educational systems almost every phase of which was framed towards repression instead of freedom. The wonder is, not that women are backwards, but that, in the circumstances, they have any mentality at all" (102). It is, therefore, not surprising that women are portrayed as the victims of his social order. His asides on women, at times crass, are often sketched in order to illustrate the ills of society—as a character comments in *The Demi-Gods*, "women and birds are able to see without turning their heads, and that is indeed a necessary provision, for they are both surrounded by enemies" (1914, 16).

Even though women are not strong heroes in Stephens's works, they are sometimes strong villains (along with men) who illustrate the evils of materialism. In "The Thieves," the rich woman's attitude to her servants goes far beyond disrespect to the servant lower class. She does not recognize their rights as individuals and regards them only as workers. She commodifies them, denying them any shared sense of human fellowship in their place of employment. Stephens's description of her resembles Krishna's description of pompous wealthy people: "[These people] regard themselves as important. They are adamant about their materialistic notions and are intoxicated by pride stemming from their power, wealth, and fame" (Raval 1990, 59). But the wealthy woman's aristocratic convictions are undermined when she later pockets another pair of silk stockings in a draper's shop and is arrested by a deferential policeman. Because of her wealth and social position, she believes, first, that she exists both beyond suspicion and incrimination and, second, that she should be treated cordially in her arraignment, which the narrator implies she will be given.

Stephens's portrayal of class as caste highlights the lack of communication and comprehension among Irish status groups. Of all of Stephens's stories, "The Boss" most memorably portrays Stephens's use of this metaphor, and gives a notable illustration of his recommendations for individual transcendence. Stephens parodies the rhetoric of classical Indian philosophy in the first vignette of the story, borrowing character and language. Here an Irish "Boss" reminds us of Brahma's all-powerful presence. Stephens parodies lines from the "Manduka Upanishad," which Stephens called "a wonderful Upanishad" (Finneran 1978, 30) and once lent to Yeats.[17] His source for "The Boss" was most likely from the *Mandukyopanishad, with Guadapada's Karikas and the Bhashya of S'ankara* (1894). In the second paragraph of the story, Stephens describes the Boss as such: "He knew all that was happening, whether near at hand or far away. . . . All the machinery of the great organization was under his hands. He touched it at any point he pleased; and there was no part of it obscure or unimportant to his mind" (1928, 179). The "Manduka Upanishad" (*upanishad* means "teaching") opens similarly: "He is beyond thought and invisible, beyond family and colour [*color* is a translation of *varna*]. He has neither eyes nor ears; he has neither hands nor feet. He is everlasting and omnipresent, infinite in the great and infinite in the small" (Mascaro 1965, 76).

Most obviously, Stephens parodies the sentence structure of the transplanted Upanishads. Starting sentences with the third-person singular personal pronoun "He" places the Boss and Brahma as *the* main subject and center of their respective realms. Furthermore, Stephens parodies Brahma's attention to both the large and the small. The line from the "Manduka Upanishad" "infinite in the great and infinite in the small" provides a source of parody for Stephens's line, "he knew all that was happening, whether near at hand or far away." The Boss is thus set up to be the hub of the "great machinery," just as Brahma is the hub of existence.[18] Furthermore, by depicting this capitalist "Boss" as a god, Stephens mocks the pomposity and self-aggrandizement of the upper class. He transfers a simplified view of classical Vedantic philosophy onto the "everyday" Dublin reality in order to set up his theme of transcendence.

The Boss in his capitalist managerial role controls "the entire vast business of his company" (1983, 179). He is a member of a higher social class or caste, like the wealthy woman in "The Thieves." Stephens's description of him reveals the importance that the Boss places upon himself and upon his position as "the manager." The Boss (like the other characters, he goes unnamed) has what seem to be inherited relations with other bosses, whom the narrator describes as "predecessors in the caste." As a member of this particular capitalist caste, the Boss's power and wealth depend upon the subjugation and commodification of the lower class. The Boss recognizes that he needs "help" from the workers to keep his organization running, but he claims that he would never use the "kindly" term *help*. Instead, he "atrociously" uses the synecdoche *hands,* which diminishes his workers' entire beings to their machinelike function. We find the Boss's ruthless perspective on the working class toward the end of the first vignette: "There is but one disposable material in the universe—it is life; and for man, when he has evolved beyond rudimentary abilities, there is but one tool to be found—and it is man. To the manager's mind man had become as common as mud; as useful as coal; as unvoiced and anonymous as either" (180). The hubris of the Boss, and others in his caste, denies not only respect for his workers, but also fundamental human rights. The Boss considers the truly commodified lower-class worker as "a legged, a mobile affair" who "must be put somewhere where his value can be used" or should be dismissed (181).

Written in the aftermath of the Easter Rising during the violent years leading up to the Anglo-Irish War, the power dynamics in this particular national analogy can also be read as indicative of colonial power struggles. Reading the Boss as the imperial power, holding the surplus of capital and the reins of control in Ireland, implicates capitalist ventures with English colonialism. The progression of the story concerns the punishment and dismissal of a lower-level manager who has become rebellious. The Boss uses every maneuver he can to force the employee to resign, but the tenacious employee will not. This forces the Boss to call him into his office to directly ask him to resign, and if that fails (which it does) to dismiss him with words as direct "as the snarl of a dog" (188). For this climactic meeting, the Boss sets the chairs in the room in a fashion that would best manipulate the power dynamics in his favor. Such knowledge seems secondhand to the Boss figure:

> The distance between this chair and the manager's desk permitted conversation, but it prohibited familiarity; and it had the effect of isolating the individual who sat on it not only from the manager's desk but almost from the room. He was marooned on it. He was segregated and indicated by it as a stranger. The person who occupies a seat thus cleverly arranged feels, though it be insensibly, that he has lost all contacts; that he is "in the air"; and his disadvantages become so immediately evident to himself that the equilibrium of his mind is disturbed and an automatic idea of inferiority awakens in him, with its logical sentiment of humility and obedience. (191–92)

The propagation of inferiority is much a part of the strategy of the Boss and signifies the larger pathology of Empire that critics such as Frantz Fanon and Ashis Nandy have explored. In Stephens's story, the Boss has obviously used this technique of alienation before. The ruling class, like the colonizer, must use such techniques in their everyday life in order to preserve the ideological "mould of society," and maintain a closed system of social hierarchy. Stephens associates such manipulations of power with the upper caste, and, in doing so, he blends Orientalist understandings of the Brahmin caste with anticolonial nationalist and labor critiques. But Stephens does not leave the situation here.

The Boss misreads this particular employee who is "not distressed by the iso-lated chair" (192). The employee has come fully prepared to momentarily overturn this hierarchy. He carries a walking stick with him, "a long, flexible whalebone," and bolts the door after he enters. Then "[h]e lifted his chair out of isolation; placed it nearer to the manager's desk, and sat upon it. Then he put on his hat; not imper-tinently, but obviously to leave his hands free" (195). Both men are determined and immovable. The employee then tells the Boss that he does not depend upon his job for his livelihood; as it turns out, the employee is not a member of the worker caste after all. The Boss had misread him. The employee continues to explain his inten-tions to the Boss: "I am thus so free that I can afford to resent ill-will, and chastise a personal antagonist. . . . You have determined to place on me a public affront, I have determined to resent it and to punish it." The Boss dryly asks how he is to be punished. The employee explains: "'You have called me here to discharge me. I,' touching his whalebone, 'have brought this here to beat you' " (196).

The Boss asks the employee if he knows what will happen to him. The em-ployee acknowledges that he will be arrested, pay a fine, and serve three months in jail, but states, "It is a matter of indifference to me." The Boss then fires him. In the following scene the mutual antagonism between the men—"cold excitement . . . cold rage" (196)—braces them for a beating. What happens, however, is totally un-expected, unless we understand Stephens's borrowings from Vedantic philosophy. The employee "reached a hand to the manager's shoulder; and the latter's hand stretched automatically forward and hovered over the bell upon his table. Thus they halted for two seconds staring fixedly at each other. Then, with a disdainful move-ment of the lips, the manager removed his hand without having touched the bell; and at once the man took his hand from the manager's shoulder." Because the Boss did not ring the bell to summon help, the man's threat of violence becomes redun-dant to the employee because the Boss accepts his punishment. Their mutual an-tagonism dissolves; almost mystically, "all anger evaporated" and they share "something magical" as they momentarily transcend the situation (197).

The employee's anger turns to pride, but not in himself nor the manager: "[H]e was proud of man; and he was extraordinarily happy" (198). His purpose, perhaps unrealized by himself until this moment, had not been to punish the Boss, but to force the Boss to realize the illusory nature of power and status in society. In the words of Stephens's favored "Manduka Upanishad," they had been longing to attain "what is above creation [which] cannot be attained by action" (Mascaro 1965, 77). After the man sets his whalebone down, the Boss's mind "was emptied of hate or disdain as if something magical had come and they had dared to await it" (1928, 198). The narrator concludes by telling us that, although the Boss soon forgets the episode, he gradually stopped dismissing workers, and "[b]efore two years had passed he resigned a position in which he took no further interest, and in which, he considered, he was leading the life of a donkey" (199). In terms of Stephens's philosophy, both the Boss and the fired employee have done what politics cannot do: through the threat of insurrection they have transcended class and caste. In 1920, four years after the Easter Rising, when Stephens first wrote this story, the colonial overtones would have been clear, with England as the materialistic Boss and Ireland as the worker not recognized as an equal. Such a peaceful resolution remained an unrealized hope, however.

Stephens excerpts his criteria for transcendence from the Bhagavad Gita, which states "one should act to harmonize the existing social order with the goal to liberate mankind" (Raval 1990, 16). Stephens summarizes a similar social philosophy on matters such as class struggle as early as his 1913 essay "Come Off that Fence!": "Only from your own prosperity can there come any assuagement for the miseries of your class or of humanity" (1983, 110). When Stephens writes of individual prosperity, he means not merely material prosperity but individual freedom, purity, and transcendence. This subversive, nonmaterialistic, and nonmodern movement in Stephens's national analogies stems from his combination of an Orientalist vision of Indian spirituality and "everyday" class politics and in many ways parallels the cross-colonial ties of many of his contemporaries.

Stephens merged rhetorical pasts with his present as a way of reimagining Ireland as it broke from England. By positing Orientalist versions of Hindu spirituality within national analogies of Irish culture and contemporaneous Dublin, Stephens critiques the ideologies of capitalists and imperialists. Indo-Irish stories such as "The Boss" reveal an imaginative link between Indian and Irish anticolonialist narratives, which built on Orientalist and Celticist understandings. Stephens's national analogies demonstrate a specifically Irish answer to Homi Bhabha's rhetorical question of how a "nation's modernity" can be written. The Orient, which has a long history as a source of allegory in Irish literature, provided Stephens with a way of representing the emerging Irish nation and a way to reconcile conflicts in Irish society. His identification with the Oriental and the Celtic reveals a relationship with the Orient similar to the sympathetic one of romantic Orientalists, perhaps the main difference being the associations that the mystical East held for each—for both, the East was traditional and antimaterialist, but for Stephens the Orient was also antisectarian and anticolonial.

8 James, Seumas, and Jayaram Cousins

London lay between Ireland and India.
>   —James Cousins, *We Two Together*

From the heights where the East and West are one. / . . . I shall step
out behind a star / And seek the quiet haunted lakes / . . . where my
De Dananns are.
>   —James Cousins, "To Ireland"

SPENDING HALF HIS LIFE in Ireland and half in India, James Cousins revamped the Oriental and Celtic, bringing their age-old semiotic pairing into a new cross-cultural synthesis. All of his work was charged with what he termed a vision of cultural syncretism, or *samadarsana,* which he translated as "same-sightedness." In order to rationalize the link between Ireland and India, two cultures that long existed on the borders of European empires, he embraced Theosophy's quasi-racial theories, which resembled the speculative work of antiquarians, who had sought to prove an Oriental origin for the Celts. Cousins rewrote this narrative by asserting that both cultures could be invigorated by reestablishing an ancient East-West spiritual connection. Historical arguments about a Phoenician colonization of Ireland held little sway (except as an origin legend) in the early twentieth century, but racial arguments about an original Indo-European, or Aryan, culture had grown influential across Europe, and were later brought to genocidal conclusions by the Third Reich. The pseudoanthropological argument asserted that the people on the margins of Indo-European cultures—the eastern and western edges being India and Ireland—retained ancient similarities and mystical understandings because they were the least modernized. In many ways, this theory merely modernized the links imagined between the "barbaric" peoples of the ancient Greeks and Romans.

Both James Cousins and his wife, Margaret, grew up Protestant in Ireland, James in Belfast, Margaret in rural Roscommon, and when both moved away from their regions, they also left their family's religion. They became interested in

Theosophy and mysticism during the Celtic Revival through the influence of George Russell (AE). Cousins wrote plays with Irish themes for the Abbey and taught geography in the High School, and Margaret became increasingly involved in the suffrage movement. After spending forty years in Ireland, in 1915 at midlife, they moved to Madras, India, where they spent most of the next forty years. Annie Besant, the president of the Theosophical Society, paid for their voyage and hired Cousins as literary editor of a newspaper in India that Besant ran. They went east to find the spiritual and cultural source that many Celtic Revivalists had sought through Theosophy, as well as to take the lessons of Irish cultural revivalism to help foment a revival in India. In India they enjoyed an influence as suffragists, European Theosophists, and Irish cultural nationalists, associating with political and cultural leaders of the day, including Rabindranath Tagore, Mohandas Gandhi, Krishnamurti, and Aurobindo Ghose. Margaret helped found the All-Asian Women's Conference and continued to devote herself to women's issues throughout her life, even being jailed for extended periods in England, Ireland, and India. James, a prolific writer, provocative cultural ideologue, and entertaining global lecturer on Ireland and India, sported a pince-nez and a painter's cravat, and was well-known for his earnest (if sometimes overearnest) personality. Inspired by AE's agrarian cooperative work and mystical vision, he promoted, in very practical ways, Indian culture through literature, education, activism, and exhibitions. Writing to Tagore once, he commented on his practical work in educational institutions: "I find there is an aesthetic for other activities than art. As soon as I find it, I take joy in it. . . . The qualities that give life to art are also inherent in the art of life. When we touch them we live" (Apr. 4, 1926, Sl. 35).[1] Throughout his career he wrote cultural criticism, drama, and poetry with Irish and Indian subjects and claimed as an old man living in northern India that he still wrote poems inspired by Celtic gods (Cousins and Cousins 1950, 698).

Cousins advocated for an international cultural exchange against Euro-American rationalism and imperial cultural dominance. As an alternative to standard responses of the colonized, especially mimicry and nativism, he proposed reviving native Indian culture and encouraged a cross-cultural renaissance to help resist both colonialism and reactionary nationalism. His cultural politics paralleled his aesthetics and his mysticism; in both, he studiously avoided reifications, emphasizing that the goal of artistic creation was not the art object, but the process itself. The same held true for education, anticolonialism, and religion, for which he argued the importance of local culture and individual experience. His writings, both critical and literary, recast the narratives of Celticism and Orientalism with a clearly stated agenda: to promote *samadarsana*. Influenced by both anticolonialist politics and Theosophical mysticism, as well as various aesthetic theories, this vision encouraged a confluence of traditions and international hybridity in the face of religious, imperial, national, and sectarian conflicts. But this vision differed enormously from the international missionary efforts of Christians, whom he hotly attacked in his collection *Heathen Essays* (1925) for distracting Asian cultural expression, arguing that "the influence of foreign religious proselytism is a denationalizing one" (67). Through Theosophy, Cousins entertained racial connections between Ireland and India, but his synthetic Irish-Indian vision did not depend upon it, and he frequently criticized racist and sexist politics. After Ireland had achieved a measure of independence in 1921, he and others theorized the inevitability of decolonization through a process of cultural awakening and revival.

Though much of his writing never reached European and American audiences, and the style of his poetry appears more Edwardian than modernist to readers and critics, his work is significant because it addresses cultural fragmentation in its many forms. His vision addressed the early twentieth century's lack of supportive cultural interchange, and, in many ways, it was a direct response to the divisive politics of colonialism, anticolonialism, nationalism, and globalization. Directly and indirectly, his work and writings influenced many prominent Indian and postcolonial critiques, particularly in the work of Rabindranath Tagore and Aurobindo Ghose, who titled his *Renaissance in India* (1946) after the work by Cousins, noting in the opening pages, "The subject matter of the book was written in a way of appreciation of Mr. James H. Cousins' book of the same name" (n.p.). But because Cousins was not Indian, his "postcolonial" writing has received little attention by postindependence Indian scholars, D. K. Chatterjee and Gauri Viswanathan being the noteworthy exceptions. His mature work was not written in Ireland, nor does it have Irish themes; Irish critics, therefore, have also largely ignored his tremendous output. Moreover, because his work pointedly differed from realist, existentialist, modernist, and postmodernist aesthetics and concerns, it has received very little attention in the European and American academy. Nevertheless, his work has tremendous value, precisely because it slips out of such categories. His cultural vision resembles a totalizing Western philosophy, but it does not promote a hierarchy based on racial, ethnic, cultural, or political divisions, nor does it advocate any program for one culture's hegemony. His spiritualist vision, with its attendant essentialism and generalities, has been understood to some degree in an Orientalist context, but to see his work as part of the unacknowledged discourse of Irish Orientalism is more accurate and revealing. Perhaps more than any other Irish writer, he developed the logic of this discourse within his own composite identity and life.

His poetry sought to unify his experiences in Ireland and India, as a sonnet from his late series "Before and After" conveys. Cousins wrote the poem in standard English, yet shadows of both Irish and Hindi emerge in the three-poem series:

> Not now, as once through swift salt-savoured rain,
> He watches men and women slowly pass

With "God and Mary to you" to early mass
By fuchsia hedges in a Kerry lane.
Here, by the azure-eyed convolvulus
He listens to loud ceremonial chants
Surging around precipitous elephants
when men in season grow God-amorous.
By other paths on the same quest he goes;
Not to the rainy peak that Patrick trod;
But hearing in strange speech the name of God
Along the selvage of Himâlayan snows,
Where, in the chaste colossal quietude,
Fades from the heart and brain[,] the human feud.
(1940, 468)

The move after the first quatrain from southwestern Irish imagery to northern Indian imagery disorients the imagery of the remote East and "hidden" Ireland. By pairing two moments, one in Ireland in 1909 and one in India in 1939, Cousins links these settings through the contrasts and represents both Irish and Indian cultures in a cross-cultural continuum that is neither cosmopolitan nor metropolitan but peripheral and circumferential. The simultaneity of the main verbs of the first two quatrains, "He watches" and "He listens," implies that both scenes occur simultaneously; only the introductory clause in the first line, "Not now," signifies that the first scene occurs in the past. The first quatrain's images of mass goers in County Kerry greeting each other in translated Irish (*Dia agus Muire dhuit*) is paired with another scene of devotion, not at Croagh Patrick, but at a religious festival in the Himalayan foothills. The third quatrain unites these "premodern" spiritual progressions in the first two quatrains into a new synthesis within the poet figure: "By other paths on the same quest he goes." Cross-cultural unity is the goal of this poet pilgrim, where even in "strange speech," he can hear the "name of God." This circumferential unity gains significance with the turn of the closing couplet, in which "the human feud" is said to fade, yet its resonance lingers, being the last words of the poem. It seems dissonant to the message of unification that leads up to it, and it counters the too easy tone of spiritual verse. Yet for Belfast-reared Cousins, human feuding took many forms, and he alternately targets the imperial and postcolonization feuds of sectarianism, nationalism, and imperialism—all of which he treats as antithetical to his vision of *samadarsana*.

Cousins and Theosophy

James Cousins's vision borrowed much from Theosophical treatises, from Madame Blavatsky to another Irishman, William Quan Judge, but his work differs in significant ways. Since the inception of Theosophy, under the guidance of Madame Helena Blavatsky, Oriental mystical "wisdom" had been at the core of the quasi-religion Theosophy. Indian philosophy, in particular, informed Blavatsky's foundational writings, especially in her major works, *The Secret Doctrine* (1888) and *Isis Unveiled* (1877). These works refashion Hindu and Buddhist ideas of karma, reincarnation, and nirvana, among others, blending them with European occult and gnostic notions about astral beings, planes, and travel—this occult mysticism in many ways dominated the philosophic. We see the dominance of European imperial traditions in the hierarchies that Blavatsky concocted: invariably, white Europeans were in control. Even on the astral plane, the supreme group of bodiless mahatmas were eerily tagged "The White Lodge" or "The Great White Brotherhood." They watched over humanity, keeping a favored eye on Theosophical students, who tended to be, particularly in the nineteenth and early twentieth centuries, European. Not surprisingly, Blavatsky was their most favored disciple.

All of this occult mysticism and Orientalism, however, was not the only attraction of Theosophy for intellectuals and artists. Theosophy also borrowed much from the scientific advances concerning atomic physics in the late nineteenth century. As Judge explains in one of the movement's most important books, *The Ocean of Theosophy* (1893), "Embracing both the scientific and the religious, Theosophy is a scientific religion and a religious science" (qtd. in C. Ryan 1975, 4). Among Theosophists, Blavatsky is reputed to have predicted the splitting of the atom before her death in 1891. Unlike primitivist and Romantic notions that rejected modernity in all of its forms, Theosophy attempted to co-opt it into a broader framework that addressed the eventual cultural fragmentation inherent in modernity. Janet Oppenheim notes in a *History Today* article (1989) that more than any single influence, it was the confluence of a number of ontologies that made Theosophy attractive to its members. "Unlike similar groups, Theosophy claimed to respect modern science and to offer, at long last, the new synthesis of science and religion that the nineteenth century had long awaited. It was largely thanks to Blavatsky's shrewd blend of Hindu and Buddhist theology, ancient hermetic lore, and echoes from contemporary science that Theosophy outlived its origins to expand round the globe and survive today" (15–16). Significantly, later adherents continued to define Theosophy as principally a synthetic movement, as Irving Cooper explains in *Theosophy Simplified* (1964): "Modern Theosophy may be defined as a synthesis of the essential truths of religion, science, and philosophy" (21). Cousins's cultural syncretism clearly borrowed tremendously from such tenets, even though he brought them in new directions toward artistic, literary, and educational goals.

Cousins and other Irish Theosophists had discovered an updated Irish version of Vallancey's argument with linguistic and Orientalist conclusions about the Indo-European languages, namely, that a unified Indo-European race and culture had once spanned East and West. For Theosophists in Ireland, this argument had considerable appeal; it helped them depict Ireland (and India) as an ancient and remote culture, untouched by Roman civilization and modern culture. Another Irish Theosophist who traveled to India, a protégé of Cousins, Pierce L. Pielou, articulates a common theory of early-twentieth-century Celticists in his pamphlet *Megalithic Remains in Ireland, Particularly Those of the Valley of the Boyne* (1937), suggesting that an early De Danaan culture had come to Ireland as mysterious "traders in gold and amber . . . introduced a new culture and even made settlements in the island" (13). In addition to telling the story of Dublin Theosophists at Cousins's house (quoted in the introduction to this section), he cites much more popularly accepted evidence in order to corroborate this origin story from an *Irish Times* article by archaeologist R. A. Stewart Macalister (who also compiled the 1938 edition of *Lebor Gabála*). Pielou continues:

> I do not hesitate to say . . . that in all Europe there is no site which in its own special way is of greater importance. Ireland remained free from any direct interference from the Roman Empire, and Ireland, therefore, preserved that European life which elsewhere was destroyed, or, at least, profoundly modified by Roman interference. Ireland, therefore, is of immense importance for the understanding of European history, as only in Ireland can we get back to the bedrock foundation of that civilisation, and we may very fairly say that in Tara we have the concentration of the Bronze Age and the early Iron Age in Ireland. The importance of Tara then, is not merely national; it belongs to the whole world. (23)

Such archaeological arguments rehashed the ideas of seventeenth-century philologists who assumed Ireland to be a primeval land with a static culture. Such well-worn perspectives of the global importance of Ireland have been frequently used to bolster assertions about Ireland's spiritual or cultural role in the world. Here Pielou uses this argument to link Tara with other Aryan cultures in the remote East and the ancient mystical past. With such evidence, Theosophists asserted that repositories of this original culture still existed at its extremities, particularly in Irish and Indian cultures, both of which had been recently suppressed by a dominant colonial culture. Theosophy sought to revive the residual and resistant cultural forms that were perceived to be equally ancient and linked across continents in racial and cultural sensibility, what Cousins and other Theosophists repeatedly referred to as "the Aryan chain" (1918, 33).

As the word *Aryan* might suggest, twentieth-century anticolonial Theosophists still had difficulty distinguishing their racial politics from imperial and totalitarian politics. Race often was the sticking point in overcoming cultural divides for Cousins and other cultural universalists and syncretists, despite assertions about affinities between Ireland and India. During that age of racial "sciences," where bloodlines determined character, advocates of cross-cultural harmony had to respond to questions of racial difference. Furthermore, in order to assert cultural affinities between the Irish "race" and the Indian and West Asian "races," Theosophists had to address differences in skin color and other supposed markers of race in their theories of an original Indo-European culture, the "Aryan chain."

For nearly a century, scholars have stayed away from such issues, but recently serious investigations have begun. In a study on Annie Besant and religious conversion in *Outside the Fold* (1998), Gauri Viswanathan comments on this process in Cousins's work:

> The mythologies of the past are preserved and reproduced by what Cousins clearly regarded as a racial imagination. Hence he could argue that the literary revival of his time was an awakened memory of what had, in epigenetic terms, been suppressed by colonial rule. But what makes the new, animated literary spirit unique is that it could be joined both to the purposes of nationalism and anticolonialism *and* a selective recasting and racial reinscription of a mythologized history as the "high" civilization of the Aryans. (207)

But this "high" Aryan civilization did more than advocate Irish and Indian literary nationalism. Cousins expanded upon theories of an ancient Aryan culture posited in Orientalism and Theosophy, as we see in his work dedicated to Rabindranath Tagore, *The Cultural Unity of Asia* (1922). Such an argument relied upon bloodlines and "racial natures" to determine unity of culture:

> So subtly, however, had the Aryan influence intermingled with the culture of Ireland that when, once again, at the beginning of the twentieth century, the ancient Asian spirit touched Ireland through the philosophy of India, as conveyed to it through the works of . . . the Theosophical Society, there was an immediate response. Two poets (AE and Yeats) found their inmost nature expressed in the Indian modes. They found also the spiritual truths that Asia had given to the world reflected in the old myths and legends of Ireland. (7–8)

Like eighteenth-century antiquarians, Yeats, and AE, James Cousins found an ancient Asian connection through Celticism. For Cousins, reviving Indian culture became an extension of reviving Irish culture.

We find further allusion to this ancient narrative in Cousins's laudatory poem "To Eire," which describes the first colonization of Ireland—by "sailers of a thousand ships"—echoing the pseudohistorical and antiquarian studies of the previous centuries, as well as the sentiments of other Celticists and Orientalists:

> To thee, beloved! of old there came
> The sailers of a thousand ships,
> Who learned to love thy hidden name,
> And love the music on thy lips.
>
> And some, who thought to build thy pyre,
> And on its ruin rear a throne,
> Have loved to sit around thy fire
> And count thy saddest songs their own.

Significantly, over the sectarian tensions of early-twentieth-century Ireland, the poem asserts the hybridizing history of Irish culture, noting how the generations of settlers, conquerors, and immigrants became Irish and loved to "count thy saddest songs their own." The second half of the poem further links these various lovers of Eire, who "love the music on thy lips," with another such group, Irish exiles, such as Cousins, around the world:

> And sons of thine, who broke love's bands
> To seek a fabled, far-off shore,
> Grope through the world with aching hands,
> And hunger for thee evermore.
>
> For, though thy sorrows may not cease,
> Though, blessing, thou art still unblest,
> Thou hast for men a gift of peace,
> O daughter of divine unrest!
>
> (1940, 11)

As this poem alludes, for seekers like Cousins, the Orient represented "a fabled, far-off shore," as Ireland had to the "sailers of a thousand ships." Unlike Anglo-French Orientalists, Cousins sought to uncover a "gift of peace" in this ancient Asian-European culture.

By resurrecting an Aryan culture, he asserted that an international and enlightened "brotherhood" would emerge. In promoting indigenous culture, Cousins was also promulgating the goals of European racial discourse and Orientalist Theosophy, which paved the way for—as Viswanathan argues—other discourses of racial and cultural superiority as well as decolonialization (see her recent essay "Spirituality, Internationalism, and Decolonization: James Cousins, the 'Irish Poet from India' " [2003]). Viswanathan also distinguishes Cousins's work from Besant's. Besant was clearly aware of the machinations of Empire and once articulated the cultural colonization process as: "The genius of the Empire is to make every nation that you conquer feel that you bring them into the Imperial Family, that they and you from that time forward are brothers" (qtd. in Viswanathan 1998, 195). Though Cousins's anticolonialism differed in degrees from Besant's, his racialism illustrates the political liminality of Irish Orientalism: subversive in intent, yet often strategically complicit within the overarching discourse.

Cousins was actually attempting to unify these cultures in opposition to European colonialism and materialism, as Viswanathan notes: "[Cousins] found himself drawn to the larger project of establishing the common foundations of Irish–Indian culture as the first step toward the overthrow of colonial rule in both countries" (205). The Cousinses' ideas on suffrage and revivalism often differed markedly with Besant's, as they repeatedly imply in *We Two Together*. Indeed, Besant publicly fired James Cousins from *New India* under the watchful eye of the British authorities, who had previously jailed Besant for sedition. Not fitting Cousins within the discourse of Irish Orientalism, Viswanathan primarily highlights Cousins's complicity with the narrative of racial hierarchy, which, she effectively argues, further paved the way for the establishment of India's place in the British Commonwealth.

As a Theosophist and revivalist, Cousins repeatedly sought to "discover" Asia's essential truth and locate the "Real India"—a project not entirely dissimilar to Anglo-French Orientalists or nativists anywhere. This task resembled the old rehearsal of colonialist narratives of the mystical Orient, mapping the "real India" through Aryan and Vedantic Hinduism (see Richard King's observations in *Orientalism and Religion* [1999]). But it had other roots in Irish culture, where the Orient long signified a source of difference for Irish culture in opposition to British hegemony. Still, such essentialism spurred nativist quests for "the Hidden Ireland" and reactionary isolation in postindependence Ireland. Cousins's Indo-Irish works promoted an autoexoticism that in twentieth-century Ireland led to the reification of "cozy homesteads" in a stifling postcolonial nativism, as many others have noted. But similarities do not make these narratives and cultural processes the same. Cousins assiduously promoted native cultural formations and activities over foreign ones and worked to develop actual political ties between Ireland and India, even lobbying De Valera at one point on Indian and international politics. Cousins opposed British stereotypes and attacked colonial images of primitive cultures. Uniting the cultural revivals in Ireland and India functioned as an element in Cousins's decolonizing strategy: unify the colonized "periphery" as a way of avoiding the center, and chart the resistant cultural circumference of "peripheral" cultures.

The Theosophical Society, with Annie Besant as its head, was responsible for James and Margaret Cousins coming to India, and Theosophy influenced them throughout their lives. Any evaluation of their writings and activism, however, should not be limited to their Theosophical work. Not only did Cousins bring a different agenda than Besant, Olcott, Judge, or Blavatsky to Theosophy, but both he and Margaret did not remain entirely within the movement as these leaders did, nor is his memory treasured in the Theosophical Society, which has not reprinted his works. Though he continued to give speeches to Theosophical groups and do work for Theosophical institutions throughout his life, his own cultural and literary activities took precedence (as did Margaret Cousins's political organizing) over recruiting for and building the Theosophical Society. Anne Taylor's biography of Besant describes Cousins in the light that Besant saw him when he came to India, that is, as "a 32-year-old Belfast man [he was actually 42 in 1915] who was more at home in Dublin where, as poet, he ranked next to Yeats and AE [a certain exaggeration]. He joined the Theosophical Society in 1902, excited by the idea that Ireland was to play a leading role in Europe's spiritual regeneration" (1992, 301). Though Taylor's picture of Cousins has some inaccuracies, her impression of his sense of Ireland's future is on target. Like James Stephens, Yeats, AE, and many other Irish cultural nationalists, he never let go of the sense of Ireland's destiny, the role "Ireland was to play" in reinvigorating the spirit of Europe and, indeed, the world. Much like the projections of zealous Orientalists, preparing the West for Eastern mystical enlightenment, such a spiritual program has not achieved its regenerative and quasi-apocalyptic missionary ideals. For Cousins, being Irish in India meant having a natural affinity with Indian culture and working against the aims of the British Empire, an identity that repeatedly landed him and Margaret (more often) in trouble with the British Raj. While Besant (herself claiming an Irish–English identity) began to work in a more concentrated fashion for Indian civil and political rights in 1913, she only worked to upgrade India's status within the British Empire to the classification of dominion. Clashing with Besant's placating perspective of the imperial family, Cousins lost his job at *New India* by voicing his support of Irish nationalism and Indian self-reliance.

New India

In 1915 in Madras, Cousins became the literary editor on the staff of *New India,* a Theosophical newspaper run by Annie Besant. Cousins used his position there primarily to promote Indian revivalism but also to write about Irish issues, and their applicability to the Indian situation as a nascent modern nation. But his voice was not the first at the paper making such connections, based on ideas of a shared sensibility within the British Empire. Other articles detailing Irish history had previously appeared in *New India;* for instance, Pestanji Dorabji Khandalavala's "Irish Trouble: A Tableau of Events" describes Ireland's Catholic population as "a proscribed and outcast race" (Mar. 23, 1916, 13). Cousins's comparisons between Ireland and India, however, were more explicit. An excerpt from a typical early article by Cousins demonstrates how he promoted his cross-colonial program and his nonsectarian ideals. On April 22, 1916, his article "A Plea for an Indian Musical Festival" welcomed the "call for an All-India Musical Congress," especially one that would treat Indian music "as a National asset." Using examples from Celtic music festivals, he indicated the nonsectarian unity that such festivals inspired in Ireland:

> I take the liberty of suggesting to the promoters of the All-India Musical Confer-ence the necessity for keeping the theoretical and practical sides of Indian music in vital touch, and I make the further suggestion that this might be done by instituting some form of the Irish or Welsh National Music Festivals, which include both the talking department of a Conference, and practical performance. The Irish festival, with which I am best acquainted, began as an annual competition in the Irish capi-tal. In a few years it had become an event of National pride and importance. It united in the service of the Nation's higher life rival elements that had hitherto only known one another through distorted distances. Catholic and Protestant singers and choirs and players vied with one another in artistic enthusiasm, and local festi-vals were the natural result, with their beneficent influence on the whole country's life. . . . The vivid memory of the exaltation and unification which the National Festival brought to Ireland, and of individuals whom I watched growing into splen-did executants and fine composers, and all with a keen sense of "Ireland," compels me to urge the consideration of such a scheme on those who have at heart the fos-tering of the musical art as one of the highest expressions of the Genius of India. (10)

Because the festivals inspired an "exaltation and unification" across religious divides of an Irish national spirit, Cousins argues that an Indian one could also help coalesce the "Genius of India" and build a broader cultural nationalism. Along with such ar-guments, Cousins advocated reforms in Indian education to promote native arts, history, and language, and he vigorously promoted the cooperative movement, which AE and Horace Plunkett had tirelessly developed in Ireland and England. Rabindranath Tagore even asked for Cousins's help in establishing cooperatives in 1923 or 1924, asking Cousins in a letter to "let us know how far its methods can be adapted to our Indian condition" (Sl. 1).[2] On May 3, 1916, in an article titled "The Art of Co-operation by an Irish Co-operator," Cousins makes another explicit comparison between the anticolonial movements that boycotted English manufac-ture: "The *Swadeshi* movement in India and the *Sinn Fein* movement in Ireland, apart from their political significances, are in essence practical co-operation" (9). In general, the politics of the paper focused on Indian issues and advocated Indian Home Rule, but not independence, the aim of both Swadeshi and Sinn Féin.

Irish nationalism had repeatedly served as a model for Indian nationalists (as his-torians such as Christopher Bayly, Michael Silvestri, and H. V. Brasted have docu-mented), and the political implications of his comments would have been clear to

Cousins's audience. Cousins's purpose, however, was not simply nationalistic; throughout his life in India, he worked to guard and strengthen Indian culture against the presumption of European superiority that accompanied the projects of British imperialism and European missionary work. He repeatedly pointed to Ireland and the Irish Revival as a model for India but not because he saw Ireland as superior, but because it had similar struggles. All of his work—journalistic, educational, literary, critical—was charged with this vision of cultural syncretism, or *samadarsana*.

At *New India,* the British governor had already pressured Besant to tone down the Home Rule agenda, and after Cousins joined the editorial staff, the pressure increased. The following year, the Anglophile press tagged Cousins as a nationalist provocateur, following his series of editorials eulogizing and praising the leaders of the Irish Easter Rising. His first article on the Rising, "The Irish Disturbances," was also printed on May 3, 1916, and began with the following interpolation: "LOVERS OF THE SACRED CAUSE OF LIBERTY the world over will read with something deeper than sorrow the account which we publish today of the outbreak of disturbances in Ireland." The opening phrase resounded like a call or a declaration and drew immediate attention in Madras. But it was the author's highlighting his personal connections with the rebels in addition to his implication that such troubles existed "the world over" that raised fear and outrage in British circles. Cousins commented in that first article that he did not condone the violence of the rebels and only supported the Home Rule movement, but he also offered the nationalists generous understanding:

> [W]hile we deplore it, we cannot shirk the plain truth that the responsibility for the tragedy lies at the doors of others than those who have borne or will bear the penalty. The outbreak is simply and solely the reaction of a quick and proud race to the vacillation and ineptitude in regard to the passing of the Home Rule Bill displayed by the Liberal Government. . . . [T]he lesson of history has been lost on the ruling caste, that frankness and generosity are the way to love and loyalty, while prevarication and shuffling are the parents of revolt. (8)

Sympathizing with the rebels, he blamed Britain and the imperial "ruling caste" (a phrase with a particular resonance in British India) for the rebellion. His emotional response as an Irish immigrant in India to the rebellion—"something deeper than sorrow"—stirred anticolonial sentiment, but, even more so, his portraits of physical-force nationalists disturbed the imperial hornet's nest.

His miniessays spanned a week and focused on Cousins's personal connections with the leaders of the uprising, relaying anecdotes about their ideals, personalities, and activities. His first tribute on May 4 commented on Countess Constance

Markievicz, Padraic Pearse, and James Connolly. Over the course of the next few days, he continued to note something about all of the executed or jailed leaders, but after the initial uproar, the pieces became more abbreviated. Overall, he humanized, instead of demonized, the leaders of the rebellion, just as the reports of their executions came out. He noted that these figures bridged the many subcultures of Irish society, revealing the "diversity in unity" of Ireland. Because these pieces have never been reprinted after their initial publication in the Madras (now Chennai) press, I quote, at length, sections from the first article on Markievicz, Pearse, and Connolly:

> The three persons named in the cables telling of the political uprising in Ireland are typical in their diversity in unity, of the democratising influence that a struggle for ideals brings with it. In my sixteen years' residence in Dublin in active participation in the literary renaissance, I touched every phase of the multifarious activities that made life in Ireland such an enchantment up to the settling in of a degenerate tendency some five years ago, and I naturally came in contact with the three leaders named.
>
> Constance Markievicz
> I first met Countess Markievicz on the committee of the Theatre of Ireland of which I was treasurer. Notwithstanding her name, she is a representative of the English colonisation that became "more Irish than the Irish themselves." Her family name is Gore-Booth, and her brother, Sir Jocelyn, owns about forty thousand acres of land in the magical district of County Sligo. It was while studying painting in, I think, Paris, that she met Count Markievicz, a painter nobleman of Poland, who married her. She and her husband have been the promoters of a Repertory Theatre in Dublin, and have written several plays. She also formed an independent Irish Corps of his "Boy Scouts," and in the strike in Dublin a couple of years ago she was unremitting in her labours to feed and clothe the wives and children of the strikers. Countess Markieviez stands for the aristocracy of Ireland. She is one of the few who have realised their obligation to the country and tried to fulfil it. I do not know in what way she has become entangled in the present upheaval, but I do know that if all of her class had endeavoured to serve Ireland as she did, in the years when I knew her prior to my leaving Ireland, the present lamentable event could not possibly have transpired.

For Cousins, Markievicz represents an elite hybrid caste in Irish society in a nonsectarian uprising; notably, he does not mention her religion, nor the religion of any of the leaders. In the next passage he relays an event in which Padraic Pearse had a difference with priests, but he does not mention Pearse's passionate Catholicism. Cousins, rather, emphasizes the connection between cultural work and nationalist politics in such passages. Coincidentally, as literary editor he had just printed a poem by Markievicz's sister Eva Gore-Booth the previous day; under his editorship, the cultural connections between literature, theater, education, language, and nationalism appear manifold.

Patrick Pearse

I met Patrick H. Pearse also in dramatic circles, and ultimately associated myself with him in educational work in a school that he ran on much the same lines as Tagore's School at Bolpure. His ideals in education were of the finest kind. His pupils got up plays in Irish and English, and he himself, one of the best scholars in the Irish language and literature, has translated much out of the heart of Ireland. My last meeting with him was "real Irish." A number of leaders of the Gaelic League had come to Clifden, in county Galway, near which I was staying on a holiday, to hold a meeting in support of the language movement. I found them in the blues because the local priest had forbidden them the use of the Parish Hall. I suggested their imitating the women suffragists and speaking from their motor in the market-place; but they would not go against the priest. I found, however, that they would willingly have a meeting beyond the local priest's province, and I set off on my cycle through my own parish and called up every human being I could find. When I got back to the cross-roads that I had arranged, I found two motor-cars surrounded by a delighted crowd. The meeting was in full swing. The people were delighted, and Pearse made what was said to be a splendid speech in "sweet Irish." The scene was beautiful beyond words. The serrated group of the Twelve Bens was purple in the setting sun. The sun itself was going down in golden magnificence across the Atlantic. Around us were bogs, and little farms, white roads, and all the hints of kindliness that are the characteristic of rural Ireland looking out of clear eyes and bubbling on friendly lips. It is, I doubt not, the touching of scenes like this, the living in an atmosphere of a native culture that is as old as the culture of Greece, and as living as the newest discovery, that has formed part of the driving force that has sent him to the supreme hazard in the cause of his beloved land. He stands for the "intellectual" class in Ireland which has not yet got over the bitter memory of centuries when the scaffold was the doom of those who sought for learning, and chains and banishment the reward of patriotism.

Cousins underscores the link between Pearse's cultural nationalism with his role as insurrectionary. Having Pearse "stand for the 'intellectual' class," he compares Pearse's school with the newly founded Santiniketan in West Bengal, which Tagore had established with his Nobel Prize money (an award that came after Yeats's endorsement). The applicability of Pearse's work to this famous Indian one would have been clear to *New India*'s readers, as would all of Cousins's allegorical readings of these rebels. The last section, on James Connolly, evokes images of an international suffrage movement and labor struggle while presenting Connolly symbolically.

James Connolly

James Connolly, the labour leader, is the very antithesis physically and mentally of the others. He is a Donegal Ulsterman, somewhat stout and small; deliberate and unrhetorical in speech. I met him frequently when the suffrage movement arose in Ireland, and the more thinking section of organised labour, including Connolly, worked with the women. Something of the epicure in me was repelled by a certain commonplaceness in his appearance; but I came ultimately to value highly the clarity and humanity of his heart, qualities which are shining through every page of his splendid book Labour in Irish History. Although his supreme devotion was to his beloved working-class, he was absolutely straight when the greatest of woman suffrage was presented to him. Would to God John Redmond had been the same, for then the treason to the sacred cause of human freedom that he perpetrated would not have permitted the present tragedy. James Connolly stands for the Irish people, shrewd, kindly, fearless, devoted, ready to lead or follow for an ideal, and totally regardless of little standards of gain or loss.

As in the two previous passages, Connolly "stands" for a distinct segment of the population: this time the masses, who are therefore motivated by national idealism. Throughout the pieces, Cousins refers to the rebellion as a tragedy, not as an insurrection and not as a piece of resolute wickedness on the part of the Irish rebels, as papers across Britain and Ireland had been doing. The Marxist implications of treating Connolly as a representative of the people was risky enough, but his closing remarks show his understanding and make his Irish-Indian analogies even more poignant.

In the time of trial of these my comrades of years gone by, my heart goes out to them in unspeakable love, and with something of a great exultation that there are still those who are not afraid to die for Ireland. Something temperamental and something arising out of a wider view of life than theirs, makes it impossible for me to give assent to specific acts that will bring down on them the dire force of unscrupulous power. My destiny is merely to live for her—to bear something of her geniality, her waywardness perhaps, her joy in beauty, her search for truth, into other lands.

I salute you, sisters and brothers of our Divine Mother land in the spirit of devotion though in acts far removed. If I cannot see eye to eye with you, I can see through you: if I cannot approve, I can at least offer you the gift of understanding. (May 4, 1916, 6)

This sympathetic portrayal of the Rising is personalized and treats these leaders as clear symbols—and as in an allegory, the meaning may be transposed onto another place and situation: India. Although he does not "assent to specific acts," he clearly implies who is the in the wrong and in whose hands "unscrupulous power" exists.

Significantly, in the closing lines, he refers to Ireland as "Divine Mother," a phrase that had unmistakable parallels with "Mother India" at the time. Such Irish-Indian analogies are at the heart of Cousins's cross-colonialism.

Cousins notes that his own "destiny" was "to live for her" and to bear attributes of Ireland—genial, wayward, joyful, searching—"into other lands"; clearly, the Indian reader could read cross-colonially and easily compare leaders such as Gurudev (Tagore), the Mahatma (Gandhi), and Bose (Subchandra) with these leaders. The affinities existing between these ends of the Empire existed as more than an allegorical exercise for his readers, however; the Irish figures stood for a common struggle. Moreover, his admission of "love" for these rebels and his "exultation" that "there are still those who are not afraid to die for Ireland" rings as a clear endorsement of, if not their rebellious actions, their rebellious spirit.

Such an interpretation, at least, existed in British and Anglocentric circles. Another newspaper, the Raj-supported *Madras Mail,* responded immediately by condemning Cousins's articles, suggesting that his articles were poisonous, that he wrote as a provocateur, and that his "private emotions" revealed clear sympathies with the rebels.[3] In a counterresponse, Besant printed a rebuttal on May 6, along with a somewhat convoluted defense from Cousins. Besant's angry tone belies her attempt to reframe the issue around Indian Home Rule:

> The *Mail,* in its virulent hatred of all who are in favour of Home Rule for India, never loses an opportunity of using its poison-fang on *New India.* We accept it as a compliment. But it should try not to misquote in its efforts to malign. Mr. James H. Cousins, writing under his own name, gave some account of his personal acquaintance with the leaders in what he called "the present lamentable event" in Ireland; he quite plainly expressed his dissent from their action, and said he could not approve their acts, but wrote of his love for "these my comrades of years gone by" *in other movements.* The *Mail,* with its instinct to strike at the fallen and its incapacity for understanding a chivalrous word for old friends in their hour of defeat, leaves out the words "of years gone by" and puts in brackets after the word, "comrades," "the leaders of the Irish rebellion." This dastardly blow is worthy of the *Madras Mail* of to-day, fallen from its once high position of fairness and honour. The editorial opinion was plainly given in our issue of May 3rd. The outbreak was foolish and criminal, the result of desperation, as former similar outbreaks had been. (9)

Besant makes plain the difference between the Irish and Indian situations by stressing that Cousins wrote of *"other movements"*—not Indian Home Rule or the possible consequences of not achieving it. Other articles in the paper that week emphasized Besant's position. For example, on May 8, an article appeared titled "Mrs. Besant on Violence and Home Rule: Report that Was Suppressed," which noted: "Mrs. Besant said that she has been convinced of the necessity of the two countries [India and Britain] remaining together all along from the moment she landed in this country in 1893" (6). Cousins continued to write his reports of the leaders but in a markedly toned-down fashion. His denial of supporting the rebels followed Besant's piece on the same day, May 6, and clearly echoed her argument. Still, he does not condemn the insurrection. She introduces his comments as such: "We had written our note on [the] shameful paragraph in the *Madras Mail* before receiving the following from Mr. James H. Cousins, but it is fair to let him speak for himself. He writes:"

> Your contemporary the *Madras Mail* gives some words of mine from *New India* the questionable distinction of attention. It does so by a method that I, a journalist of nearly a quarter of a century's experience in Ireland and England, can only describe as unworthy of a great office. It inserts a sentence in brackets in lieu of several words of mine, and omits all that follows the quotation that it makes. Thus it endeavours to give a meaning to my words which no person who was not on the hunt to get any chance of a blow, fair or foul, at the work of *New India* would stoop to insinu-ate. I referred to those whom I knew in the list of arrested leaders as "my comrades *in years gone by.*" Your mean contemporary omits the words in italics. It also omits my statement that I cannot approve of what they have done, and so tries to distil something "poisonous" out of a human being's recognition of the spirit of sacrifice for a patriotic ideal, even though it is misguided and futile. Had my destiny kept me at home, I should have strained every nerve to hold them back—though, indeed, I would hardly have been made aware of the matter. [S]ince my voice and pen were always against violence, and my comradeship with them—over three years ago, when no one would have dreamed of such a contingency—was outside the politi-cal movement. Others of my "comrades in years gone by" in the same literary and social circles, have given their lives in the trenches of Flanders in the cause of the Al-lies. They, too, have been ready "to die for Ireland" because they believed that their service would bring nearer the fulfillment of the hope that stands on the British Statute Books, signed by the King. To them too, I would offer my affection but, then, the *Madras Mail* is not interested in my "private emotions," unless their ex-pression can give its ghoulish brain something to twist into a misrepresentation.

Cousins's counterresponse expresses his surprise at the attention his piece has caused. It had invoked a much larger discourse. After noting (consciously or not) that one could receive "a blow, fair or foul" at *New India,* Cousins reasserts his non-violent perspective, something that also had a growing resonance in 1916 through the Indian concept of ahimsa. He also defends his "recognition of the spirit of sac-rifice for a patriotic ideal." He attempts to distance himself from physical-force Irish nationalism, however, with reference to Ireland's "sacrifice" for the Allies in the European war—a note rarely sounded by Irish nationalists (then or today), who opposed Irish participation and even sought aid from Germany during World War I.

New India had repeatedly highlighted Irish and Indian involvement in the war effort during this period (Besant had been asked by the Madras governor to present the war in a good light [Taylor 1992, 301]).[4] Just prior to news of the reporting of the news of the Easter Rising on May 3, Cousins had reprinted Eva Gore-Booth's poem from the Herald (London) titled "Conscientious Objectors (after a Military Tribunal)," which certainly did not promote honorable deaths in the Great War. Rather, it stressed how these conscientious objectors stood bravely at their execution:

> Before six ignorant men and blind,
> Reckless they rent aside
> The Veil of Isis in the mind. . . .
> Men say they shirked, and lied.
> (1916, 13)[5]

Clearly, New India's promotion of the war effort did not go far enough to quell suspicions of Irish or Indian nationalist sympathies. After the paper was officially charged with "exciting[,] or attempting to excite hatred, contempt or disaffection" in Madras (New India, Oct. 20, 1916, 3), Besant fired Cousins as a way to appease critics.

Partly as a result of Cousins's articles, Besant had to appear before the governor of Madras in order to continue publication of New India. Anne Taylor, a Besant biographer, comments on how the Cousinses were perceived by Governor Pentland and the Raj in general: "The Government of Madras suspected him of links to the Irish trade union activist James Larkin. Almost equally disturbing to those in charge of public order was Cousins's wife Margaret, who . . . was a militant suffragette, a veteran of the hunger strike, who had spent time in Holloway Gaol for throwing bits of flowerpot at the windows of 10 Downing Street, and in Mountjoy Prison for a similar assault on Dublin Castle." Fearing the influence of Besant and her Irish colleagues, in 1915 Pentland had requested permission from the viceroy, Lord Hardinge, to deport Besant for her publishing New India and Commonweal. Taylor continues:

> The strenuous campaign she was conducting through the Commonweal and New India, for what she now referred to as Home Rule, made her an All India problem, he ventured optimistically. Hardinge disagreed; her nuisance factor was confined to Madras, whose Government had the necessary means of restraining her; he recommended Pentland use the Press Act against New India. Under this a newspaper could be required to deposit large sums of money as a guarantee of good behaviour.[6] Pent-

land hesitated, fearing that it would only enhance Besant's standing at the forth-coming Indian National Congress. He tried to remonstrate with her instead. She was delighted at the opportunity of expressing defiance to his face. "I told the Lord Pentland that I would work with him so far as the War was concerned, but in those matters where I disagreed with him I should have to speak out, and I left him say-ing . . . whether he stopped the paper or interned me, I should keep on along the lines I had marked out because I thought that necessary for the well-being of Em-pire." (1992, 301)

Cousins's article had caused a "storm of rage" in British circles, and Taylor notes that Besant felt "obliged" to dismiss him (302). Besant worked for Indian Home Rule at the time, not for Indian independence; the paper had to reflect this fact. In Besant's own words, "*New India* stands for Indian self government within the Em-pire" (301). Cousins, with his Indo-Irish nationalist insinuations, had become a clear political liability.

The Irish rebellion may have disturbed the British Raj more than it enthused Indian nationalists. The "distinction of attention" that Cousins's pieces received was greater than many other published arguments of Indian independence at the time. Although Cousins did not explicitly recommend any course of action for In-dians, his words resonated as allegory, in part because of the existing discourse of Irish-Indian affinities. Readers generated even more analogies than the ones Cousins supplied. While *New India* attempted to amplify Irish participation in the First World War and in the British Empire (as unionists long have noted), the more spectacularly emotional discourse of Irish nationalism, with its ancient grudges and insurrectionary threat, unmistakably supplanted the narrative of Irish involvement in Empire. Likewise, for the Anglo-Indian audience, narratives of Irish and Indian affinities rang clearly and sounded dangerous. This ancient affinity, along with fears in the Raj of the disintegration of Empire, resurfaces almost atavistically within the discourse of Irish nationalism, suggesting cross-colonial ties. At the time, Irish na-tionalists were fantastically imagined to have clandestine ties to the distant East, as demonstrated in the memoirs of "Colonel Standfast," W. A. Tilney, the British of-ficer who claimed to have been taken captive by Mongols in western Ireland.[7] The fear that Ireland would "lead" other colonies into decolonizing movements ap-peared as a distinct possibility and, in many respects, proved an apt forecast.

Celticist Roots

The Cousinses' joint autobiography, or "duo-autobiography," *We Two Together*, tells how the couple attempted to manifest their ideals in their living. James Cousins was born in Belfast in 1873 to a Protestant family of what he saw as a racially mixed ancestry of the British Isles: English, Irish, Scottish, Welsh, and Huguenot. Cousins viewed his "ancestral blend" as the origin of his predisposition toward cultural synthesis in his life and work: "It may be true, as Gibbon suggested in his autobiography that we 'have lived in the persons of our forefathers,' not to mention our foremothers. But I have a suspicion that . . . my forebears, with what they had distilled from tradition and environment, came to live in me, and brought with them the temperamental burden of five nations" (Cousins and Cousins 1950, 3). As an adult, he viewed himself as an inheritor of multiple traditions in the British Isles, but his affinities to Ireland and his "Celtic heritage" were the strongest. A reading of the stereotypes of his racial blend, which Cousins certainly encouraged, is uncritically relayed in a recent study of Cousins by a supporter of Theosophy, D. K. Chatterjee, *James Henry Cousins: A Study of His Works in the Light of the Theosophical Movement in India and the West* (1994): "Thus Cousins inherited the qualities of the Celtic imagination from his mother and the practical Anglo-Saxon ability of organization through his father" (18–19). Although he did not advocate any hierarchical structure of the races, the concept of race always presupposes that such distinctions exist. Moreover, Cousins, as a European in India, certainly received the benefits of white-skin privileges. This aspect of his work has been rightly pointed out, although the criticisms have not always engendered greater understandings.

David Burleigh's 1993 essay "Rumours of the Infinite: An Irish Poet in Japan," for instance, criticizes Cousins's comments on race:

> "Race tradition" is a concept that is central to Cousins' thought, and there are several mentions of it in *The New Japan*. Earlier in life the poet had learnt, from Mrs. Besant, about "a long process of racial and cultural evolution out of which Ireland was ultimately to emerge as the spiritual mentor of Europe, even as India had long ago been to Asia." . . . Cousins' strongly held convictions with regard to racial and sexual equality, and his efforts to achieve things, remain wholly admirable still. But his refusal to modify his notions about "race tradition" even after World War II [in actuality, *The New Japan* was published in 1923], means that some passages in his writings are less easily acceptable today. His spiritual identification is with the Celtic school of Yeats and AE, his contemporaries in Ireland. . . . He seems unaware in this ascription that, as an Ulster Protetant [*sic*], he is very likely not of Celtic stock or origin, but he was seldom troubled by doubts or contradictions of this kind. (30)

As we have seen, however, Cousins actually had done some thinking on the point of his own Celtic inheritance. Moreover, in *The New Japan*, Cousins, in noting a "symbol of race superiority" immediately adds in a parenthetical remark, "(for that dangerous stupidity has been eradicated from my nature for this and all future incarnations)" (1923, 60). Also when discussing race, Cousins often included the word *culture* as a complementary, if not entirely synonymous, term, as in the passage cited by Burleigh ("a long process of racial and cultural evolution").

For Cousins, culture, "race," family, occupation, and environment were the primary determinants of an individual's outlook and social perception. As a young man, Cousins apprenticed and worked in a number of trades (as a pawnbroker, events promoter, office clerk, correspondent clerk for a coal importer, private secretary and speechwriter for Belfast's lord mayor, shorthand teacher, journalist, and shipping clerk) before he was drawn to the literary and cultural revival in Dublin and to the nationalist and suffragist causes. The main elements of his Protestant working-class identity[8] were formed before he embraced the cultural and political goals of the Celtic Revival. He notes that he had been brought up within the ideology of Protestant white supremacy and Empire. Although he later recognized such ideological positions as spurious, as an eighteen year old he did not know how to take them: "A young minister became famous for the pulpit innovation of quoting poems by somebody called Kipling, who was apparently a very superior man, as he stood up for our Empire, and gave reasons why we should put a shilling each year on the collecting card for Foreign Missions and particularly for taking the light to the darkness of the heathen in India. But these things did not touch anything inside me. I was feeling blindly and without guidance" (Cousins and Cousins 1950, 14). His accounts of his childhood often focus on his early awareness of the politics of Empire and sectarianism in Ireland and emphasize his dislike for them. In *The Faith of the Artist* (1941) he further explains how as a young man he recognized the prejudiced positions of nationalist and Unionist politics:

> When I was a boy in north Ireland, the term Nationalist was one of the most common on the platform and in the press. In my environment, fifty years ago, in Protestant Ulster, a Nationalist was (I was taught) a very wicked person, who wanted Ireland to be denied the benefit of being governed by a parliament in England, which knew nothing about Ireland, and was therefore in a position to govern it without prejudice. The slogan of the Nationalist, per contra, was "Ireland, a nation," a self-governing unit expressing a restored traditional culture. The antinationalist slogan was "Home Rule means Rome rule," which recognised the fact that the nation called Irish contained rival religious interests, and differed strongly on the nature of "kingdom come" and the way to alternative destinations therein. Early in my conscious life I discovered that Nationalism and its reverse were only shallowly rooted in reality: that they were mental abstractions, theories of government held by particular groups within a nation. (80)

The presence of sectarian politics, he implies, allowed him to recognize their limitations later in life. For him, nationalism in itself was not a solution to Ireland's "troubles" and problems in Empire; these were "theories of government" that could not address the problems of cultural and spiritual identity.

Along with the specific narratives of imperialism, he groups sectarian prejudices, noting in *We Two Together* that in Northern Ireland, sectarian differences pervaded even his childhood understanding of good and evil: "My mother was what
was believed to be a 'good Christian,' and consigned all Popish superstitions and
those who believed in them to 'the bad place.' " When Cousins discovered Theosophy for himself, he believed he had found a way to resolve these sectarian and imperial narratives and counter distrust and uncritical thinking. Like Yeats and
Stephens, Cousins's attraction to the mystical and prophetic was in some ways to
avoid sectarian tensions, which had been linked to the binarism of good and evil,
but it was also a firm belief that a resurgent nonsectarian spiritualism could unite
Irish culture. And, as with Yeats, these beliefs were not wholly imported from
Celticism and Orientalism. "[My mother] had her own private beliefs outside the
strict Wesleyan canon. One belief was prophetic dreams. This faculty I shared with
her; and her symbolical interpretations, though neither of the apocalyptic order
nor derived from penny dream-books, had the curious knack of coming true"
(Cousins and Cousins 1950, 15). As with other Protestant Revivalists—AE and
Yeats in particular—Cousins was drawn to Theosophy and Indian philosophy,
in part, as a way of addressing sectarian dilemmas in modern Ireland. But such
traditions also made sense because they encouraged this domestic Protestant spiritualism from his family. Furthermore, Theosophy had become intellectually fashionable, and its influence in Dublin was not small. William Magee (pseudonym
John Eglinton) notes in *Anglo-Irish Essays* (1918), "[I]n our own day, when so many
of our poets and novelists are agnostics, Theosophists, etc., we know that they have
done a good deal to undermine established religion" (15). Cousins did not see
himself as fashionable or as adopting sensibilities assigned to the Celtic or the Oriental; rather, he believed he was mining a tradition that had been suppressed by the
established religions.

The literary life drew Cousins as a young man, although no one in his family
had much truck with the arts; his father was a "deep-sea merchant" (Denson 1967,
19), and his mother worked at home and claimed to not be a reader of poetry. He
began to put a collection together in the early 1890s and published his first book of
poems, *Ben Madighan and Other Poems,* in 1894. This book was highly derivative
and clearly from a Wesleyan Methodist perspective. Even the author later considered it to be a "dreadfully juvenile book" filled with "unnecessary illustrations, all
but two from stock-blocks [that is, ready-made prints], its notes and footnotes, and
its photo-frontispiece of the author, signature and all, bear witness to an appalling
seriousness" (Cousins and Cousins 1950, 30–31). Nevertheless, it was received
warmly in Belfast, as much because it announced a Protestant voice in literature as
because of any other chord the poetry struck. Cousins admits it had little value as
literature: "The book disturbed no hornets. Rather it aroused much appreciation—
not as poetry, for it had none, . . . but because, in a city in which as far as I then

knew literature was a subject in Queen's College but nowhere else, a writer had apparently arrived, and had lifted the self-respect of the city by transforming the commonplace Cave Hill into the historical and romantic Ben Madighan" (32). The title of the volume reveals how attractive, exotic even, Irish cultural nationalism was becoming to the young poet—Ben Madighan being the Irish name of Cave Hill, which lies outside the center of Belfast near Coleraine. More than anything else about this volume, its centerpiece and title had provoked something in Cousins: "I discovered . . . that my nature responded in profound and inspiring affinity with a native cultural tradition more venerable and attractive than the religious bigotry of my upbringing that had nothing to do with real religion, and the grasping for money and position that had nothing to do with real wealth or eminence" (1941, 83). After this discovery of a Celtic "affinity," Cousins began to study Irish and joined the Belfast chapter of the Gaelic League. Despite such nationalist overtures, he was hailed by the Protestant press as a new poetic genius. With his mild success, Cousins did what a number of other Northern Protestant writers had done before him: he moved to the Ireland's literary capital, Dublin, and embraced the Celtic zeitgeist, to the chagrin of his Belfast supporters.

The same year *Ben Madighan* was published, Cousins read a volume of the new Theosophical and Celtic Revivalist poetry, *Homeward: Songs by the Way,* by the older Northern poet AE. According to Cousins, the book prompted his move to Dublin and transformed his sense of poetry: "I read the little book through in an interval, and went on fire with the realization that immortal poetry had been given to Ireland" (Cousins and Cousins 1950, 33). Padraic Colum comments on Cousins's move to Dublin:

> There were poets in Dublin, and this young Northerner had entered a poetic career, having already published a volume *Ben Madighan and Other Poems.* Moreover, he felt the attraction of the Gaelic Revival that was now at its most fascinating period. He looked with admiration and affection to Sir Samuel Ferguson, the Northern poet who had gone to Gaelic for his material. And in Dublin there was that poet from the North, AE, whose sources were in Theosophical ideas which were of interest to James Cousins. He discovered a Gaelic patronymic and occasionally wrote Cousins as "Mac Oisin." (Denson 1967, 3)

This passage highlights Cousins's youthful enthusiasm and the flimsiness of the au courant Celticism, which nevertheless became an integral aspect of Cousins's overall program: "I did not know what the Spirit of Ireland was; but I suspected that She was neither Catholic nor Protestant, but old enough to have preceded these historical imports to her terrain" (Cousins and Cousins 1950, 42). Like other Revivalists trying to deepen their understanding of ancient Ireland, Cousins was drawn to Theosophy and located Ireland's origins in the Orient.

In Dublin, Cousins became involved with various reform and revival movements, meeting major cultural nationalists of the day, including Yeats, the Fay brothers, Edward Martyn, Lady Gregory, AE, Frederick Ryan, Francis Sheehy-Skeffington, Padraic Colum, Alice Milligan, Maud Gonne, George Moore, James Stephens, James Joyce, Douglas Hyde, and others. Cousins felt part of something momentous, working closely with the Fay brothers; their Irish National Dramatic Company produced his two earliest plays in 1902, *The Sleep of the King* and *The Racing Lug.* The former play translated Celtic legend into a modern and poetical idiom (in the style of AE's and Yeats's symbolic dramas). The latter, which is perhaps one of his strongest works, is set in a Northern Irish fishing village and sympathetically portrays Northern Protestants in a rural setting. It was performed at the opening of the Ulster Literary Theatre in Belfast. *The Racing Lug* is a tragedy about deaths at sea, and its plot and poetic realism have prompted critics to name it as a precursor to Synge's *Riders to the Sea* (1905). Cousins's future as a playwright in Ireland, however, was soon curtailed when Yeats closed the ranks of the Dublin revivalist theater groups. Yeats had liked then disliked Cousins's plays, and soon dismissed him as a hanger-on of AE. Others never saw him as more than a follower of the larger figures in the Revival; George Moore describes him in *Vale,* the third volume of *Hail and Farewell,* as one of "AE's Canaries" (Moore 1914, 169). Although Cousins remained very close to AE, he always felt some distance between Yeats and himself, as William Dumbleton notes: "Of *The Sleep of the King,* Yeats said to Cousins, 'Splendid, my boy, splendid. Beautiful verse beautifully spoken by native actors. Just what we wanted.' The last sentence with its patronizing air, gave the company a twinge, Cousins felt, with its 'suggestion that we were contributory to him and not he to us' " (1980, 23). Cousins's later realistic comedy *Sold* did not fair well in the Dublin theater world and signaled the end of his literary career in Ireland. Significantly, he is primarily remembered in Ireland as a Theosophical dilettante and poetaster, as the man Yeats drove out, and as the butt of jokes by James Joyce, made after he had stayed as a guest in the Cousinses' home in Sandymount, before he moved to the famous Martello Tower.[9]

In 1903 James Cousins married Margaret and not long after turned to teaching in the High School, at which Yeats and Charles Johnston (founder of the first Theosophical Lodge in Dublin) had been pupils, and continued to promote the various forms of the "intellectual radicalism" of the day (as John Wilson Foster puts it), which included spiritualism, vegetarianism, antivivisectionism, anti–imperialist agitation, Irish-language revivalism, as well as supporting the woman suffrage and agricultural cooperative movements.[10] It is worth noting that sensuality and sexuality were considered base desires by Theosophists at the time, particularly by James and Margaret Cousins. Margaret writes that during the first year of her marriage, she "grew white and thin" due to the "problems of adjustment to the revelation . . . [of] the physical basis of sex" (Cousins and Cousins 1950, 108). And, like most

Theosophists, they strove toward chastity.[11] Sensuality and sexuality remained stigmatized in their overarching goals of promoting cultural revivalism. Although James taught literature in Dublin, his main subject became geography. He vigorously applied himself to teaching world geography, critiquing imperial spatial conceptions of Asia and Ireland. He continued to write verse heavily influenced by Swinburne, Shelley, Blake, and, his mentor, AE, through whom he studied the ideas of Blavatsky and Mohini Chatterjee. Both he and Margaret became active in cultural and social reform as they simultaneously began to study Indian philosophy. Margaret notes, "Dr. R.V. Khedkar of Lolhapur, in India, came to our home every Sunday evening of 1906, and often on Wednesday evenings, and read through 'The Bhagavad Gita' with us and a few friends. From his Sanskrit copy, reinforced by various translations, he tried to make us understand the Vedantic philosophy" (105). As with other Celtic Revivalists, the connection between Celticism and Orientalism was treated as part of the path to spiritual selfhood: speculation, mysticism, and creativity became antidotes to rationalism, religion, and sectarianism.

Cousins formed his ideas on cultural revivalism and national awakenings in Dublin with the architects of the Revival. Like AE, he attributes the changes in Irish culture not merely to social and political movements but to a sort of cultural awakening. In explaining these transformations, he quotes AE: "'Nationality . . . was never so strong in Ireland as at the present time. It is beginning to be felt, less as a political movement, than as a spiritual force. It seems to be gathering itself together, joining men, who were hostile before, in a new intellectual fellowship.' . . . This growth was not to be accomplished through creeds and churches, but through the setting free of the divinity that is inherent in every fragment of nature and humanity" (69). Seeing nationality as a spiritual force is a truism of nativism, and, perhaps more so than any literary Celticist except AE, Cousins treated his devotion to Ireland as spiritual vocation. Cousins recognized at a later point how the accompanying provincialism limited his initial understandings of other cultures: "Looking back to this period of my life, I am struck by the very little influence that was felt by my mind from events that were happening outside Ireland and appeared to be regarded as of importance elsewhere. I was not peculiar in this want of resonance" (68–69). Theosophy, despite its more bizarre theories and explanations of reality, offered Cousins a more international perspective than Celticism and Irish nationalism. As Cousins's literary career dissipated and the Revival became more insular, India grew more alluring. In 1908, when James and Margaret officially joined the Theosophical Society, international opportunities opened, especially in India.

The Path to India

Important to their conversion were the Theosophical works and translations of another Irishman, Charles Johnston, the school friend of Yeats who had married a niece of Madame Blavatsky and had written several "translations from the San-skrit," including a pocket abridged edition of the Bhagavad Gita. The fact that Johnston was Irish and had become a significant figure in the Theosophical move-ment encouraged the Cousinses in their Theosophical pursuits, which they took on with the zeal of converts. They recount the process by which Johnston's works came into their hands in their "duo-autobiography," which is filled with accounts of coincidence and pivots on a "dream-order" psychically projected by Madam Blavatsky herself. Their involvement in the Theosophical world soon seemed their destined vocation or, at least, a powerful psychic calling to become the rep-resentatives of a neo-Celtic spiritual sensibility. They were supposed to be the translators of an ancient mystical Celticism—to become what AE called the "in-terpreters." Their neo-Celticism brought them (James in particular) a certain amount of status in Theosophical circles. As their experiences with the Dublin Branch of Psychical Research had taught them, the mysterious, the unknown, and the exotic had cachet.

Their spiritualism was notorious and occasionally ridiculed, but it also seems to have given them a position as occult trendsetters in artistic circles. Like Yeats's wife, George, in the 1920s,[12] but much earlier, Margaret (Gretta) Cousins began to demonstrate an ability to "transmit" automatic writings from mystical beings: "We discovered that Gretta's own hand, when left free from any muscular influence save the slight grip necessary to hold the pencil, was moved in a manner entirely outside her normal volition, and wrote intelligible communications" (116). James also records the numerous visions that Gretta had of "Niav" and other Celtic "god-desses." Significantly, she does not record them in nearly as great of detail and does not mention such psychic phenomena later in life. Like a mystical ham–radio oper-ator, they transposed mysterious messages supposedly picked up from a variety of voices, from American mystics to "a Persian astrologer of many centuries ago" (107), often concerning their own future and their spiritual development. James comments in *We Two Together:* "Among the automatic communications that came through Gretta was a series purporting to be given by an 'American Adept.' The 'Adept' took up the position of teacher to us, with the special intention of devel-oping our intuitions, through which we might reach knowledge of the nature of superconscious life and its denizens. There was, he told Gretta, a group of Adepts connected with India who were higher than his own group, and he would ulti-mately lead us to them" (123). Amid these happenings, which Gretta describes as being of the "spiritually exciting kind" (134), they first met Annie Besant, then the newly instated leader of the Theosophical Society.

At a Theosophical Society convention in England, Besant shook their hands and "expressed pleasure at having someone from Ireland at the Convention": "She loved Ireland, and was thrilled by its future as the spiritual leader of Europe. She concluded the ten-minute interview by ignoring me, putting her hand on Gretta's shoulder, and saying 'Go back to Ireland, my dear, and form a Lodge of The Theosophical Society, and when it is formed I will come and lecture for you' " (126). Shortly thereafter, Besant made James her "Presidential agent" in Ireland and came to lecture in 1909. Later in December 1912, the Cousinses were asked to relocate to India by an English entrepreneur; there James would help "spread the manufacture of reformed foods" with a salary "four times" his teaching salary in the High School (214). In the midst of financial troubles with a cooperative bank (where James was an officer), they grew eager to go to India. Soon, they accepted the offer but got only as far as Liverpool and Garston due to the outbreak of the war. After working on various suffrage and vegetarian causes in England—Margaret was even jailed for a time—a call from Annie Besant came. She wanted James to help with the Theosophical Society's newspaper, *New India,* headquartered in Madras. They accepted and James got out of his obligation to the English entrepreneur. It is not without real significance that their first plan to get to India had been through a business fostered by English colonial rule and along trade routes established by the East India Company. As Cousins knowingly commented in his autobiography, "[W]hen one is intent on going somewhere, one has to take in the intervening stopping-places; and Garston and London lay between Ireland and India" (232). The center of Empire here mediates the interactions between the cultures on the periphery. If we take this process as paradigmatic, or rather recognize the correspondence between the theoretical and the actual, we might note that Besant's Theosophical operations in India might also be a form of imperially sponsored "mediation." Significantly, most opportunities for cultural exchange between Ireland and India were through either Catholic missionary work or British "concerns": mercantile, military, civil, or academic Orientalism.

Although their stay in England was longer than they anticipated, they spent their time in Garston promoting cultural and "reforming activities" (238), often taking platforms to speak on vegetarianism or women's vote or Irish drama, often displaying their "Irish humor" (236). Their time in England apparently prepared them to become comfortable in their new positions as representatives of Ireland, speaking on the Celtic Revival as well as ideas concerning social, political, educational, and cultural reform. If Cousins was not a vital member of the Irish Renaissance, he certainly was regarded as one in India, where his advice on anticolonial cultural renewal was actively sought. Their move to India seemed a culmination of the Orientalist logic of Revivalists, which Yeats summed up with his dictum in the preface to *Certain Noble Plays of Japan,* "Copy the East and live deliberately." William Dumbleton in particular has read his interest in the Orient in opposition to others:

> Yeats and Russell, along with their Irish contemporaries, derived their Eastern interests from afar, or from imported Eastern *gurus.* Cousins, distinctively, made real

his interest. His attention to the East brought him there physically and spiritually, testifying to his strong belief in the reality of his spiritual convictions. It could be said that Russell and Yeats, in the Romantic tradition, longed for, or said they longed for, an immersion in an Eastern religious and artistic pattern of thought and action; but Cousins, singularly, acted. (1980, 27)

Yeats, Stephens, and AE never went to India, and their works more often reflect the broad stereotypes of Anglo-French Orientalism. But Cousins's works are better informed and more accurate in their portrayals of the various Indian cultures.

Cousins belongs to a tradition of Irish emigrants who strayed from official imperial routes. But in many ways, his work could be understood in relation to Irish missionaries and educators.[13] As with the Irish nun Margaret Noble, who changed her name to Sister Nivedita and whose memory is revered in India, Cousins embraced Indian culture instead of attempting to merely transform it along the lines of imperial culture. The editor of a series of books titled *Modern Indian Artists* (published simultaneously in Calcultta, New York, London, and Tokyo), Ordhendra Coomar Gangoly explicitly compares Cousins to Sister Nivedita and her work promoting Indian art in the introduction to a volume, for which Cousins wrote the text:

> In issuing the second volume in this series of studies of Modern Indian Artists we are fortunate in procuring the collaboration of a critic eminently gifted with sympathy and a discriminative insight rare among the every growing circle of students and votaries of Indian Art. If the mantle of the late Sister Nivedita has fallen on anybody it is on the graceful shoulders of Dr. Cousins. And after the passing of that eminent person who "dedicated" [the meaning of] (Nivedita) her life and soul to the study of Indian culture, none has come out to India with greater reverence for the ideals that its stands for, than this poet of the new Irish Renaissance. Through the interpretation of such sympathetic minds the works of modern Indian painters reveal their hidden significance. (Gangoly 1923, unpaginated foreword)

Sister Nivedita, although her stature was much greater, provides an appropriate comparison for Cousins; she worked along similar lines in India as others did in Ireland, promoting both a new nation and an ancient culture. Two of her "Laws of Thought" aphorisms included by Aurobindo Ghose in *The Ideal of the Karmayogin* (1918) (first printed in the *Karmayogin,* no. 36, 1910) reveal part of her thinking: "As a nation, we must lead the culture of the world.""Who is it that will sacrifice and labour and build and struggle till we have grasped and mastered our intellectual heritage? Ourselves. Ourselves. Always ourselves" (68). This last quote echoes the slogan of one of Ireland's emergent political parties at the time, Sinn Féin—"ourselves"—which formed in 1907. It also echoes the famous ballad by Thomas Davis,

"Ourselves Alone" (from which Sinn Féin derived its name), which was first printed in *The Spirit of the Nation* in 1843 and was wildly popular in the second half of the nineteenth century in Ireland where Nivedita grew up as Margaret Noble.

Cousins's writings criticized those individuals who wrote about India without firsthand knowledge (see, for example, his 1918 essay "Ruskin, the Indian Race, and Indian Art"); he recognized how much ideology and emotional prejudice surrounded representations of Asian cultures. Although Cousins consciously worked against English cultural colonialism in India, he never became fluent in any of the indigenous languages, unlike Sister Nivedita who did, having come to India at a younger age. But Cousins's Indian years confirmed an Irish-Indian connection for Indian cultural nationalists such as Rabindranath Tagore. His experience in Ireland gave him a certain amount of authority to comment on issues of Indian culture; he opposed many of the narratives of Orientalism, asserting the sameness between European and Asian cultures and art forms, instead of detailing differences and positing otherness. Many of his essays (and Margaret Cousins's) take European writers to task for their misrepresentations.

Cousins later noted that he imagined himself as an Irish world citizen, a term common in this discourse that harks back to Oliver Goldsmith's pseudo-Oriental letters, *The Citizen of the World*. As the Irishness of Goldsmith and Thomas Moore lent credibility to their interpretation of the Orient, Cousin's mission of spreading cultural revivalism to India was founded upon the supposed shared sensibilities between Celtic and Oriental peoples. Cousins recounts his travels somewhat romantically, making his willing emigration into a story of spiritual exile that moves from the provincial to the international: "I ceased to be a citizen of my particular world—though that world had its own exquisite completeness—and was driven by the winds of destiny on the spiritual adventure of becoming[,] as fully as possible, a world polarized and orbited in a citizen" (Cousins 1932, v-vi). Cousins viewed his life as the "spiritual adventure" and developed a vision of geocultural formation that depended, in Catherine Nash's words, upon "both crude environmental determinism and spiritual essentialism" (1996, 406).[14]

After being dismissed from his position at *New India,* Cousins returned to education; Besant helped get him a job in Madanapalle teaching English at the Theosophical College, where he eventually became principal in 1918. For the next twenty years, he worked in education, lectured, arranged and exhibited Indian art shows, and wrote. These years, certainly his busiest, were also the time when his ideas most developed beyond Theosophy and he made a real contribution to India. When he was leaving *New India,* an article seemingly on him appeared on June 21, 1916, by an English Theosophist, Helen Veale, that echoed his earlier articles calling for reforms in Indian education. In "Educational Progress," Veale notes: "A new-comer to India from the West cannot fail to be struck by the zeal for education now being shewn here, and the great opportunity afforded to reformers along that line to build up a model system, that shall avoid the defects of western education, while uniting its practical efficiency to Indian idealism" (9). Most likely, this zeal had come from Cousins, who embarked on his new task enthusiastically. His broader approach to education, based more on Indian culture, closely followed models initiated by Rabindranath Tagore. Anglocentric models of education were promoted in India at the time, and some advocates of it feared the growing influence of Irish missionaries. Others, such as Charles Harvey, advocated a greater investment in the arts and crafts in India but with the air of a standard Orientalist:"In the West, however, the craftsman is somewhat of an artificial product, the survival of another age, and it is only in eastern countries with their less complex civilisation that in these days we may hope to see him in his natural environment" (1916, n.p.). Not only was Cousins's tone different, his approach was based on geocentric ideals, which advocated both local culture and international cross-fertilization, as his articles in *New India* and many other works suggest.[15]

Cousins and Tagore

Cousins continued to write for multiple Indian newspapers and journals as well as for an audience around the world, and he gave lecture tours outside of the Theosophical circuit. His star was rising, as evinced in his having an essay, "The Play of Brahma," printed on the front page of the *Times Literary Supplement* in 1920 (Cousins and Cousins 1950, 384). In 1922 the Theosophical College closed, and Cousins accepted the position of director at the Brahmavidya Ashrama, or School of Universal Studies, which was greatly influenced by Rabindranath Tagore's ideas on education and his Santiniketan school in the North—Cousins reports that Tagore called their school the "Santiniketan of the South" (342). They remained in contact with Besant, both James and Margaret Cousins participating in her Theosophical Educational Trust, which in 1917 merged with the Society for the Promotion of National Education, and became an official state program, but their contact with her lessened. At the first official meeting of the Board of National Education in Calcutta, Tagore was appointed its first chancellor, and both James and Margaret became senators.

Cousins's friendship with Rabindranath Tagore, unlike that of W. B. Yeats's, lasted for many years—from 1915 until Tagore's death in 1941. As their unpublished letters reveal, Cousins greatly respected "Gurudev" (as Tagore was respectfully and affectionately called), and Tagore had much admiration for Cousins, whom he even nominated for the Nobel Prize in Literature (at Cousins's prompting) in 1934, as a letter dated December 27 indicates (Sl. 63). Their letters cover many topics—translation, agricultural cooperatives, literature, travel abroad, aesthetics, and family losses—but most concern education and plans or operations for their respective schools. In 1925 Tagore even invited Cousins to come help run Santiniketan "for a year or two" as "Principal of our Department of Collegiate Studies," partly because Tagore was going abroad for an extended period in 1926 (Nov. 11, 1925, Sl. 21). In 1918, the year with the most correspondence, their topics ranged enormously. They discussed the possibility of Cousins editing a collection of Tagore's works for Macmillan, which C. F. Andrews had earlier agreed to do and eventually did (May 12, 1918, Sl. 11), as well as Yeats's 1917 marriage to Georgie Hyde Lees. Tagore wrote: "I have got a letter from Yeats in which he confesses to having been married. I wonder what will happen to the fairies with whom he was in speaking term[s]—and also to his wonderful room in Woburn" (June 17, 1918, Sl. 12). Cousins had earlier written an account of Yeats reading Tagore aloud, in which he compared them as "brother-poet[s]" in his *New Ways in English Literature* (1920); he dedicated the book to Tagore (18).[16]

They also sent one another books, and their letters shared insights about the differences between Indian and European literature, as this 1916 note from Tagore illustrates: "When a European says he fully wants to live he does not mean to say he wants to live the life of truth but that it is his wish to live the life of passion—and his literature reflects his desire. It is not light that he wants but conflagration. He consumes himself and his world.—and the present war is the best illustration of that" (Apr. 8, 1916, Sl. 4). Tagore asked advice and critique from Cousins on the translation of one of his poems, praising Cousins as a sympathetic non-English reader of Indian culture, "your mind being at home in India and having the poetic insight" (Feb. 4, 1918, Sl. 9). The poem, "Fugitive," appeared later that year in *New India*.[17] Cousins also noted his poetical kinship with Tagore in a letter dated July 7, 1918, noting that he felt "temperamentally in affinity" with Tagore: "I wrote last afternoon in my tamarind grove a sonnet—which still wants a line to complete it and lo! one of your poems says exactly the same thing. I am heartily glad to come towards you in thought and feeling, even if I stumble along far behind in expression. Next incarnation, I shall attain freedom of expression" (Sl. 33).

Later in the 1930s, Margaret Cousins, with the help of her husband, set about actively promoting Tagore's "Jana Gana Mana," which he had composed in 1911,[18] as a song to unify India. They had it printed, translated, broadcast on the radio, and arranged for schoolchildren to sing it (Sl. 18, 25, 27, 48, 50); on November 6, 1936, Tagore affectionately wrote: "We are fellow-voyagers in the same unchartered Seas and I claim to be a pioneering pilot. Visva-Bharati turned me into a beggar long before you conceived the idea of coming out to the East!! It is hopeful to know that 'Jan-Gan-Man' is getting better known every day and I myself heard it sung to the correct tune in various distant parts of the country. I know I have to feel thankful to Mrs. Cousins for her work in this connection" (Sl. 27). Significantly, the song was adopted in 1950 as the national anthem of India. Cousins's last letters to Tagore before his death reveal the closeness he felt to Tagore:"Hoping we shall have much aspiration and work together in our next incarnation" (Dec. 1940, Sl. 58). Although Tagore was of much greater stature, both felt a kinship, shared ambivalences about popular nationalism, and devoted themselves to India, education, and literature.

Like Tagore, Cousins traveled widely in Asia (lecturing on cultural revivalism, education, and literature) and around the globe—spending full years in Japan, the United States, and continental Europe. But as with Tagore, Cousins spent most of his years from 1915 until his death in 1956 in India. From 1933 to 1938, he served as principal of the new Besant Theosophical College at Mandanapalle, and from 1934 to 1948 he also served as art adviser to the government of Travancore. During the Second World War, the Cousinses stayed in northern India in the foothills of the Himalayas and offered little commentary on the war or much written support of the Allies; rather, they continued to work for Indian independence and culture. Throughout his time in India, Cousins organized a number of important exhibitions and tours of Indian art, about which he wrote numerous essays that praise local art and admonish artists that ape European standards. Also, he continued to write poetry, drama, and criticism—of European and Indian art and culture. Cousins's interest in Indian art in many ways grew more prominent than his dedication to Theosophy. In 1923, he embarked "on a tour of research into the cultural conditions of as much of India as I could cover in a limited time, and into the possibility of founding centres for the encouragement of local art . . . perhaps becoming the means of recognition of artistic and literary 'immortals' " (Cousins and Cousins 1950, 29). This work became the most important to Cousins, second only to his writing. Remarkably similar to Tagore's philosophy and thoughts, Cousins argued strenuously against cultural mimeticism and reactionary nationalism, specifically arguing that Indians should study in their native languages and not copy European standards of taste and culture.

Harmonize and Synthesize

Onto colonial India, Cousins projected Irish tensions—in particular, the tensions of Northern Ireland and Belfast. As in the antisectarian play *Mixed Marriage* (1911), written by St. John Ervine, a fellow Ulsterman who had also been drawn to Dublin to write, sectarian tensions threaten community and the nation in Cousins's literary works. The resolution, when not tragic, typically involves a process of negotiating difference and sameness and, ultimately, reforming the conflict as a syncretic union. That Cousins would posit such Irish themes and concerns onto Indian culture should not be surprising. The early theorist of postcolonialism Frantz Fanon argued a similar point in discussing British colonists in Africa: "The settler makes history and is conscious of making it. And because he constantly refers to the history of his mother country, he clearly indicates that he himself is the extension of that mother country. Thus the history which he writes is not the history of the country which he plunders but the history of his own nation" (1963, 40). A similar process worked for Irish emigrants, both imperial and anticolonial ones, in the British colonies. For Irish settlers like the Cousinses, the history they made and the one they referred to was Ireland's, itself a decolonizing culture. Indeed, Cousins was distinctly aware that he was not British and that his presence in India fundamentally differed from the British presence. Describing a dinner hosted by the British director of public instruction in his autobiography, Cousins reveals his lack of identification with Britain: "It was interesting to touch the official British mind in the place of power in Indian India. I had no antipathy to them as human beings. . . . But my freedom complex resented the circumstances that placed the directing of a peoples' education in the hands of men who were racially, religiously and temperamentally the opposite to all they should be" (Cousins and Cousins 1950, 328). Education, like spirituality, he felt should respond to and emerge from *samadarsana,* promoting cross-colonial and universal values, as well as international, national, and local criteria.

Cousins's representations of the Orient can be usefully read within the field of anticolonial and postcolonization narratives. Discussing the anticolonialist objectives of contemporary film critics, Homi Bhabha notes that "the colonial stereotype is a complex, ambivalent, contradictory mode of representation, as anxious as it is assertive" (1983, 69–70). Robert Young in *White Mythologies* (1989) argues that this point is Bhabha's main insight into colonial and anticolonial discourse: "Colonialism is identified as the discourse which betrays a dissonance implicit in Western knowledge" (146). Many strategies of colonial resistance have historically worked to expose this dissonance in the process of representation, by highlighting the artificial process of representation. But hybrid identities, and the formation of syncretic philosophies to account for them, also attempted to ease the anxieties and mollify the assertiveness of colonial and anticolonial discourse, with varying degrees of success. Working to undo the essentialized cultural differences fostered by Anglo-French Orientalism often becomes a reductive process of positing new essentialized differences to replace the old ones—for example, promoting a spiritual over material philosophy to unify Asian and European spiritual "seekers" against materialist ideologues of colonialism and nationalism. Although many Theosophists were prey to such reductive critiques, such totalizing narratives did not line Cousins's representations and critiques, which attacked stereotypes and focused on developing syncretic possibilities. As Bhabha and others have noted, strategies of "hybridization" work to embody difference in composite representations or syncretic practical identities or both. Moreover, of all of the strategies of resistance Bhabha examines, hybridization seems most akin to Cousins's syncretic perspective, borrowing narratives from both colonizer and colonized.

Any understanding of Cousins's life's contribution to literature and culture, as well as to Orientalism, must recognize his composite identity. This identity is reflected in the latter part of this chapter's title, "James, Seumus, and Jayaram Cousins"—all names that he adopted at various points in his life. But this identity does not reflect the existential crisis of the colonized like the one detailed by Frantz Fanon in *Black Skin, White Masks* (1967)—or what Patrick Hogan terms "alienating hybridity" (2000, 320); for the Irish Orientalist, such a composite identity could be a liberating and strategic advantage. His baptismal name, James Cousins, remained his primary name throughout his life, but after moving to Dublin to participate in the Revival, he translated and signed it Seumas Cuisín and, more grandly, Seumas Mac Óisin. In India, after formally converting to Hinduism (a "reformist" sect of Hinduism) and bathing in the Ganges, he was given the name Jayaram, which he translated as "victory to the light" (Cousins and Cousins 1950, 646). His immersion (such as it was) into Hindu culture reflected his allegiance to India and his desire to promote an indigenous cultural revival. Moreover, this composite or synthetic identity was one that he saw as both national and universal. One commentator on Cousins's cultural writings, Catherine Nash, distinguishes Cousins's identity as such: "While he tried to articulate a form of national identity that could be an alternative to essentialist ideas of nationhood and empty internationalism, he seemed more comfortable with harmonizing cultural differences than with cultural hybridity. However, his own philosophy was a hybrid species with roots in the Western assimilation of colonial cultures through Orientalism and exoticism as well as in genuine deference and respect" (1996, 408). But his writings on cultural revival movements also relied on centuries-old semiotic tropes of Oriental-Celtic affinities, the same that Irish Orientalists had often developed as a starting ground for discovering postcolonization cultural and political similarities.

The King's Wife: A Reading

Cousins brought Celtic narratives into an Indian context. In doing so, he did more than Celtic Revivalists who advocated cultural unity but only merged Orientalist and Irish tropes. Cousins also critiqued both imperialism and nationalism, promoting instead tolerance and syncretism. Informed by Indian folklore, Cousins's poetic drama *The King's Wife* (1919) best illustrates his contribution to both Irish and Indian drama. The play highlights similarities between colonized cultures; it has an Indian story and characters but draws on Irish themes, legends, and devices. Cousins modeled much of the play on his Irish experience, writing in *We Two To-*

gether that much of the play had been "brought from Ireland" (Cousins and Cousins 1950, 384). It echoes Yeats's "Cathleen ni Houlihan" and the jealous lovers in the legends of Deirdre and Conchubar and Etáin and Midir (the last of which Cousins wrote a version in 1922). The play, like the Indian legend from which it borrows, ahistorically links three figures from Indian history. The famous Akbar, a Mogul emperor and a Muslim, lived in the sixteenth century and attempted to create an eclectic religion for the whole of India. The Hindu queen Mirabai lived in the fifteenth century and wrote and sang renowned spiritual poetry. In the play and in some legends, she is married to a Rajput Hindu king of the same time, Kumbha. Akbar, having disguised himself as a Hindu, travels to the Kumbha's palace to hear Mira sing in the garden. Kumbha discovers their meeting and condemns Mira to death because of being "spiritually polluted" by a Muslim. The characters dramatize religious and cultural schisms familiar to both India and Ireland.

Cousins explains what he sees as their principal differences in his brief preface:

> The story on which this poem is based, though told and read all over India, is not in accordance with history. Akbar and Mira are separated by a century of time, and it does not appear to be absolutely certain that the greatest of the Rajput kings was the husband of one of the greatest of women saints and singers. The author of the poem hopes, however, that the presentation of three types of religious expression (the spiritual adventure and breadth of Akbar, the simple devotion of Mira, the inquisitorial fanaticism of Kumbha) which are contemporaneous in all lands and ages, may, by the evocation of some measure of aesthetic joy, provide compensation for historical discrepancy and such liberties as he has taken with the story itself. (1919, 4)

These "three types of spiritual expression" correspond also to responses to cultural colonialism as outlined by postcolonial theorist Patrick Hogan. The main difference is that Cousins focuses on sectarian conflicts within imperial contexts. Whereas Cousins claims these expressions to be "contemporaneous in all lands and ages," they particularly inform narratives of decolonizing cultures.

Patrick Hogan has mapped similar responses in the anglophone literatures of India, Africa, and the Caribbean in his work *Colonialism and Cultural Identity*. Hogan's analysis of the "cultural geography of colonialism" (2000, 303) greatly informs Cousins's antisectarian depiction; the three main characters correspond with three of Hogan's "standard relations to culture" in a decolonizing culture: "orthodoxy," "unreflective conformism," and "syncretism." Mira's relationship with Hindu tradition and religion might be best classed as orthodox, a position that Hogan summarizes as "[o]pen-minded, flexible adherence to indigenous culture, with particular emphasis on large ethical[, spiritual, aesthetic,][19] or social principles, rather than on specific customary practices." Kumbha can be categorized an "unreflective conformist," a position that appears opposite of orthodoxy: "[c]lose-minded, inflexible adherence to indigenous culture, with little attention to large ethical[, spiritual, aesthetic,] or social principles and with particular emphasis on specific customary practices standard in one's immediate community" (319). Kumbha dismisses spiritual principles as youthful interests; as King his priorities shifted to duty and power: "My business is with stern and present things, / Not with pale phantoms and futurity." Mira, in contrast, reads beyond the actions of characters into allegorical spiritual understandings:

> past our little reach
> I hear invisible compassionate lips
> Laugh softly, and in comprehending eyes
> Catch a far meaning to the shadow-dance
> Of children who have hurt themselves in play,
> And shall have sleep, and waken, and forget.
> (Cousins 1919, 48)

In contrast to both, Hogan defines *syncretism* as "[t]he synthesis of metropolitan and indigenous culture. This synthesis may be intentional, and aimed at the production of a new culture superior to both its precursors, or it may result spontaneously from the natural development of contact cultures" (2000, 320). Including poetry, and religion within the rubric of culture (as Cousins did), syncretism describes the ideals of both Akbar and Cousins.[20] Instead of colonial conflict, however, Cousins places ethnic and religious conflict as the play's main tension; notwithstanding, Hogan's terms apply. Such suspicious and violent sectarian conflicts exist, to a large extent, because of British colonialism and their "divide and conquer" strategies. The conflicts existed in India, Ireland, and elsewhere when Cousins wrote the play and continue to this day in postpartition India and Pakistan and elsewhere around the globe. Akbar's syncretic goals may be accurately described as antisectarian rather than as simply anticolonial. He seeks out the beautiful devotional songs of the Hindu queen Mira, and his actions advocate his famous synthesis of Hindu and Muslim aesthetics and spirituality.

Donning Hindu clothes in the first scene as a disguise, Akbar and his court poet, Tansen, actually mimic aspects of the dominant Hindu practical identity, copying their salutations and dressing in dhotis. But this mimeticism has a positive value in the drama and functions as part of Akbar's (and Cousins's) cultural hybridity and syncretism—aiming for "the production of a new culture superior to both its precursors." As they enter Chitorgarh in Rajputana, Tansen remarks to Akbar, "An hour ago / I died to Islam and was born a Hindu," then advises Akbar to take off his trousers and "take this cloth / and reincarnate quickly" (1919, 6–7). Significantly, although Akbar will "reincarnate" into Hindu clothes, he will remain Muslim:

> . . . If my limbs
> Could ape the Hindu as glibly as your tongue
> Takes on his language, I far more would fear
> To lose myself in that which we assume
> Than be unmasked; and so I rather choose
> To don the Hindu than to slough the Muslim,
> And being both, be either at the need.
>
> (7)

Instead of trading one for the other, he "be[comes] both," avoiding the "either/or" binary of standard power relations. Rather, he chooses a "both/and" strategy, transforming into an Indian identity that is both Muslim and Hindu.

Strategies of decolonization employ various devices, often allegorical or doubled. The protagonists in *The King's Wife,* Akbar, Tansen, and Mira, likewise all use disguises and doublespeak to enact their syncretism. Outside a Hindu temple, Akbar and Tansen nervously exchange greetings with two Hindu "citizens" and successfully pass as Hindus (11). Tansen in a nice moment of doublespeak tells them that Akbar was a king "one life back." Disguise also allows Mira a spiritual freedom (albeit brief); when she passes as a beggar on the road, she claims:

> For the first time in my life
> Solely and utterly I am myself,
> and go on my own way.
>
> (84)

Akbar and Tansen approach the temple and hear Mira; afterward, they meet her, and Akbar makes a low obeisance in Hindu form and praises her for having led him through song "[u]nto the vision of the Feet of God" (28). On departing he places, as a tribute, a jeweled necklace in her hands as she is praying, calling them stones. Afterward, Kumbha discovers the precious "stones," rails about Muslim "pollution," and condemns Mira to die. All ministers and citizens refuse to execute her, but Kumbha has a death warrant delivered to his wife, confident that she will obey it.

At the opening of the last act, Mira, the orthodox follower of tradition, has left the palace disguised as a beggar, having received her death warrant and intending to obey her king, after being admired by the other king. She meets a beggar on the road and gives him a royal coin out of kindness. He does not recognize her because the queen is disguised as a beggar; soon afterward, however, he wonders if she was a goddess. After she leaves, the beggar shows the coin to a guard, who rushes after her, supposing it stolen. But the beggar queen apparently commits suicide, and the text has double meanings, both tragic and transcendental, where she is described as "floating away in the moonlight" despite there being no moon in the sky and her being at the river (92–93). Various characters take her suicide and/or ascension differently: one compares it to "a lotus that slips away from muddy anchorage." Another describes it in ambivalent terms as "great sorrow that has more sweetness in it than vina-strings or dances, or the food that rich men scatter at a festival" (94). Through her end, she adheres to tradition but loses her life. This ambivalent ending is one of the "liberties" that Cousins admits in his retelling of this story. He notes in the preface: "One . . . liberty is the refusal to carry on the poem to a miraculous rescue, a reconciliation, and an ending in domestic felicity. These may, to those who require them, constitute an unwritten epilogue" (4). This unwritten epilogue might also explore Akbar's subsequent attempts to establish a syncretistic culture.

The play's ambivalent end, both tragic and redemptive, reflects this hope as well as the violent year of 1919: World War I, the Anglo-Irish War, the British massacre at Amristrar, and Hindu-Muslim riots in India. D. K. Chatterjee reads the play's conclusion in terms of its Theosophical and Orientalist cogency: "The play wants to show the victory of the spirit of Mira that she, in the intensity of her faith sought death to record her triumph. She knows that through death she finds the holy spirit of Krishna in life. The play is essentially a spiritual play and is one of the finest achievements of Cousins's interpretation of the fundamental religious spirit of India" (1994, 105). Her suicide is more problematic for other contemporary readers, in part because death or transcendence as the only viable strategy for women characters seems a poor solution. In Cousins's gaze, however, her suicide represents the tragedy of "Mother India" and works to undermine the king's authority (his ministers cease to follow his orders). Her obedience is intended to paint her as a martyr and a complicit resistor.

Like his later play, *The Hound of Uladh* (1942),[21] *The King's Wife* brings Irish and Indian drama together. The suffering and maligned Mira represents more than a type of "spiritual expression": she is a young Indian Cathleen ni Houlihan, or the more poetic iconographic image of Ireland, Erin. She represents the spirit of a nation divided by two culturally opposed "kings." The title's ambiguity suggests that either Kumbha or Akbar might be the queen's husband: Kumbha as her traditional husband, Akbar as her spiritual one. The relationship between Kumbha and Mira also clearly echoes Irish legends of jealous lovers—particularly, the stories of Deirdre and Conchubar and Étaín and Midir, both of which had been repeatedly told in Irish drama, poetry, and prose. Cousins's most acclaimed poem is his long narrative "Etain the Beloved," and he wrote a monograph, *The Story of Etain: A*

Celtic Myth and an Interpretation. For Cousins, Mira signifies the real India, as opposed to the one endorsed by Europeans and Indian nationalists. As Cousins elsewhere wrote:"The real India hovers over India's heads. . . . It lives through Indian minds and bodies on Indian soil, but it is greater far than they: it includes them, as the soul includes the senses" (1918, 24–25). Like the Irish iconographic feminine from the *spéir bhean* of the *aisling* to Cathleen ni Houlihan, Mother India signifies the nation (particularly as male writers imagined it). Mira's similarity to the Irish figure is most clear at the close of the play, when, disguised as a beggar, she walks toward a flooded river, resolved to drown herself. This moment invokes the last scene in Yeats's play; as Dumbleton notes, the queen "escapes, dressed as a beggar— a Queen with the walk of a beggar, the opposite of Yeats' Cathleen ni Houlihan, an old woman with the walk of a Queen" (1980, 66).

Geosophy

In *The Kingdom of Youth,* Cousins argues that a proper universalism[22] should promote "the declaration of one's own temperamental and racial identity as a nation or individual, coupled with a recognition of the equally valid claims of others to their own identity" (qtd. in Nash 1996, 403). Differences should be recognized as "equally valid claims" within or between cultures.[23] Cousins argues that international relations are best approached through a geocentric perspective. Having taught geography at the High School in Dublin, Cousins had developed this approach to education that began studies at the local level and continued to the regional, the national, and the universal without privileging one area (geographical or epistemological) over the other. Catherine Nash comments on Cousins's ideas of this form of education in "Geo-centric Education and Anti-Imperialism: Theosophy, Geography, and Citizenship in the Writings of J. H. Cousins" (1996). Nash differentiates Cousins's writings and cultural and educational work from the work of British imperialists in India:"While much has been written of the complicity of geography with British Imperialism and projects of the nation state, the focus of this paper is the educational writings of James H. Cousins who advocated geography as a source of ordered knowledge, mystic insight, and resistance to imperialism" (399). Exploring how Cousins's approach offers valuable insights into anticolonial and decolonizing movements, Nash outlines Cousins's manifold approach to geocentric education, which included the promotion of both physical knowledge and mystical insight. His program for developing a "Theosophical geographical imagination of non-hierarchical difference and global spiritual unity" began with studying local environments, arts, philosophies, and languages.

In both metaphysical and concrete ways, his program worked in opposition to the "largely imperialist content and ideology of education in Britain and British

colonies—specifically in Ireland and India" (400). In line with Indian cultural nationalists, Cousins advocated the "Indianisation of education for Indians in India"
(Cousins and Cousins 1950, 274). It included the argument "that textbooks should
focus on indigenous knowledge and be written in the language of the pupil an student," as well as broader spiritual and cultural arguments. Nash expands on
Cousins's involvement:

> In his extensive writings in Irish educational and Indian geography journals, Indian
> newspapers and Theosophical books and pamphlets from the early-1900s to the
> late-1930s, Cousins expounded upon the centrality of geography to civic educa-
> tion, its efficacy in reinforcing pride in the local in colonial contexts and its role in
> fostering forms of global harmony and spiritual unity. In doing so he attempted to
> reconcile ideas of anti-imperial resistance and national separatism with his belief in
> universal spiritual unity . . . [grounding] the rhetoric of inter-war internationalism
> in a dual and harmonious sense of local pride and global unity. (1996, 400)

This local and global "harmonious sense" borrowed from Indian religions and
philosophies as well as from neo-Celtic and European aesthetics. Cousins's reflections on geocentric education constitute the theoretical frame, which was often
triadic in structure and emphasized syncretism as a dialectical goal.

Although Nash does not link Cousins to other Irish Orientalists specifically, she
does acknowledge that Cousins's work was based on an "anti-imperialism Orientalism, which valued the East and especially India as the home and source of spirituality over Western imperialism" (400). His program for geocentric education
included the teaching of geography as a subject, something that owed much to the
expansion of British imperial knowledge and Orientalism. Cousins's geocentric
program promoted the study of geography, which, as Nash notes, "could be de-
ployed in the development of citizens, empowered to resist to [sic] metropolitan values and Anglocentric and Eurocentric models of world geography while avoiding
xenophobic nationalism" (401). Cousins crafted his geocentric ideas on citizenship
in resistance to metropolitan and colonizing values in the imagined geography of
Empire. Nash notes how Cousins articulated the difference between his anticolonial geography and British world geography: "[While] formal and popular forms of
geographical knowledge imagined a world where 'inferior' races were subordinated
but united with a British Empire, Cousins re-formulated the relationship between
geography and colonialism by re-working the meaning of the often imperialist notion of unity in difference" (402). Cousins's subversion of such notions, commonly
used to justify colonial rule, in the service of anticolonial projects typifies his goals
of valuing "non-hierarchical difference and global spiritual unity" (399).

Such ideological, epistemological, and programmatic subversion by anticolonialist writers cannot be reduced to being a part of reactionary colonial nativism. Luke Gibbons has critiqued this reductive process as a way of restricting decolonization by redefining "even resistance within the colonial frame and thus neutralizing the very idea of anti-colonial discourse" (1991, 104).[24] Rather than dismissing Cousins's attempts to create an indigenous and national system of education, we should note how it informed his writings and influenced later writers and thinkers. Through such geocentric and syncretistic work, Cousins helped refocus the center of India's cultural revival, moving it away from colonial, political, and economic centers of power toward local centers—from England to India. The local became the starting point for inquiry for his students, that is, their education began literally with the ground below their feet and moved to studies of their own culture and only afterward to a comparative study of other cultures. This study, moreover, was not limited to the study of English culture, but also included other cultures on the periphery. This circumferential knowledge destabilized the dynamic of metropole and periphery in the face of the imagined geography of Empire, which posited England and Europe as the international center.

Nash comments on Cousins's critique of internationalism:

> Cousins was wary of an idea of international interdependence which was organized around Western economic and political privilege and hoped the League of Nations would help to achieve international harmony through spiritual unity, self-reliance and unselfishness rather than "spurious Internationalism" of economic or political connections that worked to the advantage of the most powerful (Cousins, *Footsteps of Freedom*, 75). Local self-sufficiency and independence would be the aim of "Constructive Human Geography" (*The Kingdom of Youth* 90). (1996, 403)

Cousins's geocentric critiques extended beyond abstract discussions of culture and politics, however.

During one visit back to Ireland, after Irish independence, both James and Margaret paid a visit to Eamon de Valera, with hopes of promoting an international solidarity on woman suffrage and anticolonial issues between Ireland and India. They also asked De Valera to bring India into the League of Nations. But the Irish leader was not seeking to greatly develop Ireland's international contacts in the early decades of the century; rather, he was seeking to rebuild Ireland through an isolationist policy.

Critiques of Orientalism

Perhaps Cousins's most direct critique of Orientalist narratives came in the form of a postmortem attack on John Ruskin's lecture and essay "The Deteriorative Power of Conventional Art over Nations" (1858). Cousins's essay "Ruskin, the Indian Race, and Indian Art" in *The Renaissance in India* (1918) methodically critiques Ruskin's essay, exposing it as biased and unfounded. But his greater purpose is to validate and recommend indigenous Indian art and aesthetics:

> [Ruskin] was as ignorant of the matter on which he dogmatised to such adjectival purpose, as we are of the future. . . . there is left in Mr. Ruskin's lecture a residue of prejudice and inequitable handling of even the known facts, that does such violence to the better parts of Mr. Ruskin, and such injustice to a great and ancient people, that I am moved to rejoinder. I know that post-mortem criticism is not very profitable; nor indeed contemporary criticism. [But] . . . I believe that an intelligent, dignified and frank criticism of both past and present in literature and the arts is essential to the best interests of the Renaissance in India. (116–17)

His essay proceeds to summarize Ruskin's argument and attack "the attitude of infallibility which Mr. Ruskin could so well assume" (118). Ruskin's main argument about the "deteriorative" and unnatural art of India begins by contrasting Scottish culture with Indian culture. Indeed, this point may be where Cousins took first issue, that is, when Ruskin broke apart the Celtic-Oriental semiotic connection by opposing Scottish culture with Indian culture. Ruskin begins by opposing these cultures at the margins of Empire, which are united in their opposition: "[I]n these two great populations, Indian and Highland—in the races of the jungle and of the moor—two national capacities distinctly and accurately opposed. On the one side you have a race rejoicing in art, and eminently and universally endowed with the gift of it; on the other you have a people careless of art, and apparently incapable of it, their utmost effort hitherto reaching no farther than to the variation of the positions of the bars of colour in square chequers" (1858, 11). Ruskin defines both Scottish and Indian cultures in opposition to British culture; they are, in a sense, opposite sides of the same imperial impression. Cousins tentatively accepts this opposition, but only to develop his main critique of Ruskin, who relies upon an emotional plea to his British audience.

The rhetorical pathos of Ruskin's lecture hinges upon the British public's reaction to the Indian "Mutiny," or the Indian (or Sepoy) Revolt of 1857. Ruskin describes it hyperbolically, in accord with English sentiment and disbelief at the time: "Since the race of man began its course of sin on this earth, nothing has ever been done by it so significant of all bestial, and lower than bestial degradation, as the acts [of] the Indian race in the year that has just passed by." Ruskin bases his characterization of India on this conclusion, using "cruelty stretched to its fiercest against the gentle and unoffending," as evidence of racial character (11). He then develops his argument with this controlling question: How can a people who love art so much behave so basely? He derives his answer from his juxtaposition of the Scottish against the Indian: "Out of the peat cottage come faith, courage, self-sacrifice, purity, and piety, and whatever else is fruitful in the work of Heaven; out of the ivory palace come treachery, cruelty, cowardice, idolatry, bestiality,—whatever is fruitful in the work of Hell" (12). Though Scotland and Ireland were perceived differently in English culture, the recent Irish Famine had flooded English popular presses and informed popular understandings of the spiritual values of Gaelic "peat cottage" culture, which, in Ruskin's view at least, was imbued with ideas of "self-sacrifice" and "faith"—values easy to distinguish from the values of the "hellish" Indian "mutineers." Skin color and proximity, however, seem the unspoken differences between Scotland and India in Ruskin's argument.

Cousins devotes his essay to exposing the holes and contradictions in Ruskin's argument, beginning by noting that Ruskin claims "the Indian mutineer was 'the Indian race,' and that the race came out of the 'ivory palace!' " (1918, 121). Cousins first takes to task Ruskin's generalizations about "the Indian race," highlighting India's diverse cultures and religions as well as class inequities. Although Cousins is careful not to sympathize with the Indian "mutineers"—"it is not necessary to go into the question of the rights and wrongs of the Mutiny" (122)—he points out that other brutal killings have occurred, and he mentions, in particular, the Scottish and English massacre of Highlanders at Glencoe, Scotland, and Cromwell's brutal campaign in Ireland. Somewhat in line with what has come to be known as the "politics of otherness," Cousins suggests that Ruskin apply his generalizations first to Britain. To make his point and show the absurdity of Ruskin's statements about India, he poses a similar hasty conclusion about England: "[Ruskin] would surely not allow without protest such an argument as this: 'The English race is inartistic: a small class of that race murdered a highland clan, therefore the whole English race is a race of murderers because it is inartistic' " (121–22). Cousins continues pointing out how Ruskin's use of "race" inaccurately applies to Indian society. He reads, in short, *contrapuntally*—situating Ruskin's essay within its historical and colonial moment—and discusses the weight of prejudice and exaggeration in the tenor of Ruskin's essay and in its damaging conclusions.

In *Culture and Imperialism* (1993), Edward Said describes a mode of reading as contrapuntal when it takes into account perspectives outside the univocal metropolitan one. In a study of Said's work, Bill Ashcroft and Pal Ahluwalia describe this mode.

> In a sense, contrapuntal reading is a form of "reading back" from the perspective of the colonised, to show how the submerged but crucial presence of the empire emerges in canonical texts. As we begin to read, not univocally, but *contrapuntally*, with a simultaneous awareness both of metropolitan history and of those of other

subjected and concealed histories against which the dominant discourse acts. . . ,we obtain a very different sense of what is going on in the text. . . . Contrapuntal reading is a technique of theme and variation by which a counterpoint is established between imperial narrative and the post-colonial perspective, a "counter-narrative" that keeps penetrating beneath the surface of individual texts to elaborate the ubiquitous presence of imperialism in canonical culture. (1999, 93)

This postcolonial mode of reading is not precisely what Cousins is doing in his essay on Ruskin, but it seems remarkably close. Like Rabindranath Tagore's essays on imperialism, discussed in chapter 6 (more than W. B. Yeats's on India and the East), Cousins's essay is an anticolonial precursor to later postcolonial criticism. Cousins certainly sets up a counternarrative to Christian and European cultural history in discussing Indian history and art. This counternarrative reveals the biases of imperialism in Ruskin's canonical text on Indian art. If Cousins does not methodically outline his anticolonial criteria in his critique of Ruskin's "reasoning," he does isolate several inaccurate Orientalist tropes in Ruskin's argument. He credits Ruskin's Orientalist biases to the "disorderly emotions" of Ruskin, which, he argues, originated in his biased and limited understandings of the Indian "Mutiny."

More than anything, however, Cousins defends in his critique the diversity of Indian culture, in particular its various spiritual doctrines and religions. "'Superstition' and 'idolatry' were the softest words that Mr. Ruskin could find for the venerable faiths of the bulk of the human race. Indian art is put to the service of 'superstition, of pleasure, or of cruelty'" (1918, 125). For Cousins, the faiths of India are not so easily dismissed. Also, in a more direct address about English colonialism in India, Cousins discusses (with a measure of irony) the imperial and European bias behind Ruskin's critique of Indian culture and art.

But there is something more to be said of Mr. Ruskin's "apparent connection" of artistic success and national degradation. "You find," he tells us, "that the nations which possessed a refined art were always subdued by those who possessed none." He gives a list: Lydian subdued by Mede, Athenian by Spartan, Greek by Roman, Roman by Goth, Burgundian by Switzer. Why does he not add Indian by Britisher? The whole purport of the argument is the alleged degradation of India, as evidenced in the Mutiny. Is he afraid of the truth that "national degradation," the natural consequence of national presumption and pride, is the nemesis of conquest? Captive Greece "took captive her rude conqueror" not physically but intellectually. That captive India might in a similar way take captive *her* conqueror (all conquerors are ruder than the conquered, says Mr. Ruskin) is an unthinkable proposition, for it is not her religion superstition, her piety idolatry, her ivory palaces . . . homes of all that is fruitful in the work of Hell—though how Hell, an invention of the Christian Middle Ages, can be connected with India is not stated! (128–29)

Prejudice, preconceived ideas, and ill-fitting notions are what Cousins hopes to expose in his critique, but whether he saw them as systematic in European Orientalism is not certain. Concepts such as an "Orientalist discourse" had not emerged in 1918, but Cousins did manage to identify a process by which stereotypes (based in "emotion") and preconceived ideas (about a "race") force individuals and cultures to generate further, often dangerous, cultural projections. After dismissing Ruskin's argument as being one of an "ignorant bigot," Cousins comments on Ruskin's process of critiquing from a distance: "This view of the Indian people is, as Mr. Ruskin says, *indicated* by Indian art. It is not necessary, according to his practice, to go to a country in order to get to know it: indeed, contact with a people might have disquieting effects on one's notions: if the people do not conform to our idea of them (*indicated* by the arts . . .), clearly they *ought* to" (132–33). Although Cousins identifies the cause of this argument to be "emotional prejudice," we can see that he was also describing how a cultural "indication" gathered at a remove encourages cultural stereotyping.

Significantly, the only other critic that Cousins refers to for support is another Irishman, Oscar Wilde, who, like many literary Orientalists of the time, saw an aesthetic and spiritual escape from English Victorian conventions in "the method and spirit of the East." The Orient, stereotyped as it later was revealed to be, offered a potent antidote to the conventions of English culture and to the narratives of Empire. Cousins closes his argument with a renewed call for equitable criticism based on aesthetic geocultural principles, not on personality, emotional prejudice, or geographic distance. Nevertheless, he fears that Ruskin's essay may not be merely the "result of a passing emotion" but, rather, part of a "fixed mental attitude" (140), and he calls for future studies and critiques of Indian culture to "resist the temptation to renounce the duty of balanced thought" (148).

Although in *The Renaissance in India* Cousins hotly criticizes John Ruskin's attack on Indian culture, he continues to repeat many of Ruskin's Orientalist assumptions about the essentially different, mystical, and Vedantic India. It was not until the 1920s that Cousins began to question the dominant devices of Orientalism and the machinations of both Empire and nationalism. Later in life, he reflected on Orientalist representations of Asian cultures. In doing so, he not only further suspected the "hectic emotions" of British Orientalists and the common stereotypes of Orientals, but also began to describe the very cultural processes of acquiring them: "Whether such stories were true or false, they gave me a very sinister glimpse into the dreadful process of working up mental and emotional prejudices which ultimately become convictions and both colour and create future action" (1923, 3). His essay "Between Two Civilizations" offers a view into his perspective for improving East-West relations, one that, as Cousins notes, the Irish-Greek Orientalist Lafcadio Hearn had pioneered fifty years previously in Japan.

Although Cousins did not fully recognize the complicity of Orientalism and Empire, he began to recognize Orientalism as not just a knowledge base, but as a critical "strategy of knowing" and determining Asian cultures.

In response to imperialism and sectarianism, Cousins does not posit resignation, rebellion, sorrow, or hope—the four classical attitudes of defeated slaves. Rather, he advocates tolerance and syncretistic unity, a theme familiar to generations of Irish Orientalist writers. We can find such assertions about tolerance as far back as Thomas Moore's 1820 preface to his Oriental narrative poem *Lalla Rookh,* in which he claimed "The cause of tolerance [is] again . . . my inspiring theme" (1850, x). Significantly, tolerance has not been a dominant theme in Irish literature, until recently perhaps. But it was not uncommon in the texts of Irish literary Orientalism, in part because complicity depends upon inclusiveness. Often it is the case that tolerance as an artistic theme flourishes in spaces where cultural and ideological differences compete. Tolerance is a both/and strategy that offers a way of relaxing stereotypes and overcoming religious differences. In Cousins's syncretistic characters, such as Akbar, and his poems of cross-cultural and synthetic vision, such as his Hindu-Muslim poem "Unity,"[25] we see Cousins's hope that cultural revivalism and cultural syncretism would overcome sectarianism; he expresses this hope explicitly in his study of India's cultural revival, *The Renaissance in India:* "[I]t is not improbable that the next great movement in the religious life of India will be towards the pulling down of the walls between the shrines of Siva and Vishnu rather than the strengthening them" (1918, 57). Although this turned out not yet to be the case, and partition must have been a disappointment to Cousins, he had posited cultural solutions to these postcolonization sectarian feuds. Religious and sectarian differences were not the only resistance that *samadarsana* met. The "human feud" ran also along the East-West gulf, which Orientalism generally encouraged and Cousins generally subverted. Instead of this divide, Cousins posited a geocentric and cross-colonial universalism, as poems such as "To Ireland" evince:

> Something within this earth of me
> With yours an ancient friendship knows;
> But deeper than nativity
> My ultimate allegiance goes.
> . . . .
> I know a legend-haunted place
> Where I can wander night or day
> With quick or dead, the ancient race
> Of comrades on the upward Way;

Poets who heard a distant drum
That rallied visions to their eyes
Of holy Ireland free. . . .

These unto me Their hands will reach
Over the archway of the sun,
Speaking the single spirit-speech
From the heights where East and West are one.

Before the blinding morning breaks
I shall step out behind a star
And seek the quiet haunted lakes
And hills where my De Dananns are.

(1940, 359–60)

Having access to both the narratives of the European colonizer (or "modern-izer") and the rhetorical convictions of the colonized, Cousins could "be inside such structures in order to make [his] argument . . . [and] outside them in order to subvert them" (Young 1989, 128). Unquestionably, his argument for Indian cultural nationalism emerged from within the discourse of race, Empire, and Orientalism. His anticolonial narratives, however, make his Irish-Orientalist perspective at odds with more canonical literary and cultural Anglo-French and German Orientalists. Neither reading Cousins as solely a decolonizing critic and Irish author nor reading him as a European Orientalist gone native will reveal represent his syncretism. Indeed, either/or positions that peg Cousins and other Irish Orientalists as essentially either colonizer or colonized are exactly what the synthetic visions and composite identity of James, Seumus, and Jayaram Cousins decisively rebuke.

Conclusion

Was Fu Manchu Celtic? and Other Scrutable Speculations

Everyone who writes about the Orient must locate himself vis-à-vis
the Orient.
—Edward Said, *Orientalism:Western Conceptions of the Orient*

India and Ireland are too far apart in space, time, and historical
connection for these resemblances to be more than coincidences
due to similarity of occasion, or to some common cause acting on
the minds of men, or to chance.
—Laurence Ginnell, *The Brehon Laws:A Legal Handbook*

AT THE CENTER of the Irish diaspora, and in the bones of an international Irish
identity, has lain the unspoken suggestion that to be Irish is to differ from the norm.
What are the roots of such a difference? What is the history of a supposed Irish barbarity? What have Irish writers done with such a history? For more than a millennium Ireland has been imagined as a border culture, and for more than eighty years
it has had an internal border between Northern Ireland and the Republic of Ireland. Small wonder that Irish culture long found parallels with representations of
Asian and West Asian cultures; both long signified alterity and had colonial histories. Nevertheless, clear distinctions exist between the inheritors of the terms *Celtic*
and *Oriental*. First, *Celtic* is worn as a badge of identity and pride, whereas *Oriental*
is commonly treated as a pejorative conflation of diverse cultures.

From the Scythian Fenius Fein to the inscrutable Fu Manchu, Irish writers
have long imagined characters and tropes of Asia and West Asia. Whether "Irishness" always inflects the representation is an important question to ask. Does it matter that the early-twentieth-century creator of Fu Manchu, novelist Sam Rexhorn,
was Irish? To what extent? Is the representation identical with dominant Anglo-
Irish representations? The logic of this study would assert that it does matter, but to

371

what extent to people with Chinese or Asian heritages? Such questions are more pertinent to Irish culture and its cultural relations with British and American culture. These inquiries may also help reveal the complex dynamics of power that found and further cultural stereotypes. The hope for this book is that the discussions of Irish Orientalism will contribute to a better understanding of both how Asian and West Asian cultures were imagined in Europe and why Irish writers and thinkers long identified with Asia and West Asia through Orientalism.

This discourse has many roots and has gone in many directions. To relegate the history of an idea to a single textual moment misrepresents the reality of any discourse. Even the question of the source of the various Oriental origin legends of the Irish cannot be resolved tidily; it reveals, however, the legends' intertextuality. We may look back at Strabo or other Greeks for their scant descriptions or to Giraldus Cambrensis, who was the earliest influential non-Irish author to use the legends to establish the otherness of the Irish in relationship to the British. We may credit *Lebor Gabála* as the first extended native recording of the supposed waves of Eastern emigrants to Ireland. We may also jump ahead to the use of the Oriental origin legends in Spenser who asserted the ethnic barbarity of the Irish. We may come to the conclusion that each generation uses the myth distinctly, independently. But every author is a reader and a listener who crafts and recrafts some tradition. Cultural continuity remains the standard rather than the exception. This study has broadly approached the topic of Orientalism in Irish literature and culture, not only investigating the major Irish literary figures associated with Orientalism. The result is, purposefully, a literary and intellectual history that maps a range of texts in the hope of demonstrating the lineaments of this continuity. This history has argued for the existence of a discourse outside of the dominant one, for treating Irish Orientalism as distinct, drawing from both its own traditions and others, both contributing to and subverting imperial discourses, particularly Anglo-French Orientalism.

Critics and cultural commentators have tagged the connection between Ireland and the Orient variously: a historical truth, an enabling myth, a nationalist fiction, a lie of the land, and (perhaps most commonly) a mere response to imperial stereotypes, whether an acceptance or a rejection of them. Each of these understandings admits an aspect of this unacknowledged discourse. At times Irish texts refuted these links, especially during the nineteenth century when many Irish (Catholic, Protestant, nationalist, or unionist) vied for a share of Empire. In most literary representations, Irish writers encouraged links between Ireland's Celtic identity and the distant edges of Empire across the world. In order to best address this focus, this work has resisted the ease of dividing Irish texts into binary camps of imperial or anticolonial, nationalist or unionist, Protestant or Catholic, Anglo-Irish or Gaelic Irish. In these divisions the discourse of Empire reasserts itself with its attendant, inherent promotion of sectarianism. Historically, literary critics (primarily the ones focused on the canon) have used this easy divide when discussing Orientalism in Ireland. For instance, despite providing many insights, Carol Loeb Shloss appeals to this false divide to make sense of Joyce's Orientalism: "At the least, [Joyce's] work challenges us to see that Orientalism in Ireland has never been a singular and facilely explained phenomenon. If, in the hands of the Anglo-Irish, it was a tool of governance and mental restriction, in the hands of others it could provide the means of its release" (1998, 270). The first half of this statement accurately asserts the ambivalence of the discourse, but the second half assigns easy moral valences and ignores the evidence of a host of Anglo-Irish writers—even unionists—who wrote to subvert imperialism. This is not meant to cast aspersions on the scholar-ship of Shloss; rather, it is meant to point out that most established and careful Irish-studies scholars reference such cultural divisions as if they were absolute ideological, moral, or historical categories.

Existing in the penumbra of Anglo-French Orientalism, this Irish discourse presented images of the Orient that mirrored Ireland's own liminal situation in the British Empire. Drawing on a traditional semiotic link with the Orient, many Irish writers recognized themselves in anticolonial representations of an Oriental other, as many would do with the ancient Celts. Although the word *other* inherently sig-nifies difference, it may also signify mutual opposition and allegiance, especially in the context of Empire. In other terms, to briefly syllogize, if X does not equal Z, and Y does not equal Z, then X and Y are alike in both being not Z; such recogni-tion, if reinforced, spells the origins of cross-colonial thinking. Such is the perpet-ually emerging and dominant logic of Irish Orientalism. Alike in cultural difference and peripheral status, the adjacent Indian and Irish could draw from one another's examples, however stereotypical or reductive. In an imperial parent-child metaphor, the tropes of the Celt and the Oriental might be understood as fraternal twins, separated at birth, who could acknowledge one another only through a parent's gaze. The imperial gaze, however, was increasingly anxious at this recogni-tion in the late nineteenth century, fearing it augured imperial disintegration through successive triangulating, colonial rebellions. Imperial anxiety also signaled the possibility of a movement from the peripheral to the circumjacent, as when "barbarians" gather. In a sense, always accompanying this imperial gaze and anxiety is the foreboding anticipation of the barbarians coming to surround.

The relationship between intra-imperial and cross-colony analogies, therefore, is a tight one, and imperial comparisons greatly influenced the discourse in Irish culture. It not only reinforced the semiotic connection between the Celt and the Orient, but also narrowed and specified the conclusions of Orientalists and Celti-cists, fueling further cross-colonial aims of decolonizing nationalists around the world. Ireland, both geographically proximate to modern Europe and somehow synchronous with the ancient Orient, was repeatedly imagined as straddling East-West geography, culture, and history. The remnants of a "remote" Gaelic and Celtic culture, therefore, could be seen as embodying the seeds of antiquity and humanity; for Revivalists, the future nation would build a bridge between the Orient and the Occident, and often between the material and the spiritual. Even during the formation of the modern categories of Oriental and Celtic in the eighteenth century, their relationship to one another was debated in England but assumed in Ireland. In some ways, their connection became endemic to the collective identity of Europe; it served as a European link to the Orient that may textually unravel, cement, or reframe the hierarchical distinction between the Occident and the Orient. The contemporary Celt preserved an image of Europe's barbaric past, a semiotic message to ensure the Oriental and African colonies of Europe's own progress from barbarism to civility. Framed from a sympathetic point of view, Irish and Celtic cultures became lifelines for modern Europe to eternal truths, antiquity, and "remote" cultures. The connection between the Oriental and the Celtic is the perpetual exception to European modernity; it is a continual sign of the borders that modern civilization requires.

Alternate narratives developed when Irish-Oriental connections no longer held scholarly credibility. In the historical moments between antiquarianism and Theosophy holding cultural credibility, the semiotic connections between the Oriental and the Celt developed as literary devices for making allegorical comments on imperial and nationalist politics. This tradition developed hand in hand with nineteenth-century cross-colonial comparisons—Irish-Indian, Irish-Egyptian, and Irish-Chinese—that emerged within the decolonizing movements around the globe. In understanding developments in Ireland, the Indian nationalist recognized the problems of India's own decolonization; in understanding violence at Amristrar, the Irish nationalist historicized and contextualized violence against the Irish, moving from the particular to the systemic. By understanding Orientalism, the Irish could better understand British representations of Ireland and Celticism and exploit these narratives in creating new syncretic and resonant ones. Cross-colonial comparisons on the one hand often exposed the discourse of Anglo-French Orientalism, and Celtic-Oriental connections on the other hand attempted to reverse the negative portrayals of both Celtic and Oriental cultures and seize the value coding—significantly, both of these repeatedly referenced intra-imperial comparisons and Irish origin legends in making their points.

The belief in an ancient historical connection between Irish and Asian cultures has little justification; nevertheless, it persevered for centuries, appearing and reappearing throughout numerous discourses and epistemes. Indeed, it made sense (or was justified) through many once "reliable" modes of knowing: origin legends, pseudohistory, antiquarianism, and the many faulty and essentialist nineteenth-century arguments based in race, ethnography, and anthropology. The comparison and the discourse continued, sometimes in the penumbra of intellectual or literary culture, sometimes in the spotlight, sometimes fashionable, and other times absurd, worn out, or strange. Perhaps this discourse has not been acknowledged as such because it could never be fully justified or had been adequately historicized—the dissimilarities between India and Ireland, for example, greatly outweigh the similarities—according to standard historicist, literary, and linguistic inquiries, as well as most current cultural and postcolonial comparisons. Nevertheless, the justification for treating these impressions as a discourse and a tradition has appeared, I hope, through the examinations of its textual moments and political positions.

Irish writers brought a distinct set of considerations to their Orientalist representations, ones that varied considerably from English and other representations of the East. As the Oriental and the Celt became categorical types of the *other* in English literature, Irish writers often identified with them in order to decolonize Irish culture and create a new non-British national culture. What often makes many representations of the Orient in Irish texts seem contradictory or even confusing, as compared to English or French representations, is the presence of *both* imperial *and* anticolonial narratives. To understand Ireland's liminal place in Empire and its decolonizing culture, however, sheds light on not only Irish literary history but also the rise of postcolonial literature. If we accept that advances in anglophone or postcolonial literature written in English began with authors such as Rabindranath Tagore, then we must concede the important roles of Irish cultural nationalist writers such as W. B. Yeats, George Russell (AE), and James Cousins. English writers from William Shakespeare to Alexander Pope, Jane Austen, William Wordsworth, and C. F. Andrews certainly provided major literary models for Indian, African, Australian, and Caribbean authors through which they wrote back to the metropole and made their own traditions in English. Irish authors played a different role by being the first British colony to forge their own literary tradition in resistance to Empire, critiquing English forms and developing hybrid Irish ones. They also provided early cross-colonial exchanges through literary and cultural work, a main example being the interchanges among Rabindranath Tagore, W. B. Yeats, and James Cousins.

What else unifies the works of this school of cross-colonial writers in the early twentieth century? Literary critics and scholars in the past twenty years have taken pains to link postmodern and modernist projects, linking the breakdown of communal meaning and identity with the movement away from traditional cultural master narratives. But like many writers at the end of the nineteenth and beginning of the twentieth centuries, Tagore, Yeats, and Cousins did not embrace the experimental techniques and existentialism of modernist writers. They were drawn to syncretistic forms in literature, culture, mysticism, and re-created traditions. Perhaps the most poignant uses of Irish Orientalism in literature occurred during this period when cross-colonial sympathies were recognized. Both Irish Celticism and cross-colonialism worked to rhetorically unite the periphery of Empire and bring that discourse not to a conclusion, but to an acknowledged head, a focal point.

A common thread among this school of writers was their work to revive and revalue a culture. And many of their exchanges among literature, politics, and culture were clearly articulated in discussions also related to education. Education in countries such as Ireland and India stemmed from ideals put forward repeatedly by cultural critics, authors, and educators in England such as Matthew Arnold. Yet fundamental changes to programs happened, as in the cases of schools run by both Rabindranath Tagore and James Cousins. Arnold (in the shadow of his Celt-hating father) looked to educate the philistine middle classes in the existing literature of the British canon, whereas educators such as Cousins and Tagore wanted to create a new canon that could address both local and cosmopolitan traditions in postcolonization cultures. But not all writers interested in revivalism were interested in education as Tagore and Cousins were, but many tended to value syncretistic approaches to literature, art, and education.

A looming question remains: Can we situate such nonmodernist writers and thinkers in an aesthetic, a teleology, or an ontology outside of revivalism and decolonization? Perhaps we can classify them only as spiritualists, mystics, and humanists in opposition to existentialist moderns. We may perceive distinctions between writers who were modernists and those who were not (regardless of nationality), such as those between writers like T. S. Eliot and W. B. Yeats, James Joyce and George Russell, Virginia Woolf and Rabindranath Tagore, E. M. Forster and James Cousins. The experimentalism and existentialism of the former in each pairings contrast with the mysticism and universalism of the latter. For most of the twentieth century, these distinctions were generally understood as sound literary discretion. The experimental and technical mastery of writers such as Woolf or Joyce evinced quality, whereas the works of Tagore and AE were dismissed in much of the anglophone world as being full of unsophisticated, mystical, and nonrational cultural theories. Even an author whose technical skills cannot be denied such as W. B. Yeats has puzzled literary critics and scholars with his mysticism, which is politely dismissed by modernist and postmodernist scholars as poetic spiritualism or understood as merely signifying a floundering of Yeats amidst the loss of communal meaning, values, and traditional and essentialist master narratives in modern times. Apparently, to understand the projects of these authors is to read them according to the criteria of modernism and postmodernism, despite their avid and repeated denials of such teleologies.

Postcolonial criticism has offered other paths of inquiry and enabled us to value the works of writers such as Tagore and Yeats in terms of decolonizing narratives, but rarely have we investigated their aesthetics. Irish studies has been greatly informed by postcolonial criticism as of late, but cursory glances into essays of the early twentieth century reveal similar discussions about culture and decolonization that predate even the term *postcolonial,* and these discussions often explore form and seek new meanings. Such essays are read as nationalist, Orientalist, and revivalist but rarely as commensurate with or relevant to contemporary discussions. Were these writers attempting to mutate and reform the master narratives that attended imperialism, even as the modernists were abandoning them? If so, their course has a somewhat different trajectory than the path of modernism and postmodernism. To examine these developments in literature and culture in terms distinct from modernism and postmodernism is to disrupt the assumed cultural progression from essence to appearance to simulation, from unified identity to multiple identities, from meaning to meaninglessness to fragmentation of meaning.

Many postcolonial literatures begin with fragmentation and move to new syntheses, which are anything but modernist. They embrace new meanings, experimental spiritualisms, humanistic truths, and salvaged cultural traditions. For the postmodern reader to read the poetry of a writer such as Cousins or AE according to a modern or postmodern aesthetic is painful because the reader's criteria conflict and share few of the assumptions and hopes of the author. The egoism and romantic longing for tradition in the poetry of Yeats may enable the postmodern reader to wistfully appreciate rhyme structures as an exercise in nostalgia, fronting the implicit impossibility of going away to the wild waters with a fairy in hand to escape the weeping of the world. But contemporary readers generally cannot appreciate these early postcolonial works unless they appreciate their criteria and aesthetic goals. Reading these works for their stated goals and understanding them within a non(post)modernist field of aesthetics not only helps us understand the value of their critiques of rationalist politics and imperialist politics, but also helps us allow for a nonrational appreciation of mystical and spiritualist works beyond their seemingly naive embrace of emotion, image, and symbol. But this work is for another study, as is the progression of Irish Orientalism in the twentieth century, leading up to the advent of postcolonial theory in Ireland.

For centuries, historians and writers have emphasized the significance of Ireland's past, reaching disparate conclusions. Powerful unprovable assumptions about the sanctity of tradition suffuse Irish history and literature: the older a culture's history, the more traditional it must be; origin legends reveal a culture's character; legends, myths, and histories ground a culture's future. Generally, customs become traditions when cultures move away from their customs—or have them ripped away—and traditions always imply a level of codification and rigidity. One finding that has not been explicitly stated in this study is that traditions tend to stem from reified moments (in a text or otherwise) rather than from memories or actual customs. The history of Irish origin legends in Irish Orientalism demonstrates this. In the eighteenth century, Irish writers increasingly inherited the astigmatic lenses of British modes of representing both themselves and the Orient. But Irish representations of the East always had distortions more germane to their own cultural myopias and aspirations, more relevant to their own important textual moments from origin legends to pseudohistories to Orientalist allegories ("Everyone who writes about the Orient must locate himself vis-à-vis the Orient" [Said 1995, 20]).

The soul of the modern Celt owes a great deal to Irish culture's Oriental roots. Clearly, the rise of arguments about a Celtic heritage in Ireland paralleled the decline of a rational acceptance of Ireland's Oriental heritage. The comparison between Ireland and the Orient endured, in part, because of the complex of allegiances in Ireland; each representation reinvented this semiotic connection but carried on the tendencies that reveal and reinforce the discourse, ones that tend toward coherence, cultural syncretism, linguistic primacy, venerable origins, remoteness and borderliness, badges of sameness, exposure of representations as constructions, and characterizations of an "other consciousness" in a cross-cultural "community of sufferings." These exist not as historical truths but as strategies for representing culture and meaning—strategies that are asserted then reinterpreted and later used again in somewhat different circumstances. Sometimes they are descried; sometimes the device is turned around and redirected, swiveling like a gun on a turret or a lazy Susan on a dinner table, revealing its alternating nature. But this semiotic continuity, akin to an unacknowledged historical memory, perseveres in the discourse. The origins of this Irish-Oriental comparison are complex, having been used to both validate and denigrate the Irish—through this supposed connection to a mythical land in an ancient time in a distant place.

Notes

Introduction

1. The full text of the poem "Krishna" follows:

> *Imitated from a fragment of the Vaishnava Scriptures*
> I paused beside the cabin door and saw the King of Kings at play,
> Tumbled upon the grass I spied the little heavenly runaway.
> The mother laughed upon the child made gay by its ecstatic morn,
> And yet the sages spake of It as of the Ancient and Unborn.
> I heard the passion breathed amid the honeysuckle scented glade,
> And saw the King pass lightly from the beauty that he had betrayed.
> I saw him pass love to love; and yet the pure allowed His claim
> To be the purest of the pure, thrice holy, stainless, without blame.
> I saw the open tavern door flash on the dusk a ruddy glare,
> And saw the King of Kings outcast reel brawling through starlit air.
> And yet He is the prince of Peace of whom the ancient wisdom tells,
> And in their silence men adore the lovely silence where He dwells.
> I saw the King of Kings again, a thing to shudder at and fear,
> A form so darkened and so marred that childhood fled if it drew near.
> And yet He is the Light of Lights whose blossoming is Paradise,
> That Beauty of the King which dawns upon the seers' enraptured eyes.
> I saw the King of Kings again, a miser with a heart grown cold,
> And yet He is the Prodigal, the Spendthrift of the Heavenly Gold,
> The largess of Whose glory crowns the blazing brows of cherubim,
> And sun and moon and stars and flowers are jewels scattered forth by Him.
> I saw the King of Kings descend the narrow doorway to the dust
> With all his fires of morning still, the beauty, bravery, and lust.
> And yet He is the life within the Ever-living Living Ones,
> The ancient with eternal youth, the cradle of the infant suns,
> The fiery fountain of the stars, and He the golden urn where all
> The glittering spray of planets in their myriad beauty fall.
> (Russell 1912, 460)

2. A coherentist point of view might be applied to the rationale of this study in the sense that an Irish worldview made sense by having affinities with distant cultures. The vigorous opposition that de-

veloped between Irish culture and English culture encouraged the development of a connection between Ireland and Asian cultures. Coherentism is glossed by Sybil Wolfram as a "theory of truth according to which a statement is true if it 'coheres' with other statements" (1995, 140). Jonathan Dancy
gives a longer gloss on coherentism, within a discussion of the problem of "infinite regress of justification" in philosophy, that is, to justify something one must rely on another reason or justification:

> [A] concern with the regress of justification is a concern with the *structure* of justification. Co-
> herentism tries to show that a justified set of beliefs need not have the form of a superstruc-
> ture resting on a base; the idea here is that the foundationalist programme is bound to fail, so
> that the "base" is left groundless, resting on nothing. If this were the result, and if foundation-
> alists were right about the structure of a justified belief set, the only possible conclusion would
> be the skeptical one that none of our beliefs are in fact justified.
>
> Coherentists reject the base-superstructure distinction; there are no beliefs which are in-
> trinsically grounds, and none which are intrinsically superstructure. Beliefs about experience
> can be supported by appeal to theory (which would be going upwards in terms of the foun-
> dationalist model), as well as vice versa (theories need the support of experience). The whole
> thing is much more of a mess, and cannot be sorted neatly into layers. (1995, 246)

3. Bryan Turner also argues in his essay "Outline of a Theory of Orientalism" (2000) that Said allows for the possibility of Orientalists to critique the dominant discourse, particularly cosmopolitan
Orientalists who resisted the divide between East and West.

4. Willy Maley discusses the term *proximity* in his essay "Nationalism and Revisionism: Ambiviolences and Dissensus" (1999):

> According to Andrew Murphy, "the category of proximity is central to virtually all English
> writing on Ireland" (Murphy 1996: 19). Murphy uses the term "proximity" as employed by
> Jonathan Dollimore in *Sexual Dissidence* (1991), where Dollimore maintains that "within
> metaphysical constructions of the Other what is typically occluded is the significance of the
> *proximate*" (Dollimore 1991: 33, Murphy 1996: 33). . . . Murphy, in keeping with a certain
> critical tradition in Irish criticism, argues for the significance of Ireland's close connections
> with Britain, a "physical proximity" that "has resulted in an extended history of contact be-
> tween the two islands, stretching over many centuries" (Murphy 1996: 29). . . . Proximity can
> amount to colonialism by proxy. (13–14)

5. For example, we can see such identification as early as the late eighteenth century in Dean
Mahomed's autobiographical account of his years in Ireland in *Travels* (1794), which subverted the
Orientalist accounts of the Orient. See Fisher 1996.

6. I borrow this term from philosophy (see Quine 1960). Jan Narveson glosses it as "the status of
being somehow accessible to at least two (usually all, in principle) minds or 'subjectivities.' It thus implies
that there is some sort of communication between those minds; which in turn implies that each com-
municating mind is aware not only of the existence of the other but also of its intention to convey information to the other. The idea, for theorists, is that if subjective processes can be brought into
agreement, then perhaps that is as good as the (unattainable?) status of being *objective*" (1995, 414). In the
context of this study, I am implying cross-colony intersubjective communication differs from the type
of communication that occurs between colonizer and colonized—because it is reciprocal.

7. See Hegel 1977, particularly the "Lordship and Bondage" chapter.

8. See Ashcroft, Griffiths, and Tiffin 1989; Spivak 1990 and 1999; Bhabha 1990; Lloyd 1993; Said
1994; Gibbons 1996; and G. Smyth 1998.

9. In *Orientalism,* Said writes: "The distinction I am making is really between an almost unconscious (and certainly an untouchable) positivity, which I shall call *latent* Orientalism, and the various stated views about Oriental society, languages, literatures, history, sociology, and so forth, which I shall call *manifest* Orientalism. Whatever change occurs in knowledge of the Orient is found almost exclusively in manifest Orientalism; the unanimity, stability, and durability of latent Orientalism are more or less constant" (1995, 206).

10. Mansoor had earlier published his master's thesis as an article in *Hermathena,* "Oriental Studies in Ireland, from the Times of St. Patrick to the Rise of Islam" (1943).

11. See Marx 1963.

12. See Spivak 1990.

Part One. Continuity and Development

1. Source criticism interrogates the textual sources of knowledge of ancient times. It takes into account the sociopolitical climate in which a text was written and seeks to understand the conditions that produced the text. Before source criticism, ancient texts were take to be authoritative accounts of actual events and persons.

Chapter 1. Origin Legends and Pseudohistories

1. Although the borders of Scythia changed and were often amorphous, its territory generally centered around the north coast of the Black Sea. The Scythians were a confederation of powerful nomadic tribes that controlled (at various times) large West Asian areas stretching from the borders of Egypt to southern Russia, from Greece to the Aral Sea; they dominated these regions from the eighth century B.C.E. to the second century B.C.E., when they were overcome and routed by the Sarmatians. Archaeological evidence suggests that they operated as middlemen in the silk trade from China westward. The Greeks reported that they had many "barbaric" customs, including tattooing, beheading their enemies, drinking blood from skulls, and embalming corpses. Some corroborating evidence exists; skull cups set in gold have been found at archaeological digs of their burial mounds (see Artamonov 1969). Among the first to master horsemanship in the region, they often rapidly appeared and disappeared from areas. Some intermingled with Dahae kinsmen and became known as the Parthians, who resettled in India. Their final disappearance probably fueled speculations about their migrations to western Europe and to Ireland via Spain. They figure prominently in Greek histories, particularly in the fourth book of Herodotus's history, as the brave if brutal warriors who exterminated the Cimmerians.

2. Most of the Hebrew Bible, or the Tanakh (also called the "Written Torah"), was written between 931 and 400 B.C.E. and arranged around 450 B.C.E. Some parts were written in Aramaic, into which the whole was later translated when Aramaic became the vernacular of the Hebrews. It was also translated into Greek around 250 B.C.E.

3. Malcolm Chapman in *The Celts: The Construction of a Myth* comments on the origins of the word *barbarian,* from the Greek *barbaroi:* for the Greeks, "there was only one, or at most two, languages, worthy of attention. The rest were vulgar noises, animal cries, babble, chatter, jabber; or, indeed, barbarous—an onomatopoeic rendering of the language of those who went 'barbarbar' " (1992, 32).

4. Umberto Eco notes:

[A] long discussion lasted until the XVII century, whether Adam did or did not give names to fishes—since they are not mentioned in the Bible and it is difficult to figure out how God succeeded in bringing them into the Garden. In Genesis 11 we are told that after the Flood, "the whole earth was of one language, and of one speech." Yet, human beings in their vanity conceived a desire to rival the Lord, and thus to erect a tower that would reach up to the heavens. To punish their pride and to put a stop to the construction of the Babel tower, God confused their languages. Latin and Greek civilizations were not disturbed by the plurality of languages. They simply identified their own tongue as the language of Reason, and considered the Barbarians as stuttering people, speaking no language at all. Even the First Church Fathers did not feel a great embarrassment because of the confusion of tongues. They assumed that Hebrew was the original idiom of mankind, but they peacefully wrote in Greek and Latin. (1997, 2)

5. Basing his work on Arno Borst's eight-volume *Der Turmbau von Babel* (1957), Eco comments in a lecture based on his book *The Search for the Perfect Language* (1997; originally written in Italian in 1996) that the search for a perfect language took two directions: "Some looked backwards, trying to retrieve the language spoken by Adam. Others looked ahead, thinkng of Language of Reason as possessing the perfection of the lost speech of Eden." Some scholars, such as Irish grammarians in the seventh century, also argued that their language possessed both the Adamic spark and the necessary elements of Reason, and hence already were, in a sense, "perfect." Eco elaborates: "In the seventh century Irish grammarians, in a work titled [']The precepts of the poets,['] said that that [*sic*] the Gaelic language was created after the confusion of tongues by the 72 wise men of the school of Fenius, through a curious 'cut and paste' operation on all the languages born after the dispersion—so that the best of every language was selected and retained in Irish, which was perfect because it preserved the original isomorphism between words and things" (1997, 2).

6. The main genealogical manuscripts are located in the *Book of Glandalough* (1125–1130), the *Book of Leinster* (ca. 1150–1165), the *Book of Ballymote* (ca. 1400), the *Book of Lecan* (1397–1418), and Dubaltach Mac Fhir Bhisigh's *Great Book of Genealogies* (ca. 1650–1664); for the period of 550–1200, more than twenty-one generations, "the tracts give the names, family connections, and dynasties of some 15,000 individuals. In addition, they record over 2,000 collective names of families, dynasties, and local communities. There are also detailed genealogies for the period 1200–1700, including some Viking and extensive Anglo-Norman materials" (Welch 1996, 213).

7. John Carey, the Irish medievalist scholar, has promoted the use of the term *synthethic history* in referring to *Lebor Gabála Érenn,* alongside the similar term *pseudohistory*. I follow suit, in part because I want to argue that this sort of synthetic history and cultural syncretism is a great part of Irish culture, Celticism, and Irish Orientalism. See Carey 1993 for a broader discussion. For more on "pseudohistory," see Kelleher 1963. Also, as Carey notes, Eoin Mac Neill had used these terms, in referencing *Lebor Gabála Érenn,* back in 1921 in his *Celtic Ireland*.

8. Eco comments in *The Search for the Perfect Language:*

In a work entitled *Auracepit na n-Éces* ('the precepts of the poets' [or "The Scholar's Primer," as John Carey translates it]), the Irish grammarians refer to the structural material of the tower of Babel as follows: "Other affirm that in the tower there were only nine materials, and these were clay and water, wool and blood, wood and lime, pitch, linen, and bitumen. . . . These represent noun, pronoun, verb, adverb, participle, conjunction, preposition, interjection." Ignoring the anomaly of the nine parts of the tower and only eight parts of speech, we are meant to understand that the structure of language and the construction of the tower are analogous. This is part of an argument that the Gaelic language constituted the first and only instance of a language that overcame the confusion of the tongues. It was the first, programmed language, constructed after the confusion of tongues, and created by the seventy wise men of the school of Fenius. The canonic account in the *Precepts* shows the action of the founding of this language . . . as a "cut and paste" operation on other languages that the 72 disciples undertook after the dispersion. . . . It was then that the rules of this language were constructed. All that was best in each language, all there was that was grand or beautiful, was cut out and retained in Irish. . . . Wherever there was something that had no name in any other language, a name for it was made up in Irish. . . .

This first-born and, consequently, supernatural language retained traces of its original isomorphism with the created world. As long as the proper order of its elements was respected, this ensured a sort of iconic bond between grammatical items and referents, or states of things in the real world. (1997, 16–17)

9. Geographies, topographies, and chorographies resemble one another, especially today, but in classical times the genres were distinguished by the scope of the work. The editor of Pomponius Mela's *De Chorographia*, F. E. Romer, explains: "In Greek technical literature *khôrographia* typically designates a written description *(graphê)* covering a district or region *(khôros)*, perhaps a country, but in any case more than one individual place. A *topographia*, in contrast, was a description limited to a single place *(topos)*, while in theory a *geôgraphia* would have described the whole earth *(gê)*" (2001, 4).

10. See the work of Philip O'Leary for more on this subject, particularly his essay "'Children of the Same Mother': Gaelic Relations with the Other Celtic Revival Movements, 1882–1916," in the *Proceedings of the Harvard Celtic Colloquium* (1986) and his indispensible text *The Prose Literature of the Gaelic Revival, 1881–1921: Ideology and Innovation* (1994).

11. Edward Ledwich makes this argument in *Antiquities of Ireland* (1804), as discussed in the section on Irish historiography in chapter 2.

12. The elaborate genealogy of Noah in the Hebrew Bible traces Noah's link to Abraham and all of Judea's link, via Canaan and Ham, Noah's grandson and son. In total, Noah had three sons: Shem, Ham, and Japheth. In Jewish, Christian, and Islamic myth, these sons are the progenitors of all the world's races, although many Africans, Asians, and Native Americans were not originaly included. Of the sons who gave birth to peoples, Shem fathered Elam (Persians), Asshur (Assyrians), Arphaxad (Chaldeans), Lud (Lydians), and Aram (Syrians); Ham fathered Cush (Ethiopians), Mizraim (Egyptians), Phut (Libyans), and Canaan (Judeans); Japheth fathered Gomer (Galls), Magog (Scythians and Goths), Madai (Medes in Persia), Javan (Grecians), Tubal (Iberes in Spain), Meshech (Cappadocians in Russia), and Tiras (Thracians). The Irish were assumed to be mostly descended from Magog, but also from Gomer and Tubal.

13. Some earlier Irish copies of ancient texts that mention Asian or West Asian areas may have predated Dicuil, but no earlier works authored by Irish writers are extant. *Scela Alaxandair* offers possible evidence for this fact, being dated to the tenth century. It is based upon Orosius's fifth-century history *Historiae Contra Paganos*. The work centers around Alexander's correspondence with the Indian king Dindimus, and a letter from Alexander to Aristotle on the wonders of India.

14. J. J. Tierney's introduction to *Dicuili Liber de Mensura Orbis Terrae* comments that traveling Irish monks *(Scotti peregrinantes)* had traveled to Gaul and established monasteries there since the seventh and eighth centuries, adding, "without doubt the period of the greatest influx of Irish teachers and scholars into the Frankish kingdom was that of the late eighth and the ninth centuries" when Charlemagne ruled ([Dicuil] 1967, 4).

15. Dicuil borrowed heavily from Isidore of Seville, mostly from book 9, according to Tierney ([Dicuil] 1967, 30).

16. See note 13 in this chapter.

17. Ancient historians classified the various tribes of central and western Asia, in the environs of contemporary Iran, as Scythian. From this original use, the name spread to signify the cultures of

northern Asia, although many early historians distinguished the Seres or Chinese from them. Eventually, various branches of the Scythians account for many European peoples and, perhaps most pointedly, for the "wild" Irish.

18. See [Dicuil] 1967, 30; and Thomas Cahill's somewhat exaggerated account of this period in *How the Irish Saved Civilization* (1995).

19. A variety of disciplinary approaches have been taken in exploring the origins of the Celt: Malcolm Chapman, a sociologist, argues how the classification of the large and probably undefined population of Europe as Celts might have developed in *The Celts* (1992). Also see Joep Leerssen's introduction to *Celticism* (1996a), a collection of essays edited by Terence Brown (the collection is interdisciplinary, involving literature, history, cultural history, linguistics, and archaeology), and *The Atlantic Celts:Ancient People or Modern Invention?* (1999) by archaeologist Simon James, which argues that to refer to the ancient Irish as Celts is an anachronism.

20. Rufius Festus Avienus served in the late Roman Empire as a proconsul to Africa (A.D. 366) and Achaia (372) and wrote poetry as well as an antiquated description of the coast of Europe, *Ora Maritime,* based on Himilco and other ancient sources (Kenny 1993, 121).

21. Avienus paraphrases Himilco's text as such:

Under the head of this range the Oestrymnic gulf opens before the inhabitants, in which stand the Oestrymnides islands, widely scattered, and rich in minerals, tin and lead. Here is a vigorous people, proud in spirit, skilful at their work. Zeal for business displays itself on all the hills, and in their famous skiffs they sail widely over the turbid gulf, and the abyss of the monster-infested ocean. These people have no knowledge of building ships of pine; they do not follow the common practice of shaping bars from fir; but—a thing to marvel at—they always construct their ships of skins sewn together, and often in a hide speed over the vast deep. From thence it is a two days' voyage to the Sacred Island (so the ancients called it). This lies amid the waves, abounding in verdure, and the race of the Hierni dwell there, wide spread. (Kenny 1993, 121)

James Kenny notes that the name of the "Sacred Island" was likely a misinterpretation of a Greek designation of the island as Iverni, which has a cognate with the Latin *sacer.* We should not dismiss this appellation as a mere "mistaken etymology," however. After all, the name stuck. Philip Freeman further translates the passage in Avienius:

> The Carthaginian
> colonists and people around the Pillars
> of Hercules frequented these waters.
> Four months scarcely is enough for the voyage,
> as Himilco the Carthaginian proved
> by sailing there and back himself.
> (Koch and Carey 2000, 47)

22. The Celts often fascinated the Greeks, and we find extensive details about them in Gaul in Diodorus Siculus, but he wrote little about Ireland, in part because his Alexandrian (third century B.C.E.) sources seem to have known little about Ireland or other borderlands. The fantastic details seem to have been born mostly from hearsay, exaggerated stories, and ignorance.

23. Edmund Spenser makes these connections explicit in *A View of the State of Ireland* (see Spenser 1633, 33).

24. Either possibility allows him to contradict earlier historians, especially Pytheas and Eratosthenes. Horace Leonard Jones, in his edition of Strabo's *Geography,* notes:"The inhabited world [from India to Ireland] is thought of as an arc [of latitude], which, when produced, completes a circle," and "Even in his round numbers Eratosthenes is usually close to the truth" (1997, 240, 241).

25. Strabo notes at the outset of his *Geography* (1997) that geography belongs to the field of philosophy but involves politics and military operations.

26. Romer in his edition of *De Chorographia, Pomponius Mela's Description of the World,* interprets the genre of chorography:"[A] work like Mela's *Chorographia* in Latin falls nominally between these two theoretical poles of topography and geography," explaining that "[a] *topographia . . .* was a description limited to a single place *(topos),* while in theory a *geôgraphia* would have described the whole earth *(gê)*" (2001, 4). See also note 9 in this chapter.

27. Romer notes in his introduction:

After Mela's description of the inhabited world (the Northern *orbis*) crossed into Italy, its circulation increased steadily, even as a school text, well into the Age of Discovery. The Portuguese captain Pedro Álvares Cabral (ca. 1467–ca. 1520), often called the discoverer of Brazil, thumbed well his own copy of Mela and annotated its margins extensively with an eye toward the Southern *orbis.* In addition, when Cabral set sail on 9 March 1500 from the mouth of the Tagus River, he carried on board a Spanish physician and astronomer named Joan Faras, who in the 1490s had become the first translator of *The Chorography* into Spanish. (2001, 29)

28. Romer elaborates:

[I]t is hard to imagine that the most scientifically up-to-date and politically important world map of the early imperial era did not play some part in Mela's conception. Whether or not Agrippa's map underlies the actual outline of the world as given by Mela cannot be known with certainty, but *chorographia* was nevertheless the Roman name for public maps. If the Augustan map was known either formally or informally as the *chorographia,* then both Mela's title and his subject matter deliberately ring with echoes of the Augustan project. In a literary-theoretical sense Mela cast his work as a map . . . and it may not be stretching the point to suggest that the voice of Mela's textual *oratio* was meant at least to respond to the great *chorographia* of Augustus. (2001, 21)

29. Romer adds a note about Mela's comments on the Irish:"M[ela] shares the ancient prejudice about the savagery of the inhabitants [. . .], and M[ela]'s view of the irreligious and barbaric inhabitants thus gives a small insight into his ethnocentrism" (2001, 117).

30. Again, Romer elaborates:"[Mela's] text here was revised by an Irish hand or by a scribe favorable to the Irish. Where M[ela] wrote of the inhabitants of Ireland that they are 'ignorant of all virtue, to a greater degree than any other nation' (omnium virtutium ignari <magis> aliae gentes), the scribe added the gloss 'at least they know virtue to some degree' (aliquatenus tamen gnari). M[ela] regularly uses *virtutium* for *virtutum* in the genitive plural" (2001, 117).

31. See Eco 1997. He notes that both Irish and Chinese (as well as some of Dante's attempts to find a perfect"vulgar" language) were claimed as the original language:"It was one thing to argue that one's own national language could claim nobility on account of its derivation from an original language—whether that of Adam or that of Noah—but quite a different matter to argue that, for this reason, one's language ought to be considered as the one and only perfect language, on a par with the

language of Adam. Only the Irish grammarians . . . [who wrote *Auracepit na n-Éces*] and Dante had had, so far, the audacity to arrive at such a daring conclusion" (96). Eco also explains how the work of John Webb in 1699 argued that Noah, after landing his ark, had lived in China: "Consequently, it was the Chinese language which held primacy. Furthermore, since the Chinese had not participated in the construction of the Tower of Babel, their language had remained immune from the effects of the *confusion;* Chinese had survived intact for centuries, protected from foreign invasion. Chinese thus conserved the original linguistic patrimony" (91–92).

32. John Carey's essay "The Irish Vision of the Chinese" explains this connection. In the following quote, he refers to a passage in Julius Solinus's *Collectanea* (50), which he translates as:

> Beyond (these) uninhabited regions the first men of whom we learn are the Seres *(primos hominum Seres cognoscimus):* "I would suggest that the phrase *primos hominum Seres cognoscimus* (cf. Pliny, *primi sunt hominum qui vocantur Seres*) was at some point mistranslated 'we learn of the Seres, *first of men.*' " This interpretation, taken together with their [the Seres] absence from the genealogical system elaborated from Genesis by Isidore, would lead naturally to the idea that the Seres were descended from a son of Adam older than those mentioned in the Bible; that his child was born before the Fall would further explain the innocence ascribed to the Seres, and their avoidance of other humans. (75)

33. G. M. Bongard-Levin notes in *The Origin of Aryans: From Scythis to India* that Scythian legends often described a mystic changing into the form of a bird and other animals. He also notes: "Some legends from the *Mahābhārata* [concern] the 'flights' of divine *rishis;* about the 'travels' of honoured sages, on birds, to various quarters of the world and specially to the northern abode of the 'blessed' people" (1980, 89). Such accounts may help explain why Ireland's name of "blessed isle" was reinforced by classical scholars. Certainly, the similarities in myth in Scythia, India, and Ireland encouraged the semiotic pairing of the Irish and the Oriental.

34. Joep Leerssen further comments in *Mere Irish and Fíor-Ghael* on Solinus's accounts of Ireland and the importance of his work for medieval writers:

> Solinus embellished his account still further, and in his third-century *De mirabilibus mundi* (a.k.a. *Polyhistor*) wrote: [original in Latin, translation taken from Leerssen's footnote:] "There are no snakes at all there, only few birds, and an inhospitable and bellicose race of people. Those who are victorious in battle paint their faces with the blood shed by their victims: custom and aberration amount to the same thing. When a mother gives birth to a male child, she puts his first food on her husband's sword, and gently feeds it into the little one's mouth on the swordtip; and does so with heathen prayers that he may not meet his death but in battle and in arms. Those who aspire to refinement adorn their swordhilts with the teeth of sea animals, for these are of an ivory-white brightness—and the greatest boast of a man is to 'shine forth' in battle prowess. There are no bees there. If one throws sand or pebbles brought over from there between their beehives, they desert their combs in swarms." There is a fluid border between the genres of geography and fantasy. Solinus' work was, like the later one by Mandeville, a book of wonders full of the most fabulous monsters and miraculous phenomena. However, Solinus, like his two predecessors [Strabo and Pomponius Mela], enjoyed a tenacious reputation throughout the middle ages, and the descriptions of Ireland that these authors gave did not go unheeded in later times. (1996b, 33)

35. For more information on the place of the Milesians as intermediaries between the Mediterranean and Scythia, see Minns 1965, especially chapter 8, "Colonization and Trade."

36. Even the eighteenth-century speculative antiquarian Charles Vallancey confirmed the Latinate origin of the name (though still off a bit): "Here it must not be forgotten, that all agree that Milesius, who headed this colony from Spain, was only so named on this expedition from *mil* a champion, and that his proper name was *Gallamh*, i.e. the white hand, and this method of naming become common, as red hand, withered hand, &c." (1770–1804, vol. 2, no. 8, unnumbered 11).

37. Speculations about the links between the city of Miletus and the Irish continued through the twentieth century to today. One can find arguments asserting the connections on Web sites devoted to linking the British and the Israelites, ancient Irish mythical history, and theories predicting the Apocalypse based on the Bible. While Mary Francis Cusack's (1829–1899) *Illustrated History of Ireland: From the Earliest Period* (1868) does not discuss this connection, a number of fringe arguments reference her text as a source for it.

38. See Koch and Carey 2000 for a map of "Ancient Celtic Europe" with borders delineating the regions with archaeological and material evidence of Celtic culture or "La Tène material culture" and areas with only "ancient Celtic place- and tribal names" (418–19). The regions mentioned in Irish origin legends have linguistic evidence of Celtic culture but no material evidence: around the Black Sea, the Iberian peninsula, and the Munster region of Ireland (the Southwest). Also see entries in the *Encyclopedia Britannica* on Galatia, Scythia, Celts, Miletus, and Greek conquests.

39. Material evidence demonstrates that ancient Celtic-influenced cultures stretched across Europe from Ireland to Scythia (southern Ukraine); Celtic place-names suggest that Celtic settlements existed in Spain and Anatolia (central Turkey); and numerous references to the Galatians exist in Roman texts, not to mention Paul's letters to the Galatian Christians in the Christian Bible.

40. Considerable discussion exists on whether the "Atlantic Celts" existed in the British Isles. Archaeologist Simon James offers a popular account of this debate in *The Atlantic Celts: Ancient People or Modern Invention?* (1999). For a more scholarly discussion of the cultural origins of the Celt, see Brown 1996 and Chapman 1992.

41. The Milesians are also remembered for their sixth-century B.C.E. pre-Socratic philosophers, the first "natural philosophers," Thales, Anaximander, and Anaximenes. They are credited with founding abstract cosmology, in part because they worked to construct ideas about the nature of the universe (and the earth) as an entire entity. They are also remembered for their pioneering work in cartography.

The origins of Miletus date back to the "Ionian Revolt" of the Greco-Persian War in 499 B.C.E., after which, as Scythian tribes centered on the north side of the Black Sea lessened in power, Miletus grew in significance, especially through Black Sea trade. Having been sacked and rebuilt after its initial success, the city operated as a successful trade center and minor colonial hub for nearly ten centuries on the Aegean coast until the sixth century C.E.

42. R. Mark Scowcroft notes:

Medieval Irish historians and genealogists frequently posit eponymous ancestors for national and familial groups, as do the authors of Ireland's toponymic legends (the *dindsenchas*) eponymous founders for place-names. Hence, for example, Conn Cétchathach (XCIX), eponym and (possibly historical) ancestor-figure for Ireland's northern half *(Leith Cuinn)*, its predominant dynastic group *(Síl Cuinn)* and the Connachta. . . . This probably native habit was reinforced and extended following the example of Isidore of Seville, whose *Etymologiarum (sive Originum) Libri XX* so often go beyond eponymy into more complex forms of etymological analysis. (1988, 12)

Scowcroft continues: "Isidore says that Ireland is called *Hibernia* because of its proximity to *(H)iberia:* hence, according to the rule of eponymy observed above, the Irish would have reason to believe that their ancestors came from Spain" (14).

43. I am grateful to John Carey, who has been particularly helpful in tracing these uses. The points in this paragraph and the next are based on suggestions that he has made in private correspondence, but if their articulation is not clear, the fault is mine.

44. In "The Irish National Origin-Legend: Synthetic Pseudohistory," John Carey provides a concise overview of the theory of how this connection was originally made through specious etymology:

> In the first of the accounts of Irish origins . . . all the invaders are made to come to Ireland from Spain: A. G. van Hamel (in his "On *Lebor Gabála*" *Zeitschrift für Celtische Philologie* 10 [1914–15], [97–197]) plausibly suggested that this detail was inspired by Isidore's invocation of Spain as "mother of races" in the encomium which introduces his "History of the Goths." In the second of the accounts, the derivation of the Gaels from Scythia appears to imply an equation of *Scythae* or "Scythians" and *Scot(t)i* or "Irishmen"; this could I think have been inspired by a passage later in the same work.
>
> > Gothi de Magog Iafeth filio orti cum Scythis una probantur origine sati, unde nec longe a uocabulo discrepant. Demutata enim ac detracta littera Getae, quasi Scythae, sunt nuncupati[*sic*]. ·
>
> > The Goths, descended from Magog son of Japhet, are shown to have the same origin as the Scythians, from whom they do not differ greatly in name. For if one letter is changed and another dropped they are called *Getae* (that is, Scythians).
>
> > The same stratagem of altering one letter, dropping another—and incidentally, changing the declension—which turns Gothi to *Getae* can turn *Scythae* to Scoti; and the genealogical doctrine according to which the Gaels and Scythians descend from Magog is only a step removed from Isidore's assertion that Magog was the ancestor of the Goths and Scythians. Although the current orthodoxy appears to be that the "History of the Goths" did not circulate outside of Spain, these hints in *Historia Britonum* may provide evidence that among its many contributions to their knowledge, Isidore's work furnished seventh-century Irish scholars with a model of barbarian pseudohistory. (1994, 12–13)

45. Lloyd Laing and Jennifer Laing's study *Celtic Britain and Ireland, AD 200–800* (1990) provides an overview of the history of this period as well as a survey of the archaeological, literary, linguistic, and antiquarian studies about the peoples of Ireland in this period.

46. Carey cites the following text as his source and gives the following note: "*Corpus Genealogiarum Hiberniae,* I, ed. M.A. O'Brien (Dublin 1962; rev. imp., 1976), p. 1; on the name's formation, cf. Scowcroft, '*Leabhar Gabhála*—Part II,' p. 20, n. 53" (1994, 10).

47. Goffart also lists some of the lesser historians of the period: "Count Marcellinus (in the East Roman Empire), Victor of Tunnuna (an African, but writing in the East), Marius of Avenches (in Frankish Gaul), John of Biclar (in Visigothic Spain), and the anonymous 'Copenhagen Continuator of Prosper' (in Italy);" many translations of Greek and Roman texts also appeared (1988, 9).

48. The entry on annals in *The Oxford Companion to Irish Literature* provides a clear and concise overview of these texts. The surviving annals point to previous works: "The annals dealing with the early Middle Ages appear to share a common core of entries down to the 10th cent. It has been suggested that this conformity derives from a lost *Chronicle of Ireland* compiled in the 10th cent. from still earlier records. The wording in the earliest identifiable stratum in the common corpus of information shows that it derives from records kept at Iona. These entries deal with events from the late 6th cent. to AD 740, and were probably written down on Iona from the late 7th cent. onwards. . . . They provide historical evidence, but their dating system cannot be relied upon" (Welch 1996, 16).

49. Scowcroft uses the contemporary spelling of the text.

50. Eco in *The Search for the Perfect Language,* citing Borst 1957–1963 and Lubac 1959, describes how Hebrew was perceived:"From Origen to Augustine, almost all of the church Fathers assumed, as a matter of incontrovertible fact, that, before the confusion, humanity's primordial language was Hebrew. The most notable dissenting voice was Gregory of Nyssa *(Contra Eunomium).* God, he thought, could not have spoken Hebrew; were we to imagine, he said ironically a schoolmaster God drilling our fore-fathers in the Hebrew alphabet (cf. Borst 1957–63: I, 2, and II/1, 3.1)? Despite this, the image of He-brew as the divine language survived through the middle ages (cf. De Lubac 1959: II, 3.3)" (1997, 74).

51. Mark Scowcroft, an Old Irish scholar, has given the best overview of this important, if con-fusing, early work in two studies published in *Ériu.* See Scowcroft 1987 and 1988.

52. Carey notes:"The term 'synthetic history' seems to have been introduced by Eoin Mac Neill, *Celtic Ireland* (Dublin 1921), p. 40, where 'pseudo-history' is also mentioned; see further J.V. Kelleher, 'Early Irish history and pseudo-history,' *Studia Hibernica* 3 (1963) 113–27" (1994, 4 n. 8).

53. Carey provides other examples of other texts that record portions of the origin legends:"The Middle Irish 'tale-list,' in a section which Proinsias Mac Cana has taken to have been added in the tenth or eleventh century, includes the migrations of Partholón, Nemed, the Fir Bolg, the Tuatha Dé, and the sons of Míl Espáne among the events of which a *fili* or professional poet was supposed to be able to furnish an account; and a précis of Irish pseudohistory is included in the probably tenth-century tale, 'The Settling of the Manor of Tara' " (1994, 17–18). Carey continues to comment on the contribu-tions of four particularly influential poets of the period, "Eochaid ua Flainn *(ob.* 1004), Flann Main-istrech *(ob.* 1056), Tanaide Eólach *(ob. ca.* 1075?), and Gilla Coemáin *(fl.* 1072)" (18).

54. A number of separate annals were mostly likely copied from an original *Chronicle of Ireland,* written down sometime in the late seventh century. The later annals include *Annals of Inisfallen, Annals of Ulster, Annals of Loch Cé, Annals of Connacht,* and *Annals of Clonmacnoise,* the events of which were compiled by Mícheál Ó Cléirigh between 1632 and 1636 in his *Annála Ríoghachta Eireann (An-nals of the Kingdom of Ireland),* more commonly known as the *Annals of the Four Masters* (Welch 1996, 15–17).

55. Whitley Stokes's 1895–1896 publication of *Annals of Tigernach* (reprinted 1993) reprinted the following excerpt, which follows an entry on the previous page that notes:"Natiuitas *Conculainn* m*aic* Soaltaim" (birth of Cúchulainn son of Soaltam) (34):"KKKK. Marc*us* Antoni*us* Niger uictus ab Au-gusto i*n* Alaxandria sese propr*i*a manu int*er*fecit, *et* Cleopat*r*a uxor *cius* serpentis morsu i*n* sinist*r*a tacta exanimata *est.* Hóc an*n*o cepit regnare i*n* Emai*n* Conchobor m*ac* Nessa, q*ui* reg*n*auit an*uis.* lx. Roran*n*ad Hériu iársi*n* hi cóic, íar n-árcai*n* Co*n*are Móir m*aic* Etarsceóil hi mBrudin Dá Dergga, eti*r* Co*n*chobur m*ac* Nessa oc*us* Coip*r*e Nia fer" (35). As in this section, the blending of Irish and Latin is often seam-less; interestingly, Stokes provides translations of only the Old Irish.

56. R. A. Stewart Macalister, the 1938 editor of *Lebor Gabála,* notes:

These different histories appear to have been in existence, and (even if their combination had already been effected) to have been still available in their separate form, when Nennius wrote his *Historia Britonum,* about the end of the eighth [*sic*] century. He must have been able to refer to a literary source of information about the Pre-Milesian invasions: but for the history of the Milesians themselves he apparently had to depend on the oral information conveyed to him by persons described as *peritissimi Scottorum.* . . . [T]he only point about it which we need notice here us the single word "Damhoctor"—which Nennius wrongly supposes to be a per-sonal name, denoting the leader of one of the invading troops. . . . But evidently it is nothing but the Irish for "a company of eight persons": this misunderstood word is a valuable testi-mony that for *this* part of the history Nennius had a written text in the Irish language at his elbow. (xxviii-xxix)

57. John Carey, in "The Irish National Origin-Legend: Synthetic Pseudohistory," discusses this process, crediting Heinrich Zimmer's pioneering work in the 1890s, *Nennius Vindicatus: Über Entstehung, Geschichte und Quellen der Historia Britonum* (Berlin, 1893) (1994, 215–25). Carey comments on the borrowings in the first two sections—what he terms the "invasion-sequence":

> The three initial settlements have clear counterparts in the later literature: for *Partholomus* we find Parthólon the son of Sera; for *Nimeth* son of *Agnomen* there is Nemed the son of Agnoman; while to the three sons of the soldier of Spain there correspond the variously reckoned sons of Míl Espáne, ancestors of the Gaels themselves. Later accounts likewise tell of an attack on a tower which ends when the attackers are drowned by the sea, but it is associated with the descendants of Nemed, not the sons of Míl. The name of the settler *Builc,* included by the author of *Historia Britonum* in the list of later migrations, is in fact a population-name: the *Builg* are the same as the Fir Bolg, whose settlement occurs in the later versions between those of the people of Nemed and their successors, the Tuatha Dé. (7–8)

58. Again, to understand *Lebor Gabála Érenn* as a unified text is impossible because the text comes to us in a series of redactions from oral sources. I will be using the synthesized compilation put together by R. A. Stewart Macalister in 1938. Macalister gives the number of redactions as fifteen, but some of them are copies of one another, and so he reduces the number to eleven (ix). Scowcroft uses four major medieval recensions, distinguished by more recent scholars (1987, 84).

59. Scowcroft continues:

> The text as printed is a typographical nightmare, swarming with *sigla* denoting actual or supposed glosses, scribal and recensional additions, and extant and hypothetical MSS and texts. Some half-dozen typefaces, called on to indicate the presumptive standing of every word in the tradition, leave the reader dizzy and confused, and important, *variae lections* are buried in the footnotes under masses of trifling orthographic variants. Worse than the design of the *apparatus,* however, is the arrangement of the text itself. . . . Macalister's edition has thus inhibited rather than encouraged critical enquiry into *LG*. Until a more serviceable edition appears, however, students of the tradition must still consult this one. (1987, 82–83)

60. See Scowcroft 1988 and McCone and Simms 1996, 7–8.

61. John Carey translated this story, "Scél Tuán meic Chairill" (1984).

62. Mark Scowcroft calls this story "the common core of all recensions" (1987, 94), and Macalister speculates: "We infer that the book originally described only a single 'taking'—that of the Celtic Irish, to whom the author himself belonged, and in whom he was chiefly interested. This is why *Gabála,* in the singular number, still remains in the title of the book: it is not the 'Book of the Takings of Ireland,' but 'The Book of The Taking' " (1938, xxviii).

63. R. Mark Scowcroft comments: "The author of the conflation avoids repetition by fusing the two accounts of the Milesians, thus 'interpolating' one tract into the other. The result is a history of the Irish that pauses to present a history of Ireland, bringing them into it at their appointed time" (1988, 3).

64. Scowcroft explains that two branches of a single canon of the medieval recensions of *Lebor Gabála* exist—μ and ★. Four later texts conflate the branches in the two-part version of the Milesian invasion, but one text, *Great Book of Lecan,* holds both in uncontaminated form. The second recension of this text (b) also has as an appendix with the first branch (μ). The quote points to variations in these different texts (1988, 2).

65. See note 13 in this chapter.

66. R. A. Stewart Macalister, the editor of the most complete edition of *Lebor Gabála*, traces this sort of naming process back to an earlier text, *Liber Occupationis Hiberniae*. The original of this text no longer exists, but Macalister argues that it has been subsumed in different copies of *Lebor Gabála*. Macalister calls *Liber Occupationis Hiberniae* "a sort of quasi-historical romance, with no backing either of history or tradition; an artificial composition, professing to narrate the origin of the Gaedil onward from the Creation of the World (or the Flood), their journeyings, and their settlement in *their* 'promised land,' 'Ireland.' This production was a slavish copy, we might almost say a parody, of the Biblical story of the Children of Israel" (1938, xxx–xxxi). Macalister further suggests that the idea of the parallel story had come from the medieval writer Orosius: "The germ which suggested the idea to the writer [of *Liber Occupationis Hiberniae*] was undoubtedly the passage in Orosius (I.2.81), wrongly understood as meaning that Ireland was first seen from Brigantia in Spain, where (ibid., § 71) there was a very lofty watch-tower. This suggested a reminiscence of Moses, overlooking the Land of Promise from Mount Pisgah: and the author set himself to work out the parallel, forward and backward." But he also asserts that another Irish text, "compounded out of a number of separate sagas," must have been included in the original versions of *Lebor Gabála* (xxxi). Precisely what this "original" text included and what various scribes added cannot be determined.

67. Nennius's history is generally understood to have been compiled over a long period and probably by more than one author. The year 831 is the earliest signed date, but other versions may have included eighth-century materials. James Kenny notes: "The nucleus of the compilation was, doubtless, a legend of Germanus, and, perhaps, of the Saxon invasion. To this were added the Brut legend, material from Gildas and Bede, the Arthurian, the Saxon, and the Irish documents, etc. The whole was worked over by Nennius in the ninth century" (1993, 155).

68. Cessair sought to settle in a place where sin had not yet been committed and set sail before the Flood. Cessair and her party nearly all died, leaving only Fintan, who was preserved in a cave to become Ireland's first chronicler. See Carey 1995.

69. Nennius criticizes Ptolemy and Tacitus for distinguishing Ireland as an international site distinct from Britain: "Tacitus relates that Hibernia was more frequented by foreigners than Albion. But in that case, the ancients would undoubtedly have left us a more ample and credible account of this island. While I am writing a description of Hibernia, it seems right to add, that it was reduced under the Roman power, not by arms, but by fear: and moreover, that Ptolemy, in his second map of Europe, and other celebrated geographers, have erred in placing it at too great a distance from Britain, and from the northern part of the province Secunda, as appears from their books and maps" (1848, 461).

70. Elizabeth Rambo in *Colonial Ireland in Medieval English Literature* classifies the British images of Ireland into three categories: "the 'wild Irish' . . . the Wasteland and the Otherworld Island." She also notes that these images "are not necessarily either positive or negative, though they also reflect England's alienation from Ireland and the Irish" (1994, 119).

71. Andrew Hadfield notes in his article "Briton and Scythian: Tudor Representations of Irish Origins": "Geoffrey's purpose in writing the *Historia* is a matter of fierce scholarly debate, and it has been suggested that the work is an elaborate hoax. In the sixteenth century any such subtle nuance was lost, however, and the *Historia,* whether taken seriously or not, was read as a chronicle" (1993, 391).

72. Edmund Campion comments on this "prediction" in his 1571 *Historie of Ireland,* treating it as a sign interpreted as such only after the Norman invasion had begun: "Onely because a frogge was found living, in the Meadowes of Waterford, somewhat before the conquest, they construed it to import their overthrowe" (10; original pagination).

73. Umberto Eco in an essay called "The Force of Falsity" discusses the assumption that before Columbus, Europeans believed the earth to be flat. "Nineteenth-century secular thought, irritated by

the Church's refusal to accept the heliocentric hypothesis, attributed to all Christian thought (patristic and scholastic) the idea that the earth was flat. The nineteenth-century positivist and anticlerical [*sic*] made a meal of this cliché, which, as Jeffrey Burton Russell has demonstrated, was strengthened during the battle the supporters of Darwinian theory joined against every form of fundamentalism. It was a matter of demonstrating that, as the churches had erred about the sphericity of the earth, so they could err also about the origin of the species" (1998, 4).

74. The year 1598 was the date that Spenser's *View* was entered in the Stationer's Register in England; Spenser had begun working on it in 1596. For an overview of the work, see Hadfield and Maley 1997, xi.

75. Historian Andrew Hadfield continues in "Briton and Scythian: Tudor Representations of Irish Origins": "Scythian origins of the Irish were exaggerated either in times of political crisis and by writers who despaired of assimilating them to an English form of government, or by those keen to convince the crown administration that they had the best claim to govern Ireland" (1993, 408).

76. Campion, apparently relying on Boethius, refers to Gaedel Glass as Gathelus and has Scota as his wife, not his mother, as in other accounts (1940, 27–28). He also truncates the account and blends it with the story of Gurguntius, a Briton king, who meets the Scythians and sends them to Ireland—a variation of Bede's account in which the Irish send the Scythians to Scotland.

77. Seathrún Céitinn (Geoffrey Keating) comments in *Foras Feasa ar Érinn (The History of Ireland,* 1634) that this explanation (which he critiques in Stanyhurst's text, but was derived from Campion's) incorrectly guesses at the words' ("faro, faro") origins, which Keating asserts "is the same as 'watch, watch O,' or 'O take care,' telling the other party to be on their guard, as the Frenchman says, 'gardez, gardez,' when he sees his neighbour in danger" (1902, 43).

78. Camden writes: "And no cause have we to mervaile, that Ireland which now for the most part is rude, halfe-barbarous, and altogether voide of any polite and exquisite literature, was full of so devout, godly and good wits in that age, wherein good letters throughout all Christendome lay neglected and halfe buried" (1610, 68).

79. Andrew Hadfield and Willy Maley provide a valuable overview to the 1997 edition of *A View:*

> *A View* is a prose dialogue of some 65,000 words between Eudoxus, a rational Englishman, interested in politics but largely ignorant of Ireland, and Irenius, who is clearly speaking from a position of knowledge and probably represents one of the New English colonists, like Spenser himself. . . . [T]he two figures plunge straight into the argument with Eudoxus' perplexed observation that if Ireland is "of so goodly and commodious a soyle" as Irenius claims, why has nothing been done to transform "that nation to better government and civility"? (This question was also posed by Giraldus in the 1180s.) . . . The opening speeches set the tone for the rest of the dialogue. Eudoxus asks the questions and Irenius provides the answers, often at great length and in the form of what appear to be digressions from the subject, so that it is he who dominates the dialogue. Irenius' words also establish the fear, frequently expressed in English works on Ireland in the 1590s, that if nothing is done, then Ireland will ruin England too. (xvii)

80. Spenser's Irish representations have attracted considerable attention in the past fifteen years. The principal studies include the essay collection edited by Patricia Coughlan, *Spenser and Ireland: An Interdisciplinary Perspective* (Cork: Cork Univ. Press, 1989); a special issue of the *Irish University Review* edited by Anne Fogarty, *Spenser in Ireland: "The Faerie Queen," 1596–1996* 26, no. 2 (autumn–winter 1996); and Hadfield 1997.

81. Spenser's Irenius explains: "Also the Scythians used, when they would binde any solemne vow

or combination amongst them, to drink a bowle of blood together, vowing thereby to spend their last blood in that quarrel: and even so do the wild Scots, as you may read in Buchanan: and some of the Northern Irish" (1633, 63).

82. See Andrew Hadfield's chapter "'Ripping Up Ancestries': The Use of Myth in 'The Present State of Ireland,' " in *Edmund Spenser's Irish Experience: Wilde Fruit and Salvage Soyl* (1997), and Elizabeth Butler Cullingford's chapter "Romans and Carthaginians," in *Ireland's Others: Ethnicity and Gender in Irish Literature and Popular Culture* (2001). In order to illustrate the reputation of Scythians as barbarous cannibals, Cullingford cites the works of Herodotus, Shakespeare, Marlowe, Montaigne, and Cambrensis (102–5). She also notes: "Shakespeare, however, may have drawn on the popular legend of St Andrew, who, on finding the Scythians eating their enemies, supplied them with the Eucharist instead. (Presumably symbolic cannibalism provided a satisfactory replacement for the literal kind)" (103).

83. Irenius's "deduction" bolsters his foregone conclusion about the Irish and their need of a civilizing force. In addition to referring to contemporary Irish customs, he references (but does not cite) classical descriptions of the Scythians in Strabo (1633, 52), Didorus Siculus, Herodotus (59), Olaus Magnus, Io. Bohemus (55), Solinus (62), and others.

84. Clare Carroll explains in her essay "Spenser and the Irish Language: The Sons of Milesio in *A View of the Present State of Ireland, The Faerie Queene, Book V* and the *Leabhar Gabhála*" (in the special issue of the *Irish University Review, Spenser in Ireland: "The Faerie Queene," 1596–1996*): "In comparing Spenser's account with the versions of the invasions of Ireland recounted in the *Leabhar Gabhála* and in a *View* does the story of Gaedel (Spenser's Gathelus) occur first, and only Spenser follows the Irish spelling of Nemed." Carroll's footnote: "Roland M. Smith was the first to recognize that Spenser must have known an Irish version of the Milesian invasion story in 'Spenser, Holinshed, and the *Leabhar Gabhála*,' *Journal of English and German Philology*, 43 (1944), 390–401." She continues: "While Spenser may have drawn the story of the 'sons of Milesius, King of Spain' from Giraldus, he may just as well have taken it from the *Leabhar Gabhála*. In any case, Spenser was not dependent on Campion, Holinshed or Nennius for this story since they all refer to 'foure brethren Spaniards,' rather than to the 'four sons of Milesius,' the *'Maic Milead'* of the Irish text. . . . Roland Smith went to great lengths to show how many different Irish intertexts could have influenced Spenser's version of the story, including not only the *Leabhar Gabhála*, but also the *Benshenchas*, the *Book of Lecan,* and the *Senchas már*, or *Ancient Laws of Ireland*." Carroll's footnote: "Roland M. Smith speculates on the Irish intertexts for *The Faerie Queene* 5.4 in 'Spenser's Tale of the Two Sons of Milesio,' *Modern Language Quarterly* 3 (1942), 547–57" (1996, 286–87).

85. Spenser's conjectures lead him in several directions, one of which is African: "[T]he manner of riding on the wrong side of the horse, I meane with their faces towards the right side, as the Irish use, is (as they say) old Spanish, and some say African, for amongst them the woemen (they say) use so to ride: Also the deepe smocke sleeve, which the Irish woemen use, they say, was old Spanish, and is used yet in Barbary: and yet that should seeme rather to be an old English fashion" (1633, 65).

86. Not long after Spenser's text, Seathrún Céitinn reports in his *Foras Feasa ar Éirinn* that "the Fomorians, namely, navigators of the race of Cham, who fared from Africa . . . came fleeing to the islands to the west of Europe, and to make a settlement for themselves" (Keating 1902, 179).

87. For more on English travel and colonial writing from this period, see Leerssen 1996b and Hadfield 2001.

88. Joseph Cooper Walker later commented on these yellow shirts in *An Historical Essay on the Dress of the Ancient and Modern Irish:* "The COTA was a kind of shirt made of thin woolen stuff plaided [*sic*], or of linen dyed yellow. . . . The custom of dying this part of the dress yellow, Spencer [*sic*] thinks came from the east: 'it was dvised (says he) in those hot countries, where saffron is very common and rife, for avoiding that evil which cometh by much sweating, and long wearing of linen.' " A footnote

following this reads:" *View of the State of Irel.* Lord BACON assigns a more delicate, and perhaps as sound a reason for the universal use of linen shirts dyed with saffron, amongst the Irish. . . . [They used dye from] lichen that grows upon the rocks" (1788, 4).

89. Luke Gibbons has written insightfully on the North American connections, most recently "Towards a Postcolonial Enlightenment: The United Irishmen, Cultural Diversity, and the Public Sphere" (2003).

90. For a discussion, see Carlin 1985, especially 99–101.

91. In his introductory verse, Lithgow summarizes his travels after journeying from "Æthiop" (where he fought a mighty king) to England. Irish "defects" and Spanish cruelty are the high points of the verse:

> Well I am sped, bids England's *Court adiew,*
> *And by the way the* Hiberne *bounds I view;*
> *In whose defects, the truth like Razor sharpe*
> *Shall sadly tune, my new string'd* Irish *harpe:*
> *Then scud I* France, *and cross'd the* Pyrheneise
> *At the* Columbian *heights,* . . .
> *Then rest'd at* Malaga, *where I was shent*
> *and taken for a* Spie *crush'd rackt, and rent.*
> *Where ah! (when Treason tride) by fals position;*
> *They wrest'd on me their lawlesse* Inquisition:
> *Whichafter Tortures, Hunger, Vermine gnashes,*
> *Condemn'd me quick, stake-bound, to burn in ashes:*
> *Gods Prouidence comes in, and I'me discouered*
> *By Merchants meanes, by* Aston *last deliuered.*
>
> (1732, 424–25)

92. Joep Leerssen notes that "Lithgow was an aggressively anti-Catholic Presbyterian; his travel description, which appeared in 1622, is full of hateful remarks against the 'snakish Papists,' 'that snarling Crew'—an attitude perhaps partly explained by (or else partly explaining) the fact that [he had] been held prisoner by the Inquisition" (1996b, 55).

93. Lithgow begins his description of Ireland, having returned from Africa to England, as such:

But now having finished the two Descriptions, of my first and second adventures; it rests now most necessary, to relate the meritorious designe, and miserable effect of my third Voyage. After I had (I say) by the great Providence of God, escaped infinite dangers, by Seas suffering thrice shipwracke, by Land, in Woods and on Mountaynes often invaded; by ravenous Beasts, crawling and venomous Wormes daily incombred; by home-bred Robbers, and remote Savages; five times stripd to the skin; excessive fastidiousnesse, unspeakable adversitites, parching heates, scorching drouth, intolerable distresses of hunger, imprisonments, and cold; yet all these almost incredible sufferings past, could never abate the flame of mine austiere affection conceived; but ambitious curiosity, exposing me to a third Voyage, I may say as *Æneas* did in his penententiall mood. (1632, 425)

94. As in Solinus's *De Mirabilibus Mundi* (or *Polyhistor*). See Leerssen 1996b, 33.

95. For more on these comparisons, see Curtis 1971.

96. See Joep Leerssen's works as well as Ignatiev 1995 and Curtis 1968.

Chapter 2. Ogygia: Europe's Backyard Orient and the Rise of Antiquarianism

1. Keating was a Tipperary priest of a Hiberno-Norman family who had been educated in France in the first decades of the seventeenth century; there he earned a doctorate of divinity and began writing in Irish. Leerssen reports in *Mere Irish and Fíor-Ghael* that his name was probably a corruption of MacÉtienne, "a French name with a Gaelic patryonym" (1996b, 274). Although he signed his major work as Seithrún Céitinn, he is generally referred to by the Anglicized version, Keating.

2. Leerssen traces this process in detail, especially in his chapter "The Vindication of Irish Civility":"[O]n the Continent, Irish defence against English denigrations was . . . generally embedded in a less pessimistic, counter-reformatory attitude, and tended to concentrate on the religious dimension of the conflict. However, a more secular trend can be found within this general context, one which is at pains to disprove the English attribution of barbarism and incivility, not only by pointing at Irish religiousness past and present, but also by including its pre-Christian antiquity" (1996b, 270).

3. Source criticism (though itself criticized at times for placing too much emphasis on textual influence) explores and analyzes sources, contexts, and translations of ancient works, particularly the Bible and classical and medieval texts. See note 1 in the introduction to part 1.

4. For an overview of the discussion up to the mid-1990s, see Leerssen 1996a and W. J. McCormack's chapter on Celticism in *From Burke to Beckett:Ascendancy,Tradition and Betrayal in Literary History* (1994). Also see archaeologist Simon James's account of Celtic history in *The Atlantic Celts:Ancient People or Modern Invention?* (1999); Malcolm Chapman's more sociological and anthropological work, *The Celts:The Construction of a Myth* (1992); and the works of Hildegard L. C. Tristam, particularly his essay "Celtic in Linguistic Taxonomy," which along with Timothy Champion's essay "The Celt in Archaelogy" also appears in Brown 1996.

5. See Knox 1968.

6. See the collaborative effort of Loftus and Huntingdon in *An History of the Twofold Invention of the Cross whereon Our Savior was Crucified:Translated out of an Antient Aramœan Biologist:Together with An Account of the Conversions of the Ethiopians, out of Ecclesiastical History* (Dublin, 1686). Huntingdon did the translation, and Loftus wrote and arranged the text.

7. The Semitic languages are divided into three groups, each of which contain subgroups:Eastern, Northwestern (or Western), and Southwestern (or Southern). The Eastern branch includes Akkadian (once spoken in the geographic area of Iraq); Southwestern includes South Arabian, Arabic, and Ethiopian languages (including Amharic); and the Northwestern branch includes Amorite, Usaritic, Aramaic, and the Canaanite languages, which comprise Hebrew, Phoenician, Punic, Moabite, Edomite, and Ammonite. Note that this list is not all-inclusive; other languages and dialects, both extinct and alive, are grouped in these categories.

8. In "The Editor's Preface" to *Collectanea De Rebus Hibernicus*, vol. 1, no. 1 (1770–1804), the Anglo-Irish Vallancey argues that "our Irish druids" were "strangers" to Greek and Roman deities, claiming they were monotheists, worshiping, in the manner of the early Phoenicians, "Baal or the Sun, as the type of one Supreme Being" (xi). Vallancey expands his meaning in an earlier passage: "The pagan inhabitants of this island preserved the primitive Phœnician idolatry of the worship of the Sun and heavenly host, as types of a Supreme Being, until the arrival of the first Christian missionaries. Our druids like those of Gall, constituted academices to promote learning, and they were obliged to devote twenty years to study before they were admitted to the degree of doctor" (x).

9. Droixhe also asks rhetorically:"A mesure que s'affirmait son étroite union avec le punique ou l'éthiopien, comment pouvait se maintenir intacte sa singularité de langue originale et sacrée?" ([T]he recognition, toward the middle of the seventeenth century, of a sufficiently filled-out Semitic unity allowed [scholars] to envision Hebrew within a comparative framework that is more realistic but less fa-

vorable to Hebrew's mythical attributes. In so far as its close union with Punic and Ethiopian was affirmed, how could the singularity and sacredness of it as the original language remain intact?) (1978, 40).

10. Joep Leerssen notes in *Mere Irish and Fíor-Ghael:* "The first tentative re-grouping of European languages, performed by [Jules-César] Scaliger [1484–1558] in his 'Diatriba de Europaeorum linguis' (published in *Opuscula varia,* 1610, and influential with early philologists like [the Anglo-Irish James] Ussher) grouped certain languages, such as Romance, or Germanic ones, together into related families. In this model, Irish and Welsh were considered unrelated individual entities, radically different, each constituting a separate, problematic one-member 'fringe'-family, like Basque or Finnish" (1996b, 288). The interest in Irish, Welsh, and other Celtic languages would develop, however gradually, over the next decades.

11. See notes 48 and 54 on Irish annals in chapter 1. Also, for more detailed background information, see the introduction to the 1966 edition of the *Annals of the Four Masters.*

12. The other three of the "Four Masters" were actually lay scholars from distinguished Irish families: Cúchoigríche Ó Cléirigh, Fearfeasa Ó Maoilchonaire, and Cúchoigríche Ó Duibhgeannáin. Although other scholars contributed to the work in a lesser capacity, the work received the designation *Annals of the Four Masters* by John Colgan in his introduction to *Acta Sanctorum Hiberniae* (1645) (Welch 1996, 17).

13. See Leerssen 1996b for an extended discussion of the origin and use of these terms.

14. Leerssen, in *Mere Irish and Fíor-Ghael,* cites a poem (translated by Eleanor Knott in the second edition of *Irish Classical Poetry, Commonly Called Bardic Poetry* [1960]) that asserts the immigrant status of all in Ireland. The poem dates from the second half of the sixteenth century and is by the *fili* Tadhg Dall Ó hUiginn:

> Gi bé adéaradh gur deóraidh
> Búrcaigh na mbeart n-inleóghain—
> faghar d'fhuil Ghaoidhil nó Ghoill
> nách fuil 'na aoighidh agoinn.
>
> . . . .
> Géadeirdís sliocht Ghaoidhil Ghlais
> coimhighthe le cloinn Séarlais—
> cloche toinighthe bheann mBreagh—
> coimhighthe an dream adeireadh.
>
> (1996b, 176)

Knott translates this passage as: "Should any say that the Burkes of lion-like prowess are strangers—let one of the blood of Gael or Gall be found who is not a sojourner amongst us. . . . Though the descendants of *Gaedheal Glas* used to speak of the race of Charles, set stones of *Banbha's* hills, as foreigners—foreigners were they who spoke thus" (176).

15. O'Flaherty, unfortunately, represented the decline of a traditional Gaelic education in Ireland at the time. Born in County Galway, he was one of the last generation to be educated in both classical texts (by John Lynch) and in traditional bardic learning (by Dubhaltach Mac Fhir Bhisigh). A great deal of his family's lands were lost after the 1641 Rebellion, and later the Williamite War further ravaged his prosperity and library. The *Oxford Companion to Irish Literature* reports a story too common for Irish scholars of that century: "[B]y 1700, when Edward Lhuyd met him . . . he was living in poverty, the 'late revolution' having 'destroyed his books and papers.' [Samuel] Molyneaux, touring Connaught in 1709, found him living in virtual destitution with most of his library gone" (Welch 1996, 431).

16. Leerssen notes: "Flemish and Dutch scholars, especially around the university of Leyden, developed the concept of a Nordic language group which was called 'Scytho-Celtic.' This development—beginning with Van der Mijil's *Lingua Belgica* of 1612 and *Germania antique* by Philip Cluverius of 1616, also had its participants from further afield" (1996a, 288).

17. Ware's works began to appear in 1626, and were printed in collected form as *Irish Antiquities* (1705), edited by Ware's son Robert. In addition to exploring ancient Irish dress and armament, Ware guessed at the origins and uses of ogham script (which generally had practical uses, such as counting or naming): "Besides the common characters, the ancient Irish used various occult or artificial methods of writing, called *Ogum,* in which they wrote their secret and mysterious affairs" (qtd. in O'Flaherty 1793, 99).

18. See Deane 1997 and Luke Gibbons, "Towards a Postcolonial Enlightenment: The United Irishmen, Cultural Diversity and the Public Sphere," in Carroll and King 2003.

19. O'Flaherty continues: "What if I should be bold enough to assert, that our Fenius was that Phœnix, the author of the Greek alphabet, who devised those ancient Greek characters which the Latins use? The Irish letters are not very unlike the Latin; the name of Phœnix and Fenius, or Phœnius, are not very different, and the invention supports it; the time and place, in matters of such antiquity, are very often confounded. Besides, I have the authority of the above cited poet, Forehern, to give an air of credibility to my conjecture" (1793, 83).

20. James Parsons argues: "I have endeavoured to trace the languages of *Europe* to their source; and think I have discovered that which was previous to the *Greek* tongue, all over *Asia Minor, Scythia* and *Greece.* And this was the *Japhetan,* called afterwards the *Pelasgian,* and then the *Gomerian* and *Magogian,* or *Scythian* language; which is not found only in *Ireland,* the *Highlands* of *Scotland,* and *Wales.* . . . (Parsons, 1767: xii)" (qtd. in D. Davis 2000, xviii).

21. For Rowland Jones, "language ought not to be considered as mere arbitrary sounds, or any thing less than a part, at least, of that living soul, which God is said to have breathed into man" (qtd. in D. Davis 2000, xvi); rather, "letters or characters embody a relation of form and meaning which is rational and divinely inspired. Letters or characters combine to form more complex meanings in particles, which in turn combine to form the basis of words" (xvii). The Celtic Revivalist and mystical Orientalist George Russell (AE) of the early twentieth century argued a very similar, and equally untenable, position in his *Candle of Vision* (1918).

22. Daniel R. Davis quotes Lachlan Maclean as writing: "If it should be denied that we have proved the Adamic origin of the Celtic, it is *undeniable* that we have proved the *Natural* origin of it, and certainly *Nature* was prior to Adam (237)" (2000, xxiii). Davis also notes that Maclean claims his work will help prepare missionaries for encounters with pagans.

23. In *On the Language and Wisdom of the Indians,* Schlegel privileges Germanic languages by connecting them to classical languages and to the supposedly most ancient language: Sanskrit.

> The old Indian language, *Sanscrit,* . . . has the greatest affinity with the Greek, Latin, as well as the Persian and German languages. This resemblance or affinity does not exist only in the numerous roots, which it has in common with both those nations, but extends also to the grammar and internal structure; nor is such resemblance a casual circumstance easily accounted for by the intermixture of the languages; it is an essential element clearly indicating community of origin. It is further proved by comparison, that the Indian is the most ancient, and the source from whence others of later origin are derived.
>
> The affinity of the Indian language with the Armenian, the Sclavonian, and the Celtic, is on the contrary, very unimportant, in comparison with the striking uniformity of other languages supposed to be derived from that stock. Still that connexion, trifling as it is, must not

be completely overlooked, since in classifying these languages we discover many points of resemblance in the construction of some of the grammatical forms which cannot be numbered among the casualties to which every language is exposed, but rather appertain to its internal structure and organization. (2001, 428–29)

In a later chapter, Schlegel continued to downplay the place of "Erse" and "Bretagne" and Basque in relation to German, Indian, Latin, Greek, and Persian languages, dismissing their apparent similarities: "It is easy to discover trifling points even in such languages as are most widely removed from the Indian, Greek, and German" (464).

24. Schlegel asserted the superiority of the proto-Indo-European family, with Germanic languages at its modern head, over other world languages in *On the Language and Wisdom of the Indians.* On the Chinese language, he wrote: "In the Chinese, all particles indicating modification of time, person, &c., are monosyllables, perfect in themselves, and independent of the root. The language of this otherwise refined and civilized people stands consequently in the lowest grade; it seems possible that the highly artistic system of writing so early introduced may have contributed to the imperfection of the language, seizing it, as it were, in its infancy, and fixing its characteristics at too early a stage of their development" (2001, 448). And, on the native languages of the Americas: "These languages, in their earliest origin, are deficient in that living germ [of roots that modify] essential to a copious development; their derivations are poor and scanty, and an accumulation of affixes, instead of producing a more highly artistic construction, yields only an unwieldy superabundance of words, inimical to true simple beauty and perspicuity. Its apparent richness is in truth utter poverty, and languages belonging to that branch, whether rude or carefully constructed, are invariably heavy, perplexed, and often singularly subjective and defective in character" (449–50).

25. Joep Leerssen's comments in *Remembrance and Imagination* are again useful here:

Round Towers occur in some profusion in Ireland (nineteenth-century sources cite anywhere from fifty to a hundred specimens, either still standing or mentioned in the records), but hardly occur in other European countries. They do not have any analogues in the standard typology of mainstream European architecture and are, therefore, largely *sui generis* and practically exclusively Irish. The various comparisons that were made, in the course of the nineteenth century, with other edifices such as the Sardinian *nuraghe* or Oriental pagodas or minarets, are so far-fetched as to illustrate rather the opposite of what they intended to prove: Round Towers, we may conclude, really do not resemble anything else. Nowadays, the consensus is that Round Towers are a primitive form of fortification, current before the introduction of Norman-style castles or late-medieval siege technology, and aimed mainly (apart from possible secondary use as belfry, light-beacon or lookout-tower) to offer monastic communities some form of refuge from marauding bands of enemies. They are usually assigned to a period between 900 and 1100 AD. (1997, 108–9)

26. Thomas Leland's perspective may have been comparatively conservative (he was a Protestant, a senior fellow of Trinity College, and prebendary of St. Patrick's in Dublin); nevertheless, he relays the Scythian and Phoenician origins in *The History of Ireland from the Invasion of Henry II, with a Preliminary Discourse on the Antient State of that Kingdom* (1773). He states that it is not his "design to explore the antiquities of the Irish, to decide on the authenticity of scattered records, or to take any share in any contest relative to these points" (iv); rather, he wants to "trace the progress of the English power in Ireland, from the invasion of Henry the Second, through the conflicts of many ages, which a British reader may esteem it neither useless nor uninteresting" (i). The following quote is from his section "Preliminary of the History of Ireland Previous to the Introduction of Christianity":

If all nations have affected to deduce their History from the earliest periods, and to claim that origin which they deemed most honourable, the old Irish have been particularly tempted to indulge this vanity. Depressed from many ages, and reduced to a mortifying state of inferiority, stung with the reproaches, with the contempt, and sometimes with the injurious slander of the neighbors, they passionately recurred to the monuments of their ancient glory, and spoke of the noble actions of their ancestors in the glowing style of indignation. O'Flagherty [*sic*], their celebrated antiquarian, (in a vindication of his Ogygia against Sir George Mackenzie, which I have seen in manuscript) speaks with an enthusiastic zeal of his country, as the venerable mother of Britain, "that engendered of her own bowels one hundred and seventy-one monarchs for above two thousand years, to the year 1198, all the same house and lineage; with sixty-eight kings and one queen of British-Scotland, (omitting Bruces and Baliols) and four imperial kins and two queens of Great Britain and Ireland, sprung from her own loins." In the reign of Edward the Second, the Irish claimed a still greater antiquity. An Ulster prince of this time, boasts to the pope of an uninterrupted succession of one hundred and ninety-seven kings of Ireland, to the year 1170.

It cannot be denied, that no literary monuments have yet been discovered in Ireland earlier than the introduction of Christianity into this country; and that the evidence of any transactions previous to this period, rest, entirely on the credit of Christian writers, and their collections from old poets, or their transcripts of records deemed to have beeen [*sic*] made in times of paganism. It seems unreasonable to expect, that any other domestic evidence of Irish antiquity should subsist at this day. From these the antiquarian forms a regular history, (mixed indeed with childish and absurd fables) of a long succession of kings from the earlier ages of the world. Not to mention Partholan, his sons, his hound, and oxen; the gigantic Fomorians and their extirpation; the Nemedians, Firbolgs, Tuatha-de-Danans and their sorceries; it is generally asserted, that about a thousand, or to speak with the more moderate, about five hundred years before the Christian æra, a colony of Scythians, immediately from Spain, settled in Ireland, and introduced the Phœnician language and letters into this country; and that however it might have been people still earlier from Gaul or Britain, yet Heber, Heremon, and Ith, the sons of Milesius, gave a race of kings to the Irish, distinguished from their days by the names of Gadelians and Scuits, or Scots. Hence their writers trace a gradual refinement of their country, from a state of barbarous feuds, factions, and competitions; until the monarch celebrated in their annals by the name of Ollam-Fodla. . . . Keating, the Irish historian, who transcribed his accounts from poetical records, mentioned little more of this boasted assembly, than that its great object was to introduce civility, and to guard against those crimes which predominate in days of rudeness and violence. The magnificent detail of its grandeur and solemnity, the scrupulous attention paid by its members to the national history, annals, and genealogies, are nothing more, (as I am assured) than the interpolations of an ignorant and presumptuous translator. (vi–viii)

He undercuts this pseudohistory later in his introductory remarks, but notes that some truth is contained in the works:

They who compare this account with the progress of society in other European settlement may decide on the justness of this colouring. The Irish antiquarian deduces from it an intrinsic proof of the general authenticity of his favourite annals. Even from the idle tales of enchantments and supernatural events, a late advocate labours to prove their high antiquity. . . . But to the antiquarian I leave it to establish the authenticity of this history. It is only pertinent to my purpose to observe, that if we suppose that the old poets were merely inventors of this whole series of actions and incidents so circumstantially detailed, still they must have drawn their picture from that government and those manners, which subsisted in their own days, or were remembered by their fathers. So that we may reasonably conclude, that the state of Ireland for several centuries at least before the introduction of English power, was such as they describe it in these early periods. And this is the only conclusion which I am concerned to establish. (xvi–xvii)

27. Vallancey explained why he wrote his first major study, *Essay on the Antiquity of the Irish Language,* in a later preface in *Collectanea De Rebus Hibernicus:*

The positive assertions of all the Irish historians, that their ancestors received the use of letters directly from the Phœnicians, and the concurrence of them all in affirming that several colonies from Africa settled in Ireland, induced the author of the following essay, who had made the antient and modern language of Ireland his peculiar study for some years past, to compare the Phœnician dialect or Bearla Feni of the Irish with the Punic or language of the Carthaginians. The affinity of the language, worship and manners of the Carthaginians, with those of the ancient Irish appeared so very strong, he [Vallancey, the author] communicated his discoveries from time to time to some gentlemen well skilled in the antiquities of Ireland, and of the eastern nations; their approbation of this rude sketch induced the author to offer it to the consideration of those who have greater abilities and more leisure to prosecute such a work. (1770–1804, vol. 2, no. 8, unnumbered 13)

28. In *Orientalism and Race,* Tony Ballantyne notes the influence of these British scholars, particularly noting that Francis Wilford's work on Indian geography influenced Vallancey's *Ancient History of Ireland Proved from the Sanscrit Books of the Bramins of India* (1797) (2002, 36).

29. Vallancey praises recent Orientalist contributions and laments that such efforts have not been applied to ancient Ireland:

Mr. Richardson published his Dissertation in 1777, Mons. Anquetil Duperron obliged the world with his *Legislation Orientale.* Had these gentlemen studied to have given the picture of the Irish Brehon Laws, they could not have done it to greater perfection; and the pains they have taken to free the eastern nations from *barbarism* and *despotism,* by proving these people to have had a written law, time immemorial, reflects honour on their humanity. At this present time, that great luminary of eastern learning, Mr. *William Jones,* has in the press, *the Mahometan law of succession to the property of intestates, in Arabick, taken from an ancient MS with a verbal translation and notes.* This work will throw new lights on the history of the eastern people. . . . The Brehon laws of the ancient Irish have been passed over in shameful silence by their historians, they have been barely mentioned, but never translated or quoted. (1770–1804, vol. 3, no. 1, xii–xiii)

30. Charles O'Conor did publish *Dissertations on the History of Ireland, to which Is Subjoined a Dissertation on the Irish Colonies Established in Britain with Some Remarks on Mr. Mac Pherson's Translations of Fingal and Temora* in 1766. He also translated O'Flaherty, particularly his *Ogygia Vindicated: Against the Objections of Sir George MacKenzie* in 1775. Samuel Johnson twice wrote to O'Conor encouraging his writing of a history of Ireland, the first dated April 9, 1757, and the second dated May 19, 1777.

31. Here is the fuller quote from Vallancey on etymology:

We know the ridiculous light most etymologists are held in, the author has trod with all possible caution in this very remote path of antiquity. The arbitrary liberties taken by some etymologists have justly drawn on them the censure of the learned. Their general rule of the commutation of letters has often led many astray, and caused them to lose sight of the radical word and its primitive sense; thus for example, the word *adder* may by an etymologist unacquainted with the English language be turned to *otter,* for the *a* and *o* being both broad vowels are commutable, and the word may be written *odder;* the *d* being also commutable with *t,* the word may be formed to *otter,* an animal of a very different species from the primitive word *adder.* (1770–1804, vol. 2, no. 8, unnumbered 13–14)

32. Recent archaeological evidence suggests that the Scythians had more permanent settlements. Vallancey needed such an itinerant people, however, to account for such widespread influence. In his "Proem," Vallancey also argues that the "gypsies" are not Egyptian or Indian in origin but, like the Irish, ancient Indo-Scythian (1770–1804, vol. 6, no. 1, xiii–xv). See Burke 2002 for traveller origins.

33. In Montesquieu's earlier and well-known *Persian Letters* of 1721, the troglodytes represent an ancient people, the majority of whom were self-serving and vicious and perished because of their lack of community interest. Only two virtuous families survive and eventually choose a king but then suffer under their leader (1972, xi–xiv).

34. Vallancey's fuller argument about Thule follows:

Ireland, so properly called, was probably the first of the British isles that got the Name of Thule, as being the first the Carthaginians met with steering their course northward, when they departed from Cape Finestre the northern head-land of Spain. And this island seems to be the same said by Aristotle to have been discovered by the Carthaginians. . . . The situation of Thule has been much controverted; yet all agree it was some place towards the north, with respect to the first discoverers, and many make it to be one of the British isles. This agrees perfectly with the situation of Ireland, for the Carthaginians in sailing from Cadiz having once cleared Cape St. Vincent, had Ireland in a direct northern course before them. (1770–1804, vol. 2, no. 5, unnumbered 1–2)

Amid citations from Strabo, Pytheas Massiliensis, Catullus, Caesar, Silicus Italicus, Pliny, Tacitus, Satius ad Claud. Uxorem, Bede, Stephanus Byzantius, Holstenius, Festus Avienus, Diodorus Siculus, Arngrimus Jonas, Wernerus Ralwingus, Sir R. Sibbald, Claudian, Gildas, and Camden, Vallancey uses etymology to try to confirm his point: "Some derive the name Thule from the Arabic word *Tule,* which signifies afar off, and think it was in allusion to this the poets usually called it *ultima Thule.* Bochart derives it from a Phœnician word signifying darkness. But the words *Thual* and *Thuathal* in the Irish and probably in the Punic language signified the north, as also the left hand, agreeable to the oriental manner of naming the cardinal points with respect to their looking towards the east in their devotions" (unnumbered 6).

35. In book 1 of *On the Wisdom and Language of the Indians,* Friedrich Schlegel notes: "I close with a retrospect of the works of Sir William Jones, who by establishing the affinity between the Indian language and the Latin, Greek, German, and Persian, first threw light on this obscure study, and consequently on the earliest popular history, which before his time was every where dark and confused" (464).

36. Michael Franklin in his introduction to the 2001 republication of *On the Language and Wisdom of the Indians* (1808) notes:

Building upon the secure foundations of Sir William Jones's "Third Anniversary Discourse" (1786), he likewise rigorously shuns conjectural etymology, placing increasing emphasis, not as Jones had done, upon both "the roots of verbs and . . . the forms of grammar," but upon grammatical structure alone. In the words of Jeffrey S. Librett (from "Figuralizing the Orient, Literalizing the Jew: On the Attempted Assimilation of Letter to Spirit in Friedrich Schlegel's *Über die Sprache und Weisheit der Indier," The German Quarterly,* 69:3 [1996], 260–76, 264):"For Schlegel, similarity of *structure* indicates commonality of origin" ("gemeinschaftliche Abstammung"), and hence also commonality of essence or spirit, "whereas similarity of *roots* indicates the belated intermingling ('Einmischung') of languages that have originated separately and that share a mere contiguity of material existence." (xii)

37. Michael Franklin, the editor of the 2001 republication of Schlegel's *On the Language and Wisdom of the Indians* (1808), comments:"The fact that Schlegel and the other early German Indologists were reliant upon the publications of the British Orientalists reminds us of the very different position of Germany, anxious to define its place in Europe's destiny. There was, of course, no colonial link such as that which produced the intimate and complex interconnexions between Indology and British colonialism. If, however, the involvement of German Romanticism in Indology was not complicated by implications in external colonialism, it was certainly problematized by internal nationalistic factors" (xiv-xv).

38. Hans Aarsleff argues cogently on the influence of Jones on Schegel in his chapter titled "Sir William Jones and the New Philology," in *The Study of Language in England, 1780–1860* (1983). Also see Michael Franklin's introductions in the six-volume series *The European Discovery of India* (2001), which contains translations of Charles Wilkins, Francis Gladwin, William Jones, William Hodges, Carl W. Friedrich von Schlegel, Horace Hayman Wilson, and Henry Thomas Colebrook. The general scholarship on the influence of Schlegel and Jones on diverse fields in Europe, North America, and India is too extensive to list here.

39. See W. J. McCormack's "Varieties of Celticism," a chapter in *Burke to Beckett: Ascendancy, Tradition and Betrayal in Literary History* (1994), for a discussion of the impact of German idealism on the Gaelic Revival.

40. Both senses of the word *visionary* were in use at the time, according to the *Oxford English Dictionary.*

41. In "On the Origin and Families of Nations," Jones protests against speculative etymology for its inexact nature:

I beg leave, as a philologer, to enter my protest against conjectural etymology in historical researches, and principally against the licentiousness of etymologists in transposing and inserting letters, in substituting at pleasure any consonant for another of the same order, and in totally disregarding the vowels: for such permutations few radical words would be more convenient than *cus*or *cush,* since, dentals being exchanged for dentals, and palatials for palatials, it instantly becomes *coot, goose,* and, by transposition, *duck,* all waterbirds, and *evidently* symbolical; it next is the *goat* worshipped in *Egypt,* and, by a metathesis, the *dog* adored as an emblem of *Sirius,* or, more obviously, a *cat,* not the domestick animal, but a sort of ship, and, the *Catos,* or great sea-fish, of the *Dorians.* (qtd. in Aarsleff 1983, 130)

42. In addition to the letters of Jones, see Schlegel's *On the Language and Wisdom of the Indians,* in which he discusses the Celtic languages alongside Basque and Coptic languages and argues for their distance from Indian, Greek, and German (2001, 463–65). He references Vallancey, however, with respect.

43. Charles Saunders Peirce argued that in addition to induction and deduction, this third mode of reasoning and rhetoric exists, abduction. Whereas deduction begins with the "mental categories" and propositions of philosophy, and induction arrives at a conclusion after seeking "facts, evidence, and demonstration," abduction arrives at a conclusion based on the available evidence. Using inferences and hypotheses, it arrives at the most convincing and coherent explanation for the existence of phenomena or circumstances. A leading Peirce scholar and philosopher, Christopher J. Hookway (author of two important studies of the philosophy of Peirce, *Peirce* [1985] and *Truth, Rationality, and Pragmatism: Themes from Peirce* [2000]), succinctly summarizes abduction:

The term was introduced by Charles Peirce to describe an inference pattern sometimes called "hypothesis" or "inference to the best explanation." He used the example of arriving at a Turkish seaport and observing a man on horseback surrounded by horsemen holding a canopy over his head. He inferred that this was the governor of the province since he could think of no other figure who would be so greatly honored. In his later work, Peirce used the word more widely: the logic of abduction examines all of the norms which guide us in formulating new hypotheses and deciding which of them to take seriously. It addresses a wide range of issues concerning the "logic of discovery" and the economics of research. (Honderich 1995, 1)

Such an "inference pattern" has particular value when other modes of reasoning yield no results, perhaps following the collapse of a general theory (from which to deduce) or not having sufficient data (from which to induce a general conclusion). Hookway continues:

The logic of abduction is a logic of discovery: it studies how we are guided in constructing new hypotheses from the ruins of defeated ones; and it examines the norms guiding us in deciding which ones are worth testing. All scientific activity is grounded in the hope that the universe is intelligible, and intelligible to us. And we are to take seriously no hypothesis that "blocks the road of inquiry," forcing us to accept regularities as brute or inexplicable. It is connected to this that Peirce espouses "synechism," the doctrine that we are to expect the universe to display continuities rather than discontinuities. . . . The logic of abduction advises us to favour theories that posit continuities over those that allow from brute unmediated discontinuities. (651)

44. This souterrain and cave near Glenballythomas, south of the Rathcroghan crossroads in Roscommon, has a circular chamber that was probably an Iron Age burial chamber and a long passage. It is credited as being "discovered" by Sir Samuel Fergson in 1864, when he mapped the ogham writings in it. Obviously, Boswell and others had been there before then. The cave is also known as "Oweynagat" *(Uaimh na gcat),* or Cave of the Cat, and has been the source of much local lore because of its unique shape and the presence of two ogham stones, being seen variously as the home of the Morrígan and the Irish entrance to the otherworld.

45. Citing Herodotus, Boswell writes a piece of spectacularly absurd reasoning:

[T]he bones of the Egyptians were quite hard, and in [Herodotus's] own words, able to resist the percussion of a weighty stone; whereas those of the Persians, and other nations, could be broken with the least pebble. Now the bones which I found were not mouldered away equally all round, nor reduced to a cretaceous substance, as those of other nations would have been after remaining under ground so long, but instead thereof, had only decayed into a vast number of small holes, so as in some measure to resemble a sponge, the parts between the holes being quite hard, and perfectly preserving the figure of the bone; and this proves they must have been Egyptian, as no other bones could *have preserved any part of their surface so long.* (1790, 20)

46. Betham notes this in his privately printed publication of *Etruria Celtica* (1842, 52–53). See Leerssen 1997, 126–34, for an account.

47. See Gerry Smyth's discussion of the supplementarity of the Anglo-Irish (especially W. B. Yeats) in his excellent *Decolonisation and Criticism* (1998).

48. Joep Leerssen provides an interesting analysis of a sample of Betham's dodgy translation work, what he calls "fantastical disjointed quarks and neutrons, elementary particles without structure or cohesion or semantic identity, which could belong to any language":

[Betham] set out to hunt for similarities between the Irish language (which he did not understand) with Etruscan (which nobody understood), [decoding] . . . the Umbrian *Tabulae Iguvinae* or Gubbio Tablets, which he called the "Eugubian Tables" . . . [in] such a manner as to make it yield an account of the sea-route from Italy to Ireland. He transcribes the original PUNE CAR NE S PE TUR I E AT I I ER I E A BI E CA TE NA RA C LU M into something that he considers Gaelic: "Pune car na is be tur i e at i i er i a bi e ca ta na ra ac lu am." That, in turn, is translated in the literal English—to wit, "Phoenician to Carne (the turn) it is night voyage in it likewise in knowledge great in it the being away how it is the going with water on the ocean"; and that means, in Betham's idiomatic translation: O Phoenicians, this is a statement of the night voyage to Carne (the turn), and of the manner of going, with great science, over the waters of the ocean. (Leerssen 1997, 92)

Chapter 3. Allegory and Critique: Irish Orientalism in Eighteenth- and Nineteenth-Century Literature

1. Joep Leerssen coined this term in his important discussion of *The Wild Irish Girl* (1806) by Sydney Owenson (Lady Morgan) in *Remembrance and Imagination:* "Not only does [auto-exoticism] involve the reflex to 'see ourselves as others see us,' or in the 'cracked lookingglass of a servant,' or in an amused fascination with one's own quaintness; it is also an exoticist preoccupation with the curious, unknown nature of Ireland's other, Gaelic culture, while at the same time enshrining that culture as a central part of one's national identity. Irish cultural nationalism as a form of internalized exoticism takes its initial shape in a romantic atmosphere, as expressed most powerfully for the first time in *The [W]ild Irish [G]irl*" (1997, 67).

2. The narrator of *Hiberniæ Lachrymæ; or, The Tears of Ireland, a Poem* adds to the speculative origins of the Celt in the following passage:

> But when the Sov'reign Ruler of the sky
> Cast on his people a propitious eye,
> Brought them from Egypt; and by Joshua's hand,
> Gave them possession of the promis'd land;
> The old Philistines [that is, Ireland's ancestors], who dwelt there before,
> Were forced to migrate to a foreign shore;
> With martial force, these landed on your coast,
> And, to this day, the name Milesian boast.

(1799, 4–5)

One significant implication of this argument is that the taking of Irish land has historical precedence and theological justification.

3. See Jourdan 1996. Also see Leerssen 1996a and Watson 1996.

4. I will not begin to summarize the vast scholarship on the Ossian debates, but for more information on the continental reception of Ossian, see Gaskill 1996.

5. I am using parody in the broad sense that Linda Hutcheon defines it in *A Theory of Parody* (1985): repetition with difference.

6. *Letters from an Armenian* has been attributed to Robert Hellen, a judge of common pleas in Ireland (H. J. Smith 1926, 83). Also, written on the copy in the British Museum is "by Judge H-l-n" and the catalog has "[By R. Hellen?]." Samuel Halkett and John Laing, in their *Dictionary of the Anonymous and Pseudonymous Literature of Great Britain* (1882), however, attribute the *Letters* to Viscount Pery. Also, leading eighteenth-century scholars (such as Kevin Whelan) have expressed belief that Pery was the author. I will refer to Pery, therefore, as the author.

7. Giovanni Paolo Marana, *Letters writ by a Turkish Spy, who liv'd five and forty years . . . at Paris: giving an Account . . . of the most remarkable transactions of Europe . . . from 1637 to 1682,* translated from the French, *L'Espion Turc . . . á Paris* (1687), by W. Bradshaw and edited by Robert Midgley, 8 vols. (London, 1687–1693). This work was originally written and published in Italian in 1684. "Each subsequent edition added considerable material to the preceding one, and it is apparent that at least one-third of the completed work cannot be attributed to Marana, but is probably from the pen of Cotolendi, the author of Mlle. de Tournon. . . . Another writer who imitated Marana in this respect was Du Fresny, who in his Amusements Sérieux et comiques posed, in order to examine French conditions with critical eyes, as a Siamese traveler at Paris" (H. J. Smith 1926, 34–35). Robert Boyle's *Occasional Reflections* (1665) also had imaginary foreigners commenting on English affairs. See Conant 1908 for more on this.

8. See Mary Helen Thuente's lucid essay "William Sampson, United Irish Satirist and Songwriter" (1998).

9. Interestingly, Croker was parodying the longstanding public interest in Lord MacCartney's embassy to China, which resulted in numerous pamphlets from the Chinese emperor to King George, themselves based on the mistranslation of an actual letter. Much was made of the fact that MacCartney was Irish.

10. Louis Le Comte, S.J., *Memoirs and Observations Topographical, Physical, Mathematical, Mechanical, Natural, Civil, and Ecclesiastical. Made in a late Journey Through the Empire of China, and Published in several Letters. Translated from the French in second edition* (London, 1698). Jean-Baptiste Du Halde, *The General History of China. Containing a Geographical, Historical, Chronological, Political, and Physical Description of the Empire of China, Chinese-Tartary, Corea, and Thibet. Including an Exact and Particular Account of their Customs, Manners, Ceremonies, religion, Arts and Sciences. The Whole adorn'd with Curious Maps, and Variety of Copper-Plates* (London, 1736), translated from *Description géographique, historique chronologique, politique, et physique de l'empire de la Chine* (La Haye, 1696). Thomas Simon Gueullette, *Chinese Tales . . .* (1725), *Mongul Tales . . .* (1736), *Tartarian Tales . . .* (1759), and *Peruvian Tales . . .* (4th ed., 1764). Jean Baptiste de Boyer, Marquis D'Argens, *Chinese Letters* (London, 1741), reprinted as *The Chinese Spy* (London, 1751), translated from *Lettres Chinoises, ou Correspondance Philosophique, Historique et Critique, Entre un Chinois Voyageur et ses Correspondans à la Chine, en Moscovie, en Perse, et au Japon* (La Haye, 1739); Goldsmith borrowed significant amounts from D'Argens's French version. Joseph Addison, *Spectator* no. 50 (Apr. 27, 1711). George Lyttleton, *Letters from a Persian in England to His Friend at Ispahan* (1735). William Collins, *Persian Eclogues* (1742). Horace Walpole, *A Letter from Xo-Ho, a Chinese Philosopher at London, to his friend Lien Chi at Peking* (1757). Arthur Murphy, *The Orphan of China* (1759). John Hawkesworth, *Almoran and Hamet* (1761). Samuel Johnson, *Rasselas, Prince of Abyssinia* (1759). Thomas Percy, *Hau Kiou Choaan* (1761).

11. In Oliver Goldsmith's *The Citizen of the World* (1926), Hamilton Jewett Smith links Goldsmith's *Citizen of the World* with Marana's and Montesquieu's works and, to a lesser degree, Joseph Addison's *Spectator* no. 50 (Apr. 27, 1711), which consists of pseudoletters supposedly written by four Indian kings who were visiting London, and Samuel Johnson's *Rasselas, the Prince of Abyssinia* (1759) and his various Oriental tales in the *Rambler* (July 28, Oct. 30, 1750, May 11, 1751, Jan. 11, Feb. 29, Mar. 3, 1752) and the *Idler* (Sept. 22, 1759, Mar. 8, 22, 1760).

12. See Eco 1997 for more on early European understandings of the Chinese language, which some took to be a "perfect" language.

13. Although there is no "Selim" in Montesquieu's *Persian Letters,* there is a "Solim," a eunuch that Usbek puts in charge of his seraglio after the death of the former chief eunuch (see Montesquieu 1972, 151–61).

14. In the eighteenth century, Armenia was part of the Persian Empire.

15. Aza notes the social disparity in the Irish countryside: "Thou askest me, what are the respective Conditions of the Lord and of the Peasant in this remote World: Know therefore that they are, in general, the Conditions of the *Master* and *Vassal*. . . . [The] Way through Industry to Property and from Property to Power . . . was brought in the same Reign into Ireland. But Circumstances concurred to aid the Law in *England,* which *Ireland* hath not yet enjoyed" ([Pery] 1757, 59). Aza then takes the contrast a step further by comparing English trade and colonialism in both the East and Ireland. He concludes that the best way to alter the "Master/Vassal" inequities in Ireland is to increase Irish commerce with imperial England (a common Anglo-Irish argument at the time): "[English] Commerce soon after began to extend, it stretched to *Astracan,* crossed the *Caspian,* and reached even our World: The Riches of our *East* contributed to loosen the Shackles of the *West;* Property, when diffused, spread a Sense of Freedom, which at length destroyed the Vassalage and established a more perfect Equality in *England.* Trade would have made as compleat a Change here, if this Island had been ripe for it, more civilized, and equally unconfined in exerting its natural Advantages: But it was still barbarous, the Years of its Lordly Slavery were not completed" (59–60). While the "barbarous[ness]" of Ireland ensured Irish "Slavery," the "Riches of our East" helped bring about political liberty in England. Such an argument not only advocates colonial commerce in the Middle East and Asia but also justifies it in Ireland.

16. Goldsmith found this example of the genre to be at times unconvincing, as he notes in a review of this particular work:

> Whether the country our Author describes was deficient in materials, and had not national follies enough for general satire, we are not to determine; but certain it is, he has by no means been cautious in his endeavours to preserve the fictitious character he has assumed. This pretended Armenian espouses party, enters into the minutiæ of the politics of Ireland, explains Poynings Act, and pays not a little attention to my Lady Mayoress, the Chandler's daughter. . . . [I]t contains many things interesting to a native of Britain. The properest means of increasing our own power, by increasing that of a country which contributes to our wealth, are here explained; and the manifest error, in politics, of a government which endeavours to enrich one part of its dominions by impoverishing another, and of chusing to have but one flourishing kingdom when it might be possessed of two, is here concisely and prettily exposed. . . . It is some consolation to think, that if our calamities be as general as some would persuade us they are, our own vices alone have not brought them on; our fellow-subjects of Ireland having contributed to their share. *Iliacos intra muros peccatur et extra.* [Trojans sinned both inside and outside the walls]. (1966, 1:90–92)

Goldsmith's critic persona only discusses the Anglo-Irish in his review, which is more devoted to discussing the techniques of the letters than to discussing the one letter that paints a picture of the native

Irish. This review, which came out in August 1757, indicates Goldsmith's interest in the genre, which became manifest in his own satirical "Chinese Letters." These pseudo-Oriental letters first appeared in the *Public Ledger* in January 1760 and were published in book form in 1762 as *The Citizen of the World.* It was after examining Pery's earlier and much less successful text that Goldsmith reserved his Oriental critiques and satires for English culture; his Oriental narrator mostly avoided any mention of the "more remote" country of Ireland.

17. Like Montesquieu and Lyttleton, however, Pery finds aspects of the society to criticize, namely, that the women are handsome but not as neat (1757, 9); that they drink too much—"They are a People . . . [who] would be happier, if they followed the Command of our holy Prophet and *abstained from Wine*" (10); and that they "import" "Folly" and "Vice" from England "Duty-free" in part because they are not allowed to "trade extensively abroad" (37). Nevertheless, the Anglo-Irish retain a purity that is lost in the cosmopolitan center: "[O]ur Women are not arrived to that Ease, which prevaileth in *London,* of doing at once what they desire to do; nor doth this Place afford such Opportunities as *London;* here they are much more temperate in Fact, and though many of them promise an easy Conquest, they will hold out long" (39–40).

18. In "Letter XX," for instance, Aza complains to Abdallah about Irish intemperance in general, contrasting them with both the British and the "Easterns": "These People call us Easterns Voluptuous, *Abdallah,* yet there is no Sense ungratified by [the Irish]. . . . This People follow the Example of the *English,* yet they eat much less, for they labour less and drink much more Wine: They go to such Excesses in their intoxicating Liquors, that my Friend says, it would be no difficult Task to take any City of this Kingdom by Surprize, two Hours after the time of dining, as Half of the People are at that time usually mad" ([Pery] 1757, 85–86).

19. Nina Witoszek and Pat Sheeran's *Talking to the Dead: A Study of Irish Funerary Traditions* (1998) works over this tradition (but misses Pery's text), seeking to establish it as the primary narrative of Irish culture.

20. A footnote from Friedman's *Collected Works of Oliver Goldsmith* is of relevance here:

> Goldsmith had used this figure of the conquerors in similar contexts on two earlier occasions; see the review of Goldsmith's of Mallet's *Remains* in the *Monthly Review* for 1757: "The learned on this side the Alps have long laboured at the Antiquities of Greece and Rome, but almost totally neglected their own; like Conquerors who, while they have made in roads into the territories of their neighbours, have left their own natural dominions to desolation; ([vol.] I, p. 6);" and cf. the *Enquiry:* "The Germans early discovered a passion for polite literature; but unhappily, like conquerors, who invading the dominions of others, leave their own to desolation, instead of studying the German tongue, they wrote in Latin . . . ([vol.] I, p. 278.)." (3:24)

21. Oriental pilgrimages were similar to English travel writers going to Killarney and elsewhere in western Ireland in the nineteenth century, a primary difference being that in Ireland they generally were not seeking to recover a lost culture.

22. See Charles Stewart's *Travels of Mirza Abu Taleb [sic] Khan in Asia, Africa and Europe in the Years 1799–1803* (London, 1814; reprint, Delhi, 1972) for an account of one of the first Indian visitors to Ireland, who concluded, "The poverty of peasants or common people in [Ireland] is such that the peasants of India are rich when compared to them" (1972, 47). I am indebted to Christopher A. Bayly for this citation. For more on this, see his "Ireland, India and the Empire: 1780–1914" (2000). Also see the detailed discussion in Kabir 1961 and Cloake 1988.

23. Macaulay was reviewing Henry Neele's *Romance of History: England,* published in London in 1828.

24. A fuller quote from Ledwich's *Antiquities of Ireland* (1790) more clearly reveals his argument:

The want of literary memorials created an impenetrable obscurity, which every attempt to deduce the origin of nations, or detail early events, was unable to penetrate or dispel. How then were national honor and high-born ancestry, the love of which is most conspicuous and prominent in rude people, to be supported? The answer is by poetic tales and bardic inventions; and hence we find the wild and naked German sang the praises of his greater progenitor, Tuisco; the Highlander of Scotland the exploits of Cuchullin, and the Hibernian the wonderful peregrinations of Milesius. Bardic fictions and unfounded traditions are the oral records of every barbarous nation.

As soon as society, by the aid of regular government and the use of letters emerged from rudeness to an imperfect civilization, a new species of historic composition appeared, made up of popular tales and genuine facts, so ingeniously interwoven as not only to resemble but to pass for true history. This was the origin of romantic history, and of the Iliad, the Thebaïd, the Argonautics and similar productions. These works flattered general prejudices by embodying and identifying truth and fiction, so that it became a difficult task for subsequent writers to separate the one from the other. It was not without some struggle that people relinquished popular fables, the delight of their youth, and the constant themes of garrulous old age, however they vanished in the superior illumination of learning and criticism: wherever they are still retained, that people may be pronounced credulous and ignorant. (1804, 1–2)

25. Oliver MacDonagh comments on the representation of time in *States of Mind: A Study of Anglo-Irish Conflict, 1780–1980*: "Time was being so foreshortened that the character of druidical Ireland was being treated as validating or invalidating, in some significant fashion, the early-nineteenth-century political and social order. In part, this use of antiquity as a touchstone of the present resembled the use made of the early Church by the religious reformers and counter-reformers in the theological disputations of the sixteenth century; but with the roles reversed" (1983, 2).

26. See the scholarship of Kevin Whelan, particularly *The Tree of Liberty: Radicalism, Catholicism, and the Construction of Irish Identity, 1760–1830* (1995).

27. See the discussion of William Camden's *Annales: The True and Royall History of the Famous Empresse Elizabeth, Queene of England, France and Ireland* (1625) in chapter 1. Also see note 36 in this chapter.

28. Although Warren Hastings was acquitted, the lengthy trial, from 1788 to 1795, brought considerable public attention to the exploitative manner in which the East India Company governed much of India. See Thomas O. McLoughlin, *Contesting Ireland: Irish Voices Against England in the Eighteenth Century* (1999), for a discussion on Burke's comments on India. McLoughlin asserts that because Burke could not freely comment on Irish colonial politics, he focused on imperial abuses in India.

29. See introduction to Bernasconi 2001.

30. In *The Irish Race in the Past and the Present*, Augustus J. Thébaud, S.J., bases his discussion of the Irish on racial theories, treating the Irish as most probably a "sub-race" of the Japhetic stock, although they at one time "swarmed all over Asia" (1883, 5) and elsewhere:

[T]he posterity of Japhet is so different from that of Sem and of Cham. In each of those great primitive stocks, an all-wise Providence introduced a large number of sub-races, if we be allowed to call them so, out of which are sprung the various nations whose intermingling forms the web of human history. Our object is to consider only the Celtic branch. For, whatever may be the various theories propounded on the subject of the colonization of Ireland, from whatever part of the globe the primitive inhabitants may be supposed to have come, one thing is certain, to-day the race is yet one, in spite of the foreign blood infused into it by so many men of others stocks. Although the race was at one time on the verge of extinction by Cromwell, it has finally absorbed all the others; it has conquered; and whoever has to deal with true Irishmen, feels at once that he deals with a primitive people, whose ancestors dwelt on the island thousands of years ago. (3)

31. See Ina Ferris, *The Achievement of Literary Authority: Gender, History, and the Waverley Novels,* for a discussion of Owenson's influence on Scott's *Waverley* (1991, 122–33).

32. Traditional *aisling* and Mother Ireland images in Irish literature often link nature and the land with an image of a national feminine ideal. These feminine figures range from the archetypal sovereignty goddess, the *banfheis rígi,* to the heroines of myth (Queen Medbh, Deirdre, and Etain), to the figure in *aisling* poems, the *spéirbhean,* and to the many personae of Mother Ireland (Cathleen ní Houlihan, the Sean Bhean Bhoct, the Old Woman of Beara, Erin, Hibernica, and so on). Also, the Celtic image was often feminized, as were emblems of the Orient, in English literature, in which the imperial British were masculinized and treated as images of authority.

33. Owenson's full note in *The Wild Irish Girl* is as follows: "This was, with little variation, the general costume of the female *noblesse* of Ireland from a very early period. In the 15th century the veil was very prevalent, and was termed fillag, or scarf; the Irish ladies, like those of ancient and modern Greece, seldom appearing unveiled. As the veil made no part of the Cetic costume, its origin was probably merely oriental. The great love of ornaments betrayed by the Irish ladies of other times, 'the beauties of the heroes of old,' are thus described by a quaint and ancient author.—'Their necks are hung with chains and carkanets—their arms wreathed with many bracelets' " (1999, 48).

34. Joep Leerssen in *Mere Irish and Fíor-Ghael* writes: "[U]nless otherwise specified, the 'meere Irish' (that is, those most unlike Englishmen) are the 'real' Irish—which is nearly, but not quite, a tautology" (1996b, 55). Leerssen describes how Ireland's populations were understood, citing John Dymmok's seventeenth-century "Treatise of Ireland," which divides Ireland into four populations: "English Irish, meer Irish, degenerate English, and wild Scots"; Dymmok concentrates on describing the treacherous meer Irish, who appear as "by far the most picturesque" (50).

35. Much like the conception of the Revivalist James Stephens about ancient Ireland a century later, Owenson argues that Ireland's ancient social stratification was elaborate and distinguished; she exoticizes it, however, in comparing it to an idealization of ancient China in one of her footnotes: "In the excellent system of the ancient Milesian government, the people were divided into classes;—the *Literati* holding the next rank to royalty itself, and the *Beataghs* the fourth; so that as in China the state was so well regulated, that every one knew his place from the prince to the peasant. 'These Beataghs,' says M. O'Halleran [*sic*], 'were keepers of open houses for strangers or poor distressed natives; and as honorable stipends were settled on the Literati, so were particular tracts of land on the Beataghs to support, with proper munificence, their station" (1999, 181).

36. Although Owenson does not reference Camden or his comment, Glorvina's response to English suppositions on the "ancient modes and ancient taste" of dress specifically discusses the yellow color of clothing that Camden attributes to urine-dyed fabric:

[T]he ancient Irish, like the Israelites, were so attached to this many-coloured *costume,* that it became the mark by which the different classes of the people were distinguished. Kings were limited to seven colours in their royal robes; and six were allowed the bards. . . . But that bright yellow you now behold so universally worn, has been in all ages their favorite hue. Spenser think[s] this custom came from the East; and Lord Bacon accounts for the propensity of the Irish to it, by supposing it contributes to longevity.

"But where," said [Horatio], "do these poor people procure so expensive an article as saffron, to gratify their prevailing taste?"

"I have heard Father John say," she returned, "that saffron, as an article of importation, could never have been at any time cheap enough for general use. And I believe formerly, as *now*, they communicated this bright yellow tinge with indigeous plants, with which this country abounds." (1999, 93–94)

Glorvina then suggests that the yellow hue is gotten from "yellow lady's bed-straw" *("Galicens borum"),* "cypress moss" *("Lichen juniperinus"),* or "yellow weed" *("resida Luteola")* (94). Also see note 27 in this chapter.

37. The passage in which Horatio writes of the change in his perspective continues: "All the faculties of my taste called into exertion, yet unsated even by boundless gratification. My fancy restored to its pristine warmth, my heart to its native sensibility. The past given to oblivion, the future unanticipated, and the present enjoyed, with the full consciousness of its pleasurable existence" (Owenson 1999, 123–24).

38. For an overview of the scholarship on the Romantics' interest in Owenson's novel, see Julia Wright's introduction to the 2002 republication of *The Missionary* (42).

39. Owenson refers to Hilarion also as the apostalic nuncio (a high-ranking papal emissary) and the missionary (through most of the novel). Luxima, who calls him "Father," is also referred to as a Hindu priestess, a Christian neophyte, and an insurrectionary prophetess.

40. Julia M. Wright's 2002 introduction is the best starting place for research on the novel, although the recent interest in the novel must be credited, in part, to the 1981 republication of *The Missionary* by Scholar's Facsimiles and Reprints and edited by Dennis R. Dean, whose introduction encouraged new looks at the much forgotten text. In addition to the many essays Wright cites there, Siraj Ahmed has written a valuable critique of the novel within the context of changes in the East India Company. His essay "'An Unlimited Intercourse': Historical Contradictions and Imperial Romance in the Early Nineteenth Century" is on the Romantic Circles, Praxis Series, Web site, "The Containment and Re-deployment of English India" (http://www.rc.umd.edu/praxis). Also, Gauri Viswanathan offers a valuable commentary on *The Missionary* as a sort of anticonversion narrative in the first chapter of *Outside the Fold: Conversion, Modernity, and Belief* (1998). Another important commentary can be found in Balachandra Rajan's *Under Western Eyes: India from Milton to Macaulay* (1999).

41. Owenson's preface to the 1859 edition of *Luxima, the Prophetess: A Tale of India* points to the 1857 Indian revolt: "Vividly portraying as it does the gorgeous Scenery, the Manners, Customs, and above all, the RELIGION of that portion of the greater Indian Empire to which it relates—and these have been subject to little, if any change—the story of 'Luxima,' will, it is presumed, prefer no ordinary claims to public attention, and the more particularly on account of the recent melancholy occurrences which have distracted a country with which we have so long had extensive commercial relations. (iii–iv)" (qtd. in Owenson 2002, 53).

42. Gregory Schopen's provocative essay "Archaeology and Protestant Presuppositions in the Study of Indian Buddhism" (1997) asserts that the emphasis on textual sources by nineteenth-century European scholars excluded other valuable practices and reflected the Protestant Reformation bias toward the text of the Bible and off Catholic practices and relics.

43. See King 1999 and Said 1995.

44. Owenson earlier had written in her *Patriotic Sketches of Ireland* (1807):

The Irish, nationally considered with respect to their prevailing religion, never were a bigoted people, though the vivacity of their imagination has sometimes devoted them to superstitious illustion. When Christianity took the lead of druidism in Ireland, it was preserved and nurtured by the same mild principle of toleration, as suffered its admission; and though the druidical tenets flourished two centuries after the arrival of the first Christian missionary in the island, yet neither historical record, nor oral tradition, advances any detail of religious persecution adopted on either side. The tenets preached by the Christian missionary, or the arguments opposed by the heathen controvertist, awakened no further interest in the public consideration, than a desire to embrace that mode of faith, which came home with most force to reason, and to truth. If the arguments held out were not always attended with conviction, the doubtful superiority was never decided at the sword's point. (qtd. in Wright 2002, 284)

45. An instance of Moore's blending of Celtic and Phoenician theories can be seen in the opening lines of his second chapter in *History of Ireland* (1843): "In those parts of the Spanish coasts with which the Irish were early conversant, the Phœnicians became intermixed with the original race, or Celts; and it would appear, from the mixed character of her ancient religion, that Ireland was also peopled from the same compound source" (1835–1846, 32).

46. In a letter dated December 17, 1814, to "Messrs. Longman & Company," Moore proposes the terms of *Lalla Rookh:* "I have taken our conversation of yesterday into consideration, and the following are the terms which I propose:'Upon my giving into your hands a poem of the length of Rokeby, I am to receive from you the sum of 3000£' " (1964, 406).

47. Critics long linked Moore's Orientalism to his Irishness, as in the case of English critic Robert Sencourt, whose *India in English Literature* vigorously criticizes Moore's inaccuracies and "the grotesques with which Moore adorns the fabric of Eastern romance" but also praises the tenor of his representations:"But Moore was not always misleading; many have remarked the resemblance between the psychology of the Indian and the Irishman; and possibly the poet's nationality gave him an insight into the workings of the oriental mind; certainly he shows great skill in reproducing that compound of voluptuousness and philosophy which from earliest times has characterized the Indian" (1923, 309).

48. Howard Mumford Jones in his biography of Moore, *The Harp that Once—: A Chronicle of the Life of Thomas Moore,* writes of *Lalla Rookh*'s publication and the Orientalist atmosphere surrounding it in England:

> The book had appeared at exactly the right time. A score of travel books had whetted the appetite of readers for the glamorous East. Napoleon's exploits in Egypt and Wellesley's in India had increased the vogue of Orientalism, as had the tales of nabobs returning from the Orient with liver complaint and riches mysteriously acquired. There were Turkish ornaments above the ionic columns at Carlton House, Mameluke saddles and an effigy of Tippoo Sahib in the armory, and Chinese dresses and a palanquin in another chamber; there was an Egyptian Hall at the Mansion House; the Rosetta Stone puzzled gaping visitors in the British Museum; and under the innumerable minarets of the Pavilion at Brighton Chinese mandarins stared at green and pink marble panels on the walls. The fashionable world had yawned over *Thalaba* and *The Curse of Kehama,* but *The Giaour* and *The Bride of Abydos* restored passion to the East. James Mill began his *History of British India* the year of *Lalla Rookh,* and Shelley's *Laon and Cythna,* which became *The Revolt of Islam,* was completed in September. What matter if to the general imagination India and Egypt, the Turks and the Parsees, the Bosphorus and the Vale of Cashmere were indistinguishable parts of a vague, rich universe of color and dream? "Stick to the East"—it was the only poetical policy. *Lalla Rookh* was the culminating point in poetical Orientalism. (1937, 170–71)

49. Nigel Leask continues his valuable commentary: "Moore—A Whig 'orientalist' of the school of Jones rather than a reformer of the school of Mill or Shelley—is sympathetic to the claims of a romantic, organic nationalism which, he implies, must free itself from the imposture of Jacobin cosmopolitanism and French atheism. . . . [T]he sort of nationalism idealized by Moore in *The Fire-worshipper,* [advocates] a national independence founded on Catholic emancipation and the repeal of the Act of Union. At the same time he seeks to 'enlighten' his address by recommending 'Liberty, benevolence, peace and toleration' to the superstitious but oppressed Irish" (1992, 113).

50. Other critics have noted that Moore's commentary extended beyond a British Orientalism into discussions of Irish nationalist politics. See, for instance, Majeed 1992 and Sharafuddin 1994.

51. Luke Gibbons is discussing James Joyce's "Dead" in this section and borrows the term *double struggle* from Joyce.

52. A "Peri" corresponds to an angel in Christianity.

53. Translation theory often explores the idea that the translator, in many ways, must create a new text, in a sense betraying the original text. I use the word *traitorous* to point to this sense of the betrayal of translation.

54. The full pseudotranslated poem, "To the Ingleezee Khafir, Calling Himself Djaun Bool Djenkinzun," reads:

I

Thus writeth Meer Djafrit—
   I hate thee, Djaun Bool,
Worse than Márid or Afrit,
   Or corpse-eating Ghool.
I hate thee like Sin,
   For thy mop-head of hair,
Thy snub nose and bald chin,
   And thy turkeycock air.
Thou vile Ferindjee!
   That thou thus shouldst disturb an
Old Moslim like me,
   With my Khizzilbash turban!
Old fogy like me,
   With my Khizzilbash turban!

II

I spit on thy clothing,
   That garb for baboons!
I eye with deep loathing
   Thy tight pantaloons!
I curse the cravat
   That encircles thy throat,
And thy cooking-pot hat,
   And thy swallow tailed-coat!
Go, hide thy thick sconce
   In some hovel suburban;
Or else don at once
   The red Moosleman turban.

> Thou dog, don at once
>> The grand Kizzilbash turban!
>
> III
> Thou vagabond varlet!
>> Thou swiller of sack!
> If our heads be all scarlet
>> Thy heart is all black!
> Go on to revile
>> IRAN's nation and race,
> In thy fish-faggish style!
>> He who knows with what face
> Thou canst curse and traduce
>> Thine own Mufti, Pope Urban,
> May scorn thine abuse
>> Of the Khizzilbash turban—
> Scorn all thine abuse.
>> (Mangan 1997, 3:158–59)

55. De Vere repeatedly uses this term in *English Misrule and Irish Misdeeds* (1848).

Chapter 4. Empire, Ireland, and India

1. S. B. Cook in his essay "The Irish Raj: Social Origins and Careers of Irishmen in the Indian Civil Service, 1855–1914" makes this similar point: "Some historians have recently argued that there was not merely a dualistic Irish reaction to British culture and dominance (nationalism and Unionism), but rather a spectrum of responses which resulted from the complexity of the imperial relationship with Britain and the cultural, ethnic and political heterogeneity of Ireland" (1987, 507).

2. See David Lloyd's groundbreaking work *Anamolous States: Irish Writing and the Post-colonial Moment* for a discussion of Ireland's anomalous position, which Lloyd argues stems from its "uneven process of assimilation" by colonizing forces (1993, 111).

3. Although the title page of *The Story of Irish Orientalism* gives "M. Mansoor" as the author's name, the British Library lists Mansoor's name as "Menaham Mansūr." Complicating matters, Carol Loeb Shloss has given his name as "Mallikarjun Mansoor" in her essay "Joyce in the Context of Irish Orientalism" (1998, 264)—this is the same name as a famous Indian musician and raga singer, who died in 1992. I will refer to the author by the 1944 spelling on his own title page.

4. See Babington 1991.

5. William Keogh's argument concerning discrimination against Irish advancement in the Indian Civil Service also seems to have been personal. Keogh abandoned the Irish Party and its reform efforts four years later in 1852, out of what historian Alvin Jackson describes as "personal ambition," and accepted a post as a junior minister in the Aberdeen coalition (1999, 91). Clearly, for Keogh, advancement in Empire was important and not only for the Irish in the Indian Civil Service. His personal advancement, however, signifies what he desired for the whole of Ireland—a greater and more powerful place in the Empire.

6. Sir Patrick Cadell comments: "These figures show that about half of the soldiers were of Irish birth or descent. The percentage of Irish recruits was, however, far larger towards the end of the period, that is, in the late forties. This was doubtless due to the famine years in Ireland. . . . In 1846, for

example, the 67th obtained from 400 to 500 Irish recruits, and was able to form a second battalion" (1950–1951, 78–79).

7. For his information, Michael Holmes cites both Cook 1993 and Flanagan 1977.

8. George Thomas's story has been detailed in Hennessy 1971.

9. Suspicion frequently raises a fear that is often easily confused with guilt, as many interrogators know. Edward Said focuses on the Orientalist assumptions that create such incidents and misunderstandings and foster colonial control, reading commentary by Egypt's first British master, Lord Cromer. In the following lengthy quote, Cromer explains a central piece of Orientalist wisdom:

Sir Alfred Lyall once said to me: "Accuracy is abhorrent to the Oriental mind. Every Anglo-Indian should always remember that maxim." Want of accuracy, which easily degenerates into untruthfulness, is in fact the main characteristic of the Oriental mind.

The European is a close reasoner; his statements of fact are devoid of any ambiguity; he is a natural logician, albeit he may not have studied logic; he is by nature sceptical and requires proof before he can accept the truth of any proposition; his trained intelligence works like a piece of mechanism. The mind of the Oriental, on the other hand, like his picturesque streets, is eminently wanting in symmetry. His reasoning is of the most slipshod description. Although the ancient Arabs acquired in a somewhat higher degree the science of dialectics, their descendants are singularly deficient in the logical faculty. They are often incapable of drawing the most obvious conclusions from any simple premises of which they may admit the truth. Endeavor to elicit a plain statement of facts from any ordinary Egyptian. His explanation will generally be lengthy, and wanting in lucidity. He will probably contradict himself half-a-dozen times before he has finished his story. He will often break down under the mildest process of cross-examination. (qtd. in Said 1995, 38)

10. Bayly mentions the Conlans:

There were, of course, families of longer term residence in India such as the Conlans of Allahabad, many of them associated with the uncovenanted service, posts and railways. The Conlans appear to have followed one of the familiar paths of upward mobility in eighteenth century Ireland moving from commerce into professions and from Catholicism to Protestantism. A Conlan became leader of the Allahabad Bar in the 1880s. Only in later generations did Australian and American Conlans rediscover their Catholicism. Indo-Irish families were prominent among Eurasians who were also to throw up Indian labour activists and early nationalists. (2000, 18)

11. The standard work on Hearn is Dawson 1990.

12. See Koizumi and Ronan 1992 and Watarai 1996.

13. The possessions of Britain at the time included Maritius, Demarara, Trinidad, Jamaica, Natal, Réunion, Gaudeloupe, Cayenne, and Martinique.

14. A fuller version of Grierson's quote from his *Report on Colonial Emigration from the Bengal Presidency* follows:

A glance at the map prefixed to this report will show that the colonies importing Indian labour are in the belt of the tropics. The only exception is Natal, which is subtropical. The conditions of life in these colonies are much the same, viz. an equable climate, free from sudden or extreme variations, and an amazing fertility. The original natives of these countries, living for generations where life without labour was easy and pleasant, have developed into a type of human beings peculiarly unfitted for the higher forms of cultivation of the soil. When, therefore, European enterprize attacked these countries with the hope of carrying off the richer products of the earth, the indigenous natives were found unsuited for aiding them in the work. Cooly labour had, accordingly to be imported; and the only places where suitable labor was found to be available were India and China. Both these countries are subtropical, the greater portion being outside the tropical belt. Here the conditions of life are very different. The climate is anything but equable, and is subject to sudden and extreme variations. At one time the country is deluged by rain, at another parched for months together. Here life is impossible without labour. The most elaborate precautions have to be taken to obtain even a probably chance of raising a moderate crop; and the result is that the inhabitants of India and China have, in the course of generations, developed into human beings possessing considerable agricultural skill and a wonderful capacity for continuous hard work. The Indian's whole life is one long labour—he never has a moment's rest. The difference therefore between the tropical indogen of the colonies, and the cooly imported from India is that the former has developed, in the course of centuries, into an animal incapable of protracted labour, and the latter into an animal naturally industrious, and skilled in the arts of agriculture.

When an Indian cooly is transported to a tropical colony, he finds himself in a place quite beyond his experience. He finds a soil capable of yeilding [sic] good crops with hardly any cultivation, and he naturally applies to it all the labour and all the skill and industry which is inherent in him. The result is an outturn such as would be impossible in India, and such as he had never even dreamed of before. (1883, 36)

15. Edward Said comments in *Orientalism* on Rudyard Kipling's ideas of whiteness in the British colonies:

Kipling's White Man, as an idea, a persona, a style of being, seems to have served many Britishers while they were abroad. The actual color of their skin set them off dramatically and reassuringly from the sea of natives, but for the Britisher who circulated amongst Indians, Africans, or Arabs there was also the certain knowledge that he belonged to, and could draw upon the empirical and spiritual reserves of, a long tradition of executive responsibility towards the colored races. . . . Yet in the end, being a White Man, for Kipling and for those whose perceptions and rhetoric he influenced, was a self-confirming business. One became a White Man because one was a White Man. (1995, 226)

16. For instance, Akbar is given somewhat backhanded praise as a brilliant soldier and general with a genius for organization that is "rare among eastern potentates and not common in any part of the world" (V. A. Smith 1966, 257). Smith praises the emperor for his original mind but criticizes his inability to conceive of a form of government other than autocracy (with himself as emperor), which could qualify Akbar to be classed an Oriental despot, but Smith does not say so. Also, throughout the study, Akbar is treated as a somewhat devious and often hubristic leader.

17. W. Nassau Lees's letter was reprinted in *Indian Musalmans: Being Three Letters Reprinted from the "Times" with an Article on Education, Reprinted from the "Calcutta Englishman" with an Appendix Containing Lord Macaulay's Minute* (1871).

18. Cook does not treat Ireland as a colony per se, but he discusses how Ireland had an anomalous identity within the United Kingdom, distinct from Wales or Scotland (1993, 21–26): "Commonly re-

garded as the third realm of the United Kingdom Ireland was, at the same time, seen as sharing in the colonial experience in ways that the English core of the metropolitan state did not. Even though Ireland was not actually considered by policy-makers a colony in its own right, the well-formed habit of analogy and exchange suggests a complicated view by contemporaries of a land whose integration into the rest of the United Kingdom was imperfect and which in some ways occupied what may be described as an anomalous intermediary relationship between Britain and its empire" (136).

19. These conservative Irish scholars have called for the end of postcolonial criticism in Irish studies. The subfield of postcolonial thought in Irish studies has become so extensive that Oxford University Press recently published a full-length history and critique of it: Stephen Howe's controversial *Ireland and Empire,* which has been reviewed, attacked, and criticized widely in Irish studies circles (see my review in the *Irish Literary Supplement* [fall 2001], from which the following comments are gleaned). Howe argues that a recently revitalized Irish nationalist and postmodernist/postcolonial critique has overstated the case of Irish colonization and decolonization. He rigorously surveys the past twenty or so years of Irish studies scholarship and concludes that postcolonial arguments amount to nationalist revisionism of Irish culture and history. He justly concludes of Irish history: "A colonial past, then, yes; though one that took unique hybrid forms, involving extensive integration and consensual partnership as well as exploitation and coercion" (2000, 232). He also persuasively argues that the domination of Ireland more closely resembles other European states (Albania, Czechoslovakia, Estonia, Finland, Poland, and so on) than Bengal, Egypt, or Ghana. He asserts that cross-colony ties (factual or imagined or both) between Ireland and other British colonies, such as India, have little categorical validity, yet he points to their pervasive use now and in the Irish past. In doing so, Howe points to more than he suspects, and reveals more than he can dispel. He dismisses the significant recognition that cross-colony ties between Ireland and India have a much wider and richer cultural history than ties, say, between Ireland and Poland, Estonia, or Sicily.

20. The Irish government had appointed Eugene O'Curry (1794–1862) and John O'Donovan (1806–1861) as coeditors of the publication. They commissioned a distinguished panel that included Sir George Petrie (1789–1866) and James Henthorn Todd (1805–1869) (Welch 1996, 425). After O'Donovan's and O'Curry's deaths, the work was completed under the editorship of Robert Atkinson.

21. Sir Henry Sumner Maine borrows from an imperial description of the Celts in Gaul for his understanding of the ancient Irish: "Cæsar supplies an answer, which must, I think, contain a portion of the truth. He says that if a Celt of Gaul refused to abide by a Druid judgment he was excommunicated: which was esteemed the heaviest of penalties" (1966, 39).

22. Maine projects how Irish history might have been different if the English had either further colonized Ireland or not done so at all:

> I do not know that the omission of the English, when they had once thoroughly conquered the country, to enforce the Brehon law through the Courts which they established, has ever been reckoned among the wrongs of Ireland. But if they had done this, they would have effected the very change which at a much later period they brought about in India, ignorantly, but with the very best intentions. . . . The Anglo-Norman settlement on the east coast of Ireland acted like a running sore, constantly irritating the Celtic regions beyond the Pale, and deepening the confusion which prevailed there. If the country had been left to itself, one of the great Irish tribes would almost certainly have conquered the rest. All the legal ideas which, little conscious as we are of their source, come to us from the existence of a strong central government lending its vigour to the arm of justice would have made their way into the Brehon law; and the gap between the alleged civilization of England and the alleged barbarism of Ireland during much of their history, which was in reality narrower than is commonly supposed, would have almost wholly disappeared. (1966, 53–55)

23. Maine provides the following example of the "strong air of fancifulness and unreality":

It seems as if the Brehon lawyer, after forming (let us say) a conception of a particular kind of injury, set himself, as a sort of mental exercise, to devise all the varieties of circumstance under which the wrong could be committed. . . . The indulgence of his imagination drew frequently into triviality or silliness, and led to an extraordinary multiplication of legal detail. Four pages of the Book of Aicill (a very large proportion of an ancient body of law) are concerned with injuries received from dogs in dog-fights, and they set forth in the most elaborate way the modification of the governing rule required in the case of the owners—in the case of the spectators—in the case of the "impartial interposer"—in the case of the "half-interposer," *i.e.* the man who tries to separate the dogs with a bias in favour of one of them—in the case of an accidental looker on—in the case of a youth under age, and in the case of an idiot. The same law-tract deals also with the curious subjects of injuries from a cat stealing in a kitchen, from women using their distaffs in a woman-battle, and from bees, a distinction being drawn between the case in which the sting draws blood and the case in which it does not. Numberless other instances could be given; but I repeat that all this is mixed up with that even now has juridical interest, and with much which in that state of society had probably the greatest practical importance. (1966, 45–46)

24. Maine argues the Brehon and the Brahmin relied on religious authority:

The Brehon could not, like the Brahmin, make any such portentous assertion as that his order sprang from the head of Brahma, that it was an embodiment of perfect purity, and that the first teacher of its lore was a direct emanation from God. But the Brehon did claim that St. Patrick and other great Irish saints had sanctioned the law which he declared, and that some of them had even revised it. Like the Brahmin, too, he never threw away an opportunity of affirming the dignity of his profession. In these law-tracts the heads of this profession are uniformly placed, where Cæsar placed the Druids, on the same level with the highest classes of Celtic society. The fines payable for injury to them, and their rights of feasting at the expense of other classes (a form of right which will demand much attention from us hereafter), are adjusted to those of Bishops and Kings. (1966, 50–51)

25. The title page of the third edition (1917) reads: "Revised in accordance with matter found in the Fifth Volume of the Ancient Laws of Ireland, issued since the first edition was written, and with matter gleaned elsewhere."
26. Derived from the Irish word *brethem,* "a judge."
27. Below is a fuller quotation of Dan Breen's autobiography, beginning with the imprisonment of nationalist prisoners after their arrest following a Volunteer meeting:

[Seán Treacy] was summarily tried and sentenced to six month's imprisonment. Such trials had become a mere formality; the political prisoners refused to recognize the British courts, and turned the proceedings into a farce by reading newspapers or singing treasonable ballads while the evidence was being produced. At the end of August or early September, Seán and a number of other prisoners were transferred from Cork to Mountjoy jail, Dublin. On 20 September Seán and his comrades went on hunger-strike in protest against the treatment meted out to them by their jailers. It was one of the first occasions on which Irish political prisoners made use of this procedure. Five days after the hunger-strike began, Tom Ashe died as a result of the efforts made by the prison doctor and his attendants to use forcible feeding.

The tragedy enfuriated the whole Irish nation, and two days afterwards the British gave in and accorded prisoners in Mountjoy the conditions for which they had campaigned. Forcible feeding of political prisoners on hunger-strike was never again attempted. (1991, 18–19)

28. Michael Silvestri quotes the leaflet "The Youths of Bengal" as such: "This is how a nation awakes. Flare up with the fire of vengeance for the annihilation of foreign enemies. You will find that the victory is yours. History bears testimony to this. Read and learn the history of Pearse—the gem of young Ireland—and you will find how noble is his sacrifice; how he stimulated new animation in the nation, being mad over independence. . . . Pearse died and by so dying he roused in the heart of the nation an indomitable desire for armed revolution. Who will deny this truth?" The footnote reads: "'The Youths of Bengal' (1929), cited in Hale, *Terrorism in India*, p 214" (2000b, 469).

29. Silvestri cites Nirad C. Chaudhuri, *Thy Hand Great Anarch! India, 1921–1952* (1987), for this quote (2000b, 469).

Part Two. The Oriental and the Celt: The Syncretism of the Revival

1. Luke Gibbons insightfully discusses Sophie Bryant's work in his essay "The Sympathetic Bond: Ossian, Celticism, and Colonialism" (1996).

2. In her chapter "Phoenician Genealogies and Oriental Geographies: Language and Race in Joyce and His Successors," Elizabeth Butler Cullingford notes, "Whether it is serious or strategic, Joyce's Orientalist assertion of exotic (and factually dubious) Phoenician-Semitic and Egyptian-African origins balances his condemnation of Irish insularity" (2001, 138).

3. The *James Joyce Quarterly*'s special double issue of winter and spring 1998, "ReOrienting Joyce," contains a number of valuable essays for a discussion of Irish Orientalism, including essays by R. Brandon Kershner, Zack Bowen, Heyward Ehrlich, Carol Loeb Shloss, and Aida Yared. Both Ehrlich and Shloss note that Joyce followed a tradition of Irish Orientalism developed by Moore and Mangan. In "Joyce in the Context of Irish Orientalism," Shloss notes:

> In aligning the Celtic with the Phoenician, Joyce followed the example of Charles Vallancey and Thomas Moore; thus, it is in tracing this affinity that we can see the most distinctive features of Joyce's Orientalist strategy, for he wished to exploit the similarities of Ireland and the East as part of the claim that Irish civilization was more ancient and more distinguished than its contemporary demeaned position within the British Commonwealth would indicate. He was interested in an Irish connection to the Orient that preceded Orientalism, which had inspired Mansoor to write about the contributions of the Anglo-Irish to the study of the East. In the hands of Joyce, Orientalism became part of an anti-imperialist strategy that could buttress a sense of Irish identity founded neither on the English language nor on the expansionism in British rule. (1998, 266–67)

4. Brigadier General F. P. Crozier notes in *A Word to Gandhi: The Lesson of Ireland:* "The 'Black-and-Tans,' a nickname given to the new English recruits of the old R.I.C., on account of their green caps and khaki clothing and their similarity to the famous pack of hounds of that name, not for its ability to hunt and kill anything, and later extended to all the police in Ireland outside Ulster, began to submerge the military in September 1920 and went from bad to worse, till they kicked the dust of Ireland off their boots for ever in 1922, on account of the futility of the whole régime" (1931, 27–28).

5. A copy of *The Leslies of Tarbert, Co. Kerry, and Their Forebears* by Pierce Leslie Pielou (Dublin: Brindleys, 1935) exists in the Adyar Theosophical Library in Chennai, India. The copy is inscribed to

James and Margaret Cousins, "To Jim and Gretta, From Leslie," and reinscribed in a different hand, "Presented to the Adyar Library on the 8th of January 1950 by Dr. J.H. Cousins." Cousins, a friend of the Pielous, later wrote a tribute in memory of Annie Pielou, who died in 1940.

6. In a story of W. P. Ryan's, once at a Dublin séance Yeats requested a glass of water and a sword but had to make do with a saw, which he waved about madly but summoned no spirits until an old soldier produced a bayonet. "The bayonet, unlike the saw, passed muster. Then the passes, signs, summonings, and all the modern magic began. But what presences really manifested themselves the audience never knew, for rising into sheer and whirling ecstasy, the poet and wonder-worker began to slash on all sides with the bayonet, and amid shrills, screams and laughter the auditors dashed helter-skelter from their places and took fearful refuge under a large table till the worst was over" (1912, 203).

7. In another pamphlet, *The Growth of the Theosophical Society in Ireland,* which contains prints of paintings by AE and Yeats done on the walls of the Theosophical Society's Lodge House, Pielou details this history, noting the positions of its chief Irish members, including one of the "formers" William Quan Judge of the Theosophical Society in 1875. He tells how Claude F. Wright founded the Dublin Lodge in 1885 and of the involvement of Charles Johnston, and one of Yeats's aunts, Isabella Varley, daughter of William Pollexfen of Sligo. He ends the pamphlet with a missionary call: "Let us keep Dr. Annie Besant's ideal of the future and purpose of Ireland before us, and work so that Ireland may become once again a spiritual force in Europe" (1947, 81).

Chapter 5. Uniting the Circumference: Cross-Colonialism

1. For an extended discussion of the *Nation,* see Cairns and Richards 1988.

2. Following Chen Pu Sze's speech, he continued to contribute to *An Phoblacht:* "China's Struggle for Political and Economic Freedom" (Jan. 28, 1927, 3) and "The Rise of China as a Great Power" (Feb. 4, 1927, 3), which was continued the following week (Feb. 11, 1927, 3). In addition, many articles presented the Chinese nationalist position; for example, "Chinese Claims Outlined" (Jan. 21, 1927, 4); "Voice of Resurgent China" (Feb. 25, 1927, 2); "British Policy in China" (Feb. 4, 1927, 3); and "The Unequal Treaties and the Chinese Revolution" (Apr. 1, 1927, 2).

3. Chinese rebels kidnapped Irish missionaries in 1827. The capture raised quite a stir in the British and Irish presses for weeks, although the missionaries were reported released unharmed on February 8, 1927, after being reported as "Stabbed and Bound to Trees in China [in] All-Night Agony," as a headline in the *Irish Independent* (similar to many other papers) read (Feb. 5, 1927, 7). To be fair to the *Irish Independent,* which certainly played up the reports, on February 10, 1927, the following note was printed with the headlines: "Exaggerations: Priests Deny Stories": "'Rev. Fathers O'Connell and McDonald, of St. Columba's Mission, Hanyang, concerning whom sensational reports had been sent out in connection with their arrest in West Hupeh, deny the exaggerations, according to a Hankow cablegram, received by the Orient Press Service,' says the 'Daily Herald.' 'Our clothes and boots were not taken off,' they say; 'neither were we stabbed, nor were we tied to poles nor to a tree' " (7). *An Phoblacht,* characteristically, had its own particular take on the situation, as a letter to the editor by "Cave Hill" demonstrates: "If Irish missionaries are ill-treated in China it is because they are looked on as Britishers; if convents are razed it will be because they are regarded as buildings housing members of the race that has forced opium on China, looted Chinese commerce for years, and to-day turns machine guns on defenceless women and children" (Jan. 21, 1927, 3).

4. A number of recent critics, such as Ashis Nandy and Patrick Hogan, have rightly questioned some Eurocentric assumptions and conclusions of arguments such as Brasted's, particularly assertions that attribute most of Indian nationalist thought to Europeans. As a case in point, Brasted writes, "Since the Hindu past was unable to supply a suitable foundation on which to unite the peoples of

India in devotion to the cause of self-determination, Indian nationalists turned to European history" (1985, 24).

5. Bayly's work highlights parallels between the anticolonial movements in these countries, especially between Ireland and India, in which, despite significant differences, he has found striking parallels in regard to the effects of colonialism and the resistance to it.

6. See Said's very relevant comments on the Orientalist wisdom of Lord Cromer in Egypt in *Orientalism* (1995, 31–40).

7. The 1879 poster calls for an April 20 "Great Tenant Right Meeting in Irishtown." I thank Kevin O'Neill for bringing this poster to my attention.

8. Christopher Harvie has commented on James Connolly's pan-Celtic socialism in his essay "The Scottish Intellectuals, 1760–1930." He notes that Scottish "proletarian nationalism" co-opted the memory of James Connolly in the early twentieth century: "Connolly was . . . assumed to represent a Celtic socialism, and remained a significant influence on the Scottish left in the inter-war period" (1992, 254).

9. Ireland needed alliances in order to break from the British Empire, but, as Casement knew, they needed not be German. France might have helped break Ireland from England at one time; "Napoleon, too late, in St. Helena, realized his error: 'Had I gone to Ireland instead of Egypt the Empire of England was at an end' " (1958, 19). Casement attributes a moment when modern Ireland could have gained its freedom (if the French had invaded) to the moment that Said views as the "birth of modern Orientalism" and its nexus of historical specificity, knowledge, and power (see 1995, 87, 388). In other words, Napoléon's acquisition of Egypt, through the use of Orientalist knowledge in 1798, may have temporarily added to the French Empire, but it did not undermine the British one, which could have aided Ireland and saved Napoléon's empire from British defeat. Again, Casement seeks arguments that prove that if Europe had helped Ireland, Irish victory would have been certain.

10. For instance, Casement does not always treat India coevally; he compares his contemporary India with Ireland at the end of the eighteenth century, noting that if one "[s]ubstitute[s] India for Ireland . . . the Grattan of 1780 becomes the Indian patriot of to-day" (1958, 82).

Chapter 6. W. B. Yeats's Celtic Orient

1. I follow Patrick Colm Hogan's lead in using the more descriptive term *postcolonization* for a culture such as Ireland's instead of *postcolonial*. Hogan explains the use of this more accurate term in *Colonialism and Cultural Identity* (2000).

2. Homi Bhabha uses this term in his essay "DissemiNation: Time, Narrative, and the Margins of the Modern Nation" (see Bhabha 1990). Bhabha's use of the term *national narrative* signifies a narrative in the broadest cultural sense, that is, a narrative that permeates a culture, embodying its identity and hegemony.

3. AE adopts this term in his nationalist exploration of Irish identity, *The National Being* (1916). AE differentiated the terms *national ideal; national soul; the body* or *State of the nation;* and *the national being.* On the last of these terms he wrote: "In the highest civilizations the individual citizen is raised above himself and made part of a greater life, which we may call the National Being. He enters into it, and it becomes an oversoul to him, and gives to all his works a character and grandeur and a relation to the works of his fellow-citizens, so that all he does conspires with the labors of others for unity and magnificence of effect" (11–13).

4. Yeats and other Revivalists were also fascinated by the fashionable modernist works of French symbolists, who were also interested in "Asiatic" cultures. But like the French poets and Ezra Pound (with his "ideograms"), many modern artists grossly misunderstood their "material." Yeats was no ex-

ception: for his Celtic Noh dramas, he believed he had found an authentically trained Japanese Noh dancer in Michio Ito, a modern dancer trained in Paris; the irony of his mistake is significant.

5. It is important to note, however, that in "The Celtic Element in Literature," Yeats is not merely making Celtic-Oriental comparisons; rather, he is arguing for recognition of the "Celtic element" in world literature and the importance of national epics for nations, Finnish and "Mahomedan" as well as Irish.

6. The preface to *The Cat and the Moon* continues: "It cannot be because of the books we have read, for we have all read such different books. . . . That is the kind of insoluble problem that makes the best conversation, and if you will come and visit me, I will call the Dublin poets together, and we will discuss it until midnight" (Yeats 1923, 854).

7. Charles Johnston recalled his school days with Yeats in his essay "Yeats in the Making" (1977).

8. Roy Foster comments lucidly on Yeats's Protestant occultism in his biography:

[Yeats] might be located in a particular tradition of Irish Protestant interest in the occult, which stretched back through Sheridan Le Fanu and Charles Maturin, took in WBY's contemporary Bram Stoker, and carried forward to Elizabeth Bowen: all figures from the increasingly marginalized Irish Protestant middle class, from families with strong clerical connections, declining fortunes and a tenuous hold on landed authority. An interest in the occult might be seen on one level as a strategy for coping with contemporary threats (Catholicism plays a strong part in all their fantasies), and on another as a search for psychic control. (1997, 50)

9. Edward Larrissy argues, "There is much truth in the suggestion that many Anglo-Irish writers are ambivalently haunted by the power of the Catholic faith professed by their social inferiors. Both Yeats and Wilde, in their different ways, seem at times to be supplying a deficiency which is measured by Catholicism. One of the chief differences was that Wilde was ready to toy with and eventually succumb to the Catholic Church, while Yeats's attitude to official Catholicism always contained a large quota of mistrust and a sense of superiority" (1994, 21).

10. Larrissy continues:

Yeats was born into a caste and family with strong Masonic connections. And although by his day the "egalitarian overtones" had been moderated, the sense of being a rational mean between sectarian extremes persisted. This fact makes a contribution towards Yeats's sense of his capacity to mediate between Irish extremes in general. But so also does the supposed character of Freemasonry, as of Rosicrucianism, for their mystical doctrines were supposed to derive from the Orient, a location which, as we have seen, was thought throughout the nineteenth century to have strong associations with the Celtic, with Ireland, and more especially with Ancient Ireland, and her temper and wisdom. (1994, 18)

11. Foster provides the following commentary:

While [Yeats] was discovering the world of the nationalist intelligentsia, he was serving another apprenticeship—spiritual rather than political. Like his literary explorations, it began as he finished at the High School, and some of the inspiration came from family example. In late 1884 WBY's aunt Isabella Pollexfen Varley, married to an artist in London and more intellectually modish than her sisters, sent WBY a copy of A.P. Sinnett's *Esoteric Buddhism*. This was a founding text of the fashionable New Age religion, Theosophy, blending East and West in a spiritual synthesis readily absorbed by its devotees, WBY probably first heard about it at one of Dowden's Sundays: Dowden had ordered Sinnett's work for the National Library. After obtaining it, WBY lent the book to his friend Charles Johnston, still at the High School. Johnston, handsome and enterprising all his life, had been considering a career in the Church; instead he went to London to interview the founders of the movement, and on his return introduced Theosophy to Dublin. A craze began, to the chagrin of the Headmaster, who saw "his most promising students [touched] [*sic*] with the indifference of the Orient to such things as college distinction and mundane success." For some of them, notably Johnston and WBY, the "craze" continued into the time spent at art school and far beyond. (1997, 45)

12. Foster comments that "[Mir Alaud Ali] represented a local reflection of the fashion for Indian things which infused intellectual avant-garde circles in the 1880s" (1997, 47). His footnote to this comment is also instructive: "This was encouraged by the work of Max Muller [*sic*] (notably his editions of *The Sacred Books of the East*, 1879–1910) and English versions of *The Buddhist Sutras* (1881), *The Bhagavad-Gita* (1882) and *The Upanishads* (1884). But it had been anticipated by Goethe, and Indian philosophy also influenced Emerson, Whitman and other writers devoured by WBY at this time. Andrew Lang's *Myth, Ritual and Religion* (2 vols., 1887) was the inescapable vade-mecum" (552 n. 80).

13. Foster provides further commentary on Chatterjee and his place in the Theosophical movement:

He supplied Madame Blavatsky with the tenets of Hindu mystical thought, which she fed into the mysteriously derived "Mahatma" letters to her disciple Sinnett. From 1884 Mohini Chatterjee acted as Theosophy's roving ambassador in Europe. Rather than expounding Sinnett's ideas (which owed more to Western occultism), he broadcast the more existentialist principles of Samkara, a mystical approach which queried much accepted religion and stressed the need to extinguish "action": the end of Samkara philosophy was to express the supreme in the individual self. Souls, moreover, were emanations from four divine spirits, endlessly incarnated and endlessly returning to their source. Thus in Dublin, during April 1886, he preached the necessity to realize one's own individual soul by contemplation and the illusory nature of the material world. (1997, 47–48)

14. First, in act 1, Anusuya questions the king about who he is and why he is in their "pious grove"; as she pries answers from the king, Śakantulā says in an aside: "Be brave my heart. Anusuya speaks your very thoughts" (Yeats 1973, 12). Second, during act 4, Anusuya questions Śakantulā about her love aches—"I have heard old, romantic stories, and I can't help thinking that you are in a state like that of a lady in love. Please tell us what hurts you. We have to understand the disease before we can even try to cure it"; the amorous king, listening in the bushes, echoes Śakantulā's earlier aside: "Anusuya expresses my own thoughts" (Kalidasa 1959, 29).

15. Looking back from 1925, after he was the established poet of the Revival and the new Irish Free State, Yeats elaborated on the origins of the poems in a note to *Crossways*:

Many of the poems in *Crossways,* certainly those upon Indian subjects or upon shepherds and fauns, must have been written before I was twenty, for from the moment when I began *The Wanderings of Oisin,* which I did at that age, I believe, my subject-matter became Irish. Every time I have reprinted them I have considered leaving out most, and then remembered an old school friend who has some of them by heart, for no better reason, as I think, than that they remind him of his own youth. The little Indian dramatic scene was meant to be the first scene of a play about a man loved by two women, who had the one soul between them, the one woman waking when the other slept, and knowing but daylight as the other only night. It came into my head when I saw a man at Rosses Point carrying two salmon. "One man with two souls," I said, and added, "O no, two people with one soul." I am now once more in *A Vision* busy with that thought, the antithesis of day and of night and of moon and of sun. (1973, 489)

16. Foster argues that Chatterjee's influence can also be seen here: "Some of the poems [of *Wanderings*] looked back to his Theosophist induction of 1885 and 1886, using the language of Indian mysticism: Mohini Chatterjee's Vedantic teachings were reproduced in quatrains enjoining 'Long thou for nothing, neither sad nor gay,' and 'Kanva on Himself,' never republished in WBY's lifetime, turned Mohini's injunctions straight into poetic form" (1997, 85).

17. The dinner was sponsored by the India Society and the influential Irish publication the *Nation* (Foster 1997, 469).

18. Tagore's family were wealthy zamindars, or landowners, and although they were Brahmos, they still wore their Brahmin thread. See Dutta and Robinson 1996 for more discussion.

19. Tagore even performed the role of the "Fakir" in his play *The Post Office*, just as Yeats occasionally took the stage in the Abbey.

20. Many studies explore this "Oriental" fashion in Europe; one particularly relevant and erudite essay is Sylvia C. Ellis's chapter on the popularity of "things Japanese" in her book *The Plays of W. B. Yeats: Yeats and the Dancer* (1995). The essay, "Japan, *Japonisme,* and *Japonaiserie,*" traces this influence on Yeats and on European culture as a whole.

21. Postcolonial critics may place much of Yeats's cultural nationalism in the category or mode of "liberal decolonisation" (see G. Smyth 1998). Smyth writes: "Yeats's attempt to discover/construct a valid culture to equal metropolitan culture and thus form the basis for an equal political relationship (a hallmark of liberal decolonisation) was disabled at its conceptual moment, because the drive to assert equality in fact reinforced the structure of inequality" (75). This disablement, however, did not prevent Yeats's ideas and writings from being widely influential in Irish cultural nationalist circles.

22. Cousins, who is the main subject of chapter 8, had moved to India with his wife, Margaret, early in the century and often wrote about the similarities between Irish cultural nationalism and Indian cultural nationalism, having participated in dramatic revivals in both countries. Much of their lives is recorded in their "duo-autobiography," *We Two Together* (1950).

23. In his essay "Yeats and Decolonization," Edward Said discusses Yeats's rivaling allegiances and one of his techniques for resolving sectarian and political tensions: "For Yeats the overlappings he knew existed between his Irish nationalism and the English cultural heritage that both dominated and empowered him as a writer were bound to cause an overheated tension, and it is the pressure of this urgently political and secular tension that one may speculate caused him to try to resolve it on a 'higher,' that is, nonpolitical level. (1990, 80).

24. This is not to say that Yeats was never involved in politics (he later was a senator in the Irish Free State), only that he often treated politics as a distasteful necessity.

25. Yeats first discussed witnessing this man arranging Asian prints in the British Museum in his autobiographies. Significantly, Yeats states that it was a Japanese man arranging the prints, not a Chinese man, as he implies in the introduction to *Gitanjali:* "I saw a Japanese at a great table judging Chinese and Japanese pictures. 'He is one of the greatest living authorities,' I was told, 'the Mikado's hereditary . . . ' " (1995, 548). By not identifying the Japanese man's nationality, whom Yeats refers to in the introduction only as "a little dark-skinned man," and by stating that he was arranging only Chinese prints, Yeats demonstrates how he conflated the cultures of the "Orient." He probably did so to

simplify the story, but his elisions are still significant; they demonstrate that he presented such cultural differences in the "Orient" as not that important, to him or to his audience.

26. Tagore expressed such images and ideas in longer form in essays in *Nationalism* and in "A Poet's School" (1926). A fuller version of the quote from 1912 cited in the text reads: "As I stand by the open window I find streams of people running in various directions. They seem to me like so many tools in the hands of an invisible mechanic. . . . I stand outside this giant engine and see the living pistons, propelled by the steam of hunger, moving up and down with an indomitable energy. . . . Nobody knows the goal of this incessant drive, what latent power is in the process of being manifested" (qtd. in Dutta and Robinson 1996, 163–64).

27. Tagore's criticism of colonialism and imperial culture also parallels his criticisms of "civilized man" in later essays such as "A Poet's School" (1997b, 251).

28. Edward Said's *Orientalism* discusses how the European academic discipline of Orientalism, in conjunction with European colonialism, "Orientalized" the self-perceptions of Near Eastern and Asian cultures.

29. *Kalevala* is a collection of Finnish oral poetry that was touted as a type of national story or the Finnish national epic. Yeats was interested in developing an Irish equivalent. For an insightful and critical exploration of the construction of national epics (the Finnish *Kalevala* in particular) during the nation building of the eighteenth and nineteenth centuries, see André Lefevere's "The Gates of Analogy: The *Kalevala* in English," in *Constructing Cultures: Essays on Literary Translation* (Bristol, Pa.: Multilingual Matters, 1998).

30. Yeats remarks in the notes to *At the Hawk's Well* about the first large audience attending his "aristocratic form" of drama: "And round the platform upon three sides were three hundred fashionable people including Queen Alexandra" (1969, 416).

31. In "Studying a New Science: Yeats, Irishness, and the East," Rickard has detailed much of Yeats's personal relationship with Swami. He also explores what he calls Yeats's "'Indo-Irishness'—his conjunction of Irish and Indian ethnicity and culture—in order to demonstrate some of the ways that 'India' functioned as a construct for Yeats in larger historical and ideological struggles" (1997, 97).

32. Rickard notes: "Yeats worked to 'translate' and popularize elements of Indian culture that he hoped would invigorate contemporary writers, especially Irish writers, and serve as a poetic last will and testament or a cultural blueprint for constructing a non-modern, antimaterialist Irishness that would owe no debt to political and cultural forces that Yeats found obnoxious in the Ireland of the 1930s" (1997, 103).

33. Rickard elaborates:

Yeats was sensitive to India as an oppressed colony of England, but his actual knowledge of contemporary India was limited; again, whatever he saw in India politically seemed to mirror Irish realities. English colonization of India was leading to the same ills and deterioration that Yeats felt he was witnessing in contemporary Ireland, though he seems to have felt that while India was threatened by Western development and modernization, it was less affected than Ireland, still closer to its original native culture. (Yeats seems to have been ignorant of the many divisions and tensions within modern India.) In 1932, Yeats wrote that he had been told by "an exceedingly religious Mohammedan" that "India would never organise" and that this is what made India an "eternal nation" *(Essays and Introductions* 427). (1997, 102)

Chapter 7. Theosophy and the Nation: George Russell (AE) and James Stephens

1. Other original prose works, particularly *The Charwoman's Daughter* (1912), *The Crock of Gold* (1912), *Here Are Ladies* (1913), and *The Demi-Gods* (1914), also mix whimsy and fantasy with harsh social conditions. These conditions mostly result from the characters' poverty.

2. Irish novelists such as James Joyce, Flann O'Brien, and Liam O'Flaherty also disrupted the English form of the novel. The immediate critical result was often that their works were seen as poorly constructed attempts at a novel (by English standards). But later, because modernism also affected their novelistic forms and narrative devices, these writers' innovations have often been considered not as Irish novels, per se, but as modernist novels. It is important to remember that critics rarely identify an Irish novelistic tradition in the nineteenth century (excluding Anglo-Irish writers in the "Big House" tradition, such as Maria Edgeworth, and Romantic writers such as Sidney Owenson, who distinguished their work as Irish long before Joyce and O'Brien). These modernist Irish writers made a conscious distinction between Irish novels and English novels. Their innovations might, therefore, also be considered as breaks with a colonially imposed literary standard.

3. Peter Kuch cites this from an unpublished letter to Charles Weekes (Dec. 14, 1926), which was in Kuch's possession at the time of writing *Yeats and A.E.: The Antagonism that Unites Dear Friends.* He also points to a 1932 dissertation by Grace E. Jameson titled "Mysticism in AE and Yeats in Relation to Oriental and American Thought" (Ohio State Univ.) for evidence (1986, 46–47).

4. See Nicholas Allen's excellent biography *George Russell (Æ) and the New Ireland, 1905–30* (2003), Brown 1988, Kuch 1986, Kain and O'Brien 1976, Summerfield 1975, and Abinash Chandra Bose 1970.

5. In 1907 *Sinn Féin* essays such as "The Seoinin," "The Builders," "Patriotism and Parochial Politics," and "Irish Englishmen," Stephens defines and sharply attacks the "Seoinini," or the west Briton, "caste."

6. Stephens wrote in 1930:

The article for the Irish worker had afterwards an history. It was entitled "Get off that Fence [*sic*]," and was addressed to the Irish clergy. At this time an agitation still referred to as the "Great Strike["], under James Larkin, was paralysing Dublin. Feeling in the city, and, by extension, in the whole country was extraordinarily high. The animation on both sides was actually murderous and some clerical remarks quoted in the Freemans Journal, the journal of Mr Murphy against whom the strike was directed[,] goody-goody, temporazing [*sic*] ineptitudes (such as harassed clergymen in difficult times must perhaps use) annoyed me. My article was an ill-timed invitation to the Irish clergy to "get off that fence," and it created a stir. Some good clergymen, apparently as young as I was, were as annoyed with my article as I was with what I considered the Church's backing and filling. I was surprised in a weeks time to find that I was dubbed "Anti-Christ" in some Irish papers, and was even more surprised, a few years later, to find that the reason giving [*sic*] for the murder of a man on the steps of the Pro-Cathedral (Dublin's principal Catholic house of worship) was that he was "known" to be the author of this article, which was nevertheless signed by me. (1974, 98)

7. Stephens later recounted this story in a talk on "St. Patric [*sic*]" on BBC radio in 1946 and switched the locations of the men to Leix and Offaly. Other changes exist, but, on the whole, the story is along the same lines as "For St. Patrick's Day." A transcript of this talk appears in Stephens 1964, 34–39.

8. M. N. Srinivas writes in "Varna and Caste" on the complexities of the caste system in India:"To [the layman] varna means simply the division of Hindu society in four orders, viz., Brahmana (Brahmin, traditionally, priest and scholar), Kshatriya (ruler and soldier), Vaishya (merchant) and Shudra (peasant, labourer and servant)" (1992, 28). But Srinivas warns us, "The varna model has been the cause of misinterpretation of the realities of the caste system [today]. A point that has emerged from recent field research is that the position of a caste in the hierarchy may vary from village to village" (32). Srinivas also notes, "One of the most striking features of the caste system as it actually exists is the lack of clarity in the hierarchy, especially in the middle regions" (31). It is important to understand that Stephens would have only had an understanding of the hierarchical *varna* system of caste, not of any of the complex ethnographic realities in Indian society.

9. Patricia McFate in *The Writings of James Stephens* notes, "By 1913 AE thought of Stephens as his 'boon companion': he advised Stephens to read the *Bhagavad-Gita* and *The Upanishads*" (1979, 14).

10. Editor Richard Finneran reports that "Stephens's edition of the Mahābhārata in twelve volumes was translated by Pratap Chandra Roy and published from 1883 to 1896" (Stephens 1974, 398). In the just mentioned 1938 letter to William Rothenstein, which thanks him for sending a new book of Rothenstein's, Stephens commented:"I'm in the mid-sea of the vast Mahabharata, on my 9th volume, with three more to go. There is a book to thank the Dragons for! All the names, ten thousand, Bhisma, Drona, Yudhishthira, & the Twins, are of my household" (398).

11. Both *Hunger:A Dublin Story* and "The Boss" were later reprinted in *Etched in Moonlight* (1928).

12. Andre Beteille distinguishes at length between the class system and the caste system in *Caste, Class, and Power:*

> Castes, as status groups, are defined essentially in terms of styles of life. Property and occupation enter as important elements in the style of life of a status group, but they need not be decisive. . . . Together with this there are ritual prescriptions with regard to the manner of dress, the caste mark, and so on. . . . Another distinctive feature of the caste system as a system of status groups is its extreme proliferation, or the multiplicity of castes. Social classes, defined in terms of ownership or nonownership of the means of production, tend to be reduced to a few broad divisions—ultimately, according to Marx, to two. Status groups, on the other hand, show a tendency to multiply. Nowhere has this tendency manifested itself in a more extreme form than in the caste system. (1965, 188–89)

13. I am indebted to Mary Mitchell Lennon, my grandmother, for this point.

14. In a book review of James Cousins's *Wisdom of the West* in the *Irish Review,* Stephens comments on the influence of print culture on Irish society:"There is a safety also connected with orally descending wisdom which it is well not to lose sight of. Printing is really the great transformer and disturber of thought—for, as the necessity of relying solely on memory becomes less imperative, and the fact that artificial memory of books may be relied on, wisdom ceases to be the intimate holy thing it was, and becomes only an intellectual curio which any person may tamper with or misuse as he pleases" (1912c, 100).

15. In his recent study *Ornamentalism: How the British Saw Their Empire* (2001), David Cannadine asserts that the British relied on established hierarchies to govern colonies such as India.

16. I am borrowing the term *practical identity* from Patrick Hogan's *Colonialism and Cultural Identity,* in which he defines the term as follows:

> *Practical Identity.* The set of habits or competencies that guide one's ordinary interactions with other people, along with the communal responses one relies on in those interactions. These

interactions range from "personal" practices of greeting or table manners to more obviously collective practices of work or religious ceremony. They involve implicit knowledge of when, where, and how to participate in such interactions. One's habits or competencies define the "cognitive" component of practical identity. They are completed by a set of predictable communal responses to one's actions—standard replies to greetings, coordinated or corresponding actions necessary to the progress and resolution of religious ceremonies, and so on. These communal responses define the "social" component of practical identity. An "intrinsic" view of practical identity sees the cognitive component as fixed early on. An "extrinsic" view sees it as more flexible and open to significant transformation or augmentation, as in response to changing socio-economic conditions. (2000, 322).

17. Translated by Manilal N. Dvivedi. This source is Richard Finneran's guess in *The Olympian and the Leprechaun* (1978, 16). In a 1935 letter to Yeats, Stephens reveals his thoughts on the Manduka Upanishad: "I saw an essay by you today in a quarterly on the Manduka Upanishad. I think I lent that to you years ago. Tis a wonderful Upanishad. My copy had the Guadapada and Shankara commentaries. It is strange to think that an Upanishad can be enriched—but these enrich that" (1974, 388). It is also interesting to note that the only Yeats book that Yeats inscribed in Stephens's library was *The Ten Principal Upanishads* (1937). The inscription reads: "James Stephens from W B Yeats April 19 1937" (30).

18. Stephens's story "The Boss" opens as a mock heroic. Augustine Martin and others, including Yeats, have noted that Stephens used the mock heroic often. While discussing other works of Stephens, Martin writes: "[H]is influence has been substantial . . . in exploiting the mock heroic possibilities of Gaelic prose patterns; or in blending the mythic and the fabulous with the quotidian and realistic" (1980, 8). In "The Boss" the blend of Indian myth and employer-employee relations is also the blend of "the fabulous with the quotidian."

Chapter 8. James, Seumas, and Jayaram Cousins

1. The Tagore-Cousins letters are housed at Visva-Bharati at Santiniketan, West Bengal. "Sl." indicates the sleeve number of the letter within the Tagore-Cousins collection.

2. In an unpublished letter from Tagore to Cousins, probably sometime in 1923 or early 1924.

3. For more on this article in the *Madras Mail,* see Denson 1967, 142–43.

4. Irish and Indian loyalty to the British was emphasized the same days that Cousins's "Irish Leaders" articles appeared. On Thursday, May 4, 1916, for example, some headlines read: "Mrs. Besant on Loyalty" followed by "India and Confederacy of Empire" (about Indian efforts in the war). Also the day after his rebuttal was printed on May 6, 1916, Cousins had printed in *New India* a book review that he either wrote or commissioned (as literary editor) titled "Ireland's Fight in the Empire's Cause," which gave a favorable review of Michael MacDonagh's *Irish at the Front* (1916).

5. The entire poem "Conscientious Objectors (after a Military Tribunal)," from "The World of Literature" section, references religions in addition to Christianity. The full poem, reprinted on May 3, 1916, reads:

> For the Hidden One in every heart,
> Lost star of the world's night,
> Fire that burns in the soul of art,
> The Light within the light.
> For the gentleness of Buddha's dream
> And Christ's rejected truth,

The treasure under the world's stream,
Pearl of pity and ruth.
Before six ignorant men and blind,
Reckless they rent aside
The Veil of Isis in the mind. . . .
Men say they shirked, and lied.

(3)

6. An article in *New India,* "'New India' in the High Court," provided more details of the situation:

The Offg. Chief Justice in his judgement, said:—This is an application under section 17 of the Indian Press Act of 1910 by Mrs. Annie Besant, the keeper and printer of the "New India" Printing Works and the editor of the newspaper, "New India." The applicant seeks to have set aside an order of the Chief Presidency Magistrate of Madras, dated 22nd May, 1916, requiring her to deposit security of Rs 2,000 under section 3 (1) of the Act and an order of the Governor-in-Council, dated 25th August 1916, declaring under section 4 (1) the security to be deposited and all copies of "New India" wherever found to be forfeited to His Majesty. No copies of "New India," it may be mentioned, have actually been seized. (Oct. 19, 1916, 3)

7. For more on this account, see the introduction to this section, or see Tilney 2001, 147–49.

8. I am referring to his "reflective identity" here. I borrow the terms *practical identity* (see note 16 in chapter 7) and *reflective identity* from Patrick Hogan's *Colonialism and Cultural Identity,* in which he defines the latter as follows:

Reflective Identity. A hierarchized set of properties and relations which one takes to define oneself. This set prominently includes sex, race, ethnicity, family position, and so forth. This set of properties and relations is first of all a matter of social attribution, not introspection. The hierarchy appears to be a function of practical identity. One's practical place in the activities of society is in part of function of attributed categories such as sex. For example, little girls play some games with some toys, while little boys play other games with other toys. The practical identity that results from the repetition of such activities is what appears to determine which properties we take to be most definitive of ourselves in reflective identity. For example, sex is almost always high in one's reflective identity, probably because it is crucial to one's practical identity. (2000, 322)

9. In a footnote, Richard Ellmann in *James Joyce* (first published in 1959) cites a February 1907 letter from Joyce to his brother Stanislaus in describing Joyce's appraisal of Cousins: "For Joyce, Cousins was synonymous with amateur writer. When, in Rome, his literary ambitions began to fall away from him, he wrote:'I hve [*sic*] come to the conclusion that it is about time I made up my mind whether I am to become a writer or a patient Cousins. I foresee that I shall have to do other work as well but to continue as I am at present would certainly mean my mental extinction' " (1965, 249).

10. Cousins's earnest involvement in various movements made him a prime target for lampoons. Padraic Colum's essay relays an anecdote from the time: "James Cousins was a man devoted to good causes, and like many such men he sometimes brought out derisiveness. I recall a discussion when he spoke too earnestly against the drinking of unpurified water. A squib went round about this rejection. 'Standing water breeds corruption.' (Blake). 'Water; I never drink it.' (Cousins). Still, he had humour.

There is a coarseness distinctively of Belfast and I heard him on occasions put a dash of it into his talk" (Denson 1967, 5).

11. Margaret continues discussing the topic of sex:

> Every child I looked at called to my mind the shocking circumstance that brought about its existence. My new knowledge, though I was lovingly safeguarded from it, made me ashamed of humanity and ashamed for it. I found myself looking on men and women as degraded by this demand of nature. Something in me revolted then, and has ever since protested against, certain of the techniques of nature connected with sex. Nor will I and many men and women of like nature, including my husband, be satisfied, be purified and redeemed, life after life, until the evolution of form has substituted some more artistic way of continuance of the race. (Cousins and Cousins 1950, 108–9)

12. Yeats knew of Margaret's automatic writing and her mediumship in 1912 (if not before) when Maud Gonne invited the Cousinses, who were vacationing in France, to come stay with herself, Iseult, and Yeats in her house in France. James Cousins reports in *We Two Together,* "After dinner we gathered around a large open fire. Yeats got onto astrology with Mrs. Cousins, and this and mediumship kept us awake till after midnight" (Cousins and Cousins 1950, 159). Interestingly, Maud Gonne asked the Cousinses to take Yeats to the train station when they were all leaving.

13. See Holmes and Holmes 1997, especially Anne Maher's chapter, "Missionary Links: Past, Present, and Future."

14. Catherine Nash acknowledges some of the limits of Cousins's "theorizing of difference" in her article "Geo-centric Education and Anti-imperialism: Theosophy, Geography, and Citizenship in the Writings of J. H. Cousins." She provides an example of Cousins's "[c]rude environmental determinism and spiritual essentialism": "In writing on the geography of Karma, for example, Cousins suggested that nations could be spiritually dull, mixed or awake, and that the 1923 Japanese earthquake been [*sic*] a positive force in shaking Japan out of its dull and inert condition (J. H. Cousins and L. E. Tristram, 'Some Geographical Aspects of Karma,' *Theosophist* 45 [1924], 423–36)" (1996, 406).

15. Two particular articles in *New India* demonstrate his aims: "The Place of Geography in the Teaching of Civics" (Oct. 20, 1916, 9) and "Geo-economics: The New Science" (Nov. 1, 1916, 9). Other works on the subject include *The Social Value of Arts and Crafts* (Bangalore: Bangalore Press, 1924); *Geosophy: The Philosophy of Geography* (Adyar: Brahmavidya Ashrama, 1927); *Oriental Ideals in Education* (Karachi: Seva Kunj, 1928); and *Three Lectures on Educational Principles & Practice* (Palghat: Scholar Press, 1935).

16. See chapter 6 on W. B. Yeats.

17. Tagore's humility is evident in the letter, in which he downplays his skills in English:

> I have been told by some of my critics that my English is not modern and therefore it sounds strangely remote and inadequate to the present day readers. As I can have no conscious choice in my English style, never having the advantage of an analytical training in the acquirement of your language, I cannot judge my own performance in English. I am not even sure of my grammar, and I have no doubt that I make absurd mistakes in my English which would be tragic in a university examination paper. Of course, I know that a mere absence of mistakes is not vital in literature, being aware that my own Bengali is only too often incorrect from the schoolmaster's point of view. Yet your language being foreign to me I cannot fully trust my instinct about the atmosphere of the words I use and I am still more uncertain whether my ideas assume their aspect of truth to an English reader of an average receptivity of mind. This

is the reason why I send you the accompanying translation. Please tell me if the English is appropriate, if the meaning is clear enough to be attractive to an English reader, not judging them from your own standard, your mind being at home in India and having the poetic insight. Please know, I am genuinely sincere when I ask you to be unsparingly frank with me and to have the full revenge against myself for the trouble I am giving you. Yours very sincerely[,] Rabindranath Tagore. (Feb. 4, 1918, Sl. 9)

18. Krishna Dutta and Andrew Robinson's fine biography, *Rabindranath Tagore: The Myriad-Minded Man* (1996), neglects to mention the Cousinses' work in promoting "Jana Gana Mana." See pp. 161 and 409 on the origins of "Jana Gana Mana."

19. To better fit both Mira and Kumbha in these categories, I have added "spiritual and aesthetic principles" to Hogan's categories.

20. A significant difference remains between his character and Hogan's definition concerning the power relations between metropolitan and indigenous cultures. Although Muslims held, historically, the "seat / of India's sovereignty" (Cousins 1919, 59) at the time of the action of the play, the relationship between the imperial Muslim and the conquered Hindu cultures was not exactly one of metropolitan to indigenous culture, especially in Cousins's play.

21. Cousins sought to "catch the inner import" of myths, particularly "the Exile of the sons of Doel Dermait," in *The Hound of Uladh*. William Dumbleton provides relevant commentary: this central import Cousins also saw in Indian myth, for "the realities which the old Celtic deities symbolized were eternally valid both in the constants of universal life and in the flux of human concepts of that life from religion to religion and era to era" (1980, 71). Cuchulain, then, is the Irish parallel to the Hindu Atman, the divine spark, the Will; Laeg, Cuchulain's charioteer, is Krishna, the receptacle of knowledge and intuition that carries Will to fulfillment; Lugaidh, the knight-compatriot of Cuchulain in the play, is Monas, the active Mind that adjusts external details to fulfillment, as they become explicitly defined in the play (68).

22. Not surprisingly, Akbar's antisectarian, syncretistic, and national goals are similar to Cousins's and are based in types of universalism. Kumbha reacts strongly against the cultural and spiritual universalism of Akbar in the play, just as Cousins faced opposition to his universalism and syncretism from both Indians and Europeans. In *Colonialism and Cultural Identity*, Hogan delineates the different "components of universalism" as: "descriptive universalism," "experiential or empathic universalism (versus projection)," "ethical universalism and the politics of otherness," and "cultural universalism" (2000, 323–24). Descriptive universalism is perhaps the most basic in what it asserts: "The view that cultures share a broad range of specifiable properties and structures—in language, literature, music, and so on" (323). The second, experiential or empathic universalism, Hogan argues, involves an amount of imaginative identification in assisting an individual to empathetically adopt "another viewpoint." Hogan carefully and assertively contrasts this empathic universalism with the "projection of one's own viewpoint" onto the other, a process that characterizes much of Orientalist and other colonial discourses. The third component, ethical universalism, has also been applied in "a non-universal way"—that is, it has been historically applied in support of colonialist projects. Hogan defines it as "the view that there are general ethical principles that apply cross-culturally and can be invoked cross-culturally to defend or condemn specific cultural practices." It was generally applied, as numerous studies have indicated, unequally in the colonial world through missions, colonial governments, trade practices, and education, to name a few areas that rigorously "reformed" traditional cultures, altering them to fit European cultural norms. The "politics of otherness" seeks to correct this historical trend of unequal application by emphasizing the critic's need to examine his or her own culture's ethical problems before critiquing another culture's unethical practices.

23. What Hogan calls "cultural universalism" parallels the point of view that Cousins's character Akbar builds upon, "[t]he view that cultures are not, in principle, tied to any particular ethnic or racial group, but are the common property of all people. This aspect of universalism implies that we all have equal obligation to and interest in the preservation of diverse cultures, though diverse cultures divested of putative racial or ethnic ownership" (2000, 324). Kumbha responds violently to Akbar primarily because of Akbar's cultural universalist actions, through which he hoped to manifest his new syncretistic religion. Akbar reads the mingling of cultures as beneficial, whereas Kumbha sees it merely as a recipe for spiritual pollution. Cousins's belief that culture, especially spirituality, philosophy, and art, belonged to all is evidence of his cultural universalism, as well as his Theosophy, which required its adherents to investigate and study cultures comparatively. Unfortunately, Theosophists rarely recognized their own inherited biases of Orientalist and imperial discourse.

24. Willy Maley's essay "Nationalism and Revisionism: Ambiviolences and Dissensus" points to Gibbons's useful formulation (1999, 14).

25. The following is an example of his synthetic vision in his poem "Unity":

> High on the rock-paved praying-ground
> the sons of Allah stand,
> Then in obeisance soul-profound
> Bend earthward head and hand.
> In robe and turban many-hued
> they bloom upon the mind,
> A bank of flowers in prayerful mood
> Bending before a wind.
> And here, beside the white-towered shrine,
> God Shiva's ancient seat,
> Field-blossoms in the sunlight shine
> About my wandering feet;
> And, as a breeze across my brow
> On some glad errand runs,
> They bow, as in devotion bow
> Allah's and Shiva's sons.
> So calm the encircling hills, so sweet
> The jasmine-scented air,
> God, man and nature seem to meet,
> And cancel *here* and *there;*
> And show that, underneath their mask,
> One holy impulse stirs
> Those flowers that grace from Allah ask,
> These clay-born worshippers.
> In such clear glimpses of the Whole
> Our foolish barriers fall;
> for who finds kinship with the soul
> Is kindred unto all.
>
> (1940, 191–92)

Bibliography

Aarsleff, Hans. 1983. *The Study of Language in England, 1780–1860.* Minneapolis: Univ. of Minnesota Press.

Ahmad, Aijaz. 1992. *In Theory: Classes, Nations, Literatures.* New York: Verso.

Ahmed, Siraj. N.d. "'An Unlimited Intercourse': Historical Contradictions and Imperial Romance in the Early Nineteenth Century." Romantic Circles Web site, Praxis Series: "The Containment and Re-deployment of English India." http://www.rc.umd.edu/praxis. Downloaded on Aug. 15, 2003.

Allen, Nicholas. 2003. *George Russell (Æ) and the New Ireland, 1905–30.* Dublin: Four Courts.

"Answers to Questions about the Missions." 1937. *Far East* 20, no. 6 (June): 123.

"Answers to Questions about the Missions." 1938. *Far East* 21, no. 4 (Apr.): 75.

Arnold, Matthew. 1973a. *The Complete Prose Works of Matthew Arnold: English Literature and Irish Politics.* Edited by R. H. Super. Vol. 3. Ann Arbor: Univ. of Michigan Press.

————. 1973b. *The Complete Prose Works of Matthew Arnold: Lectures and Essays in Criticism.* Edited by R. H. Super. Vol. 9. Ann Arbor: Univ. of Michigan Press.

Artamonov, M. I. 1969. *The Splendor of Scythian Art: Treasures from Scythain Tombs.* New York: Frederic A. Praeger.

Ashcroft, Bill, and Pal Ahluwalia. 1999. *Edward Said: The Paradox of Identity.* New York: Routledge.

Ashcroft, Bill, Gareth Griffiths, and Helen Tiffin. 1989. *The Empire Writes Back: Theory and Practice in Post-colonial Literature.* New York: Routledge.

Atkinson, Joseph. 1798. *Killarney: A Poem.* Dublin: Wm. Porter.

Babington, Anthony. 1991. *The Devil to Pay: The Connaught Rangers Revolt in the Punjab, 1920.* England: Leo Cooper Pen and Sword Books.

Baggett, Jeffrey Scott. 2000. "Celticism, Orientalism, and Irish Identity, 1829–1916: Ferguson, Mangan, and Yeats." Ph.D. diss., Emory Univ.

Ballantyne, Tony. 2002. *Orientalism and Race: Aryanism in the British Empire.* New York: Palgrave.

Barfoot, C. C. 1998. "English Romantic Poets and the 'Free-Floating Orient.' " In *Oriental Prospects: Western Literature and the Lure of the East,* edited by C. C. Barfoot and Theo D'haen, 65–96. Atlanta: Rodopi.

Bartlett, Thomas. 1997. "The Irish Soldier in India, 1750–1947." In *Ireland and India: Con-*

nections, Comparisons, Contrasts, edited by Michael Holmes and Denis Holmes. Dublin: Folens.

Bayly, Christopher. 2000. "Ireland, India and the Empire: 1780–1914." *Transactions of the Royal Historical Society,* 6th ser., 10 (Dec.): 377–98.

Beckett, Samuel. 1957. *Murphy.* 1938. Reprint, New York: Grove Press.

Bede. 1994. *Historical Works.* Translated by J. E. King. Vol. 1. 1930. Reprint, Cambridge: Harvard Univ. Press.

Bernasconi, Robert, ed. 2001. *Concepts of Race in the Eighteenth Century.* Chicago: Univ. of Chicago Press.

Beteill, Andre. 1965. *Caste, Class, and Power.* Berkeley and Los Angeles: Univ. of California Press.

Betham, Sir William. 1842. *Etruria Celtica: Etruscan Literature and Antiquities Investigated; or, The Language of that Ancient and Illustrious People Compared and Identified with the Iberno-Celtic, and Both Shown to Be Phœnecian.* Dublin: Hardy.

Bhabha, Homi. 1983. "The Other Question." *Screen* 24, no. 6: 18–35.

———, ed. 1990. *Nation and Narration.* London: Routledge.

———. 1994. *The Location of Culture.* New York: Routledge.

Blavatsky, Helen Petrovna. 1888. *The Secret Doctrine: The Synthesis of Science, Religion, and Philosophy.* 2 vols. London: Theosophical Publishing.

Blunt, Wilfrid Scawen. 1907. *The Secret History of the English Occupation of Egypt.* London: T. Fisher Unwin.

———. 1999. "The Arabi Trial." In *Imperialism and Orientalism: A Documentary Sourcebook,* edited by Barbara Harlow and Mia Carter, 147–59. Malden, Mass.: Blackwell.

Boehmer, Elleke. 1995. *Colonial and Postcolonial Literature: Migrant Metaphors.* New York: Oxford Univ. Press.

Bongard-Levin, G. M. 1980. *The Origin of Aryans: From Scythis to India.* Translated by Harish C. Gupta. New Delhi: Arnold Heinemann.

Borde, Andrew. 1870. *The Fyrst Boke of the Introduction of Knowledge: A Compendyous Reyment or a Dyetary of Helth: The Treatyse Answerynge the Boke of Berdes.* Early English Text Series, no. 10. London: Early English Text Society.

Borst, Arno. 1957–1963. *Der Turmbau von Babel: Geschichte der Meinungen Über Ursprung und Vielfalt der Sprachen und Völker.* 6 vols. Stuttgart: Hiersemann.

Bose, Abinash Chandra. 1970. *Three Mystic Poets: A Study of W. B. Yeats, A.E., and Rabindranath Tagore.* 1945. Reprint, Folcroft, Pa.: Folcroft Press.

Boswell, John Whittley. 1790. *Syllegomena of the Antiquities of Killmackumpshaugh, in the County of Roscommon, and Kingdom of Ireland, in which It Is Clearly Proved that Ireland Was Originally Peopled by Egyptians.* Dublin: Privately printed.

Bourke, U[lick] J. 1887. *Pre-Christian Ireland.* Dublin: Browne and Nolan.

Boyle, Frank. 2000. *Swift as Nemesis: Modernity and Its Satirist.* Stanford: Stanford Univ. Press.

Brasted, H. V. 1985. "Irish Models and the Indian National Congress, 1870–1922." *South Asia* 8, no. 2 (June–Dec.): 24–45.

Breckenridge, Carol A., and Peter van der Veer, eds. 1993. *Orientalism and the Postcolonial Predicament.* Philadelphia: Univ. of Pennsylvania Press.

Breen, Dan. 1991. *My Fight for Irish Freedom*. 1924. Reprint, Dublin: Anvil Books.

Brewster, Scott, Virginia Crossman, Fiona Becket, and David Alderson. 1999. *Ireland in Proximity: History, Gender, Space*. New York: Routledge.

Brown, Terence, ed. 1988. *Ireland's Literature: Selected Essays*. Totowa, N.J.: Barnes and Noble.

————. 1996. *Celticism*. Atlanta: Rodopi.

Brown, Thomas. 1813. *Intercepted Letters; or, The Twopenny Post-Bag: To which Are Added Trifles Reprinted*. 10th ed. London: J. Carr.

Bryant, Sophie. 1913. *The Genius of the Gael: A Study in Celtic Psychology and Its Manifestations*. London: T. Fisher Unwin.

Burke, Edmund. 1999. "On the Impeachment of Warren Hastings, 15–19 February." In *Imperialism and Orientalism: A Documentary Sourcebook,* edited by Barbara Harlow and Mia Carter, 31–38. Malden, Mass.: Blackwell.

Burke, Mary. 2002. " 'Phoenician Tinsmiths' and 'Degenerated Tuatha De Danaan': The Origins and Implications of the Orientalization of Irish Travellers." *Australian Journal of Irish Studies* 2:22–34.

Burleigh, David. 1993. "Rumours of the Infinite: An Irish Poet in Japan." *Ferris Studies* no. 28 (Mar.).

Cadell, Sir Patrick. 1950–1951. "Irish Soldiers in India." *Irish Sword* 1, no. 2: 76–79.

Cahill, Thomas. 1995. *How the Irish Saved Civilization: The Untold Story of Ireland's Heroic Role from the Fall of Rome to the Rise of Medieval Europe*. New York: Doubleday.

Cairns, David, and Shaun Richards. 1988. *Writing Ireland: Colonialism, Nationalism, and Culture*. Manchester: Manchester Univ. Press.

Cambrensis, Giraldus. 1982. *The History and Topography of Ireland*. Translated by John O'Meara. 1951. Reprint, London: Penguin.

Camden, William. 1610. *Britain; or, A Chorographicall Description of the Most Flourishing Kingdomes, England, Scotland, and Ireland, and the Ilands Adioyning, out of the Depth of Antiqvitie: Beavtified With Mappes of the Several Shires of England: Written first in Latine by William Camden; Translated newly into English by Philémon Holland. Doctour in Physick: Finaly, Revised, Amended and Enlarged with Sundry Additions by the Said Author*. London: George Bishop and Ioannis Norton.

————. 1625. *Annales: The True and Royall History of the Famous Empresse Elizabeth, Queene of England, France and Ireland, &c., True Faith's Defendresse of Diuine Renowne and Happy Memory. Wherein All Such Memorable Things as Happened During Hir Blessed Raigne, with Such Acts and Treaties as Past Betwixt Hir Majestie and Scotland, France, Spaine, Italy, Germany, Poland, Sweden, Denmark, Russia, and the Netherlands, are Exactly Described*. London: B. Fisher.

Campbell, Mary. 1936. *Lady Morgan: The Life and Times of Sydney Owenson, Lady Morgan (1776–1859)*. New York: Russell.

————. 1988. *Lady Morgan: The Life and Times of Sydney Owenson*. London: Pandora Press.

Campion, Edmund. 1940. *A Historie of Ireland*. Edited by Rudolf B. Gottfried. 1571. Reprint, New York: Scholars' Facsimilies and Reprints.

Cannadine, David. 2001. *Ornamentalism: How the British Saw Their Empire.* New York: Oxford Univ. Press.

Carey, George W. 1976. Introduction to *Popular Government,* by Sir Henry Sumner Maine, 13–20. Indianapolis: Liberty.

Carey, John. 1984. "Scél Tuáin Meic Chairill." *Eriu: Founded as the Journal of the School of Irish Learning Devoted to Irish Philology and Literature* 35: 93–111.

———. 1987. "The Irish Vision of the Chinese." *Eriu: Founded as the Journal of the School of Irish Learning Devoted to Irish Philology and Literature* 38: 72–79.

———. 1993. "A New Introduction to *Lebor Gabála Érenn: The Book of the Taking of Ireland,*" edited and translated by R. A. Stewart Macalister. London: Irish Texts Society.

———. 1994. "The Irish National Origin-Legend: Synthetic Pseudohistory." In *Quiggin Pamphlets on the Sources of Medieval Gaelic History.* Cambridge: Univ. of Cambridge, Department of Anglo-Saxon, Norse, and Celtic.

———. 1995. "Native Elements in Irish Pseudohistory." In *Cultural Identity and Cultural Integration: Ireland and Europe in the Early Middle Ages,* edited by Doris Edel. Portland, Oreg.: Four Courts.

Carlin, Norah. 1985. "Ireland and Natural Man in 1649." In *Europe and Its Others: Proceedings of the Essex Conference on the Sociology of Literature, July 1984,* edited by Francis Barker et al., 2:91–111. Colchester: Univ. of Essex Press.

Carroll, Clare. 1996. "Spenser and the Irish Language: The Sons of Milesio in *A View of the Present State of Ireland, The Faerie Queene, Book V* and the *Leabhar Gabhála.*" Edited by Anne Fogarty. *Irish University Review: A Journal of Irish Studies.* Special issue, *Spenser in Ireland: "The Faerie Queene," 1596–1996* 26, no. 2 (autumn-winter): 281–90.

———, ed. 2003. *Ireland and Postcolonial Theory.* Cork: Cork Univ. Press.

Casement, Roger. 1958. *The Crime Against Europe: The Writings and Poetry of Roger Casement.* Edited by Herbert O. Mackey. 1914. Reprint, Dublin: C. J. Fallon.

[Cecil, Robert, Lord Salisbury]. 1883. "Disintegration Art: VIII." *Quarterly Review* 156 (Oct.): 559–95.

Champion, Timothy. 1996. "The Celt in Archaelogy." In *Celticism,* edited by Terence Brown, 61–78. Atlanta: Rodopi.

Chapman, Malcolm. 1992. *The Celts: The Construction of a Myth.* New York: St. Martin's.

Chatterjee, Dilip Kumar. 1994. *James Henry Cousins: A Study of His Works in the Light of the Theosophical Movement in India and the West.* Delhi: Sharada.

Chaudhuri, Nirad C. 1987. *Thy Hand Great Anarch! India, 1921–1952.* Reading, Mass.: Addison-Wesley.

Clifford, James. 1987. "Of Other Peoples: Beyond the Salvage Paradigm." In *Discussions in Contemporary Culture,* edited by Hal Foster. Seattle: Bay Press.

Cloake, Margaret Morris, ed. and trans. 1988. *A Persian at the Court of King George, 1809–10: The Journal of Mirza Abul Hassan Khan.* London: Barrie and Jenkins.

Coleman, James. 1908. "A Tipperary Adventurer in India." *Journal of the Waterford & South-East of Ireland Archæological Society* (Apr.-June): 109–10.

Conant, Martha Pike. 1908. *The Oriental Tale in England in the Eighteenth Century.* New York: Columbia Univ. Press.

Connolly, James. 1973. *James Connolly: Selected Writings.* Edited by P. Berresford Ellis. New York: Monthly Review.

Cook, Scott B. 1987. "The Irish Raj: Social Origins and Careers of Irishmen in the Indian Civil Service, 1855–1914." *Journal of Social History* 20, no. 3: 507–29.

————. 1993. *Imperial Affinities: Nineteenth Century Analogies and Exchanges between India and Ireland.* New Delhi: Sage Publications.

Cooper, Irving. 1964. *Theosophy Simplified.* Wheaton, Ill.: Theosophical Press.

Corkery, Daniel. 1941. *The Hidden Ireland: A Study of Gaelic Munster in the Eighteenth Century.* Dublin: Gill and Son.

Cousins, James H. 1894. *Ben Madigan and Other Poems.* Belfast: Marcus Ward.

————. 1916. "A Plea for an Indian Musical Festival." *New India* (Apr. 22): 10.

————. 1918. *The Renaissance in India.* Madras: Ganesh.

————. 1919. *The King's Wife.* Madras: Ganesh.

————. 1920. *New Ways in English Literature.* Madras: Ganesh.

————. 1922a. *The Cultural Unity of Asia: A Study of the Tendency to Unification in Asian Cultural Movements.* Adyar, Madras: Theosophical Publishing House.

————. 1922b. *The Play of Brahma (an Essay on the Drama in National Revival).* Bangalore City: Amateur Dramatic Association.

————. 1923. *The New Japan: Impressions and Reflections (with Seventy-four Illustrations).* Madras: Ganesh.

————. 1925a. *Heathen Essays.* Madras: Ganesh.

————. 1925b. *Samadarsana (Synthetic Vision): A Study in Indian Psychology.* Madras: Ganesh.

————. 1929. *The Girdle.* Madras: Ganesh.

————. 1932. *A Wandering Harp: Selected Poems.* New York: Roerich Museum Press.

————. 1934. *A Study in Synthesis.* Madras: Ganesh.

————. 1940. *Collected Poems (1894–1940).* Madras: Kalâkshetra.

————. 1941. *The Faith of the Artist.* Madras: Kalâkshetra.

————. 1970. "The Racing Lug." In *Lost Plays of the Irish Renaissance,* edited by Robert Hogan and James Kilroy. Dublin: Proscenium.

————. 1973. *"The Sleep of the King: A One Act Poetic Drama" and "The Sword of Dermot: A Three Act Tragedy": Introduction by William A. Dumbleton.* Chicago: De Paul Univ. Press.

Cousins, James H., and Margaret E. 1950. *We Two Together: A Duo-Autobiography.* Madras: Ganesh.

[Croker, John Wilson]. 1804. *An Intercepted Letter from J—T—, Esq., Writer at Canton, to His Friend in Dublin, Ireland.* Dublin: M. N. Mahon.

Cromer, Lord (Sir Evelyn Baring). 1999. "The Mutiny of the Egyptian Army: January–September 1881." In *Imperialism and Orientalism: A Documentary Sourcebook,* edited by Barbara Harlow and Mia Carter, 140–47. Malden, Mass.: Blackwell.

Crozier, F. P. 1931. *A Word to Gandhi: The Lesson of Ireland.* London: Williams and Northgate.

Cullingford, Elizabeth Butler. 1996. "British Romans and Irish Carthaginians: Anticolonial Metaphors in Heaney, Friel, and McGuinness." *PMLA* 111, no. 2 (Mar.): 222–39.

————. 2001. *Ireland's Others: Ethnicity and Gender in Irish Literature and Popular Culture.* Cork: Cork Univ. Press and Field Day.

Cunningham, Bernadette. 1986. "Native Culture and Political Change in Ireland, 1580–1640." In *Natives and Newcomers: Essays on the Making of Irish Colonial Society, 1534–1641,* edited by Ciaran Brady and Raymond Gillespie, 148–70. Dublin: Irish Academic Press.

Curtis, L. Perry. 1968. *Anglo-Saxons and Celts: A Study of Anti-Irish Prejudice in Victorian England.* New York: Conference on British Studies, Univ. of Bridgeport.

———. 1971. *Apes and Angels: The Irishman in Victorian Caricature.* Washington, D.C.: Smithsonian Institution.

Cusack, Mary Francis. 1868. *An Illustrated History of Ireland: From the Earliest Period.* London: Longmans, Green.

Dalmia, Vasudha. 1996. "'The Only Real Religion of the Hindus': Vaisnava Self-Representation in the Late Nineteenth Century." In *Representing Hinduism: The Construction of Religious Traditions and National Identity,* edited by Vasudha Dalmia and Heinrich Von Stietencron, 176–210. Thousand Oaks, Calif.: Sage.

Dancy, Jonathan. 1995. "Problems of Epistemology." In *The Oxford Companion to Philosophy,* edited by Ted Honderich, 245–48. New York: Oxford Univ. Press.

Davis, Daniel R. 2000. Introduction to *The Antiquities of Nations,* by Paul Perzon. Vol. 1 of *Celtic Linguistics, 1700–1850,* edited by Daniel R. Davis. New York: Routledge.

Davis, Robert Bernard. 1977. *George William Russell ("AE").* Boston: Twayne.

Dawson, Carl. 1992. *Lafcadio Hearn and the Vision of Japan.* Baltimore: Johns Hopkins Univ. Press.

Dean, Dennis R. 1981. Introduction to *The Missionary (1811) by Sydney Owenson, Lady Morgan: A Facsimile Reproduction,* v–x. Delmar, N.Y.: Scholar's Facsimiles and Reprints.

Deane, Seamus. 1985. *Celtic Revivals.* London: Faber.

———. 1997. *Strange Country: Modernity and Nationhood in Irish Writing since 1790.* New York: Oxford Univ. Press.

Deane, Seamus, Terry Eagleton, Fredric Jameson, and Edward W. Said. 1990. *Nationalism, Colonialism, and Literature.* Minneapolis: Univ. of Minnesota Press.

Denson, Alan, ed. 1967. *James H. Cousins (1873–1956) and Margaret E. Cousins (1878–1954): A Bio-Bibliographical Survey: Compiled by Alan Denson: Family Reminiscences and an Autobiographical Note by William D. Cousins: Foreword by Padraic Colum.* Kendal, England: Alan Denson.

De Vere, Aubrey. 1877. *Antar and Zara, an Eastern Romance: Inisfail and Other Poems Meditative and Lyrical.* London: King.

———. 1970. *English Misrule and Irish Misdeeds: Four Letters from Ireland, Addressed to an English Member of Parliament.* 1848. Reprint, Port Washington, N.Y.: Kennikat.

[Dicuil]. 1967. *Dicuili Liber de Mensura Orbis Terrae.* Edited by J. J. Tierney. Dublin: Dublin Institute for Advanced Studies.

Dinnis, Enid. 1936. "A Mystic Journey: How a School-Mistress Went to China." *Far East* 39, no. 1 (Jan.): 16–18.

Diodorus of Sicily. 1993. *The Library of History: Books IV.59-VIII.* Translated by C. H. Oldfather. 1939. Reprint, Cambridge: Harvard Univ. Press.

Droixhe, Daniel. 1978. *La Linguistique et l'appel de l'histoire (1600–1800).* Geneva: Droz.

———. 1996. "Ossian, Hermann, and the Jew's Harp." In *Celticism,* edited by Terence Brown, 21–33. Atlanta: Rodopi.

Duffy, Reverend T. Gavan. 1921. "An Irish Missionary Episode: The Bishops Fennelly." *Irish Ecclesiastical Record,* 5th ser., 42 (May): 464–84.

Dumbleton, William A. 1980. *James Cousins.* Boston: Twayne.

Dunsany, Edward Lord. 1996. *The Hashish Man and Other Stories.* Edited by John Longhi. San Francisco: Manic D Press.

Dutta, Krishna, and Andrew Robinson. 1996. *Rabindranath Tagore: The Myriad-Minded Man.* New York: St. Martin's.

Eagleton, Terry. 1998. "The Ryan Line." In *Crazy John and the Bishop and Other Essays on Irish Culture,* 249–72. Notre Dame: Univ. of Notre Dame Press.

Eco, Umberto. 1997. *The Search for the Perfect Language.* Translated by James Fentress. Cambridge, Mass.: Blackwell.

———. 1998. *Serendipities: Language and Lunacy.* Translated by William Weaver. New York: Columbia Univ. Press.

Editors of Ireland's Mirror. 1804. *A New and Impartial History of Ireland from the Landing of Partholan to the Present Times, Faithfully Extracted from the Most Received Authorities.* Dublin: Holmes and Charles.

Ehrlich, Heyward. 1998. "'Araby' in Context: The 'Splendid Bazaar,' Irish Orientalism, and James Clarence Mangan." *James Joyce Quarterly* 35, no. 2–3 (winter-spring): 309–31.

Ellis, P. Berresford. 1973. Introduction to *James Connolly: Selected Writings,* edited by P. Berresford Ellis. New York: Monthly Review.

Ellis, Sylvia C. 1995. "Japan, *Japonisme,* and *Japonaiserie.*" In *The Plays of W. B. Yeats: Yeats and the Dancer.* New York: St. Martin's.

Ellmann, Richard. 1965. *James Joyce.* New York: Oxford Univ. Press.

Fanon, Frantz. 1963. *The Wretched of the Earth.* New York: Grove Press.

Fenollosa, Ernest Francisco, and Ezra Pound. 1916. *Certain Noble Plays of Japan.* Churchtown, Dundrum, Ireland: Cuala Press.

Ferguson, Samuel. 1865. *Lays of the Western Gael.* London: Bell and Daldy.

———. 1867. *Publication of the Royal Irish Academy* 9: 168.

———. 1872. *Congal: A Poem, in Five Books.* Dublin: E. Ponsonby.

Ferris, Ina. 1991. *The Achievement of Literary Authority: Gender, History, and the Waverley Novels.* Ithaca: Cornell Univ. Press.

Finneran, Richard J. 1978. *The Olympian and the Leprechaun: W. B. Yeats and James Stephens.* Dublin: Dolmen.

Fisher, Michael H. 1996. *The First Indian Author in English: Dean Mahomed (1759–1851) in India, Ireland, and England.* New York: Oxford Univ. Press.

Flanagan, Kieran. 1977. "The Rise and Fall of the 'Celtic Ineligible': Competitive Examinations for the Irish and Indian Civil Services in Relation to the Educational and Occupational Structure of Ireland, 1853–1921." Ph.D. diss., Univ. of Sussex.

Flynn, Joyce. 1981. "The Route to the Táin: James Stephens' Preparation for His Unfinished Epic." *Proceedings of the Harvard Celtic Colloquim* 1: 15–57.

Foster, John Wilson. 1991. *Colonial Consequences: Essays in Irish Literature and Culture.* Dublin: Lilliput.

Foster, R. F. 1997. *W. B. Yeats: A Life: I: The Apprentice Mage, 1865–1914.* New York: Oxford Univ. Press.

Franklin, Michael. 2001a. Introduction to "On the Language and Wisdom of the Indians," by Carl Wilhelm Friedrich von Schlegel. In *The European Discovery of India: Key Indological Sources of Romanticism,* edited by Michael Franklin, 4:vii–xviii. London: Ganesha and Edition Synapse.

———. 2001b. Introduction to "Sacontalá: On the Mystical Poetry of the Persians and Hindus: Gítagóvinda," by William Jones. In *The European Discovery of India: Key Indological Sources of Romanticism,* edited by Michael Franklin, 3:vii–xxxiii. London: Ganesha and Edition Synapse.

Fraser, T. G. 1984. *Partition in Ireland, India, and Palestine.* London, Macmillan.

Gangoly, Ordhendra Coomar, ed. 1923. *Modern Indian Artists.* Calcutta: H. Mukhurji.

Gaskill, Howard. 1996. "Herder, Ossian, and the Celtic." In *Celticism,* edited by Terence Brown, 257–71. Atlanta: Rodopi.

[Ghose], Sri Aurobindo. 1946. *The Renaissance in India.* 3d ed. Calcutta: Arya Publishing House.

Gibbons, Luke. 1991. "Race Against Time: Racial Discourse and Irish History." *Neocolonialism* (special double issue with title). *Oxford Literary Review* 13, no. 1–2: 95–117.

———. 1996a. "The Sympathetic Bond: Ossian, Celticism, and Colonialism." In *Celticism,* edited by Terence Brown, 273–91. Atlanta: Rodopi.

———. 1996b. *Transformations in Irish Culture.* Notre Dame: Univ. of Notre Dame Press.

———. 2003. "Towards a Postcolonial Enlightenment: The United Irishmen, Cultural Diversity, and the Public Sphere." In *Ireland and Postcolonial Theory,* edited by Clare Carroll and Patricia King, 81–91. Cork: Cork Univ. Press.

Ginnell, Laurence. 1894. *The Brehon Laws: A Legal Handbook.* London: T. F. Unwin.

———. 1917. *The Brehon Laws: A Legal Handbook.* Dublin: O'Callaghan.

Goffart, Walter. 1988. *The Narrators of Barbarian History (A.D. 550–800): Jordanes, Gregory of Tours, Bede, and Paul the Deacon.* Princeton: Princeton Univ. Press.

Gogarty, Oliver St. John. 1994. *As I Was Going Down Sackville Street.* 1937. Reprint, Dublin: O'Brien Press.

Goldring, Maurice. 1993. *Pleasant the Scholar's Life: Irish Intellectuals and the Construction of the Nation State.* London: Serif.

Goldsmith, Oliver. 1840. *Letters from a Citizen of the World to His Friends in the East.* 1762. Reprint, London: Charles, Knight.

———. 1966. *Collected Works of Oliver Goldsmith.* Edited by Arthur Friedman. 5 vols. New York: Oxford Univ. Press.

Goonetilleke, D. C. R. A. 1988. *Images of the Raj: South Asia in the Literature of Empire.* London: Macmillan.

Gore-Booth, Eva. 1916. "Conscientious Objectors (after a Military Tribunal)." *New India* (May 3): 13.

Graham, Colin. 1998. *Ideologies of Empire: Nation, Empire, and Victorian Epic Poetry.* New York: Manchester Univ. Press.

Gregory, Lady Augusta. 1882. "Arabi and His Household." *Times* (London), Oct. 23, 4.

Grierson, George. 1883. *Report on Colonial Emigration from the Bengal Presidency.* [Calcutta: Miscellaneous Official Publications].

———. 1885. *Bihār Peasant Life, Being a Discursive Catalogue of the Surroundings of the People of that Province, with Many Illustrations from Photographs taken by the Author.* Calcutta and London: Trübner.

———. 1895. *Curiosities of Indian Literature: Selected and Translated by G.A. Grierson, of the Indian Civil Service Edited with the Translator's Kind Permission by Maharaja Kumara Babu Ramadina Sinha.* Bankipore: Khadgavilas Press.

Gupta, Dipankar, ed. 1992. *Social Stratification.* New York: Oxford Univ. Press.

H. F. N. 1945. Review of *The Story of Irish Orientalism,* by Menahem Mansoor. *Dublin Magazine* 20, no. 4 (Oct.-Dec.): 59–60.

Hadfield, Andrew. 1993. "Briton and Scythian: Tudor Representations of Irish Origins." *Irish Historical Studies* 28, no. 112 (Nov.): 390–408.

———. 1997. *Edmund Spenser's Irish Experience: Wilde Fruit and Salvage Soyl.* Oxford: Clarendon Press.

———, ed. 2001. *Amazons, Savages, and Machiavels: Travel and Colonial Writing in English, 1550–1630: An Anthology.* New York: Oxford Univ. Press.

Hadfield, Andrew, and Willy Maley, eds. 1997. *A View of the State of Ireland: From the First Printed Edition (1633).* Malden, Mass.: Blackwell.

Hale, H. W. 1974. *Terrorism in India, 1917–1936.* Delhi: Deep Publications.

Halkett, Samuel, and John Laing. 1882. *A Dictionary of the Anonymous and Pseudonymous Literature of Great Britain, Including the Works of Foreigners Written in, or Translated into, the English Language.* Vol. 2. Edinburgh: W. Paterson.

Harlow, Barbara, and Mia Carter, eds. 1999. *Imperialism and Orientalism: A Documentary Sourcebook.* Malden, Mass.: Blackwell.

Harvey, Charles R. 1916. *The Arts-Crafts of India: A Suggestion to the Government.* Pamphlet reprinted from *Commonweal* (Jan. 28).

Harvie, Christopher. 1996. "The Scottish Intellectuals, 1760–1930." In *Celticism,* edited by Terence Brown, 231–56. Atlanta: Rodopi.

Hearn, Lafcadio. 1894. *Glimpses of Unfamiliar Japan.* Vol. 1. Boston: Houghton and Mifflin.

———. 1923. *Life and Letters of Lafcadio Hearn Including the Japanese Letters.* Edited by Elizabeth Bisland [Wetmore]. Vol. 15 of *The Writings of Lafcadio Hearn.* Boston: Houghton Mifflin.

Hegel, G. W. F. 1977. *Phenomenology of Spirit.* Translated by A. V. Miller. Oxford: Clarendon.

Hennessy, Maurice. 1971. *The Rajah from Tipperary.* London: Sidgwick and Jackson.

Herbert, Algernon. 1853. "Article 1." Review of *Annals of the Kingdom of Ireland, by the Four Masters, from the Earliest Period to the Year 1616,* edited and translated by John O'Donovan. *London Quarterly Review* 93, no. 185 (July): 1–14.

Hiberniæ Lachrymæ; or, The Tears of Ireland, a Poem. 1799. Dublin, n.p.

Higden, Ranulphi [Ralph]. 1865. *Polychronicon Ranulphi Higden Monachi Cestrensis, Together with the English Translations of John Trevisa and of an Unknown Writer of the Fifteenth Century.* Edited by Churchill Babington. Vol. 1. London: Longman.

Hobsbawm, Eric, and Terence Ranger. 1983. *The Invention of Tradition.* Cambridge: Cambridge Univ. Press.

Hogan, Edmund M. 1990. *The Irish Missionary Movement: A Historical Survey, 1830–1980.* Washington, D.C.: Catholic Univ. of America Press.

Hogan, Patrick Colm. 2000. *Colonialism and Cultural Identity: Crises of Tradition in the Anglophone Literatures of India, Africa, and the Caribbean.* Albany: SUNY Press.

Holmes, Michael. 2000. "The Irish and India: Imperialism, Nationalism, and Internationalism." In *The Irish Diaspora,* edited by Andy Bielenberg, 235–50. New York: Longman.

Holmes, Michael, and Denis Holmes, eds. 1997. *Ireland and India: Connections, Comparisons, Contrasts.* Dublin: Folens.

Honderich, Ted, ed. 1995. *The Oxford Companion to Philosophy.* New York: Oxford Univ. Press.

Hookway, Christopher. 1985. *Peirce.* Boston: Routledge.

————. 2000. *Truth, Rationality, and Pragmatism: Themes from Peirce.* New York: Oxford Univ. Press.

Howe, Stephen. 2000. *Ireland and Empire.* Oxford: Oxford Univ. Press.

Hutcheon, Linda. 1985. *A Theory of Parody: The Teachings of Twentieth-Century Art Forms.* New York: Routledge.

Hutchinson, John. 1987. *The Dynamics of Cultural Nationalism: The Gaelic Revival and the Creation of the Irish Nation State.* Boston: Allen & Unwin.

Ignatiev, Noel. 1995. *How the Irish Became White.* New York: Routledge.

The Imperial Epistle from Kien Long, Emperor of China, to George the Third, King of Great Britain, &c. &c. &c. in the Year 1794: The Fifth Edition. 1799. Dublin: J. Milliken.

Inden, Ronald B. 1990. *Imagining India.* Cambridge, Mass.: Basil Blackwell.

Ireland in Past Times: An Historical Retrospect, Ecclesiastical and Civil, with Illustrative Notes. 1826. London: Hatchard.

An Irish Officer in the Service of Persia. 1819. *The History of Mirza Abul Hassan Khan, the Persian Ambassador, with Some Account of the Fair Circassian.* Dublin: Thomas Christopher Clifford.

Jackson, Alvin. 1999. *Ireland, 1798–1998: Politics and War.* Malden, Mass.: Blackwell.

James, Simon. 1999. *The Atlantic Celts: Ancient People or Modern Invention?* Madison: Univ. of Wisconsin Press.

Jeffrey, Keith. 1996. *"An Irish Empire"? Aspects of Ireland and the British Empire.* Manchester: Manchester Univ. Press.

Johnston, Charles. 1977. "Yeats in the Making." In *W. B. Yeats, Interviews and Recollections,* edited by E. H. Mikhail, 1:6–13. New York: Barnes & Noble Books.

Jones, Howard Mumford. 1937. *The Harp that Once—: A Chronicle of the Life of Thomas Moore.* New York: Holt.

Jones, William. 1799a. "The Preface [to] Institutes of Hindu Law; or, The Ordinances of Menu, According to the Gloss of Callúca. Comprising the Indian System of Duties,

Religious and Civil." In *The Works of Sir William Jones,* 3:53–63. London: G. G. & J. Robinson and R. H. Evans.

———. 1799b. "Third Anniversary Discourse: On the Hindus, Delivered 2d of February, 1786. By the President." In *The Works of Sir William Jones,* 1:19–34. London: G. G. & J. Robinson and R. H. Evans.

———. 1970. *The Letters of Sir William Jones.* Edited by Garland Cannon. 2 vols. Oxford: Clarendon.

Jourdan, Annie. 1996. "The Image of the Gaul During the French Revolution: Between Charlemagne and Ossian." In *Celticism,* edited by Terence Brown, 183–206. Atlanta: Rodopi.

Joyce, James. 1959. *Critical Writings.* Edited by Ellsworth Mason and Richard Ellmann. New York: Viking.

———. 1985. "Dubliners." In *The Portable James Joyce,* edited by Harry Levin. 1914. Reprint, New York: Penguin.

———. 1986. *Ulysses,* edited by Hans Walter Gabler. 1922. Reprint, New York; Random House.

Kabir, Humayun. 1961. *The Russell Lecture: Mirza Abu Talib Khan.* Patna, Bihar, India: Patna Univ.

Kain, Richard M., and James H. O'Brien. 1976. *George Russell (A.E.).* Lewisburg, Pa.: Bucknell Univ. Press.

Kalidasa. 1959. *Shakuntala and Other Writings.* Translated by Arthur W. Ryder. New York: Dutton.

Kapur, Narinder. 1997. *The Irish Raj: Illustrated Stories about Irish in India and Indians in Ireland.* Antrim: Greystone Press.

Kearney, Richard, ed. 1985. *The Irish Mind: Exploring Intellectual Traditions.* Dublin: Wolfhound Humanities.

Keating, Geoffrey. 1902–1914. *Foras Feasa ar Éirinn; The History of Ireland.* Edited by David Comyn and Patrick S. Dineen. 4 vols. London: Irish Texts Society.

Kelleher, John V. 1963. "Early Irish History and Pseudo-history." *Studia Hibernica* 3: 113–27.

Kelleher, Margaret. 1997. "Literary Connections: Cultural Revival, Political Independence, and the Present." In *Ireland and India: Connections, Comparisons, Contrasts,* edited by Michael Holmes and Denis Holmes, 100–119. Dublin: Folens.

Kenealy, Edward Vaughan. 1867. *The Book of God: The Apocalypse of Adam-Oannes.* London: Reeves and Turner.

Kenny, James F. 1993. *The Sources for the Early History of Ireland: Ecclesiastical, an Introduction and Guide.* 1929. Reprint, Dublin: Four Courts.

Keogh, William. 1851. "Government Patronage at Home and Abroad." *Irish Quarterly Review* 1, no. 3 (Sept.): 485–522.

Kiberd, Declan. 1995. *Inventing Ireland: The Literature of the Modern Nation.* Cambridge: Harvard Univ. Press.

King, Richard. 1999. *Orientalism and Religion: Postcolonial Theory, India, and "the Mystic East."* New York: Routledge.

Kirkpatrick, Kathryn. 1999. Introduction to *The Wild Irish Girl,* by Sydney Owenson (Lady Morgan), vii–xviii. New York: Oxford Univ. Press.

Knott, Eleanor. 1960. *Irish Classical Poetry, Commonly Called Bardic Poetry.* 2d ed. Cork: Published for the Cultural Relations Committee of Ireland by Colm O Lochlainn.

Knox, R. Buick. 1968. *James Ussher: Archbishop of Armagh.* Cardiff: Univ. of Wales Press.

Koch, John T., and John Carey, eds. 2000. *The Celtic Heroic Age: Literary Sources for Ancient Celtic Europe & Early Ireland & Wales.* Andover: Celtic Studies Publications.

Koizumi, Toki, and Sean G. Ronan. 1992. *Lafcadio Hearn: His Life, Work, and Irish Background.* Dublin: Ireland Japan Association.

Komesu, Okifumi. 1984. *The Double Perspective of Yeats's Aesthetic.* Totowa, N.J.: Barnes and Noble.

Kosok, Heinz. 1996. "Charles Robert Maturin and Colonialism." In *Literary Inter-Relations: Ireland, Egypt, and the Far East,* edited by Mary Massoud. Gerrards Cross: Colin Smythe.

Kuch, Peter. 1986. *Yeats and A.E.: The Antagonism that Unites Dear Friends.* Totowa, N.J.: Colin Smythe.

Kushigian, Julia A. 1991. *Orientalism in the Hispanic Literary Tradition.* Albuquerque: Univ. of New Mexico Press.

Laing, Lloyd, and Jennifer Laing. 1990. *Celtic Britain and Ireland, AD 200–800.* Dublin: Irish Academic Press.

Lane-Poole, Stanley. 1896. "Preface and Notes." In *Selections from the Prose Writings of Jonathan Swift.* New York: D. Appleton.

Larrissy, Edward. 1994. *Yeats the Poet: The Measures of Difference.* New York: Harvester Wheatsheaf.

The Lawrences in India. 1911. "Irish Literary Society." *Irish Book Lover* 2 (Feb.): 113–14.

Leask, Nigel. 1992. *British Romantic Writers and the East: Anxieties of Empire.* Cambridge: Cambridge Univ. Press.

Ledwich, Edward. 1804. *Antiquities of Ireland.* 1790. Reprint, Dublin: John Jones.

Leerssen, Joep. 1996a. "Celticism." In *Celticism,* edited by Terence Brown, 1–20. Atlanta: Rodopi.

———. 1996b. *Mere Irish and Fíor-Ghael: Studies in the Idea of Irish Nationality, Its Development and Literary Expression prior to the Nineteenth Century.* 1986. Reprint, Notre Dame: Univ. of Notre Dame Press.

———. 1997. *Remembrance and Imagination: Patterns in the Historical and Literary Representation of Ireland in the Nineteenth Century.* 1996. Reprint, Notre Dame: Univ. of Notre Dame Press.

———. 1998. "Irish Studies and *Orientalism:* Ireland and the Orient." In *Oriental Prospects: Western Literature and the Lure of the East,* edited by C. C. Barfoot and Theo D'haen, 161–73. Atlanta: Rodopi.

Lees, W. Nassau. 1871. *Indian Musalmans: Being Three Letters Reprinted from the "Times" with an Article on Education, Reprinted from the "Calcutta Englishman" with an Appendix Containing Lord Macaulay's Minute.* London: Williams and Norgate.

Leland, Thomas. 1773. *The History of Ireland from the Invasion of Henry II, with a Preliminary Discourse on the Antient State of that Kingdom.* Vol. 1. Dublin: R. Moncrieffe.

Lennon, Joseph. 2001. "Postcolonial Ireland? The Battle over a Label." Review of *Ireland and Empire,* by Stephen Howe. *Irish Literary Supplement* 20, no. 2 (fall): 30–31.

Lithgow, William. 1632. *The Totall Discourse, of the Rare Adventures of Nineteene Yeares Travayles.* London, n.p.

Litvak, Leon, and Glenn Hooper, eds. 2000. *Ireland in the Nineteenth Century: Regional Identity.* Dublin: Four Courts Press.

Lloyd, David. 1987. *Nationalism and Minor Literature: James Clarence Mangan and the Emergence of Irish Cultural Nationalism.* Berkeley and Los Angeles: Univ. of California Press.

———. 1993. *Anamolous States: Irish Writing and the Post-colonial Moment.* Durham: Duke Univ. Press.

———. 1996. "Discussion Outside History: Irish New Histories and the 'Subalternity Effect.' " In *Subaltern Studies: IX. Writings on South Asian History and Society,* edited by Shahid Amin and Dipesh Chakrabarty. Delhi: Oxford.

Longenbach, James. 1988. *Stone Cottage: Pound, Yeats and Modernism.* New York: Oxford Univ. Press.

Longley, Edna. 1994. *The Living Stream: Literature and Revisionism in Ireland.* Newcastle upon Tyne: Bloodaxe.

Lowe, Lisa. 1991. *Critical Terrains: French and British Orientalisms.* Ithaca: Cornell Univ. Press.

Lubac, Henri de. 1959. *Paradoxes: Suivi de nouveax paradoxes.* Paris: Éditions du Seuil.

Luce, J. V. 1945. Review of *The Story of Irish Orientalism,* by Menaham Mansoor. *Hermathena* 65: 113–14.

Lyttleton, George. 1735. *Letters from a Persian in England to His Friends at Ispahan.* London: Harrison.

Macalister, R. A. Stewart, ed. and trans. 1938. *Lebor Gabála Érenn: The Book of the Taking of Ireland.* Dublin: Irish Texts Society.

———. 1970. *Ireland in Pre-Celtic Times.* 1925. Reprint, New York: B. Blom.

Macaulay, Thomas Babington. 1897. *The Works of Lord Macaulay Complete in Ten Volumes.* Vol. 5. New York: Longmans Green.

MacDonagh, Oliver. 1983. *States of Mind: A Study of Anglo-Irish Conflict, 1780–1980.* Boston: George Allen and Unwin.

MacDonnell, Eneas. 1828. *Speech Delivered by Eneas MacDonnell, Esq., at a Meeting of the Inhabitants of Mayo, Held, July 16th, 1826, Wherein the Ancient Fame of Ireland, and Her Liberal Contributions to the Diffusion of Religion, Science, and Civilization, Throughout Great Britain and Other Nations, Are, in Part, Illustrated.* Leeds: Edward Baines.

MacGeoghegan, Abbé James. 1844. *The History of Ireland, Ancient and Modern, Taken from the Most Authentic Records and Dedicated to the Irish Brigade.* Dublin: Duffy.

Mac Neill, Eoin. 1921. *Celtic Ireland.* Dublin: M. Lester.

Magee, William Kirkpatrick [John Eglinton]. 1968. *Anglo-Irish Essays.* 1918. Reprint, Freeport, N.Y.: Books for Libraries Press.

Mahaffy, John Pentland. 1869. *Twelve Lectures on Primitive Civilizations and Their Physical Conditions (Delivered at Alexandra College).* London: Longmans, Green.

Maher, Anne. 1997. "Missionary Links: Past, Present, and Future." In *Ireland and India: Con-*

nections, Comparisons, Contrasts, edited by Michael Holmes and Denis Holmes, 29–51. Dublin: Folens.

Maine, Sir Henry Sumner. 1864. *Ancient Law: Its Connection with the Early History of Society, and Its Relation to Modern Ideas.* 1861. Reprint, New York: Scribner.

———. 1883. *Dissertations on Early Law and Custom, Chiefly Selected from Lectures Delivered at Oxford.* London: J. Murray.

———. 1889. *Village Communities in the East and West: Six Lectures Delivered at Oxford to which Are Added Other Lectures, Addresses and Essays.* 1871. Reprint, New York: Holt.

———. 1966. *Lectures on the Early History of Institutions.* 1875. Reprint, Port Washington, N.Y.: Kennikat Press.

Majeed, Javed. 1992. *Ungoverned Imaginings: James Mill's "History of British India" and Orientalism.* Oxford: Clarendon Press.

Maley, Willy. 1999. "Nationalism and Revisionism: Ambiviolences and Dissensus." In *Ireland in Proximity: History, Gender, Space,* edited by Scott Brewster, Virginia Crossman, Fiona Becket, and David Alderson, 12–26. New York: Routledge.

Mangala, Ci. Na. 1995. *A Wandering Harp: James H. Cousins, a Study.* Delhi: B. R. Publishers.

Mangan, James Clarence. 1997. *The Collected Works of James Clarence Mangan: Poems.* Edited by Jacques Chuto, Rudolf Patrick Holzapfel, and Ellen Shannon–Mangan. 4 vols. Portland, Oreg.: Irish Academic Press.

Mani, Lata, and Ruth Frankenberg. 1985. "The Challenge of *Orientalism.*" *Economy and Society* 14, no. 2 (May 2): 174–92.

Mansergh, Nicholas. 1997. "The Prelude to Partition: Concepts and Aims in Ireland and India." In *Nationalism and Independence: Selected Irish Papers,* edited by Nicholas Mansergh. Cork: Cork Univ. Press.

Mansoor, M[enahem]. 1943. "Oriental Studies in Ireland, from the Times of St. Patrick to the Rise of Islam." *Hermathena* 62, no. 62: 40–60.

———. 1944. *The Story of Irish Orientalism.* Dublin: Hodges, Figgis.

Martin, Augustine. 1977. *James Stephens: A Critical Study.* Totowa, N.J.: Rowman and Littlefield.

———. 1980. Introduction to *Desire and Other Stories by James Stephens,* by James Stephens. Dublin: Poolbeg.

Marx, Karl. 1963. *The Eighteenth Brumaire of Louis Bonaparte.* 1852. Reprint, New York: International Publishers.

Mascaro, Juan, trans. 1965. *The Upanishads.* Baltimore: Penguin.

Matless, David. 1991. "Nature, the Modern and the Mystic: Tales from Early Twentieth Century Geography." *Transactions of the Institute of British Geographers* 16: 272–86.

McCone, Kim, and Katharine Simms. 1996. *Progress in Medieval Irish Studies.* Maynooth: St. Patrick's College.

McCormack, W. J. 1985. *Ascendancy and Tradition in Anglo-Irish Literary History from 1789 to 1939.* Oxford: Clarendon.

———. 1994. *From Burke to Beckett: Ascendancy, Tradition and Betrayal in Literary History.* Rev. ed. Cork: Cork Univ. Press.

McFate, Patricia. 1979. *The Writings of James Stephens: Variations on a Theme of Love.* New York: Macmillan.

McLoughlin, Thomas O. 1999. *Contesting Ireland: Irish Voices Against England in the Eighteenth Century.* Dublin: Four Courts Press.

Mehrotra, S. R. 1971. *The Emergence of the Indian National Congress.* Delhi: Vikas.

Mill, John Stuart. 1860. *England and Ireland.* London: Longmans, Green, Reader, and Dyer.

Minns, Ellis H. 1965. *Scythians and Greeks: A Survey of Ancient History and Archeology on the North Coast of the Euxine from the Danube to the Caucasus.* 1913. Reprint, New York: Biblo and Tannen.

A Missionary. 1936. "Some Types in a Chinese Congregation." *Far East* 39, no. 1 (Aug.): 184–85.

Molony, J. Chartres. 1970. *The Riddle of the Irish.* 1927. Reprint, Port Washington, N.Y.: Kennikat.

Montesquieu, Charles de Secondat, Baron de. 1972. *Persian Letters.* Translated by John Ozell. 2 vols. New York: Garland.

Montmorency-Morres, Hervey. 1821. *A Historical and Critical Inquiry into the Origin and Primitive Use of the Irish Pillar-Tower.* London: Sherwood, Neely, and Jones.

Mooney, Thomas. 1845. *A History of Ireland, from Its First Settlement to the Present Time, Including a Particular Account of Its Literature, Music, Architecture, and Natural Resources, with Upwards of Two Hundred Biographical Sketches of Its Most Eminent Men, Interspersed with a Great Number of Irish Melodies, Original and Selected, Arranged for Musical Instruments, and Illustrated by Many Anecdotes of Celebrated Irishmen, and a Series of Architectural Descriptions.* 2 vols. Boston: Patrick Donahoe.

Moore, George. 1911–1914. *Hail and Farewell.* 3 vols. London: Heinemann.

Moore, Thomas. 1835–1846. *The History of Ireland.* 4 vols. London: Longman.

———. 1850. *Lalla Rookh.* Buffalo: Derby.

———. 1875. *Poetical Works of Thomas Moore.* London: William Nimmo.

———. 1964. *Letters of Thomas Moore.* Oxford: Clarendon.

Morgan, Hiram. 1994. "An Unwelcome Heritage: Ireland's Role in British Empire-Building." *History of European Ideas* 19, no. 4–6: 619–25.

Moryson, Fynes. 1907. *An Itinerary Containing His Ten Yeeres Travell.* 4 vols. 1617. Reprint, Glasgow: MacLehose.

Murphy, L. D. 1925. "Indian Vignettes." *Irish Monthly* 53 (Oct.): 527–31.

Narveson, Jan. 1995. "Intersubjective." In *The Oxford Companion to Philosophy,* edited by Ted Honderich, 414. New York: Oxford Univ. Press.

Nash, Catherine. 1996. "Geo-centric Education and Anti-imperialism: Theosophy, Geography, and Citizenship in the Writings of J. H. Cousins." *Journal of Historical Geography* 22, no. 4: 399–411.

Nennius. 1848. *Leabhar Breathnach Annso Sis: The Irish Version of the "Historia Britonum" of Nennius.* Translated by James Henthorn Todd. Dublin: Irish Archaeological Society.

"'New India' in the High Court." 1916. *New India* (Oct. 19): 3–7.

Ní Chuilleanáin, Eiléan. 1996. "'Forged and Fabulous Chronicles': Reading Spenser as an

Irish Writer." *Irish University Review: A Journal of Irish Studies.* Special issue, *Spenser in Ireland: "The Faerie Queene," 1596–1996* 26, no. 2 (autumn–winter): 281–90.

Nivedita, Sister (Margaret Noble). 1966. "The Laws of Thought." In *The Ideal of the Karmayogin,* by Aurobindo Ghose. 1918. Reprint, Pondicherry: Sri Aurobindo Ashram.

O'Conor, Charles. 1766. *Dissertations on the History of Ireland. To which is Subjoined A Dissertation on the Irish Colonies Established in Britain With Some Remarks on Mr. Mac Pherson's Translations of "Fingal" and "Temora."* 2d ed. Dublin: Printed by G. Faulkner.

O'Donovan, John, ed. and trans. 1845. *A Grammar of the Irish Language Published for the Use of the Senior Class in the College of St. Columba.* Dublin: Hodges and Smith.

———. 1851. *Annals of the Kingdom of Ireland, by the Four Masters, from the Earliest Period to the Year 1616.* Dublin: Hodges and Smith.

O'Driscol, John. 1827. *The History of Ireland.* London: Longman.

Ó Duilearga, Séamus. 1948. *Leabhar Sheáin Í Chonaill: Sgéalta Agus Seanchas Ó Íbh Ráthach.* Dublin: Folklore of Ireland Society.

O'Flaherty, J. T. 1810. *Thoughts on the Origin and Language of the Ancient Scots, Addressed to a Friend in Cork, with a View to His Project of Establishing an Irish School in that City: To this Letter Is Affixed a Heroic Poem in the Original Irish, with a Beautiful Translation by Miss Brooke.* Cork: J. Conner.

O'Flaherty, Roderic. 1685. *Ogygia; seu, rerum Hibernicorum chronologia.* London: R. Everingham and Ben Tookle.

———. 1775. *Ogygia Vindicated Against the Objections of Sir George Mac Kenzie, King's Advocate for Scotland in the Reign of King James II (A Posthumous Work).* Translated by Charles O'Conor. Dublin: G. Faulkner.

———. 1793. *Ogygia.* Translated by James Hely. Vol. 1. London: R. Everingham.

O'Grady, Standish James. 1999. *All Ireland.* 1898. Reprint, Washington D.C.: Woodstock Books.

O'Leary, Philip. 1986. "'Children of the Same Mother': Gaelic Relations with the Other Celtic Revival Movements, 1882–1916." *Proceedings of the Harvard Celtic Colloquium* 6: 101–30.

———. 1994. *The Prose Literature of the Gaelic Revival, 1881–1921: Ideology and Innovation.* University Park: Pennsylvania State Univ. Press.

Olender, Maurice. 1992. *The Languages of Paradise: Race, Religion, and Philology in the Nineteenth Century.* Translated by Arthur Goldhammer. Cambridge: Harvard Univ. Press.

———. 1997. "From the Language of Adam to the Pluralism of Babel." Translated by Sharon Neeman. *Mediterranean Historical Review* 12, no. 2 (Dec.): 51–59.

Oppenheim, Janet. 1989. "The Odyssey of Annie Besant." *History Today* no. 39 (Sept.): 12–18.

Oshima, Shotaro. 1965. *W. B. Yeats and Japan.* London: Luzac.

Owenson, Sydney (Lady Morgan). 1999. *The Wild Irish Girl.* Edited by Kathryn Kirkpatrick. 1806. Reprint, New York: Oxford Univ. Press.

———. 2002. *The Missionary: An Indian Tale.* Edited by Julia M. Wright. 1811. Reprint, Orchard Park, N.Y.: Broadview Press.

Paine, Jeffery. 1998. *Father India: How Encounters with an Ancient Culture Transformed the Modern West.* New York: Harper Collins.

Pasha, Arabi. 1999. "Appeal to Gladstone, *The Times,* July 2, 1882." In *Imperialism and Orientalism: A Documentary Sourcebook,* edited by Barbara Harlow and Mia Carter, 147. Oxford: Blackwell.

[Pery, Edmund]. 1757. *Letters from an Armenian in Ireland to His Friends at Trebisond, &c. Translated in the Year 1756.* London: Printed for Robert Owen.

Philip, Kavita. 2002. "Race, Class, and the Imperial Politics of Ethnography in India, Ireland, and London, 1850–1910." *Irish Studies Review* 3 (Dec. 10): 289–302.

Pielou, Pierce Leslie. 1935. *The Leslies of Tarbert, Co. Kerry, and Their Forebears.* Dublin: Brindleys.

———. 1937. *Megalithic Remains in Ireland, Particularly Those of the Valley of the Boyne.* [Adyar, Madras]: Theosophical Publishing House.

———. 1947. *The Growth of the Theosophical Society in Ireland.* Adyar, Madras: Adyar Library.

———. 1955. "Ireland's Link with Egypt, Crete, and the Middle East." *Theosophy* 34, no. 2 (May-Aug.): 27.

Poliakov, L. 1974. *The Aryan Myth: A History of Racist and Nationalist Ideas in Europe.* Translated by Edmund Howard. London: Chatto and Windus.

Pollock, Sheldon. 1993. "Deep Orientalism?" In *Orientalism and the Postcolonial Predicament,* edited by Carol A. Breckenridge and Peter van der Veer, 76–133. Philadelphia: Univ. of Pennsylvania Press.

Pound, Ezra, and Ernest Fenollosa. 1959. *The Classic Noh Theatre of Japan.* New York: New Directions.

Prichard, James Cowles. 1857. *The Eastern Origin of the Celtic Nations Proved in a Comparison of Their Dialects with the Sanskrit, Greek, Latin, and Teutonic Languages: Forming a Supplement to Researches into the Physical History of Mankind.* London: Houlston and Wright and Bernard Quaritch.

Pyle, Hilary. 1965. *James Stephens: His Work and an Account of His Life.* New York: Barnes and Noble.

Quine, W. V. 1960. *Word and Object.* Cambridge: Technology Press of the Massachusetts Institute of Technology.

Rajan, Balachandra. 1999. *Under Western Eyes: India from Milton to Macaulay.* Durham: Duke Univ. Press.

Rambo, Elizabeth L. 1994. *Colonial Ireland in Medieval English Literature.* Selinsgrove, Pa.: Susquehana Univ. Press.

Ratton, J. J. L. 1911. "The Bishop's Cash-Chest: A True Story." *Irish Monthly* 61 (Feb.): 80–84.

Raval, Hasmukh M. 1990. *Bhagavad-Gita: A Philosophical System.* St. Louis: Warren H. Green.

Rawson, Claude. 2001. *God, Gulliver, and Genocide: Barbarism and the European Imagination, 1492–1945.* New York: Oxford Univ. Press.

Renan, Ernest. 1896. *The Poetry of the Celtic Races, and Other Studies.* Translated by William G. Hutchinson. London: W. Scott.

———. 1990. "What Is a Nation?" In *Nation and Narration,* edited by Homi K. Bhabha. New York: Routledge.

Rickard, John. 1997. "Studying a New Science: Yeats, Irishness, and the East." In *Represent-*

ing Ireland: Gender, Class, Nationality, edited by Susan Shaw Sailer, 94–112. Gainesville: Univ. Press of Florida.

Rigney, Ann. 1996. "Immemorial Routines: The Celts and Their Resistance to History." In *Celticism,* edited by Terence Brown, 159–81. Atlanta: Rodopi.

Robbins, William. 1947–1948. "Matthew Arnold and Ireland." *University of Toronto Quarterly* 17: 52–67.

Romer, F. E. 2001. *Pomponius Mela's Description of the World.* Ann Arbor: Univ. of Michigan Press.

"The Round Towers of Ireland." 1899. *The Irish Builder: A Journal Devoted to Architecture, Archæology, Engineering, Sanitation, Arts and Handicrafts* 41, no. 957 (Dec. 1): 201–3.

Ruskin, John. 1858. "The Deteriorative Power of Conventional Art over Nations." In *The Two Paths,* 9–36. Boston: Dana Estes.

Russell, George (AE). 1895. "The Legends of Ancient Eire." *Irish Theosophist.*

———. 1908. *Homeward: Songs by the Way.* New York: John Lane.

———. 1912. "Krishna: Imitated from a Fragment of Vaishnava Scriptures." *Irish Review* 2, no. 22: 460.

———. 1913. *Collected Poems.* London: Macmillan.

———. 1915. *Imaginations and Reveries.* Dublin: Maunsel.

———. 1918. *The Candle of Vision.* London: Macmillan.

———. 1920. *The Economics of Ireland and the Policy of the British Government.* New York: B. W. Huebsch.

———. 1923. *The Interpreters.* New York: Macmillan.

———. 1930. *The National Being.* 1916. Reprint, New York: Macmillan.

———. 1933. *The Avatars: A Futurist Fantasy.* New York: Macmillan.

———. 1988. *The Descent of the Gods: Comprising the Mystical Writings of G. W. Russell—A.E.* Edited by Raghavan Iyer and Nandini Iyer. Gerrards Cross: Colin Smyth.

Ryan, Charles. 1975. *H. P. Blavatsky and the Theosophical Movement.* Pasadena: Theosophical Univ. Press.

Ryan, Frederick. 1911. "The Persian Struggle." *Irish Review* 1, no. 6: 281–86.

Ryan, W[illiam] P[atrick]. 1912. *The Pope's Green Island.* Boston: Small and Maynard.

Said, Edward. 1985. "Orientalism Reconsidered." In *Europe and Its Others: Proceedings of the Essex Conference on the Sociology of Literature, July 1984,* edited by Francis Barker et al., 1:14–27. Colchester: Univ. of Essex Press.

———. 1990. "Yeats and Decolonization." In *Nationalism, Colonialism, and Literature,* by Seamus Deane, Terry Eagleton, Fredric Jameson, and Edward Said. 1988. Reprint, Minneapolis: Univ. of Minnesota Press.

———. 1993. *Culture and Imperialism.* New York: Knopf.

———. 1995. *Orientalism: Western Conceptions of the Orient.* Rev. ed. 1978. Reprint, New York: Vintage.

Sailer, Susan Shaw, ed. 1997. *Representing Ireland: Gender, Class, Nationality.* Gainesville: Univ. Press of Florida.

Sawyer, Roger. 1984. *Casement, the Flawed Hero.* Boston: Routledge and Kegan Paul.

———. 1997. *Roger Casement's Diaries, 1910: The Black and the White.* London: Pimlico.

Schlegel, Carl Wilhelm Friedrich von. 2001. "On the Language and Wisdom of the Indians." In *The European Discovery of India: Key Indological Sources of Romanticism,* edited by Michael Franklin, 4:425–526. London: Ganesha and Edition Synapse.

Schopen, Gregory. 1997. "Archaeology and Protestant Presuppositions in the Study of Indian Buddhism." In *Bones, Stones, and Buddhist Monks: Collected Papers on the Archaeology, Epigraphy, and Texts of Monastic Buddhism in India,* 1–22. Honolulu: Univ. of Hawaii Press.

Schwab, Raymond. 1984. *Oriental Renaissance: Europe's Rediscovery of India and the East, 1680–1880.* New York: Columbia Univ. Press.

Schwarz, A. 1913. *Man: Whence, How and Whither.* London: Theosophical Society.

Scowcroft, R. Mark. 1987. "*Leabhar Gabhála,* Part I: The Growth of the Text." *Eriu: Founded as the Journal of the School of Irish Learning Devoted to Irish Philology and Literature* 38: 80–142.

———. 1988. "*Leabhar Gabhála,* Part II: The Growth of the Tradition." *Eriu: Founded as the Journal of the School of Irish Learning Devoted to Irish Philology and Literature* 39: 1–66.

Sekine, Masaru, and Christopher Murray, eds. 1990. *Yeats and the Noh: A Comparative Study.* Gerrards Cross: Colin Smyth.

Sencourt, Robert. 1923. *India in English Literature.* London: Simpkin, Marshall, Hamilton, Kent.

Sharafuddin, Mohammed. 1994. *Islam and Romantic Orientalism: Literary Encounters with the Orient.* New York: I. B. Tauris.

Shaw, George Bernard. 1984. *John Bull's Other Island.* 1907. Reprint, New York: Penguin.

Sheridan, Frances. 1767. *The History of Nourjahad: The Persian.* London: Cook.

Shloss, Carol Loeb. 1998. "Joyce in the Context of Irish Orientalism." *James Joyce Quarterly* 35, no. 2–3 (winter-spring): 264–71.

Sidney, Sir Philip. 1989. *An Apology for Poetry; or, The Defence of Poesy.* Edited by Geoffrey Shepherd. Revised by R. W. Maslen. New York: Manchester Univ. Press.

Silvestri, Michael. 2000a. "'An Irishman Is Specially Suited to Be a Policeman': Sir Charles Tegart and Revolutionary Terrorism in Bengal." *History-Ireland* (winter): 40–44.

———. 2000b. "'The Sinn Féin of India': Irish Nationalism and the Policing of Revolutionary Terrorism in Bengal, 1905–1939." *Journal of British Studies* 39 (Oct.): 454–86.

Simpson, D. P., ed. 1960. *Cassell's New Latin Dictionary.* New York: Funk and Wagnalls.

Skelton, Robin. 1990. *Celtic Contraries.* Syracuse: Syracuse Univ. Press.

Smith, Anthony D. 1986. *The Ethnic Origins of Nations.* New York: Blackwell.

Smith, Hamilton Jewett. 1926. *Oliver Goldsmith's "The Citizen of the World."* New Haven: Yale Univ. Press.

Smith, Vincent Arthur. 1966. *Akbar: The Great Mogul, 1542–1605.* Delhi: S. Chand.

S[mith], W. 1801. *Historical Explanations of Emblematic Cards: For the Use of Young Persons.* Dublin: Marchbank.

Smyth, George Lewis. 1844. *Ireland: Historical and Statistical.* London: Whittaker.

Smyth, Gerry. 1998. *Decolonisation and Criticism: The Construction of Irish Literature.* Sterling, Va.: Pluto Press.

Soulif, Samje [pseud.]. 1804. *Conspiracy Detected and Converted.* Dublin: Graisberry and Campbell.

Spenser, Edmund. 1633. "A View of the Present State of Ireland." In *The Historie of Ireland,*

Collected by Three Learned Authors Viz. Meredith Hanmer, Edmund Campion and Edmund Spenser, edited by James Ware. Dublin: Societie of Stationers.

Spivak, Gayatri. 1990. *The Post-colonial Critic: Interviews, Strategies, Dialogues*. Edited by Sarah Harasym. New York: Routledge.

———. 1999. *A Critique of Postcolonial Reason: Toward a History of the Vanishing Present*. Cambridge: Harvard Univ. Press.

Srivivas, M. N. 1992. "Varna and Caste." In *Social Stratification*, edited by Gupta Dipankar. New York: Oxford Univ. Press.

Stanihurst, Richard. 1808. "A Treatise Conteining a Plaine and Perfect Description of Ireland, with an Introduction to the Better Understanding of the Histories Appertaining to the Iland." In *Holinshed's Chronicles of England, Scotland, and Ireland*, edited by Raphaell Holinshed. Vol. 6. 1586. Reprint, London: Johnson.

Stephens, James. 1912a. *The Charwoman's Daughter*. London: Macmillan.

———. 1912b. *The Crock of Gold*. New York: Macmillan.

———. 1912c. "The Wisdom of the West." Review of *Wisdom of the West*, by James Cousins. *Irish Review* 2 (Apr.): 100–102.

———. 1914. *The Demi-Gods*. London: Macmillan.

———. 1916. *The Insurrection in Dublin*. London: Macmillan.

———. 1923. *Deirdre*. London and New York: Macmillan.

———. 1924. *In the Land of Youth*. London: Macmillan.

———. 1928. *Etched in Moonlight*. New York: Macmillan.

———. 1962. *A James Stephens Reader*. Edited by Lloyd Frankenberg. Preface by Padraic Colum. New York: Macmillan.

———. 1964. *James, Seumas, & Jacques: Unpublished Writings of James Stephens*. Edited by Lloyd Frankenberg. New York: Macmillan.

———. 1974. *Letters of James Stephens*. Edited by Richard J. Finneran. New York: Macmillan.

———. 1983. *Uncollected Prose of James Stephens*. Edited by Patricia McFate. 2 vols. New York: St. Martin's.

Stewart, Charles. 1972. *The Travels of Mirza Abu Taleb [sic] Khan in Asia, Africa and Europe in the Years 1799–1803*. 1814. Reprint, Delhi: Sona.

Strabo. 1997. *The Geography of Strabo*. Vol. 1, *Geography: Books 1–2*. Translated by Horace Leonard Jones. 1917. Reprint, Cambridge: Harvard Univ. Press.

Summerfield, Henry. 1975. *That Myriad-Minded Man: A Biography of George William Russel "A.E.," 1867–1935*. Totowa, N.J.: Rowman and Littlefield.

Swift, Jonathan. 2001. *Gulliver's Travels*. Edited by Robert DeMaria Jr. New York: Penguin.

Synge, J. M. 1921. *In Wicklow and West Kerry*. Dublin: Maunsel and Roberts.

Tagore, Rabindranath. 1916. *Gitanjali (Song Offerings): A Collection of Prose Translations Made by the Author from the Original Bengali, with an Introduction by W. B. Yeats*. New York: Macmillan.

———. 1995a. *Gora*. Delhi: Macmillan.

———. 1995b. *Nationalism*. Delhi: Macmillan.

———. 1997a. "East and West." In *Rabindranath Tagore: An Anthology*, edited by Krishna Dutta and Andrew Robinson, 203–14. New York: St. Martin's.

———. 1997b. "A Poet's School." In *Rabindranath Tagore: An Anthology*, edited by Krishna Dutta and Andrew Robinson, 248–61. New York: St. Martin's.

———. 1997c. "Poet Yeats." In *Rabindranath Tagore: An Anthology*, edited by Krishna Dutta and Andrew Robinson, 215–21. New York: St. Martin's.

———. *Rabindranath Tagore: An Anthology*. 1997d. Edited by Krishna Dutta and Andrew Robinson. New York: St. Martin's.

Taylor, Anne. 1992. *Annie Besant: A Biography*. New York: Oxford Univ. Press.

Thébaud, Augustus J., S.J. 1883. *The Irish Race in the Past and the Present*. New York: Excelsior Catholic.

Thuente, Mary Helen. 1998. "William Sampson, United Irish Satirist and Songwriter." *Eighteenth-Century Life: Ireland, 1798–1998: From Revolution to Revisionism and Beyond* 22, no. 3 (Nov.): 19–30.

Tigernach. 1993. *The Annals of Tigernach*. Vol. 1. Reprinted from *Revue Celtique*. 1895–1896. Reprint, Felinfach: Llanerch Publishers.

Tilney, W. A. 2001. *Colonel Standfast: The Memoirs of W. A. Tilney, 1868–1947: A Soldier's Life in England, India, the Boer War, and Ireland*. Edited by Nini Murray-Phillipson. Wilby: Michael Russell.

Trevor-Roper, Hugh. 1984. "The Invention of Tradition: The Highland Tradition of Scotland." In *The Invention of Tradition*, edited by Eric Hobsbawm and Terence Ranger, 15–41. Cambridge: Cambridge Univ. Press.

Tristam, Hildegard L. C. 1996. "Celtic in Linguistic Taxonomy." In *Celticism*, edited by Terence Brown, 257–71. Atlanta: Rodopi.

Turner, Brian S., ed. 2000. *Orientalism: Early Sources*. Vol. 1, *Readings in Orientalism*. New York: Routledge.

Vallancey, Charles. 1770–1804. *Collectanea De Rebus Hibernicus Published from Original Manuscripts*. Vols. 1–6. Dublin: T. Ewing.

———. 1772. *Essay on the Antiquity of the Irish Language: Being a Collation of the Irish with the Punic Language*. Dublin: S. Powell.

———. 1786. *An Essay Towards Illustrating the Ancient History of the Britannic Isles: Containing An Explanation of the Names Belgae, Scythae, Celtae, Brittani, Albanich, Eirinnich, Caledonii, Siluri, &c. &c. Intended as a Preface to a Work Entitled, A Vindication of the Ancient History of Ireland*. London: John Nichols.

———. 1797. *Ancient History of Ireland Proved from the Sanscrit Books of the Brahims of India*. Dublin: Graisberry and Campbell.

———. 1812. *An Account of the Ancient Stone Amphitheatre Lately Discovered in the County of Kerry with Fragments of Irish History Relating Thereto, &c, &c, &c*. Dublin: Graisberry and Campbell.

Van Hamel, A. G. 1914–1915. "On *Lebor Gabála*." *Zeitschrift für Celtische Philologie* 10: 97–197.

Veale, Helen. 1916. "Educational Progress." *New India* (June 21): 9.

Vindex, Julius [pseud.]. 1802. *Vindication of the Irish Nation, and Particularly of the Roman Catholics, Against the Calumnies of Libellers*. Pt. 4. Dublin: James Fletcher.

Viswanathan, Gauri. 1998. *Outside the Fold: Conversion, Modernity, and Belief*. Princeton: Princeton Univ. Press.

———. 2003. "Spirituality, Internationalism, and Decolonization: James Cousins, the 'Irish Poet from India.' " In *Ireland and Postcolonial Theory,* edited by Clare Carroll, 158–76. Cork: Cork Univ. Press.

Wade, Allan. 1954. *The Letters of W. B. Yeats.* London: Hart-Davis.

Walker, Joseph Cooper. 1788. *An Historical Essay on the Dress of the Ancient and Modern Irish: Addressed to the Right Honourable the Earl of Charlemont to which Is Subjoined, a Memoir on the Armour and Weapons of the Irish.* Dublin: George Grierson.

Ware, James, ed. 1633. *The Historie of Ireland, Collected by Three Learned Authors Viz. Meredith Hanmer, Edmund Campion and Edmund Spenser.* Dublin: Societie of Stationers.

Watarai, Yoshiichi. 1996. "Lafcadio Hearn's *Kwaidan* and Japanese Mythologies of the Dead." In *Literary Inter-relations: Ireland, Egypt, and the Far East,* edited by Mary Massoud, 73–76. Gerrards Cross: Colin Smyth.

Watson, George J. 1994. *Irish Identity and the Literary Revival: Synge, Yeats, Joyce, and O'Casey.* Washington, D.C.: Catholic Univ. Press.

———. 1996. "Celticism and the Annulment of History." In *Celticism,* edited by Terence Brown, 207–20. Atlanta: Rodopi.

Welch, Robert, ed. 1996. *The Oxford Companion to Irish Literature.* Oxford: Clarendon.

Whelan, Kevin. 1995. *The Tree of Liberty: Radicalism, Catholicism, and the Construction of Irish Identity, 1760–1830.* Cork: Cork Univ. Press.

———. 2000. "Writing Ireland: Reading England." In *Ireland in the Nineteenth Century: Regional Identity,* edited by Leon Litvak and Glenn Hooper, 185–98. Dublin: Four Courts Press.

Windschuttle, Keith. 1999. "Edward Said's 'Orientalism' Revisisted." *New Criterion* 17, no. 5 (Jan.): 30–38.

Witoszek, Nina, and Pat Sheeran. 1998. *Talking to the Dead: A Study of Irish Funerary Traditions.* Atlanta: Rodopi.

Wolfram, Sybil. 1995. "Coherence Theory of Truth." In *The Oxford Companion to Philosophy,* edited by Ted Honderich, 140. New York: Oxford Univ. Press.

Wright, Dennis. 1988. Introduction to *A Persian at the Court of King George, 1809–10: The Journal of Mirza Abul Hassan Khan,* edited and translated by Margaret Morris Cloake. London: Barrie and Jenkins.

Wright, Julia M. 2002. Introduction to *The Missionary: An Indian Tale,* by Sydney Owenson (Lady Morgan), 9–57. Orchard Park, N.Y.: Broadview Press.

Yeats, William Butler. 1916. Introduction to *Gitanjali (Song Offerings): A Collection of Prose Translations Made by the Author from the Original Bengali, with an Introduction by W. B. Yeats,* by Rabindranath Tagore. New York: Macmillan.

———. 1934. *Letters to the New Island.* Edited by Horace Reynolds. Cambidge: Harvard Univ. Press.

———. 1961. *Essays and Introductions.* New York: Macmillan.

———. 1969. *The Variorum Edition of the Plays of W. B. Yeats.* Edited by Russel K. Alspach. New York: Macmillan.

———. 1970. *Uncollected Prose.* Edited by John P. Frayne. Vol. 1. New York: Columbia Univ. Press.

————. 1973. *The Variorum Edition of the Poems of W. B. Yeats.* Edited by Peter Allt and Russel K. Alspach. New York: Macmillan.

————. 1976. *Uncollected Prose.* Edited by John P. Frayne and Colton Johnson. Vol. 2. New York: Columbia Univ. Press.

————. 1986. *The Collected Letters of W. B. Yeats.* Vol. 1, *1865–1895.* Edited by John Kelly. Oxford: Clarendon.

————. 1987. *The Early Poetry.* Vol. 1, *Mosada and the Island of Statues: Manuscript Materials by W. B. Yeats.* Edited by George Bornstein. Ithaca: Cornell Univ. Press.

————. 1989. *Yeats's Poems.* Edited by A. Norman Jeffares. London: Macmillan.

————. 1994a. *The Collected Letters of W. B. Yeats.* Edited by John Kelly and Ronald Schuchard. Vol. 2. Oxford: Clarendon.

————. 1994b. *The Collected Works of W. B. Yeats.* Vol. 4, *Later Essays.* Edited by William H. O'Donnell. New York: Scribner's.

————. 1995. *Autobiographies: Memories and Reflections.* 1955. Reprint, London: Bracken.

Young, Robert. 1989. *White Mythologies: Writing History and the West.* New York: Routledge.

Zimmer, Heinrich. 1893. *Nennius Vindicatus: Über Entstehung, Geschichte und Quellen der "Historia Britonum."* Berlin: Weidmann.

Index

459